The Rise and Fall of Modern Empires, Volume I

The Rise and Fall of Modern Empires
Series Editor: Philippa Levine

Titles in the Series:

**The Rise and Fall of Modern Empires, Volume I
Social Organization**
Owen White

**The Rise and Fall of Modern Empires, Volume II
Colonial Knowledges**
Saul Dubow

**The Rise and Fall of Modern Empires, Volume III
Economics and Politics**
Sarah Stockwell

**The Rise and Fall of Modern Empires, Volume IV
Reactions to Colonialism**
Martin Shipway

The Rise and Fall of Modern Empires, Volume I
Social Organization

Edited by

Owen White

University of Delaware, USA

LONDON AND NEW YORK

First published 2013 by Ashgate Publishing

Published 2016 by Routledge
2 Park Square, Milton Park, Abingdon, Oxon OX14 4RN
605 Third Avenue, New York, NY 10017

First issued in paperback 2022

Routledge is an imprint of the Taylor & Francis Group, an informa business

Copyright © Owen White 2013. For copyright of individual articles please refer to the Acknowledgements.

All rights reserved. No part of this book may be reprinted or reproduced or utilised in any form or by any electronic, mechanical, or other means, now known or hereafter invented, including photocopying and recording, or in any information storage or retrieval system, without permission in writing from the publishers.

Notice:
Product or corporate names may be trademarks or registered trademarks, and are used only for identification and explanation without intent to infringe.

Publisher's Note
The publisher has gone to great lengths to ensure the quality of this reprint but points out that some imperfections in the original copies may be apparent.

British Library Cataloguing in Publication Data
The rise and fall of modern empires.
   Volume I, Social organization.
   1. Colonies–Administration–History–19th century–
   Case studies. 2. Colonies–Administration–History–20th
   century–Case studies. 3. Imperialism–Social aspects.
   4. Indigenous peoples–Social conditions–19th century–
   Case studies. 5. Indigenous peoples–Social conditions–
   20th century–Case studies.
   I. White, Owen, Dr.
   325.3'2-dc23

The Library of Congress has cataloged the printed edition as follows: 2012953506

ISBN 13: 978-1-4094-3397-2 (hbk)
ISBN 13: 978-1-03-240265-9 (pbk)

DOI: 10.4324/9781315237343

Contents

Acknowledgements vii
Series Preface ix
Introduction xi

PART I   LAND AND LABOUR

1 Sara Berry (1992), 'Hegemony on a Shoestring: Indirect Rule and Access to Agricultural Land', *Africa: Journal of the International African Institute*, **62**, pp. 327–55.   3
2 R.E. Elson (1986), 'Sugar Factory Workers and the Emergence of "Free Labour" in Nineteenth-Century Java', *Modern Asian Studies*, **20**, pp. 139–74.   33
3 Allen Isaacman and Arlindo Chilundo (1995), 'Peasants at Work: Forced Cotton Cultivation in Northern Mozambique, 1938–1961', in Allen Isaacman and Richard Roberts (eds), *Cotton, Colonialism, and Social History in Sub-Saharan Africa*, Portsmouth, NH: Heinemann, pp. 147–79.   69
4 Thaddeus Sunseri (2003), 'Reinterpreting a Colonial Rebellion: Forestry and Social Control in German East Africa, 1874–1915', *Environmental History*, **8**, pp. 430–51.   103
5 Warwick Anderson (2000), 'Geography, Race and Nation: Remapping "Tropical" Australia, 1890–1930', *Medical History. Supplement*, **20**, pp. 146–59.   125
6 William Cunningham Bissell (2011), 'Between Fixity and Fantasy: Assessing the Spatial Impact of Colonial Urban Dualism', *Journal of Urban History*, **37**, pp. 208–29.   139
7 Brenda S.A. Yeoh (1991), 'The Control of "Sacred" Space: Conflicts Over the Chinese Burial Grounds in Colonial Singapore, 1880–1930', *Journal of Southeast Asian Studies*, **22**, pp. 282–311.   161

PART II   MECHANISMS OF RULE

8 Eugene L. Rogan (1994), 'Bringing the State Back: The Limits of Ottoman Rule in Jordan, 1840–1910', in Eugene L. Rogan and Tariq Tell (eds), *Village, Steppe and State: The Social Origins of Modern Jordan*, London: British Academic Press, pp. 32–57.   193
9 Gerard Sasges (2012), 'State, Enterprise and the Alcohol Monopoly in Colonial Vietnam', *Journal of Southeast Asian Studies*, **43**, pp. 133–57.   219
10 David Omissi (1991), '"Martial Races": Ethnicity and Security in Colonial India, 1858–1939', *War and Society*, **9**, pp. 1–27.   245

11 Emily Lynn Osborn (2003), '"Circle of Iron": African Colonial Employees and
the Interpretation of Colonial Rule in French West Africa', *Journal of African
History*, **44**, pp. 29–50. 273
12 Elizabeth Schmidt (1990), 'Negotiated Spaces and Contested Terrain: Men,
Women, and the Law in Colonial Zimbabwe, 1890–1939', *Journal of Southern
African Studies*, **16**, pp. 622–48. 295
13 Iain R. Smith and Andreas Stucki (2011), 'The Colonial Development of
Concentration Camps (1868–1902)', *Journal of Imperial and Commonwealth
History*, **39**, pp. 417–37. 323
14 Maryinez Lyons (1988), 'Sleeping Sickness Epidemics and Public Health in the
Belgian Congo', in David Arnold (ed.), *Imperial Medicine and Indigenous
Societies*, Manchester: Manchester University Press, pp. 105–24. 345
15 William R. Roff (1982), 'Sanitation and Security: The Imperial Powers and the
Nineteenth Century Ḥajj', *Arabian Studies*, **6**, pp. 143–60. 365

PART III THE SOCIAL WORLD OF EMPIRE

16 Charles Hirschman (1986), 'The Making of Race in Colonial Malaya: Political
Economy and Racial Ideology', *Sociological Forum*, **1**, pp. 330–61. 385
17 Ann L. Stoler (1989), 'Making Empire Respectable: The Politics of Race and
Sexual Morality in 20th-Century Colonial Cultures', *American Ethnologist*, **16**,
pp. 634–60. 417
18 Barbara N. Ramusack (1990), 'Cultural Missionaries, Maternal Imperialists,
Feminist Allies: British Women Activists in India, 1865–1945', *Women's Studies
International Forum*, **13**, pp. 309–21. 445
19 Robert Crews (2003), 'Empire and the Confessional State: Islam and Religious
Politics in Nineteenth-Century Russia', *American Historical Review*, **108**,
pp. 50–83. 459
20 James P. Daughton (2001), 'Kings of the Mountains: Mayréna, Missionaries, and
French Colonial Divisions in 1880s Indochina', *Itinerario*, **25**, pp. 185–217. 493
21 Jun Uchida (2011), 'A Sentimental Journey: Mapping the Interior Frontier of
Japanese Settlers in Colonial Korea', *Journal of Asian Studies*, **70**, pp. 706–29. 527

Name Index 551

Acknowledgements

My understanding of empire has benefitted greatly from discussion with graduate students at the University of Delaware, with special thanks on this occasion to Jeffery Appelhans and Laura Muskavitch. I am also grateful to Philippa Levine and Patricia Sloane-White for their valuable suggestions.

Owen White

Ashgate would like to thank our researchers and the contributing authors who provided copies, along with the following for their permission to reprint copyright material.

American Anthropological Association for the essay: Ann L. Stoler (1989), 'Making Empire Respectable: The Politics of Race and Sexual Morality in 20th-Century Colonial Cultures', *American Ethnologist*, **16**, pp. 634–60.

Cambridge University Press for the essays: Sara Berry (1992), 'Hegemony on a Shoestring: Indirect Rule and Access to Agricultural Land', *Africa: Journal of the International African Institute*, **62**, pp. 327–55. Copyright © 1992 International African Institute; R.E. Elson (1986), 'Sugar Factory Workers and the Emergence of "Free Labour" in Nineteenth-Century Java', *Modern Asian Studies*, **20**, pp. 139–74. Copyright © 1986 Cambridge University Press; Warwick Anderson (2000), 'Geography, Race and Nation: Remapping "Tropical" Australia, 1890–1930', *Medical History. Supplement*, **20**, pp. 146–59. Copyright © 2000 Cambridge University Press; Brenda S.A. Yeoh (1991), 'The Control of "Sacred" Space: Conflicts Over the Chinese Burial Grounds in Colonial Singapore, 1880–1930', *Journal of Southeast Asian Studies*, **22**, pp. 282–311. Copyright © 1991 National University of Singapore; Gerard Sasges (2012), 'State, Enterprise and the Alcohol Monopoly in Colonial Vietnam', *Journal of Southeast Asian Studies*, **43**, pp. 133–57. Copyright © 2012 National University of Singapore; Emily Lynn Osborn (2003), '"Circle of Iron": African Colonial Employees and the Interpretation of Colonial Rule in French West Africa', *Journal of African History*, **44**, pp. 29–50. Copyright © 2003 Cambridge University Press; James P. Daughton (2001), 'Kings of the Mountains: Mayréna, Missionaries, and French Colonial Divisions in 1880s Indochina', *Itinerario*, **25**, pp. 185–217. Copyright © 2001 Research Institute for History, Leiden University; Jun Uchida (2011), 'A Sentimental Journey: Mapping the Interior Frontier of Japanese Settlers in Colonial Korea', *Journal of Asian Studies*, **70**, pp. 706–29. Copyright © 2011 Association for Asian Studies, Inc.

Copyright Clearance Center for the essay: Robert Crews (2003), 'Empire and the Confessional State: Islam and Religious Politics in Nineteenth-Century Russia', *American Historical Review*, **108**, pp. 50–83. Copyright © 2003 University of Chicago Press.

Elsevier for the essay: Barbara N. Ramusack (1990), 'Cultural Missionaries, Maternal Imperialists, Feminist Allies: British Women Activists in India, 1865–1945', *Women's Studies International Forum*, **13**, pp. 309–21. Copyright © 1990 Pergamon Press Plc.

Allen Isaacman and Arlindo Chilundo (1995), 'Peasants at Work: Forced Cotton Cultivation in Northern Mozambique, 1938–1961', in Allen Isaacman and Richard Roberts (eds), *Cotton, Colonialism, and Social History in Sub-Saharan Africa*, Portsmouth, NH: Heinemann, pp. 147–79. Copyright © 1995 Allen Isaacman and Arlindo Chilundo.

Maney Publishing for the essay: David Omissi (1991), '"Martial Races": Ethnicity and Security in Colonial India, 1858–1939', *War and Society*, **9**, pp. 1–27. Copyright © 1991 University of New South Wales.

Oxford University Press for the essay: Thaddeus Sunseri (2003), 'Reinterpreting a Colonial Rebellion: Forestry and Social Control in German East Africa, 1874–1915', *Environmental History*, **8**, pp. 430–51.

William R. Roff (1982), 'Sanitation and Security: The Imperial Powers and the Nineteenth Century Ḥajj', *Arabian Studies*, **6**, pp. 143–60. Copyright © 1982 William R. Roff.

Sage Publications for the essay: William Cunningham Bissell, (2011), 'Between Fixity and Fantasy: Assessing the Spatial Impact of Colonial Urban Dualism', *Journal of Urban History*, **37**, pp. 208–29. Copyright © 2011 Sage Publications.

Springer for the essay: Charles Hirschman (1986), 'The Making of Race in Colonial Malaya: Political Economy and Racial Ideology', *Sociological Forum*, **1**, pp. 330–61. Copyright © 1986 Eastern Sociology Society.

I.B. Tauris & Co Ltd for the essay: Eugene L. Rogan (1994), 'Bringing the State Back: The Limits of Ottoman Rule in Jordan, 1840–1910', in Eugene L. Rogan and Tariq Tell (eds), *Village, Steppe and State: The Social Origins of Modern Jordan*, London: British Academic Press, pp. 32–57.

Taylor & Francis Group for the essays: Elizabeth Schmidt (1990), 'Negotiated Spaces and Contested Terrain: Men, Women, and the Law in Colonial Zimbabwe, 1890–1939', *Journal of Southern African Studies*, **16**, pp. 622–48. Copyright © 1990 Editorial Board of the Journal of Southern African Studies; Iain R. Smith and Andreas Stucki (2011), 'The Colonial Development of Concentration Camps (1868–1902)', *Journal of Imperial and Commonwealth History*, **39**, pp. 417–37. Copyright © 2011 Taylor & Francis.

Every effort has been made to trace all the copyright holders, but if any have been inadvertently overlooked the publishers will be pleased to make the necessary arrangement at the first opportunity.

Publisher's Note

The material in this volume has been reproduced using the facsimile method. This means we can retain the original pagination to facilitate easy and correct citation of the original essays. It also explains the variety of typefaces, page layouts and numbering.

Series Preface

In the modern world, empires have been a constant and characteristic element of the political landscape. While the fact of colonial conquest is by no means unique to the modern period, the empires of the past three hundred years or so share some fundamental characteristics. These were empires much of whose dominance was based on technological prowess; they were principally the province of Western nations; and they frequently claimed a humanitarian impulse connected to the technology that also helped them succeed in conquering other lands. They were also, for the most part, white empires ruling principally over peoples considered inferior, not least because of their racial difference from their European overlords.

We can trace some critical changes in the nature of empire over time, a shift from colonies of settlement intended to absorb population from Europe to colonies of extraction never intended as sites where large numbers of Europeans would settle permanently. There is no simple linear chronology to this: the two always co-existed but at the same time, there is no doubt that in the nineteenth century there was a growing emphasis on the model of extraction, especially where raw materials for industrial production were available, even while settlement continued.

The colonized adopted a variety of tactics in the face of conquest. Many chose to collaborate, a tactic that could certainly enrich and empower a lucky or canny few. Collaboration came in many forms ranging from enforcement of colonial laws to securing a Western education or converting to Christianity. Just as many, however, adopted the opposite route of resistance, and this, too, had many guises from outright rebellion to slow work routines. We need to remember, too, that many people remained unaware or barely cognisant of a colonial presence, especially in places where colonial officials were sparse on the ground. There was a world of difference between colonies such as French Algeria or British India, where a substantial European population influenced everything from available foodstuffs to architecture, from labour opportunities to town planning, and much of sub-Saharan Africa where a mere handful of colonial officials housed in modest dwellings, and often itinerant, was often the only visible manifestation of colonial rule.

These four volumes are closely concerned with all aspects of modern colonial rule. We have divided the volumes into four broad but inevitably overlapping areas. The four overarching themes that we thought best captured the breadth and depth of this critical historical phenomenon are Social Organization, Colonial Knowledges, Economics and Politics, and Reactions to Colonialism. All four volumes offer analyses of the experience of both the colonized and the colonizer, and pay as much attention to ideas as to events, to the materiality of politics and economics as to the cultures that developed around colonial practice. All take seriously the need to explore the impact of empires locally and globally – that is, in the places which were colonized, in the places responsible for that colonization and in the complex and multiple global ramifications of empire-building. For at every level, the fact of empire shaped political and diplomatic relations, the pursuit of both knowledge and profit, the contours of resistance as well as the quotidian rhythms of life in many parts of the world.

We should recognize, moreover, that while the age of formal imperialism may be over, its consequences have been tenacious. The legacies of colonialism haunt a considerable number of our contemporary political conflicts and have shaped the economics of many locations around the world. Policy debates in the early twenty-first century have been profoundly shaped by a neo-imperialist lobby that argues for a continued relevance for a humanitarian imperialism. These four volumes offer a comprehensive assessment of the impact, effects and legacies of modern imperialism.

PHILIPPA LEVINE
University of Texas at Austin, USA

Introduction

> The history of empires is that of the miseries of humankind.
>
> Edward Gibbon, *An Essay on the Study of Literature*

In 1761 Edward Gibbon had not yet visited Rome, much less decided to write about the empire whose ruins would strike him so forcefully during his 'grand tour' of Europe. Yet, as the quotation above – the opening line of his first book – demonstrates, empires were already on his mind. Published in the midst of a war among empires that would come to be known as the Seven Years' War, Gibbon's piercing judgement might have served as a warning to over-ambitious contemporaries. A few years later, his *Decline and Fall of the Roman Empire* would elaborate a similarly despondent view of empire as a type of political organization 'adverse to nature and reason' (Gibbon, 1901, vol. 5, p. 302).[1] Even as Gibbon wrote, however, industrialization was expanding the capabilities of his own country, England, as well as its needs and appetites. The era of modern empires was only just beginning.

The essays in the present volume, published over 250 years after Gibbon's summary verdict, reveal some of the ways that more recent generations of historians have aimed to capture and analyse the impact of modern empires on societies across the globe. This historiography has indeed catalogued a good deal of misery, but it has also provided an intensely varied picture of imperial activity. The coloured shadings on maps of the world – pink for the British Empire, blue for the French and so on – encompassed territories that were fought over and vigorously exploited, as well as regions whose inhabitants rarely saw representatives of imperial power. There were many losers in the contest of empire, but the spoils did not accrue solely to colonizers. Meanwhile, though there were stronger imperial powers and weaker imperial powers, even the strongest often had to concede limits to their capacity to transform the territories they ruled.

In the few decades since the decline and fall of the formal empires that did so much to shape the contemporary world, historians have gone well beyond the questions of high politics that seemed especially to preoccupy an older breed of scholars. Sometimes aided by practices or concepts developed by social scientists or cultural theorists, historians have sought to bring social dimensions of empire more plainly into view. Specialists in the history of particular colonized regions and peoples, often far removed from imperial metropoles, have led the way in focusing attention on how empire transformed local economies or social practices.[2] Many historians have taken up the challenge to produce a more ethnographically precise picture of the people who did the colonizing.[3] There is broad understanding, too, of

---

[1] *Decline and Fall* was first published between 1776 and 1788.
[2] For a recent example by one pioneering scholar, see Vansina (2010).
[3] The challenge was laid down especially influentially in Stoler and Cooper (1997).

the way that developments 'on the ground' could be shaped by dominant discourses relating to categorizations of human difference such as race, gender and class.

'Difference', as many historians of empire have noted, is a concept that must stand close to the centre of any consideration of how modern empires operated. Empires were inherently diverse spaces – territorially, demographically and culturally – but they were premised on a relationship of dominance. This dominance was often demonstrated at the outset by some display of military force. Yet the initial conquest frequently proved to be the easy part of empire. To translate dominance into the institution of effective and stable regimes, empire-builders had to develop techniques to manage the diversity around them (and of which they themselves represented a new component). Divide-and-rule tactics might work for a time, and differentiating ideologies such as racial thought might influence the fashioning of social hierarchies. But lived experience ran the risk of exposing the hollowness of imperialist claims to mastery over colonized peoples, while even the most self-confident and well-resourced colonialists knew that they needed some local help for their rule to work at all. The problem, then, became how to sustain a rule that was necessarily collaborative without undermining the authority and distinctiveness of the rulers, or building up indigenous elites to a level that might threaten the integrity of the empire itself.[4]

M.K. Gandhi asserted in 1909 (and innumerable times thereafter) that India's imperial overlords were not as powerful as they wanted their subjects to think, and nor were Indians so weak; thus the British were 'not in India because of their strength, but because we keep them' (1997, p. 39). Gandhi notwithstanding, anti-colonial nationalist historiography, which had its own reasons for emphasizing the heroism of counter-imperial struggles, did not allow much space for an image of modern imperialists as relatively weak. A historiographical trend in recent decades, however, has involved an effort to establish a sense of proportion in terms of what empires either were or were not able to achieve. In India, it is clear that the British truly did possess a considerable coercive apparatus, a function in large part of a military presence that even in peacetime absorbed as much as 40 per cent of India's annual budget (Killingray, 1999, p. 4). But in other parts of the empire, British resources were but a fraction of those available to the rulers of the Raj. In situations where colonizers were trying to enact 'hegemony on a shoestring', in Sara Berry's phrase from Chapter 1, the delegation of power to approved local elites was a virtual necessity. For that reason, one historian characterizes the colonial administrator Frederick Lugard's famous elaboration of the principles of 'indirect rule' in Northern Nigeria as 'a rationalization of comparative impotence' (Burroughs, 1999, p. 196).[5] It should be emphasized that to say imperial rulers could not organize a given territory in the way they wanted is not at all to suggest they had no impact. As Berry shows, even plans and structures developed 'on a shoestring' could institute novel political formations and generate new social conflicts (see also Spear, 2003). But many of the essays in this collection do reinforce the now commonplace view that the social history of empires is to some extent a story of interaction or 'negotiation' between ostensibly stronger and weaker parties. Though empires were coercive and exacting, the history of empires is by no means a straightforward story of 'organizers' and 'organized'.

---

[4]   Stimulating discussions of imperial problems of 'difference' may be found in Barkey (2008, ch. 1), Cooper (2005, ch. 1) and Metcalf (1995).

[5]   The best study of how modern empires ruled through indigenous leaders is Newbury (2003).

Land and Labour

The opening section of this volume groups essays that address fundamental determinants of social organization: the ways people attempt to provide for themselves, their families and their communities, and the uses made of different environments. In terms of land and labour, it could be argued that the age of modern empires did not offer any innovation more dramatic than an earlier imperial era's plantation complex and long-distance trade in slaves from Africa. As Robin Law has pointed out, the abolitionist movement that attacked this system in the nineteenth century could itself be seen as 'inherently imperialist', insofar as it 'implicitly asserted a supposed responsibility and right of Europeans' to determine Africa's future, and relied on 'coercion and intimidation of other states' to help make the end of the trade a reality (2010, p. 150). If the suppression of the Atlantic Slave Trade reflected European self-confidence, however, hesitation to tackle the institution of slavery within colonized territories often stemmed from the perception that such a change could spark conflict with local elites and reveal Europeans' weakness. It was for this reason that when substantial numbers of slaves in French West Africa began to leave their masters in 1905, the reaction of French republican administrators was nervously 'ambivalent' (Roberts and Klein, 1980, p. 388; see also Klein, 1998).

Modern empires nonetheless proved adept at mobilizing labour for their own needs. The Dutch 'cultivation system' for the production of sugar in nineteenth-century Java, as discussed in Chapter 2 by R.E. Elson, and Portuguese forced cotton cultivation in Mozambique a century later, documented by Allen Isaacman and Arlindo Chilundo in Chapter 3, both depended on brute force against local populations (see also Bosma *et al.*, 2007; Isaacman and Roberts, 1995). In other instances the labour was brought from further afield. Workers on fixed-term contracts – notably Indians, of whom over 1.3 million signed contracts of indenture from the 1830s to the 1920s – filled the demand for plantation labour from the Caribbean and the Guianas to South Africa and islands in the Indian and Pacific oceans (Northrup, 1995, pp. 156–57).[6] Commenting in 1901 on the development of the Assam tea industry, India's viceroy, Lord Curzon, described indenture as 'an abnormal system' that could nonetheless be tolerated as part of an 'effort to open up by capital and industry the resources of a distant and backward province' (quoted in Behal, 2010, p. 31). The 'abnormality' of much colonial labour organization flowed from the differential treatment of colonial workers compared with their counterparts in colonial metropoles. Such could be said of the notoriously severe disciplinary regime imposed on rubber plantation workers in French Indochina or the way that master-and-servant laws affording minimal protection to employees were introduced in British territories like Kenya several decades after similar laws had been scrapped as unacceptable for British labour. Moreover, though these types of organization may have stemmed from economic considerations, racial ideologies were often close at hand to shape and provide justification for interactions on the ground between workers, employers and magistrates (Anderson, 2000; Brocheux, 1975; Hay and Craven, 2004).

Though colonial powers were prepared in many cases to deploy much more than verbal persuasion as they introduced forms of production that they hoped would make their territories profitable, the success or failure of agricultural change was rarely if ever entirely in their

---

[6] For a different type of labour migration, see Yang (2003) and Carter and Bates (2010).

hands. In West Africa, for example, the expansion of groundnut production in Senegal or cocoa in the Gold Coast and Ivory Coast highlight the fact that as often as not the 'cash-crop revolution' of the late nineteenth and early twentieth centuries depended on the willingness of indigenous producers to take risks with new forms of cultivation, while top-down schemes like the French effort to make the French Soudan a major cotton exporter were liable to fail miserably if they could not attract local support (Austin, 2009; Groff, 1987; Roberts, 1996). Much the same point could be made of territories where there was substantial European settlement. In French Algeria, for example, several government attempts to promote cash crops failed before settlers took it upon themselves to plant vineyards on a massive scale and thereby brought unprecedented investment capital to the colony. That Algeria became for a time the third-biggest wine producer in the world was in spite of some of the colony's founding figures, who had warned that Algeria should not develop products that might place it in competition with metropolitan France (Isnard, 1951/54, vol. 2, pp. 11–28).

For the French statesman Jules Ferry, writing in 1892, Algeria's vineyards – despite their location within a Muslim-majority territory – represented 'the peaceful and permanent seizure of the African land in the name of France' (1892, p. 8).[7] He was being far too optimistic, of course: most of the vineyards, let alone the million-strong European settler population, did not remain for long after Algerian independence in 1962. But, if the imperial presence was not permanent, colonial regimes certainly left their mark on the environments they encountered (Beinart and Hughes, 2007). Sometimes the colonizers exploited natural resources, while at other times they turned towards conservation; but in either case modern empires often over-rated their own knowledge and capacity for mastery, and, whether they knew what they were doing or not, their actions had social effects. Thus French scientists in Morocco, seeing themselves as heirs to the Romans, founded part of their environmental policy on a belief that the control of local nomadic populations was a prerequisite for making the deserts bloom again (the deserts did no such thing) (Davis, 2005). British irrigation schemes in India were genuinely transformative, yet explicitly took place at the expense of 'troublesome' pastoralists, damaged some apparently successful indigenous forms of water management and stubbornly failed to eradicate famine (Beinart and Hughes, 2007, pp. 133–39; D'Souza, 2006; Gilmartin, 1994). In Chapter 4, Thaddeus Sunseri describes how a German desire to control and conserve forest resources in East Africa ran up against long-standing local practices and unwittingly fed a serious rebellion against colonial rule.

Such resistance was always a risk as colonialists conjured with the new spaces before them. In Chapter 5, Warwick Anderson observes that in a region with an unusually low population density like northern Australia it did not seem unreasonable to dream of a world reserved for whites. Plans to re-imagine space in urban settings, however, were liable to be much more fraught. In an intensely mixed urban environment like that of Zanzibar, the idea of socially or racially segregated space (justified, as in Australia, on grounds of public health) remained an impractical idea for an under-resourced colonial government, as William Bissell points out in Chapter 6. Colonial planners in Singapore, meanwhile, found that they could not so easily redevelop burial grounds as their counterparts in European cities had done in previous decades. As Brenda Yeoh explains in Chapter 7, instead they encountered a culturally unfamiliar notion of 'sacred' space that forced municipal authorities into a period

---

[7] For the French impact on the land, see Heffernan and Sutton (1991).

of negotiation and compromise with the various Chinese communities in the city. In short, to think like the journalist who in 1911 described Australia as 'a big blank map' (p. 138 this volume) was a luxury that most colonial rulers quickly realized they could not afford.

Mechanisms of Rule

Modern empires nonetheless had to make their control effective. As demonstrated by the essays in the second section of this volume, the builders of empire deployed numerous strategies towards that end. Encouraging settlement was one possibility. If the home country could not supply a sufficient quantity of settlers, then migrants from other countries might do. Levels of out-migration from nineteenth-century France did not match those from other European countries, so 'French Algeria' made up the shortfall with a mix that included substantial numbers of Spanish, Italians and Maltese (Smith, 2006, pp. 66–71). Curiously, as Eugene Rogan documents in Chapter 8, a number of Algerians displaced by the French conquest found their way to Jordan, where Ottoman authorities hoped that these migrants might help secure and develop what at the time was a tenuously controlled frontier territory. The case of late nineteenth- and early twentieth-century Jordan, indeed, underlines the salience of the historiographical trend to incorporate the Ottoman experience alongside more familiar European histories of empire (Mikhail and Philliou, 2012). The decision of Ottoman leaders to build new roads, railways and telegraph lines in Jordan mirrored the developmental approach that French empire-builders at the time called *mise en valeur* and tied to the broader notion of a 'mission to civilize' (cf. Conklin, 1997 and Deringil, 2003).

The overall rationality of colonial development can often appear obscure, unless one reduces it to the lowest common denominator of the imperative to dominate. Thus in Vietnam the French operated an alcohol monopoly that produced minimal net revenue but, as Gerard Sasges explains in Chapter 9, the invasive apparatus required to enforce it served a logic of control over local communities quite effectively. Elsewhere in the French Empire at the same time, one governor determined to impose his will on the territory he ruled was following a broadly similar rationale in promoting not alcohol consumption but temperance, even though on the surface this stood to undercut the colonial state's tax receipts (White, 2007). Such examples help to underline the fact that there was very often a close connection between colonialist economic initiatives and attempts at social organization. Taxation itself, especially in the form of direct taxes, was perceived by colonial governors as a means to shape social behaviour – for example by inculcating desirable work habits and simply placing colonial subjects in a more direct relationship to colonial authority – as much as an instrument of economic transformation (Bush and Maltby, 2004).

Attempts at transformation of any kind required indigenous assistance. For their initial conquests and subsequent security, modern empire-builders relied on troops found mostly in territories they had already conquered but sometimes from outside their boundaries, as in the case of the Gurkhas who first impressed the British with their resistance in the Anglo-Nepali War of 1814–16. The great Indian rebellion that began with a mutiny among units of the Bengal Army in 1857 made recruitment strategy a subject of urgent importance, as David Omissi notes in Chapter 10, in the very same year (though entirely coincidentally) that a governor eager to expand French rule in West Africa secured official approval for a new military corps called the Senegalese *tirailleurs*. Class (or caste) was a key factor in these colonial armies; the British became especially wary of enlisting higher-caste Brahmins after the rebellion, for example, while many of the West African *tirailleurs* were former slaves or of slave status, contributing to a negative image of the corps in local society (Echenberg, 1991, p. 18; Mann, 2006). But recruitment decisions came to be influenced particularly strongly by racial ideology, as colonial powers formulated notions about 'martial races' that valorized the qualities of supposedly more 'hardy' (as well as more 'masculine') peoples like the Sikhs of the Punjab (Lunn, 1999; Streets, 2004).

Such divide-and-rule strategies, of course, could easily foster wounded feelings of exclusion among certain groups. Yet colonialists were often unsure how far they could trust the loyalty even of those they rewarded. Individual colonial administrators tended not to remain in any one post for long, and were accordingly prone to knowledge deficits in terms of local politics and local languages. Especially in areas with a sparse imperial presence, this sometimes allowed room for locally recruited intermediaries – interpreters, clerks, scribes – to find a role that went beyond their subordinate job descriptions, as Emily Osborn illustrates in Chapter 11 (see also Jeater, 2001; Lawrance *et al.*, 2006).

Colonial law opened up further arenas of contestation, sometimes in a way that held out the possibility of gains for less powerful members of society. But when colonial administrators aimed to uphold what they understood to be indigenous law they were liable, even if unwittingly, to become the instruments of local interests.[8] In the early decades of British rule in Southern Rhodesia, for example, as documented by Elizabeth Schmidt in Chapter 12, some African women and girls benefited from European administrators' squeamishness about allowing practices such as forcible marriage to be legally permissible on the basis of 'custom'. Over time, however, the colonialists' concern to avoid alienating local male elders influenced them to restore the patriarchal basis for what became codified as 'customary law'. The subject of law and empire is a complex one and naturally varies from place to place and empire to empire. The legal protection that backed the Russian Empire's ascription of rights to different ethnic and religious communities, for instance, allowed imperial subjects 'to decide some matters of local but significant importance with the sanction of the state' (Burbank, 2006, p. 400; see also Crews, 2004). In matters that directly implicated the authority of the colonialists themselves, however, colonial law could appear little more than an arbitrary and self-serving instrument of rule. Legal regimes for colonial subjects like the Portuguese *indigenato* or the French *indigénat* – under which an administrator could send a subject to jail for 'any act of a nature to weaken respect for French authority' – were, as Gregory Mann puts it, 'perhaps the most important element of the administrative tool kit' (2009, p. 334). When Europeans committed crimes in colonial territories, meanwhile, their punishments (if convicted) rarely matched those meted out to colonial subjects for similar offences (Bailkin, 2006).

Colonial disciplinary techniques had a tendency, whether under the influence of racial thinking or a simple lack of resources, to lump and consolidate groups of people the colonialists considered threatening. The British in India, for example, identified so-called 'criminal tribes', whose members they registered and whose movements they restricted (Metcalf,

---

[8] For a good introduction, see Roberts and Mann (1991).

1995, pp. 122–25). In French Vietnam, most prisoners were incarcerated indiscriminately in crowded communal cells, even though it eventually became clear that this 'facilitated conspiratorial plotting among inmates' and helped to spread radical anti-colonial ideologies (Zinoman, 2001, p. 157). This type of aggregating strategy, which implicitly rested on the denial of individual rights, found a particular application as colonial regimes confronted armed opposition. As Iain Smith and Andreas Stucki note in Chapter 13, the concentration of civilians in camps was first applied in Spanish Cuba but the method would be a feature of colonial wars for decades to come, from South Africa at the start of the twentieth century through to Malaya, Kenya and Algeria in the 1950s and 1960s. In Chapter 14, Maryinez Lyons describes how the same principle of sweeping measures for whole populations led to the creation of a *cordon sanitaire* covering about 300,000 square kilometres of the northern Congo, as agents of first the Congo Free State and then the Belgian Congo tackled trypanosomiasis or sleeping sickness. This type of civilian concentration seemed if anything to make the problem worse, while the drug atoxyl that doctors forcibly administered to the sick turned many Africans blind.[9]

Strategies of concentration and confinement were attempts to manage the emanations of a world on the move. Modern empires were themselves responsible for much of this movement, for example as a consequence (as we have seen) of their labour needs in different parts of the world; modern forms of transportation speeded the process. This imperially contoured globalization forged new paths for the spread of disease, as in the case of the plague pandemic that hit ports around the world after 1894 (Beinart and Hughes, 2007, pp. 167–83; Echenberg, 2007). The Muslim *hajj*, or pilgrimage to Mecca, was another impetus to movement, and one that imperial powers whose territories contained substantial numbers of Muslims came in the nineteenth century to see as a source of concern – notably as a vector for 'Asiatic' cholera, but also for potentially dangerous ideas such as pan-Islamic ideology, as discussed by William Roff in Chapter 15. European interest in the *hajj*, however, also extended to the desire to make money from all of this movement. Surveillance worked especially well for a country like Britain, which placed itself in a better position to take advantage of the Ottoman Empire's crumbling position in the Middle East while helping at the same time to secure the profits of European shipping companies (Low, 2008; Miller, 2006).

The Social World of Empire

The essays in the final part of the volume allow us to develop a fuller understanding of the way modern empires' strategies of differentiation shaped human interaction. We have already seen that the imperial recruitment of workers and soldiers often drew on the perception that some populations were inherently more valuable (or more compliant) than others. But European racial ideologies then had the effect of magnifying and sustaining differences among subject groups. In Chapter 16, for example, Charles Hirschman shows that the multiethnic composition of the population of the modern nation of Malaysia has its roots in an imperial drive to maximize the production of commodities such as tin and rubber, but racial ideas then

---

[9] For more on scientific interventions in colonial settings, see, for example, Tilley (2011).

structured relations among the Malay, Chinese and Indian populations in ways that remain relevant to the present.

Colonizers were also constantly defining and redefining the boundaries of their own community. Europeans were conscious of being 'islands of white' in all but the most extensively settled territories, but race was not the only factor that influenced the way colonial societies organized themselves. Class-based prejudices, for example, determined to a significant degree the membership of the clubs that provided a focus for European social life in places like British India, just as they did in similar institutions 'back home'. The particular circumstances of colonial society, however, led sometimes to arrangements that were much less common in the metropole. Thus a concern not to abandon European women to the company of native servants encouraged their inclusion, albeit with restrictions, in previously male-dominated social spaces. Moreover, while many who belonged to associations like the Freemasons would have preferred to maintain the ethnic homogeneity of their membership, imperial 'civilizing' ideals and metropolitan Masons' insistence on making the Masonic ideal of fraternity a reality made it possible for increasing numbers of Indians to join lodges from the late nineteenth century (Bickers, 2010; Harland-Jacobs, 2007; Kennedy, 1987; Sinha, 2001).

What came to seem a special preoccupation of virtually all colonial regimes was 'respectability'. The precise content of this concern varied from place to place; at times, for example, the focus was on groups like European paupers or vagrants, who might undermine colonial claims to racial superiority. To a remarkable degree, however, anxieties about the successful maintenance of colonial rule revolved around sex. In some earlier colonial settings – the North American fur trade is the classic example – relations between European men and local women formed part of a complex negotiation of access to resources (see, for example, Whaley, 2007). Even in a more settled and 'conventional' colonial situation, as late as the 1850s a French governor of Senegal lived openly and fathered a child with a young African woman. Such arrangements, of course, do not demonstrate an absence of racial thinking, much less an egalitarian approach to women.[10] Yet they do provide a contrast to the generalized concern that emerged among colonial regimes by the early twentieth century to attempt to regulate sex as an increasingly crucial element of 'the politics of Empire' (Levine, 2004, p. 134). The new norm, as prescribed in guides to correct colonial behaviour, promoted a sort of bourgeois domesticity founded on a clear racial hierarchy, with European women cast in the role of both moral guardians of imperial 'prestige' and the needy objects of European male protection, as Ann Stoler illustrates in Chapter 17. The existence of people of ethnically mixed parentage served as one reminder, however, that this was a difficult norm to uphold, and that colonial social boundaries were always shifting and permeable (Clancy-Smith and Gouda, 1998; Stoler, 2002; White, 1999).

The study of sexuality in colonial contexts is just one of the ways that gender has become an especially productive interest among historians of empire. It is a theme, of course, that cuts across many of the essays in this volume, from the way the Portuguese demand for cotton reshaped the gender-based division of labour in Mozambique, to the response of women in Southern Rhodesia to new social influences, to the discursive gendering of whole peoples as 'masculine' or 'effeminate' (see Chapters 3, 10 and 12; see also Sinha, 1995). There was often a

---

[10] Ghosh (2006) cautions, for example, against viewing early colonial India as a sort of 'golden age' of easy mixture before a hardening of social and racial boundaries.

direct line between such gendered constructions and attempts to influence social organization. The campaign that developed in Britain against *sati*, or widow-burning, in India figured Hindu women as in need of the kind of protection that only a more socially interventionist colonial power could deliver; when the practice was banned in 1829 it made a statement that British notions of civilization should assert themselves and not cower before the possibility of local opposition (Hall, 2004, pp. 52–54). In Chapter 18, Barbara Ramusack reveals how efforts to influence the lives of Indian women from afar continued into the twentieth century through the work of individuals like the British MP Eleanor Rathbone, who well before her sole brief visit to India decided to campaign for a higher minimum age of marriage for Indian women.

Reformers like Rathbone, as well as other British women who developed a commitment to the status of Indian women, could be seen as players in what we might now call 'culture wars'. Modern empires, indeed, set the stage for a potentially limitless range of cultural conflicts as peoples who often had a very limited understanding of each other now found themselves in close contact. Sometimes colonialists in effect chose to cause cultural offence, as in the decision of the British in Burma never to remove their shoes when entering a Buddhist pagoda: they knew the outrage this caused, but decided that the need to act like rulers took precedence over hurt feelings. At other times the offence was inadvertent: the zoo the British opened in Rangoon in 1906 seemed to them a fine addition to a modern city, whereas for Burmese Buddhists the very concept of putting animals behind bars was appalling (Cangi, 1997, p. 89). But colonial interventions in the religious or cultural sphere sometimes worked. The idea that an early twentieth-century British architect could design mosques in a fanciful 'Indo-Saracenic' style that had no precedents in local architecture might be judged a plan with a poor chance of success, yet A.B. Hubback's Masjid Jamek in Kuala Lumpur and Masjid Ubadiah in Kuala Kangsar were embraced and remain integral to the religious landscape of modern-day Malaysia (Metcalf, 2007, pp. 56–67).

Religion, in fact, often developed in unpredictable ways under modern empires. The Russian state, for example, accepted and protected the religious diversity of an empire that contained more Muslims even than the Ottoman Empire. The tsarist regime's desire to avoid conflict, however, led it to promote 'orthodoxy' within its various religious communities, and as Robert Crews explains in Chapter 19, an imperial power that took an ostensibly 'neutral' religious stance thereby ended up having quite an impact on religion itself. In Chapter 20, James Daughton considers the case of the French in 1880s Indochina. French governments after 1870 mostly took a secular view of how best to organize colonial territories, yet despite deeply held suspicion among many republicans about the loyalties of missionaries they often had little option but to make use of them in 'civilizing' works such as education and medical care. Missionaries, moving beyond national and colonial boundaries as members of multinational religious organizations, by no means guaranteed to work with colonial administrations, remaining for prolonged periods in colonial territories yet generally standing at some remove from the colonizers' social worlds, truly were a wild card in relation to empire, sometimes to the degree that they seem to have been building empires of their own (Cox, 2008; Daughton, 2006; Etherington, 2005; White and Daughton, 2012).

As the example of missionaries makes clear, any conception of colonial society that rests on neatly bounded categories of 'rulers' and 'ruled' does not adequately reflect the lived reality of empire. Jun Uchida, in Chapter 21, presents the case of Japanese settler children in Korea, who provide a good example of a relatively privileged group of people, educated with a view to maintaining their identity as rulers, who nonetheless frequently came to feel caught between the demands of loyalty to the mother country and their emotional attachment to the place they lived (see also Caprio, 2009). In an earlier century, Europe's empires in the Americas had been brought down by such people. We do not refer to the Japanese born in Korea or Europeans born in Algeria as 'creoles' (though in the latter case the term *pied-noir* perhaps hints in that direction); nor do twentieth-century empires provide any real equivalents to Simón Bolívar, Miguel Hidalgo or George Washington.[11] But perhaps this was only a matter of time, or a consequence of events like the Second World War, which brought Japan's empire to such an abrupt end. Of course the subjective experience of empire differed greatly for Koreans. Far from the nostalgia felt by former Japanese settlers, Korean memories of insult and violence make the history of empire a subject of peculiar sensitivity to the present.

This collection aims not only to inform readers about a complex and crucial topic in modern world history, but also to inspire further contributions that will enhance our understanding of what Edward Gibbon recognized so long ago as one of the defining dramas of human existence.

References

Anderson, David M. (2000), 'Master and Servant in Colonial Kenya, 1895–1939', *Journal of African History*, **41**, 3, pp. 459–85.

Austin, Gareth (2009), 'Cash Crops and Freedom: Export Agriculture and the Decline of Slavery in Colonial West Africa', *International Review of Social History*, **54**, 1, pp. 1–37.

Bailkin, Jordanna (2006), 'The Boot and the Spleen: When was Murder Possible in British India?', *Comparative Studies in Society and History*, **48**, 2, pp. 462–93.

Barkey, Karen (2008), *Empire of Difference: The Ottomans in Comparative Perspective*, Cambridge: Cambridge University Press.

Behal, Rana (2010), 'Coolie Drivers or Benevolent Paternalists? British Tea Planters in Assam and the Indenture Labour System', *Modern Asian Studies*, **44**, 1, pp. 29–51.

Beinart, William and Hughes, Lotte (2007), *Environment and Empire*, Oxford: Oxford University Press.

Bickers, Robert (ed.) (2010), *Settlers and Expatriates: Britons over the Seas*, Oxford: Oxford University Press.

Bosma, Ulbe, Giusti-Cordero, Juan and Knight, G. Roger (eds) (2007), *Sugarlandia Revisited: Sugar and Colonialism in Asia and the Americas, 1800 to 1940*, New York: Berghahn.

Brocheux, Pierre (1975), 'Le prolétariat des plantations d'hévéas au Vietnam méridional: aspects sociaux et politiques (1927–1937)', *Mouvement Social*, **90**, pp. 55–86.

Burbank, Jane (2006), 'An Imperial Rights Regime: Law and Citizenship in the Russian Empire', *Kritika: Explorations in Russian and Eurasian History*, **7**, 3, pp. 397–431.

Burroughs, Peter (1999), 'Imperial Institutions and the Government of Empire', in Andrew Porter (ed.), *The Oxford History of the British Empire*, Vol. 3: *The Nineteenth Century*, Oxford: Oxford University Press.

---

[11] The Afrikaner leader Jan Smuts might represent one counter-argument to this proposition.

Bush, Barbara and Maltby, Josephine (2004), 'Taxation in West Africa: Transforming the Colonial Subject into the "Governable Person"', *Critical Perspectives on Accounting*, **15**, 1, pp. 5–34.

Cangi, Ellen Corwin (1997), *Faded Splendour, Golden Past: Urban Images of Burma*, Kuala Lumpur: Oxford University Press.

Caprio, Mark E. (2009), *Japanese Assimilation Policies in Colonial Korea, 1910–1945*, Seattle: University of Washington Press.

Carter, Marina and Bates, Crispin (2010), 'Empire and Locality: A Global Dimension to the 1857 Indian Uprising', *Journal of Global History*, **3**, 1, pp. 51–73.

Clancy-Smith, Julia and Gouda, Frances (eds) (1998), *Domesticating the Empire: Race, Gender, and Family Life in French and Dutch Colonialism*, Charlottesville: University of Virginia Press.

Conklin, Alice L. (1997), *A Mission to Civilize: The Republican Idea of Empire in France and West Africa, 1895–1930*, Stanford, CA: Stanford University Press.

Cooper, Frederick (2005), *Colonialism in Question: Theory, Knowledge, History*, Berkeley: University of California Press.

Cox, Jeffrey (2008), *The British Missionary Enterprise since 1700*, New York: Routledge.

Crews, Robert D. (2004), 'Islamic Law, Imperial Order: Muslims, Jews, and the Russian State', *Ab Imperio*, no. 3, pp. 467–90.

Daughton, J.P. (2006), *An Empire Divided: Religion, Republicanism, and the Making of French Colonialism, 1880–1914*, Oxford: Oxford University Press.

Davis, Diana K. (2005), 'Potential Forests: Degradation Narratives, Science, and Environmental Policy in Protectorate Morocco, 1912–1956', *Environmental History*, **10**, 2, pp. 211–38.

Deringil, Selim (2003), '"They Live in a State of Nomadism and Savagery": The Late Ottoman Empire and the Post-Colonial Debate', *Comparative Studies in Society and History*, **45**, 2, pp. 311–42.

D'Souza, Rohan (2006), 'Water in British India: The Making of a "Colonial Hydrology"', *History Compass*, **4**, 4, pp. 621–28.

Echenberg, Myron (1991), *Colonial Conscripts: The Tirailleurs Sénégalais in French West Africa, 1857–1960*, Portsmouth, NH: Heinemann.

Echenberg, Myron (2007), *Plague Ports: The Global Urban Impact of Bubonic Plague, 1894–1901*, New York: New York University Press.

Etherington, Norman (ed.) (2005), *Missions and Empire*, Oxford: Oxford University Press.

Ferry, Jules (1892), *Le gouvernement de l'Algérie*, Paris: Armand Colin.

Gandhi, M.K. (1997), *Hind Swaraj and Other Writings*, ed. Anthony J. Parel, Cambridge: Cambridge University Press.

Ghosh, Durba (2006), *Sex and the Family in Colonial India: The Making of Empire*, Cambridge: Cambridge University Press.

Gibbon, Edward (1764), *An Essay on the Study of Literature*, London: T. Becket and P.A. De Hondt (first published in French in 1761).

Gibbon, Edward (1901), *The History of the Decline and Fall of the Roman Empire*, ed. J.B. Bury (7 vols), London: Methuen.

Gilmartin, David (1994), 'Scientific Empire and Imperial Science: Colonialism and Irrigation Technology in the Indus Basin', *Journal of Asian Studies*, **53**, 4, pp. 1127–49.

Groff, David H. (1987), 'Carrots, Sticks, and Cocoa Pods: African and Administrative Initiatives in the Spread of Cocoa Cultivation in Assikasso, Ivory Coast, 1908–1920', *International Journal of African Historical Studies*, **20**, 3, pp. 401–16.

Hall, Catherine (2004), 'Of Gender and Empire: Reflections on the Nineteenth Century', in Philippa Levine (ed.), *Gender and Empire*, Oxford: Oxford University Press, pp. 46–76.

Harland-Jacobs, Jessica (2007), *Builders of Empire: Freemasonry and British Imperialism, 1717–1927*, Chapel Hill: University of North Carolina Press.

Hay, Douglas and Craven, Paul (eds) (2004), *Masters, Servants, and Magistrates in Britain and the Empire, 1562–1955*, Chapel Hill: University of North Carolina Press.

Heffernan, Michael J. and Sutton, Keith (1991), 'The Landscape of Colonialism: The Impact of French Colonial Rule on the Algerian Rural Settlement Pattern, 1830–1987', in Christopher Dixon and Michael Heffernan (eds), *Colonialism and Development in the Contemporary World*, London: Mansell, pp. 121–52.

Isaacman, Allen and Roberts, Richard (eds) (1995), *Cotton, Colonialism, and Social History in Sub-Saharan Africa*, Portsmouth, NH: Heinemann.

Isnard, H. (1951/54), *La vigne en Algérie: étude géographique* (2 vols), Gap: Ophrys.

Jeater, Diana (2001), 'Speaking Like a Native: Vernacular Languages and the State in Southern Rhodesia, 1890–1935', *Journal of African History*, **42**, 3, pp. 449–68.

Kennedy, Dane (1987), *Islands of White: Settler Society and Culture in Kenya and Southern Rhodesia, 1890–1939*, Durham, NC: Duke University Press.

Killingray, David (1999), 'Guardians of Empire', in David Killingray and David Omissi (eds), *Guardians of Empire: The Armed Forces of the Colonial Powers, c. 1700–1964*, Manchester: Manchester University Press, pp. 1–24.

Klein, Martin A. (1998), *Slavery and Colonial Rule in French West Africa*, Cambridge: Cambridge University Press.

Law, Robin (2010), 'Abolition and Imperialism: International Law and the British Suppression of the Atlantic Slave Trade', in Derek R. Peterson (ed.), *Abolitionism and Imperialism in Britain, Africa, and the Atlantic*, Athens: Ohio University Press, pp. 150–74.

Lawrance, Benjamin N., Osborn, Emily Lynn and Roberts, Richard L. (eds) (2006), *Intermediaries, Interpreters, and Clerks: African Employees in the Making of Colonial Africa*, Madison: University of Wisconsin Press.

Levine, Philippa (2004), 'Sexuality, Gender, and Empire', in Philippa Levine (ed.), *Gender and Empire*, Oxford: Oxford University Press, pp. 134–55.

Low, Michael Christopher (2008), 'Empire and the Hajj: Pilgrims, Plagues, and Pan-Islam under British Surveillance, 1865–1908', *International Journal of Middle East Studies*, **40**, 2, pp. 269–90.

Lunn, Joe (1999), '"Les Races Guerrières": Racial Preconceptions in the French Military about West Africans during the First World War', *Journal of Contemporary History*, **34**, 4, pp. 517–36.

Mann, Gregory (2006), *Native Sons: West African Veterans and France in the Twentieth Century*, Durham, NC: Duke University Press.

Mann, Gregory (2009), 'What was the *Indigénat*? The "Empire of Law" in French West Africa', *Journal of African History*, **50**, 3 pp. 331–53.

Metcalf, Thomas R. (1995), *Ideologies of the Raj*, Cambridge: Cambridge University Press.

Metcalf, Thomas R. (2007), *Imperial Connections: India in the Indian Ocean Arena, 1860–1920*, Berkeley: University of California Press.

Mikhail, Alan and Philliou, Christine M. (2012), 'The Ottoman Empire and the Imperial Turn', *Comparative Studies in Society and History*, **54**, 4, pp. 721–45.

Miller, Michael B. (2006), 'Pilgrims' Progress: The Business of the Hajj', *Past and Present*, **191**, pp. 189–228.

Newbury, Colin (2003), *Patrons, Clients, and Empire: Chieftaincy and Over-rule in Asia, Africa, and the Pacific*, Oxford: Oxford University Press.

Northrup, David (1995), *Indentured Labor in the Age of Imperialism, 1834–1922*, Cambridge: Cambridge University Press.

Roberts, Richard L. (1996), *Two Worlds of Cotton: Colonialism and the Regional Economy in the French Soudan, 1800–1946*, Stanford, CA: Stanford University Press.

Roberts, Richard and Mann, Kristin (1991), 'Law in Colonial Africa', in Richard Roberts and Kristin Mann (eds), *Law in Colonial Africa*, Portsmouth, NH: Heinemann, pp. 1–58.

Roberts, Richard and Klein, Martin A. (1980), 'The Banamba Slave Exodus of 1905 and the Decline of Slavery in the Western Sudan', *Journal of African History*, **21**, 3, pp. 379–94.

Sinha, Mrinalinhi (1995), *Colonial Masculinity: The 'Manly Englishman' and the 'Effeminate Bengali' in the Late Nineteenth Century*, Manchester: Manchester University Press.

Sinha, Mrinalinhi (2001), 'Britishness, Clubbability, and the Colonial Public Sphere: The Genealogy of an Imperial Institution in Colonial India', *Journal of British Studies*, **40**, 4, pp. 489–521.

Smith, Andrea L. (2006), *Colonial Memory and Postcolonial Europe: Maltese Settlers in Algeria and France*, Bloomington: Indiana University Press.

Spear, Thomas (2003), 'Neo-Traditionalism and the Limits of Invention in British Colonial Africa', *Journal of African History*, **44**, 1, pp. 3–27.

Stoler, Ann Laura (2002), *Carnal Knowledge and Imperial Power: Race and the Intimate in Colonial Rule*, Berkeley: University of California Press.

Stoler, Ann Laura and Cooper, Frederick (1997), 'Between Metropole and Colony: Rethinking a Research Agenda', in Frederick Cooper and Ann Laura Stoler (eds), *Tensions of Empire: Colonial Cultures in a Bourgeois World*, Berkeley: University of California Press, pp. 1–56.

Streets, Heather (2004), *Martial Races: The Military, Race, and Masculinity in British Imperial Culture, 1857–1914*, Manchester: Manchester University Press.

Tilley, Helen (2011), *Africa as a Living Laboratory: Empire, Development, and the Problem of Scientific Knowledge*, Chicago: University of Chicago Press.

Vansina, Jan (2010), *Being Colonized: The Kuba Experience in Rural Congo, 1880–1960*, Madison: University of Wisconsin Press.

Whaley, Gray (2007), '"Complete Liberty"? Gender, Sexuality, Race, and Social Change on the Lower Columbia River, 1805–1838', *Ethnohistory*, **54**, 4, pp. 669–95.

White, Owen (1999), *Children of the French Empire: Miscegenation and Colonial Society in French West Africa, 1895–1960*, Oxford: Oxford University Press.

White, Owen (2007), 'Drunken States: Temperance and French Rule in Côte d'Ivoire, 1908–1916', *Journal of Social History*, **40**, 3, pp. 663–84.

White, Owen and Daughton, J.P. (eds) (2012), *In God's Empire: French Missionaries and the Modern World*, Oxford: Oxford University Press.

Yang, Anand (2003), 'Indian Convict Workers in Southeast Asia in the Late Eighteenth and Early Nineteenth Centuries', *Journal of World History*, **14**, 2, pp. 179–208.

Zinoman, Peter (2001), *The Colonial Bastille: A History of Imprisonment in Vietnam, 1862–1940*, Berkeley: University of California Press.

Part I
Land and Labour

[1]

HEGEMONY ON A SHOESTRING: INDIRECT RULE AND ACCESS TO AGRICULTURAL LAND

Sara Berry

Struggles over access to and control of land have a long history in sub-Saharan Africa. For a long time, cultivable land was regarded by students of African economic and agrarian history as abundant and therefore immune from both market competition and political conflict. Recent scholarship suggests that this view is oversimplified. Since precolonial times, Africans have attached both material and symbolic significance to land, and rights in land have been exchanged, negotiated and fought over in the course of political and religious as well as demographic and economic change. This article will examine changing patterns of struggle over access to and the meaning of land rights during the early decades of colonial rule, when Africans' relations to land and to each other were being reshaped both by the process of colonial domination and by the accelerating pace of agricultural commercialisation.

Commercialisation, together with colonial regimes' exactions of taxes, labour, and provisions, increased Africans' demand for land and labour, and intensified their efforts to appropriate a share of the increased flow of income from cash crops and wage employment. Competition over land, labour, and income gave rise, in turn, to struggles over the terms on which people gained access to productive resources and/or controlled both income and processes of production and exchange. Patterns of agricultural commercialisation and conditions of access to land were both, in turn, affected by colonial policies aimed directly at regulating rural economic activity, and by colonial regimes' overall strategies of surplus appropriation and social control. Administrators' efforts to collect taxes, keep order, and mediate disputes shaped the legal and institutional conditions under which farmers sought access to land and labour, whether or not they were explicitly designed for that purpose. The effects of land legislation or of agricultural officers' efforts to introduce new methods of cultivation and animal husbandry must be understood in the context of colonial processes of governance in general.

Recent literature on the colonial state in Africa has attempted to move beyond the dominant liberal and Marxist paradigms of the 1960s and '70s. These paradigms, articulated in part as reactions against the laudatory or apologetic historiography of the colonial era, depicted colonial states as external agents, seeking to govern or exploit African societies according to the interests and political philosophies of European powers. The liberal or neoclassical paradigm portrayed the state as an arbiter of conflicting interest groups, existing outside the social and economic system, and capable of impartial intervention to advance the 'public interest', while Marxist writers played a series of variations on the theme of the state as an executive committee of the metropolitan (or local settler) bourgeoisie. (For reviews of some of this literature see Lonsdale, 1981; Kitching, 1985; Jessop, 1977.)

More recently, several authors have tried to unpack these arguments: to look at the state as a complex institution, made up of individuals and interest groups with diverse links to the societies they seek to govern (see, for example, Bates, 1983; Jessop, 1977; Chazan *et al.*, 1988). Lonsdale and Berman (1979) and Berman and Lonsdale (1980) argued, for example, that the colonial state in Kenya was drawn into increasingly coercive patterns of labour control through officials' efforts to cope with the contradictions of capitalist accumulation in a colonial context. Others have suggested that the state plays several roles, serving as an agent of capitalist or other class interests; as an arbiter of social conflict; and as an arena within which social groups struggle to advance their interests through alliances with elements in the state apparatus (Joseph, 1984; Beinart *et al.*, 1986; Chazan *et al.*, 1988).

Scholars' interest in disaggregating the state, conceptually speaking, has intersected with a growing interest, among students of political economy and social history, in the role of culture in shaping social and economic processes. Colonial rule and capitalist accumulation generated conflicts of interest, among Europeans and Africans as well as between them. The outcome of those conflicts was shaped not only by the material and political resources which different groups could marshal in support of their interests, but also by the terms in which people understood their interests and expressed them (Peters, 1988; Carney, 1988; Carney and Watts, n.d.). Historians such as Beinart (1984), Anderson (1984), and Vaughan (1987) have shown how major events, such as famine or soil erosion, become focuses of multiple explanations which, in turn, shape people's responses to the events themselves. Similarly, Peters (1984), Comaroff (1980), and other anthropologists have explored the role of struggles over meaning in shaping governments' policies and interactions between colonised peoples and colonial regimes. In particular, a growing body of literature has shown that 'customary' laws were not static perpetuations of precolonial norms, but new systems of law and adjudication based on colonial administrators' interpretation of African tradition (Colson, 1971; Moore, 1975, 1986; Ranger, 1983; Chanock, 1985; Snyder, 1981).

The present discussion is intended as a contribution to ongoing efforts to draw these strands of argument together. I will look at the early decades of British colonial rule in Africa, when administrators struggled to establish effective control with extremely limited resources. Scarcity of money and manpower not only obliged administrators to practise 'indirect rule' but also limited their ability to direct the course of political and social change. In effect, I will argue, colonial regimes were unable to impose either English laws and institutions or their own version of 'traditional' African ones on to indigenous societies. Colonial 'inventions' of African tradition (Ranger, 1983) served not so much to define the shape of the colonial social order as to provoke a series of debates over the meaning and application of tradition which in turn shaped struggles over authority and access to resources.

The article is organised in four sections. The first presents my general argument about the impact of colonial rule on conditions of access to agricultural resources. The second describes the kinds of debate which arose under indirect rule over the meaning and uses of 'custom', while the third and fourth illustrate their implications for the organisation of native administration, and for changing conditions of access to land. Examples are drawn from rural areas in four British colonies, selected to reflect different histories of colonial domination and agricultural commercialisation.[1] Because of the time period covered, African countries are referred to by their colonial names.

HEGEMONY ON A SHOESTRING: THE ARGUMENT

As they moved to assert military and political control over most of sub-Saharan Africa, colonial administrators faced from the outset a continual struggle to make ends meet. As self-declared rulers of the African continent, Europeans assumed responsibility for governing extensive territories inhabited by scattered and diverse peoples—a vast and potentially expensive project. The British exchequer was, however, reluctant to subsidise either the recurrent costs or the capital costs of colonial administration (Frankel, 1938; Pim, 1940, 1948; Hailey, 1957: 1307 ff.; Hopkins, 1973: 190–1). Partly because of financial stringency, the number of European personnel posted to colonial administrations was limited, and officials were expected to raise enough revenue from their colonies to cover the costs of administering them. However confidently administrators might share Earl Grey's conviction that 'the surest test for the soundness of measures for the improvement of an uncivilized people is that they should be self-sufficient' (quoted in Pim, 1948: 226) the daily struggle to wrest revenue, labour and provisions from reluctant, hostile or scattered subjects was not an easy one (Asiegbu, 1984; Munro, 1975; cf. Weiskel, 1975).

To live within their means, officials worked both to raise revenue and to keep down the costs of maintaining order and running the day-to-day business of administration. One obvious way to cut costs was to use Africans, both as employees and as local agents of colonial rule. African clerks and chiefs were cheaper than European personnel; also, by integrating existing local authorities and social systems into the structure of colonial government, officials hoped to minimise the disruptive effects of colonial rule (Hailey, 1957). In other words, for reasons of financial and administrative expediency, most colonial regimes in Africa practised indirect rule, whether or not they had articulated it as their philosophy of imperial governance.

Although, over time, colonial administrators did evolve an elaborate set of principles and institutions for formalising the conception and practice of indirect rule, in fact they not only failed to preserve (or restore) stable systems of traditional social order, but actually promoted instability in local structures of authority and conditions of access to productive resources. My argument differs from those of authors who have suggested that European 'inventions' of African tradition served to rigidify jural norms and practices, and hence social structures, in Africa (Chanock, 1985; Ranger, 1983; Snyder, 1981; MacGaffey, 1970).[2] Colonial officials certainly tried to govern according to fixed rules and procedures which were based on what they imagined to be the stable political and jural systems of the African past. But they rarely exercised enough effective control to accomplish exactly what they set out to do.

This was so for several reasons. First, colonial administrators' own economic and political interests often had contradictory implications for their strategies of exploitation and control. Second, contrary to British expectations, African societies were not divided into neatly bounded, mutually exclusive, stable cultural and political systems, but were dynamic, changing communities, whose boundaries were fluid and ambiguous and whose members were often engaged in multiple contests for power and resources. And, finally, officials' efforts to learn about indigenous societies in order to build on them frequently elicited conflicting testimony about the nature of 'native law and custom'. I shall elaborate each of these points in turn.

The contradictions of colonial interests in African agriculture
The financial viability of a colonial regime was likely to be both threatened and enhanced by successful African participation in cash cropping and wage employment. Whether or not a particular episode of conquest was motivated by the desire to promote European capitalist interests in Africa, once colonial rule was established, officials counted on European enterprise to generate taxable income and wealth. Trading firms, concessionaires, mining companies, and European settlers were all expected to increase the volume of commercial activity and hence the flow of taxable income generated by the colonial economy. European profits depended, in turn, on ready access to cheap African labour—as farm and mine workers, as porters and dock hands, and as producers of commodities for export or for the direct provisioning of Europeans in Africa. Africans were, in turn, more likely to offer their labour cheaply if they were hard pressed to meet their own needs independently of trade with or employment by Europeans. In short, African prosperity threatened the profits of European enterprise on African soil.

However, Africans also paid taxes and bought European goods, and their ability to do so increased with their income. Thus colonial regimes walked a tightrope between encouraging Africans to become involved in labour and commodity markets and attempting to prevent them from becoming economically independent enough to ignore the opportunities afforded by European-controlled markets and jobs. Officials did not want to stifle the flow of African labour, produce, and tax revenue on which the fiscal and economic health of the colony depended, but they were equally anxious to minimise the cost of African labour and produce, and to limit Africans' ability to influence the terms of exchange.

Colonial administrators' ambivalence towards African agricultural growth and commercialisation was expressed differently in different colonies, depending on the particular local configuration of economic activities and interests. In settler economies, such as Kenya, officials faced conflicting pressures to encourage increased African production for sale, in order to generate taxable income, supply the home market, and keep down wage costs, and to suppress it, in order to force out labour and protect European farmers from African competition. Officials advocated the creation of African reserves both to limit Africans' access to land and augment the flow of labour to European farms, and to 'protect' Africans from dispossession or excessive exploitation. On the issue of labour recruitment, they shifted their strategy, first using African headmen as recruiters in order to forestall the abuses of commercial recruiters; then shifting to professional recruiters, or even acting as recruiters themselves, as popular discontent threatened to undermine the authority of headmen and, hence, their effectiveness as agents of indirect rule (Lonsdale and Berman, 1979; Heyer et al., 1976; Cowen, 1981).

In Northern Rhodesia large tracts of land were cleared for settlers, but so few ever arrived that their labour needs were insignificant, and colonial authorities never faced the issue of restricting African cultivation in order to generate labour supplies. Instead they wrestled with the issue of settlement patterns. For administrative purposes, it was convenient to have people concentrated in large settlements under the effective control of powerful chiefs. From the earliest years of British South Africa Company rule, officials waged a series of unsuccessful campaigns to prevent the dispersal of Bemba settlements. However, concentrated settlements soon led to deforestation and soil erosion. No sooner had the colonial administration moved people into newly demarcated native reserves, in the 1930s, than the resultant overcrowding led to visible signs of environmental degradation, and villagers had to be resettled within a few years (Allan, 1965: 109 ff.).

In West Africa there were no settlers to speak of, and colonies prospered from the rapid expansion of tree-crop and other agricultural production for export. Even here, however, officials worried that farmers would neglect food crops in their rush to produce for export; that African methods of production resulted in poor-quality produce which brought low prices in Europe; and that European traders' efforts to protect themselves against African competition would provoke disturbances that might threaten the smooth flow of trade (Kay, 1972; Hopkins, 1973). Here, too, official policy towards agriculture and commerce wavered between encouraging export crop production and African commerce and limiting it, as administrators struggled to balance competing interests and manage the contradictions of agricultural development.

The dynamics of African political economies
For much of the colonial era, many Europeans assumed that African communities consisted of mutually exclusive socio-cultural units—tribes, villages, kin groups—whose customs and structures had not changed very much over time. Officials could see, of course, that there was conflict among Africans at the time of colonial conquest, but they assumed they could restore order by reconstituting what they believed to have been the 'closed, corporate, consensual systems' of the past (Ranger, 1983: 249). Accordingly, colonial administrators set out to discover the boundaries and customs of 'traditional' communities, and the 'original' relations between them, in order to use tradition as the basis of their own administrative structures and practices.

In attempting to construct stable, workable administrative systems in

Africa, officials sometimes sought to preserve traditional structures of authority, sometimes to reorganise or completely recreate them. In northern Nigeria colonial officials found a system of Muslim emirates, complete with written legal codes, courts, and administrative structures, which were almost ideally suited to their purposes. Also, since a majority of the Fulani aristocracy agreed to accept British overrule in exchange for confirmation of their own authority, the process of conquest was brief and relatively smooth. However, few other systems of local government proved as comprehensible or congenial to British notions of administrative efficiency (Perham, 1938; Hailey, 1957; Coleman, 1960). Most African chiefs kept no tax rolls or law books; few made any attempt to separate either the principles or the practice of adjudication from those of politics or diplomacy; and many were vague about the exact boundaries of their domains. In decentralised societies, such as those of central Kenya or south-eastern Nigeria, where colonial administrators were unable to find strong chiefs or hierarchical systems of authority, they created them.

In more centralised polities, chiefs who resisted or challenged colonial domination were deposed and their government sometimes reorganised as well, to prevent renewed dissent. For example, the British deliberately weakened Asante hegemony after 1896 by signing separate treaties with chiefs and communities formerly subordinate to Kumase and disregarding Kumase's claims to 'customary' overlordship. In western Nigeria, where Yoruba states had been engaged in a series of battles and shifting alliances for most of the nineteenth century, British officials insisted on assigning them to positions in a fixed hierarchy under the supreme authority of the Alafin of Oyo, despite the fact that, since the 1850s, Ibadan had been stronger than Oyo, and Ibadan's principal opponent (the Ekitiparapo or Ekiti–Ijesha alliance) was quite independent of Oyo (Johnson, 1921; Atanda, 1973; Akintoye, 1971).

In the early years of colonial conquest and 'pacification' officials dealt with each area *ad hoc*, responding pragmatically, sometimes ruthlessly, to local conditions in their efforts to establish control and mobilise resources. By the end of the First World War, however, official thinking was converging towards a standard 'mental map of an Africa comprised of neatly bounded, homogeneous tribes' (Ambler, 1987: 32) and an increasingly uniform conception of their own imperial mission and how best to realise it. Lugard's *The Dual Mandate in Tropical Africa* (1923) laid out the philosophy of indirect rule and, during the next twenty years, officials laboured to replicate a common system of native administration across the map of colonial Africa. In 1929 the Secretary for Native Affairs in Northern Rhodesia noted with satisfaction that, when the Colonial Office took over administration of the colony in 1924, ' "the tribes were in a very disorganised state", but since then a tribal organisation had been "created" ' (Chanock, 1985: 112).

In fact precolonial communities were neither static nor internally cohesive. In central Kenya during the nineteenth century 'men and women throughout the region moved in a complex world of overlapping, layered and shifting associations' (Ambler, 1987: 32) formed through migration, marriage, trade, and blood brotherhood. 'As agricultural settlement steadily expanded, the patterns of [social] identity were continually recast by the evolving relations among communities' (*ibid.*: 35). Nor were fluid, overlapping or contested social boundaries and lines of authority peculiar to acephalous polities such as those of the Kikuyu, Igbo, or Tiv. Even as British missionaries moved into Northern Rhodesia, followed in 1895 by agents of the British South Africa Company, a major realignment was taking place among Bemba chieftaincies. As Roberts (1973) has shown in detail, the 'strength' of Bemba chiefs and the cohesiveness of the tribe under the central authority of the Chitimukulu, which so impressed early British observers, rested not on any institutionalised system of central authority, but rather on a particular conjuncture of historical circumstances. In the 1860s and '70s shifting alliances and conflicts among neighbouring peoples combined with a realignment of long-distance trade patterns to reward Bemba skills at ivory hunting and slave raiding without bringing dissident groups into their territory (Roberts, 1973: 198–9). This led to a temporary consolidation of Bemba power within the region, but also promoted competition among Bemba chiefs. By the 1880s the power of the Chitimukulu was declining and several smaller chieftaincies were switching their allegiance to the increasingly powerful Mwamba (Roberts, 1973: 211–4; Werbner, 1967). With the establishment of BSAC control in 1895, large fortified Bemba settlements dispersed, leaving much room for subsequent debate over which chiefs had traditional claims to authority over whom.

In Asante, since the eighteenth century, successive Asantehenes had manipulated the allocation of rights over land and people in order to consolidate and extend the power of Kumase (McCaskie, 1980, 1984; Tordoff, 1965; Wilks, 1975). In 1889 Yaa Kyaa secured the throne of Kumase for her son, Agyeman Prempe I, by promising his supporters to restore to them all the land and subjects 'who had been sold, pawned, confiscated or otherwise alienated' from their ancestors by previous Asantehenes. After more than a century of confiscation and redistribution by several Asantehenes, Yaa Kyaa's promises left much room for debate over who was entitled to what (McCaskie, 1984). Similarly, in western Nigeria, much of the nineteenth century was taken up by warfare, migration, and shifting alliances among Yoruba states which generated multiple, conflicting precedents for demarcating 'traditional' social boundaries and chiefly jurisdictions.

In general, colonial regimes imposed themselves on societies already engaged in struggles over power and the terms on which it was exercised. By announcing their intention to uphold 'traditional' norms and structures of authority colonial officials were, in effect, declaring their intention to build colonial rule on a foundation of conflict and change. The result was 'a blizzard of claims and counterclaims' to rights over land and people which served as 'a mechanism for generating factional struggle' rather than eliminating it (Dunn and Robertson, 1973: 73).

The search for tradition
The debates and tensions provoked by European efforts to construct stable governing structures on top of volatile African social realities were exacer-

bated by colonial administrators' methods of implementing indirect rule. To build colonial administration on a foundation of 'native law and custom', officials needed information about traditional systems of law and authority. But few African societies, apart from those with established traditions of Islamic scholarship, possessed written bodies of legal and historical knowledge from which such information might be drawn. Officials had therefore to rely on travellers' accounts (sketchy and dated, at best) and on oral testimony.

Oral evidence was gathered informally at first; later, more systematically, by official commissions of inquiry and by professional anthropologists hired by colonial regimes for the purpose (Hailey, 1957: 54–6). But the search for oral tradition was fraught with difficulties. Like scholars who collect oral history, colonial administrators who set out to gather information on local laws and customs were told multiple, often conflicting stories. Whichever version of customary rights and practices an official chose to believe, people were sure to challenge it—both because the past was in fact complex and changing, and because Africans took advantage of officials' interest in tradition to offer evidence favourable to their own interests.

When tensions rose over a particular aspect of colonial policy, the Colonial Office convened commissions of inquiry, both to investigate immediate grievances and to amass information about local customs. Though the work of these commissions often contributed to the emergence of an official orthodoxy concerning 'native law and custom', the evidence they collected was often full of varied and conflicting testimony. For example, in southern Nigeria and the Gold Coast, after recurring protests both from influential Britons opposed to commercial concessionaires and from Africans who objected to the proposed enactment of a Crown Lands Ordinance for these territories, the Colonial Office convened the West African Lands Committee in 1912, to consider the 'laws in force' concerning 'the conditions under which rights over land or the produce thereof may be transferred', and whether those laws needed amending (WALC, 1916: correspondence, 2). Perhaps unintentionally, the committee's draft report (which was never published) summed up the colonial administrator's dilemma: 'natives have rights under their own laws and customs', and, for the courts to protect them, 'the appropriate custom or law must be brought to the knowledge of the court'. In practice, however, the testimony offered to the courts 'is often very unsatisfactory and untrustworthy' (*ibid.*).

Partly because the evidence they collected was frequently confusing or contradictory, administrators sought common rules by which to interpret customary practices and apply them to the business of governance. In the 1920s colonial regimes began to employ professional anthropologists to help them discover the rules and practices of traditional African cultures. In keeping with the intellectual currents of the time, anthropologists such as Rattray, Meek and Gluckman assumed that traditional African societies were well ordered, self-reproducing systems, whose natural evolution had been disrupted by the trauma of colonial conquest. Often they saw it as their mission to discover or reconstruct these 'original' systems through fieldwork, and then persuade colonial authorities to restore them, in order to put African societies back on their normal evolutionary path towards civilisation (Kuklick, 1979: 50).

For Rattray, the 'true Ashanti' was to be found among elderly people in remote forest settlements, isolated from the corrupting influences of commerce and colonial politics, where social interaction was still ordered according to traditional religious precepts (McCaskie, 1983). In Nigeria, Meek concluded from his investigation of the Aba women's war in 1929, colonial rule had weakened the religious basis of traditional law and order, undermining 'what was before a well-ordered community', and threatening to replace it with 'a disorganized rabble of self-seeking individualists' (quoted in Chanock, 1985: 26). And Gluckman's writings (1941, 1965) present a picture of the Lozi kingdom as a cohesive system, in which economic, political, social and religious practices complemented and reinforced one another in harmonious and well-ordered fashion.

By the 1920s the study and interpretation of African custom were becoming institutionalised as part of the routine activity of colonial administration. Beginning in 1922, District Officers in the Gold Coast were 'obliged to take examinations in native custom, although apparently they were not required to pass them' (Kuklick, 1979: 51). In general, anthropological research served to reinforce the official view of African societies as clearly bounded and coherently organised (Crook, 1986: 89–90; Kimble, 1963: 486). To be sure, some administrators were well aware that tradition could be invented as well as recalled. 'After a review of fifty years' disputes' in the coastal Ghanaian stool of Ada, one official commented sarcastically that the Adas' 'knowledge of ancient traditions is, in fact, small, but the manufacture of new ones has been raised by them to the status of a rural industry' (quoted in Sutton, 1984: 42–3). Indeed, some saw distinct advantages in the confusion: in Ahafo, one official pointed out in 1930, 'as a result of the system of indirect rule in vogue it is extremely unlikely that any riot or disturbance should be directed against Government authorities. What disturbances occur are invariably in the nature of "faction fights"' (quoted in Dunn and Robertson, 1973: 87).

However, multiple and conflicting testimonies were more likely to be dismissed as evidence of Africans' venality or obtuseness than to be examined for the possibility that the homogeneous systems of primordial law and culture which officials had painstakingly pieced together to serve as the basis of the colonial order might never have existed in the first place. In Brong Ahafo 'it was the conventional wisdom of the administration, apt to be produced without noticeable irony after the recital of the most baroque confusions, that in unravelling disputes about traditional issues, one must "always be governed by well established Akan custom"' (Dunn and Robertson, 1973: 169).

In summary, colonial rule affected conditions of access to land and labour through the interplay of administrators' ambivalence towards African farmers' prosperity, their efforts to govern through indigenous rules and authorities, and on-going debates over the meaning of 'native law and custom'. As agricultural commercialisation and labour migration gave rise to disputes over the means of production officials insisted on resolving them in terms of 'native law and custom'. Their insistence served, in turn, to reinforce existing linkages between farmers' access to resources, their position in local structures of power, and their ability to win arguments over customary rules and practices. Ongoing struggles over power and the interpretation of tradition were incorporated into the rules and procedures through which officials sought to 'cope with the contradictions' and 'crises of accumulation' which accompanied colonial rule (Lonsdale and Berman, 1979; Berman and Lonsdale, 1980). Struggles over the meaning of traditional rules and structures of authority shaped struggles over resources, and vice versa (Peters, 1984).

In general, the effect of indirect rule was neither to freeze African societies into precolonial moulds, nor to restructure them in accordance with British inventions of African tradition, but to generate unresolved debates over the interpretation of tradition and its meaning for colonial governance and economic activity. In seeking to maintain social and administrative stability by building on tradition, officials wove instability —in the form of changing relations of authority and conflicting interpretations of rules—into the fabric of colonial administration.

THE INTERPRETATION OF CUSTOM: RULES AND SOCIAL IDENTITIES

In their respective attempts to enhance the power and exploit the resources of colonial regimes, Europeans and Africans debated both the nature of customary rules and the demarcation of social groups to which they should apply. For European officials, the second question arose because they assumed that Africans belonged to distinct, mutually exclusive groups, each with its own set of rules and institutions for enforcing them. Whether or how a particular rule should apply to a given individual depended on what group s/he belonged to. For example, the right to cultivate land or the obligation to pay tribute for doing so was held to depend on the social origin of the person in question. The rights and obligations of 'strangers' were commonly held to be different from those of indigenes, and much effort was accordingly devoted to determining who was a stranger by classifying people according to descent group, or 'tribal' affiliation. How 'the law' was applied then followed from the decision as to who a person was.

In the Gold Coast, for example, by endorsing the view that a chief's right to collect cocoa rents depended on the social origin of the farmer the colonial authorities helped to intensify disputes over boundaries between stools, and the designation of 'paramount' and subordinate chiefs (Hill, 1963; Austin, 1987). In Kenya and Northern Rhodesia, where African reserves were demarcated on tribal lines, land rights were similarly linked to social identity. Needless to say, this created many anomalies, since existing settlement patterns were often multi-ethnic (Sorrenson, 1967: 37–8).

For Africans, the interpretation of rules also depended on who was involved, but for different reasons. In most precolonial African societies, status and wealth depended on accumulating dependants or followers. 'Strangers' were welcomed—as wives, clients, 'blood brothers', settlers or disciples—because they enhanced the prestige and often the labour force of the head of a household, kin group or community. Access to land and labour thus followed from negotiations over a person's relationship with other individuals or groups. Negotiations could take a long time. Payment of bridewealth, for example, sometimes took years: an adult son might still be paying part of his mother's bridewealth after his own sons were eligible for marriage and/or his mother had died (Comaroff, 1980). In the event of divorce or separation the disposition of a couple's children and property depended not on whether or not the couple were married but on how married they were at the time of separation—which depended in turn on the interpretation of transactions and other events in the history of their relationship (see also Comaroff, 1980).

As commercialisation led to new demands for land and labour, Africans increased their efforts to negotiate new relationships in order to gain access to additional productive resources. In Akan, Yoruba, and Kikuyu societies, marriage gave men various claims on the labour of their wives, while women (and, in matrilineal Akan communities, men) gained the right to cultivate land belonging to the husband's lineage. In central Kenya in the nineteenth century, people participated in rituals of 'blood brotherhood' in order to augment the portfolio of kin-like relationships through which they could organise trade or seek refuge in other communities in times of famine or disease (Ambler, 1987).

As cocoa farming spread in southern Ghana and Nigeria during and after the 1890s, would-be farmers sought access to suitable uncultivated forest land by negotiating with heads of local families or chieftaincies. Often they acquired rights to plant tree crops or even to the land itself in exchange for money, labour services, and/or annual 'gifts' of produce or cash which served to acknowledge the continued authority of local leaders. Similar processes occurred in Kenya, where migrants (*ahoi*) 'begged' permission to settle and farm in a new area. *Ahoi* might work for local elders or marry into their families in order to get established. As they accumulated herds and formed their own domestic establishments they advanced to full membership of the *mbari* or settlement of their hosts (Kanogo, 1987: 26). Also, in Northern Rhodesia, access to land or labour followed from a decision to marry or join a new community (Richards, 1939; Pottier, 1985; Watson, 1958).

In general, then, people tended to negotiate access to land and labour in the process of joining a new household or community. Negotiations often included transfers of goods or money in exchange for rights of access or control, but the meanings of such transfers were not fixed—as colonial officials assumed them to be. For example, the sale of land or other assets did not necessarily extinguish the rights of the seller: in central Kenya, land sold in exchange for cash might be reclaimed by the seller or his kin on the grounds that custom dictated that land belonged to the 'family' or that sales were redeemable (Sorrenson, 1967; Fisher, 1954). Similarly, in both Ghana and Nigeria, purchasers of cocoa farms might be held responsible for paying tribute (or rent) to the landholders who had given the original farm owner permission to plant permanent crops in the first place (Berry, 1975; Hill, 1963). In both cases, terms of access were negotiable, and the outcome in any particular transaction depended on the history of relations between the persons involved, and the way they were interpreted at the time of the land acquisition. As Chief Kinyanjui told the Kenya Land Commission, when questioned about his role in a past land dispute, 'I do not remember what I said before the District Commissioner eight years ago. Tell me who summoned me to give evidence. What I said depends on whose witness I was' (Kenya Land Commission, 1934: 282).

In short, administrators sought information on traditional social structures and identities in order to know how to apply customary rules in governing colonial peoples, while African colonial subjects renegotiated rules and social identities in order to cope with or take advantage of colonial rule and commercialisation. Together they debated the nature of linkages between customary law and social identity. But the debates remained unresolved, partly because European officials were struggling with conflicting evidence about social processes which they misunderstood, and partly because Africans' efforts to take advantage of the colonial economic and political order led them to keep redefining the rules and institutions on which colonial officials predicted their strategies of governance. Whatever conclusions officials reached about the content of customary laws or the boundaries of traditional societies were either challenged by Africans offering a different version of tradition, or outpaced by changing social and economic practices. Both processes tended to keep the debates going, rather than give rise to a new set of fixed rules or social relations. In the following section I will illustrate the process of debate with two examples: the periodic reorganisation of chiefly jurisdictions and native administrations under colonial rule, and debates over customary land tenure.

THE 'ORGANISATION AND RE-ORGANISATION' OF NATIVE ADMINISTRATION

After World War I colonial regimes across Africa moved to codify customary law and formalise the structures of indirect rule, in keeping with the general trend towards rationalisation and professionalisation of the colonial service (Young, 1988: 45 ff.). Chieftaincies—often recognised in accordance with British ideas of administrative efficiency—were legally constituted as 'Native Authorities'. Chiefs were empowered (and required) to raise revenue, spend money on public facilities such as roads, latrines, and clinics, and adjudicate cases according to customary law—all under the supervision of British officials, who also had the power to appoint and depose chiefs themselves. In principle, British officials sought to create permanent structures for the consistent and disinterested enforcement of fixed rules. In practice, both the structures and the boundaries of native administrations were periodically readjusted—in some cases practically up to the eve of independence.

For example, in the Gold Coast, native authorities were not even fully established until 1944, less than a decade before they were abolished altogether. From the nineteenth century, British officials had found it expedient to negotiate with Akan stools as semi-autonomous states, rather than subsume them under the formal apparatus of indirect rule. This did not stop the British from working actively to undermine the power of Asante, first by military attack and, in 1896, by negotiating a series of treaties with neighbouring states which placed them on an equal footing with Kumase in the eyes of the colonial regime.

During the early decades of colonial rule, as the spread of cocoa raised the value of land and the volume of litigation over access to it, chiefs manoeuvred to maximise their revenues from cocoa 'rents' and judicial fees and fines—by asserting claim to land and subjects which the British had allocated to other jurisdictions, and by reinterpreting customary rules concerning their prerogatives. Citizens and aspiring candidates to chiefly office responded with a flood of protests and destoolment proceedings which kept administrators busy and led to periodic adjustments of stool boundaries and hierarchies. One of the most dramatic cases was the decision, in 1935, to restore Kumase hegemony over a number of neighbouring stools, in response to prolonged agitation by Kumase chiefs and their supporters. 'With the restoration of the Ashanti Confederacy in 1935 reasonably clear . . . titles to land in return for regular payments gave way to a massive Kumasi *Reconquista*', in which Kumase chiefs tried to reassert their 'customary' right to collect tribute on land which, since the British occupation, had been extensively planted in cocoa and had accordingly increased in value many times over (Dunn and Robertson, 1973: 53).

In western Nigeria, early treaties between colonial agents and Yoruba chiefs were supplanted, after 1916, by the designation of Yoruba obas as native authorities. The colonial regime also attempted to establish hierarchies of superior and subordinate chiefs, both within pre-existing Yoruba states and between them. Since Yoruba states had been engaged for much of the nineteenth century in a series of struggles over hegemony, 'tradition' offered a poor guide in demarcating these hierarchies. As in the Gold Coast, Yoruba communities regularly questioned their assigned status *vis-à-vis* their neighbours, and administrators were confronted with countless petitions from communities seeking autonomy from a neighbouring chief, or groups of people within a town or state seeking to depose a chief, in the hope of enthroning a successor who would be more favourable to their interests. During the 1930s District Officers prepared a series of 'Organisation and Re-organisation Reports' in which fresh batches of local testimony were presented in defence of preserving or redrawing boundaries and relations between communities (Nigerian National Archives, 1934–50; see also Hailey, 1957: 462).

In the settler colonies, the former demarcation of social boundaries was guided by issues of land appropriation as well as local administration. In Kenya, where administrators had to contend with the absence of 'any Chief who could command the respect accorded to the Kabaka of Uganda' or any 'ready-made organisation which could be converted into an administrative machine',[3] British officials appointed headmen, often on the basis of their willingness to collaborate with the colonial authorities rather than any traditional claims to power.[4] Local native councils were created in 1925, modelled on Kikuyu *kiama* (councils of elders), but drawn from administrative districts designated by the colonial administration and comprised of individuals selected or approved by District Officers. In practice, spheres of authority were not clearly defined, and the councils and the native tribunals (customary courts) functioned more as arenas of struggle over control of land, revenue, jobs and influence than as guardians of Kikuyu custom (Kitching, 1980: 198; Glazier, 1985: 82 ff.).

Native reserves were not formally demarcated until 1926, largely because settlers objected to being cut off from potential access to land within them (Sorrenson, 1967: 19). Once established, however, the reserves were organised on tribal lines, thus linking land rights firmly with social identity, and provoking prolonged debate over the relative weight of 'tribal', 'family', and individual rights (Sorrenson, 1967; Sillitoe, 1962; Kenya Land Commission, 1934). Within the reserves, migration and changing economic opportunities led to new demand for access to land, which intensified debate over which communities had the right to allocate use rights to individuals.

In Northern Rhodesia, British officials waged a series of unsuccessful campaigns to control settlement patterns and shape Bemba chieftaincies to the needs of orderly administration. When agents of the British South Africa Company first moved into the new protectorate, in the late 1890s, they were favourably impressed with the apparent power of Bemba chiefs, who presided over large fortified settlements, and even worried that they might have a tendency to abuse their power. *Pax Britannica* obviated the need for such encampments, however, and people lost no time in dispersing themselves over the countryside, in order to practise their extensive system of *citemene* agriculture. Company officials were afraid the dispersal of the population would erode the authority of Bemba chiefs, making them useless as agents of Company rule. In 1907 the company banned the practice of *citemene* and forcibly rounded people up into villages, 'but the famine which followed led to a change of mind' (Hellen, 1968: 203; see also Kay, 1964). Colonial officials who succeeded the company pursued similar ends with less draconian means, but their efforts to establish a minimum size for Bemba villages were no more successful. When admonished that their authority would dwindle if they permitted their 'subjects' to scatter, Bemba chiefs blandly countered that 'the greater the number of villages, the greater the prestige of the chief' (Ranger, 1971: 27).

When indirect rule was formally established, in 1929, four out of thirty-odd Bemba chiefs were designated native authorities; the rest were relegated to subordinate status. Elsewhere in the colony, chieftancies were created outright. In both cases, colonial restructuring provoked numerous disputes over chiefly ranking, prerogatives, jurisdictions and succession (Meebelo, 1971: 195–219). As in other colonies, efforts by the Colonial Office to implement 'national self-determination on a tribal level' resulted in African complaints about the rankings of native authorities, and British complaints about Africans' 'failure' to follow custom (Gann, 1963: 230). Native administrations were reorganised periodically, up to the eve of independence.

In short, British efforts to build stable systems of native administration on customary foundations had the effect of maintaining fluid, flexible social boundaries and structures of authority. In practice, British officials' efforts to impose fixed rules in the name of tradition (Chanock, 1985; Glazier, 1985; Ranger, 1983) served to 'institutionalise' struggle and debate over the meaning of customary rules and structures of authority—an outcome which

INDIRECT RULE AND ACCESS TO LAND: THE LIMITS OF COLONIAL CONTROL

Debate over customary land rights and the meaning of ownership was joined in the Gold Coast over a series of Land and Forestry Bills proposed by the colonial government between 1894 and 1911 (Kimble, 1963: chapter 9; Crook, 1986: 88). To create a legal basis for future government control over the allocation of land for public or private use, the Governor proposed in 1984 that all 'vacant' land be declared the property of the colonial state. A public outcry followed, in which the central argument advanced by African chiefs, merchants, lawyers and clergymen was that there was no vacant land in the colony—'all land is owned' (Kimble, 1963: 336; Crook, 1986: 88). To avoid unrest, the government dropped the Bill but, in 1897, put forward a new version, under which the state would act as 'trustee' for the African population. The Bill stipulated, further, that any farmer who developed 'vacant' stool land could, on application to the Governor, be given 'settlers' rights' of individual ownership (Kimble, 1963: 340; Asante, 1975: 33).

The 1897 Bill provoked a storm of opposition. J. Mensah Sarbah and other African lawyers and clergymen organised the Aborigines' Rights Protection Society to lobby against any measure which even appeared to threaten Africans' land rights. Though not always sympathetic to 'traditional rulers', in this case the ARPS was supported by a number of chiefs eager to appropriate a share of rising cocoa incomes in the name of customary chiefly prerogative. Led by spokesmen for the ARPS, opponents of the Bill reiterated the argument that 'all land is owned' and hence exempt from appropriation by the colonial state. When officials and judges asked, 'Owned by whom?' they received a variety of answers, but the one which proved mutually acceptable was 'by the community' (Sarbah, 1897; Hayford, 1969; Crook, 1986: 89).

The Lands Bill of 1897 was shelved indefinitely, but the debate continued. In 1910 rumours that colonial authorities planned to enact Crown Land Ordinances for the Gold Coast and southern Nigeria reawakened African suspicions that this was simply a manoeuvre to alienate their land. Public meetings were held in both colonies at which people denounced the proposed legislation (Kimble, 1963; Hayford, 1969; Berry, 1975: 120). Asked by the Governor to prepare a report on Yoruba customs, a committee of Lagosians headed by Henry Carr affirmed that 'every piece of land, cultivated or uncultivated, including forests, has an owner' (Hopkins, 1969: 85). Fearing unrest, officials in Nigeria demurred at requests for concessions. When Lever Bros. applied for a large palm oil concession in southern Nigeria in 1908 the government agreed, on condition that the company negotiated separate agreements with every community or descent group which claimed jurisdiction over any part of the land in question. Lever Bros. decided it would be too much trouble and moved their operations to the more hospitable terrain of the Congo Free State (Great Britain, 1914).

In 1912 the West African Lands Committee was convened to collect evidence on customary land tenure in West Africa, and to make recommendations for codifying and enforcing it. The committee sat for three years, collecting oral and written testimony from hundreds of witnesses. The committee's report was never published, but its findings were well known among colonial officials. Although the evidence and correspondence included statements that land sales had occurred in the Gold Coast since the 1870s, that Yoruba chiefs had no claims to land other than that belonging to their own families, etc., the committee's work appears to have strengthened the growing consensus that land was communally owned in Africa. The draft report endorsed the Yoruba chief who declared, 'I conceive that land belongs to a vast family, of which many are dead, few are living, and countless numbers are yet unborn', adding that land was 'God-given' in Africa and 'cannot be alienated' (WALC, 1916: 31–2). Quoting the testimony of E. D. Morel, R. E. Dennett and the Commissioner of Lands in Southern Nigeria, C. W. Alexander, the committee stressed the political importance of upholding 'pure native tenure'. Land tenure, they asserted, was the foundation of native rule: 'together they stand or fall' (*ibid.*: 3).

As indirect rule evolved from a successful compromise in northern Nigeria to a blanket prescription for colonial rule in all contexts, officials articulated an increasingly confident and uniform understanding of 'pure native tenure'. Chief Justice Maxwell's ruling on a Kenyan land case, in 1919, was typical: he avowed with 'absolute certainty' that 'the theory of individual ownership of land is absolutely foreign to the mind of any African until he has begun to absorb the ideas of an alien civilization' (Kenya Land Commission, 1934: 32). Occasionally official documents sounded a note of realism: a 1947 report on land tenure in Adansi (Gold Coast) concluded that, because native court judgements 'turned on questions of historical fact . . . rather than Court decisions on legal principles . . . it has not proved possible to abstract . . . any general principles of Akan land tenure' from court records (Matson, 1947, quoted in Kyerematen, 1971: 36). Such cautionary tales did not, however, stem the tide of codification of 'native law and custom'.[5]

By linking land 'ownership' to community membership, administrators opened a Pandora's box which ultimately undermined their own efforts at codification. As Crook (1986: 89) has pointed out, 'the irresoluble ambiguity in th[e] doctrine [of community ownership] was—which community?' and the answer depended on 'vexed questions of historical precedent and jurisdictional claims'. As we have seen, debates over chiefly jurisdiction were difficult if not impossible to resolve from oral testimony. Similarly, chieftaincy disputes and periodic reorganisation of native administrations occurred with undiminished frequency throughout the colonial period. The 'doctrine' of community ownership of land meant, in effect, that such reorganisations affected not only the conduct of government business but also the definition of property rights—as in the case of the Kumase reconquest of Ahafo lands which followed the restoration of the Asante Confederacy in 1935.

The linking through 'customary law' of land access to community membership also meant that individual farmers' efforts to negotiate access to land for purposes of cash cropping could influence issues of social identity and administrative structure. In 1913, for example, the chief of Akwapim claimed authority over parts of Akyem Abuakwa, on the grounds that farmers from Akwapim, who had migrated to Akyem Abuakwa to plant cocoa, were still his 'subjects'. The ensuing dispute was still not resolved in 1926 (Hill, 1963: 154–7). In addition, official recognition of chiefs' traditional right to allocate land to 'strangers' and collect tribute from anyone who derived anything valuable from the land opened a window of opportunity for Akan chiefs to profit from the growth of cocoa production. Disputes arose over who should be considered a 'stranger' and therefore liable to pay tribute on his or her cocoa farms; whether chiefs' traditional claim to one-third of any game, gold, or forest products derived from their territory entitled them to one-third of the proceeds from strangers' cocoa farms; and whether cocoa tribute, or 'rent' as it came to be called, should be treated as the personal income of the chief or the public revenue of the stool (Hill, 1963: 147; Austin, 1987: 262). In general, struggles over access to land provoked reinterpretations of jurisdictional boundaries and vice versa, leading in some cases to disputes which dragged on for fifty years or more (Sutton, 1984: 42; Dunn and Robertson, 1973: 225).

In western Nigeria land rights were vested in families (*idile*, lit. houses) rather than chieftaincies, but this did not isolate them from local politics or render them any less subject to debate. As in the Gold Coast, 'strangers' were expected to make annual payments (*isakole*) in exchange for the right to use land. On any given family's land, a 'stranger' could be a person from another house within the same town (Berry, 1975: 91; Lloyd, 1962: 64–5). In Ibadan some enterprising hunters familiar with the uninhabited forests surrounding the town 'showed' fellow townsmen where to plant cocoa, then claimed jurisdiction over the land and the right to collect *isakole* from the farmers to whom they had served as guides. Some accumulated hundreds of 'tenants' in this way, advancing their status within their own lineages and their claims to political prominence in the town (Jenkins, 1965; Berry, 1975: 94, 117–21).

Another example was a case in Ife in the late 1940s when an Ife family sued several tenants for back payments of *isakole*.[6] The tenants belonged to a group of Ife residents known as Modakekes, whose ancestors had fled to Ife from Oyo during the nineteenth-century wars, and the suit stirred old tensions between the Modakekes and the indigenes. As tension mounted, Ife chiefs and families began to insist that all Modakekes farming in Ife were 'strangers', liable to pay *isakole* to an Ife family, whether or not they had ever done so in the past. The native court, controlled by the Oni, upheld the Ifes' claim, ordering the Modakekes to pay or lose their farms (Berry, 1975: 114–15; Oyediran, 1974). As in Ahafo in 1935, social identities—based on traditions of origin or nineteenth-century political allegiances—were invoked to redefine land rights in an area where cash cropping had spread extensively.[7]

In Kenya debates over customary land tenure were, of course, shaped from the start by the administration's decision to bring in European settlers and provide them with land and cheap labour. A Crown Lands Ordinance was enacted in 1902, without reference to African opinion, in order to facilitate land allocation to settlers. The earliest settlers staked claims in what is now Kiambu District, receiving English-style leasehold titles which could be bought and sold. The law stated that land appropriations were to be made 'with due regard to African interests', but in practice little effort was made to ascertain the nature of Africans' claims to land before it was alienated to settlers, or to ensure that Africans displaced by settlers received compensation (Sorrenson, 1967: 18). By 1907 a thriving market had emerged in land titles, and prices rose four- or five-fold in the next few years (Lonsdale and Berman, 1979; Kenya Land Commission, 1934: 323).

Kikuyus' resentment at being denied access to land they had used in the past for cultivation, grazing, water, etc., was intensified by the knowledge that Europeans were reaping large profits from speculative land sales, and they pressured local administrators for redress. District Officers, responsible for maintaining order in their districts at minimal cost, were anxious to mitigate African discontent. The first serious attempt to collect information on traditional Kikuyu land tenure was made by a District Officer named Beech in 1911. He amassed testimony from several hundred Kikuyu *mbari* who asserted that land appropriated by settlers had formerly belonged to them and that, in agreeing to let Europeans settle there, they had had no intention of forfeiting all future rights to the land. Their claims to compensation were largely ignored until the late 1920s, when growing demand for land in the Kikuyu reserves led both to frequent litigation in local courts and to renewed pressure on administrators to address Kikuyu grievances.

Within a few years of the beginning of European settlement in Kenya, settlers were beginning to move beyond Kiambu to the Rift Valley, where they found vast tracts of land inhabited mostly by nomadic pastoral groups such as the Maasai, who did not interfere with Europeans' appropriations of land but did not provide a usable source of labour either. Beginning in 1909, however, Kikuyu who had been displaced by European settlers, or simply wanted more land, also began to migrate into the Rift Valley. They also came as settlers—expecting to 'beg' for land in the traditional manner (*ahoi*), performing services and professing subordination to their hosts until they had established homesteads and herds of their own, then graduating to full membership of the host community (Kanogo, 1987: 26; Wambaa and King, 1975). At first, European settlers welcomed the extra labourers and gave Kikuyu migrants liberal access to land in exchange for minimal amounts of work. However, they considered the Kikuyu to be squatters or tenants, with no permanent rights to land which the settlers had acquired from the government or purchased from other Europeans.

Many Kikuyu squatters prospered during their early years in the Rift Valley; some accumulated substantial herds and established large communities of kin and followers, in a manner reminiscent of migrant cocoa farmers in West Africa (Kanogo, 1987: 17–27; Wambaa and King, 1975). Just before and after World War I, and again in the late 1920s, however, when European settlers' profits were being squeezed by rising land values, fluctuating market conditions and competition from successful squatters, settlers put pressure on the colonial administration to tighten restrictions on squatters' assets and conditions of service. In 1929 the government carried out a 'sweep' (*kifagio*) of squatters' livestock, slaughtering thousands of animals and offering little or no compensation to their owners.[8] In 1937 the government enacted a new Resident Native Labourers Ordinance which empowered settlers to eliminate squatters' herds and demand up to 270 days' labour annually from Africans resident on their land.

Beginning in 1929, some squatters left the 'White Highlands', hoping to escape further official and settler inroads into their assets and incomes. Some returned to the Kikuyu reserves; others sought access to land in reserves earmarked for other 'tribes'. Both forms of migration led to increased population density, tension over land access, and debate over the interpretation of customary land rights within the reserves. Colonial officials acknowledged that land within the Kikuyu reserve was controlled by individual *mbari*, and even recognised that some returned squatters were unable to get land from their *mbari*. Nonetheless, the government accepted the recommendation of the Kenya Land Commission that 'legitimate' Kikuyu claims for compensation could be satisfied by adding blocks of land to the 'tribal' reserve rather than to dispossessed individuals or *mbari*. In short, government policies towards Kikuyu land claims incorporated multiple interpretations of 'customary' land tenure, and served to exacerbate tension and litigation rather than resolve Kikuyu grievances.

In Sorrenson's trenchant phrasing, 'the "final solution" of the Kikuyu–European land conflict was seen in tribal terms' (1967: 24). Administrators did indeed cling to their belief in the primacy of tribes and tribal tenure, but the 'solution' turned out to be anything but final. Within a few years the colonial government decided to open up additional blocks of land to displaced squatters, but to exercise close control over the way they used the land, in order to forestall problems of overgrazing and soil erosion, which were already serious in some of the African reserves. The controls greatly angered Kikuyu settlers (some of them displaced for the third or fourth time), as did the government's refusal to grant them full *githaka* rights to land allocated them in the settlements. The resulting tensions contributed directly to the Mau Mau uprising of the early 1950s (Throup, 1988; Kanogo, 1987; Sorrenson, 1967; Ochieng and Janmohamed, 1977).

CONCLUSION

Colonial efforts to exercise hegemony on a shoestring did not block the commercialisation of agricultural production and resource mobilisation in Africa but did shape the way in which rights of access to land and labour were defined and transacted, and the way people used resources to establish and defend rights of access. Under indirect rule, colonial regimes incorporated on-going struggles over power and social identity into the structure of colonial administration, and elicited conflicting testimonies from their African subjects concerning the meaning of 'native law and custom'. As a result, property rights and labour relations were neither transformed according to the English model nor frozen in anachronistic 'communal' forms, but instead became subjects of perpetual contest. Under indirect rule, British officials sought to make rights of access contingent on people's social identity. At the same time, Africans sought to negotiate new social identities in order to take advantage of commercial or political opportunities. The combined result was an on-going debate about how rules of access were linked to social identity, and vice versa.

My conclusions differ from those of scholars who have argued that, by codifying customary law and using fixed rules to adjudicate disputes, colonial governments incorporated custom, transforming it from a flexible idiom of dispute to an instrument of authoritarian rule. According to this view, power was transferred from traditional communities to appointed chiefs and their literate clerks, and fixed rules, based on British inventions of African tradition, replaced the flexible, negotiable arrangements of the past. In turn 'legalization led to a freezing of rural status and stratification, henceforth defined and not negotiated' (Chanock, 1985: 47; MacGaffey, 1970; Snyder, 1981).[9]

The literature on customary law and dispute settlement does not entirely support this interpretation. Writing of Zambia, Chanock himself points out that the effects of commercialisation on social relations were contradictory. People ignored traditional obligations to kin in order to save money for other uses, and at the same time intensified the exploitation of family labour in order to expand production for the market. '[C]onflicts about what was and what was not customary were intense' (Chanock, 1985: 236). Such conflict underlay many of the cases heard in customary courts, where they were argued from multiple perspectives. In the courts of Bemba chiefs, Richards observed in the mid-1930s, 'the composition of the court varied according to the issue discussed' (Richards, 1971: 111). Infractions of regulations imposed by the colonial regime (such as sanitation laws or tax liabilities) were frequently heard only by the chief and court clerk, but disputes over land, marriage, chiefly succession or protocol attracted large, varying groups of participants, who debated each case at length (*ibid.*: 112–3, 116–20; see also Perham, 1936: 21–4).

Forty years later, Canter (1978) studied disputing processes in a Lenje chieftaincy near Lusaka. He found that, while local court proceedings were brief, formal, and authoritarian, enforcement of court rulings was left to informal negotiations between the parties involved. Moreover, a large number of disputes were heard in family or village moots, where attendance was open and there were no limits to the number of issues which might be raised, the number of people who might speak, or the length of time they might discuss a case. From observations in a rural district near Chipata, Van Donge (1985: 69) concluded that 'life in Mwase Lundazi was not so much shaped by "development policies" and their intended and unintended consequences as by arbitration sessions, which were chaired by the chief, in which land and headmanships were discussed and by local court sittings which mostly dealt with disputes between co-wives' (see also Bond, 1987).

In her study of customary law in Ada, Sutton (1984: 47 ff.) argues that, throughout the colonial period, there was also confusion over which laws applied in what contexts. 'It was not a question merely of "two systems of jurisprudence . . ."—African and English—but of English law and many African systems' (*Ibid.*: 47). It was unclear, for example, whether a case on appeal from a native to a superior court was to be heard according to

English or customary law and, if the latter, whether English judges were qualified to hear it. There were also endless possibilities for reopening cases on the grounds that previous rulings had misinterpreted customary law, or for moving cases back and forth between courts and informal moots for the same reason (see also Dunn and Robertson, 1973).

The continual renegotiation of rights of access and control which occurred under indirect rule affected both the significance of market transactions and farmers' strategies of investment. Much of the literature on the nature of African property rights and their implications for economic development postulates a universal dichotomy between individual and communal rights: then deduces behaviour from the supposed logic of whichever system appears, from available evidence, to have gained the upper hand in a particular colonial context (Feder and Noronha, 1987; cf. Collier, 1983). In fact, individual and community rights frequently coexisted, and more than one community might claim rights to a particular resource. Structures of access to productive resources involved 'bundles of rights' (Gluckman, 1965) and bundles of right-holders. The way in which a particular resource was managed depended on relations among right-holders as well as on the jural content of the rights they held.

Under indirect rule, membership of a community came to be considered the primary basis for claiming rights to productive resources. Hence the delineation and exercise of property rights became enmeshed in conflicting testimony over community boundaries and structures. Indirect rule affected the management of resources not by preserving communal property rights, with their attendant problem of 'free riders' (people who misuse resources because they cannot be held accountable for conserving them), but by assigning property rights to social groups whose structures were subject to perennial contest.

The fact that land rights were subject to an on-going debate over the interpretation and application of 'custom' helps to explain why agricultural surplus was often channelled into ceremonies or redistributed among farmers' kin, clients and/or patrons.[10] As we have seen, farmers' ability to gain or retain access to land for purposes of cultivation depended as much on their relationships with other people as on the specific terms under which they claimed land rights. Consequently, farmers often found it advisable to invest part of any available surplus in the means of contesting access to resources, leaving less for investment in directly productive capital. Such investments included not only the actual costs of litigation but also marriage payments, funeral ceremonies, loans and various forms of patronage. These kinds of outlay served to reinforce or advance people's standing in social networks, or helped to promote interpretations of custom which might strengthen their claims to productive resources. People invested in the means of access to productive resources—including social identities or forms of status through which they could claim rights to productive resources—as well as in the means of production *per se*.

NOTES

[1] This article is part of a larger study of changing conditions of access to productive resources and their implications for patterns of resource use in African agriculture. The study

is built on a comparison of agrarian change in one rural area in each of four anglophone countries, from the late nineteenth century to the present. The case study areas were selected to represent a range of variations in both agro-ecological conditions and political–economic history. Among other things, the cases represent the major variant patterns of European and African interest in land during the colonial period. They include two agricultural economies on the 'traders' frontier' in West Africa—namely, the cocoa-growing areas of central Ghana and south-western Nigeria—and two in settler colonies—the predominantly Kikuyu areas of Kenya's Central Province, and the ecologically and commercially marginal agrarian systems of north-eastern Zambia. In the Kikuyu reserve in Kenya, African farmers expanded agricultural production for the market throughout the colonial period, despite losing substantial amounts of land to European settlers. In north-eastern Zambia, by contrast, there were only a handful of European settlers and almost no agricultural commercialisation occurred until after independence.

[2] Ranger (1983) points out that some groups of people who were oppressed or subordinated as a result of the invention of tradition resisted, but implies that the outcome usually favoured those groups (such as chiefs, elders, men) who claimed superiority under the rubric of tradition—rather than remaining fluid or indeterminate.

[3] Hailey (1957: 446) gives the source of this statement as the *Report of the Commission appointed to look into the Financial and Economic Position* . . . (Nairobi, 1948).

[4] Tignor (1976), Kenya Land Commission (1934).

[5] For examples of efforts to codify customary law in western Nigeria see Ward Price (1939), Elias (1951), Rowling (1952, 1956), Lloyd (1962). For the Gold Coast, Asante (1975), Kyerematen (1971).

[6] Before the spread of cocoa cultivation *isakole* was a gift of produce given by a 'stranger' to the owners of the land he farmed on. As cocoa raised cash returns to farming, 'tenant' farmers were expected to pay a certain amount of cocoa, or its equivalent in cash, each year. The amounts were not insignificant—1 cwt per annum was common—but neither were they exorbitant. Moreover, a land-holding family usually collected the same amount from each tenant regardless of the size of his farm. In this respect *isakole* was closer to a form of tribute than a pure economic rent (Berry, 1975: 104–11).

[7] In both Ghana and Nigeria cocoa farms were brought and sold and, in Ghana, farmers also purchased land, often well in advance of their ability to bring it under cultivation (Hill, 1963; Berry, 1975, 100–4; Galletti *et al.*, 1956, 138 ff.; Lloyd, 1962, 128–9). Yet the meaning of land and farm sales was open to debate. In the Gold Coast the High Court ruled, in 1907, that a farm pledged as security for a loan could be attached and sold if the borrower defaulted (Asante, 1975: 41–2). A decade later, however, the West Africa Lands Committee criticised this ruling as contrary to 'pure native tenure'. By the 1920s the courts were insisting that customary tenure precluded individual ownership (Asante, 1975; 45 ff.). In Nigeria sales of cocoa farms did not affect landholders' continuing right to the land on which they stood. Farm buyers still owed *isakole* to the owners of the land and, in areas such as Ibadan, where owners and tenants came from the same town, sales of trees were not recognised in the customary courts for fear they would undermine the landholder's claim (Berry, 1975: 112–13). In both Ghana and Nigeria all cocoa farms, including purchased ones, tended to become family property in time (Lloyd, 1962: 295–6, 305–7; Hill, 1963: 127; Berry, 1975: 102; Okali, 1983: 115 ff.).

[8] Colonial officials rationalised the slaughter of squatters' stock as necessary to prevent overgrazing and deterioration of pasture land. The rise of conservationist thinking among colonial officials in the 1930s will be discussed in a forthcoming paper.

[9] Kitching (1980) points out the irrelevance of European concepts of ownership for understanding precolonial Kikuyu practice, but argues that 'settler colonialism' effected a transition 'from simultaneous to exclusive land use' (p. 286). I am arguing that simultaneous and overlapping claims on land and labour persisted under colonial rule, and that the nature of property rights was not transformed but left unresolved.

[10] It is beyond the scope of this article to describe in detail the effects of contested rights in land on patterns of land use and agricultural investment. I have discussed social investments out of agricultural surplus elsewhere (Berry, 1985, 1989) and will also treat them in more detail in a forthcoming study.

REFERENCES

Afigbo, A. E. 1982. 'The Native Revenue Ordinance in the Eastern Provinces: the adventures of a colonial legislative measure', in B. Obichere (ed.), *Studies in Southern Nigerian History*. London: Frank Cass.

Akintoye, S. A. 1971. *Revolution and Power Politics in Yorubaland, 1840–93*. Ibadan History Series. London: Heinemann.

Allan, W. H. 1965. *The African Husbandman*. New York: Barnes & Noble.

Ambler, Charles. 1988. *Kenyan Communities in the Age of Imperialism*. New Haven: Yale University Press.

Anderson, David. 1984. 'Depression, dustbowl, demography, and drought', *African Affairs* 83, 332: 321–44.

Aronson, Dan. 1978. *The City is our Farm*. Cambridge, Mass.: Schenkman.

Asante, S. K. B. 1975. *Property Law and Social Goals in Ghana. 1844–1966*. Accra: Ghana Universities Press.

Asiegbu, A. J. 1984. *Nigeria and its British Invaders*. New York: Nok.

Atanda, J. A. 1973. *The New Oyo Empire: indirect rule and change in western Nigeria, 1894–1934*. London: Longman.

Austin, Gareth. 1987. 'The emergence of capitalist relations in south Asante cocoa-farming, c. 1916–33', *Journal of African History* 28 (4), 259–79.

Baldwin, R. E. 1966. *Export Growth and Economic Development in Northern Rhodesia*. Berkeley and Los Angeles, Cal.: University of California Press.

Bates, Robert. 1983. *Essays on the Political Economy of Rural Africa*. Cambridge: Cambridge University Press.

Beinart, William. 1984. 'Soil erosion, conservationism and ideas about development: a southern African exploration, 1900–60', *Journal of Southern African Studies* 11 (1), 52–83.

Beinart, William, and Bundy, Colin. 1987. *Hidden Struggles in Rural South Africa*. London: James Currey.

Beinart, William, Delius, Peter, and Trapido, Stanley., eds. 1986. *Putting a Plough to the Ground*. Johannesburg: Ravan.

Berman, Bruce, and Lonsdale, John. 1980. 'Crisis of accumulation, coercion, and the colonial state: the development of the labor control system in Kenya, 1919–29', *Canadian Journal of African Studies* 14 (1), 37–54.

Berry, Sara. 1975. *Cocoa, Custom and Socio-economic Change in rural Western Nigeria*. Oxford: Clarendon Press.

—— 1985. *Farmers Work for their Sons*. Berkeley and Los Angeles, Cal.: University of California Press.

—— 1988. 'Property rights and rural resource management: the case of tree crops in West Africa', *Cahiers des Sciences Humaines* 24 (1), 3–11.

—— 1989. 'Social institutions and access to resources in African agriculture', *Africa* 59 (1), 41–55.

Bond, G. C. 1987. 'Religion, ideology and property in northern Zambia', in I. Markovitz (ed.), *Studies in Class and Power in Africa*. New York and Oxford: Oxford University Press.

Brokensha, David. 1966. *Social Change in Larteh, Ghana*. Oxford: Clarendon Press.

Bruce, John. 1986. *Land Tenure Issues in Project Design and Strategies for Agricultural Development in sub-Saharan Africa*. Madison, Wis.: Land Tenure Center.

Bullock, R. A. 1975. *Ndeiya: Kikuyu frontier*. Waterloo, Ont.: Department of Geography, University of Waterloo.

Canter, R. S. 1978. 'Dispute settlement and dispute processing in Zambia', in L.

Nader and H. Todd (eds), *The Disputing Process*. New York: Columbia University Press.

Carney, Judith. 1988. 'Struggles over crop rights and labour within contract farming households in a Gambian irrigated rice project', *Journal of Peasant Studies* 15 (3), 334–49.

Carney, Judith, and Watts, Michael. n.d. 'Disciplining Women? Rice, Mechanization and Production Politics in West Africa' (mimeo).

Chanock, Martin. 1985. *Law, Custom and Social Order*. Cambridge: Cambridge University Press.

Chazan, Naomi, Mortimer, R., Ravenhill, J., and Rothchild, D., 1988. *Politics and Society in Contemporary Africa*. Boulder, Colo.: Lynne Rienner.

Clayton, A, and Savage, D. 1974. *Government and Labour in Kenya, 1895–1963*. London: Frank Cass.

Coleman, James. 1960. *Nigeria: background to nationalism*. Berkeley and Los Angeles, Cal.: University of California Press.

Collier, Paul. 1983. 'Malfunctioning of African rural factor markets: theory and a Kenyan example', *Oxford Bulletin of Economics and Statistics* 45 (2), 141–72.

Colson, Elizabeth. 1971. 'The impact of the colonial period on the definition of land rights', in V. Turner (ed.), *Profiles of Change: African society and colonial rule*. Vol. 3 of L. Gann and P. Duignan (eds), *Colonialism in Africa*. Cambridge: Cambridge University Press.

Comaroff, John. 1980. *The Meaning of Marriage Payments*. London: Academic Press.

Coquery-Vidrovitch, Catherine. 1969. 'Recherche sur un mode de production africain', *La Pensée* 1 (144), 61–78.

Cowen, Michael. 1981. 'Commodity production in Kenya's Central Province', in J. Heyer, P. Roberts and G. Williams (eds), *Rural Development in Tropical Africa*. New York: St Martins Press.

Crook, Richard. 1986. 'Delocalization, the colonial state and chieftaincy in the Gold Coast', *African Affairs* 85, 75–105.

Cruise O'Brien, Donal. 1971. *The Mourides of Senegal*. Oxford: Clarendon Press.

Dunn, John, and Robertson, A. F. 1973. *Dependence and Opportunity: political change in Brong Ahafo*. Cambridge: Cambridge University Press.

Eades, Jeremy. 1979. 'Kinship and entrepreneurship among Yoruba in northern Ghana', in William Shack and Elliott Skinner (eds), *Strangers in Africa*. Berkeley and Los Angeles, Cal.: University of California Press.

Edsman, Bjorn. 1979. *Lawyers in Gold Coast Politics*. Stockholm: Almqvist and Wiksell.

Elias, T. O. 1951. *Nigerian Land Law and Custom*. London: Routledge.

Fallers, Lloyd A. 1956. *Bantu Bureaucracy*. Cambridge: Heffer.

—— 1961. 'Are African cultivators to be called "peasants"?' *Current Anthropology* 2, 108–10.

Feder, Gershon, and Noronha, R. 1987. 'Land rights systems and agricultural development in sub-Saharan Africa', *World Bank Research Observer* 2 (1), 143–69.

Fisher, Jeanne. 1954. *The Anatomy of Kikuyu Domesticity and Husbandry*. London: Department of Technical Co-operation.

Fortes, Meyer. 1975. 'Strangers', in M. Fortes and S. Patterson (eds), *Studies in African Social Anthropology*. London: Academic Press.

Francis, Paul. 1981. 'Power and Order: a study of litigation in a Yoruba community'. Ph.D. thesis, University of Liverpool.

Frankel, S. H. 1938. *Capital Investment in Africa*. London: Oxford University Press.

Galletti, R., Baldwin, K. D. S. and Dina, I. O. 1956. *Nigerian Cocoa Farmers.* London: Oxford University Press.

Gann, L. H. 1963. *A History of Northern Rhodesia to 1953.* London: Chatto and Windus.

Glazier, Jack. 1985. *Land and the Uses of Tradition among the Mbeere of Kenya.* New York: University Press of America.

Gluckman, Max. 1941. *The Economy of the Central Barotse Plain.* Livingstone, Northern Rhodesia: Rhodes-Livingstone Institute.

—— 1965. *The Ideas in Barotse Jurisprudence.* Manchester: Manchester University Press.

Goody, Jack. 1971. *Technology, Tradition and the State.* Cambridge: Cambridge University Press.

Great Britain. 1914. 'Correspondence concerning Palm Oil Grants in West Africa', Colonial Office Confidential Print 1023.

Grier, Beverly. 1987. 'Contradictions, crises and class conflict: the state and capitalist development in Ghana prior to 1948', in I. Markovitz (ed.), *Studies in Class and Power in Africa.* New York: Oxford University Press.

Guyer, Jane. 1978. 'The food economy and French colonial rule in central Cameroon', *Journal of African History* 19 (4), 577–98.

Hailey, Lord. 1957. *An African Survey*, revised edition. London: Oxford University Press.

Hart, Keith. 1978. 'The economic basis of Tallensi social history', in G. Dalton (ed.), *Research in Economic Anthropology* I, 185–216. Washington, D.C.: American Anthropological Association.

Haugerud, Angelique. 1983. 'The consequences of land tenure reform among smallholders in the Kenya highlands', *Rural Africana* 15/16, 65–90.

—— 1989. 'Land tenure and agrarian change in Kenya', *Africa* 59 (1), 61–90.

Hayford, J. C. 1969. *The Truth about the West African Land Question*, revised edition. New York: Negro Universities Press.

Hellen, J. A. 1968. *Rural Economic Development in Zambia, 1890–1964.* Munich: Weltforum-Verlag.

Heyer, Judith, Maitha, J., and Senga, W. 1976. *Agricultural Development in Kenya.* Nairobi: Oxford University Press.

Hill, Polly. 1963. *Migrant Cocoa Farmers of Southern Ghana.* Cambridge: Cambridge University Press.

—— 1968. 'The myth of the "amorphous peasantry": a northern Nigerian case study', *Nigerian Journal of Economics and Social Studies* 10, 239–60.

Hopkins, A. G. 1969. 'A report on the Yoruba, 1910', *Journal of the Historical Society of Nigeria* 5 (1), 67–100.

—— 1973. *An Economic History of West Africa.* London: Longman.

Hunter, John. 1963. 'Cocoa migration and patterns of land ownership in the Densu valley near Suhum, Ghana', *Transactions and Papers, Institute of British Geographers* 31, 61–87.

Iliffe, John. 1979. *A Modern History of Tanganyika.* Cambridge: Cambridge University Press.

Jenkins, G. D. 1965. 'Politics in Ibadan'. Northwestern University Ph.D. thesis.

Jessop, Bob. 1977. 'Recent theories of the capitalist state', *Cambridge Journal of Economics* 1 (4), 353–74.

Johnson, Samuel O. 1921. *A History of the Yorubas.* Lagos: Church Missionary Society.

Jones, Christine. 1988. 'The Mobilization of Resources for Agricultural Development in sub-Saharan Africa: an economic perspective' (mimeo).

Joseph, Richard. 1984. 'Class, state and prebendal politics in Nigeria', in Nelson Kasfir (ed.), *State and Class in Africa*. London: Frank Cass.
Kanogo, Tabitha. 1987. *Squatters and the Roots of Mau Mau*. London: James Currey.
Kay, Geoffrey. 1972. *The Political Economy of Colonialism in Africa*. Cambridge: Cambridge University Press.
Kay, George. 1964. 'Aspects of Ushi settlement history', in R. W. Steele and R. M. Prothero (eds), *Geographers and the Tropics*. London: Longman.
Keegan, Tim. 1985. 'Crisis and catharsis in the development of capitalism in South African agriculture', *African Affairs* 84 (336), 371–98.
Kenya Land Commission. 1934. *Evidence and Memoranda* I. London: HMSO.
Kimble, David. 1963. *A Political History of Ghana*. Oxford: Clarendon Press.
Kitching, Gavin. 1980. *Class and Economic Change in Kenya*. New Haven, Conn.: Yale University Press.
—— 1985. 'Politics, method and evidence in the "Kenya debate"', in H. Bernstein and B. Campbell (eds), *Contradictions of Accumulation in Africa*. Beverly Hills, Cal.: Sage.
Klein, Martin. 1967. *Islam and Imperialism in Senegal*. Palo Alto, Cal.: Stanford University Press.
—— (ed.), 1980. *Peasants in Africa*. Beverly Hills, Cal.: Sage.
Kuklick, Henrika. 1979. *The Imperial Bureaucrat: the colonial administrative service in the Gold Coast, 1920–39*. Stanford, Cal.: Hoover Institution.
Kyerematen, A. A. Y. 1971. *Inter-state Boundary Litigation in Ashanti*, African Social Research Documents 4. Cambridge: African Studies Centre, University of Cambridge.
La Rue, George Michael. 1989. 'The *Hakura* System: land and social stratification in the social and economic history of the sultanate of Dar Fur (Sudan), ca. 1785–1875'. Ph.D. thesis, Boston University.
Lewis, John van Dusen. 1981. 'Domestic labor-intensity and the incorporation of Malian peasant farmers into localized descent groups', *American Ethnologist* 8 (1), 53–73.
Lloyd, Peter C. 1962. *Yoruba Land Law*. Ibadan: Oxford University Press.
Lonsdale, John. 1981. 'States and social processes in Africa: a historiographical survey', *African Studies Review* 24 (2/3), 139–225.
Lonsdale, John, and Berman, Bruce. 1979. 'Coping with the contradictions: the colonial state in Kenya, 1895–1914', *Journal of African History* 20 (4), 487–506.
Lugard, Frederick D. 1923. *The Dual Mandate in Tropical Africa*, second edition. Edinburgh: Blackwell.
McCaskie, Thomas. 1980. 'Office, land and subjects in the history of Manwere fekuo', *Journal of African History* 21 (2), 189–208.
—— 1983. 'R. S. Rattray and the construction of Asante history', *History in Africa* 10, 187–206.
—— 1984. '*Ahyiamu*—"a place of meeting": an essay on process and event in the history of the Asante state', *Journal of African History* 25 (2), 169–88.
MacGaffey, Wyatt. 1970. *Custom and Law in the Lower Congo*. Oxford: Clarendon.
Mackenzie, Fiona. 1989. 'Land and territory: the interface between two systems of land tenure, Murang'a District, Kenya', *Africa* 59 (1) 91–107.
Mandala, Elias. 1982. 'Peasant cotton agriculture, gender and intergenerational relationships: the Lower Tchiri Valley of Malawi, 1906–40', *African Studies Review* 25, 27–44.
Meebelo, H. S. 1971. *Reaction to Colonialism*. Manchester: Manchester University Press.
Miles, John. 1978. 'Rural protest in the Gold Coast: the cocoa hold-ups', in C.

Dewey and A. G. Hopkins (eds), *The Imperial Impact*. London: Institute of Commonwealth Studies.
Moore, Sally Falk. 1975. *Law as Social Process*. Berkeley and Los Angeles, Cal.: University of California Press.
—— 1986. *Social Facts and Fabrications*. Cambridge: Cambridge University Press.
Moseley, Paul. 1983. *The Settler Economies*. Cambridge: Cambridge University Press.
Munro, J Forbes. 1975. *Colonial Rule and the Kamba*. Oxford: Clarendon Press.
Nigerian National Archives. 1934–50. 'Organization and Reorganization Reports' for various districts. CSO 26 series.
Njonjo, Apollo. 1978. 'The Africanisation of the "White Highlands": a study in agrarian class struggles in Kenya, 1950–74'. Ph.D. thesis, Princeton University.
Nkadimeng, Malete, and Relly, Georgina. 1983. 'Kas Maine: the story of a black South African agriculturalist', in B. Bozzoli (ed.), *Town and Country in the Transvaal*. Johannesburg: Ravan.
Ochieng, W. R., and Janmohamed, K. K. (eds). 1977. 'Some perspectives on the Mau Mau movement', special issue of *Kenya Historical Review* 5 (2), 173–384.
Okali, Christine. 1983. *Cocoa and Kinship: the matrilineal Akan*. London: Kegan Paul for the International African Institute.
Okoth-Ogendo, H. W. O. 1976. 'African land tenure reform', in J. Heyer, J. Maitha and W. Senga, *Agricultural Development in Kenya*. London: Oxford University Press.
Olson, Mancur. 1971. *The Logic of Collective Action*, revised edition. New York: Schocken.
Oyediran, O. O. 1974. 'Modakeke in Ife', *Odu*, new series, 7, 68–82.
Parkin, David. 1972. *Palms, Wine and Witnesses*. San Francisco: Chandler.
Peel, J. D. Y. 1983. *Ijeshas and Nigerians*. Cambridge: Cambridge University Press.
Perham, Margery, (ed.). 1936. *Ten Africans*. London: Faber.
—— 1938. *Native Administration in Nigeria*. London: Oxford University Press.
Peters, Pauline. 1984. 'Struggles over water, struggles over meaning', *Africa* 54 (3), 29–49.
—— 1988. 'Understanding Resource Mobilization in Arable Agriculture in sub-Saharan Africa' (mimeo).
Pim, Alan. 1940. *The Financial and Economic History of the African Tropical Territories*. London: Oxford University Press.
—— 1948. 'Mining, commerce and finance', in Margery Perham (ed.), *The Economics of a Tropical Dependency* II. London: Faber.
Pottier, Johan. 1985. 'Reciprocity and the beer pot: the changing pattern of Mambwe food production', in J. Pottier (ed.), *Food Systems in Central and Southern Africa*. London: School of Oriental and African Studies.
Ranger, Terence. 1971. *The Agricultural History of Zambia*, Historical Association of Zambia pamphlet 1. Lusaka. National Educational Company.
—— 1983. 'The invention of tradition in colonial Africa', in E. Hobsbawm and T. Ranger (eds), *The Invention of Tradition*. Cambridge: Cambridge University Press.
Richards, A. I. 1939. *Land, Labour and Diet in Northern Rhodesia*. London: Oxford University Press for the International African Institute.
—— 1971. 'The conciliar system of the Bemba', in A. I. Richards and A. Kuper (eds), *Councils in Action*. Cambridge: Cambridge University Press.
Roberts, Andrew. 1973. *A History of the Bemba*. London: Longman.
Robertson, A. F. 1987. *The Dynamics of Productive Relationships: African share contracts in comparative perspective*. Cambridge: Cambridge University Press.
Ross, Paul. 1986. 'Land as a right to membership: land tenure dynamics in a

peripheral area of the Kano close settled zone', in M. Watts (ed.), *State, Oil, and Agriculture in Nigeria*. Berkeley, Cal.: Institute of International Studies.

Rowling, C. W. 1952. *Report on Land Tenure in Ondo*. Ibadan: Government Printer.

—— 1956. *Report on Land Tenure in Ijebu*. Ibadan: Government Printer.

Sarbah, J. M. 1897. *Fanti Customary Laws*. London: Clowes.

Shipton, Parker. 1989. 'The Kenyan land tenure reform: misunderstandings in the public creation of private property', in R. E. Downs and S. P. Reyna (eds), *Land and Society in Contemporary Africa*. Durham, N.H.: University Press of New England.

Sillitoe, K. K. 1962. 'Local organization in Nyeri', *Conference Proceedings, East African Institute of Social Research*. Nairobi: East African Institute of Social Research.

Snyder, Francis G. 1981. *Capitalism and Legal Change: an African transformation*. New York: Academic Press.

Sorrenson, M. P. K. 1967. *Land Reform in the Kikuyu Country*. Nairobi: Oxford University Press.

—— 1968. *Origins of European Settlement in Kenya*. Nairobi: Oxford University Press.

Southall, Roger. 1978. 'Farmers, traders and brokers in the Gold Coast cocoa economy', *Canadian Journal of African Studies* 12, 185–211.

Suret Canale, Jean. 1971. *French Colonialism in Tropical Africa, 1900–45*, trans. T. Gottheiner. London: Hurst.

Sutton, Inez. 1984. 'Law, chieftaincy and conflict in colonial Ghana: the Ada case', *African Affairs* 83 (330), 4162.

Swindell, Ken. 1985. *African Farm Labour*. Cambridge: Cambridge University Press.

Throup, David. 1988. *Economic and Social Origins of Mau Mau*. London: James Currey.

Tignor, Robert. 1976. *The Colonial Transformation of Kenya*. Princeton, N.J.: Princeton University Press.

Tordoff, William. 1965. *Ashanti under the Prempehs, 1888–1935*. London: Oxford University Press.

Vail, Leroy. 1976. 'Ecology and history: the example of eastern Zambia', *Journal of Southern African Studies* 3, 129–55.

Van Donge, J. Kees. 1985. 'Understanding rural Zambia: the Rhodes–Livingstone Institute revisited', *Africa* 55 (1), 60–75.

Vaughan, Megan. 1987. *The Story of an African Famine*. Cambridge: Cambridge University Press.

Wambaa, Rebman, and King, Kenneth. 1975. 'The political economy of the Rift Valley: a squatter perspective', in B. A. Ogot (ed.), *Hadith 5: Economic and social change in East Africa*. Nairobi: East African Literature Bureau.

Ward Price, H. L. 1939. *Land Tenure in the Yoruba Provinces*. Lagos: Government Printer.

Watson, William. 1958. *Tribal Cohesion in a Money Economy*. Manchester: Manchester University Press.

Weber, Jacques. 1977. 'Structures agraires et évolution des milieux ruraux: le cas de la région cacaoyère du centre-sud Cameroun', *Cahiers ORSTOM*, Série Sciences Humaines, XIV (4), 361–81.

Weigel, Jean Yves. 1982. *Migration et production domestique des Soninke de Sénégal*. Paris: ORSTOM Travaux et Documents.

Weiskel, Timothy. 1975. *French Colonial Rule and the Baule Peoples*. Oxford: Clarendon Press.

Werbner, Richard. 1967. 'Federal administration, rank and civil strife among Bemba royals and nobles', *Africa* 31 (1), 22–48.
West African Lands Committee. 1916. *Minutes of Evidence*. London: Colonial Office.
West, Henry. 1972. *Land Policy in Buganda*. Cambridge: Cambridge University Press.
Wilks, Ivor. 1975. *Asante in the Nineteenth Century*. Cambridge: Cambridge University Press.
Young, Crawford. 1988. 'The African colonial state and its political legacy', in N. Chazan and D. Rothchild (eds), *The Precarious Balance*. Boulder, Colo.: Westview.

Abstract

In their efforts to govern African colonies through traditional rulers and customary law, British officials founded colonial administration on contested terrain. By committing themselves to uphold 'native law and custom' colonial officials linked the definition of Africans' legal rights with their social identities, which were, in turn, subject to conflicting interpretations. As agricultural growth and commercialisation intensified demand for land, competition for access to land and control over agricultural income gave rise to disputes over customary jurisdictions and structures of authority. Using evidence from colonial Nigeria, the Gold Coast, Kenya and Northern Rhodesia, this article argues that, under indirect rule, the commercialisation of transactions in rights to rural land was accompanied by, and served to promote, unresolved debate over their meaning.

Résumé

En s'efforçant de gouverner les colonies africaines à travers les dirigeants traditionnels et le droit en usage, les représentants officiels britanniques ont fondé l'administration coloniale sur un terrain contentieux. En choisissant de maintenir 'le droit et la coutume indigènes', les représentants coloniaux ont lié la définition des droits légaux des africains à leurs identités sociales, qui à leur tour, étaient sujettes à des interprétations contradictoires. Comme le développement de l'agriculture et de la commercialisation ont intensifié la demande d'acquisition de terres, la concurrence pour accéder à la propriété et contrôler le revenu agricole ont engendré des controverses sur les juridictions usuelles et les structures de l'autorité. En prenant les exemples des colonies du Nigéria, de la Côte-d'Or, du Kenya et de la Rhodésie du Nord, cet article soutient que sous une représentation indirecte, la commercialisation des opérations dans les droits fonciers ruraux a contribué à engendrer un débat non résolu sur leur sens.

[2]

Sugar Factory Workers and the Emergence of 'Free Labour' in Nineteenth-Century Java

R. E. ELSON

The Australian National University

The Cultivation System and Coercion

THE Cultivation System, introduced by the Dutch in Java in 1830, was grounded on peasant coercion. Capitalizing on the colonial government's ability to force peasants to produce large, cheap and regular quantities of tropical agricultural goods and to labour unrelentingly at a great variety of other tasks, the System succeeded in its aim of transforming Java from a financial millstone around Holland's neck into a highly profitable resource.[1] Coercion, in the eyes of the Cultivation System's founder and guiding light, Governor-General Johannes van den Bosch (1830–33), was the most appropriate and effective means of creating wealth from Java's peasant masses. The power of incentive alone, he argued, had failed in the recent past to spur the Javanese to greater productive activity because the peasant had not reached the required stage of social development. 'Never forget', he remarked in 1830, 'that the Javan has progressed no further in intellectual terms than our children of 12 or 13 years old, and possesses even much less knowledge than they do. They must be led and governed as children.'[2] Van den Bosch's branch of coercion, however, was not a

I should like to thank Dr J. G. Butcher, Dr M. R. Fernando, Dr J. Ingleson, Dr G. R. Knight and Mr R. Hatley for their comments and advice, and the Australian Research Grants Scheme and the School of Modern Asian Studies, Griffith University, for research funding. This is a substantially revised version of a paper presented at the Eighth International Economic History Congress, Budapest, 1982.

[1] C. Fasseur, *Kultuurstelsel en Koloniale Baten* (Universitaire Pers, Leiden, 1975), ch. VIII, esp. pp. 118–20.

[2] 'Rapport van den Gouverneur-Generaal van den Bosch aan den Minister van Kolonien', in J. P. Cornets de Groot van Kraaijenburg, *Over het Beheer onzer Kolonien* (Gebroeders Belinfante, 's Gravenhage, 1862), p. 358. See Van den Bosch, 'Verslag

blunt instrument. It was based upon the time-worn notion of domesticating the indigenous elite and employing its customary authority over the peasantry to achieve Dutch ends. Under the overall direction of the colonial authorities and their officials, then, peasants were to be 'led and governed' by their own leaders, for whom, Van den Bosch claimed, they possessed a 'childlike respect'.[3] According to J. C. Baud, Van den Bosch's successor and a man who shared his general views,[4] it was this 'habit of submission and obedience, so characteristic of the Javanese', which made 'many things possible here which elsewhere would be fraught with great difficulties'.[5] By adroitly appropriating this authority, the Dutch were able to press huge numbers of peasants to the task of creating profits for Holland's treasury from the soil of Java.

The Sugar Industry, Factory Labour, and the Problem

The export sugar industry was one of the cornerstones of this great project of exploitation. At the orders of their chiefs and under the general management of local Dutch officials, peasants put large tracts of their village rice land to cane, tended the crop to maturity, and harvested and transported it to the factories which dotted the rural landscape in Java's sugar regions. This work did not exhaust their obligations, however. The colonial government had contracted private entrepreneurs to mill cane grown by peasants under compulsion and to deliver manufactured sugar to government warehouses for export. Making the contracts had been a tiresome and difficult undertaking for the government. The troubled economic history of the Java sugar industry—a story of fluctuating prices, transport problems, and oscillating government policies[6]—made many potential private manufacturers

mijner verrigtingen in Indie gedurende de jaren 1830, 1831, 1832 and 1833', *Bijdragen tot de Taal-, Land- en Volkenkunde* [hereafter *BKI*], vol. 7 (new series), 1864, pp. 390ff, for a similar formulation.

[3] 'Rapport van den Gouvernor-Generaal', p. 358.

[4] Writing to John Crawfurd many years later, Baud explained that 'the experience acquired [after 1816] tended to prove that native industry, unless propelled by the ruling power, seldom leaves the narrow circle of the very limited want of the people' (letter Baud to Crawfurd, 2 October 1857, Collectie Baud, no. 889, Algemeen Rijksarchief, The Hague [hereafter ARADH]).

[5] 'Rapport van den gouverneur-generaal ad interim, aan den minister van kolonien, omtrent eene inspektie-reis over Java' [1834], in S. van Deventer, *Bijdragen tot de Kennis van het Landelijk Stelsel op Java* (Joh. Noman en Zoon, Zalt-Bommel, 1865–1866), vol. 2, p. 677.

[6] See H. Ch. G. J. van der Mandere, 'De Suikerindustrie op Java, hare geschiedenis en ontwikkeling', *Indie*, vol. 5 (1921–22), pp. 121–3, 139–41, 187–8, 229–30.

'FREE LABOUR' IN NINETEENTH-CENTURY JAVA 141

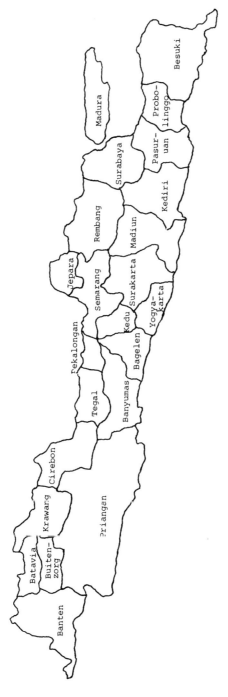

Map 1. Residencies of Java, c. 1850

wary of getting their fingers burnt by this latest scheme to revitalize the industry; as a result, the authorities had to resort to all manner of blandishments and concessions (and sometimes to threats) to recruit the entrepreneur-manufacturers they needed.[7] The attractive conditions the government felt obliged to offer manufacturers included not only interest-free loans for factory construction and running expenses, cheap materials and labour for construction work, and inexpensive supplies of firewood, but also gangs of forced labourers for heavy manual work in the factories during the milling season and beyond. Peasants, therefore, found themselves pushed into a schedule of duties that involved not just cultivating, harvesting and transporting cane, but also building, woodcutting and hauling, and long hours of sweaty labour within the stifling confines of the sugar factories.

My purpose here is to analyse how the sugar industry gradually dispensed with forced labour over the succeeding half-century or so and replaced it with a system of ostensibly voluntary wage labour. For the sake of economy, coherence and convenience, I shall confine my attention purely to the sphere of factory labour, but even this narrow focus reveals interesting facets of the changing nature of labour organization in the context of Javanese adaptation to an increasingly intrusive colonial presence. In essence I shall argue that the largely non-economic coercion upon which Van den Bosch founded his System and which remained the key feature of labour recruitment and control in the early decades of the government sugar industry gradually gave way in the later nineteenth century to a new, more subtle and more purely economic form of coercion, grounded in the deepening poverty and dependence of the Javanese peasantry.

Redressing Imbalances in the Early Contracts

By about 1834 the government sugar system was more or less fully operational. Already, however, the authorities were discovering that their eagerness to entice potential manufacturing agents into the scheme

[7] Van Deventer, *Bijdragen*, vol. 2, pp. 356ff. The government's anxiety to attract manufacturers is exemplified by the circular of the Director of Cultivations, J. van Sevenhoven, 9 February 1832, published as Bijlaag B of *Stukken betreffende het Onderzoek der (bij besluit van den Gouverneur-Generaal van Nederlandsch Indie van 8 December 1853, No 10) benoemde Commissie voor de Opname der Verschillende Suikerfabrieken op Java* (n.p., n.d.), p. 3. For an example of an early contract, see that made with T. B. Hofland in Van Deventer, *Bijdragen*, vol. 2, p. 176. The generous conditions are attested to in a 'Nota' written by E. A. van Vloten, owner of the Pangka factory in Tegal Residency (Archive of the Minister of Colonies [hereafter AMK], Verbaal [hereafter V] 21 April 1849/9, ARADH).

'FREE LABOUR' IN NINETEENTH-CENTURY JAVA 143

had resulted in contracts which 'left much to be desired as far as the interests both of peasants and government were concerned'.[8] The wide range of tasks required of peasants under forced labour was seen to be 'oppressive'.[9] More important, as far as the government's aims were concerned, was that it found itself subsidizing manufacturers' milling operations through its provision of cheap forced labourers while at the same time it was contractually bound to accept low grade sugar from the factories at prices well above those obtaining on world markets.[10] As a result, especially in those parts of East Java where sugar production exceeded all expectations, manufacturers were amassing huge fortunes on the basis of government largesse. Beginning in 1834, the government moved to redress this unequal and embarrassing situation and at the same time lessen the peasantry's burdens. Early that year Van den Bosch laid down that 'the work . . . in the factory itself should, as much as possible, be done by voluntary workers'.[11] In the same year the government stipulated that all new sugar contracts require manufacturers to provide their own factory labourers.[12] It formalized its position in 1836 by drawing up a model contract which restricted its responsibilities purely to having peasants cultivate cane to maturity and placed all aspects of harvesting, transport and manufacture squarely on the shoulders of manufacturers. As new contracts were made and old ones renewed after expiration in the light of these conditions, manufacturers concerned were bound to recruit and manage their factory labourers on the basis of free agreements with peasants (or, in practice, with their village chiefs) and wage payments.[13]

These measures reflect the fact that voluntary wage labour was an established fact of Javanese rural life. Earlier in the century, for example, John Crawfurd had noted the existence of a 'class of

[8] [J. van Sevenhoven] 'Over de Kultures op het Eiland Java en voornamelijk van Producten voor de markt van Europa', Exhibitum [hereafter Exh] 8 August 1840/265 Geh, ARADH.
[9] 'Kultuur Verslag', 1834, AMK, Exh 15 October 1835/MI Kab Geh, ARADH.
[10] Fasseur, *Kultuurstelsel*, pp. 66–7.
[11] 'Eenige Zakelijke Extracten uit een Algemeen Overzigt, door Zijne Excellentie den Commissaris-Generaal van den Bosch zamengesteld, gedagteekend 24 Januarij 1834', in Anon., *Blik op het Bestuur van Nederlandsch-Indie onder den Gouverneur-Generaal J. van den Bosch, voor zoo ver het door denzelven ingevoerde Stelsel van Cultures op Java betreft* (Kampen, 1835), p. 174.
[12] 'Kultuur Verslag', 1834.
[13] 'Kultuur Verslag', 1837, AMK, V 2 April 1840/M5 Kab, ARADH; K. van Gorkom, 'Historische Schets van de Suikerindustrie op Java', *Tijdschrift voor Nijverheid en Landbouw in Nederlandsch-Indie* [hereafter *TNLNI*], vol. 23, 1879, pp. 300–1.

ambulatory labourers',[14] while Van den Bosch himself spoke of a 'numerous class of proletarians' among the Javanese.[15] Nonetheless, the government was far from confident that there was a sufficient stock of workers who would voluntarily and reliably present themselves for wage work at the factories, especially given the need for wages there to be kept at the lowest possible levels. Fully conscious of the general problem of wage-labour shortages, Van den Bosch had even dabbled with solutions which ranged from the establishment of barracks of permanent coolies (*koelie-etablissementen*) to the importation of wage labourers from China.[16] These considerations tempered the government's drive to shift a greater onus for labour recruitment and control to the manufacturers. While it was clearly in the government's interest to redress the uneven division of responsibilities and benefits enshrined in the early contracts, it would serve no useful purpose if manufacturers found themselves unable to recruit sufficient voluntary workers and were forced therefore to suspend operations. Consequently, the government's policy settled to one of blurry compromise whereby it sought to encourage manufacturers to employ as many voluntary workers as possible, while at the same time making good any labour shortfalls by providing manufacturers with cheap forced labourers conscripted from villages proximate to the factories.[17] While stated government policy did not allow this practice until 1847,[18] the fact was that the provision of forced labourers remained a customary feature of factory operations throughout this period and was even spelled out in a number of contracts officially approved after 1836.[19] *Koloniaal Verslag* summed up the government's pragmatic approach in 1852 in suitably matter-of-fact tones: 'The difficulties... which manufacturers experienced, and still experience here and there, in obtaining the required means of transport and [factory] coolies, have made it necessary that the government lend assistance in that area'.[20]

[14] *History of the Indian Archipelago* (Frank Cass & Co. Ltd, London, 1967, reprint), vol. 1, p. 110.
[15] 'Verslag mijner verrigtingen in Indie', p. 401.
[16] Van Deventer, *Bijdragen*, vol. 2, pp. 159, 339–40.
[17] To ease manufacturers' recruitment problems, the 1836 model contract allowed that voluntary workers employed during the season be exempted from compulsory public works labour (*herendiensten*) provided manufacturers reimburse the government for the costs of the labour foregone (Van Gorkom, 'Historische Schets', pp. 304–5).
[18] Van Gorkom, 'Historische Schets', p. 310.
[19] See the conditions of contract for the factories Pangka and Comal in Tegal in 'Staat der verschillende kultuur-inrigtingen op Java onder ultimo 1848. Suiker Kultuur. La. B.', AMK, Exh 9 May 1851/4, ARADH.
[20] *Koloniaal Verslag* [hereafter *KV*], 1852, p. 88.

'FREE LABOUR' IN NINETEENTH-CENTURY JAVA 145

Voluntary Wage Labour in the 1850s

These arrangements ensured that, by the mid-1850s, forced labourers still constituted an integral component of the factory workforce. At the same time, however, most factories had responded to government encouragement[21] and taken on significant numbers of voluntary wage labourers. As had always been the case, each factory maintained a core of skilled workers—carpenters, smiths, experienced factory hands and overseers—who worked on contract. Some of them were permanently attached to the enterprise but most were hired only for the duration of the milling 'campaign' at monthly wages ranging from f10 to as much as f30.[22] Manufacturers probably recruited most of them from local urban centres which normally provided a haven for their skills and to which they returned in the off season. In addition, there was the all-important 'sugar-cooker', nearly always Chinese, practised in the secrets of the sugar manufacturing process. He and the bevy of assistants in his train were usually paid on the basis of the amount of sugar they were able to produce from the cane provided them: since this was the key to the manufacturer's prosperity, the sugar-cooker was always lucratively reimbursed for his labour and skill. The Chinese cooker at the Paiton factory in Probolinggo, for example, received 30 *duit* [1 *duit* = 1/120 guilder] for every picul [= 62 kilograms] of sugar he produced, giving him an annual income of around f6,000.[23] All the men in this core group were professionals, accustomed to trading their skills for a wage, fully-fledged members of Java's still insignificant proletariat.

In addition, factories also employed varying numbers of unskilled voluntary wage labourers. A few factories, indeed, such as Tulis in Rembang and Jakatra-Oost and Dankbaarheid in Pasuruan could already boast a wholly voluntary workforce.[24] In some places, such as Surabaya, Cirebon and Kediri Residencies, voluntary workers made up a sizeable proportion of factory employees,[25] and in Pasuruan Resi-

[21] See, eg, *KV*, 1850, p. 65.
[22] Based on information contained in the monographs of individual sugar factories in Probolinggo and Pasuruan Residencies. These form a small part of the voluminous materials compiled by the Umbgrove Commission of Inquiry into the government sugar system, AMK, Exh 30 April 1859/50, ARADH [hereafter Umbgrove Commission].
[23] From the money he paid each of his 19 assistants a monthly wage of f8.50 ('Monographie van Paiton', Umbgrove Commission).
[24] *Stukken betreffende het Onderzoek*, Bijlaag IJ (Pasoeroean), p. 4; Bijlaag IJ (Rembang), p. 2.
[25] *Ibid.*, Bijlaag IJ (Soerabaija), p. 4; Bijlaag IJ (Cheribon), p. 4; Bijlaag IJ (Kedirie), p. 3.

dency's 17 government factories they comprised as much as three-quarters of the unskilled workforce.[26] In other sugar regions, however, such as Probolinggo and Banyumas, they were in a minority,[27] and it is probably fair to say that most manufacturers throughout the rest of Java were still heavily reliant on the government to provide significant and regular numbers of cheap forced labourers for factory work.[28]

This local unevenness in the recruitment of labour sprang from a combination of factors—the density of the local population and the amount of land available for farming, the proximity of factories to towns, the availability of other forms of employment, to name just a few—but in a significant degree it probably stemmed from the varying degrees of enthusiasm with which local government officials pressed manufacturers to emancipate themselves from the need for government assistance. Some Residents, for example, were sympathetic to the difficulties manufacturers claimed to experience in recruiting labourers, and provided assistance without demur or delay; others were slow to press for the greater use of voluntary labour.[29] By contrast, a number chafed at the notion that the provision of conscripted labourers was a matter of right for their manufacturers and continually agitated for them to assume a greater weight of responsibility in procuring their own workers. In Surabaya, for instance, the Resident in 1852 proposed a step-by-step reduction in the number of forced labourers used for factory work, while five years later his successor laid down strict guidelines for the delivery of forced workers which included regulation of their numbers, higher wages and a ban on factories using them during the period of planting the main rice crop.[30] The most noteworthy case of

[26] 'Beantwoording der 12 vraagpunten opgenomen in de kabinetsmissive van Zijne Excellentie den Gouverneur Generaal dd. 14 Julij 1854, No 113b' [Pasuruan Residency], Umbgrove Commission.

[27] *Stukken betreffende het Onderzoek*, Bijlaag IJ (Probolinggo), p. 2; Bijlaag IJ (Banjoemas), p. 1.

[28] See, e.g., *ibid*., Bijlaag IJ (Bezoekie), pp. 2–3; Bijlaag IJ (Samarang), pp. 3–4; Bijlaag IJ (Japara), p. 3.

[29] According to the Resident of Jepara, it was not until 1862 that his predecessor made the first serious attempt to obtain voluntary labourers in the Residency (letter to Governor-General, 29 April 1864, AMK, Exh 3 August 1864/44, ARADH). Again, the Resident of Probolinggo argued in the strongest terms in 1861 that it was simply impossible for manufacturers to dispense with the government's assistance in obtaining the necessary number of workers (letter to Governor-General, 9 November 1861, AMK, Exh 8 August 1863/22, ARADH).

[30] Letter Resident of Surabaya to Director of Cultivations, 26 August 1858, AMK, Exh 28 November 1861/41, ARADH. See also 'Residentie Pasoeroean. Kultuur Verslag, 1855', Local Archive [hereafter AD], Pasuruan 23, Arsip Nasional, Jakarta [hereafter ANJ]; *KV*, 1850, p.65; *KV*, 1856, p. 103.

'FREE LABOUR' IN NINETEENTH-CENTURY JAVA 147

opposition to the manufacturers was the decision of the Resident of Tegal in 1848 to limit the number of conscripted workers provided by the government and to restrict their activities to the manufacturing process (and thereby prevent their being used, as happened in one factory, for such things as tending flower beds in the factory surrounds).[31]

The very existence of a significant corps of voluntary wage workers indicates an often unrecognized complexity in Javanese social and economic life at this time. Unfortunately, our knowledge of the patterns of their lives is far from complete. Some, as we have seen, were permanently employed at the factories, while others, in the majority, found work on a seasonal basis. A third category comprised those who worked for short periods of time for daily wages (*daglooners*).[32] By one account, permanent workers tended to be drawn from far afield, while more temporary labourers were normally resident in areas adjacent to the factories.[33] Some indication of the composition of a factory's unskilled voluntary workforce may be gained from a contract I came across in the local archives of Pasuruan Residency. It provides the names and origins of 83 'coolies' who had contracted for work in the factory De Goede Hoop in 1863. Of that number, 41 came from the Residency capital, Kota Pasuruan, 17 resided at the factory, 11 lived in the district in which the factory was situated, 13 were from neighbouring lowland districts, and one came from the nearby hill district of Tengger.[34]

Seasonal or shorter term workers seem to have comprised two distinct groups of people. The first was a collection of highly mobile seasonal labourers who pursued employment where they could find it. In East Java, for example, labourers from the neighbouring (and economically depressed) island of Madura commonly crossed the straits to seek dry

---

[31] Letter Resident of Tegal to H. P. Hoevenaar, 19 May 1848 (and Van Vloten's accompanying Nota), AMK, V 21 April 1849/9, ARADH; 'Kultuur Verslag', 1848, AMK, Exh 26 August 1850/8, ARADH; letter O. C. Holmberg de Beckvelt to Minister of Colonies, 8 May 1849, AMK, V 23 May 1849/1, ARADH; 'Nota' accompanying letter Governor-General to Minister of Colonies, 14 September 1849, AMK, V 5 December 1849/3, ARADH; letter Governor-General to Minister of Colonies, 19 June 1850, AMK, V 4 November 1850/3, ARADH; letter Director of Cultivations to Governor-General, 28 April 1853, AMK, V 27 March 1856/5, ARADH; Fasseur, *Kultuurstelsel*, pp. 72–3, 162–3.

[32] Letter Resident of Surabaya to Director of Cultivations, 26 August 1858; letter Resident of Pekalongan to Director of Internal Administration, 20 February 1869, AMK, Exh 7 March 1870/82, ARADH.

[33] Letter Resident of Surabaya to Director of Cultivations, 26 August 1858.

[34] 'Contract', AD, Pasuruan 9, ANJ.

season work in both domestic and export agriculture.[35] In Central Java, workers travelled from the Residencies of Rembang and Semarang for jobs at factories in neighbouring Jepara Residency.[36] Most of these 'foreign' seasonal workers were probably circular migrants who returned home with a portion of their earnings at the end of the season. Some of them, however, were more transient and rootless people, colourfully described by one sugar manufacturer in the following terms:

... wanderers, vagabonds, who through want, misdeed or tyranny have had to leave their village, and have now given themselves over to a wandering life, here today, there tomorrow, leaving debts behind in the markets, at night lying together like animals in so-called coolie-sheds, or in any shelter they can get, each cent they earn immediately gambled away or spent on opium, and never doing more work than they need to in order to satisfy their base desires.[37]

Seasonal workers, whether circular migrants or transients, often lived in squalid *kampung* on the outskirts of local towns and travelled back and forth to the factories each day. In some cases, factory owners or managers allowed them to establish settlements on the factory grounds, something especially common in Cirebon. Some of the *kampung* there were very large indeed—Cileduk factory's worker compound numbered nearly 2,000 inhabitants and Arjowinangun more than 1,400—and housed not just the workers but their families as well. Manufacturers sometimes arranged for workers to cultivate small plots of land to augment their incomes; at Arjowinangun, for example, they had the opportunity of working about 70 hectares of rice land in neighbouring villages.[38] When it became evident that provision of compounds for wage labourers facilitated their recruitment, they became quite common throughout Java's sugar regions.[39]

[35] 'Nota omtrent de aangelegenheden der Suikerkultuur in de residentie Pasoeroean (opname 1863)', Archive of the Director of Cultivations [hereafter ADK], no. 525, ANJ.

[36] *Stukken betreffende het Onderzoek*, Bijlaag IJ (Japara), p. 3; 'Rapport, betreffende de Suikerkultuur in de Residentie Japara', AMK, Exh 16 May 1864/62, ARADH.

[37] B. R. P. Hasselman, *Mijne Ervaring als Fabrikant in de Binnenlanden van Java* (Martinus Nijhoff, 's Gravenhage, 1862), p. 27. Hasselman added that some manufacturers were not above providing their itinerant workers with opportunities to dispose of their wages recklessly, especially through gambling, thereby keeping them penniless and dependent upon the manufacturer for further income (p. 28). See also D.H. Burger, *Sociologisch-Economische Geschiedenis van Indonesie* (Koninklijk Instituut voor de Tropen, Amsterdam, 1975), vol. 1, p. 110.

[38] *Stukken betreffende het Onderzoek*, Bijlaag IJ (Cheribon), pp. 4–5.

[39] 'Nota omtrent de aangelegenheden der Suikerkultuur in de residentie Pasoeroean'; letter Resident of Semarang to Director of Internal Administration, 15 February 1869, AMK, Exh 7 March 1870/82, ARADH; G. R. Knight, 'Capitalism, Commodities and the Transformation of Java', paper presented at the Third National Conference of the Asian Studies Association of Australia, Griffith University, 1980, p. 22.

'FREE LABOUR' IN NINETEENTH-CENTURY JAVA 149

The second group of seasonal or daily labourers was based on villages in the districts surrounding the factories. Nearly all of them came from that large segment of the peasantry who possessed insufficient land to feed themselves and their families or no land at all, and who were therefore dependent for income from labour opportunities provided by others.[40] Women and children formed an important component of this local group, performing a variety of allegedly less onerous tasks in the factories.[41] The 15–20 cents a day they earned was doubtless a prized supplement to the 25 cents which a voluntary unskilled male could expect, and which was barely sufficient for individual subsistence.[42]

Manufacturers recruited their voluntary workers in a number of ways. One common practice was to send a trusted employee, usually a foreman (*mandur*), to local urban centres and communities of seasonal workers where those accustomed to wage labour resided. The foreman carried with him a large sum of cash, used for making advance payments (*voorschot*)—usually a month's wages—to those he could entice to contract their services to the factory. Judging from later evidence,[43] it seems highly likely that potential workers often organized themselves into labour gangs whose leaders carried on the necessary negotiations with the foreman and agreed to provide and control workers at the factories. Doubtless, too, these arrangements frequently took on an enduring character, as foremen established links with pools of workers

[40] Indications are that these people were often in a majority in Javanese villages in the mid-nineteenth century. M. R. Fernando has calculated that more than half the farmers in Cirebon Residency in 1858 were landless ('Peasants and Plantation Economy: The Social Impact of the European Plantation Economy in Cirebon Residency from the Cultivation System to the End of the First Decade of the Twentieth Century', PhD dissertation, Monash University, 1982, p. 160). Even in the sugar districts of Pasuruan Residency, allegedly one of the most prosperous regions of Java, 40 per cent of peasant households had no shares in village rice lands (calculated from statistics contained in the monographs for Pasuruan Residency, Umbgrove Commission). The author of the article 'Rijst' in P. J. Veth (ed.), *Aardrijkskundig en Statistisch Woordenboek van Nederlandsch Indie* (P. N. van Kampen, Amsterdam, 1869), vol. 3, pp. 45–96, while using an admittedly crude measuring stick, comes to similar conclusions for most Residencies of Java.

[41] 'Algemeen Verslag der Residentie Besoeki over het jaar 1834', AD, Besuki 15, ANJ; *Stukken betreffende het Onderzoek*, Bijlaag IJ (Probolingo), p. 3; Bijlaag IJ (Bezoekie), p. 2; *KV*, 1856, p. 104; J. Hageman, 'Over de Nijverheid in Zuidoostelijk Java', *TNLNI*, vol. 8, 1862, p. 44.

[42] 'Residentie Pasoeroean. Bijlagen behoorende tot het Kultuur Verslag van 1859', AD, Pasuruan 23, ANJ.

[43] 'Contract Fabriekskoelies' in 'Copie-Arbeidsenquete Suikerindustrie van het Algemeen Syndicaat van Suikerfabrikanten in Ned.-Indie. Fabrieksarbeid', Koloniale Bank Archives, no. 1258, ARADH. See also Ph. Levert, *Inheemsche Arbeid in de Java-Suikerindustrie* (H. Veenman & Zonen, Wageningen, 1934), p. 119, and Burger, *Sociologisch-Economische Geschiedenis*, vol. 2, p. 72.

who returned to the same factories each season. Outside these formal networks, of course, unattached individuals or small groups might also be recruited if their paths crossed those of the foreman and they showed an inclination to offer their services.

The *voorschot* system was a key method of recruitment. Its aim was to induce prospective employees to bind themselves for a period of service by offering them a large cash sum to be worked off bit by bit through the season. To this end it was usually touted about in those months of the year immediately preceding the rice harvest—November to March—when rice prices were high and non-landholders had difficulty in securing employment in domestic agriculture.[44] Many workers were eager to pocket the sums involved, but as we shall see, less ready to honour their commitments when their circumstances changed. Money in the form of a *voorschot*, of course, was not the only inducement to factory labour. Many manufacturers attracted workers by offering them strong drink or, more often, access to opium (a number of Chinese sugar manufacturers at the same time held licences for local opium farms).[45] According to James Rush, 'it was widely believed that the large number of labourers required to maintain commercial agriculture would flee any enterprise not providing opium'.[46]

The foreman-centred style of recruitment was most appropriate to secure the services of workers who were accustomed to the practices and demands of regular wage labour. While it was also used to procure peasant labourers from villages near the factories, and appears to have enjoyed success when village resources were strained by crop failure, famine or overpopulation,[47] it was not the most popular or efficient

[44] Letter Resident of Pasuruan to Director of Internal Administration, 2 November 1868, AMK, Exh 7 March 1870/82, ARADH.

[45] 'Suikerkontrakten te Passoeroean' [by H. J. Lion], AD, Pasuruan 20, ANJ; letter Van Delden to Governor-General, 4 August 1868, AMK, Exh 7 March 1870/82 ARADH; H. van Alphen, *Java en het Kultuurstelsel* (W. P. van Stockum, s' Gravenhage, 1869–1870), vol. 1, pp. 25–6. It may be relevant in this regard that in Pasuruan Residency, Chinese manufacturers used the least numbers of forced labourers ('Nota omtrent de aangelegenheden').

[46] 'Opium Farms in Nineteenth-Century Java: Institutional Continuity and Change in a Colonial Society, 1860–1910', PhD dissertation, Yale University, 1977, p. 54. Rush suggests that opium was sought after for its stimulative as much as its relaxative qualities; if so, its widespread use would have been highly appropriate for sugar factory labour with its requirements for great physical exertion and long hours which sometimes involved a 12-hour night shift.

[47] The Resident of Jepara noted in 1846 that when the price of rice was high, manufacturers had little difficulty getting voluntary wage workers (Anon., 'Algemeen overzigt van den toestand van Nederlandsch Indie, gedurende het jaar 1846', *Tijdschrift voor Nederlandsch-Indie* [hereafter *TNI*], vol. 10, 1847, p. 383). Knight ('Capitalism and Commodity Production in Java', in H. Alavi *et al.*, *Capitalism and Colonial Production*

'FREE LABOUR' IN NINETEENTH-CENTURY JAVA 151

method of obtaining 'free labour'. More commonly manufacturers exploited the power of village chiefs and other influential figures in the rural areas, official and unofficial, indigenous and European. In the case of Pakis factory in Jepara Residency, for example, villagers in the districts of Jepara and Mantoop, far from the mill, and who had previously been forced to undertake factory labour there, were now found to 'volunteer' for it with some 'encouragement' from the local government administration.[48] In the same Residency it was reported that village chiefs had been co-opted to recruit 'voluntary' workers for the Besito factory; for every labourer they delivered they received a payment of two cents from the manufacturer.[49] In Pasuruan in 1860 the Resident ordered that arrangements be made with village chiefs so that they would organize and deliver specified numbers of 'voluntary' labourers to the factories each day.[50] The Resident of Surabaya was moved to remark in 1858 that he could see no way of procuring voluntary labourers from villages on any large scale 'without chiefs and government officials involving themselves in the matter, making arrangements and giving orders, so that what is free labour in name is in fact the opposite.'[51] This method of recruitment, frequently in force as well among the growing number of private sugar enterprises, reflected a characteristic set of social circumstances which regulated village life, and to which I shall shortly return.

The Continuing Importance of Forced Labour

Notwithstanding these developments in the area of so-called free labour, manufacturers in the 1850s and early 1860s preferred to continue receiving regular consignments of forced labourers for the milling season and sometimes outside it.[52] There were obvious benefits for them in the

(Croom Helm, London and Canberra, 1982), p. 140), cites evidence from Pekalongan about 1857 when crop failure seems to have had the same effect.

[48] *Stukken betreffende het Onderzoek*, Bijlaag IJ (Japara), p. 3.
[49] 'Rapport, betreffende de Suiker Kultuur in de Residentie Japara'.
[50] 'Residentie Pasoeroean. Kultuur Verslag 1860', AD, Pasuruan 24, ANJ.
[51] Letter Resident of Surabaya to Director of Cultivations, 26 August 1858.
[52] In 1862 and 1863 there were cases reported of forced labourers being delivered before the milling season for such things as factory repair ('Advies van den Raad van Nederlandsch Indie uitgebragt in de vergadering van den 19den Augustus 1864', AMK, Exh 11 February 1865/1, ARADH. See also Resident of Surabaya to Director of Cultivations, 26 August 1858). The practice was not in force everywhere. In 1835, for example, the Resident of Pasuruan had stopped the provision of forced labourers to factories in Bangil Regency when the season ended so that peasants could devote themselves fully to the tasks of wet season rice cultivation (letter Resident of Pasuruan to Bangil Sugar Manufacturers, 8 February 1835, AD, Pasuruan 1835 (bundle otherwise unnumbered), ANJ).

maintenance of this scheme of things. In the first place it gave them a guarantee that they would always have sufficient workers to keep their factories operating uninterruptedly through the season.[53] One manufacturer claimed, indeed, that if the government ceased to provide this service his enterprise would collapse for want of labour.[54] Secondly, while some manufacturers were of a mind that voluntary labour was more efficient than forced labour, most seem to have felt that forced labourers, delivered at artificially contrived wage levels, kept wage costs lower and were less expensive in other ways.[55] Thirdly, the provision system reduced the administrative and supervisory tasks and costs associated with recruiting and managing voluntary labourers; it was far preferable simply to call on the government for assistance than to expend time and energy in the search for workers whom many manufacturers believed did not exist in sufficient quantities or suffer the vexation and financial loss caused by workers who failed to honour their agreements.[56] Manufacturers' reluctance to dispense with the government's support was tellingly expressed in one Resident's report in 1862: 'The inclination to obtain free labour does not exist, or if it does, it is of little significance; free labour is the unknown, the dark future . . .'.[57]

Their antipathy towards 'free labour' was shared by peasants, but for different reasons. Peasants found it singularly unattractive because of the long hours, the hard physical work in sweltering conditions, the continual supervision and control to which they were subject, and the low returns.[58] Moreover there was generally an abundance of alternative employment opportunities available—assisting landed peasants with the rice harvest or the planting of dry season crops, work on European private agricultural enterprises, and even harvesting and

---

[53] Letter Resident of Madiun to Governor-General, 28 March 1866, AMK, Exh 31 July 1866/46, ARADH; 'Kultuur Verslag. Residentie Pasoeroean 1866', AD, Pasuruan 31, ANJ.

[54] Letter Holmberg de Beckvelt to Minister to Colonies, 8 May 1849.

[55] *Stukken betreffende het Onderzoek*, Bijlaag IJ (Cheribon), pp. 4–5; 'Rapport over de Suiker Kultuur in de residentie Cheribon. Inspectie gedaan in de maand Augustus 1863', ADK, no. 525, ANJ; letter Resident of Madiun to Governor-General, 28 March 1866; 'Memorie van de vereeniging van suikerfabriekanten in de residentie Pasoeroean', reproduced in letter Resident of Pasuruan to Director of Cultivations, 4 April 1866, AMK, Exh 10 July 1866/50, ARADH.

[56] Letter Resident of Surabaya to Governor-General, 14 March 1861, AMK, Exh 28 November 1861/41, ARADH, and sources mentioned in note 55.

[57] 'Residentie Pasoeroean. Politiek Verslag over 1862', AD, Pasuruan 1, ANJ.

[58] Letter Assistant-Inspector of Cultivations to Director of Cultivations 30 November 1835, Collectie Baud, no. 457, ARADH; *Stukken betreffende het Onderzoek*, Bijlaag IJ (Japara), p. 3; letter Resident of Surabaya to Director of Cultivations, 26 August 1858; Levert, *Inheemsche Arbeid*, pp. 79–80.

transport work for the factories—against which factory labour ran a poor last in terms of conditions, pay, status and social rewards.[59] The only marginal benefit—and one generally available only for a short time from the early 1860s—was the remission from *herendiensten* and other compulsory services which was granted to those who volunteered for factory work.[60] Even this benefit was somewhat illusory in the sense that those most likely to take on voluntary factory labour were landless peasants who, in theory, were not normally liable for corvée work anyway, who in practice often found themselves pressed into it, and who lacked the political muscle to give the remission any practical validity.[61] As a consequence of all this, local government officials were customarily required to make up deficiencies in the workforces of nearly every factory contracted to the government through conscripting peasants from surrounding villages for factory work.[62]

Generally, the task of organizing the required numbers of forced labourers was delegated to the district head, an indigenous official, who arranged with village chiefs to call up workers needed by the factories. Like most other arrangements governing the operation of the Cultivation System in Java, local circumstances and decisions dictated the precise method of conscription. The most common practice, in force especially throughout the eastern corner of Java, was for local officials to designate the villages within a five or ten kilometre radius of each factory as liable for service to the government sugar industry. This meant that their inhabitants were obligated to numerous different duties. A peasant landholder, for example, might find himself liable not only to plant and

[59] Letter Resident of Surabaya to Director of Cultivations, 26 August 1858; 'Rapport over de Suiker Kultuur in de residentie Cheribon'; letter Resident of Banyumas to Governor-General, 6 July 1867, AMK, Exh 20 October 1868/2, ARADH; Knight, 'Capitalism and Commodity Production', p. 140.

[60] As far as I can ascertain, this remission was available only in Pasuruan before the 1860s. From 1864 it became much more widespread and appears to have facilitated the recruitment of contracted labourers somewhat, if only because wealthier peasants sometimes volunteered for factory work, gained their remission, and then employed poorer villagers to take their place at the factory ('Nota omtrent de aangelegenheden'; letter Resident of Jepara to Governor-General, 12 April 1864, AMK, V 9 November 1864/193 Geh, ARADH; letter Resident of Cirebon to Director of Internal Administration, 4 March 1869, AMK, Exh 7 March 1870/82, ARADH; Bijblad 1748 (1865); Van de Mandere, 'De Suikerindustrie op Java', p. 283).

[61] [J. van Sevenhoven], 'Over de Heerendiensten waaraan de Javaan onderworpen is, en de middelen om dezen last te verminderen', AMK, V 8 August 1840/268 Geh; *Stukken betreffende het Onderzoek*, Bijlaag IJ (Cheribon), p. 5; letter Resident of Surabaya to Director of Cultivations, 26 August 1858; letter Resident of Probolinggo to Director of Cultivations, 6 January 1864, V 25 November 1865/211 Geh, ARADH; Knight, 'Capitalism and Commodity Production', p. 134.

[62] *KV*, 1860, pp. 118–19.

tend cane for the government but also to work in the factory during the milling season.[63] Less commonly, as occurred in parts of Cirebon, Pekalongan Semarang, and throughout Jepara, the government set aside villages for specific purposes.[64] Some were designated as cane-growing villages, some to provide transport facilities, while others—sometimes long distances from the factories[65]—were required to deliver labourers for harvesting and factory duties. Most often, these tasks were formally the responsibility of landholding villagers because of the customary notion that the right of access to land carried with it concurrent responsibilities for the performance of service for supra-village authorities. In fact, while landholders usually performed their cultivation duties—usually with help from the landless[66]—they tended to shunt their other assignments, particularly the despised factory labour, onto poorer elements within the village. It was extremely common for landholders—sometimes with the co-operation of village chiefs who drew a profit from the undertaking—to devise arrangements which led to poorer villagers carrying the brunt of factory labour. Sometimes it was a matter of sending a peasant who stood in a client or dependent relationship to the landholder to substitute for him at the factory; sometimes it was purely a matter of paying another villager a sum of money, in addition to the factory wage, to take one's place. Whatever the case, it was nearly always the less privileged who made up the required quota of forced labourers, freeing landholders from the hardships of factory work and relieving them for more profitable pursuits within the economic life of the village.[67]

[63] Monographs for Pasuruan and Probolinggo Residencies, Umbgrove Commission; Fasseur, 'Organisatie en sociaal-economische betekenis van de gouvernementssuikerkultuur in enkele residenties op Java omstreeks 1850', *BKI*, vol. 133, 1977, pp. 282–3; letter Resident of Surabaya to Director of Cultivations, 26 August 1858; letter Director of Cultivations to Governor-General, 2 March 1865, AMK, V 2 October 1865/H15 Kab, ARADH.

[64] *Stukken betreffende het Onderzoek*, Bijlaag IJ (Samarang), pp. 3–4; Bijlaag IJ (Pekalongan), p. 2; Fasseur, 'Organisatie', p. 280; 'Rapport over de Suiker Kultuur in de residentie Cheribon'.

[65] The Cileduk factory in Cirebon, for instance, used 350 forced labourers a day from the district of Ciawi, 20 kilometres away across hills and valleys (G. H. van Soest, 'De vrijwillige suikerkultuur in de residentie Cheribon', *TNI*, vol. 23, pt 2, 1861, p. 103). A similar situation obtained in Jepara. See Fasseur, 'Organisatie', p. 280, and Van Deventer, *Bijdragen*, vol. 3, p. 123.

[66] O., 'De suikerkultuur in 't oosten en westen van Java', *TNI*, vol. 14, pt 1, 1852, pp. 237–8.

[67] Letter Resident of Surabaya to Director of Cultivations, 26 August 1858; letter Resident of Semarang to Governor-General, 5 April 1861, AMK, Exh 25 November 1865/211 Geh, ARADH; letter Resident of Jepara to Director of Cultivations, 29 March 1864, AMK, V 9 November 1864/193 Geh, ARADH; 'Kultuur Verslag. Residentie

Structural and Other Impediments to Voluntary Labour

The government's tolerance over the first three decades of the sugar system of the demands made upon it by manufacturers to deliver conscripted labourers sprang from its desire not to prejudice the factories' operations and its own profits. Underpinning this tolerance, as we have seen, was the commonly held view that the Javanese peasant was mentally unfit for regular and reliable service in a wage labour economy, that existing social usages and modes of organization within the indigenous sphere were inappropriate for a fully-fledged system of wage labour. Through the 1850s and early 1860s, however, with a growing disenchantment with the system of forced cultivations as a whole and a concomitant re-emergence of liberal ideas,[68] the colonial authorities began to take the question of 'free labour' more seriously. As they did so, it seems that government officials began to realize that the 'character' or 'nature' of Javanese villagers was not necessarily an immutable given but a result of the way in which their lives were organized. This realization had important ramifications for future policy and practice, so it is therefore worthwhile to pursue the notion further.

Peasants in the sugar regions of Java generally lived in villages centred around wet-rice cultivation. Land was the heart of their existence and those in the village who controlled access to it built a complex web of political, social and economic relationships which reflected the disposition of wealth and rank within the village and recognized at the same time the right of supra-village authorities to exact a portion of villagers' produce and labour in return for protection and status. There were few mechanisms for social and economic survival and advancement outside this structure, and success was normally a function of attaching oneself to a regular village patron. Most landless villagers, for example, had no choice but to cultivate their village betters

Pasoeroean 1866'; Knight, 'Capitalism and Commodity Production', pp. 138–9. There were other arrangements, of course, which had the same goal. In Semarang, for example, a certain number of landholders arranged with their peers to bind themselves to the factories for the duration of the season. In return, the remaining landholders took over their compulsory public works labour duties and granted them a share of the crop payments received for the village's cane. In the same Residency, four villages set aside for the provision of factory labourers regularly employed unattached workers from Pekalongan and elsewhere to replace them in the factories. This allowed them to pursue uninterrupted their livelihood as fishermen (*Stukken betreffende het Onderzoeg*, Bijlaag IJ (Samarang), pp. 3–4).

[68] See Fasseur, *Kultuurstelsel*, especially ch. VII and following chapters.

in order to gain the food, shelter and employment opportunities they needed; landholders, by the same token, jostled for the favour of village ruling cliques who managed such important matters as the apportionment of rice fields, the assessment of taxation and the organization of labour.

Under these circumstances, and in the absence of ready alternatives, the important and sustaining values were enduring loyalty, deference, reciprocity and mutual sensitivity, not those normally associated with capitalistic individualism. More important than this, however, was that the formal and informal round of obligations and duties required of villagers allowed few people the regular and uninterrupted opportunity to pursue a wage-based livelihood outside the village. In addition to *herendiensten* there were the tasks of compulsory export cultivation, the conduct of domestic agriculture (requiring the greatest labour inputs for harvesting mature rice crops and preparing the land for new ones at times which coincided with the beginning and latter stages of the milling season), village community work such as guarding crops and repairing village roads, the performance of ceremonials (most commonly at the end of the rice harvest), and also complying with the levies of indigenous aristocrats who often clung desperately to their customary privileges despite government attempts to control them.[69]

The weight of these burdens fell most heavily on the landholding group within the village, but as we have seen, landholders were everywhere successful in redistributing a good measure of their assigned tasks to poorer villagers whose social and economic dependence left them little say or choice in the matter.[70] These labour-sharing techniques were admirably suited to maximizing landholders' agricultural and other interests, but they placed severe limits on the availability

---

[69] Letter Resident of Surabaya to Director of Cultivations, 26 August 1858; letter Resident of Surabaya to Governor-General, 14 March 1861; letter Resident of Cirebon to Governor-General, 19 November 1861, AMK, Exh 8 August 1863/22, ARADH; 'Residentie Pasoeroean. Kultuur Verslag over het jaar 1863', AD, Pasuruan 24, ANJ; letter Resident of Probolinggo to Director of Cultivations, 6 January 1864; letter Resident of Pekalongan to Governor-General, 12 June 1867, AMK, Exh 30 June 1868/38, ARADH.

[70] 'Nota, betrekkelijk het verrigten van Diensten door de bevolking in de Residentie Banjoemaas, ten behoeve van Gouvernements werken of voor den arbeid bij de suiker fabriek Kalibagor gedurende den maaltijd, zoo ten opzigte de dienstpligtigheid, als betaling, welke de bevolking hier voor erlangt', AMK, V 24 January 1859/17, ARADH; 'Residentie Pasoeroean. Bijlagen behoorende tot het kultuur verslag van 1859', AD, Pasuruan 23, ANJ; letter Resident of Tegal to Director of Cultivations, 11 May 1861, AMK, V 5 February 1864/Pl Kab, ARADH; Anon., 'Wat is waarheid? Vrije arbeid blijkens officiele stukken', *TNI*, vol. 22, pt 2, 1860, p. 226.

TABLE 1
Number of Days of Forced Factory Labour in Java's Sugar Factories, 1862–1872

Residency	1862	1863	1864	1865	1866	1867	1868	1869	1870	1871	1872
Cirebon	55766	142055	?	?	0	0	0	0	0	0	0
Tegal	198119	253374	111793	2050	0	0	0	0	0	0	0
Pekalongan	93426	159948	70946	62609	0	0	0	0	0	0	0
Semarang	99235	254115	?	15961	770	0	0	0	0	0	0
Jepara	185072	309292	?	134202	0	0	0	0	0	0	0
Rembang	21600	21240	19560	181000	2400	0	0	0	0	0	0
Surabaya	447854	532299	555964	14160	195300	161547	123730	105508	42076	0	0
Pasuruan	234000	236280	220082	553692	130952	98533	71981	7833	0	0	0
Probolinggo	193080	243240	264200	213939	31554	15255	8085	7975	0	0	0
Besuki	181060	220520	175560	237600	87600	87610	58869?	?	?	6101	0
Banyumas	34971	46015	36015	159600	28600	0	0	0	0	0	0
Madiun	6000	20185	15000	33000	9477	995	1250	4875	7624	0	0
Kediri	83347	116527	?	15000	0	0	0	0	0	0	0
				±57650							
TOTALS	1833530	2536090	?	1680463	486653	363940	263915	?	?	6101	0

? = Information unavailable or in doubt.
Source: *KV*, 1867–68, Bijlage MM; *KV*, 1870, Bijlage LL; *KV*, 1871, Bijlage JJ; *KV*, 1872, Bijlage MM; *KV*, 1873, p. 217.

TABLE 2
Number of Factories Using Forced Labourers, 1862–1872

Residency	Number of factories contracted to government	1862	1863	1864	1865	1866	1867	1868	1869	1870	1871	1872
Cirebon	10	8	9	?	1	0	0	0	0	0	0	0
Tegal	9	7	7	6	6	0	0	0	0	0	0	0
Pekalongan	3	2	2	2	2	0	0	0	0	0	0	0
Semarang	4	4	4	?	4	1	0	0	0	0	0	0
Jepara	9	8	9	?	8	0	0	0	0	0	0	0
Rembang	1	1	1	1	1	1	0	0	0	0	0	0
Surabaya	18	18	18	18	18	12	13	13	11	9	0	0
Pasuruan	17	15	15	14	14	12	11	10	2	0	0	0
Probolinggo	10	10	10	10	10	6	2	3	1	0	0	0
Besuki	5	5	5	5	5	4	4	3	?	4?	2	0
Banyumas	1	1	1	1	1	1	0	0	0	0	0	0
Madiun	2	1	1	1	1	1	1	1	1	1	0	0
Kediri	6	6	6	?	3	0	0	0	0	0	0	0
TOTALS	95	86	88	?	74	38	31	30	?	14?	2	0

? = Information unavailable or in doubt.
Source: *KV*, 1867–68, Bijlage MM; *KV*, 1870, Bijlage LL; *KV*, 1871, Bijlage JJ; *KV*, 1872, Bijlage MM; *KV*, 1873. p. 217.

'FREE LABOUR' IN NINETEENTH-CENTURY JAVA 159

of less prosperous peasants for regular extra-village wage labour. The result, as one Resident complained, was that 'voluntary day-wage-workers [could] be obtained only at certain times of the year and even then very irregularly'.[71] These structural impediments, together with the manufacturers' reluctance to dispense with forced labour, the inherent unattractiveness of factory labour and the availability of alternative means for poor and landless peasants to earn a livelihood, greatly inhibited the growth of 'free labour' in the factories. 'A great obstacle in the obtaining of free labour', lamented *Koloniaal Verslag* in 1857, 'remains the fact that, except for the capital cities of the regions, a proper class of day-wage-workers has not been established everywhere'.[72]

The 'Transition' to 'Free Labour'

Notwithstanding this imposing array of impediments, by 1872 every government sugar factory in Java had dispensed with the use of factory labourers conscripted and delivered by the government.[73] Why did the transition come about so abruptly and completely? The answer is to be found almost solely in a hardening of the government's attitude to the general issue of forced labour. From about 1850, the government moved, at first in fits and starts and eventually with increasing determination and purposefulness, towards the emancipation of the peasantry from formal compulsion. By 1870, the great edifice of the Cultivation System had been more or less dismantled, to be replaced by a system of production based on free enterprise and voluntary labour. The government's attack on forced factory labour was a leading edge of this campaign; by the early 1860s the official line of 'encouraging' manufacturers to employ more voluntary labourers in their factories and thereby reduce their calls upon government assistance was giving way to legislative *fiat* which pushed the manufacturers towards voluntary labour. For example, the 1863 regulations revising the guidelines laid down in 1860 for the government sugar system removed the stipulation that manufacturers could use forced labourers provided by the government if they could not recruit sufficient voluntary workers.[74] In 1864, the government forebade the use of forced factory labourers outside the milling season and decreed that 'the provision of

---

[71] 'Residentie Pasoeroean. Kultuur Verslag over 1854', AD, Pasuruan 23, ANJ.
[72] *KV*, 1857, p. 36.   [73] See tables 1 and 2.
[74] Staatsblad 1863, no. 118, cf Bijblad 945 (1860).

forced labourers ... must decrease gradually each year, so that when the present contracts expire this practice will have stopped entirely'.[75] In 1865, it ordered that 'the provision of forced labourers for those sugar factories which operate on contracts based on the 1863 sugar regulation must stop unconditionally; for all others whose contracts still include a promise of some assistance from the government, it must stop as soon as possible'.[76] These legislative measures culminated in a decree of May 1866 which not only required local government officials to justify to Batavia their assistance to manufacturers in the delivery of conscripted workers but also stipulated rates of payment for forced labourers which were significantly higher than those made to voluntary workers.[77] This rapid whittling away of their privileges left many manufacturers—particularly those who had recently purchased contracts in the hope of rapid and high returns—dismayed and angry, after holding the line against 'free labour' for so long.[78] In the end, however, they had no option but to capitulate to the government's demands and set to procuring their workers through their own means.

'Freedom', Eduard Douwes Dekker pointed out, 'cannot be decreed'.[79] It was one thing to prevent manufacturers using government-supplied forced labourers; quite another to provide immediately an environment in which voluntary wage labour could flourish. How, then, was the transition to 'free labour' achieved so rapidly in circumstances of social structure, custom and attitude which had previously militated against the formation of a class of voluntary wage workers? In the first place, the colonial authorities took steps to modify some of those inhibiting features. In the late 1850s following an intensive enquiry the government refined and lessened the demands of *herendiensten* on the peasantry[80] and thereafter periodically reviewed the system of compulsory public works labour with a view to its eventual abolition.[81] About the same time it undertook an escalating and generally successful attempt to restrict further the customary rights of indigenous leaders to

[75] Bijblad 1602 (1864).   [76] Bijblad 1748 (1865).

[77] Bijblad 1844 (1866). Forced labourers were to be paid at rates about 10 cents per day higher than the prevailing rates for voluntary labourers.

[78] See, eg, Letter Resident of Jepara to Director of Internal Administration, 15 February 1869, and letter Resident of Surabaya to Director of Internal Administration, 13 May 1869, both in AMK, Exh 7 March 1870/82, ARADH.

[79] *Indonesia: Once More Free Labour* (Exposition Press, New York, 1948), p. 13.

[80] *KV*, 1856, p. 37; *KV*, 1859, p. 19.

[81] See Bijblad 1580 (1864); Staatsblad 1865 no. 69; *KV*, 1870, p. 47. Ironically, the slow pace with which these measures proceeded in practice was a result of the notion that *herendiensten* had to be retained because there were insufficient voluntary workers for the required tasks (letter Resident of Tegal to Director of Cultivations, 11 May 1861).

'FREE LABOUR' IN NINETEENTH-CENTURY JAVA

demand produce and services from the peasantry.[82] The intention of these reforms was to regularize and rationalize the often arbitrary levies of produce and labour made upon the peasantry as part of an overall scheme of modernization. Despite their often shoddy implementation,[83] they doubtlessly helped create conditions more conducive to the performance of regular paid work outside the village. Secondly, there is some evidence to suggest that villages in some regions were beginning to encounter deepening economic difficulties with static or declining resources and increasing population pressure. Factories' use of local water supplies for milling cane and irrigating new cane stands certainly limited peasants' abilities to adapt to pressing circumstances by intensifying dry season food production, but this highlighted rather than created the problem of constricting economic opportunity within village agriculture. The poor were the first victims of this situation. Unable to survive as before on a share of domestic resources, they were pushed out of the village in search of extra income. In 1864, for example, the Resident of Pekalongan noted the significant numbers of landless people in his Residency which resulted in large numbers of people vying for factory work.[84] In 1865, the Resident of Tegal pointed to 'the annual lack of food, the prevailing poverty, the lack of opportunity to earn money and the yearly failure of a large part of the *sawah* [wet rice] fields' in the Regency of Pemalang.[85] In 1867 a Surabaya manufacturer claimed that his experiences and observations showed that persistent poverty was a stimulus for the recruitment of factory labourers.[86] According to Fernando's assessment of the Cirebon situation at this time, 'landholding peasants could not always accommodate the landless people into the existing economic structure of the village'.[87] Even in Pasuruan Residency, which many Europeans described as the most

---

[82] Three regulations gazetted in 1867 (Staatsblad 1867 nos 122, 123 and 125) forbade the delivery of goods to indigenous chiefs above the level of village head, limited and specified more closely the personal services due to them from the population, and increased their salaries in compensation.

[83] Letter Resident of Tegal to Director of Cultivations, 11 May 1861.

[84] Letter Resident of Pekalongan to Governor-General, 26 March 1864, AMK V 9 November 1864/193 Geh, ARADH; Knight, 'Capitalism and Commodity Production', pp. 140-1. It was probably due to these factors that the Sragi factory had been able to operate without forced labourers since at least 1859 (letter Resident of Pekalongan to Director of Internal Administration 20 February 1869).

[85] Letter Resident of Tegal to Director of Cultivations, 13 February 1865, AMK, V 2 October 1865/H15, ARADH.

[86] Letter G. F. C. Rose to Governor-General, 6 August 1867, AMK, Exh 30 June 1868/38, ARADH.

[87] 'Peasants and Plantation Economy', p. 263.

prosperous in Java, the Resident admitted that in the villages, 'where for a relatively large population there is only a small area of cultivated land', agriculture alone could not provide a livelihood for all, adding that there existed 'plentiful opportunity to earn a living in other ways—on plantations (*ondernemingen*) and so on'.[88] Most revealing of all, perhaps, is the Resident of Jepara's remark that as early as 1860, even with a good harvest, voluntary factory workers could be obtained without much difficulty.[89] As we have seen, problems with domestic production had always brought an upturn in the numbers of those seeking factory work, but this latest development was new and important in the sense that it provided a *continuing* impetus for peasants to look beyond the strained resources of their villages for their sustenance.

Neither of these factors, however, is sufficient to explain the rapidity and completeness of the transition throughout Java, because their impact was either too locally variable or too superficial to represent a thorough and widespread transformation of villages' usages and circumstances. The only conclusion, therefore, is that the transition to 'free labour', at least at this stage, was a matter of appearance rather than of fact. In the past, the sole reliable means of securing sufficient numbers of factory labourers had been to rely upon the government to provide workers through its tried and tested method of using indigenous rural leaders to mobilize peasants bound to them by allegiance or dependence. In the present circumstances, manufacturers simply followed the government's example. They strove to control peasants by domesticating their leaders, exploiting the vertical ties which remained an essential feature of rural life. They created and co-opted networks of locally influential people—especially district chiefs and village heads but sometimes even Chinese[90]—who could be relied upon to deliver workers to the factories on a regular basis. There were certainly segments of rural officialdom in a position to be compromised by the

[88] 'Residentie Pasoeroean. Algemeen Jaarlijksch Verslag over het jaar 1876', AD, Pasuruan 21, ANJ.

[89] Letter Resident of Jepara to Director of Internal Administration, 15 February 1869. It was perhaps no coincidence that the Resident reported that, beginning in 1860, one factory had been able to engage voluntary workers without resorting to the enticement of *voorschot*.

[90] Kruseman, the manufacturer at Waru factory in Surabaya, obtained most of his voluntary labourers through the agency of a Chinese who employed 'all sorts of artful means, which no respectable European would wish to perpetrate'. Doubtless a man with strong rural links, he received a fixed amount from Kruseman for every worker he delivered ('Beschouwingen over eenige punten betreffende de Suikerkultuur' [by Kruseman, 14 February 1869], AMK, Exh 7 March 1870/82, ARADH).

manufacturers. Good numbers of the lesser aristocracy were relatively poor and prey to the financial rewards which came from liaising with sugar interests, despite its illegality. The field was even more open among village chiefs for such 'corrupt' practices, distanced as they were from European control.[91] What gradually emerged, then, through the 1860s and early 1870s, was a pattern of labour management that bore many of the characteristics of that in force before the government began to place serious pressure upon manufacturers to dispense with forced labourers. Manufacturers continued and expanded the practice of foreman-centred recruitment which offered inducements, especially the *voorschot*, to attract voluntary workers.[92] At the same time, however, they increasingly adopted the old government system of conscripting peasants from surrounding villages by employing the 'persuasive' powers of rural leaders. One manufacturer, apparently exasperated with his more orthodox efforts to recruit and manage a voluntary workforce, described his predicament in unusually cold-blooded terms:

He [speaking in the third person] sees for himself no other means to lessen the difficulty which he experiences with the coolies who have tied themselves to him, than to make agreements in relation to the native officials or village chiefs for the delivery of free labourers or by dispensing opium or strong drink to entice coolies to the factory, or even to engage some persons who are feared by the people because of their previous activities, in order to bring coolies more or less voluntarily to work.[93]

Problems of Labour Control

Despite the employment of these tested measures, things did not always work out for the manufacturers as neatly as they might have expected. In the late 1860s, a number of them encountered serious problems in continuing their milling operations without government support. In Surabaya, for example, the Resident reported that some of his

[91] This frankly speculative assertion is mostly grounded in information contained in 'Inlandsche ambtenaren en hoofden in 1866', AMK, Exh 23 February 1869/10, ARADH.

[92] Letter Director of Cultivations to Governor-General, 2 October 1866, AMK, Exh 20 October 1868/2, ARADH; letter Resident of Pasuruan to Director of Internal Administration, 2 November 1868.

[93] Letter G. F. C. Rose to Minister of Colonies, 22 February 1868, AMK, Exh 30 June 1868/38, ARADH. See also Levert, *Inheemsche Arbeid*, p. 100, and Fernando, 'Peasants and Plantation Ecomomy', pp. 261, 271–2. These sorts of arrangements paid scant regard to the provisions of Stbl. 1863, no. 152, which outlawed agreements made by village chiefs on behalf of their villages and recognized only agreements with individuals.

manufacturers had experienced so little success in recruiting workers that they had been forced to make up the numbers with 'weak children and many women',[94] and one manufacturer claimed that the consequences of government policy threatened many factories with closure.[95] In Pasuruan, one manufacturer closed down his factory because he felt he could not continue without the government-provided workers which the Resident refused to supply.[96] In Semarang, factories were often forced to suspend milling operations because of absenteeism among their workers.[97] One problem was that it took time, skill and endeavour to build the links needed to carry on as before, and some factory owners, their initiative and enterprise dulled by government cossetting, and still resentful of the turn of government policy, had little of these to invest.[98] A second and sometimes related problem was that manufacturers seem frequently to have encountered difficulties in recruiting agents from the ranks of the influential in the rural areas. To a large extent that was probably a result of the tough competition between themselves and also that offered by European private enterprises in the search for labour,[99] but in some places there are suggestions that rural elites resented manufacturers making inroads on the labour power to which they felt entitled by their rank, and manufacturers had to fight hard to reach an accommodation with them.[100] Thirdly, there are reasons for thinking

[94] Letter Resident of Surabaya to Governor-General, 19 June 1866, AMK, Exh 7 October 1868/34, ARADH.

[95] Letter Van Delden to Governor-General, 4 August 1868.

[96] Letter former Chief Inspector of Cultivations to Minister of Colonies, 2 October 1867, AMK, Exh 7 October 1867/137 Geh, ARADH.

[97] Letter Assistant-Resident of Kendal to Resident of Semarang, 5 February 1869, AMK, Exh 7 March 1870/82, ARADH.

[98] In 1862, for example, the Inspector of Cultivations criticized some Cirebon factories whose administrators 'show little skill in dealings with the native and scarcely understand and speak Malay, let alone Sundanese' ('Rapport over de Suiker Kultuur in de residentie Cheribon'). A few years later the Resident of Surabaya emphasized the importance of personal qualities in forging links with peasants: 'The humane man who deals tactfully with the common native shall achieve the desired goal far more easily and quickly than one who lacks these qualities' (letter to Director of Internal Administration, 20 February 1869, AMK, Exh 7 March 1870/82, ARADH. See also *KV*, 1878, p. 190).

[99] Letter Administrator Arjosari factory [Pasuruan] to Assistant-Resident of Bangil, 5 April 1868, AD, Pasuruan 5, ANJ; letter Resident of Surabaya to Director of Internal Administration, 20 February 1869.

[100] Knight, 'Capitalism and Commodity Production', pp. 144–7. Knight has pursued this theme of the tenacity of indigenous aristocrats in retaining control of rural production in a highly enlightening discussion, 'The Indigo Industry and the Organisation of Agricultural Production in Pekalongan Residency, North Java, 1800–1850', paper presented at the Fourth National Conference of the Asian Studies Association of Australia, Monash University, 1982.

that the power of some rural leaders to provide the liaising and controlling services required of them was waning. This was partly because the government's reforms had checked their more or less arbitrary powers of disposal over peasant labour, but perhaps more importantly because it was seen that the government—perceived more and more clearly as the ultimate source of power and authority—was not controlling this particular operation and indeed was sometimes at odds with the manufacturers.[101] In the past, the government had relied not just on a wide range of incentives—power, status, wealth—to co-opt locally legitimate rural elites but also on reinforcing that co-option with an iron hand of coercion. While it had preferred to eschew the use of physical force, it had been evident to everyone that it possessed both the will and the means to coerce reluctant or wayward officials, and through them, peasants. Manufacturers, by contrast, had no such powers to bend rural leaders or channel through them as agents; they relied almost entirely on incentives to build and service local labour networks, and their agents, in turn, had few reliable sanctions to police those networks. Correspondingly, this more tenuous control of the rural populace was indicative of an emerging and increasingly important reality in many parts of the countryside. Villagers in greater numbers were generally taking advantage of their changing circumstances to throw off some of the shackles with which their indigenous chiefs had bound them. As early as 1859 the Director of Cultivations had remarked that 'the native has not remained as childish and simple as people might think. He does not allow himself easily to be threatened . . .'.[102] Four years later the Resident of Probolinggo remarked that

> already the little man often makes evident the feeling of independence that is stirring in him ... Just as the little man is already at present slowly withdrawing himself from the power and influence of his village chief, so shall he quickly become unwilling to assist him in the working of his fields, and furthermore to carry out those small services and provide those little benefits [103]

In Pekalongan, the Resident claimed that the people had begun to understand their rights and obligations in relation to the village chiefs, and were ready to complain to higher authority if those chiefs went too

---

[101] Letter Van Delden to Governor-General, 4 August 1868.

[102] Letter Director of Cultivations to Governor-General, 22 February 1859, AMK, V 13 March 1861/28, ARADH.

[103] 'Politiek Verslag der Residentie Probolingo over den jare 1863', AD, Probolinggo 1, ANJ.

far with their demands.[104] Perhaps not too much should be made of these remarks,[105] but there was certainly a sense that the tightening economic situation which had forced numbers of people out of the previously secure realm of domestic production had at the same time lessened their dependence upon it and the leaders who controlled it. Especially with the burgeoning of private enterprise in the late 1860s and 1870s and the rapid growth of extra-village employment which went with it, more and more peasants were finding that they could make their own way free—at least to some extent—from the cramping need for village patrons. In 1870, for example, the Resident of Pasuruan reported a 'shortage of manual labourers in factories and especially for coffee-picking where, in addition to the present number, thousands of people can find a good livelihood'.[106]

Labour shortages, indeed, in some places were for a time so acute that work takers enjoyed a brief and unusual interlude of supremacy over their employers. The Resident of Besuki reported somewhat ruefully in 1869 that factory labourers were aware of the situation and as a consequence knew to raise their wage demands high.[107] Again, in one part of Pasuruan, an Assistant-Resident opined that transport workers and factory labourers 'feel themselves in a position of strength, make large demands and set the wages'.[108] This prevailing scarcity of supply was often reflected in the scale and rate of wage payments through the 1870s.[109]

All these circumstances made for a much changed environment from that of the high period of the Cultivation System. For manufacturers, the black and white simplicities of the past were often replaced by the grey uncertainties of unreliable or impotent rural agents, independent-minded villagers no longer bound by ties to their chiefs, demand for

[104] Letter Resident of Pekalongan to Governor-General, 7 October 1867, AMK, Exh 23 February 1869/10, ARADH.

[105] See the cautionary note struck by an anonymous author about similar examples of apparently increasing independence enjoyed by villagers (*De Indische Gids* [hereafter *IG*], vol. 11, pt 2, 1889, pp. 1200–3).

[106] Letter to Governor-General, 2 April 1870, AMK, Exh 14 January 1871/40, ARADH.

[107] Letter Resident of Besuki to Director of Internal Administration, 21 February 1869, AMK, Exh 7 March 1870/82, ARADH.

[108] Letter Assistant-Resident of Bangil to Resident of Pasuruan, 5 October 1868, AMK, Exh 7 March 1870/82, ARADH.

[109] A good example of this was the fact that manufacturers had to raise their wages to unheard-of levels in East Java in the 1870s to prevent workers being lured away to construction sites for the state railway then being built between Surabaya and local centres of export cultivation (*KV*, 1877, p. 197).

labour outstripping supply, higher wage payments and the ramifications thereof,[110] and a sometimes less than sympathetic set of local government administrators. New conditions of life for peasants were providing new opportunities which did not always sit happily with customary mechanisms of labour recruitment and management, and which, while not yet denying them their essential importance, tended to lessen their efficacy and efficiency.

The consequence of these developments was a multiplication of manufacturers' labour problems which continued into the early 1880s.[111] High wages, the liberal use of the *voorschot* system, and the continuing exploitation of vertical ties of customary allegiance ensured, at least by the early 1870s, that manufacturers could contract the labourers they needed.[112] Retaining them, however, was an entirely different matter. While manufacturers had long experienced difficulties in managing their contracted workers,[113] things came to a head when the government withdrew the accustomed supply of conscripted labourers and manufacturers had to rely on workforces composed entirely of 'volunteers'. From the late 1860s onwards, the colonial records are well-stocked with anguished letters of complaint from manufacturers who found it impossible to manage their employees. A Surabaya manufacturer, for example, who had recruited 220 voluntary labourers saw two-thirds of them disappear as the season wore on. Another, who needed only 34 workers, hired 48 to be on the safe side and found to his chagrin that only 12 turned up regularly. While many workers (or agents purportedly acting on their behalf) were eager to bind themselves for a stint of factory work in return for a large cash advance, great numbers of them simply failed to keep to their agreements. Some failed to turn out for work at all, others absconded after a few days or weeks, others still were highly irregular in their attendance at the workplace. Some workers, indeed, entered contracts

[110] One alleged ramification: a Surabaya manufacturer claimed that increased wages meant that the Javanese did not need to work so often; indeed, 'he earns so much in one day that he can then be idle for three' (letter Van Oven to Resident of Surabaya, 10 February 1869, AMK, Exh 7 March 1870/82, ARADH).

[111] This and the following paragraph, except where otherwise noted, are based on the extensive materials found in the following files: AMK, Exh 30 June 1868/38, Exh 20 October 1868/2, Exh 7 March 1870/82, ARADH.

[112] See also *KV*, 1875, p. 187. *KV*, 1880, p. 169.

[113] Letter Resident of Surabaya to Director of Cultivations, 26 August 1858; letter Saportas (a Cirebon manufacturer) to Resident of Cirebon, 31 August 1858, AMK, Exh 14 June 1859/W2 Kab, ARADH; 'Residentie Pasoeroean. Bijlagen behoorende tot het kultuur verslag van 1859'; letter Resident of Probolinggo to Governor-General, 9 November 1861.

with two or three different manufacturers for the same period of time, collected their salary advances and then disappeared with the large sums they had accumulated. In other cases, as we have already seen, workers demonstrated a shrewd appreciation of their own value by stipulating wages far in excess of anything previously paid. Manufacturers even found themselves suffering the excruciating humiliation of having to put up with work stoppages brought about through the activities of so-called 'hotheads' among factory employees. As a result of all this, many factories found it difficult to continue regular operations during the season and most were forced to write off substantial amounts lost in cash advances paid out to workers which were never honoured or honoured only in part.

Apart from venting their spleens at what they saw as peasants' laziness, trickery and general untrustworthiness, manufacturers had virtually no defence against these practices. Some devised bonus schemes to secure greater reliability among their workers. One manufacturer in Tegal, for instance, provided higher payments to workers who attended at least 24 days a month; another adopted the practice of granting the *voorschot* as a gift to those who worked regularly through the season. Other measures were more defensive. Some factory owners attempted to screen their employees, relying on information provided by local government officials to ensure that notorious contract-breakers were not taken on. Foremen were despatched to chase up recalcitrant workers and return them to the job. Most commonly, manufacturers cast about for sanctions to apply against those who did not keep agreements. While government officials were supposed to 'urge' those who did not keep to their obligations to do so, it is doubtful whether many expended much time or effort in so thankless a task; only a few Residents who sympathized with the manufacturers' plight were prepared to stretch the law to harass and punish offenders.[114] Apart from this, there were no legal sanctions available. Contracts were considered a civil matter, and enforcing them meant initiating civil proceedings through the courts—a long, expensive and ultimately fruitless endeavour against offenders who, even if judgement were made against them, were invariably found to have nothing with which to pay compensation. Once this became generally known, of course, it encouraged still higher levels of contract-breaking. Although a penal

---

[114] Generally they did this by interpreting a breach of contract as deliberate fraud, which was a punishable offence. It seems that the weight of legal opinion by the mid-1860s was that such an interpretation was invalid and in any case almost impossible to prove in law.

'FREE LABOUR' IN NINETEENTH-CENTURY JAVA 169

sanction was imposed in 1872 against indigenous labourers who failed to keep agreements, it proved of little value in policing contracts and was soon removed after liberals in Holland exerted considerable political pressure against it.[115] Under these circumstances, manufacturers found it impossible to recruit a docile and reliable workforce for their factory operations. With rapid economic development outside the village and the concomitant surge in demand for labour, workers had numerous clients bidding for their services, This, together with the weakening of vertical ties which had previously worked so smoothly for the government's advantage, brought an unprecedented volatility to labour relations which worked to the benefit of the labourer.

Crisis and Docility

Around 1884, a period of severe international economic depression began to affect the Indies. One of its major features was the collapse of the world sugar market resulting from the growth of a heavily protected beet sugar industry in Europe. Within a year, the price fetched by good quality Java sugar was halved, and stood well below the costs of production.[116] In their attempts to revive profitability, manufacturers sought among other things to reduce their costs, especially in the sphere of labour. They succeeded by introducing new labour-saving machinery, increasing the proportion of cheaper female and child labour among their workforces, and generally reducing wages by as much as one-third.[117]

However necessary these measures may have been for the economic viability of the sugar industry, they could scarcely have been introduced

[115] Tjoeng Tin-Fong, *Arbeidstoestanden en Arbeidsbescherming in Indonesie* (Verzijl, Gouda, 1947), pp. 38–40; A. D. A. de Kat Angelino, *Colonial Policy* (University of Chicago Press, Chicago, 1931), vol. 2, pp. 497–500.

[116] Van der Mandere, 'De Suikerindustrie', p. 537; 'Opgave der productie kosten van een picol suiker zoowel bij de fabrieken op contract met het Gouvernement werkende als bij eenige vrije fabrieken op Java', AMK, V 25 September 1885/25, ARADH.

[117] *Onderzoek naar de Mindere Welvaart der Inlandsche Bevolking op Java en Madoera* [hereafter *MWO*]. *Overzicht van de Uitkomsten der Gewestelijke Onderzoekingen naar den niet-Inlandschen Handel en Nijverheid en daaruit gemaakte gevolgtrekkingen* [hereafter *HN*]. Deel IV, Eigenlijk Overzicht (Drukkerij Papyrus, Batavia, 1912), pp. 16–17; P. Brooshooft, *De Ethische Koers in de Koloniale Politiek* (J. H. de Bussy, Amsterdam, 1901), p. 74: H. E. B. Schmalhausen, 'Waaraan heeft Java behoefte?', *IG*, vol. 24, pt 2, 1902, p. 1042; H. van Kol, *Uit onze Kolonial. Uitvoerig reisverhaal* (A. W. Sijthoff, Leiden, 1903), p. 693; E. de Vries (quoting from the 1906 landrent monograph for the district of Wangkal, Pasuruan Residency), *Landbouw en Welvaart in het Regentschap Pasoeroen* (H. Veenman, Wageningen, 1931), vol. 1, p. 111.

so quickly and sweepingly in the labour environment prevailing in the 1870s, with its fierce competition for workers, high wages, and undisciplined workforce. Clearly, the volatile situation of the 1870s had given way to something new. But how had things changed and why? The 1882 *Koloniaal Verslag* reported two important pieces of information about factory labour. The first was that, with very few exceptions, there were no complaints from manufacturers about factory labourers failing to observe their contracts. The second was that wages were static.[118] These matter-of-fact observations were important because they ran so contrary to the general pattern of labour relations in the sugar industry from the 1860s onwards. More important still, evidence from succeeding years indicated that these new circumstances had become more or less permanent.[119] Factory workers were no longer able to command high wages, they were much more disciplined and reliable in their undertakings. These fragments of data, however, shed no light on why there had apparently been so radical a reshaping of the forces which determined the reliability and price of factory labour.

Part of the answer is doubtlessly to be found in manufacturers growing more practised and skilled in the arts of labour management, in assembling and servicing the agents and labour networks to meet their needs. Partly, too, we need to take account of the greater stock of wage labourers made available to the factories through a continuation and intensification of the emancipatory trends outlined above, a general growth in the numbers of poor and landless, and the development of transport infrastructures, particularly railways, which provided labourers with a greatly enhanced potential for long-range mobility.[120] Again, there is evidence that the difficult times of the Depression, with cash scarcities, poor prices for domestic and export commodities, slack domestic trade and tightening employment opportunities[121] contributed to a general impoverishment of the Javanese which made them more ready and malleable workers, eager to accept any opportunity to increase their incomes. All of these were operative, but together or

[118] *KV*, 1882, p. 182.
[119] *KV*, 1883, p. 181; *KV*, 1884, p. 173; *KV*, 1885, p. 165; *KV*, 1887, p. 168; *KV*, 1888, p. 207; *KV*, 1889, p. 210.
[120] See, for example, Irawan, 'Het vervoer via de Spoorlijn Semarang-Vorstenlanden als Welvaartsindicator voor de bevolking in Java's Vorstenlanden (1874–1883)', in F. van Anrooij *et al.*, *Between People and Statistics: Essays on Modern Indonesian History* (Martinus Nijhoff, The Hague, 1979), esp. p. 61. The Semarang-Vorstenlanden line carried 374,427 'fourth class' passengers in 1874; by 1883, the number had risen to 509,218.
[121] See, e.g., *KV*, 1888, p. 3.

'FREE LABOUR' IN NINETEENTH-CENTURY JAVA 171

singly, their fail satisfactorily to explain this quite dramatic transformation. It is difficult, for example, to believe that manufacturers of themselves could so rapidly master a situation in which they had floundered so long. And how, given that the manufacturers' major problem was one of the disciplining labour rather than merely recruiting it, could a simple increase in the number of labourers change the situation so drastically? As for the Depression, its effects were not generally felt until some time after the changed labour climate had become apparent, and were not apparently economically devastating for the Javanese.[122]

In my view, the underlying solution to the problem lies in more far-reaching and slowly-developing structural trends in Javanese peasant society which were beginning to manifest themselves for the first time on a general scale in the last two decades of the nineteenth century. The essence of the situation was this: the relentless natural increase of the Javanese was at least seriously threatening the island's historically-conditioned ability to feed and employ them at prevailing levels of prosperity. In the past, the Javanese had always faced a variety of economic problems—famine, apparently capricious rice-price fluctuations, local overcrowding and so on. Such problems, however, had been purely regional or temporary phenomena, correctible by such things as local migration, government policy, or just the passage of time. While, as we have seen, they had affected the availability and reliability of wage labourers, they had not had much impact on the structure and organization of society as a whole, at least not beyond their periphery. Now, however, Java's demographic dilemma was not isolated just in places like Pekalongan or Semarang, and not a passing phase. It was something beginning to grip most of Java, sparing, if only for the meantime, the island's southwestern edge and its easternmost corner, still largely a frontier region.[123]

[122] 'Overzicht betreffende den oeconomischen toestand van de verschillende gewesten van Java en Madura en van een vijftal gewesten der buitenbezittingen', KV, 1892, Bijlage C. In this regard it is important to note that persistently low rice prices through the 1880s (KV, 1886, p. 206; KV, 1887, p. 172; KV, 1888, p. 252) would have been something of a boon for non-landholders, from whom the greatest number of factory labourers were drawn.

[123] This region, still thinly populated and largely uncultivated by the early 20th century, enjoyed something of an economic boom at this time, especially with the establishment of large European-financed plantations like the Jatiroto sugar factory. As a result, labour relations were similar to those which had so confounded manufacturers elsewhere in Java half a century before. See AMK, Mail report no. 1331/1909, V 25 November 1909/17, ARADH, for an interesting file on Jatiroto's labour difficulties, and also L. G. C. [astens], 'De regeling van het werkcontract op Java', *Archief voor de Java-*

This phenomenon, its emergence and its impact at the period of the turning of the century are difficult to pin down and document. The intensity of the emerging economic crisis varied from place to place, as did its immediate effects. Moreover, its outlines are clouded by the concurrent impact of the Depression which highlighted the problems, probably brought on their effects prematurely, and certainly exacerbated them. But the signs of its underlying presence are clear: Java's loss of its customary self-sufficiency in rice, a swelling population, growth in the proportion of peasants who had no access to land, larger numbers of marginal landholders who needed off-farm employment to survive, a greater propensity for women and children to seek income-producing employment, escalating problems of rural credit, large movements of people from the crowded areas of Central Java to the eastern frontier in search of land and employment, the extraordinary intensification of agriculture especially in dry season crops.[124]

In terms of our particular discussion, the impact was felt in terms of a decreasing general availability of employment. The sugar manufacturers' problems in disciplining their factory labourers in the 1860s and 1870s flowed from the prevailing slack in the overall labour market. There were still sufficient—sometimes superfluous—labour opportunities to allow people to move from job to job as wages and other circumstances dictated. By the end of the nineteenth century, things were very different indeed. Even with the notoriously unattractive conditions of factory labour, and with static or falling wage levels, people who had employment in the factories sought to retain it, and not just for the duration of the season but for seasons to come.[125] Options had narrowed with the shrinking of available economic resources, a

Suikerindustrie [hereafter *AJS*], vol. 16, 1908, Bijblad, pp. 683–4. In general, East Java remained much less economically constricted than other parts of Java; sugar factories in places like Pasuruan, Surabaya and Kediri still experienced labour supply and discipline problems into the early 20th century. See, eg, 'Copie-Arbeidsenquete... Algemeene Vragen [Gending]', Koloniale Bank archives, no. 1258, ARADH.

[124] This picture is freely drawn from the following sources: H. E. B. Schmalhausen, *Over Java en de Javanen* (P. W. van Kampen, Amsterdam, 1909); A. Neijtzell de Wilde, *Een en Ander omtrent de Welvaartstoestand der Inlandsche Bevolking in de Gouvernements-landen van Java en Madoera* (Boekh. Visser, Weltevreden, 1911–1913), vol. 1; *MWO, De Volkswelvaart op Java en Madoera. Eindverhandeling van't onderzoek naar de mindere welvaart der inlandsche bevolking.* Deel 1 (Drukkerij Ruygrok & Co, Batavia, 1914); J. W. Meyer Ranneft, *Laporan-Laporan Desa (Desa-Rapporten)* (Arsip Nasional Republik Indonesia. Penerbitan Sumber-sumber Sejarah. no. 6, Jakarta, 1974); D. H. Burger, *Sociologisch-Economische Geschiedenis*, vol. 2.

[125] This regularity of employment seems to have become increasingly prevalent at this time. See J. W. Ramaer, 'De grondhuurprijzen en de loonen bij de Java-Suiker-Industrie', *IG*, vol. 32, pt 2, 1910, p. 1316; Levert, *Inheemsche Arbeid*, p. 119.

point put quite bluntly by a report from Rembang in 1892: 'Workers can always be obtained in large numbers . . . As a rule, supply exceeds demand, and as a result, the day-wage is low.'[126] In other words, discipline no longer needed to be exerted from without by means of physical coercion or moral persuasion; it developed from the workers themselves as they came to understand the harsh realities embedded in gradually changing economic circumstances.

The result of these Java-wide tendencies, therefore, was the transformation of the factory labour force into a reliable and servile corps of employees, regularly undertaking the rigours of factory work despite significantly lower returns. By the early twentieth century, the barrage of complaint that harassed manufacturers had earlier directed to the government had lifted. The manufacturers had precious little to complain about, evidenced by a survey of most of Java's factories made around 1906 which revealed that only a little more than one per cent of wages advanced had not been honoured at the end of the season.[127]

In this situation of growing numbers, scarcer resources and failing opportunity, peasants' dependence upon manufacturers had intensified remarkably. This gave manufacturers the sanction they had been craving since the 1860s, and provided them with previously unavailable power over their workers. Sometimes it meant that manufacturers could dispense wholly with the services of influential rural brokers and recruit and control their workers wholly through factory-employed foremen who had their own ties to pools of workers.[128] Much more commonly, however, manufacturers chose to retain the services of district heads and village chiefs to mobilize, deliver and discipline their labourers;[129] many of these rural leaders, indeed, probably rejoiced in the chance to act as the manufacturer's agent, for it was a valuable supplement to their

---

[126] *KV*, 1882, Bijlage C-10, p. 1.

[127] S. C. van Musschenbroek and J. F. A. C. Moll, 'Het arbeidscontract op Java en de wettelijke regeling daarvan', *AJS*, vol. 14, Bijblad, 1906, p. 105. See also Schmalhausen, *Over Java*, p. 40.

[128] 'Notulen van eene op den 16 December in de Kaboepaten gehouden vergadering' [Pasuruan], Mail report no. 417/1893, V 22 June 1893/25, ARADH; 'Copie-Arbeidsenquete. . . . Algemeene Vragen [Gending]'; *MWO–HN*, Deel IV, pp. 17–18; Deel V, p. 3.

[129] Letter Governor-General to Heads of Regional Administration in Java, 5 February 1894, in *AJS*, vol. 2, p. 232, 1894; Anon., 'De Vrije Suikercultuur in de Residentie Bezoeki', *IG*, vol. 16, pt 1, 1894, pp. 84–5; *Nota over de 'Werk- en Leveringscontracten' ten behoeve van Ondernemingen van Landbouw en Nijverheid op Java en Madoera* (Landsdrukkerij, Batavia, 1900), Bijlage VI, pp. 28–9; *Verslag van de Suiker-Enquete Commissie* (Fuhri, Surabaya, 1921), pp. 238ff.

purses and more importantly to their otherwise waning personal control over the rural masses in the rapidly modernizing colonial state.[130]

While forms and styles of management and recruitment endured,[131] appearing, indeed, very similar to the vertically-shaped arrangements which had lubricated the operations of the Cultivation System seventy or so years before, their basis and substance were very different. Where before they had been an amalgam of customary allegiance, the fear of physical and social sanctions, and economic dependence, now they rested much more surely on the economic supremacy of the manufacturer. Old methods remained, but that was simply a matter of administrative convenience. Peasants partook of wage labour at the factories not because their indigenous superiors required it or because colonial officials physically coerced them. They did it because in the circumstances of developing crisis, there were no reliable alternatives. Their subservience to a village chief or lesser government official in keeping to the monotonous drudgery of factory work came not from an appreciation of the customary ties, concerns and rewards of village life—which, fragile and exhausted, had proved unable to sustain them—but rather from the dictates of economic survival. Their gradual consolidation into a docile class of 'voluntary workers' was signal evidence of the transformation of the bases of village life and livelihood which had occurred in nineteenth-century colonial Java.

[130] Van Kol, *Uit onze Kolonien*, pp. 694–5.

[131] Even the *voorschot* system retained its vitality, although its use declined somewhat (*Nota over de 'Werk- en Leverings-contracten'*, pp. 26–7). It became, however, much more a tool for reinforcing worker dependence than for enticing new recruits.

[3]
*Peasants at Work: Forced Cotton Cultivation in Northern Mozambique 1938–1961**

ALLEN ISAACMAN AND ARLINDO CHILUNDO

The cotton revolution transformed the rural landscape of northern Mozambique. Between 1938, when Portugal imposed a system of forced cultivation, and 1961, when Lisbon ordered its abolition, cotton output increased by almost sixfold (see Figure 7-1). By 1961 cotton represented 58 percent of the agricultural income of peasants in the north as a whole and a whopping 87 percent in the district of Niassa.[1] The Mozambican cotton scheme thus provides an ideal case study to explore the interrelated issues of labor organization, state power, and the impact of petty commodity production. No cotton scheme in colonial Africa was built upon a more repressive or sustained work regime, nor was any more completely predicated on state intervention than in Mozambique. And while artificially depressed prices throughout most of this period meant that most Mozambican cotton producers did not benefit from new market opportunities, as some theorists would suggest,[2] neither were growers simply the passive victims of surplus extraction. Their story is far more complex.

This essay examines the ways in which the Portuguese colonial state sought to organize peasant labor in northern Mozambique, the center of the cotton re-

---

* We are grateful to the Social Science Research Council, the National Endowment for the Humanities, the Rockfeller Foundation, and the Graduate School of the University of Minnesota for research and writing support. We benefited from the critical comments of Heidi Gengenbach and Barbara Isaacman on an earlier draft of this article.

[1] These figures are derived from *Estatística Agrícola* (Lourenço Marques) and annual reports from the Cotton Board.

[2] See Nelson Saraiva Bravo, *A Cultura Algodoeira na Economia do Norte de Moçambique* (Lisbon, 1963).

148   Cotton Cultivation in Northern Mozambique 1938–1961

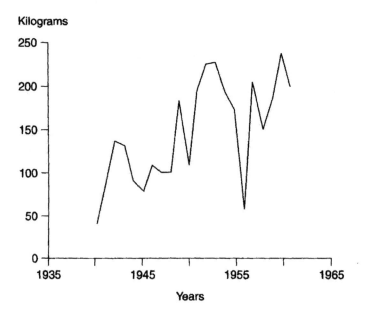

FIGURE 7-1. Productivity: Kilograms per Inscribed Producer: Northern Mozambique
Based on Nelson Saraiva Bravo, *A Cultura Algodeira na Economia do Norte de Moçambique*
(Lisbon, 1963), 135, 139.

gime,[3] and the ways in which peasants sought to organize themselves in response to state intervention. It seeks to determine how the imposition of cotton restructured the organization of work, or, more precisely, restructured the peasant labor process. The labor process provides a framework within which to explore the multiple ways work was organized in different peasant societies. By the labor process we mean the composition and organization of the peasant labor force, the degree to which work obligations are secured through political-legal institutions and supervised by external agents, and the extent to which peasants are forced to assume the risks of production. By focusing on the way different peasantries negotiated their position in relation to the labor process, we highlight the fact that peasants existed only as part of a larger social order, where ruling-class strategies of accumulation, state initiatives, and international markets infringed on their daily lives.

One of the central premises of this essay is that even within the tightly regimented Mozambican labor regime, peasants retained a degree of autonomy. The uniqueness of peasants lay in the degree of autonomy they had in relation to the colonial state and the appropriating classes. This partial autonomy was inextricably linked both to their ability to mobilize their own labor through the household and to their access to land, which together gave them command over subsistence.

---

[3] Peasants were also forced to cultivate cotton in central and southern Mozambique, but in neither regime did it dominate the economy as it did in the north.

That they were not totally locked into the market offered peasants additional freedom to act. While this space was limited, it enabled growers to cope with and at times to struggle against the efforts of the capitalist colonial state to divert labor from the food economy and to privilege commodity production over peasant consumption and the requirements of long-term social reproduction.

This essay further argues that the effects of commodification on northern communities were not uniform. The cotton regime impoverished, but it impoverished differently by region, by household, and by gender. Within some communities, it also exacerbated nascent class differences, especially in the 1950s after the state's price reforms.

The Antecedents of the Mozambican Cotton Regime: Northern Mozambique to 1938

Portuguese interest in transforming Mozambique into a major cotton-producing colony did not begin in 1938. It actually dated back at least to the middle of the eighteenth century.[4] Until the middle of the nineteenth century, however, metropolitan demand for cotton was limited. Imports from Brazil easily satisfied the nascent Portuguese textile industry.

The gradual expansion of the Portuguese textile industry in the second half of the nineteenth century, combined with Lisbon's search for alternatives to American cotton in the aftermath of the "cotton famine" caused by the U.S. Civil War, elevated interest in Mozambique's cotton potential. State officials offered subsidies, special allocations, and bonuses to European settlers who agreed to cultivate the staple. At the same time, the governor general of Mozambique ordered that cotton seeds be distributed to Africans. The governor of Tete went one step further, demanding that all peasants and ex-slaves cultivate "50 feet of cotton per hut."[5] Both the settler option and the peasant strategy failed miserably. Declining world prices, labor shortages, and lack of familiarity with the technical demands of the crop, as well as the absence of a rural infrastructure, reduced the short-lived planter interest. For their part, peasants opted to grow foodstuffs and, where conditions permitted, more profitable cash crops such as peanuts and sesame seeds.[6] Contemporary accounts make no reference to cotton production in northern Mozambique, or for that matter in any part of the colony, during the latter part of the nineteenth century and the early years of this century.[7]

With the formal annexation of Mozambique after the Congress of Berlin, Lisbon could in principle begin to reinforce its fragile hold over the north and to exploit the region's cotton potential. In reality, the Portuguese government lacked the mili-

---

[4] Direcção dos Serviços de Agricultura, *Algodão* (Lourenço Marques, 1934), 1; M. Anne Pitcher, "Sowing the Seeds of Failure: Early Portuguese Cotton Cultivation in Angola and Mozambique, 1820–1926," *Journal of Southern African Studies* 17 (1991), 43–70.

[5] Moçambique, *Boletim Oficial do Governo Geral da Província de Moçambique* (April 19, 1862), 61; Pitcher, "Sowing the Seeds of Failure," 47.

[6] Arlindo Chilundo, "Quando Começou o Comércio das Oleaginosas em Moçambique," *Relação Europa-Africa no 3e Quartel do Século XIX* (Lisbon, 1988), 511–23.

[7] Direção dos Serviços de Agricultura, *Algodão*, 1; Pitcher, "Sowing the Seeds," 46.

150 COTTON CULTIVATION IN NORTHERN MOZAMBIQUE 1938–1961

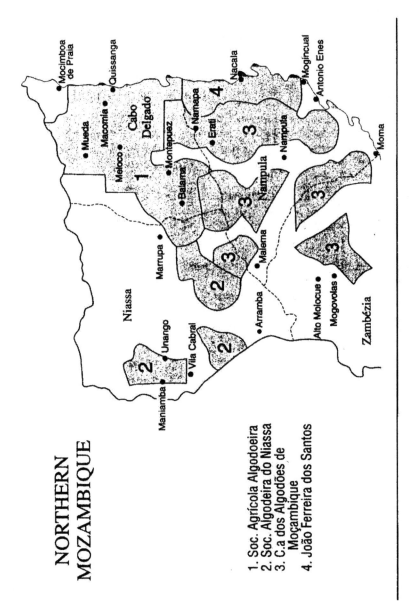

Cotton Concessionary Companies in Northern Mozambique, 1946

tary and financial resources to do either. As a result, it ceded control of a large portion of northern Mozambique (the contemporary provinces of Niassa and Cabo Delgado; see map) to the Nyassa Company, which governed this "backwater" area from 1894 until its charter expired in 1929. Much has been written about the failure of this undercapitalized company to develop the economy of the north.[8] Suffice it to say that the Nyassa Company derived most of its income by exporting conscripted labor[9] and by using its monopoly of police power to extract taxes from Africans living within its domain.[10] Nevertheless a sharp increase in the world price of cotton between 1919 and 1923[11] did stimulate some interest in the crop, primarily among European planters who leased land from the Nyassa Company. Company officials simply used their police power to pressgang laborers to work these estates. Cotton production, negligible before the War, jumped from 129 tons in 1924 to 255 tons in 1927 before declining to 197 tons in the Company's final year of activity. These figures represented less than 5 percent of the total production of cotton in the colony.[12]

In that part of the north remaining under direct government rule, cotton output was even less significant. A handful of European planters employed state-commandeered African labor to cultivate the staple. Peasants who failed to pay taxes or who were charged with other crimes were also subject to corvée labor. In a few regions, such as Mogovolas, the state also began to promote free peasant production.[13] Nevertheless, output in the north remained minuscule, as it did throughout the rest of the colony.

This failure to stimulate cotton production carried serious consequences for the Portuguese economy. Beginning with the last quarter of the nineteenth century, the metropolitan textile industry had experienced unprecedented mechanization and growth. In 1880 the textile industry operated 108,000 spindles and 1,000 looms. By 1901 this number had grown to 230,000 spindles, and six years later the textile industry utilized more than 11,000 looms.[14] Increased urbanization in and around Lisbon and Porto led to an expansion of domestic markets. The newly acquired African colonies offered additional market opportunities. This boom, however, combined with low cotton production in the colonies, required Portugal to increase the amount of ginned cotton it purchased on the world market. In 1926 approximately 5 percent of the 14.6 million kilograms that Portugal imported came from the colonies and only one-third of this amount came from Mozambique. The remainder,

---

[8] Barry Neil-Tomlinson, "The Nyasa Chartered Company: 1891–1929," *Journal of African History* XVIII (1977), 109–28; Leroy Vail, "Mozambique's Chartered Companies: The Rule of the Feeble," *Journal of African History* XVII (1976), 389–416.

[9] In the period between 1909 and 1913, thousands of young men living within the company's territory were sent to the gold mines of South Africa, the copper mines of Katanga, the port of Mombasa, the sugar estates of the lower Zambezi, and the cocoa plantations of São Tomé. After 1913 labor exports to South Africa ceased; they continued to the other locations, although the scale was reduced.

[10] Vail, "Mozambique's Chartered Companies," 401.

[11] Direcção dos Serviços de Agricultura, *Algodão*, 10.

[12] *Ibid.*, 6.

[13] José Torres, "A Agricultura no Distrito de Moçambique," *Boletim da Sociedade de Estudos da Colónia de Moçambique* (1932), 74.

[14] S. J. Chapman, *The Cotton Industry, and Trade* (London, 1905), 170; Armando Castro, *A Economia Portuguesa do Século XX 1900–1925* (Lisbon, 1973), 96.

152 Cotton Cultivation in Northern Mozambique 1938–1961

acquired on the world market, cost almost 178 million escudos, thus exacerbating a growing balance of payments deficit.[15] Despite Lisbon's effort to promote cotton, including building a northern railroad line linking the interior to the coast,[16] self-sufficiency remained illusory, and the metropolitan textile industry was still dependent upon foreign sources.

The failure of the Republican government (1910–1926) to exploit the colony's economic potential and thereby decrease Portugal's national debt was one of the factors that paved the way for the right-wing dictator, António Salazar, to take power in 1928. Fiercely nationalistic, Salazar declared that the colonies were to be the preserve of the nascent Portuguese capitalist class and were to provide raw materials and markets for the metropole. The expansion of cotton production became one of the cornerstones of Salazar's neomercantile project.

From the outset, the Salazar government rejected the previous plantation strategy. Instead, it promoted a highly regimented peasant labor regime requiring little capital investment. Modeled on the Belgian cotton system,[17] the colonial government would grant concessions to commercial interests, which would receive an exclusive right to purchase at low fixed prices cotton that peasants within the region would be compelled to grow. The concessionary companies would then sort and gin the cotton and sell it overseas, preferably to the Portuguese textile industry. The first decade yielded few tangible results. By 1931 production was actually less than half the tiny 1926 level, and the Portuguese textile industry had to purchase 99 percent of its ginned cotton abroad.[18] To help remedy this situation and to attract new concessionary companies, the Salazar government temporarily reversed its cheap cotton policy in 1932 and guaranteed a base price, a figure above the depressed international market, for all colonial cotton shipped to the metropole on Portuguese vessels.

Although this fiscal policy lured some new investors, most notably the Societé Coloniale Luso-Luxembourgeoise[19] and the Sociedade Agrícola Algodoeira,[20] the inability of the state to attract a significant number of new concessionary companies undermined Mozambican cotton production. Most peasant communities re-

---

[15] (A.I.A.), J.E.A.C., Propaganda Moçambique, "Elementos Para o Século," Gastão de Melo Furtado, June 15, 1954.

[16] As early as 1906, Massano de Amorim, governor of Mozambique district, noted that the development of the northern interior was dependent on the construction of a railroad. Distrito de Moçambique, *Relatório do Governador 1906–1907* (Lourenço Marques, 1908). Construction on the line began in 1913, and it opened for traffic in 1924 with only 94 kilometers.

[17] Portuguese officials noted enviously that the Belgians had achieved "brilliant results raising cotton production from 4 to 4,000 tons within a ten-year period." (See Boletim Oficial de Moçambique [B.O.M.], Serie 1, No. 37, September 11, 1926). Decree 11.944 was actually passed shortly after the 1926 coup but was only implemented in a serious way once Salazar came to power.

[18] In 1931 Portugal imported 15,884,841 kilograms of cotton, of which only 150,251 came from Mozambique. A.I.A., J.E.A.C., "Propaganda Moçambique," 720/0-6/34, unsigned, n.d.

[19] The Societé Coloniale Luso-Luxembourgeoise, founded in 1929, received a concession for the densely populated northern region extending from Nampula, Ribáuè, and Murrupula in Nampula Province to Alto Molócuè, Ile, Lugela and Pebane in Zambézia Province.

[20] SAGAL received a concession in 1934. Its initial grant was for 45,000 hectares in the fertile and densely populated region of Montepuez.

[21] The figure of 80,000 is based on the assumption that productivity per peasant in the middle 1930s was roughly equivalent to the 1940–1943 average of about 90 kilograms per producer.

mained outside the cotton regime. By 1937 approximately 80,000 peasants, out of a rural population of more than 4 million, had been incorporated into the system.[21] A handful of settlers using conscripted labor also continued to cultivate cotton. Production from these estates, however, was minimal.[22]

A year later the Salazar regime initiated a vigorous campaign to capture the peasantry and restructure the labor process by placing the full power of the state behind the newly formed Colonial Cotton Board (Junta de Exportação de Algodão Colonial). The Board was authorized to intervene at the point of production. It designated vast zones where peasants would be forced to cultivate cotton; it fixed mandatory dates by which rural communities had to plant, reseed, and harvest their cotton crop; it determined the number of times fields had to be weeded; and it defined the various qualities of cotton and helped to set the price paid to the peasants by the concessionary companies and to the concessionary companies by the Portuguese textile industry. Unlike the earlier system, the state agency also prohibited the export of Mozambican cotton to foreign countries. Within a few years the Board signed agreements with SAGAL, João Ferreira dos Santos, the Sociedade Agrícola Algodoeira and the Companhia dos Algodões de Moçambique,[23] who collectively received concessions and de facto police power over a substantial part of northern Mozambique (see map).

Peasants at Work: Northern Mozambique, ca. 1938–1950

Colonial planners, realizing that northern Mozambique was the only part of the country not already incorporated into the colonial capitalist economy, and viewing the region as a backwater zone with a large pool of "unproductive labor,"[24] immediately designated it as the geographic core of the forced cotton scheme. This decision only compounded their problems. The state and concessionary companies lacked even the most rudimentary scientific data about the region. It was not until 1950 that the first soil and vegetation survey was completed under the auspices of the Cotton Board's Center for Scientific Research of Cotton (CICA).[25] The absence of reliable data concerning something as elementary as day-time temperature fluctuations had considerable adverse effect on the project. When cultivated in conditions of less than 60 degrees Fahrenheit and sustained sunlight, cotton is very slow to germinate and grow and is susceptible to seed damage. In such an environment yields tend to be low. As late as 1953 a government report criticized the continued "cultivation of cotton in inappropriate climatic zones with poor soils."[26] The lack of familiarity with the latest procedures to

---

[22] In 1940 the northern settler estates produced approximately 60 tons. *Repartição Técnica de Estatística, Recenseamento Agrícola De 1939–1940* (Lourenço Marques, 1944), 22.

[23] In 1942 the Companhia dos Algodões de Moçambique (CAM) took over the concessionary areas of Granducol.

[24] Bravo, *A Cultura Algodoeira*, 247.

[25] D. H. Godinho Gouveia and Ario L. Azevedo, "A Preliminary Soil Map of Moçambique," *Trabalhos do Centro de Investigação Científica Algodoeira* 2 (1951), 141–44.

[26] J.E.A.C, "Esboço do Reconhecimento Ecológico Agrícola de Moçambique," *Moçambique Documentário Trimestral* 76 (1953), 10–11.

combat pests and treat cotton diseases placed an added burden on the incipient cotton scheme.[27]

Serious as these lapses in knowledge and preparation were, they were not nearly as deleterious as the complete absence of reliable rainfall records.[28] Cotton can be cultivated under a fairly wide range of conditions in the tropics provided there is regular and uninterrupted rainfall over approximately a five-month period.[29] If the rains are late or insufficient, growers face the prospect of poor germination or total crop failure. Too much rain, on the other hand, can result in flooding. Without these data Cotton Board officials had no scientific basis for determining where or when peasants should cultivate the crop. As it turned out, the rainy season in the north is fairly short and quite unpredictable, thus increasing peasant risk. "From one part of the region to another and from one year to the next there were great variations in rainfall," recalled A. Quintanilha, director of CICA. He concluded that "we would have needed two decades of systematic research in order to determine these precipitation patterns."[30] Neither the textile industry nor the Salazar regime was willing to wait.

The absence of a transportation system connecting prospective producers to scattered inland markets and these markets to coastal ports compounded the cotton companies' problems. By 1933 there were only 6,500 kilometers of road serving an area of more than 275,000 square kilometers in the north. Niassa district, for example, which extended over 114,000 square kilometers, had less than 1,000 kilometers of road.[31] Most of these roads were little more than upgraded trails, the best of which were surfaced with a fine gravel. In the dry season these roads were suitable for porterage (foot traffic), *machilas* (hand-held hammocks), and rickshaws, which were the principal modes of transport. During the rainy period most roads were impassable. The small number of bridges, and dependence on a variety of makeshift rafts, further hindered commerce across this inaccessible region. Compounding these difficulties was the acute shortage of cars and trucks. By the middle of the decade there were only 450 cars and trucks in all three northern provinces combined.[32] This fleet was hardly sufficient to transport a bulk commodity such as cotton.

The lack of mechanized transport and all-weather roads no doubt deterred many rural households from becoming fully integrated into a market economy. In substantial parts of Cabo Delgado, Niassa, and more remote regions of Nampula District, rural communities allocated most of their labor to the food economy. Peas-

---

[27] Direcção dos Serviços de Agricultura, *Algodão*, 14.

[28] Professor Quintanilha, who was the colony's leading agronomist and expert on cotton, recalled that "we did not have any scientific data on rainfall. All we had were some vague impressions." (Interview with A. Quintanilha, March 7, 1979; confirmed by Faria Lobo, a former concessionary company official, in an interview on May 26, 1987). It was only in 1942 that the state established CICA to begin basic research on climate, soils, and seed types, as well as the threats posed by a variety of plant diseases. It was only a decade later before meteorologists could begin to make informed estimates of the range and variability of rainfall (interview with A. Quintanilha, *ibid.*).

[29] J. D. Acland, *East African Crops* (London, 1987), 97–98; A. N. Prentice, *Cotton, with Special Reference to Africa* (London, 1972), 148–50.e]

[30] Interview with Professor A. Quintanilha, March 12, 1979, in Maputo.

[31] Manuel Correia da Silva, "Importância Económica das Principais Culturas e Meios de Transporte na Baixa Zambézia," *Primeiro Congresso de Agricultura Colonial* (Porto, 1934), 49.

[32] Correia da Silva, "Importância," 47.

ants recall that prior to 1938, the allocation of tasks within the food economy was gendered. Men cut the trees and cleared the fields. Women tended to be the principal cultivators, aided by children. They planted, thinned, and weeded millet and sorghum.[33] The latter was the principal staple and was also brewed into an alcoholic beverage drunk on important religious and social occasions. To maximize food security and labor output, women often intercropped these staples with a variety of beans and cultivated some pumpkins as well as drought-resistant manioc.[34] Men helped in the harvest and hunted and gathered forest products in the postharvest period from June through September.

To pay their taxes and to purchase a small number of consumer goods many rural producers sold a portion of their agricultural surplus, as well as wild rubber, gum, and wax, to itinerant traders or at scattered Asian- and Portuguese-owned shops notorious for price gouging.[35] "We carried our crops to the *cantineiros*, and all we received was a bit of tea, sugar, a hoe and ten escudos [35 cents] each. We got nothing."[36] This view, held widely throughout the North, probably helps to explain why in 1937 two million peasants sold only 30,000 tons of produce, or less than 15 kilograms per person.[37]

Because many rural growers had not fully internalized commodity production and had not become dependent on consumer goods, state officials could not simply entice them into cotton production by convincing them to switch from another cash crop. Colonial officials faced a difficult task even in those areas adjacent to the major coastal towns, such as Pemba, or to the inland administrative and commercial centers like Nampula and Montepuez, where rural communities produced peanuts on an appreciable scale for the market.[38] There were no compelling reasons why peasants would voluntarily shift from peanuts, which were both edible and more profitable, to cotton. The risks were just too daunting.

In the face of peasant reluctance to cultivate the fiber, the state concluded that a show of force was necessary. The absence of a strong and well-organized state apparatus in the north complicated Lisbon's agenda.[39] In many parts of this area, the only

---

[33] Christian Geffray and Mogens Pedersen, *Transformação da Organização Social e do Sistema Agrário do Campesinato No Distrito do Eráti: Processo de Socialização do Campo e Diferenciação Social* (Maputo, 1985); Dias, *Os Macondes de Moçambique* I, 97–115; António Pires, *A Grande Guerra em Moçambique* (Porto, 1924), 57–58; Soares de Castro, *Os Achirimas* (Lourenço Marques, 1941), 43–45; Group interview with Aridhi Mahandha et al., July 23, 1979, in Balama; Interview with Artur Dias, July 24, 1979, in Montepuez; Group interview with Nanjaia Taibo et al. in Namapa, May 2, 1979; Group interview with Saide Mascalane et al., August 16, 1980, in Maniamba; Joint interview with Goodwin Alsane Nzama and Saide Buana Chilombe, August 16, 1980, in Metangula.

[34] Group interviews as cited in the preceding footnote.

[35] Group interview Aridhi Mahanda et al.; Group interview with Romeu Mataquenha et al., July 17, 1979, in Montepuez; interview with Artur Dias.

[36] Group interview with Nanjaia Taibo et al.

[37] Bravo, *A Cultural Algodoeira*, 222. This figure includes sales from the fertile central region of Zambézia, where commercial production was probably higher than the adjacent northern regions. A.H.M., Secção Reserva, cx.77, "Inspecção dos Serviços Administrativos e dos Negócios Indígenas, "Relatório da Inspecção Ordinária no Distrito de Nampula da Província do Niassa: Imala," III; Hortêncio Estevão de Sousa, 1948.

[38] Group interview with Aridhi Mahanda et. al.; Interview with Artur Dias.

[39] Large parts of Mozambique, Niassa, and Cabo Delgado districts had remained outside formal Portuguese control until the period from 1910 to 1920. Throughout the next two decades Lisbon made some futile gestures to bolster its authority, but in many areas state power was nominal at best.

156 Cotton Cultivation in Northern Mozambique 1938–1961

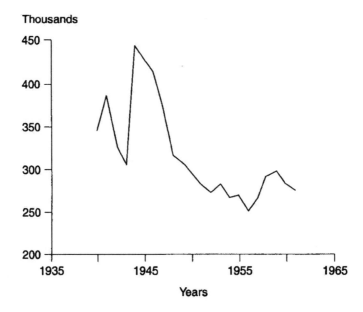

FIGURE 7-2. Numbers of Producers in Forced Cotton Regime in Northern Mozambique, 1939–1961

Based on Nelson Saraiva Bravo, *A Cultura Algodeira na Economia do Norte de Moçambique* (Lisbon, 1963), 135, 139.

Portuguese presence was a local *chefe de posto* who administered vast areas with the assistance of loyalist chiefs and a handful of African police, or *sepais*. Because of the lack of all-weather roads and mechanized transport, these local administrators were often cut off from the rural population for several months a year during the rainy season, just when cotton cultivation was getting under way.[40] And even during the remainder of the year, the primitive transport system limited their capacity to oversee peasants or lock them into the market. Despite these obstacles, once the Board unveiled its cotton project, it would tolerate no obstacles. Rural cultivators were not simply to be encouraged to grow cotton; they were to be coerced. State intervention at the point of production had three overarching objectives: (1) to increase exponentially the number of peasants compelled to grow cotton, (2) to ensure that peasants legally required to grow the crop actually did so, and (3) to expand the number of hours per day that rural producers allocated to the crop.

The simplest way for the Board to meet its objectives was to designate vast regions of the north as cotton zones and distribute concessions to the cotton companies en masse. Since the primary objective of the undercapitalized concessionary companies was to expand total output, even marginal lands held some attraction for them. More territory meant more cultivators and greater total output. On this point colonial

---

[40] For a general description of the rural administrative system, see Allen and Barbara Isaacman, *Mozambique: From Colonialism to Revolution 1900–1982* (Boulder, 1983), 28–38.

authorities were clear. "Without an infusion of new technology or sufficient knowledge of rainfall and soils, the only way to increase total output is by increasing the area under cultivation since we will not be able increase output per hectare."[41]

State officials, increasingly aware of the limits of their ability simply to impose solutions by the public threat of force, tried to instill new attitudes towards work and voluntary participation in the cotton economy. Throughout the north officials held *banjas*, or public meetings, at which they stressed the benefits cotton production offered. "The chief gathered all the people in the center of the village," recalled a group of elders in Balama, "and then the administrator explained how cotton would end nudity and give us money."[42] Most chiefs echoed the promises of their European superiors and often took the lead in becoming model cotton farmers.[43] Roman Catholic and Protestant missionaries, seeking to instill the work ethic among recent converts, reiterated this message from their pulpits and in their classrooms. Indeed, many saw no inherent contradiction between evangelization and compelling African students and teachers to work on church-owned cotton fields.[44]

In an effort to make cotton more palatable and to reduce rural skepticism, local officials initially offered a number of compromises. To alleviate peasant concerns that cotton cultivation would take valuable time away from food production, they permitted peasants to plant cotton in fields located near their gardens.[45] Also, many concessionary employees and state officials did not rigorously enforce production requirements. Some looked the other way when households cultivated less than the minimal acreage; others did not force both members of a husband-wife team to cultivate the cotton fields. These ad hoc arrangements revealed the inherent contradictions in the system. That local administrators bent some rules, and peasants reluctantly cultivated some cotton, must be seen as part of an ongoing process of jockeying and negotiating over power in the countryside.

Nevertheless, by 1940 the state—concessionary company alliance had achieved its first objective. The number of northern peasants brought into the system had jumped from under 80,000 in 1937 to approximately 350,000 in 1940, and to 445,000 three years later (see Figure 7-2). This figure represented fully one-quarter of the adult population and it did not include the large, though indeterminant, number of children who, although not formally registered, aided their parents.[46]

Peasant antipathy toward cotton increased in direct proportion to the numbers forced to grow the crop. Instead of the promised prosperity, low yields and artificially depressed prices set by the state impoverished most rural households. In some of the more marginal regions, income for a year of labor was less than twenty-

---

[41] A.H.M., J.E.A.C., "Relatório Anuário 1939–1941," Relatório de Posto de Porto Amélia, Faria Leal, November 30, 1940.

[42] Group interview with Aridhi Mahanda et al., July 23, 1979.

[43] Group interview with Amasse Nuitha et al., July 10, 1979, in Montepuez; Interview with Chico Nhulialia and Costa Nampire, May 2, 1979, in Namapa; Group interview with Romeu Mataquenha.

[44] Group interview with Maulane Samate et al, July 23, 1979, in Balama; interview with Eduardo José Macore, August 19, 1980.

[45] Interview with Faria Lobo, May 1987, in Nampula.

[46] A.I.A, J.E.A.C., "Esboço Estatístico Referente a 1941," I, João Contreiras, 1942. Statistics collected by Bravo indicate that the rise was somewhat more gradual, with 496,000 inscribed in the system by 1940; only in 1944 did the number reach 660,000. Bravo, *A Cultura*, 135.

158 COTTON CULTIVATION IN NORTHERN MOZAMBIQUE 1938–1961

five cents.[47] In 1940 the average producer received slightly more than two dollars for his or her entire crop. In response, many peasants withdrew land and diverted labor[48] to their food crops. Between 1939 and 1940 per capita acreage actually dedicated to cotton production declined by 40 percent.[49] In the north less than 1 percent of the arable land had been committed to the staple.[50] Lisbon's goal of cotton self-sufficiency remained illusory.

From the state's perspective, the partial subordination of growers was obviously not sufficient. It was not adequate just to bring thousands of new producers into the cotton regime. The challenge was to rationalize production and narrow the peasants' partial autonomy still further. This required a reconfiguration of the labor force, restructuring the work day and work space, and more vigorously enforcing work obligations.

The most pressing task was enlarging the work force and making certain all cultivators legally required to grow cotton actually did so. State and company officials ordered all men, as well as women living within the concessionary zones, to cultivate cotton. The only exceptions were adults with severe physical impairments, elders over fifty-five, and men conscripted to work on state projects or on European plantations. Even women in the final stages of pregnancy were not exempt. "Women worked right up until they gave birth," recalled Rosa Ernesto, "and a week later they had to be back in the fields."[51] Unlike the earlier period, each adult was also required to cultivate a minimum plot. In most parts of the north, a husband and his first wife had to grow a hectare of cotton. Each junior wife, single woman, or widow had to work half that area.

This legislation undercut the gendered division of labor. Throughout the north, husband-wife work teams working on a conjugal plot constituted the principal unit of production. Men were forced to sow, thin, and weed cotton, tasks previously considered "women's work." Although in some cotton zones men tried to avoid these tasks, the pressure on them was relentless.[52] In regions as diverse as the rich cotton zone of Mogovolas and the marginal Makonde highlands, these teams initially constituted 90 percent of the labor force.[53] Children worked both in the cot-

---

[47] Bravo, *A Cultura Algodeira*, 138–45.

[48] Colonial officials explained peasant antipathy toward cotton as yet another indication of the "indolence of the blacks." See A.I.A., J.E.A.C., Papéis Diversos, F. Barbosa to Rafael Guerreiro, October 28, 1939.

[49] According to Contreiras, the number of hectares of cotton increased minimally, from 142,289 to 155,925, while the number of peasants nearly doubled, from 345,581 to 636,481. Thus, although peasants could not avoid, cotton they cultivated dramatically less. A.I.A., J.E.A.C., "Esboço Estatístico Referente a 1941," I, João Contreiras, 1942.

[50] A.H.M., J.E.A.C., Relatório Anuário "Cultivadores, Indígenas áreas Semeadas Empregadas, Campanha de 1939/1940," João Contreiras, n.d.

[51] Interview with Rosa Ernesto, July 11, 1991, in Nampula.

[52] Interview with Paulo Roque.

[53] A.I.A., J.E.A.C., "Relatório Sobre a Campanha de 1944–1945 na Circunscrição de Mogovolas," João Esteves de Souza, March 12, 1946; A.I.A., J.E.A.C., 601/8, Secretaria do Posto Administrativo do Eráti, November 2, 1945; A.H.M, Secção Reserva, Cx. 77, Província do Niassa, Inspecção dos Serviços Administrativos dos Negócios Indígenas, "Relatórios e Documentos Referentes à Inspecção Ordinária Feita na Província do Niassa," 2nd parte, Capitão Carlos Henriques Jones da Silveira, Inspector Administrativo, 1944; A.H.M., Cx. 77, Inspecção dos Serviços Administrativos e dos Negócios Indígenas, "Relatório da Inspecção Ordinária ão Distrito de Nampula da Província do Niassa," III, Hortênsio Estevão de Sousa, 1948.

ton fields and in family food gardens. Perspective sons-in-law often labored on these plots as part of their bride-service responsibility.[54]

Colonial officials sought to divide the peasants' work day in both time and space in order further to privilege cotton production and to channel labor away from food crops. In most regions administrators imposed a fixed work schedule. Peasants were expected to spend the morning in their cotton field, but at peak periods they were required to work through the afternoon.[55] In some areas officials lengthened the work day by increasing the size of the cotton plots or by establishing minimum production requirements.[56] They also prohibited intercropping of basic staples in the cotton fields to prevent food crops from competing with cotton for labor time, land area, and soil nutrients. As a result many cultivators only had time to grow food in the late afternoons, in the evenings when there was a full moon, and on those Sundays when they were not forced to work on the chief's cotton fields.[57]

Recognizing the need to reinforce this separation of labor and restructure the work day, company overseers imposed a new system of land distribution. Whereas officials originally allowed individual households to select cotton plots adjacent to their gardens, after 1940 they increasingly forced peasants to grow cotton in specifically marked blocks far from their villages.[58] Because these cotton blocks were often several kilometers from their gardens, peasants could not easily sneak off and work their food crops when they were supposed to be cultivating cotton.[59] Regrouping cultivators into relatively concentrated areas adjacent to bush roads also facilitated greater labor supervision.

For all these measures to control growers, the labor regime ultimately rested on selective but particularly brutal, disfiguring, and public violence. No one was immune and no excuse was tolerated. "If a woman laid down her hoe to feed her hungry baby," recalled Rosa Ernesto, "and the overseer saw her, he would beat her with a hippo whip and force her immediately to resume her labor."[60] Grim stories, personal narratives, idle chit-chat, rumors, gossip, and songs depicting this state-sanctioned violence spread out through the Mozambican countryside. Colonial authorities, concessionary company officials, and African police committed such horrendous public acts to serve as a warning in situations where they lacked the manpower to oversee growers on a daily basis. These stories of brutality took on a

---

[54] Geffray and Pedersen, *Transformação de Organização*, 28.

[55] Joint interview with Chico Nhulialia and Costa Gaio Nampire, May 2, 1979, in Nampula; Interview with Eugénio Niquaria, July 24, 1979, in Montepuez; Interview with Pruan Hassan in Montepuez, July 20, 1979; Joint interview with Daima Magaga Mbela, et al., July 30, 1979, in Montepuez.

[56] In Namapa the local administrator expanded the basic plot by 15 percent (A.I.A., J.E.A.C., 605/8, Pasta 48, 1946, "Relatório Mensal," Augusto Guilherme Alves, Agente de Fiscalização, October 1946). In Niassa District, local officials declared in 1951 that any male who failed to produced 400 kilograms of cotton would be sent to work without remuneration on European tea estates–a powerful incentive to spend longer hours in the cotton fields (A.I.A., J.E.A.C., "Papéis Diversos," A Figueira e Sousa to Governador de Niassa), February 21, 1952).

[57] Interview with Romeu Mataquenha.

[58] Interview with Faria Lobo; Jorge Dias, *Os Macondes de Moçambique*, 112.

[59] A.I.A., J.E.A.C., 901, "Despacho," unsigned and undated. Interview with Paulo Roque, May 27, 1987, in Nampula; Interview with Fátima Konkonko, May 30, 1987, in Pemba.

[60] Interview with Rosa Maria Ernesto, July 11, 1991, in Nampula.

160 Cotton Cultivation in Northern Mozambique 1938–1961

life of their own and began to create a sense of terror that became deeply ingrained in the collective consciousness of the peasants. They reminded growers of their vulnerability and helped to create feelings of despair and powerlessness among at least a portion of the rural population.

The burden of supervising the rural population fell, in the first instance, on the shoulders of the concessionary company field agents (*propagandistas*) and overseers (*capatazes*), in whom the state vested de facto police power and on whom the state turned a blind eye when irregularities and abuses occurred. For all their brutality,[61] however, there was never a sufficient number of company agents to oversee the peasants under their control. The lack of motorized transport further complicated this task. To compensate, the concessionary companies came to rely on local state administrators (*chefes de posto*) who were under great pressure from their superiors to increase cotton production within their jurisdiction. Given their vast discretionary power, their desire for promotion, and the monetary rewards which they received from the cotton firms, most administrators rigorously enforced the cotton regime.[62] At meetings held during the dry season, they cajoled, harangued, and threatened the local population to produce more cotton. "If our fields had not been sufficiently weeded or were not the right size," remembered one elder, "he ordered the *sepais* to whip us. If someone refused to grow cotton he ordered that person arrested, put in chains, and sent to a place from where he didn't come back."[63]

While there has been a tendency in the literature to highlight Portuguese brutality, it is important to stress the massive involvement of Africans linked to the cotton regime. There simply were not enough European officials to saturate the countryside. Administrators, who had to oversee vast regions, regularly dispatched *sepais* to thrash and intimidate peasants whose cotton fields were not judged to be in appropriate condition. "They were always on our backs, beating with *palmatórias* [paddles],"[64] recounted a former grower from Macomia. For the *sepais*, these unsupervised visits also offered an opportunity to plunder the peasants and supplement their meager salaries. In some instances they let it be known that members of the rural population could avoid the most excessive punishments by offering them grain, beer, and goats, as well as sexual favors. In other cases they simply seized what they wanted.[65]

Although a clearly defined chain of European authorities and African functionaries was given the role of subduing and controlling cotton growers, on a daily basis it was the chiefs (*régulos*) who played the most critical role. They accompanied the *propagandistas* to make certain that all eligible adults had been registered and had received a designated parcel of land to work. They and subordinate vil-

---

[61] Interview with Marcelina Joaquim, April 25, 1979, in Mueda; Group interview with Arridhi Mahanda et al.; Group interview with Daima Magaga Mbela et al. See also A.H.M., Secção Reserva, Cx. 77, Inspecção dos Serviços Administrativos e dos Negócios Indígenas, "Relatório da Inspecção Ordinária ão Distrito de Nampula da Província do Niassa," III, Hortêncio Estevão de Sousa, 1948; Vail and White, *Capitalism and Colonialism*, 314–25.

[62] A number of administrators refused to enforce the cotton legislation. Their reasons ranged from moral outrage at the naked exploitation to profitable labor recruiting agreements they had made with the planter community.

[63] Quoted in Eduardo Mondlane, *The Struggle for Mozambique* (London, 1975), 71.

[64] Interview with Jonas Nakutepa, July 30, 1979, in Macomia.

[65] Interview with Amasse Nuitha.

COTTON CULTIVATION IN NORTHERN MOZAMBIQUE 1938–1961

lage headmen patrolled the fields, often on state-supplied bicycles, ensuring that cotton was planted, weeded, and harvested at the appropriate time. Chiefs also checked village homesteads and food gardens in search of "loiterers" who covertly worked their own fields to try to meet household food requirements. Those whom they discovered were often beaten, fined, arrested, or forced to work an extra stint in the chief's cotton field.[66] The indigenous authorities were both the eyes and ears of the administration and the first line of defense against peasant defiance. "In our present condition," concluded one inspector in 1943, "the chiefs and their counselors are the critical agents of white authority."[67]

This salutary statement obscures as much as it reveals. Investing power in the chiefs and promising them cotton bonuses often led to a more complicated relationship than officials had bargained for. While they were often able to shift much of the responsibility for social control and for overseeing cotton production to the local chiefs, they did not entirely foresee the threat such strong chiefs could pose. As a result the colonial regime often bypassed powerful northern authorities in favor of either pliant members of the royal family, or *sepais* and other state functionaries who had demonstrated their loyalty.[68] This ambiguous relationship between the colonial regime and the chiefs helped to structure an equally ambiguous relationship between the chiefs and their subjects. As local government representatives, chiefs could protect and reward their closest followers. And as state functionaries, they could also speak out on behalf of their communities. *Régulos* complained of abuses by *sepais* and company overseers, price gouging at the markets, and the failure of the cotton companies to provide promised technical assistance. Outside the gaze of their European superiors, a number of chiefs even organized covert acts of defiance.[69] But these were the exception. Although it is misleading to suppose that as a group the chiefs expressed unwavering allegiance to the colonial state, most chiefs regularly opted for the colonial order in order to perpetuate their own relatively privileged position.[70]

Unlike their chiefs, former growers were quite emphatic that it was not only the repressive work regime but also the particularly harsh demands of cotton production that left them reeling. Cotton cultivation demanded most of their time most of the year. Typically, peasants in the north began to open up new lands in late September or early October. Men, working together in assigned groups, cut the trees and removed the stumps and heavy shrubbery. When their husbands were press-ganged to work for the state, women brewed beer and invited people to help them; as a last resort, they performed the task by themselves.[71] With only axes and

---

[66] Group interview with Adelina Cedo et al., July 21, 1979, in Montepuez; Group interview with Romeu Mataquenha et al.; Group interview with Arridhi Mahanda et al.; Group interview with Daima Magaga Mbela et al., July 30, 1979, in Chai Chai.

[67] A.H.M., Secção Reserva, Cx. 20, "Inspecção dos Serviços Administrativos e dos Negócios Indígenas," Relatório e Documentos Referentes à Inspecção Ordinária Feita na Província do Niassa, 1a parte, 1943," Carlos Henriques Jonas da Silveira, 1943.

[68] Allen Isaacman "Chiefs, Rural Differentiation, and Peasant Protest: The Mozambican Forced Cotton Regime, 1938–1961," *African Economic History* 14 (1985), 32–33.

[69] Ibid.

[70] For a discussion of the ambiguous and contradictory position of the chiefs, see Isaacman, "Chiefs, Rural Differentiation, and Peasant Protest," *passim*.

[71] Group interview Armando Nicula, Liassa Lohaninté, and Murinvona Mpemo, July 8, 1991, in Nampula.

hoes for tools, this was exhausting work that "almost all the natives detested."[72] Women and children did most of the weeding, with some help from men. Because it took between four to six weeks to complete this arduous task, peasants tried to use the same plots several years in a row, even though they understood that tired lands yielded less cotton. To prevent this from happening, state officials insisted that rural communities plant new fields every three or four years. That peasants were reluctant to clear new cotton fields but opened up new plots for food suggests that the underlying issue was not merely one of labor but control over what the labor produced.

This preference notwithstanding, household members had to have their cotton plots cleared and ready for seeding by the time of the first rains in late November. Food gardens often had to wait. Because of the relatively short growing season and the tendency of late-sown cotton to be of poorer quality, chiefs, *sepais*, and company overseers forced them to cease other agricultural activities after the first downpour. Men marked and prepared seed beds in straight rows, scraping small hollows at prescribed intervals, while women and older children placed seeds in each hole. To reduce risks of crop failure, they dropped several seeds in each hole. Seeding generally took four to five days and was considered the least onerous task. If the rains were insufficient, however, and the plants did not germinate, or if there was excessive rainfall, the fields had to be reseeded. Since rainfall was unpredictable, reseeding occurred frequently in late December and through the month of January.[73]

Almost immediately after planting, rural households had to begin weeding their crops. Cotton could not compete with faster growing vegetation for nutrients, moisture, and sunlight, and if weeding was delayed or done poorly, the plant became drawn, spindly, and susceptible to a range of diseases.[74] Thus local officials ordered the producers to weed a minimum of three times in the period from late January to early April. Children and older family members nominally exempted from cotton assisted the registered adults.[75] Since young seedlings were particularly vulnerable, peasants had to spend up to three weeks completing the initial weeding and thinning of the cotton stands. Gabriel Nhantumbo remembered that this phase was particularly demanding: "We didn't have time to look after our other crops; cotton needs constant attention; you have to keep weeding the field and thinning out the plants."[76] In addition to caring for their cotton and food crops, peasants were called upon to repair roads and bridges washed out by the rains.[77]

If there was ever a moment when the nearly unending demands of cotton on the peasants seemed to abate, it was during April when the plants were maturing but were not quite ready for harvest. During this period, however, young children

---

[72] Bravo, *A Cultura Algodeira*, 114.

[73] Interview with Faria Lobo; Interview with Paulo Roque.

[74] Prentice, *Cotton*, 80.

[75] Group interview with Alberto Momola et al.; Joint interview with Muariri Tocola and Licúrio Makalawila; Joint interview with Fátima Spaneke et al.; Interview with Fátima Konkonko; Interview with Paulo Roque; Interview with Faria Lobo.

[76] Quoted in Mondlane, *Struggle for Mozambique*, 86.

[77] Group interview with Semble Roldão, LaFaite Daglasse, Moniz Kapete, and Uassu Subau, July 16, 1991, in Nicoadala.

spent the entire day protecting the maturing plants against monkeys. Their parents and older siblings picked the crop. Hand picking was a difficult task, especially in the hot sun. Men, women, and older children worked from the mid-morning until late afternoon. On a good day adults could pick between 30 and 40 pounds.[78] A deft picker, who could empty all the compartments of a cotton boll with one snatch of the fingers, could collect appreciably more. When possible, the peasants avoided harvesting on rainy or cloudy days, since excessive moisture discolored the lint, reducing its value. After they picked the cotton, men and women separated the lint by quality and stacked it into large piles, where it was left outside to dry for a month. Since the cotton plant did not flower all at once, growers had to repeat this set of tasks several times. Harvesting took up most of the months of May and June, and often extended into July.

In the months of July and August, northerners brought their cotton to market. Without trucks or other motorized transport, producers were transformed into conscripted porters. Manuel Baptista remembered seeing peasants "carrying 50 kilogram sacks on their head. Women carried their babies as well. Sometimes they had to walk nearly 75 kilometers."[79] Until the 1950s the limited number of markets and trucks meant that women and elders as well as younger men had to carry their heavy loads substantial distances on poorly cleared paths. The journey to the markets normally lasted two days and peasants often had to make several trips, depending on the size of their harvest.[80] After they had brought all their cotton to the market, they had to wait in long-lines until their cotton was classified and weighed, when they received their meager payment in cash. Although state officials were supposed to oversee the transactions and protect the interests of the peasants, abuses were flagrant. As one Portuguese scholar bluntly put it, "the local administrators simply shut their eyes in return for bribes."[81] And even after peasants had suffered indignities at the market, they still had to return to their cotton fields and chop and burn the stalks lest these become a host for parasites that could jeopardize the following year's crop.

Four conclusions emerge out of this cursory description of the work calendar. The first is that cotton production was a long and arduous task, almost always involving all productive members of the household. The unwillingness of the concessionary companies to invest in modern technology exacerbated the labor demands. Without plows, tractors, pesticides, trucks, or accessible markets, the entire burden of production was literally shifted onto the backs of the northern cultiva-

---

[66] Group interview with Adelina Cedo et al., July 21, 1979, in Montepuez; Group interview with Romeu Mataquenha et al.; Group interview with Arridhi Mahanda et al.; Group interview with Daima Magaga Mbela et al., July 30, 1979, in Chai Chai.

[67] A.H.M., Secção Reserva, Cx. 20, "Inspecção dos Serviços Administrativos e dos Negócios Indígenas," Relatório e Documentos Referentes à Inspecção Ordinária Feita na Província do Niassa, 1a parte, 1943," Carlos Henriques Jonas da Silveira, 1943.

[68] Allen Isaacman "Chiefs, Rural Differentiation, and Peasant Protest: The Mozambican Forced Cotton Regime, 1938–1961," *African Economic History* 14 (1985), 32–33.

[69] Ibid.

[70] For a discussion of the ambiguous and contradictory position of the chiefs, see Isaacman, "Chiefs, Rural Differentiation, and Peasant Protest," *passim*.

[71] Group interview Armando Nicula, Liassa Lohaninté, and Murinvona Mpemo, July 8, 1991, in Nampula.

tors. The initial land preparation began in September and the final destruction of the cotton stalks occurred the following August, when peasants planted manioc. Apart from the brief respite between one cotton season and another, only in the month of April were peasants largely free from cotton. Yet in that period thousands of northerners were conscripted to clear paths and rebuild the cotton markets.[82]

The second conclusion this review of the work calendar offers is that cotton production was highly labor-intensive. State and cotton concessionary officials estimated that rural households had to spend between 110 and 175 person-days just to cultivate one hectare of cotton properly.[83] In practice the minimum input varied, depending on whether cotton was grown in forests, bush savanna, or on fallow lands, and how a typical "working day" was defined. To our knowledge, contemporary household surveys for this period are virtually non-existent. There is, however, one fairly detailed report collected by agronomists at the Nacaroa experimental station in northern Mozambique;[84] when adjusted to account for the cultivation of a full hectare, a third weeding, marketing, and plant destruction, this report suggests that a figure of approximately 150 days per hectare would seem quite reasonable.[85]

The substantial number of days peasants were required to devote to cotton looms even larger when juxtaposed against the number of actual workable days. In the rainy seasons from the middle of November to the middle of March, heavy downpours and wet fields reduced by as much as a half the amount of time peasants could farm.[86] These environmental constraints placed an added burden on households often unable to mobilize adequate labor to work their cotton plots when conditions permitted.

Third, the appreciable number of days peasants worked in their fields was matched by the length of their work day. It was not uncommon for peasants to labor from sunrise to sunset and sometimes beyond.[87] Romeu Mataquenha, who planted cotton for much of his adult life recalled that "there were times when I

---

[78] See Prentice, *Cotton*, 185; Acland, *East Africa Crops*, 102.

[79] Group interview with Manuel Baptista and Joaquim Carajola, July 9, 1991, in Nampula.

[80] Interview with Manuel Baptista.

[81] Armando Castro, *O Sistema Colonial Português em África* (Lisbon, 1980), 286.

[82] Interview with Paulo Roque; Bravo, *A Cultura Algodeira*, 118.

[83] Bravo, *A Cultura Algodeira*, 201. For a comparative analysis, see Dietrich von Rotenhan, "Cotton Farming in Sukumaland," in Hans Ruthenberg, ed., *Smallholder Farming and Smallholder Development in Tanzania* (Munich, 1974), 73–75. Zairian colonial officials reached a similar conclusion (Archives Regionals de Haut-Zaire, Kisangani, Dossiers Z65). According to one study, labor requirements in Azire varied from 184 to 287 days per hectare of cotton, depending on whether the crop was cultivated in forests, fallow, lands, or savanna. Osumaka Likaka, "The Social Organization of Work," unpublished paper, 13.

[84] A.I.A., J.E.A.C., Delegação de Moçambique, Brigada Técnica de Nampula, "Relatório do Campo Experimental de Nacarôa Campanha de 1942/43, Augusto Guilherme Alves, ÃO Agente da Fiscalização, n.d.

[85] A team of researchers from the Centro dos Estudos Africanos who did a survey in Nampula during the 1978/79 campaign also concluded that peasants spent 150 days to cultivate one hectare. Although the survey was done in the postcolonial period, peasants were still using manual instruments, so we would not expect a great difference. See Centro Estudos Africanos, *A Transformação da Agricultura Familiar na Província de Nampula* (Maputo, 1980), 21–24.

[86] We are grateful to Mr. Paulo Zucula, a Mozambican agronomist, for this point.

[87] Interview with Murinvona Mpemo, July 8, 1991, in Centro Piloto de Deslocados, Nampula.

didn't sleep."[88] Women experienced this burden most acutely since they also continued to assume responsibility for such critical domestic chores as cooking, carrying firewood, and caring for infants. Listen to the words of Murinvona Mpemo:

> When I woke up it was still dark. Before going to my cotton field, I had to fetch water. As soon as I returned home, I had to pound manioc so that it could be made into porridge. I left my oldest daughter in charge of this task. I then went directly to the field for fear of being late. I spent the entire morning weeding cotton. Only in the afternoon could I go to my garden, which was far from the cotton field. I was only able to spend a short time there because I had to return home to gather wood, and prepare food for my children. . . . After eating I went to bed exhausted.[89]

Finally, because peasants had to allocate the bulk of their labor to satisfy cotton requirements, they jeopardized their food security. The problem was twofold. Even under the most favorable conditions, it was difficult to maintain two fields far apart. To complicate matters even more, the cycle of cotton production coincided almost identically with the cultivation of basic cereals and legumes. As a result, from January to March northern Mozambicans confronted an acute labor crisis. They had to weed their maize and sorghum and prepare their bean fields, precisely at the moment when cotton demands were greatest.[90] For most households this was an impossible burden.

Food production plummeted throughout the north, and shortages occurred with great regularity. There was hardly a time, especially during the first fifteen years of forced cotton production, when malnutrition and famines were not noted by colonial authorities and contemporary observers.[91] And even when cotton cultivation was not the sole cause of hunger, it was always a contributing factor. Former producers in Imala remember with great clarity how the tyranny of the cotton regime combined with a particularly bad cold spell one year to leave them without any food. The consequences were devastating. "Many people died. Some days more than 20, 30, or even 40. Everyone was afraid. So many people perished."[92] In the cotton region of Mogovolas there are reports that several thousand peasants died during the 1951 famine.[93] A senior concessionary company official, who spent thirty years in the north, acknowledged that "a great deal of hunger was caused by our insistence that peasants cultivate cotton at all costs."[94] Because the income cotton producers received was so small, many households found it difficult to purchase foodstuffs from rural Asian and European merchants. To quote from a recent study, "famine was particularly acute in the districts where the income from cotton represented the highest percentage of the family's revenue."[95]

---

[88] Group interview with Romeu Mataquenha et al., July 17, 1979, in Montepuez.

[89] Ibid.

[90] There was another, less acute bottleneck in June and July, when peasants needed to harvest beans, sorghum, and cotton, which also had to be brought to market.

[91] A.I.A, J.E.A.C., Gastão de Melo Furtado to Governador Geral, August 15, 1951; A.I.A., J.E.A.C., "Confidências 1957–59," Gastão de Melo Furtado to Presidente de J.E.A., September 1, 1959.

[92] Group interview with Imala, May 4, 1979.

[93] Armando Castro, *O Sistema Colonial* (Lisbon, 1978), 286.

[94] Interview with Faria Lobo, May 26, 1987, in Nampula.

[95] Fortuna, "Threading Through," 245.

166   COTTON CULTIVATION IN NORTHERN MOZAMBIQUE 1938–1961

In addition to the human tribulations, cotton further undermined food security by devastating the ecosystem. The introduction of the staple brought such problems as soil erosion and the spread of new plant diseases and pests, particularly red bollworm. A confidential 1947 report to the president of the Cotton Board concluded "that there is increasing evidence linking plant diseases and pests associated with cotton to the decline in food crops."[96] The labor regime exacerbated these problems. Soil exhaustion occurred, in part, because overworked peasants chose, when possible, to farm tired land rather than to spend a month clearing virgin land. Similarly, official reports indicate widespread peasant opposition to burning their plants after the harvest. While the rural cultivators recognized that these steps would improve the quantity and quality of future cotton and would eliminate an ecological niche for parasites, they were also aware that the time spent could be used more productively growing food and cash crops.[97]

The refusal of many growers to burn their cotton stalks was not an isolated phenomenon. Rather it was one of a multitude of ways in which peasants willing to take risks defied the cotton regime. In the process they helped to thwart Lisbon's goal of cotton self-sufficiency and forced colonial authorities to contemplate reforming the regime.

Reforming the System:
Rationalizing the Labor Process, ca. 1950–1961[98]

From the outset of the cotton regime, there were some officials who had favored a policy of "guiding the peasants" by using a combination of moral and material incentives and not just relying on brute force. They were concerned that growers were being squeezed too hard and sought to control the most rapacious practices of the concessionary companies.[99] They gained support from agricultural extension officers, labor inspectors, and agronomists who argued that the cotton regime was archaic, inefficient, and badly in need of reform. Textile interests in Lisbon, angry about the poor quality of the cotton, concurred.[100] In response to this criticism, the government promulgated Decree 35,844 of 1946,[101] which envisioned a more ratio-

---

[96] A.I.A., J.E.A.C., Copiador Geral de Notas 4 trimestre, Gaspar to J.E.A.C., December 11, 1947.

[97] Interview with A. Quintanilha; A.I.A., J.E.A.C. Confidencial 1947, Jose da Cunha Dias Mendes, Regente Agrícola to Chefe do Posto da J.E.A.C., December 7, 1947; A.I.A., J.E.A.C., 952, "Brigada Técnica de Cabo Delgado," Vasco Sousa de Fonseca Leone, September 30, 1949.

[98] The chronology we have adopted is somewhat different from that M. Anne Pitcher uses in her article above. In part the different approaches reflect the fact that periodization is often somewhat arbitrary and fluid. The different temporal markers also reflect her emphasis on state policy as opposed to our emphasis on the actual impact of that policy on the ground, which necessarily implies a time lag.

[99] We need to remember that paternalism and coercion were not necessarily incompatible. Research on a variety of economic and social institutions from plantations to industrial workplaces suggests that they were often integrally connected parts of a larger strategy of social control. For a discussion of the paternalist ingredients in the Mozambican cotton regime, see Allen Isaacman, "Coercion, Paternalism and the Labor Process: The Mozambican Cotton Regime 1938–1961," *Journal of Southern African Studies* 18 (1992), 487–525

[100] See, for example, E. de Queiroz Ribeiro, *O Algodão: Da Colheita à Industrialização* (Porto, 1946); and M. Anne Pitcher in this volume.

[101] *Diário do Governo*, Série 1, Decreto-Lei 35,844, August 31, 1946. For a discussion of this legislation, see the article by M. Anne Pitcher in this volume.

nal and less coercive cotton regime. Over the next decade the Board implemented this reformist project in fits and starts. Its overarching objective was to rationalize production by harnessing the most energetic labor to the best cotton lands and by introducing principles of "scientific farming." In addition to raising the prices growers received quite substantially,[102] the Board introduced four structural changes in the cotton regimes that were designed to improve the living and working conditions of the cotton producers. The results were mixed at best.

By far the most ambitious piece of social engineering was the state's project to transform the most productive peasants into progressive cotton farmers. The plan anticipated a division of the rural population into two gendered categories, *agricultores do algodão* and *cultivadores do algodão*. The former were men eighteen to fifty-five who cultivated one hectare of cotton plus an additional half-hectare per wife beyond the first spouse. They became eligible for technical assistance, production bonuses, and the possibility of relocating into planned cotton communities (*concentrações de algodão*). Most important, they were shielded from forced labor and theoretically could not be conscripted to work on European plantations. Women, the majority of producers, were not offered this choice. Instead they were lumped together as *cultivadores de algodão* with older men (fifty-five to sixty-five), men with physical handicaps, and those considered less motivated. They were required to cultivate half a hectare of cotton and a food plot of equal proportions. In colonial discourse, the classification *cultivadores de algodão* slipped easily into "subsistence producers" and "recalcitrant nomads," social categories synonymous with economic stagnation.

This bifurcation of rural communities theoretically carried far-reaching implications for the organization of rural work. In practice the distinction between *agricultores* and *cultivadores* was often circumscribed by realities on the ground. Throughout the 1950s the cotton regime still rested on force. Production bonuses, administered through the Cotton Fund, were minuscule. State technical assistance was also quite limited. Even the guarantee that *agricultores* would not be press-ganged was often violated. The provincial government of Niassa declared in 1951 that, regardless of his cotton status, any male who failed to produce 400 kilograms of cotton would be sent to work on European tea plantations.[103] Eight years later the governor of Nampula required *agricultores de algodão* to sell a minimum of 750 escudos worth of cotton to retain their exemption from contract labor.[104] The effect of these labor policies was not only to blur the legal distinction between *agricultores* and *cultivadores*, but to precipitate a contentious debate within the state apparatus, with critics protesting that this short-sighted policy would undercut the larger vision of the creation of a class of petty commodity producers.

To further this agenda, the Board promoted the construction of a network of planned cotton communities throughout the north. First proposed in 1947, these new complexes were multi-crop agricultural units organized around "scientific" principles of rotation and crop management, and located on the best available land.

---

[102] The average price paid to peasants per kilogram of cotton was 0.92 escudos in 1939, as compared to 3.45 escudos in 1961. In real terms this represented approximately a 75 percent increase, almost all of which came in the 1950s. Bravo, *A Cultura Algodoeira*, 183.

[103] A.I.A., J.E.A.C., "Papéis Diversos," A. Figueira e Sousa to Governador de Niassa, February 21, 1952.

[104] A.I.A., J.E.A.C., "Confidências 1957–1959," Júlio Bossa, September 14, 1959.

168 Cotton Cultivation in Northern Mozambique 1938–1961

Registered *cultivadores* were encouraged to join the *concentrações* voluntarily. Single women, widows, and unproductive male *agriculturalists* were rarely given this option. Each household received between a five- and seven-hectare block of land, half of which would be allowed to lie fallow at any time. On the remainder, peasants would cultivate a hectare of cotton, a hectare of corn or sorghum and other food crops, and a hectare of manioc often intercropped with peanuts. Out of these communities was to be forged a whole new class of commodity producers tied to the Portuguese material and cultural world.

The *concentrações* seemed to offer many advantages. For peasant producers, a system of crop rotation that incorporated food crops could relieve production bottlenecks and hunger. Situating peasant plots in one concentrated block adjacent to their homes, officials argued, would also allow household members to spend more time in their food gardens, since they would not have to travel from one field to another. Access to tractors, better seeds and lands, and the opportunity to grow other cash crops were all intended to increase household income still further. Finally, peasants who registered were assured that they would be exempt from contract labor.[105] This latest effort to restructure production was equally attractive to both concessionary interests and the state. Officials believed scientific farming would alleviate food crises, reduce soil erosion, convince peasants to "abandon their natural pneumatism," and increase cotton productivity without requiring substantial new investments.[106]

The cost of this social experiment was borne almost entirely by peasants. Government planners selected sites without any reference to historical residence patterns. In principle, land quality was the overarching consideration. As a result, those households and communities forced to relocate lost the protection of the ancestor spirits who resided on the historic land and who were the guardians of fertility. When skeptical peasants had second thoughts or changed their minds, they were often pressured or coerced into moving.[107] Once resettled, they found that they often had to work longer and harder than before. Opening up a hectare of new land each year and farming upwards of three to four hectares was very demanding. Above all else, the bevy of company overseers, chiefs, and *sepais* who regularly patrolled this confined space drastically reduced their autonomy. As one official bluntly put it, "within the *concentrações* we had more or less perfect control over the work of each peasant every day. We could never have exercised such power when their cotton fields were dispersed."[108]

By the end of the 1950s, the planned communities had failed to live up to Lisbon's expectations. After more than a decade of official hyperbole, the government acknowledged that only 11,000 families had been relocated in the northern three provinces.[109] This figure represented less than 2 percent of the rural popula-

---

[105] Interview with Faria Lobo.

[106] A.I.A., J.E.A.C., "Relatório Técnico," Fonseca Jorge, Chefe de Secção de Fomento, April 10, 1947.

[107] Interview with Faria Lobo; A.H.M., Secção Reserva, Cx. 89, Inspecção dos Serviços Administrativos e dos Negócios Indígenas, "Relatório da Inspecção Ordinária a Circunscrição de la Montepuez e posto de Ancuabe, do Concelho de Porto Amélia e Posto de Ocua, e Chiure, da Circunscrição de Mecúfi, Realizada no Ano de 1950/51," António Policarpo de Sousa, Inspector Administrativo.

[108] Interview with Faria Lobo.

[109] Cited in Fortuna, "Threading Through," 336.

tion.[110] While there were some complexes that were successful, they were the exceptions. In their haste to try to construct as many cotton communities as possible, officials often selected locations with poor soils and a lack of water.[111] As a result, many peasants became disillusioned; some dropped out.[112] Lisbon's social engineering neither stemmed the problems of soil erosion nor alleviated the food crises. A 1959 government memorandum concluded that the "majority of the population is underfed," and warned that "it is absolutely necessary that cotton producers have sufficient food surpluses to enable them to work."[113]

Ill-advised and unsuccessful as the attempt to create organized cotton communities was, it was far more successful than Lisbon's attempt to promote peasant-based cotton cooperatives. For the purposes of our analysis, the most significant clause of the 1955 legislation on cooperatives is that the state left the organization of production firmly in the hands of the members. With this reform in mind, Cotton Board officials predicted that the cooperatives would play a critical role "incorporating the Africans into the productive activity of the region."[114] The concessionary companies did not share their optimism. They feared a sharp reduction in output if peasants were no longer forced to cultivate cotton under a highly regimented labor regime. For their part, many local administrators opposed the cooperatives on the grounds that they would become hotbeds of social unrest, as in neighboring Tanzania. Together administrators and company officials stifled most local initiatives to organize cooperatives. By 1957 not a single one had been registered. In that year a dozen Makonde peasants led by Lázaro Kavandame formed the Mozambique African Voluntary Cotton Society. With fifteen hundred peasant members it was one of the few successful cooperative in northern Mozambique.[115]

Ironically, the most significant action the state took was to allow peasants who lived on poor lands to withdraw from the cotton system. The 1946 decree called for the elimination of cotton production on unsuitable lands and barred concessionary companies from expanding into marginal regions.[116] Throughout the rest of the decade, this policy was erratically implemented, with company officials bribing state authorities in an effort to blunt these reforms.[117] With the completion of the first agroecological study of Mozambique in 1953, the Board began to enforce the land withdrawal policy more vigorously. Between 1954 and 1955 alone, approximately 110,000 hectares of marginal lands, or approximately 15 percent of the total

---

[110] According to official government reports the 11,000 households constituted approximately 55,000 people. The population of the three northern provinces in 1950 was slightly more than 2 million.

[111] A.I.A., J.E.A.C., 901, "Plano do Trabalho," unsigned; A.H.M., J.E.A.C., Delegação de Moçambique, Brigada Técnica de Moçambique, "Relatório Anual Referente ão Ano de 1957," Manuel de Oliveira Barros, Regente Agrícola de 2a classe, January 4, 1958.

[112] A.I.A, J.E.A.C., "Confidências 1957–1959," Administrador do Mogincual, January 6, 1958.

[113] A.I.A., J.E.A.C., "Confidências 1957–1959," Gastão do Melo Furtado to Presidente de J.E.A.C., September 1, 1959.

[114] B.O.M., No. 51/55, Decreto 40:405, November 24, 1955.

[115] See Allen Isaacman, "The Mozambique Cotton Cooperative: The Creation of a Grassroots Alternative to Forced Commodity Production," *African Studies Review*, XXV (1982), 5–25.

[116] Decree number 35,8444 called for the establishment of cotton zones and elimination of unsuitable lands. Boletim Oficial de Moçambique [B.O.M.], série 1, No. 45, November 9, 1946.

[117] Interview with A. Quintanilha.

170   COTTON CULTIVATION IN NORTHERN MOZAMBIQUE 1938–1961

acreage, were taken out of the system.[118] By the end of the decade more than 200,000 hectares of land were free from the cotton regime (see Figure 7-2).

Cotton, Rural Differentiation, and Internal Conflict, 1938–1961

The fact that thousands of northern Mozambicans withdrew from cotton production reflected not only a shift in state policy but also peasant unwillingness to continue assuming the risks of production inherent in the cotton regime. In the process of restructuring the labor process, the state-concessionary alliance had impoverished most peasants; only the degree of impoverishment varied. During the first five years of the regime, government reports indicated that the annual income per producer was under one dollar in cotton centers such as Macomia, Maconde, Vila Cabral, and Mocímboa de Praia.[119] During the war years the price of "basic" consumer goods such as blankets and cloth increased by as much as 300 to 400 percent while the price peasants received for cotton showed little improvement.[120] In 1949 a survey in the Lourenço Marques *Guardian* found that on average a peasant had to produce 115 kilograms of raw cotton to be able to purchase 1 kilogram of finished cotton.[121] Virtually every elder to whom we spoke emphasized that cotton was "the mother of poverty."

If cotton impoverished, it did not impoverish equally. Nor did it impoverish everyone. A few cotton producers prospered, and a few more, through hard work and good fortune, were able to make ends meet. With land readily available, prices fixed, and technology generally underdeveloped, differentiation in the north was based ultimately on access to labor. Those producers who were able to mobilize extra-household labor fared relatively well. Conversely, those households, particularly female-headed ones, that had to rely on their own labor, and did not have access to migrant earnings, suffered the most.

No one understood the value of extra-familial labor better than the chiefs. From the outset they utilized their position of authority to appropriate their subjects' labor. As early as 1939 colonial officials noted the number of "large cotton fields belonging to the indigenous authorities but worked by their subjects."[122] Since this utilization of peasant labor enabled the loyalist chiefs to fulfill their twin obligations as labor supervisors and model farmers, colonial officials not only sanctioned but enforced this practice. A peasant from the north recalled:

> The chiefs never worked in the cotton fields. Instead they requested assistance from the local administrator who sent his *sepais* to apprehend people to work the chief's land. They cleared, seeded, and weeded it. In this way

---

[118] Department of State, "Economic Review, 1955," R. Smith Thompson, American Counsel General, March 6, 1956.

[119] *Ibid.*

[120] Blankets increased from 15 to 60 escudos, and cloth from 5–6 to 20–25 escudos. Fortuna, "Threading Through," 258.

[121] *Guardian* (Lourenço Marques), April 8, 1949.

[122] A.I.A., J.E.A.C.,"Notas Recebidas," Palma Galião to Chefe da Delegação da J.E.A.C. em Moçambique, May 12, 1939.

the chiefs could collect 20 or 30 sacks of cotton. He earned much more than anyone else.[123]

Cotton producers from virtually every major region of the north told a similar story.[124] What varied in their accounts was the amount of labor extracted.

By the 1950s the growing disparitiy in income between chiefs and their peasant subjects was increasingly reflected in lifestyle and access to the Portuguese material and cultural world. In 1951 a Native Affairs officer paid homage to Chief Megama of Mecúfi "for the way he had learned to live as a European, purchasing a truck, teaching his children to speak Portuguese . . . . carrying himself with the appropriate comportment and dressing meticulously."[125] The son of Chief Niquaria, a prosperous northern cotton producer, bragged "that we lived in a stone house and owned two motorcycles, while the rest of the population lived in huts and only had bicycles."[126]

In addition to chiefs, there were also a small number of cotton producers who profited by employing laborers from a pool of impoverished peasants living in adjacent regions. Consider the case of Lázaro Kavandame. Kavandame had been a successful labor recruiter for the Tanzanian sisal plantations before he returned home and became a leader of an autonomous cotton cooperative.[127] As president of the Mozambique African Voluntary Cotton Society, Kavandame used his position of authority as well as his entrepreneurial skills to recruit vulnerable members of the rural community to work his expanded holdings. Contemporaries report that in the late 1950s Kavandame sold between 150 and 300 bags of cotton per annum, generating profits of more than $1,000.[128] Although Kavandame's entrepreneurial skills were probably unique, there were teachers, itinerant merchants, returning migrant laborers, prosperous peasants, and highly paid cotton gin workers who pursued a similar strategy, but on a smaller scale.[129]

There are enough scattered accounts of individuals profiting inside the cotton regime that their experiences cannot simply be dismissed as a historical anomaly. These accounts of success, however, do not outweigh the evidence that for most cotton producers in northern Mozambique, access to extra-familial labor was a necessity for survival, not a precondition for accumulation. In the peak planting periods the typical household required at least eighty labor days per month. There were no doubt families who by virtue of their size, demographic composition, and the capacity of their members to work could meet this demand and even produce

---

[123] Interview with Amasse Nuitha et al.

[124] Group interview Armando Nicula, Liassa Lohaninté et al., July 8, 1991, in Nampula; Interview with Paulo José and Manuel Pacheleque, July 10, 1991, in Nampula, Group interview with Communal Village Odenepe, May 2, 1979, in Nampula.

[125] A.H.M., Secção Reserva, Cx. 89, "Inspecção dos Serviços Administrativos e dos Negócios Indígenas," Relatório da Inspecção Ordinária a Circunscrição de Montepuez e Posto do Ancuabe do Concelho de Porto Amélia, e Posto de Ocur, e Chiure da Circunscrição de Mecufi, Realizada no ano de 1950/51," António Policarpo de Sousa, Inspector Administrativo.

[126] Interview with Niquaria.

[127] Group interview with Zimu Cocote et al., July 23, 1979, in Cabo Delgado; Interview with João Cornélio Mandande, July 30, 1979, in Mueda.

[128] Interview with João Cornélio Mandande, July 30, 1979, in Mueda; Group interview with Zimu Cocote et al., July 23, 1979, in Cabo Delgado.

172 COTTON CULTIVATION IN NORTHERN MOZAMBIQUE 1938–1961

a sizable surplus. But these were the exceptions. Throughout the north peasants relied on a variety of reciprocal labor agreements with other members of their community to cope with the heavy demands of cotton. By combining resources, many peasants not only alleviated production bottlenecks but satisfied state cotton production requirements for becoming full-time cotton producers or *agricultores de algodão*. By 1959 somewhat more than half the growers managed to be eligible for this legal status.[130] Most managed to survive, however tenuously, within the cotton regime. At the same time there was an appreciable number of poorer peasants, or *cultivadores*, who were unable to meet minimum state cotton production requirements.[131]

The failure of so many of these northern households to eke out a living in cotton was linked to increased capitalist encroachment and the partial transformation of the rural work force in the aftermath of the Second World War. The postwar period witnessed the resurgence of the moribund northern sisal industry, the expansion of tobacco and tea plantations, increased settler farms, the growth of a timber industry and a major expansion of state programs to build all-weather roads, bridges, and railroad lines. The result was a quantum leap in the number of male peasants press-ganged into service for six-month stints under notoriously bad conditions.[132]

One result of labor recruitment was the progressive feminization both of cotton production and of poverty in many parts of the north. Whereas before World War II most men and women worked together on conjugal plots, many northern families were forced to send husbands and older sons to the colonial plantations and farms. In 1948, 5,070 of the 5,328 able-bodied men in Malema were compelled to work on tobacco farms in Ribáuè, while in the concelho of António Enes more than 80 percent of the 24,000 males had to work on European plantations.[133] Throughout the next decade more and more cotton zones were drawn into this labor system. By 1957 an agronomist traveling through Cabo Delgado observed "that cotton is cultivated only by women, children, elders, and the handicapped."[134]

---

[129] *Ibid.*, Group interview with Jonas Nakutepa et al., July 31, 1979, in Communal Village Micalela; Group interview with Tanga Karinga de Tangadica, July 31, 1979, in Communal Village Imbo; Jorge Dias, *Os Maconde de Moçambique* (Lisbon, 1970).

[130] In 1959, 45 percent of cotton growers in Niassa, 61 percent in Nampula, and 63 percent in Cabo Delgado had become *cultivadores*. A.I.A., J.E.A.C., Gastão de Melo Furtado to Governador de Niassa, February 24, 1959.

[131] With so many men absent, it is hardly surprising that the south had the highest percentage of *cultivadores* in the colony. Fully 80 percent of all southern producers fell into this marginal category. Most were women. What is more surprising is that in the cotton north, more than 40 percent of the growers also failed to achieve *agricultor* status.

[132] Workers on sisal and tobacco plantations received less than three dollars a month. Colonial labor inspectors reported that most estates did not provide housing or health facilities, and the daily rations of porridge was insufficient and often contaminated. A.H.M., Secção Reserva, Cx. 77 Inspecção dos Serviços Administrativos e dos Negócios Indígenas, "Relatório da Inspecção Ordinária ao Distrito: Nacala, N.D., p. 776, Hortêncio Estevão de Sousa, 1948.

[133] A.H.M., Secção Reserva, Inspecção dos Serviços Administrativos dos Negócios Indígenas, "Relatório da Inspecção Ordinária do Distrito de Nampula da Província do Niassa," Hortêncio Estevão de Sousa, 1949.

[134] A.I.A., J.E.A.C., Delegação de Moçambique, Brigada Técnica de Moçambique, "Relatório Anual Referente ao Ano de 1957 (Campanha Algodoeira de 1956–57)," Manuel de Oliveria Barros, Regente Agrícola de 2a classe), January 4, 1958.

A senior cotton official writing a year later complained that throughout the north "the contract labor system robbed households of male labor just when planting began."[135]

By the end of the cotton regime, the most destitute households were trapped in a vicious cycle. The poorer the family, the more likely that the husband was gone. His absence exacerbated the shortages of labor and increased poverty. Consider 1960 income statistics from Litúndia in northern Mozambique. In that year there were 403 cotton producers. The poorest earned $6 or less a year and "all were women and elders."[136] The income for the vast majority barely reached $30 , while a handful of chiefs and prosperous growers earned almost $200.[137] While cotton income increased with the price reforms of the 1950s, substantial disparities between communities persisted as they did within communities. By 1960 peasants in Montepuez, for example, were earning $20 from cotton, or roughly five times as much as their counterparts in Mudimbe located in the same province. Disparities within Montepuez were even greater.[138]

This uneven impact, in turn, accentuated rivalries and divisions at the community and domestic levels, which were based on intraclass as well as interclass tensions. Often these tensions antedated the introduction of cotton. The most pronounced and best-documented conflict was between loyalist chiefs and their subject populations.[139] Throughout the colonial period, chiefs were placed in a contradictory position vis-a-vis both the colonial state and the peasantry. To the extent that chiefs opted for collaboration, their actions intruded on the peasant labor process and posed a threat to the partial autonomy of their subjects. And to the extent that they were perceived as the vacillating executers of an unjust colonial policy, they often became a focal point of rural discontent. Elsewhere we have documented the contempt peasants held for most loyalist chiefs and the challenges to their authority.[140]

Because cotton production transformed the labor process, as well as the income relations between male and female peasants and between generations, the household often became an arena of conflict. At stake was who would control and distribute these critical resources. For households at risk in which women increasingly assumed the onus of managing the rural economy but had very little control over the resources, the potential for frustration and marital strains was enormous.

> Together with our husbands we carried the cotton to market. Because our husbands were the ones registered, they received the money. When we returned home, they showed it to us. The next day we took our children and went to the shop to buy clothing, wine, and a few other things. Our

---

[135] A.I.A., J.E.A.C., "Confidências 1957–1959," Gastão de Melo Furtado to Presidente da J.E.A.C., September 1, 1959.

[136] Bravo, *A Cultura Algodoeira* 198.

[137] *Ibid*, 197.

[138] A.H.M., Cx. 91, "Relatório da Inspecção Ordinária ão Concelho de Mocímboa da Praia no Distrito de Cabo Delgado, Anos De 1951–1961," Amadeu Pacheco de Amorim, May 25, 1962; A.H.M., Cx. 91, "Relatório da Inspecção Ordinária ão Concelho de Montepuez no Distrito de Cabo Delgado Anos de 1951–1960," Amadeu Paceho de Amorim, February 13, 1962.

[139] See Isaacman, "Chiefs, Rural Differentiation and Peasant Protest," 15–56.

[140] *Ibid.*, 32–36.

174 COTTON CULTIVATION IN NORTHERN MOZAMBIQUE 1938–1961

husbands asked us what we needed but it was they who decided what was bought. If we were unhappy we could complain, but there was nothing we could do.[141]

Such accounts tend to highlight the dependency and vulnerability of women. But the narrative of male domination was often only one part of the story. Fragmentary evidence suggests that many peasant women were able to shield some portion of their labor or other valued resources from expropriation by male household heads. The strategies they adopted were similar to those employed against the cotton regime. There is ample evidence of women fleeing the intensified pressures within the household.[142] Their options were relatively limited, however. They could buy out of an unhappy marriage, seek refuge at missionary stations, flee with a lover who might ultimately become a new husband, or clandestinely migrate to the cities. Rosa Ernesto remembered that "many women escaped to Nampula and Nacala in order to avoid being beaten by their husbands in disputes over cotton, money, and alcohol."[143] Murinvona Mpemo separated from her husband for three years until he agreed to divide the cotton income with her.[144] Other women simply hid money from their absentee husbands so that they could not squander it on liquor or on other frivolous items.[145] Such insurgent acts aroused fierce opposition among chiefs, male elders, and state officials, who often worked in unison to preserve shared notions of gender hierarchies.[146]

Many young men also contested the claims of elders to control their labor. Some fled to the towns, but because there were appreciably fewer opportunities for wage employment than in other parts of the colony, labor flight as a means of escape was more problematic.[147] There is evidence, primarily from the region of Eráti, that young males began to manipulate the cotton regime to their own advantage in the 1950s. Until then northern elders had used the historic institution of brideservice to secure youth labor for several years, in effect creating unpaid cotton growers out of their future sons-in-law. By the time young men had satisfied this labor requirement and married, they were already in their mid- to late twen-

---

[141] Group interview with Fátima Spaneke et al.

[142] The absence of large cities in the north, where runaway women could easily find employment, probably made urban migration a less attractive alternative. Additional research needs to be conducted on the subject.

[143] Interview with Rosa Maria Ernesto, July 11, 1991, in Nampula.

[144] Interview with Murinvona Mpemo.

[145] Ibid.

[146] A.H.M, Cx. 26, Inspecção do Serviços Administrativos e dos Negócios Indígenas, "Inspecção A Circunscrição de Guijá," António Policarpo de Sousa Santos, O Inspector Administrativo, March 12, 1957; A.H.M., Cx. 28, Inspecção dos Serviços Administrativos e dos Negócios Indígenas da Província de Moçambique, "Relatório da Inspecção Ordinária à Extinta Circunscrição dos Muchopes," António Policarpo de Sousa Santos, Inspector Administrativo, December 1957; A.H.M., Secção Reserva, Cx. 20, "Inspecção ao Concelho de Gaza e Circunscriçoes do Bilene, Manhiça e Magude, 1953," António Policarpo de Sousa Santos, Inspector Concelho de Gaza, n.d.

[147] Urban employment in the administrative capitals such as Nampula and Porto Amélia was limited and wages were appreciably lower than in Lourenço Marques. Because the agricultural and transportation sectors were so undercapitalized, they tended to rely on conscripted workers who earned less than $20 for six months labor. This was not a particularly attractive wage for most young men.

Cotton Cultivation in Northern Mozambique 1938–1961   175

ties. During the last decade of the cotton regime, an increasing number rejected this practice. Instead of providing brideservice, they worked their own cotton and peanut fields and planted cashew trees as well.[148] By reclaiming a measure of control over their own labor, they were often able to accumulate enough brideprice to start families earlier and to assert their independence from the elders.[149] The availability of unused land, increased prices for cotton and other agricultural commodities, and encouragement from state authorities anxious to increase the number of cotton producers facilitated this strategy. There are also indications that young men joined the state-organized cotton *concentrações* to be free from their household obligations.[150]

Coping and Struggling:
The Contest Over the Labor Process

Just as disgruntled wives and younger adults found ways to contest the claims of male elders, so thousands or perhaps hundreds of thousands of cotton producers at one time or another contested the state's effort to restructure the labor process. The available data suggest that in a multitude of ways, often beyond the gaze of colonial authorities, peasants drawn from all sectors of the cotton-producing population coped with, and at times struggled against, the most abusive demands of the cotton scheme.[151] In particular, they sought to minimize the amount of work they would put into the cotton regime.

For the purposes of this discussion we want to distinguish between coping with the harsh policies outlined here and resisting them. The distinction lies in the intent behind the act. Coping was aimed at muting the adverse effects of the cotton regime. These tactics enabled producers to survive and to reproduce themselves within a very harsh and brutal system. This was not an insignificant accomplishment. But these acts often had the unintended consequences of sustaining the system. Such was the case when peasants elongated their work day to meet consumption as well as cotton requirements. Resistance, on the other hand, was about the struggle over power and the appropriation of scarce resources. The intent was to block or to undermine the claims of the colonial regime and of the textile interests.

Of course, using intentionality to differentiate between coping and resistance poses several problems. While in some cases, such as sabotage, the motive may be inscribed in the act itself, in less precise and specific instances it is often extremely difficult, unless we attend critically to other voices of the actors to infer intent. This problem of intention is compounded because the intent may have been polyvalent. When peasants intercropped in their cotton fields they were both defying the state-concessionary company alliance and meeting basic consumption requirements. Cotton producers fleeing the regime were of-

---

[148] Geffray and Pedersen, *Transformação da Organização*, 61–62.
[149] *Ibid*.
[150] Interview with Alberto Momola, May 27, 1987, in Nampula. A similar point was made by Faria Lobo.
[151] Allen Isaacman and Michael Stephen, et al., "Cotton is the Mother of Poverty," *International Journal of African Historical Studies* 13 (1980), 606–608.

ten driven by multiple concerns. Although the question of multiple motives creates a certain analytical ambiguity, in real life people act ambiguously and historians need to grapple with this ambiguity.

Planting manioc instead of more labor-demanding food crops was the easiest and probably most common way to cope with the production bottleneck. Manioc was the perfect complement to cotton. It could be planted on marginal lands, required relatively little field work, and was harvested after cotton. It also had the virtue of being drought-resistant, and it did not have to be fully ripe to be edible. Manioc quickly became the basic staple in most household diets, even though it had very limited nutritional value.[152] In some regions it is estimated that cotton growers came to rely on manioc for 60 percent to 80 percent of their food intake, replacing sorghum.[153]

Many cotton producers also entered into labor exchanges to alleviate heavy work demands, particularly weeding. In some cases producers drew on kinship networks and in other cases on the labor of their neighbors. Supporting this type of mutual aid was the notion that shared labor was the only way to survive. Fátima Konkonko was adamant on this point.

> There were times when I could not possibly have finished alone. Others were in a similar situation. We agreed to work together, weeding one field after another. Sometimes, if we were still behind schedule, the *sepais* would force others who had already finished their fields to help us.[154]

These coping mechanisms were essential for the poorest households which could not afford to hire casual labor to help alleviate production bottlenecks. Female-headed households without wage remittances from absent males, in particular, relied on this strategy to survive. As Fátima Spaneke put it, "they had no other choices."[155] Their limited options stood in sharp contrast to the possibilities that better-off "married couples had of arranging work parties in their fields."[156] Typically, the organizers of such parties would invite anywhere from ten to fifty neighbors, friends, and relatives. They worked from morning to late afternoon in exchange for large quantities of beer and food, as well as the opportunity to visit, sing, dance, and gossip with their neighbors. Muariri Tocola and Licúrio Makalawila recalled that:

> Here in the Pemba region we had two types of work parties. The first we called *ipopwete*. We would prepare beer for all those who aided us with our cotton. Sometimes we would plan a big feast. We would kill some chickens and goats and brew beer. We would invite all our neigh-

---

[152] Bravo, *A Cultura Algodoeira*, 97; *Notícias*, July 19, 1941; A.I.A., J.E.A.C., 952, "Relatório da Brigada Técnica de Nampula," J. Costa Rosa, Regente Agrícola, October 1949; A.I.A., J.E.A.C., "Confidências 1957–1959," Vasco de Sousa da Fonseca Lebre to Chefe da Delegação de J.E.A.C., March 10, 1958; A.I.A., J.E.A.C., 952, Brigada Técnica de Inhambane, Vasconde Sousa de Fonseca Lebre, O Regente Agrícola, May 30, 1961; Group interviews with Pruan Hassan et al.; Group interview with Daima Magaga Mbela et al.; Joint interview with Chico Nhulialia and Costa Gaio Nampire.

[153] See, for example, Geffray and Pedersen, *Transformação da Organização*, 45.

[154] Interview with Fátima Konkonko.

[155] Group interview with Fátima Spaneke et al., May 28, 1987, in Nampula.

[156] *Ibid.*

bors. They helped us and then we had a big party. We called the celebration *nkumi*.[157]

Other households hired casual laborers in exchange for food and salt to alleviate short-term production bottlenecks.[158] However, a necessary precondition for organizing work parties and employing casual laborers was that households had to have an appreciable surplus of beer and food. Thus access to coping mechanisms was itself a marker of rural differentiation.

Joining autonomous cotton cooperatives offered a small number of peasants yet another way to increase control over their own labor. Under the 1955 legislation, peasants themselves controlled the entire production and marketing process. Gone were the company overseers. Gone were the hated sepais. Gone were the chiefs. It is hardly surprising that one of the first policies the members of the Mozambique Africans Voluntary Cotton Society implemented was restructuring the labor process. By agreeing to work only three days a week on the cotton fields rather than six, *cooperativistas* minimized the risks of food insecurity. Unlike peasants outside the cooperative, they avoided the dilemma of either being beaten or incarcerated for covertly working their food plots or facing serious food shortages.

Finally, a number of African women entered into long-term relationships with European and African overseers to escape the worst abuses of the cotton regime. Because the state never sanctioned these relationships, it is difficult to determine how frequently they occurred. Interviews with elderly women as well as local officials suggest, however, that they were fairly common.[159] And while their accounts often stress sexual violence and the victimization of women, other passages suggest that for at least some African women, and perhaps their families, cohabitation offered a way out of impoverishment and even out of cotton.[160]

While many peasants attempted to minimize the deleterious effects of the cotton regime, others resisted. Despite efforts to intimidate and terrorize them, many producers could and did find ways to contest the amount of labor they would put into the cotton system.

Three possibilities existed for withholding labor. Peasants could attempt to withdraw permanently from the cotton regime, periodically to withhold a portion of their labor, or to boycott the system at strategic moments.

Flight was both long and dangerous. Peasants sometimes had to walk several hundred kilometers through unfamiliar surroundings, often with children on their backs. They faced a number of difficulties, including lack of food and shelter, attacks from marauding bandits, and the ever-present threat of capture by police patrols. Many were not deterred by these substantial considerations. The cumula-

---

[157] Joint interview with Nuariri Tocola and Licúrio Makalawila, May 30, 1987, in Pemba.

[158] Interview with Faria Lobo, May 26, 1987, in Nampula; Interview with Murinvona Mpemo; Interview with Fátima Konkonko, May 30, 1987, in Pemba.

[159] Interview with Armando Cardoso, July 10, 1991, in Nampula; Interview with Nsaio Joaquim, July 16, 1991, in Nicoadala; Interview with Maria Sindique; Group interview with Celeste Cossa et al., July 31, 1991, in Matola.

[160] Interview with Maria Sindique.

[161] See Sebastião Soares de Resende, *Ordem Anti-Comunista* (Lourenço Marques, 1950), 140–42.

tive effect of these clandestine migrations is reflected in the 1951 observations of the bishop of Beira: "The exodus of Africans to the neighboring countries is an uncontestable fact and it is provoked by the rigorous demands of cotton."[161] Still other runaways created permanent refugee communities in remote zones, primarily the northern frontier regions, which bore striking similarities to the maroon communities in the Americas.[162]

Other cultivators managed to extract themselves from the cotton regime without fleeing. Instead they convinced state and concessionary company officials that their lands were inappropriate for cotton and should be dropped from the system. They deceived the Europeans by covertly cooking a substantial part of their cotton seeds before going through the motions of planting and weeding the crop. At harvest time they feigned surprise when few plants had germinated. Testimony from peasant producers as well as from colonial officials confirms that this type of sabotage occurred throughout northern Mozambique, although it is difficult to determine its frequency.[163]

Covertly circumventing the state-imposed work schedule was probably the most widespread way to reclaim some measure of control over the labor process. Clandestinely withholding a portion of their daily labor was considerably less risky than sabotage or flight; at the same time it increased the possibility of meeting household food requirements. There is ample evidence that thousands of producers cultivated less than the minimum plots, secretly intercropped on their reduced cotton fields, planted after the designated dates, and weeded fewer times or less thoroughly than was required.[164] The time they recaptured could be more productively used growing food and cash crops. Similar calculations drove a number of peasants to scatter or destroy poor quality lint rather than to make repeated journeys to distant markets for low returns.[165]

Thus faced with an attack on their food security, many peasants fought back in quiet but effective ways.[166] Since women, more than any segment of the rural population, understood the precarious balance between household production and commodity production, it is not unreasonable to assume that such illegal acts as intercropping and circumventing state-imposed work schedules were not simply directed against the cotton regime, but also against male elders, who controlled the cotton income that women worked so hard to produce.

Control over labor was the principal, but not exclusive, terrain of rural conflict. Cotton producers also pursued a variety of evasive tactics to minimize surplus extraction and to reduce the risks they were forced to assume. Some adulterated the cotton they sold.[167] Others smuggled their crops across international borders.

---

[162] Interview with Pruan Hassan; interview with Eugénio Maguaria.

[163] Interview with Amélia Macuácua, February 10, 1979, in Chibuto; Group interview with Marcos Changa et al.; Group interview with Romeu Mataquenha et al.; Group interview with Pruan Hassan et al.; Interview with Engineer Ferreira de Castro, September 25, 1978, in Maputo; Interview with Manuel Alves Salvador, February 12, 1979, in Xai-Xai.

[164] A.I.A., J.E.A.C., Papéis Diversos, F. Barbosa to Rafael Agapito Guerreiro, October 28, 1939.

[165] Interview with Amasse Nuitha, Communal Village Nacate, July 20, 1979, in Montepuez.

[166] For a discussion of peasants circumventing the state-imposed work schedule, see Isaacman et al., "Cotton is the Mother of Poverty," 599–602.

[167] Group interview with Marcos Chango et al.; Group interview with Makwati Simba, et al.; Group interview with Romeu Mataquenha et al.

Still others robbed company warehouses and resold their produce at interior markets.[168] These actions were inextricably linked to the state's inability to supervise their daily labor.

In the final analysis, the partial autonomy of the peasants, as well as the realization of their limited power, helps to explain why cotton producers were prone to engage in these localized or hidden forms of resistance rather than in broader social movements. Nevertheless, the sum total of these seemingly insignificant acts could and, at times, did have far-reaching consequences. To the extent that peasants achieved their objectives, they improved their living and working conditions, which often meant the difference between starvation and the chance to lead their lives with a certain measure of control and dignity. At a systemic level, their acts of defiance undercut total production, which did increase, but which fell far short of its potential and failed to achieve the Salazar regime's objectives of self-sufficiency for the Portuguese textile industry. In 1949 the minister of the colonies bemoaned "the stagnation in cotton production over the past years," which he attributed in great part "to the disinterest of the native population."[169] This shortfall continued throughout the 1950s. In 1961 the textile industry had to purchase 30 percent of its cotton abroad at a cost of $15 million.[170] The same year the state, facing growing international pressure and the threat of a rural insurgency, abolished the cotton regime and shifted once again to a settler-based plantation system.

---

[168] A.I.A., J.E.A.C., Papéis Diversos, C. Pedro Carvalho, Regente Agrícola ao Director de C.I.C.A., January 9, 1958.; Arquivo de Corpo Policial de Moçambique, Montepuez.

[169] Notícias, November 1, 1949.

[170] Bravo, A Cultura Algodoeira, 70.

[4]
reinterpreting a colonial
REBELLION:
FORESTRY AND SOCIAL CONTROL IN GERMAN EAST AFRICA, 1874-1915

THADDEUS SUNSERI

IN 1874, WHEN the British officer Frederic Elton visited the southeast coast of Tanzania around the Rufiji delta, he noted how important the region's forests were to local commerce. Rufiji people obtained a wide variety of forest products, including wax, rubber, ivory, mangroves, and "immense quantities" of copal to trade with Indians and Arabs who settled on the coast. Elton traveled north and south of the delta and crisscrossed the land in between, and thus provided a view of the region ten years before German colonial rule began. Observing how local people guarded access to copal diggings and other forest tracts jealously, Elton wrote "the natives are only too ready to unite against the slightest encroachment on their monopoly."[1] In one instance while camped along the Rufiji, Elton's party was surrounded by "about 800 men, more than half of whom were armed with guns, the rest carrying spears and bows." The leader made it clear that they were there to guard local trade against interlopers and "they heard there was to be a fight, and they would join the fight." Thirty years later the German colonial administration made the Rufiji delta and a one hundred mile stretch of coastal mangroves into a forest reserve, severely circumscribing African rights of access. With the advent of German rule, state-regulated forestry had arrived in Tanzania for the first time. In 1905, peoples of the Rufiji basin, wearing the same blue *kaniki* cloth around their hips as those whom Elton encountered, attacked representatives of German authority, including many involved in the declaration of forest reserves, in what is known as the Maji Maji rebellion.[2]

The Maji Maji rebellion (1905-1907) has been considered a pivotal event in the history of early colonial Tanzania and Africa. According to the nationalist historiography that was written in the first decade of Tanzanian independence after 1961, Maji Maji was the first manifestation of a united, interethnic opposition to colonial rule in Africa.[3] In particular, the rebellion has been portrayed as a sudden reaction to a policy of forced labor on cotton plantations that the German administration implemented shortly after the turn of the century. Named after a water medicine (*maji*) that purportedly gave African fighters immunity to the bullets of German colonizers, the dissemination of the *maji* ideology spread a message of common opposition and resistance to symbols of

German rule. Though the rebellion failed to oust Germans from East Africa, it led the colonial administration to implement a series of reforms after the war that some historians have called the "age of improvement."[4] It furthermore created a proto-nationalist tradition that could be tapped into during the 1950s decade of independence from the British colonial rulers who supplanted Germany during World War I. As one modern study put it, the rebellion "provided the beginnings of a tradition upon which national unity would one day be built in Tanzania."[5]

The nationalist historiography of Maji Maji went unchallenged for a generation.[6] The weight of the nationalist discourse and its permeation of textbooks and surveys of African history made it into a historical tradition that has not been friendly to more nuanced interpretations of early Tanzanian colonial history. The story of a purposeful, ideologically oriented anti-colonial rebellion that was "a response of Africans to the brutal conditions under which they were forced to work" has not allowed room for analyses of long-term continuities in African patterns of warfare that predated German rule, of gendered interpretations of the rebellion, or of fuller investigations of African resource use before and after the rebellion. For example, one study notes that land was not an African grievance on the eve of the Maji Maji war, because Germans guaranteed Africans ample access to land.[7] However, this assertion errs by severing land as an economic resource from its surrounding environment, something that African peasants and pastoralists would not have done. When considered as part of a larger landscape that includes mountains, forests, streams, shrines, animal habitats, and myriad resources and threats, land takes on a different meaning, and so does the rebellion.

This article examines the Maji Maji rebellion through the lens of environmental history. In particular I am interested in the intersection between German forest and wildlife policies and African resource use in the coastal districts where the rebellion broke out in the middle of 1905. In the decade before the rebellion, German officials enacted policies that dramatically circumscribed African access to forests and forest products that rural people used in their commercial networks, subsistence economies, and cultural life. Colonialists furthermore mandated hunting proscriptions that impaired the ability of African peasants to protect their fields from crop pests, and that brought the decades-old ivory trade to an end. In the year before the rebellion, Germans began a forest-reserve policy that severed the peasant economy from forests, making them virtually off limits to African use, often requiring people to relocate villages and farms and to abandon fruit trees, ancestral shrines, and hunting frontiers. The Maji Maji rebellion looks different when considered in the context of colonial environmental controls.

Forest history furthermore challenges both the nationalist view of the post-rebellion period as an era of improvement and recent interpretations of imperial environmentalism that view forest conservation as an unequivocal benefit bestowed on colonized peoples.[8] In the course of putting down the rebellion, Germans and Tanzanian peasants were drawn deeper into the forests, which acted both as places of refuge and battle sites. Once the war was over, patterns of fighting and refuge provided the colonial government with a blueprint for

Figure 1. German East Africa with Rufji and Kilwa districts shaded.

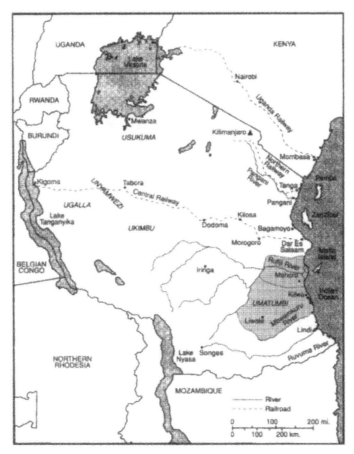

extended forest controls. These post-Maji Maji forest controls channeled rural dwellers to colonial economic pursuits and provided a template for the conservation and population-control policies of subsequent governments in Tanzania. Far from simply conserving the forest landscape for the benefit of the commonweal, as German colonial foresters asserted, forest reserves provided a mechanism for the state to control people, especially those who did not easily submit to its economic ventures.

AFRICAN FOREST USE IN EARLY COLONIAL TANZANIA

ALMOST IMMEDIATELY after effective German control in East Africa began, the colonial state enacted laws circumscribing peasant access to forests and use of their products. (See Figure 1.) German rule in East Africa witnessed a steady expansion of state control over forest use, beginning with the DOAG (German East Africa) concession company's efforts to usurp the coastal trade in forest products after 1885. The nascent colonial state introduced forest laws in 1893, leading to the creation of forest reserves shortly after the turn of the century. Then, after 1907, the number of reserves burgeoned. Indeed, just three years after the German East Africa Corporation began to occupy all the main coastal trading ports, including those surrounding the Rufiji delta, Africans of the mainland rose up in what has been dubbed the Abushiri rebellion.[9] While most scholarly attention has concentrated on the northern coast, during this rebellion the entire Rufiji delta was occupied by Yao ivory and rubber traders whose allies most likely included the armed Rufiji men whom Elton encountered just fifteen years earlier.[10]

That the colonial control of forests would elicit resistance should not be surprising given the multifaceted uses, cultural and economic, that forests held for southeastern Tanzanians. The best examples come from Uzaramo, just north of the Rufiji River, and Ungindo on the southern periphery of the Rufiji-Matumbi forest complex.[11] Among the Zaramo and related peoples, the spirits of the deceased resided in forests as *mwenembago*, which the German missionary Martin Klamroth translated as *Waldherr*—"master of the forest." Ancestral spirits selected individuals as mediums by possessing them in the forests. One informant named the *mvule* (the East African teak) and *mhogwe* trees as the locales where the initial spirit possession took place: The person so chosen returned to the living after the "forest mother" called him or her back. Klamroth's informant identified seven principal "holy trees" as important to spirit possession, including *mbuyu* (the baobab) and *mpongwe*. The forests were thus important locales for spiritual and physical healing, since mediums who derived their authority and power from the forests were called upon to remedy a variety of sicknesses and social ills. Forests were also feared places, the abodes of malevolent spirits such as the *kinyamkela*, who resided in the hollows of large trees owned by ancestral spirits. Local norms strongly prohibited the felling of such trees, otherwise, unwelcome spirits might come and reside in one's house. Spirit mediums and their adherents built "spirit huts" near trees that were necessary to propitiate malevolent spirits. Common people honored the graves of their ancestors with wooden figurines and by constructing replicas of spirit huts in their fields. This phenomenon speaks to the role of forest spirits as guardians of fields and general social health. Forests were furthermore sites of initiation and circumcision rituals that connected youth with their ancestors. Medicine used in circumcision rituals stemmed from the *mkumbi* tree, which was also the word for circumcision itself. Klamroth, a principal adviser to the German colonial administration and member of the Governor's Council, understood this cultural role of the forests, which is important in considering the post-Maji Maji period when the administration asserted control of the forests aggressively, sometimes targeting forests that had a particular spiritual meaning. Before the rebellion, in contrast, German authorities were more inclined to allow Africans to maintain the graves of the deceased in forests that they declared as reserves.[12]

A. R. W. Crosse-Upcott's study of the Ngindo also speaks to the immense economic and cultural importance of the forests to southeastern Tanzanians.[13]

There is evidence that the Ngindo emerged as a people in the mid-nineteenth century in part as forest refugees fleeing warfare. Referring to the Ngindo as being "at home in the forest," Crosse-Upcott demonstrated how important the interconnected agrarian and forest environments were to Ngindo survival. The forest was an important source of gathered food in times of famine, and important for a cash economy as the location of wild rubber, honey, wax, ivory, and game.[14] Ngindo patterns of shifting agriculture paralleled their use of the forests, with clans holding de facto ownership of trees through a "theory of recognized forest zones."[15] Crosse-Upcott's work demonstrated that the creation of boundaries between forests and agrarian lands was an artificial colonial construction that the Ngindo continuously violated in spite of forest laws. Ngindo homesteads themselves were located in close proximity to trees, and there was a tendency for "owned" trees "to stream behind the huts in a gradual movement of shifting cultivation, like the tail of a meteor."[16] Such patterns reflected movement over generations, showing the guardianship that individual clans held over forests. There was thus a "maximum diffusion" of Ngindo forest use, because concentrated use of trees (or of any resource) increased insecurity. The Ngindo exhibited a clear conservation ethic by refraining from chopping green wood for fuel and by thinning trees needed for construction purposes rather than cutting wide swaths.

Throughout the Rufiji-Kilwa region, specific forests had widespread reputations as centers of religious activity. Most important in the Rufiji region appears to have been Kipambawe kwa Kungulio, located on the upper Rufiji River near Mpanga, which Germans called the Pangani Falls. Mpanga itself was the base of a *mganga* spirit medium named Mkumbiro (or Mzee Mkando), who dispensed agricultural and rain medicines to people who often traveled for days for this purpose. German authorities believed that this was the spiritual center of the Maji Maji rebellion.[17] Furthermore, the hot spring located at Utete, south of the river midway between Mpanga and the coast, was also a likely site of medicine dispensation. A decade before Maji Maji, the spring was a site where trials by ordeal were administered.[18] Both the Mpanga and Utete hot springs were located in forests that the state would control as reserves.

Besides regional religious centers that people resorted to in times of crisis such as drought, locust plagues, and famine, most areas had local centers where people could go for medicines to protect their fields. Such was the case at Mtondo, a few hours walking distance south of the Rufiji district capital of Mohoro, which, in late 1905, witnessed a great deal of pilgrimage activity.[19] People from the region of the Rufiji delta traveled to Mtondo to receive medicines to protect their fields from wild pigs and birds—wild pigs had become especially destructive by 1905.[20] The description given by a local district secretary, Otto Stollowsky, suggests that the people were acting according to the *kinyamkela* rituals by placing the medicines in "a small building" near their fields.[21]

Apart from their deep spiritual significance, forests and their products played—and continue to play—a central role in the daily lives of southeast Tanzanians. Local household and commercial industries that predated the colonial period were oriented to the forest. Charcoal production, for which people favored the *mtondo* tree, was essential for household cooking and local industries.[22] While the charcoal demand in 1900 was doubtless not what it is today, specialists needed charcoal for iron smithing, and for salt, sugar, and coconut oil production.[23] About six logs were needed to boil a drum of cane juice for five hours to produce about one hundred pounds of jaggery (brown sugar), an important regional trade product. Salt production that relied on coastal mangroves as fuel was a commercial activity that coastal dwellers and Matumbi people of Kitope (Naminangu) forest occasionally fought over in the early 1890s.[24]

Rufiji people used wood for many other local pursuits, such as building watchtowers in rice fields to protect crops from birds, baboons, and pigs. North of the river was a vast floodplain that seasonally joined other rivers to create a wet-rice agriculture that required people to live in stilt huts and get about by canoe during the rainy seasons. One hut required some fifteen hundred poles, especially *boriti* from mangroves for hut frames and roofing beams.[25] A variety of household utensils and tools were made from wood, such as clapper systems to scare birds, and mortars and pestles for pounding grain. Along the Rufiji River a canoe-building industry was widespread. Indeed, far from seeing the river as an impermeable barrier, some local residents lived in villages on one side of the river and farmed on the other, relying on *mitumbwi* dugouts to traverse the river daily. Hans Paasche, a German officer, came across a canoe being constructed some ten kilometers south of the Rufiji River in the high forest of the Kichi hills.[26] Some people lived on river islands in the delta and farther upriver as well. Farming and forest activities were symbiotic, and villagers lived close to forests to take advantage of their resources.

The forests were essential to commercial activity before the German arrival in the 1880s, as Elton and other visitors observed. The mangrove wood industry was centuries old.[27] Rufiji and coastal peoples cut trees and transported them to wood stations awaiting the arrival of ocean-going dhows that carried the timber to Zanzibar or Arabia. Migrants to the delta carved rice and cassava fields out of delta islands while supplying mangrove trees to the many cutting stations that dotted the arms of the Rufiji. Coastal dwellers also constructed *ngalawa* outrigger canoes and *mtepe* boats for fishing and coastal transport, and built and repaired dhows and larger *jahazi* at construction stations located up and down the coast. The commercial wood industry was an important means for local people to obtain commodities like muskets and cloth, or even a cash income that they held in reserve to purchase grain in times of scarcity.[28] Aside from timber itself, products of the forest such as wild rubber, copal, wax, and honey found steady markets on the coast, attracting Indian trading diasporas to the region. European and Indian traders were particularly keen to obtain copal, ivory, and rubber in the period from about 1880 to 1914, and many Rufiji people earned cash incomes in this way.[29]

Ivory also must be added to the list of commercial forests products. Ivory was the single most valuable trade commodity along the coast at the time of the German arrival in the 1880s, when the DOAG struggled to compete with established Indian traders for this commodity. Until 1894, ivory accounted for half the value of all exports from the colony.³⁰ Many chiefs of rural Tanzania had emerged as "big men" in the nineteenth century as elephant hunters who monopolized the ivory trade to the coast and created patronage networks in rural society by distributing cotton cloth and other imported goods. In southern Uzaramo, just north of the Rufiji, a generations-old tradition of elephant hunting for trade to the coast had preceded German rule, and had been a path to power of many local *mapazi* chiefs.³¹ Such men had widespread reputations in the Rufiji-Kilwa region during the period of early colonial rule.

FOREST POLICY IN SOUTHEAST TANZANIA, 1890-1905

A HINT OF the intersection between colonial forest policy and the Maji Maji rebellion comes from the northern border of Kilwa district in southeastern Tanzania. On 5 September 1904, a colonial land commission that included a reviled German cotton planter and local Arab elites met at the coastal trading town of Samanga to declare the entirety of coastal mangroves as Crown Land, forbidding wood cutting in the forests without explicit government permission.³² The commission acted according to the 1895 Crown Land ordinance and a revised Forest Protection Ordinance (actually enacted the following week on 9 September 1904) that empowered the colonial state to create forest reserves.³³ In the next few months, land commissions met elsewhere along the Tanzanian coast to inform local people of the prohibitions against mangrove cutting. On 8 September 1904, a government commission furthermore demarcated as a forest reserve one thousand hectares of high forest at Naminangu about ten kilometers inland, demonstrating to the villagers present that colonial forest controls would not be confined to the coast.³⁴ The Naminangu reserve was taken over as "unoccupied Crown Land" and declared to be devoid of settlements and free of any African claims to its resources. The people present were instructed that henceforth the forest parcel would be under the protection of the district office and that the colonial government reserved the right to cut wood and obtain any forest product from the parcel. Transgressions of the ordinance would be punished with a one thousand rupee fine or three months labor in chains. A year after it was declared as a forest reserve, Naminangu became the site of several battles of the Maji Maji rebellion, and a place of refuge for local villagers during wartime.³⁵

The culmination of a decade-long effort to bring forests under state control, the forest reserve policy in German East Africa sought to allow the colonial state to benefit from the fiscal exploitation of forests through scientific management.³⁶ German scientific forestry had been developed in the eighteenth century, at a time when officials worried that their forests were being fast depleted, threatening the industrial development of German states.³⁷ State control of forests aimed to regulate forest use by creating long-term cycles of tree planting and harvesting that would allow for a sustainable forest management. The ideal forest, according to this model, would be one of uniform tree species and size that could be quantified and harvested in set rotations to meet fiscal and industrial needs. By the end of the nineteenth century, conservationism also played a role in German scientific forestry. Scientists recognized the importance of forests for climate and watersheds, and some considered biodiversity itself to be an important facet of forest policy. In German East Africa, Governor Adolf von Götzen articulated these concerns when he argued that forest reserves were necessary to maintain water sources in order to create an environment conducive to white settlement.[38] Nevertheless, the environmentalist argument always took a back seat to fiscal concerns. Toward this end the colonial state sought to supplant African forest use with its own. Forest policy most immediately aimed to curtail African wood cutting in designated forests and to prohibit bush fallowing (which Germans called "wild burning"), whereby peasants annually burned grasslands and forests to open up new lands for agriculture and to control weeds and vermin. Indeed, Germans considered Africans to be a clear threat to forests because of their *kulturfeindliche Gepflogenheiten*–"practices antithetical to culture" –a double entendre that implied that peasant land and resource use endangered cultivation of trees and land and also deterred a civilizing mission that came with German colonialism. African land and forest use was, in the colonial mind, responsible for the scarcity of forests in the colony and for a lack of water and moisture. Colonialists contrasted German *Kulturwälder*–cultivated or civilized forests– with African *Urwälder*–jungles or "aboriginal" forests–and German *Kulturmenschen*–civilized people–with African *Naturkinder*–children of nature.[39] German foresters argued that the estimated 1 percent forest cover in Tanzania was a result of regressive African agriculture. In contrast, Germany's tree cover had increased to 26 percent in the nineteenth century as a result of scientific forest management.[40]

Even with modest state control in much of the colony, forest policy hemmed in rural dwellers of the Rufiji-Kilwa region markedly during the decade before the Maji Maji rebellion. From the early 1890s, the colonial administration sent forest experts to the Rufiji to prepare it for scientific forestry. Most immediately, this meant curtailing African use of mangroves and other trees that had a fiscal value while recruiting German concession companies to market mangrove timber and bark.[41] In 1894, the government proscribed the cutting of "strong, straight *boritis* (mangroves)" as firewood in the Rufiji forests.[42] By 1897, the district officer recommended that the cutting fee for wood in the delta be raised 60 percent to 100 percent and that Africans be allowed to collect only fallen wood for their household construction needs.[43] Local district authorities also sought to curtail African settlements in the delta mangrove forests to deter further cutting. In 1898, the colonial government made the Rufiji delta into "a regulated state forest economy on the European model," and two years later Rufiji became the only administrative district in the colony to originate as a state forest, allowing for greater enforcement of forest ordinances.[44] The creation of the political district was a sign of creeping state control of this otherwise inaccessible region. Altogether some sixteen thousand hectares of mangrove stands in the Rufiji delta were under firm state control by 1900, and Rufiji was in effect designated as a wood reserve for the capital city of Dar es Salaam.[45] During this time, the governor leased forest stands to German businessmen interested in marketing mangrove logs to Zanzibar, Dar es Salaam, and South Africa, and enlisted German chemical firms as buyers of mangrove bark for leather dye.⁴⁶ While wood cutting was not totally prohibited to Africans, limits were set on quantities of fuel and construction wood, and the state designated where cutting could take place. In the view of Governor Götzen, "the hitherto irregular, irrational and insufficiently supervised wood cutting needs to be made orderly, planned and rational."⁴⁷ After 1904, when the state's creation of forest reserves made whole parcels virtually off-limits to African use, villagers could have concluded only that an essential part of their economic and cultural existence was being taken away.

One further forest declaration on the eve of Maji Maji warrants attention, that of the Liwale forest reserve in the southwest corner of Kilwa district, the home of the Ngindo people. Liwale town was the site of a government rubber plantation that struggled to make profits in a region well known for its wild rubber trade. In 1904, the government adjoined the rubber plantation to a tract of forest and bush land, which in April 1905 was demarcated as Liwale forest reserve.⁴⁸ Located on a 7,500 hectare expanse north of Liwale town, the forest reserve was a sudden and dramatic encroachment that carried with it all the prohibitions on forest use that applied to other reserves. This meant that forest economies, including the trade in wild rubber, copal, wax, ivory, and timber, were effectively circumscribed. Historians have for some time suspected that the outbreak of Maji Maji in this region was connected to the decline of the rubber trade, but have failed to tie that thesis to the curtailment of forest access that had wider social, economic, and cultural ramifications.⁴⁹ While many forests were left outside of effective state control, forest and hunting regulations implemented by 1905 meant that the era of free forest access was over, even in areas where reserves were yet to be declared.

Apart from forest controls, colonial regulations sharply circumscribed elephant hunting and ivory procurement at the turn of the century. It is difficult to tease out the role of ivory in the economy of the Rufiji and its environs during the German period since most of the sources describe the northern coast. Ivory exports from mainland Tanzania declined sharply with the assumption of formal German rule in 1891, as the following table shows:

Ivory exports from DOA selected years, 1890-1913:

	Value in marks	Weight in Kilograms
1890	4,582,000	204,000
1893	2,163,000	110,000
1898	1,226,000	38,000
1901	882,000	53,573
1905	486,000	23,060
1908	606,000	27,818
1909	1,026,000	51,134
1910	743,000	36,245
1911	485,000	25,793
1913	231,000	n.d.

Rainer Tetzlaff, *Koloniale Entwicklung- und Ausbeutung: Wirtschafts- und Sozialgeschichte Deutsch-Ostafrikas, 1885-1914* (Berlin, Duncker und Humblot: 1970), 293. These figures correspond roughly to those in T. Siebenlist, *Forstwirtschaft in Deutsch-Ostafrika* (Berlin, Paul Parey: 1914), 64; "Elfenbein," in Schnee, *Deutsches Kolonial-Lexicon*, 1:558-59.

While historian John Iliffe believes that this decline occurred because elephants were becoming hunted out in Tanzania by the end of the nineteenth century, evidence points to German conservationist policies as an important factor in the decline in the ivory trade.[50] In 1898, the administration of Eduard von Liebert enacted an ordinance that required elephant hunters to purchase a five hundred rupee hunting license and pay an additional one hundred rupees, or one tusk, for every elephant bagged.[51] This ordinance is perhaps responsible for the sudden drop in ivory exports over the next few years from a value of about 1.2 million marks in 1898 to about a third of that by 1905. While the amount of ivory from the south is not clear in these figures, it is clear that the Rufiji-Kilwa region had at one time been a major conduit for the export of elephant and hippo ivory to the coast.[52] Hans Paasche noted that during Maji Maji Rufiji villagers still obtained hippo teeth to sell.[53] The forests of the region certainly at one time teemed with elephants, and there is also no doubt that elephants remained in the coastal regions at the turn of the century and recovered rapidly once the state curtailed hunting. Paasche came across five elephants near Mohoro town just south of the delta in 1905.[54] In 1913, Rufiji planters complained of elephant devastations of their estates and African fields, as did Rufiji villagers shortly after World War I and throughout the British colonial period.[55] The 1898 hunting ordinance apparently led to a dramatic exodus of elephant hunters from coastal districts seeking to avoid colonial controls, and that exodus exposed villagers' fields to elephant incursions.[56] When the colonial state began its rapid declaration of forest reserves after 1904, it created islands of refuge for elephants within the agrarian economy where villagers were prohibited from freely hunting crop predators. In 1902, Governor Götzen reported that fauna in the hunting reserve created on the upper Rufiji in 1896 had increased significantly. Ten years later German planters of the region suggested that the reserve be abolished owing to elephant incursions.[57] Colonialism curtailed the profits of ivory hunting, usurped elephant hunters of the influence they once had, and exacerbated the destruction caused by elephants and other crop predators by protecting them from villagers.

MAJI MAJI AND THE FORESTS

MAJI MAJI in Rufiji region was a struggle for access to the forests and their resources. The opening battles of the war have a close connection to the forest reserves. R. M. Bell's account of Maji Maji around Liwale is telling. The "moving spirit" of the rebellion around Liwale was an elephant hunter named Abdullah Mapanda, whose village of Kitandangangora lay close to the Liwale forest reserve, thus establishing a direct connection between state control of forest resources and local grievances.[58] By mid August 1905, a rebel force that included Mapanda converged on the Liwale military station under a sergeant named Faupel, and attacked the Liwale rubber plantation administered by a German named Aimer. Both men sat on the land commission that had created the Liwale forest reserve four months earlier. Two sons of Jumbe Rihambi (Lihambe), who also sat on the land commission, willingly or not, eventually killed Aimer on his rubber plantation as he sought to escape from Liwale.[59] Faupel was killed after a rebel siege of the

Liwale fort. The rubber plantation itself was all but destroyed. Before the rebellion the plantation had possessed 49,000 rubber trees on 164 hectares. By December 1906, there were 2,000 trees left on 12 hectares.

The other major opening episode of Maji Maji occurred at Samanga town on the coast, about twenty kilometers south of the Rufiji delta. On 31 July, a German settler named Steinhagen, who sat on the commissions that established the mangrove and Naminangu reserves, sent a letter to Mohoro requesting aid against Matumbi rebels who were besieging his cotton plantation.[60] Rebels also destroyed property of influential Arab planters and Indian traders at Samanga and its environs, and threatened the area for about two weeks.[61] Many members of the Kilwa and Samanga land commissions that established the mangrove and Naminangu forest reserves were targets of rebel attacks, as were scores of other influential people. While we cannot know the reasons rebels targeted these individuals and their property, this new evidence points to colonial control of the forests as one of the motivating factors.

Members of the German commission sent to investigate causes of the rebellion believed that forest controls were a major grievance leading people to rebel. The Dar es Salaam District Officer Gustav Boeder thought that the forest ordinances were a heavy burden, especially the requirement to buy an expensive permit to cut wood intended for sale. Africans complained of difficulties in cutting and procuring wood, and Boeder concluded that the ordinances were part of the "general dissatisfaction of the natives with the existing conditions" at the time of the rebellion.[62] One member of the Maji Maji commission, a commercial beer brewer named Schultz, believed that the end of free access to the mangrove forests of the coast caused great discontent and led some people to rebel.[63] The wood business was no longer profitable because fees were higher than in times past, and much time was lost obtaining permits, especially for those who lived far from forest stations. As a result, dhow construction on the south coast had virtually ceased, and in Dar es Salaam housing construction was sharply curtailed since rural dwellers no longer could market wood in the city without burdensome oversight. Schultz, whose beer brewery was the biggest industry in the colony at the time and a major consumer of wood, asserted that all industries were adversely affected by the scarcity of fuel wood in light of forest ordinances: "I have no question that the natives, since olden days accustomed to the free use of the mangrove forests, have a strong ground for discontent owing to the rigorous closing of the mangroves" as well as inland forest reserves. In Lindi district in the far south as well it was reported that the closing of the mangrove forests and the creation of inland forest reserves coupled with wood cutting fees "endangered the economic existence of definite circles of natives and fed a general discontent."[64]

In the case of Abdullah Mapanda of Liwale, leadership of the rebellion came in part from elephant hunters who had lost their prestige owing to the collapse of the ivory trade and their inability to protect rural society from crop predators as a result of hunting ordinances.[65] The most prominent Zaramo chief to participate in Maji Maji, Kibasira, was the last among a line of *mapazi* chiefs whose power stemmed from elephant hunting. The forests near Kibasira's village of Kissangire had been targeted as a reserve by 1904, and the nearby game reserve of the upper Rufiji (the future Selous reserve) had been virtually closed to African hunting by the turn of the century.[66] Hans Paasche, sent to fight rebels along the Rufiji River, also was confronted by a rebel group led by a renowned hunter, whom Paasche himself killed. While frequently mentioned individually in accounts of the rebellion, hunters have not been integrated into analyses of the rebellion's outbreak. The colonial administration apparently took the role of hunters seriously by overturning some limitations on ivory trading in November 1905, a few months after the rebellion broke out. At that time, Governor Götzen directed local district officials to treat all ivory brought for sale by Africans as "found," even if it might have been obtained by hunting, which allowed the seller to keep the proceeds from both tusks. As Götzen's successor, Albrecht von Rechenberg, pointed out, this amelioration was more generous than the African "ground tusk" custom of relinquishing one tusk as tribute to local chiefs. One report claimed that the ameliorated rule led to a revival of ivory caravans; one arrived in Lindi in early 1907 with forty-six tusks, some freshly hunted.[67] The relaxation of ivory fees perhaps was responsible for a jump in ivory exports from a value of 443,000 marks in 1906 to 663,000 marks in 1907, and steady growth over the next few years.[68] Nevertheless, in response to criticism of the ameliorated policy, Rechenberg directed local authorities to treat tusks as a product of the hunt unless sellers could prove they had been found.

The evidence of connections between German conservationism and social rebellion demonstrates that the declaration of forest reserves and the introduction of hunting laws were not simply innocuous facets of German colonialism. Forest laws and reserves hurt rural dwellers, and led many to resist representatives of colonial forest commissions. Germans belatedly realized the damage that the rebellion inflicted on their colonial venture. Maji Maji was a black eye on German colonialism, and forced the colonial state to back off some of the policies that officials believed fed discontent. For example, the colonial administration dropped its objective of eliminating African field burning and bush fallowing, mainstays of forest policy in the 1890s. However, Germans did not back away from forest reserve declarations once the war was over. On the contrary, the end of the war ushered in a rapid creation of forest reserves. To explain this we need to examine how forests intersected with settlement patterns during the war.

FORESTS AND REFUGEES IN THE RUFIJI BASIN

THE FORESTS of Rufiji-Kilwa districts had been used at least since the mid-nineteenth century as havens for people in times of conflict.[69] As a highway into the southwestern interior, or, conversely, from the interior to the coast, the Rufiji River's navigability by dugout canoe exposed local villagers to often unwanted outside forces, including slave raiders and grain plunderers. The insecurity caused by this exposure led Rufiji dwellers to depend on the forests as hideouts, which often meant long-term occupancy. This was clearly the case in the last quarter of the nineteenth century when Mbunga (also called Mahenge) people of the upper tributaries of the Rufiji raided downriver periodically both to plunder grain and to capture people as dependent laborers to be taken back into the interior.[70] William Beardall learned of these Mbunga raids during his trip up the river in 1880 and wrote of how Rufiji people lived on river islands surrounded by reeds that they used to hide and store grain. While some regional chiefs dealt with Mbunga raids by establishing relationships of tribute with them, others, such as the villagers of Kigumi, situated themselves in "a patch of thick jungle," well stockaded, that offered a haven for diverse peoples of the river basin.[71]

Fifteen years after Beardall's journey, the German explorer Z. S. Fromm made a similar trip up the Rufiji.[72] At that time, the effects of a generation of Mbunga raids were more noticeable, as Fromm described an environment of greater insecurity. Whereas Beardall noted that most people of the central Rufiji plain lived in well-populated villages along the river, Fromm described how the fear of kidnaping and plundering of grain led many people to completely evacuate their villages, move into the forests or bush, or build huts in less visible locales among the reeds. Fromm wrote that agriculture had become extremely difficult owing to the Mbunga danger, and many people had completely abandoned fields in a region that was exceptionally fertile. Well-established villages that also served as trading centers for caravans, such as Kologelo and Mloka, had by then been abandoned. A few years later the situation showed signs of reversing as German conquest of the interior and the establishment of military posts at Ulanga and Kisaki brought the Mbunga under temporary control.[73]

Paasche's account of how Rufiji peoples used the river and the forests during the Maji Maji war is the most thorough. Paasche observed how Rufiji villagers made use of the forests as sanctuaries for the duration of the conflict. Indeed, one of Paasche's primary goals in fighting the war was to destroy all signs of forest habitation, since he believed that huts in the forest were proof of complicity in the rebellion. During the war, Rufiji people simply were repeating a pattern of using the forests for refuge learned during the late-nineteenth-century conflicts. A couple of weeks after Paasche's arrival in early August 1905, he noticed "dispersed settlements in the forests" with cassava and beans planted nearby.[74] It seems unlikely that this was evidence of a rebellion that was only one month old at the time. More likely it was a semi-permanent forest settlement that was a reaction to fifteen years of German rule and the burdens that came with it, including corvee labor, taxation, and hunting and forest controls. Loyalist spies learned from local people that women and children were hidden in the forests of the Kichi mountains just south of the Rufiji River.[75] The decision of Rufiji people to find refuge in the forests was validated by German actions in burning and plundering all forest villages they came across as rebel hideouts. Once the war was over, peasants, particularly women, continued to seek refuge in forests to avoid colonial development policies, especially a concerted drive to get householders to plant cotton or work on German plantations. Germans came to identify forest habitation as a rebellious act at worst, and an obstacle to colonial development at best.

German perceptions by the end of Maji Maji were that forests *and* people must be brought under the control of the colonial state in order for development to take place. While the goal of protecting forests was articulated frequently in published articles and colonial correspondence, not as pronounced was the connection between forest control and social control. Germans believed that only by controlling the forests would it be possible to relocate people in a manner that facilitated agricultural development. This relationship between forest control and social control was repeated under British rule in Tanganyika following World War I, and became an ongoing legacy of colonial rule that continues to this day in independent Tanzania.

CONTROLLING FORESTS AND PEOPLE

THE ACTIONS and movements of southeast Tanzanians during the war provided Germans with a template for social control that intersected with forest policy following the war. Between 1907 and 1914, the administration demarcated four additional reserves in Kilwa district. In Rufiji district the state extended preexisting reserves and created an additional nineteen, encompassing some 53,305 hectares in 1913, triple the extent of 1909.[76] Rufiji reserves would grow by another 20,000 hectares by the end of German colonial rule during World War I. These reserve declarations frequently targeted forests used as havens for rebels and villagers during the war as well as locales of cultural significance, particularly bases of spirit mediums who offered medicines of protection to rebels. Thus, preventing villagers from escaping colonial controls and using forests as bases of resistance must be considered alongside conservation and fiscal management as goals of colonial forestry practices.

The use of forest reserves for social control is seen in the vast highland forest complex along the Rufiji-Kilwa border that in 1911 was made into the Namuete, Nerumba, Kumbi, and Nadunda forest reserves.[77] This region was used as a refuge during Maji Maji. Incorporating nine forested mountains surrounded by settlements, the forest declarations were the beginning of the erasure of forest settlements from the landscape as people were forced to settle along open roads near administrative centers. While German-era maps demonstrate that peasant settlements were closely integrated into the forest landscape, modern maps of the forest complex show it to be completely devoid of settlements. Another case is the Mpanga forest reserve on the upper Rufiji River, which a land commission demarcated in 1910 on the site that Germans believed to be the main ritual center of spirit mediums involved in the Maji Maji war.[78] Two areas of intense fighting during Maji Maji on the north bank of the Rufiji—Kipo and Mtanza—also were taken over as forest reserves in 1908 and 1910 respectively.[79] Throughout the Rufiji basin, forest reserves were created or extended in areas of Maji Maji conflict.[80] The same can be said of Selous game reserve, which began as a German hunting preserve before Maji Maji. A major refuge for villagers during Maji Maji, the region since the war has been marked by removal of villagers in order to enlarge the wildlife domain.[81] While the administration demarcated many forest reserves because of their proximity to government stations and their value as sources of timber, others were chosen because they were points of refuge where people could avoid colonial controls.

Population movements after the war also contributed to German designs for forest controls, and here there is a strongly gendered pattern.[82] Following the war, German policy makers sought a quick recovery from wartime devastation by inaugurating a peasant cotton policy throughout the southeast. Peasants of the region—especially women whose husbands or sons were away as migrant laborers in the northeast, penal laborers from regions of conflict, or workers on the Central Railway—sought to escape the pressure to grow cotton by carving out niches in the bush and forests away from colonial supervision, just as they did during Maji Maji and other times of conflict. In the mountainous Matumbi landscape, for example, women practiced an agriculture using *matimbe* strips along rivulets that trickled down from the mountains.[83] Creating a hidden, dispersed agriculture that was subsistence oriented, women evaded the intense cotton program of the open lands. Colonial officials complained frequently about this pattern, which one traveler referred to as *pembeni*, living "in the corners" of the landscape.[84] In 1910, a lone widow was discovered farming a small parcel hidden in a forest reserve just outside the capital city of Dar es Salaam.[85] The unabated declaration of forest reserves that pronounced forests to be ownerless, uninhabited, and off-limits to peasant use was aimed in part at forcing villagers out into the open where they could be taxed, regulated, and channeled to cash-crop production. Villages that show up clearly on detailed maps of forest parcels during the German period were erased in subsequent years. Social control and directed population movement were conscious aims of forest policy in East Africa in part because the colonial state was frustrated by the low population of the colony (about 4 million people excluding Rwanda-Burundi, regions virtually closed to labor recruitment under German rule), which had stymied colonial development for twenty years.

CONCLUSION

THE INTERSECTION between the colonial control of forests in German East Africa and social conflict should not be surprising given the almost formulaic connection between forests and rebellion in other parts of the world throughout history.[86] As a long literature on European moral economies has shown, a major feature of the bureaucratization of the forests since the Middle Ages was the struggle between the state and peasants over access to forests for pasture, game and other food, farmland, cooking fuel, fodder, and construction materials.[87] Conflict over forest use was not confined to Europe. When European colonial regimes established forest administrations in Asia in the nineteenth century, they attacked indigenous practices of shifting agriculture that they deemed to be a threat to forests, particularly to the teak forests desired for their commercial value.[88] The earliest days of European rule in Africa also were marked by state regulation of forests and their use. Most cases of African social protest aimed at forest restrictions had a religious dimension, as local people sought to protect their access to sacred shrines located in forests.[89] Despite these cases, there are few studies of the effects of colonial forest policies on local communities in Africa, and fewer still that look for peasant reaction to forest regulations. This absence is puzzling given that in most parts of Africa colonial control of forests was a sudden and dramatic departure from past practices, in contrast to the parallel growth of states and forest controls in Europe, and state curtailment of forest access in India and Southeast Asia that predated colonial rule.[90]

This examination of the social history of Rufiji forests demonstrates that the Maji Maji rebellion had direct connections to German forest policy that have escaped the attention of historians. When the resource landscape of Rufiji peoples is examined, many features of the established Maji Maji historiographic tradition are found wanting. Considered to be a sudden reaction to German cash-crop campaigns after the turn of the century, backed by an innovative proto-nationalist ideology of resistance, the rebellion's connection to long-term historical change has escaped the attention of nationalist historians. This article began with an episode that showed the willingness of Rufiji people to fight to maintain their rights to forest resources ten years before German rule began. Fifteen years after that event, coastal people rose up in the Abushiri rebellion to maintain African control over trade in forest and other products. The interpretation here of the Maji Maji rebellion as a similar attempt by Rufiji and related peoples to maintain access to the forests in light of outside encroachment places it squarely in a long-standing tradition of coastal resistance rather than a sudden event of the turn of the century.

The lens of forest history also suggests a different outcome of the Maji Maji war than that handed down by the nationalist historiography. That interpretation sees the war as having led to a period of reform and improvement in the last decade of German rule. Denied the right to grow cash crops on their own fields before the war, African peasants, assumed to be modernizing "men of improvement," embraced cash crop regimes following the war. At the same time, forced labor regimes were ameliorated after the war. Forest history revises that view. While initially the colonial government eased forest reserve declarations and obstacles to hunting, by 1907 reserve declarations reemerged with a vengeance, and revised hunting laws reinstituted previous bans on African hunting. Indeed, in many respects the last decade of German rule can be characterized as a battle for the forests, as the German regime sought to clear reserves of settlements and to police forests to prevent illegal cutting of trees and collecting of forest produce, such as wild rubber and beeswax. Many cases of arson in the forests preoccupied authorities; most seemed to be cases of negligence in field preparation, but many were suspected to be premeditated and intentional acts of protest.[91] Forests also became hideouts for unsavory characters and malcontents, including rubber collectors and elephant hunters seeking to evade colonial controls.[92] The easing of colonial authority seen in some cases under the Rechenberg regime was not noticeable in forest policy, in spite of the clear connections that existed between colonial forestry and the Maji Maji rebellion.

German scientific forestry was couched in a rhetoric of development and modernization. The "pressing task" of colonial forestry included protecting, increasing, and improving forests.[93] Scientifically and economically managed forests were expected to provide environmental benefits, making an arid land blossom once again, providing fiscal benefits and enabling colonial officials to substitute local for imported timber and to export timber to overseas markets without damaging the forests. This rhetoric of the benefits of colonial forestry sounds familiar to those versed in the colonial forest histories of Asia, especially Indonesia and India, and, indeed, German experts were at the forefront of those forest policies.[94] However, modern environmentalist concerns about a vanishing forest landscape in Africa and elsewhere should not blind historians to the intent and outcome of early colonial environmentalism.[95] The colonial conservationist rhetoric must be placed in the context of wider development policies, just as the motives and outcomes of contemporary environmental and forest policy in Tanzania and elsewhere should be similarly scrutinized. Imperial scientific forestry in German East Africa severed rural societies from their economic and cultural links to the forests, inaugurating a twentieth-century pattern of forced population movement and social control.

Thaddeus Sunseri received his Ph.D. in African history from the University of Minnesota. An associate professor of history at Colorado State University, he is the author of Vilimani: Labor Migration and Rural Change in Early Colonial Tanzania (Portsmouth, N.H.: Heinemann, 2001) and many articles on the social history of Tanzania. He currently is working on a history of forest use in the Rufiji region of Tanzania.

NOTES

My thanks to James C. McCann, Lorne Larson, the anonymous reviewers of Environmental History, and my colleagues in the history department of Colorado State University for their critical comments on an earlier draft of this paper.

1. Frederic Elton, "On the Coast Country of East Africa, South of Zanzibar," Journal of the Royal Geographical Society 44 (1874), 227-51 (here 228).
2. Elton, "On the Coast," 248-49; Hans Paasche, Im Morgenlicht: Kriegs-, Jagd-, und Reise-Erlebnisse in Ostafrika (Berlin: C.A. Schwetschke und Son, 1907), 82, 96, 112, 118, 134.
3. John Iliffe, A Modern History of Tanganyika (Cambridge: Cambridge University Press, 1979), 168-202; G. C. K. Gwassa, "Kinjikitile and the Ideology of Maji Maji," in The Historical Study of African Religion, ed. T. O. Ranger and I. N. Kimambo (Berkeley: University of California Press, 1972), 202-17; G. C. K. Gwassa and John Iliffe, eds., Records of the Maji Maji Rising (Dar es Salaam: East African Publishing House, 1967); John Iliffe, "The Organization of the Maji Maji Rebellion," Journal of African History 8 (1967), 495-512.
4. John Iliffe, "The Effects of the Maji Maji Rebellion of 1905-06 on German Occupation Policy in East Africa," in Britain and Germany in Africa: Imperial Rivalry and Colonial Rule, ed. Prosser Gifford and William Roger Louis (New Haven, Conn.: Yale University Press, 1967), 557-75; Walter Rodney, "The Political Economy of Colonial Tanganyika 1890-1930," in Tanzania under Colonial Rule, ed. M. H. Y. Kaniki (London: Longman, 1979), 128-63.
5. C. George Kahama, T. L. Maliyamkono and Stuart Wells, The Challenge for Tanzania's Economy (London: James Currey, 1986), 1.
6. Recent analyses of the rebellion include Marcia Wright, "Maji Maji: Prophecy and Historiography," in Revealing Prophets: Prophecy in Eastern African History, ed. David

Anderson and Douglas H. Johnson (London: James Currey, 1995), 124-42; Thaddeus Sunseri, "Famine and Wild Pigs: Gender Struggles and the Outbreak of the Maji Maji War in Uzaramo (Tanzania)," *Journal of African History* 38 (1997), 235-59; Thaddeus Sunseri, "Statist Narratives and Maji Maji Ellipses," *International Journal of African Historical Studies* 33 (2000), 567-84; Jamie Monson, "Relocating Maji Maji: The Politics of Alliance and Authority in the Southern Highlands of Tanzania, 1870-1918," *Journal of African History* 39 (1998), 95-120.

7. Harald Sippel, "Aspects of Colonial Land Law in German East Africa: German East Africa Company, Crown Land Ordinance, European Plantations and Reserved Areas for Africans," in *Land Law and Land Ownership in Africa*, ed. Robert Debusmann and Stefan Arnold (Bayreuth: D. Gräbner, 1996), 32.

8. Gregory Barton, "Empire Forestry and the Origins of Environmentalism," *Journal of Historical Geography* 27 (2001), 529-52.

9. Iliffe, *Modern History*, 88-98; Jonathon Glassman, *Feasts and Riot: Revelry, Rebellion, and Popular Consciousness on the Swahili Coast, 1856-1888* (Portsmouth, N.H.: Heinemann, 1994); Robert D. Jackson, "Resistance to the German Invasion of the Tanganyikan Coast, 1888-1891," in *Protest and Power in Black Africa*, ed. Robert Rotberg and Ali Mazrui (New York: Oxford University Press, 1970), 36-79.

10. On the role of Yao as ivory traders see Edward Alpers, *Ivory and Slaves in East Central Africa* (Berkeley: University of California Press, 1975). The occupation of the Rufiji delta during the rebellion is mentioned in K. Grass, "Forststatistik für die Waldungen des Rufiyideltas," *Berichte über Land- und Forstwirtschaft* (hereafter *BLF*) 2 (1904-06), 167.

11. The following discussion is based on Martin Klamroth, "Beiträge zum Verständnis der religiösen Vorstellungen der Saramo im Bezirk Daressalam (Deutsch-Ostafrika)," *Zeitschrift für Kolonialsprachen*, Vols.1-3 (1910-1913), 37-70, 118-53, 189-223.

12. Examples include Tanzania National Archives (hereafter TNA) G8/663, Massangania Forest Reserve, 4 February 1904; TNA G8/632, Vikindu Forest Reserve, 28 January 1904.

13. A. R. W. Crosse-Upcott, "Social Aspects of Ngindo Bee-keeping," *Journal of the Royal Anthropological Institute of Great Britain and Ireland* 86 (1956), 81-108.

14. A. R. W. Crosse-Upcott, "Ngindo Famine Subsistence," *Tanganyika Notes and Records*, 50 (1950), 1-20; Crosse-Upcott, "Social Aspects"; W. A. Rodgers, "Past Wangindo Settlement in the Eastern Selous Game Reserve," *Tanzania Notes and Records* 77 & 78 (1976), 21-26.

15. Crosse-Upcott, "Social Aspects," 84.

16. Ibid., 87-88.

17. Gilbert Gwassa, "The Outbreak and Development of the Maji Maji War, 1905-1907," (Ph.D. dissertation, University of Dar es Salaam, 1973), 151-60; Bundesarchiv Berlin (hereafter BAB) R1001/726, Winterfeld report, 4 December 1905, 91b-92a; Otto Stollowsky, "On the Background to the Rebellion in German East Africa in 1905-1906," trans. John East, *International Journal of African Historical Studies* 21 (1988), 677-97 (693).

18. BAB/R1001/214, Berg report, 12 June 1895, 12.

19. Stollowsky, "On the Background," 684-86.

20. Thaddeus Sunseri, *Vilimani: Labor Migration and Rural Change in Early Colonial Tanzania* (Portsmouth, N.H.: Heinemann, 2001), 76-112.

21. Stollowsky, "On the Background," 685-86.

22. TNA G8/652, Kilwa Waldreservate "Naminangu" 1904-1914.

23. The following discussion draws largely from Kjell J. Havnevik, *Tanzania: The Limits to Development from Above* (Motala: Nordiska Afrikainstitutet, 1993), 146, 161-65, 169-70; Alexander Wood, Pamela Stedmann-Edwards and Johanna Mang, eds., *The Root Causes of Biodiversity Loss* (Sterling, Va.: Earthscan: 2000), 309-36.

24. TNA G8/19, Schroeder to Imperial Government, 7 September 1893, 40-41.
25. TNA G8/630, Boeder to Government, 21 December 1907.
26. Paasche, *Im Morgenlicht*, 109.
27. British Institute in Eastern Africa, "Kilwa: A History of the Ancient Swahili Town," in *Azania* 33 (1998), 113-69; Abdul Sheriff, *Slaves, Spices and Ivory in Zanzibar* (London: James Currey, 1987); Erik Gilbert, "Sailing from Lamu and Back: Labor Migration and Regional Trade in Colonial East Africa," *Comparative Studies of South Asia, Africa and the Middle East* 19 (1999), 9-15. According to Baumann, wood for the Chole shipbuilding industry came from the Msala mouth of the Rufiji delta. Wood for the keels came from west Mafia and Bwejuu island. Oskar Baumann, *Der Sansibar-Archipel. Erstes Heft: Die Insel Mafia und ihre kleineren Nachbarinseln* (Leipzig: Duncker und Humblot, 1896), 20.
28. In 1881, Rufiji people approached the explorer William Beardall desiring to buy rice with Maria Theresa dollars. William Beardall, "Exploration of the Rufiji River under the order of the Sultan of Zanzibar," *Proceedings of the Royal Geographical Society* 11 (November, 1881), 641-56.
29. Elton, "On the Coast," 227-30, 244. Juhani Koponen discusses the demand and use of these products in *People and Production in Late Precolonial Tanzania* (Jyväskylä: Finnish Society for Development Studies, 1988), 66-68.
30. Bruno Kurtze, *Die Deutsch-Ostafrikanische Gesellschaft* (Jena, Gustav Fischer: 1913), 95, 98-99; Heinrich Schnee, ed., *Deutsches Kolonial-Lexicon* (Leipzig: Quelle & Meyer, 1920), 1:390.
31. BAB/R1001/726, Booth report to Götzen, 16 January 1906, 126.
32. TNA G8/651, Waldreservate Bezirk Kilwa, 5 September 1904.
33. BAB/R1001/7681, Götzen memorandum, 27 July 1904, 125-26. The Crown Land ordinance has been analyzed by Sippel, "Aspects of Colonial Land Law." Sippel omits how the ordinance affected forest policy.
34. Several montane forests had by then been taken as forest reserves in nearby Dar es Salaam district, affecting the Zaramo people discussed above. TNA G8/632, Vikindu Forest Reserve, 28 January 1904; TNA G8/633, Massangania Forest Reserve, 4 February 1904.
35. BAB/R1001/721, Back to Berlin admiralty, 6 August 1905, 11. The rupee was the currency of German East Africa. One rupee equaled 1.33 marks or 32 cents.
36. For an overview of German forest policy in East Africa, see Hans G. Schabel, "Tanganyika Forestry under German Colonial Administration, 1891-1919," *Forest and Conservation History* (July 1990), 130-41. On German forest policies in the Usambara Mountains of northeast Tanzania see Christopher Conte, "Nature Reorganized: Ecological History in the Plateau Forests of the West Usambara Mountains, 1850-1935," in *Custodians of the Land: Ecology and Culture in the History of Tanzania*, ed. Gregory Maddox, James Giblin and Isaria Kimambo (London: James Currey, 1996), 96-121.
37. Henry E. Lowood, "The Calculating Forester: Quantification, Cameral Science, and the Emergence of Scientific Forest Management in Germany," in *The Quantifying Spirit in the 18th Century*, ed. Tore Frängsmyer, J.L. Heilbron, and Robin E. Rider (Berkeley: University of California Press, 1990), 315-42; Ravi Rajan, "Imperial Environmentalism or Environmental Imperialism? European Forestry, Colonial Foresters and the Agendas of Forest Management in British India 1800-1900," in *Nature and the Orient: The Environmental History of South and Southeast Asia*, ed. Richard H. Grove, Vinita Damodaran, and Satpal Sangwan (New Delhi: Oxford University Press, 1998), 324-71; James Scott, *Seeing Like a State: How Certain Schemes to Improve the Human Condition Have Failed* (New Haven, Conn.: Yale University Press, 1998), 11-12.
38. BAB/R1001/7681, Götzen to Foreign Office, 8 March 1904, 111-112.

39. M. Büsgen, "Forstwirtschaft in den Kolonien," *Verhandlungen des Deutschen Kolonialkongresses* (Berlin: Dietrich Reimer, 1910), 804.
40. Büsgen, "Forstwirtschaft," 802; "The Forest Lands of Germany," *Indian Forester* 31, 6 (1905), 729-30. The German estimate of 1 percent tree cover omitted savanna woodlands that covered much of the colony.
41. BAB/R1001/7680, Die Wald- und Culturverhältnisse in Deutsch-Ost-Afrika, 3 October 1894, 29-43. This report was published in edited form in *Deutsches Kolonialblatt* 1894/ 5, 623-29.
42. BAB/R1001/7680, Rundererlass Governor von Schele an Bezirks- und Bezirksnebenaemter sowie die Zolldirektion, 5 December 1894, 52.
43. BAB/R1001/7722, Liebert to Hohenlohe-Schillingsfurst, 14 May 1897, 10-11.
44. "Forstwesen," in Schnee, *Deutsches Kolonial-Lexicon* Vol. I, 652; Karl Grass, "Forststatistik für die Waldungen des Rufiyideltas," *BLF* 2 (1904-06), 165-96.
45. Grass, "Forststatistik," 168-69. On the importance of Rufiji region for the growth of Dar es Salaam, see Thaddeus Sunseri, "Fueling the City: Dar es Salaam and Colonial Forest Policy, 1892-1915," (London: James Currey, forthcoming).
46. BAB/R1001/7722, Stuhlmann to Foreign Office, 5 May 1898, 82; German Consul, Johannesburg, to Consul Schuckmann, German Consul, Cape Town, 29 April 1898, 83-85; BAB/R1001/7723, Mangrove Bark in DOA, 1900-1901.
47. TNA G8/651, Götzen to Kilwa and Lindi, 25 July 1905.
48. TNA G8/653, Waldreservate Bezirk Kilwa "Liwale," 1899-1909.
49. On Maji Maji and the decline of the rubber trade, see Juhani Koponen, *Development for Exploitation: German Colonial Policies in Mainland Tanzania, 1884-1914* (Berlin/ Helsinki: Lit Verlag, 1995), 237-40; Wright, "Maji Maji: Prophecy and Historiography," 137. On the wild rubber economy of the Kilombero Valley (the upper Rufiji) during German rule, see Jamie Monson, "From Commerce to Colonization: A History of the Rubber Trade in the Kilombero Valley of Tanzania, 1890-1914," *African Economic History* 21 (1993), 113-30.
50. Iliffe, *Modern History*, 130.
51. BAB/R1001/7776, Verordnung betreffend die Schonung des Wildstandes in Deutsch-Ostafrika, 17 January 1898, 56-57.
52. Elton notes this in "On the Coast," 229, 234, 244, 246. He believed that ivory was an irregular trade commodity to the coast at the delta, but was part of a thriving trade at Samanga. Pfund met a Greek rubber and ivory trader on the upper Rufiji at Kungulio in 1899. Kurt Pfund, *Kreuz und Quer durch Deutschostafrika* (Berlin: n.p., 1912), 25.
53. Paasche, *Im Morgenlicht*, 152.
54. Ibid., 126.
55. TNA G8/589, Gouvernementsrat, Wald- und Jagdreservate und gesunde Eingeborenenpolitik, June 1913; TNA AB94 Rufiji Annual Report 1924, Colonial Secretary to Forest Conservator, 23 May 1925; TNA AB 97, Rufiji Annual Report 1925; TNA 274/G1.1, Mwenyenzi Kikale Rufiji to D. C. Utete Rufiji, 26 December 1946, 278.
56. BAB/R1001/726, Westhaus testimony, 21 December 1905, 122b. Westhaus testified that since the enactment of hunting ordinances, only two to three permits were issued, compared to fifty to sixty in earlier years. Permits were necessary for large game, but not for "vermin" like wild pigs.
57. BAB/R1001/7776, Götzen to Foreign Office, 15 July 1902, 135; TNA G8/589, Gouvernementsrat, June 1913.
58. R. M. Bell, "The Maji Maji Rebellion in Liwale District," *Tanganyika Notes and Records* 28 (1950), 38-57; TNA G8/653, Waldreservat Liwale, 9 April 1905; Lott to Government, 20 December 1906.
59. Bell, "Maji-Maji," 47-48. The first names of Aimer and Faupel are unavailable.
60. Stollowsky, "Background," 689.

61. BAB/R1001/721, Back telegram, 10 August 1905, 29. Claims for compensation for losses from rebel attacks are found in TNA G3/101, Kilwa Entschädigung, 83-84.
62. BAB/R1001/726, Boeder report, 21 December 1905, 119.
63. BAB/R1001/726, Schultz report, 23 December 1905, 121a-b. Also see BAB/R1001/726, Causes of the Uprising in Dar es Salaam District, 11 December 1905, 111b.
64. BAB/R1001/726, Haber report, 9 September 1906, 88a.
65. BAB/R1001/726, Booth report, 16 January 1906, 126; Paasche, *Im Morgenlicht*, 108.
66. A map designating Kibasira's forests as "projected forest reserves" is found in TNA G8/581, Waldkarte des Bezirks Dar es Salaam, 1904, 40.
67. BAB/R1001/7682, Rechenberg to Colonial Department, 17 May 1907, 22-23; "Sonderbare Finanzpolitik," *Deutsch-Ostafrikanische Zeitung* 9 (26 January 1907), 1-2.
68. Tetzlaff, *Koloniale Entwicklung*, 293.
69. Crosse-Upcott emphasizes that the Ngindo used forests and thickets in like manner as havens from Ngoni raids. Crosse-Upcott, "Social Aspects," 84-85.
70. The Mahenge (or Mbunga) raids are discussed in Lorne Larson, "A History of the Mbunga Confederacy ca. 1860-1907," *Tanzania Notes and Records* 81 & 82 (1977), 35-42.
71. Beardall, "Exploration," 647-48.
72. "Bericht des Lieutenants Z. S. Fromm über eine Rekognierungsfahrt nach dem Rufiji," *Deutsches Kolonialblatt* 4 (1893), 291-94.
73. "Zur Reise des Kaiserlichen Gouverneurs," *DKB* (1896/97), 247-48, Larson, "History of the Mbunga," 40.
74. Paasche, *Im Morgenlicht*, 94, 106, 109.
75. Ibid., 96.
76. Siebenlist, *Forstwirtschaft*, 7.
77. The files on these declarations include: TNA G8/683, Namuete; TNA G8/684, Nerumba; TNA G8/685, Kumbi; TNA G8/686, Nadunda.
78. TNA G8/677, Waldreservat Mpanga, 26 August 1910. Mpanga was the gateway for the game reserve that was to become Selous south of the Rufiji.
79. TNA G8/674, "Kipo," 31 October 1908; TNA G8/676, "Mtanza," 12 November 1910. On the wartime role of these forests see Paasche, *Im Morgenlicht*, 111-15, 282, 292-92.
80. A sense of where conflict took place can be gained by examining locations where compensation had to be paid following the war in TNA G3/101, Kilwa Entschädigung. Paasche, *Im Morgenlicht*, mentions other locations, as do reports from the battlefield during the war.
81. Paasche mentions the area of the upper Rufiji as a hunting preserve in *Im Morgenlicht*, 150; Gordon Matzke, "The Development of the Selous Game Reserve," *Tanzania Notes and Records* 79 & 80 (1976), 37-48.
82. Sunseri, *Vilimani*, 113-35.
83. "Die Entwicklung Kilwas im Jahre 1908," *Deutsch-Ostafrikanische Rundschau*, 6 November 1909, 1.
84. "Die Reise des hochwürdigen Herrn Bischof Thomas Spreiter nach Matumbi and Kwiro," *Missions-Blaetter von St. Ottilien*, 13, 4 (1909), 131.
85. TNA G8/882, Holtz to District Office, 21 February 1910.
86. For an overview of historical intersections between forest regulations and social protest, see Richard Grove, *Ecology, Climate and Empire: Colonialism and Global Environmental History 1400-1940* (Cambridge: White Horse Press, 1997), 195-223.
87. John F. Freeman, "Forest Conservancy in the Alps of Dauphiné, 1287-1870," *Forest and Conservation History* 38 (October 1994), 171-180; Josef Mooser, "Property and Wood Theft: Agrarian Capitalism and Social Conflict in Rural Society, 1800-50. A Westphalian Case Study," in *Peasants and Lords in Modern Germany*, ed. Robert G. Moeller (Boston: Allen and Unwin, 1986), 52-80; Douglas Hay, "Poaching and the Game

Laws on Cannock Chase," in Douglas Hay, et al., *Albion's Fatal Tree: Crime and Society in Eighteenth-Century England* (New York: Pantheon Books, 1975), 189-253; Peter Sahlins, *Forest Rites: The War of the Demoiselles in Nineteenth-Century France* (Cambridge, Mass.: Harvard University Press, 1994); Regina Schulte, *Das Dorf im Verhör: Brandstifter, Kindsmörderinnen und Wilderer vor den Schranken des bürgerlichen Gerichts Oberbayern 1848-1910* (Reinbek bei Hamburg: Rowohlt, 1989); Tom Scott and Bob Scribner, eds. and trans., *The German Peasants' War: A History in Documents* (Atlantic Highlands, N.J.: Humanities Press, 1991), 67, 69-71, 79-81; Julia J. Serovayskay, "People's Struggle Against the Institution of Royal Forest Reserves in England in the 11th-14th Centuries," in *Forest History*, ed. M. Agnoletti and S. Anderson (Wallingford: CAB International, 2000), 253-61; E. P. Thompson, *Whigs and Hunters: The Origin of the Black Act* (New York: Pantheon Books, 1975); Tamara Whited, *Forests and Peasant Politics in Modern France* (New Haven, Conn.: Yale University Press, 2000).

88. Raymond L. Bryant, *The Political Ecology of Forestry in Burma 1824-1994* (Honolulu: University of Hawaii, 1996), 67-76, 117-26; Madhav Gadgil and Ramachandra Guha, *This Fissured Land: An Ecological History of India* (Berkeley: University of California Press, 1993), 146-80; Ramachandra Guha and Madhav Gadgil, "State Forestry and Social Conflict in British India," *Past and Present* 123 (1989), 141-77; David Hardiman, "Power in the Forests: The Dangs, 1820-1940," in *Subaltern Studies VIII: Essays in Honour of Ranajit Guha*, ed. David Arnold and David Hardiman (Delhi: Oxford University Press, 1994), 89-147.

89. Grove, *Ecology, Climate and Empire*, 147-52, 215; Terence Ranger, *Voices from the Rocks: Nature, Culture and History in the Matopos Hills of Zimbabwe* (Oxford: James Currey, 1999).

90. Examples of precolonial state regulation of forests in Africa and elsewhere include James McCann, *Green Land, Brown Land, Black Land* (Portsmouth, N.H., Heinemann: 1999), 79-107; Nancy Lee Peluso, *Rich Forests, Poor People: Resource Control and Resistance in Java* (Berkeley: University of California Press, 1994), 32-36; Chetan Singh, "Forests, Pastoralists and Agrarian Society in Mughal India," in *Nature, Culture, Imperialism: Essays on the Environmental History of South Asia*, ed. David Arnold and Ramachandra Guha (Delhi: Oxford University Press, 1996), 21-48.

91. "Sonderberichte der Forstverwaltung von Deutsch-Ostafrika für das Jahr 1909," *BLF* 3 (1911), 294.

92. "Videant Consules," *Deutsch-Ostafrikanische Zeitung*, 8 January 1913, 1-2.

93. Büsgen, "Forstwirtschaft," 810.

94. Indra Munshi Saldanha, "Colonialism and Professionalism: A German Forester in India," *Environment and History* 2 (1996), 195-219; Gregory Barton, "Keepers of the Jungle: Environmental Management in British India, 1855-1900," *The Historian* 62 (2000), 557-74 (558); Rajan, "Imperial Environmentalism," 324-371; Peluso, *Rich Forests*, 63, 65; Peter Boomgaard, "Forest Management and Exploitation in Colonial Java, 1677-1897," *Forest and Conservation History* 36 (1992), 4-14 (11); Raymond L. Bryant, "From Laissez-faire to Scientific Forestry: Forest Management in early Colonial Burma, 1826-85," *Forest and Conservation History* 38 (1994), 160-70 (164).

95. For a critical examination of developmentalist views of African forest use, see Melissa Leach and Robin Mearns, *The Lie of the Land: Challenging the Received Wisdom in African Environmental Change and Policy* (Oxford: International African Institute, 1996). For a critique of forest policy in British Tanganyika and in modern Tanzania see Roderick Neumann, *Imposing Wilderness: Struggles over Livelihood and Nature Preservation in Africa* (Berkeley: University of California Press, 1998).

[5]
Geography, Race and Nation: Remapping "Tropical" Australia, 1890–1930

WARWICK ANDERSON

In March 1885, the government Resident of the Northern Territory of Australia issued a report on the problem of tropical development. "To the ordinary English emigrant", wrote J Langdon Parsons, "the bare mention of 'the tropics' is sufficient to create a scare, and conjure up visions of pasty-faced children, delicate women, and men with bad livers".[1] But in 1925, Sir James Barrett, a leading figure in the medical school of the University of Melbourne, could declare: "The deliberate opinion of the vast majority of medical men and physiologists is, that so far as climate is concerned, there is nothing whatever to prevent the peopling of tropical Australia with a healthy and vigorous white race."[2] It is between these two quotations, between the voice of the administrator and the voice of the medical expert, between environmental determinism and cultural autonomy, between colonial pessimism and national optimism, that I would like to frame this essay.

What had happened to ideas of man and ideas of nature in northern Australia during this period? Throughout the nineteenth century medical geographies of northern Australia had reiterated that the tropics were no place for permanent European settlement. And yet, with the federation of the colonies in 1901, Australia was committed politically to the exclusion of non-Europeans and to the forced repatriation of the Pacific Islanders who had been compelled to labour in tropical

---

Warwick Anderson, Centre for the Study of Health and Society and History and Philosophy of Science Department, University of Melbourne, Parkville 3052, Australia.

An earlier version of this paper appeared in *Historical Records of Australian Science*. I am grateful to Martin Gibbs and Matthew Klugman for research assistance. I would like also to thank Hugh Anderson, Conevery Bolton Valenčius, Rod Home, Jan Sapp, Richard Gillespie, Nicolaas Rupke and Charles Rosenberg for advice and guidance. Versions of this paper were presented in the History and Philosophy of Science Department, University of Melbourne, and at the Institut für Geschichte der Medizin, Georg-August Universität, Göttingen.

[1] J Langdon Parsons, 'Quarterly Report on the Northern Territory, March 31, 1885', *South Australian Parliamentary Papers*, 1885, no. 54: 7. William J Sowden, in *The Northern Territory As It Is: A Narrative of the South Australian Parliamentary Party's Trip* (Adelaide, W K Thomas, 1882), confirms Parsons's fears. He reports that "with regard to the effect of the climate upon labour, there seems to be a consensus of opinion that Europeans cannot do the hewing and the drawing. That must be undertaken by coloured folk", pp. 146–7.

[2] Sir James Barrett, 'Can Tropical Australia be Peopled by a White Race?', *The Margin*, 1925, 1: 28–35, p. 30.

canefields. How then to develop the north? As medical scientists in the new nation increasingly emphasized the actual plasticity of the tropics as an pathogenic site, we find the elaboration of a discourse of tropical development—a new frontier—that proposed the settling there, under medical supervision, of a "working white race". During this period, medicos had become ever less inclined to relate disease and degeneration to climate and physical surroundings, preferring to attribute these conditions to the minute organisms that researchers at the Australian Institute of Tropical Medicine, established in 1913, located especially in insects and non-European races. A medical remapping of tropical Australia occurred, one that traced an anthropomorphic mobilization of pathology—it was a remapping that, in effect, erased pathology from the landscape. (It was the case record, more than the map, that now interested bacteriologists.) Scientists like Barrett trumpeted the inevitable conclusions of their laboratory and field investigations at the 1920 Australasian Medical Congress: a working white race could flourish in the north, despite the uncomfortable climate, but only so long as the apparently "natural" carriers of dangerous tropical pathogens—those races that had evolved with supposedly tropical disease organisms—were rigorously excluded from the geographically whitened nation.[3]

Such a brief introduction necessarily over-simplifies the politics of geographical, medical and ethnographic research in colonial and proto-national Australia. In this essay I will try to provide a more circumstantial and complex account, but there are a few broad themes I should sketch at the outset. First, a static, diminished, and increasingly dated medical geography could, in the early twentieth century, be represented as a removable impediment to racial expansion and progress, one that further investment in modern laboratory research would certainly overcome. Deprecation of the old succubus of environmental pathogenesis thus became a means of securing support for laboratory science. Second, it can be said that during this period biological and medical scientists sought a dominion over tropical nature. Gradually, the tropical environment was reconfigured from a place inimical to civilization, to a place that a relatively autonomous white civilization could modernize and exploit. Climate and vegetation had been reduced, disarmed, and exonerated; "nature" appeared ever less determinate and implacable. Instead, local and foreign race cultures were identified as the chief threat to white corporeal security, although their menace, too, when not actively excluded seemed ever more reformable—that is, available to modernization. In the laboratories and in the field, "tropical nature"

---

[3] On the development of the new speciality of tropical medicine in Australia, see R A Douglas, 'Dr Anton Breinl and the Australian Institute of Tropical Medicine', *Medical Journal of Australia*, 1977, i: 713–16; 748–51; 784–90; Lorraine Harloe, 'Anton Breinl and the Institute of Tropical Medicine', in Roy MacLeod and Donald Denoon (eds), *Health and Healing in Tropical Australia and Papua New Guinea*, Townsville, James Cook University Press, 1991, pp. 35–46; and Douglas Gordon, *Mad Dogs and Englishmen Went out in the Queensland Sun: Health Aspects of the Settlement of Tropical Queensland*, Brisbane, Amphion Press, 1990. More generally, see Michael Worboys, 'The Emergence of Tropical Medicine: A Study in the Establishment of a Scientific Specialty', in G Lemaine et al. (eds), *Perspectives on the Emergence of Scientific Disciplines*, The Hague, Mouton, 1976, pp. 75–98.

and "tropical culture" were thus reframed as separable and then brought into modernity together.[4]

In trying to locate the point at which medicine becomes less an environmental discourse and more a vocabulary for modern citizenship, I am drawing together a number of historical studies that previously were distinct. In particular, I want to connect the history of medical geography and the history of biomedical sciences with our knowledge of Australian race and settlement policy.[5] Early accounts of Australian racialism emphasized the efforts of organized white labour to exclude, for economic reasons, Asians and Pacific Islanders who could not, it seemed, be unionized.[6] More recently, some historians have argued that the white Australia policy merely codified the underlying racism of all sections of Australian society.[7] But if the labour movement's rationalization of the policy was economic, how did the middle-class explain their support for this national goal? A few scholars have pointed to a liberal political justification for the exclusion of races deemed impossible to enfranchise.[8] Yet the scientific argument for racialist policy, with its capacity to appeal to all groups in Australian society in the early twentieth century, has been

---

[4] Warwick Anderson, 'The Natures of Culture: Environment and Race in the Colonial Tropics', presented at a conference on 'Environmental Discourses in South Asia and Southeast Asia', Social Science Research Council, USA, Hilo, Hawaii, December 1995. In a sense I am describing the end of the medical discourse on settlement analysed by Conevery Bolton Valenčius, 'The Geography of Health and the Making of the American West: Arkansas and Missouri 1800–1860', Chapter 7 in this volume.

[5] On the history of medical geography, see Mirko Grmek, 'Géographie médicale et histoire des civilisations', *Annales: Economies, Sociétés, Civilisations*, 1963, **18**: 1071–87; and Philip D Curtin, 'The Promise and the Terror of a Tropical Environment', in idem, *The Image of Africa: British Ideas in Action, 1780–1850*, Madison, University of Wisconsin Press, 1964. For Australia, see J M Powell, 'Medical Promotion and the Consumptive Immigrant to Australia', *Geographical Review*, 1973, **63**: 449–76; and Helen R Woolcock, ' "Our salubrious climate": attitudes to health in colonial Queensland', in Roy MacLeod and Milton Lewis (eds), *Disease, Medicine and Empire: Perspectives on Western Medicine and the Experience of European Expansion*, London and New York, Routledge, 1988, pp. 176–93. For brief accounts of literature on climate and character in Australia, see Chris Tiffin, 'Imagining Countries, Imagining People: Climate and the Australian Type', *Span*, 1987, **24**: 46–62; and Jon Stratton, 'Deconstructing the Territory', *Cultural Studies*, 1989, **3**: 38–57. On the development of biomedical science in Australia, see F C Courtice, 'Research in the Medical Sciences: the Road to National Independence', in R W Home (ed.), *Australian Science in the Making*, Cambridge, Cambridge University Press, 1988, pp. 277–307.

[6] Myra Willard, *The History of the White Australia Policy to 1920*, Melbourne, Melbourne University Press, 1923; N B Nairn, 'A Survey of the White Australia Policy in the Nineteenth Century', *Australian Quarterly*, 1956, **28**: 16–31; and A C Palfreeman, *The Administration of the White Australia Policy*, Melbourne, Melbourne University Press, 1967.

[7] Humphrey McQueen, *A New Britannia: An Argument Concerning the Social Origins of Australian Radicalism and Nationalism*, Ringwood, Penguin, 1970; Kay Saunders, 'The Black Scourge: Racial Responses toward Melanesians in colonial Queensland', in Raymond Evans et al. (eds), *Race Relations in Colonial Queensland: A History of Exclusion, Exploitation and Extermination*, St Lucia, University of Queensland Press, 1988 [1975], pp. 147–234; Verity Burgmann, 'Capital and Labour: Responses to Immigration in the Nineteenth Century', in Ann Curthoys and Andrew Markus (eds), *Who are our Enemies? Racism and the Australian Working Class*, Sydney, Hale and Iremonger, 1978, pp. 20–34; and Ann Curthoys, 'Racism and Class in the Nineteenth-Century Immigration Debate', in Andrew Markus and M C Ricklefs (eds), *Surrender Australia? Essays in the Study and Uses of History*, Sydney, Allen and Unwin, 1985.

[8] For example, J A La Nauze, *Alfred Deakin: A Biography*, 2 vols, Melbourne, Melbourne University Press, 1965.

relatively neglected.⁹ This essay, then, is a novel exploration of a local medical effort to produce, and re-produce, flexible and plausible typologies of race and environment in order to shape public policy.¹⁰ In this project we see the ending of medical geography and the beginning of medical government; we find that the citizen, as much as the continent, has become scientifically legible.

Distribution of Disease

I am, in a sense, describing the interaction of advocates of two rather different organizing principles for the distribution of disease. An older generation of medical doctors, along with a younger group of anthropologists and geographers, retained a more static model of the spatial distribution of disease, based on physical cause and (more importantly) on physiological effect. Their medical geography, built around assumptions of racial and constitutional predisposition, sought primarily to explain endemicity of disease. In other words, disease was located securely in a specific environment, and humans—whether through evolutionary processes, God's beneficence, or temperate behaviour—were either accustomed to it or not. But in a settler society, such as Australia, migration had stimulated medical interest in the process of becoming racially adjusted to a foreign disease environment: the process called seasoning, or acclimatization. In this conventional medical geography, race and environment were everywhere inseparable as an etiological complex. But a younger generation of medical doctors, often committed to laboratory research and afire with enthusiasm for the new bacteriology and parasitology, was developing during this period a more ontologically independent model for the spatial distribution of disease. It is, in part, the difference between a clinical orientation and a more reductionist logic of laboratory research. The new votaries of the medical laboratory sought to trace the mobilization of disease organisms, the dynamics of biological cause, across a landscape, as much as to identify clinical effect within a landscape. And when disease becomes mobile in this way, it is much easier, as we shall see, for humans to stay put.¹¹

⁹ But see Raymond Evans, 'Keep White the Strain: Race Relations in a Colonial Setting', in Evans et al. (eds), op. cit., note 7 above, pp. 1–24; and Michael Roe, 'The Establishment of the Australian Department of Health: Its Background and Significance', *Historical Studies* (Australia), 1976, **67**: 176–92.

¹⁰ On metropolitan race science during this period, see Nancy Stepan, *The Idea of Race in Science: Great Britain, 1800–1960*, Hamden, CT, Archon Press, 1982; and George M Fredrickson, *The Black Image in the White Mind: The Debate on Afro-American Character and Destiny 1817–1914*, Middletown, CT, Wesleyan University Press, 1987. For other studies of the local generation of colonial race theory, see C L Bacci, 'The Nature-Nurture Debate in Australia 1900–1914', *Australian Historical Studies*, 1980, **75**: 199–212; and David Johnson, 'Aspects of a Liberal Education: late 19th Century Attitudes to Race, from Cambridge to the Cape Colony', *History Workshop Journal*, 1992, **36**: 162–82. For a preliminary account of the connections of medicine, race, and settlement policy in the tropical colonial world during this period, see Warwick Anderson, 'Disease, Race, and Empire', *Bulletin of the History of Medicine*, 1996, **70**: 62–7. On the need for such comparative studies, see Donald Denoon, *Settler Capitalism: The Dynamics of Dependent Development in the Southern Hemisphere*, Oxford, Clarendon Press, 1983.

¹¹ Warwick Anderson, 'Immunities of Empire: Race, Disease, and the New Tropical Medicine', *Bulletin of the History of Medicine*, 1996, **70**: 94–118. On acclimatization, see David N Livingstone, 'Human Acclimatization: Perspectives in a Contested Field of Inquiry in Science, Medicine and Geography', *History of Science*, 1987, **25**: 359–94; and Dane Kennedy 'The Perils of the Midday Sun: Climatic Anxieties in the Colonial Tropics', in John M MacKenzie (ed.), *Imperialism and the Natural World*, Manchester, Manchester University Press, 1990, pp. 118–40.

Warwick Anderson

Attempts to settle whites in the north had been made since the late 1830s, first at Port Essington and later at Darwin, but despite a brief mining boom and the construction of an overland telegraph, the rest of the Northern Territory, then attached to the colony of South Australia, failed to attract many white settlers. When it was transferred to the federal government in 1911, the territory contained only 2,846 non-Aboriginal inhabitants, and of these 1,182 were Europeans.[12] Settlement along the humid north Queensland coast had begun later, but swelled by a gold rush, it was more successful than in the territory. Although opened up primarily for pastoral purposes, the country was soon turned over to sugar cane plantations.[13] From the 1860s, the planters imported almost 65,000 Melanesian labourers, called Kanakas, from nearby Pacific islands, usually the Solomons and New Hebrides. Toward the end of the century almost one-third of the coastal population was from the Pacific islands.[14] (By this time most of the Aboriginal population was dead, imprisoned, driven inland, or clustered in a few shanty towns—it was presumed that racial competition would inevitably render the race extinct.) Independent producers indentured the Pacific Islanders, deemed cheap and reliable labourers, on small, relatively inefficient plantations. Social dislocation, inadequate housing, and medical neglect meant that the Islanders, supposedly adapted to the exigencies of a tropical climate, had a death rate four times higher than that of Europeans in the north.[15] And yet, even this great disparity was not sufficient to shake the prevailing assumption that they were racially immune to tropical disease.

The notion that tropical races were relatively resistant to the diseases of their ancestral realm lasted, as we shall see, just so long as tropical races were required to labour on the northern plantations. The sugar industry was reconstructed in the 1890s: the costs of recruiting Islander labour had risen in the previous decade with the depopulation of nearby islands; the Islanders whose contracts had expired began demanding higher wages; and the international sugar market collapsed in the late 1880s.[16] As a result, the industry shifted from labour-intensive plantation agriculture to a capital-intensive central milling arrangement. The Queensland government encouraged white agricultural workers to take up land to supply the mills. "The

---

[12] Gordon Reid, *A Picnic with the Natives: Aboriginal-European Relations in the Northern Territory to 1910*, Melbourne, Melbourne University Press, 1990.

[13] On Queensland history, see Raphael Cilento and Clem Lack, *Triumph in the Tropics: An Historical Sketch of Queensland*, Brisbane, Smith and Paterson, 1959; and Geoffrey C Bolton, *A Thousand Miles Away: A History of North Queensland to 1920*, Canberra, Australian National University Press, 1963. See also idem, *Spoils and Spoilers: Australians Make Their Environment, 1788–1980*, Sydney, Allen and Unwin, 1981.

[14] On the history of the labour trade, see Peter Corris, *Passage, Port and Plantation: A History of the Solomon Islands Labour Migration, 1870–1914*, Melbourne, Melbourne University Press, 1973; Kay Saunders, *Workers in Bondage: The Origins of Unfree Labour in Queensland, 1824–1916*, St Lucia, University of Queensland Press, 1982; and Ralph Schlomowitz, 'Epidemiology of the Pacific Labor Trade', *Journal of Interdisciplinary History*, 1989, 19: 585–610. Clive Moore's *Kanaka: A History of Melanesian Mackay* (Port Moresby, University of Papua New Guinea Press, 1985) emphasizes a continuing Pacific Islander presence. More generally, see Evans et al. (eds), op. cit., note 7 above.

[15] Ross Patrick, *A History of Health and Medicine in Queensland, 1824–1960*, St Lucia, University Queensland Press, 1987, p. 531.

[16] For more details on the sugar economy, see H T Easterby, *The Queensland Sugar Industry*, Brisbane, F Phillips, 1936.

most highly important economic and social result of this change", reported Dr Walter Maxwell, the American director of the Sugar Experiment Stations, in 1901, "is found in the circumstance that the ownership and occupancy embrace a large number of strong, responsible, and progressive white settlers, with families of coming men and women, who are being planted over the sugar growing areas".[17] Pacific Islanders, no longer indentured labourers, soon became part-time farm-workers competing with white farmers who cut their own cane and with white workers drawn to the cane fields after the collapse of the mining and pastoral industries in the 1890s' depression.

After federation of the colonies in 1901, the new Australian parliament had passed the Pacific Islanders Labourers Act which stipulated that no more indentured labourers would be brought into the northern tropics after 1904, and those already in the country would be deported by 1907, at the end of their agreements. Part of the common aspiration to keep the whole continent for a white race, this legislation would render the sugar industry dependent on white labour.[18] Along with the Immigration Restriction Act of the same year, it comprised the legislative core of the white Australia policy, preserved more or less intact until the 1960s.[19]

But elements of the medical profession lagged behind national policy. In late 1900, Dr Joseph Ahearne wrote to the most chauvinist and popular of magazines, the *Bulletin*, warning that "the white race of Queensland is undergoing modification physically, morally and mentally". In comparison with English boys, the currency lads were more narrow in the chest and two inches taller than they ought to be. Furthermore, "the tropical resident of some years standing possesses less endurance than his fellow workman imported from a more bracing locality"—this was because "an intelligent God equipped Man so that he should be suitable to his environments".[20]

---

[17] Walter Maxwell, 'Report on the Cane Sugar Industry of Australia', *Votes & Proceedings, Queensland Parliamentary Papers*, 1901, pp. 275–90, p. 275.

[18] Alan Birch, 'The Implementation of the White Australia Policy in the Queensland Sugar Industry, 1901–12', *Australian Journal of Politics and History*, 1965, 11: 198–210; and Peter Corris, 'White Australia in Action: The Repatriation of the Pacific Islanders from Queensland', *Historical Studies* (Australia), 1972, 15: 170–5. For explanations that emphasize economics over ideology, see Adrian Graves, 'The Abolition of the Queensland Labour Trade: Politics or Profits?', in E L Wheelwright and Ken Buckley (eds), *Essays in the Political Economy of Australian Capitalism*, vol. 4, Sydney, Australia and New Zealand Book Co., 1980, pp. 41–57; and idem, 'Crisis and Change in the Queensland Sugar Industry, 1863–1906', in Bill Albert and Adrian Graves (eds), *Crisis and Change in the International Sugar Economy, 1860–1914*, Norwich and Edinburgh, ICS Press, 1984, pp. 261–80.

[19] Sean Brawley, *The White Peril: Foreign Relations and Asian Immigration to Australasia and North America 1918–78*, Sydney, University of New South Wales Press, 1995; Burgmann, op. cit., note 7 above; and Curthoys, op. cit., note 7 above.

[20] J Ahearne, 'The Australian in the Tropics', Red Page, *Bulletin* (29 September 1900). Ahearne was merely echoing a medical convention of the late nineteenth century. In 1893, Dr E A Birch had asserted that "under the circumstances of ordinary life, a tropical climate (of which India is a type) is inimical to the European constitution". He could cite expert opinion that European children in such a depleting climate grow up "slight, weedy, and delicate, over-precocious" (Birch, 'Influence of warm climates on the constitution', in Andrew Davidson (ed.), *Hygiene and Diseases of Warm Climates*, Edinburgh and London, Young J Pentland, 1893, pp. 1–24, on pp. 4 and 5). The reform Darwinist, Benjamin Kidd, was perhaps the most pessimistic of foreign commentators, and the most widely cited in Australia. "The attempt to acclimatize the white man in the tropics", he advised, "must be recognized as a blunder of the first magnitude. All experiments based on the idea are mere idle and empty enterprises doomed to failure" (*Control of the Tropics*, London, Macmillan, 1898, p. 48).

Warwick Anderson

A G Stephens, the literary editor of the *Bulletin*, had felt that the article warranted publication on the grounds that the "appeal differed from the appeals of other colored labour apologists in that it assumed a scientific foundation. But it has been shown that Dr Ahearne's foundation is no foundation in as much as his data are insufficient to yield a conclusion". Indeed, was not Ahearne a "Townsville medico in healthy condition with a spouting kidney and not too enlarged a liver who ... shows none of the signs of race deterioration which he attributes to other North Queenslanders".[21] Mitty from Mackay wrote in, after "a hard day's work in the canefield", to point out that the white man was more than equal to the Kanaka when it came to tropical labour.[22] And S J Richards, the government medical officer at Mt Morgan, found the children there a little darker in skin colour but no less robust than their cousins down south: "So welcome Federation and a White Australia."[23]

And yet, as late as 1915, in the *Medical Journal of Australia*, we find M.B. drawing the readers' attention to an article by Leonard Hill, the professor of physiology at the London Hospital, that had appeared the year before in the *British Medical Journal*. "Evolution", according to Hill, "had settled the dark-skinned man in the tropics and the white in the temperate zones of the earth". The white man's body heat regulating mechanism was less efficient in the tropics, requiring more energy of the heart and disinclining him for muscular work. Therefore he "can be the organizer and the overlooker, and the handicraftsman working in fan-cooled buildings protected from the sun, but he can only live at the expense of the dark-skinned races whose field labor is exploited by him".[24] Hill's conclusions had inspired M.B. to suggest that the "White Australia policy is poor business, bad science, and worse morals ... the laborers in the field must have the protection of pigment". He warned that the "votaries of a White Australia claim that the white man has only gradually to acclimatize. To acclimatize is either to pigment or to enervate or both".[25] But James Merrillees of Roma, Queensland, was critical of Hill's "pious opinions". "I am open to learn of one case, scientifically asserted, where a white-skinned man acquired pigmentation and transmitted it to his offspring as a fixed character". The curse of hot climates occupied only by whites was alcohol; where there was a mixture of races, "the dangers are alcohol and syphilis".[26]

Cosmos continued the sparring in the *Medical Journal of Australia*, claiming that the "so-called science of our universities is too limited to deal adequately with the policy of a White Australia". Whatever the new laboratory experts might argue, "man—black or white—is in tune with the universe when he is in that environment which called forth his characteristics. Abundant evidence exists that the people of

---

[21] A G Stephens, 'The Australian in the Tropics', Red Page, *Bulletin* (13 October 1900).

[22] Mitty from Mackay, 'The Australian in the Tropics', Red Page, *Bulletin* (24 November 1900).

[23] S J Richards, 'The Australian in the Tropics', Red Page, *Bulletin* (29 December 1900).

[24] Leonard Hill, 'The Working Power of the White Man in the Tropics and the Electric Fan', *British Medical Journal*, 1914, i: 325.

[25] M.B., 'Correspondence—White Australia Policy', *Medical Journal of Australia*, 1915, i: 277–8, p. 277.

[26] James F Merrillees, 'Correspondence—White Australia Policy', *Medical Journal of Australia*, 1915, i: 345–6, p. 345.

the northern parts of Australia are colored".[27] But in response to these assertions, Richard Berry, the professor of anatomy at Melbourne University (and later a prominent British eugenicist), wrote that "the 'White Australia Policy' is not a policy at all, but is in reality a medical problem of the first magnitude". As such it had not yet been subject to a proper test. In Professor Berry's opinion, though, given suitable railway facilities, housing on "physiological lines", rational hours of work, proper diet, individual observation of the laws of hygiene, and elimination of the vectors of specific diseases, there was no scientific reason why the Australian tropics could not be settled by white labour that would remain "white and healthy".[28] In Berry's opinion, the torrid zone was no longer an inherently pathological site for the white race.

That a number of young geographers, anthropologists and historians also came to contribute to this medical debate indicates the still rather inchoate character of disciplinary boundaries during this period.[29] Prominent among these contributions, the work of the geographer Ellsworth Huntington marks perhaps the high tide of climatic determinism as applied to medicine. In 1915, he proposed a "climatic hypothesis of civilization" as the basis for the "new science of geography".[30] From his analysis of the records of hundreds of white United States males, Huntington, a professor of geography at Yale, found that "mental activity reaches a maximum when the outside temperature averages 38 degrees [F], that is, when there are mild frosts at night" (p. 8). From this data he drew a map showing how human energy was distributed throughout the world. It was, in effect, a physiological projection of the white male body onto whole of the globe. The tropics were redefined as an "unstimulating environment" (p. 38) where it would be impossible to sustain "European and American energy, initiative, persistence, and other qualities upon which we so much pride ourselves" (p. 41). Not surprisingly, Huntington found that the level of white energy in northern Australia was generally dismally low, causing him to express his reservations about white settlement there. "Man", according to Huntington, was "much more closely dependent upon nature than he has realized"

---

[27] Cosmos, 'Correspondence—White Australia Policy', *Medical Journal of Australia*, 1915, ii: 43–4, p. 43.

[28] R J A Berry, 'Correspondence—White Australia Policy', *Medical Journal of Australia* , 1915, ii: 93.

[29] I plan to discuss elsewhere the congruence of the older style of medical reasoning with an evolutionary anthropology that was emerging in Australia during this period. The contribution of historians to this discourse on race and environment also deserves investigation, but not here. It is worth noting, though, that the liberal historian and politician Charles H Pearson had written his influential *National Life and Character: A Forecast* (London, Macmillian, 1893) while at Melbourne University. In this book he predicted that "the black and yellow belt, which always encircles the globe between the Tropics, will extend its area, and deepen its color with time". Pearson's work influenced Theodore Roosevelt, William Gladstone, and Houston Stewart Chamberlain. During the parliamentary debate on the Immigration Restriction Bill, Edmund Barton, the first Prime Minister, quoted two passages from Pearson's book to justify efforts to hold back coloured races. Alfred Deakin, Australia's second Prime Minister, later praised Pearson for first warning of the "Yellow Peril to Caucasian civilization, creeds, and politics" (quoted in J M Tregenza, *Professor of Democracy*, Melbourne, Melbourne University Press, 1968, p. 234).

[30] Ellsworth Huntington, *Civilization and Climate*, New Haven, Yale University Press, 1915, p. v. For Huntington's defence of his Australian predictions, see 'Natural selection and climate in northern Australia', *Economic Record*, 1929, **5**: 185–201; and in response, C H Wickens, 'Dr Huntington and low lattitudes', *Economic Record*, 1930, **6**: 123–7; and R W Cilento, 'Rejoinder to Professor Huntington', *Economic Record*, 1930, **6**: 127–32. (Wickens was the Commonwealth statistician.)

Warwick Anderson

(p. 298). Inspired by Huntington's work, Griffith Taylor, then at Sydney University and later professor of geography at Toronto, constructed a "white race climograph" to delimit the physiological tropics in northern Australia.[31]

But it would be wrong to assume that all geographers were environmental determinists. For example, J W Gregory, the professor of geology at Melbourne (and later at Glasgow), had learnt much from his colleagues in the Melbourne medical faculty. When he was appointed in 1900 he was already well-known for his book that had demonstrated a great rift valley through east Africa. His exploratory zeal led him to spend as much time off the beaten track as in the classroom, and from one of these excursions had come his influential book *The Dead Heart of Australia*. As a result of his study of Australian conditions, he predicted that the whole of the country would eventually be occupied by a healthy white race. In 1910, from Glasgow, he wrote that even in tropical Queensland the white children were "not weak anaemic degenerates, while the increased output of sugar since the deportation of the Kanakas shows that white men are willing and able to work there".[32] This achievement had required isolation from inferior tropical races. Later, in his book *The Menace of Colour*, Gregory would expatiate on the dangers to health not from a foreign environment but from contact with disease-dealing coloured races.[33]

But to a large extent, all these environmental arguments—whether advocated by doctors or geographers—hinged on the definition of "tropical". Just as a racial typology was difficult to define out of a mass of individual peculiarities, so too were the simplifications necessary in the classification of an environment controversial. Books of adventure and travel described the northern coast as a place of impenetrable jungle, mangrove swamps, and unrelenting heat.[34] Others pointed to a cartographic demarcation. Thus Frederick Goldsmith at the 1902 Australasian Medical Congress had observed that "taking the tropic of Capricorn as the dividing line, more than one third of the continent of Australia lies within the tropics".[35] But this definition did not coincide with isothermal charts, so other medical doctors suggested that the

---

[31] Thomas Griffith Taylor, *The Control of Settlement by Humidity and Temperatures*, Melbourne, Commonwealth Bureau of Meteorology, 1916; idem, 'Geographical factors concerning the settlement of tropical Australia', *Proceedings of the Royal Geographical Society of Queensland*, 1917, 32/33: 1–64; and idem, 'The Distribution of Future White Settlement: A World Survey based on Physiographic Data', *Geographical Review*, 1922, 12: 375–402. On Taylor, see J M Powell, 'National Identity and the Gifted Immigrant: A Note on T. Griffith Taylor, 1880–1963', *Journal of Intercultural Studies*, 1981, 2: 43–54; and idem, 'Protracted reconciliation: society and the environment', in Roy MacLeod (ed.), *The Commonwealth of Science: ANZAAS and the Scientific Enterprise in Australasia, 1888–1988*, Melbourne, Oxford University Press, 1988, pp. 249–71.

[32] J W Gregory, 'White Labor in Tropical Agriculture: A great Australian Experiment', *The Nineteenth Century*, 1910, 67: 368–80, p. 379. On Gregory, see David Branagan and Blaine Lim, 'J.W. Gregory, traveller in the dead heart', *Historical Records of Australian Science*, 1984, 6: 71–84.

[33] J W Gregory, *The Menace of Colour*, London, Seeley Service, 1925.

[34] See, for example, Alfred Searcy, *In Australian Tropics*, London, Kegan Paul Trench Trubner, 1907. Searcy, a collector of customs at Darwin, did not believe that "white men should actively engage in the cultivation of tropical products on the coast, or rivers, or swamps", for he was "of the opinion that that can only be carried out by coloured labour", p. 366.

[35] F Goldsmith, 'The Necessity for the Study of Tropical Medicine in Australia', *Transactions of the Intercolonial Medical Congress of Australasia*, 6th session, 1902, Hobart, John Vail, 1903, pp. 178–9, on p. 178. See also G H Frodsham, *A Bishop's Pleasaunce*, London, Smith Elder, 1915, p. 238.

tropical zone should be limited to the region between the two mean isotherms of 68 degrees Fahrenheit, a temperature that permitted palms to flourish.[36] Such meteorological mapping still presented difficulties. One geographer pointed out that "the sustained high tropical temperatures of our northern areas is not that of the dangerous intensity created by the more humid conditions of the tropics".[37] So just how "tropical" were the Australian tropics? No one could agree. Sir James Barrett, ever a staunch promoter of white settlement in the north, dismissed this geographical pedantry: "The tropics has generally been associated with a temperature of 75 degrees in winter. The whole of Australia is below 75 degrees in winter; at least two-thirds, if not three-fourths, is below 70 degrees in summer; so the region which can properly be termed 'tropical' is comparatively small".[38]

For tropical pessimism about the planting of a healthy white race in the north to compel assent it was necessary, first, for the "tropics" to exist, and second, for this type of environment to produce degeneration and disease. The first proposition was uncertain, and the second came to appear increasingly suspect.

Mobilizing Pathology

Tropical pessimists in the early twentieth century generally focused on an environmentally determined lowered white resistance rather than on increased exposure to tropical disease. The foreign environment, they argued, rendered formerly robust whites degenerate and vulnerable to disease organisms; it no longer was thought, even by older medical doctors, actually to give rise to specific disease. But this persisting concern with disposition—while not exactly heretical—was increasingly out of step with a new medical enthusiasm for tracing each exciting cause of tropical disease. Modern medical scientists were less interested in adaptation and adjustment to disease environments, and more concerned with the control of an animated disease fauna, with the reform or circumvention of nature through medicalized culture. Lacking this advanced enthusiasm for tracing patterns of biological agency and transmission, the older doctors, along with most evolutionary anthropologists and geographers, had come to sound decidedly old-fashioned and irrelevant by 1920. A geographical perspective on disease by this time had been reduced to an indefensibly dated concentration on constitutional disposition. As a result, medical pessimism about a white conquest of the tropics seemed ever more spurious.[39]

If the chief medical concern was now the presence of distinctive tropical disease organisms, then there was not much to worry about. It had been clear for some time that no matter how uncomfortable one felt in northern Australia, no matter

---

[36] Anton Breinl, 'Influence of Climate, Disease and Surroundings on the White Race living in the Tropics', *Medical Journal of Australia*, 1915, i: 595–600, p. 595.

[37] A Duckworth, 'Notes on a "White Australia"', *Journal and Proceedings of the Royal Society of New South Wales*, 1910, **44**: 226–51, p. 250.

[38] James Barrett in 'Tropical Australia Discussion', *Transactions of the Australasian Medical Congress*, 11th session, 1920, Brisbane, A J Cumming, 1921, p. 63.

[39] On the development of this critique in contemporary United States tropical medicine and public health, see Warwick Anderson, 'Colonial Pathologies: American Medicine in the Philippines, 1898–1920', PhD dissertation, University of Pennsylvania, 1992.

Warwick Anderson

how far beyond Taylor's "white race climograph" one had ventured, there was little risk of meeting a tropical disease organism. This is not to claim that none existed. Joseph Bancroft in Queensland in 1876 had isolated the adult filarial worm; and in the early 1900s, his son Thomas described the development of *filaria* larvae in mosquitoes, and also incriminated *Aedes egypti* as the vector of dengue.[40] Between 1900 and 1902 at Port Darwin, Frederick Goldsmith had encountered a few cases of filariasis and dengue; and some of his patients had malaria, dysentery, beriberi, or leprosy. But he admitted that distinctively tropical diseases were still scarce in the north.[41] In a series of disease surveys of Queensland and the Northern Territory in 1910, 1911 and 1915, Dr Anton Breinl confirmed that tropical diseases, with the exception of hookworm, were rare and easily controlled with attention to personal hygiene. Virtually all of the supposed malaria he encountered turned out to be the sort that comes from glass bottles.[42]

But there remained that old canard: racial degeneration and increased susceptibility to disease. "The most prominent arguments advanced against the colonization of tropical Australia by a white race", observed Dr J S C Elkington in 1905, "have been those of probable ill-health and racial deterioration". Elkington, the son of a Melbourne University history professor, and a bellicose nationalist and Nietzschean, was then Tasmania's chief health officer, though in the 1920s he became the federal director of tropical public health. In his paper, *Tropical Australia: Is it Suitable for a Working White Race?*, published by the federal parliament, Elkington pointed out that tropical disease in Australia was so rare that "its eventual extinction is mainly a question of money". But the effects of an allegedly tropical climate "uncomplicated with malaria, bad diet, and other influences adverse to health and longevity, have never been thoroughly ascertained". Still, Elkington was sure of a few things. "The co-existence of a considerable native population undergoing the natural penalties of their insanitary ways of living will, of course, increase the danger to white residents." In the context of the new white Australia policy, one can see where this is heading. "On the whole", continued Elkington, "the evidence is against the half-caste, and the experience of other countries goes to show that it is advisable to keep the white stock pure, particularly with respect to the black races, and to the less vigorous brown peoples".[43]

Sir James Barrett, a prolific writer on tropical medicine, empire affairs, immigration, decimalization, neglected children, venereal disease, pure milk, baby clinics, national parks, and a world calendar, in 1910 joined in the academic clamour for more research. "Is there any reason", he asked in the columns of the Melbourne *Argus*, "to think that mere heat will cause physical deterioration? This is the question that

---

[40] E Ford, 'The Bancroft Memorial Lecture: The Life and Influence of Joseph Bancroft', *Medical Journal of Australia*, 1961, i: 153–70.

[41] Goldsmith, op. cit., note 35 above.

[42] For a summary, see Anton Breinl and W J Young, 'Tropical Australia and its Settlement', *Annals of Tropical Medicine and Parasitology*, 1920, 13: 351–412.

[43] J S C Elkington, *Tropical Australia: Is it Suitable for a Working White Race?*, Melbourne, Government Printer, 1905. For other accounts which touch on medical aspects of the White Australia policy, see Evans, op. cit., note 9 above; and Michael Roe, 'The Establishment of the Australian Department of Health: Its Background and Significance', *Historical Studies* (Australia), 1976, 67: 176–92.

requires answer by the experimental method. The probabilities are that life in such conditions will be vigorous, active and normal; but the experiment has never been made, or in Australia even tried, or seriously considered".[44] Barrett, a utopian rationalist if ever there was one, went on to contend that the scientific method should underpin politics and social planning, and the new tropical medicine would explain the past and predict the future of a white Australia. He wrote to the minister for home affairs, Senator J H Keating on the matter. "It was in the interests of science and their own country", he claimed, "that they had asked for an attempt to be made to secure a scientific solution to a problem by no means settled. It had been said that the Anglo-Saxon race could not live in the tropics". (Of course Barrett previously had argued that little if any of Australia was in fact tropical, but clearly the notion that disease and degeneration could derive from a mismatch of race and environment retained some rhetorical force.) In reply, the minister, later the author of *White Australia: Men and Measures in its Making*, noted that the work of Gorgas in the Panama Canal "was an object-lesson to the world that medical science properly applied to existing conditions could convert and transform them so as to make it possible for white people to continue living in places where, without the application of medical science, ... it would not be possible".[45]

Melbourne medical scientists, desperate for government support for laboratory research, thus were able to use the dispositionist remnants of a medical geography, which they thought was trivial or inconsequential, to establish Australia's first institute for medical research.[46] The campaign to establish the institute has been described elsewhere.[47] In 1913, Sir William McGregor, expert in tropical medicine and governor of Queensland, officially opened the Australian Institute of Tropical Medicine (AITM) in Townsville.[48] The first director, Anton Breinl, an expert in the chemotherapy of trypanosomiasis, had arrived from the Liverpool School of Tropical Medicine a few years before, and he was soon joined by a parasitologist, a bacteriologist, and a biochemist. The institute in 1930 was incorporated into Sydney

---

[44] James Barrett, 'White Men for the North. The Problem of Colonization, a Plea for Research Work', *Melbourne Argus*, 17 September, 1910, p. 4. See also Barrett, *The Twin Ideals: An Educated Commonwealth*, 2 vols, London, H K Lewis, 1918. On Barrett, see Michael Roe, *Nine Australian Progressives: Vitalism in Bourgeois Social Thought, 1890–1960*, St Lucia, University of Queensland Press, 1984, chapter 3.

[45] 'Tropical Australia: Deputation from Congress to the Prime Minister', *Transactions of the Australasian Medical Congress*, 8th session, 1908, 4 vols, Melbourne, J Kemp, 1909, vol. 4, pp. 101 and 103.

[46] In 1903 the University staff included five fellows of the Royal Society, but they were over-burdened with teaching and had little research equipment. When Richard Berry took up his post in the anatomy department in 1906 he complained that the building "contained literally nothing, not even a skeleton, though later I discovered quite a lot in the cupboard". Like many others, he felt that research "was practically deleted from university work" (quoted in K F Russell, *The Melbourne Medical School, 1862–1962*, Melbourne, Melbourne University Press, 1972, p. 104).

[47] Lori Harloe, 'White Man in Tropical Australia: Anton Breinl and the Australian Institute of Tropical Medicine', BA (hons) thesis, James Cook University of North Queensland, 1987; Harloe, op. cit., note 3 above; Douglas, op. cit., note 3 above; and Robert Douglas, 'One Day in the Medical Life of Queensland: The Opening of the Australian Institute of Tropical Medicine', in John Pearn (ed.), *Pioneer Medicine in Australia*, Brisbane, Amphion Press, 1988, pp. 135–44.

[48] William McGregor, 'Some Problems of Tropical Medicine', *Lancet*, 1900, ii: 1055–61. McGregor had previously been governor of Nigeria. See R B Joyce, *Sir William McGregor*, Melbourne, Oxford University Press, 1971.

University as the School of Public Health and Tropical Medicine, now the Australian Institute of Health and Welfare.[49]

"Only careful and detailed research carried on in the populated coastal districts of tropical Australia, where several generations have been reared", wrote Breinl in 1914, "will indicate whether the great experiment of populating tropical Australia by a white working community, can be accomplished".[50] But of course it did not take nearly that long. In 1920, the subject of the Australasian Medical Congress was 'Tropical Australia'. After reviewing the physiological research of the AITM, the conference declared that "the opinion of the medical practitioners present was overwhelmingly in favor of the suitability of North Queensland for the successful implantation of a working white race". They found no "inherent or insuperable obstacles" in the way of white occupation, and thought that on microbial grounds, "the absence of semi-civilized colored peoples in northern Australia simplifies the problem very greatly".[51] In an address to the Congress, W A Osborne, the professor of physiology at Melbourne, author of *Science and National Efficiency* and of *The Laboratory and Other Poems*, biographer of the bushranger Captain Moonlight and master of the art of boomerang throwing, confirmed that "one particular advantage is the absence of a large native population, for such always acts as a reservoir of infection from which epidemics spill over into the surrounding white population". Accordingly, "the white Australia policy may become more difficult, but it will become more desirable". Within this continental citadel, "may we look to improved conditions and eugenic safeguards rejuvenating the white races and starting a new epoch in their progress".[52]

Thus tropical settlement and development was, the Congress declared, "fundamentally a question of applied public health in the modern sense".[53] Dr J H L Cumpston, the first director of the federal Department of Health and among those progressives "who dream of leading this young nation of ours into a paradise of

---

[49] Douglas, op. cit., note 3 above; and Lori Harloe, 'From North to South: The Translocation of the Australian Institute of Tropical Medicine', in Pearn (ed.), op. cit., note 47 above, pp. 145–58.

[50] Anton Breinl, 'The Influence of Climate, Diseases and Surroundings on the White Race living in the Tropics', in J W Springthorpe (ed.), *Therapeutics, Dietetics and Hygiene*, 2 vols, Melbourne, James Little, 1914, vol. 2, p. 996. Elsewhere in his remarkable textbook—which mixes the latest physiology with the race theories of Charles Pearson and Houston Stewart Chamberlain—Springthorpe, a lecturer in the Melbourne Medical Faculty, implied that results were already available: "Contrary to previous beliefs", he reported, "the acclimated non-alcoholic European can maintain mental and bodily activity without any inhibitory influence", vol. 1, p. 214.

[51] 'Tropical Australia Discussion', *Transactions of the Australasian Medical Congress*, 11th session, 1920, Brisbane, A J Cumming, 1921, pp. 39–69, p. 45. See also A Grenfell Price, *White Settlers in the Tropics*, New York, American Geographical Society, 1939; R W Cilento, *The White Man in the Tropics with Especial Reference to Australia and its Dependencies*, Melbourne, H J Green, Government Printer, 1925, and idem, 'The Conquest of Climate', *Medical Journal of Australia*, 1933, i: 421–32. (Cilento was a later director of the AITM.) The physiological research of the AITM generally replicated the work of the American Bureau of Science in the Philippines: see Warwick Anderson, '"Where every prospect pleases and only man is vile": Laboratory Medicine as Colonial Discourse', in Vicente L Rafael (ed.), *Discrepant Histories: Translocal Essays on Filipino Cultures*, Philadelphia, Temple University Press, 1995, pp. 83–112.

[52] W A Osborne, 'Physiological Factors in the Development of an Australian Race', *Transactions of the Australasian Medical Congress*, 11th session, 1920, Brisbane, A J Cumming, 1921, pp. 71–82, on pp. 76 and 72.

[53] 'Tropical Australia Discussion', note 51 above, p. 45.

physical perfection",[54] agreed with this formulation. "It is all very well to have a white Australia", he announced, "but it must be kept white. There must be immaculate cleanliness".[55] The working white citizens required ceaseless supervision and discipline. "It is desirable", advised Barrett, "to arrange for several experimental stations, at which settlers could be accommodated. Each station would be under the charge of a health officer".[56] Foucault's "carceral archipelago" in the so-called tropics, perhaps?[57] "In the future", advised Anton Breinl, "the pioneer should not be the settler, but the scientifically trained man".[58]

Conclusion

By 1933, Barrett could confidently assert two medical facts, both antithetical to an older geographical understanding of disease. First: "The colored man working in the tropics has no physiological advantage over the white man, the bodily processes are the *same* in both cases." And second: "If tropical Australia had an indigenous infected population it would be in all probability scourged with tropical diseases."[59] With this anthropomorphic mobilization of pathology, a white Australia finally could be represented as a medical necessity, not just a national goal.

In 1911, the journalist C E W Bean wrote that "Australia is a big blank map, and the whole people is constantly sitting over it like a committee, trying to work out the best way to fill it in".[60] Medical geographies had proposed obstacles to white settlement, but laboratory methods altered this terrain, removing environmental obstacles and constructing in their place a thriving, obedient white citizenry. The demise of environmental determinism had sanctioned the birth of white Australia. Thus medicine was not just a means of knowing a territory, it offered in this case an opportunity to reshape it. As medicine was less obviously part of an environmental discourse, it became more centrally an element in the discourse of modernity and citizenship, where it has remained.

---

[54] J H L Cumpston, 'Presidential Address: Public Health and State Medicine', *Transactions of the Australasian Medical Congress*, 11th session, 1920, Brisbane, A J Cumming, 1921, pp. 77–87, on p. 77.

[55] J H L Cumpston, in 'Tropical Australia Discussion', note 51 above, p. 49.

[56] Sir James Barrett, 'The Problem of the Settlement of Topical Australia',," in idem, *Twin Ideals*, note 44 above, vol. 2, pp. 286–91, on p. 288. See also his 'Tropical Australia', *United Empire*, 1925, 16: 37–43.

[57] Michel Foucault, *Discipline and Punish: The Birth of the Prison*, trans. Alan Sheridan, Harmondsworth, Penguin, 1991.

[58] Anton Breinl, 'The Object and Scope of Tropical Medicine in Australia', *Transactions of the Australasian Medical Congress*, 9th session, 1911, 2 vols, Sydney, W A Gullick, 1913, vol. 1, pp. 524–35, on p. 526. See also his 'Facts and Figures regarding Health and Disease in Northern Australia', *Transactions of the Australasian Medical Congress*, 11th session, 1920, Brisbane, A J Cumming, 1921, pp. 558–69.

[59] Sir James Barrett, 'Tropical Australia', *Australian Quarterly*, 1934, 24: 64–72, p. 72.

[60] C E W Bean, *The Dreadnought of the Darling*, London, Alston Rivers, 1911, p. 318.

[6]

Between Fixity and Fantasy: Assessing the Spatial Impact of Colonial Urban Dualism

William Cunningham Bissell

Abstract
This essay seeks to historicize shifting views of colonial urbanism since the 1960s. Dualistic oppositions once dominated scholarly understandings of colonial cities, but more recently postcolonial visions of hybridity and indeterminacy have come to the fore. More than shifts in academic paradigms are at stake; indeed, such divergent discourses raise critical questions as to how we should interpret urban forms and processes more generally. Instead of championing either side, the author seeks to bring these ostensibly divergent perspectives together, arguing for a more integrated historical and analytic approach to urban landscapes. Rather than opposing colonial accounts and postcolonial narratives, materialism and discourse, social sciences and humanities, the real and the ideal, we need to articulate these frameworks in order to grasp the actual complexities of colonial urban dynamics. Analyzing flawed urban interventions in East Africa, the author shows how colonial dualities were often asserted but rarely imposed, simultaneously informed by fantasies and yet all too real.

Keywords
colonialism, dual cities, urban planning, postcolonial space, Africa

The scholarship on colonial cities has come quite a long way. Indeed, since the 1970s, what was once a rather specialized interest (and sparsely covered topic) has grown into a burgeoning literature—more than enough, as Anthony King has noted, to fill several graduate seminars, cutting across a broad range of fields from history to anthropology, geography, cultural studies, architecture, urban planning, and area studies.[1] Given the pace and direction of recent growth, it seems worthwhile at this point in time to step back and assess where things stand, seeking to historicize colonial urban analysis so as to understand where we've come from and to lay out new directions for future work. More than just retrospective interest is involved here; indeed, by examining the shifting parameters of discourse within the field it becomes possible to highlight key epistemological and methodological issues while also elucidating crucial aspects of colonial state, space, and society that have remained somewhat obscured.

From the outset, urban scholars have devoted critical attention to colonial sites as zones of difference and division. Less noted, however, is the way that the terms of discussion about these

---
[1]Lafayette College, Easton, PA, USA

distinctions have shifted significantly in recent years. From the 1960s onward, dualism (in both social and spatial senses) was treated as a defining feature of colonial cities; analysts discussed various modalities of segregation and separation as quintessential hallmarks of these sites. But as the range of colonial urban studies has grown in both scope and detail of late, a more ambiguous picture has emerged. As with the discussion of colonialism more generally, so too with colonial space: the outlines of the phenomenon no longer appear quite so definite or distinct as they once seemed. In particular, many scholars have begun to question the reality of the dual city model, arguing that this problematic conceals much more than it actually reveals. But while the impact of colonial dualism has been cast in doubt, its meaning and significance has yet to be fully explored. If colonial milieus were hardly so neatly divided as it once was assumed, how exactly do we account for the dramatic shift in perspective that has taken place with the rise of postcolonial studies? Evidence for colonial dualism used to be widely cited in the literature and with a high degree of certainty. Did an earlier generation of urbanists and scholars simply get it wrong? If so, can we say with absolute confidence that recent invocations of colonial hybridity and indeterminacy rest on more unassailable epistemological grounds? On what basis could such a claim be advanced?

A "Definitive Look": Colonial Division and Duality

Colonial cities of the modern imperial age were spread across a vast geographical space, with widely divergent social forms, cultural contexts, power dynamics, environments, and modes of economy. In the face of this diversity, it is important to keep in mind that colonial spaces were never singular or monolithic, conforming to a single type. At the same time, numerous theorists have found it useful over the years to establish common features, laying out the distinctive patterns of colonial urbanism on a wider scale.[2] And indeed from the beginnings of scholarship on the subject, there seemed to be a remarkably widespread and deep consensus about the dualistic nature of colonial space and society. In fact, it proves difficult to find even a single account that does not echo this finding in one form or another.

In the mid-1960s, Janet Abu-Lughod first took note of what she described as a widespread phenomenon: "The major metropolis in almost every newly industrializing nation is not a single unified city but, in fact, two quite different cities." Given the prevalence of this pattern, she wrote, it was truly remarkable that it had remained "almost unstudied."[3] Drawing on Cairo as her example, she argued that by the end of the nineteenth century, the city had been split into two zones, with separate but juxtaposed communities, cultures, and temporalities of development. "To the east lay the native city, still essentially preindustrial in technology, social structure and way of life; to the west lay the 'colonial' city with its steam-powered techniques, its faster pace and wheeled traffic, and its European identification."[4] These cleavages were by no means restricted to Cairo or even to the British imperial sphere. Indeed, as the literature soon reflected, sharp spatial and social divisions were characteristic of colonial cities in the French domain as well.

In Morocco Hubert Lyautey initiated a set of influential urban policies that emphasized both spatial containment of indigenes and paternalist preservation. Existing urban spaces (the "casbah," the medina) would be reified as cultural monuments to tradition and changed as little as possible. Surrounding them, and set up in pointed contrast, would be *villes nouvelles*, modern cities for European settlers, planned and structured with wide boulevards, ornamental parks and gardens, and the latest infrastructure: an object lesson in European modernity and the alleged march of progress.[5] Moreover, this model proved influential throughout much of the French African sphere, as Raymond Betts observed: "The development of dual cities, such as Casablanca and Fez in Morocco, where European and 'native' lived worlds apart, was seen by more than one French West African colonial administrator as a system worth emulating" in Dakar and elsewhere.[6]

In the Belgian Congo, Jean La Fontaine identified strikingly similar colonial urban patterns, as did Phyllis Martin in the context of Brazzaville.[7]

Colonial dualism was also found to be characteristic of most of British East and Southern Africa.[8] Indeed, throughout the continent, segregation and separation of Africans and Europeans, colonized and colonizers, black and white, seemed to be the inflexible rule.

> The period preceding the First World War gave colonial cities their definitive look: . . . most cities in Africa became characterized by a sharp contrast between the "white city" and the African districts or so-called "villages." This dualism . . . became the main element in the definition of colonial cities. At the same time, it symbolized colonial domination and gave a concrete aspect to the duality of colonial society by creating a visual distance between the colonizers and the colonized.[9]

Few analysts evinced any equivocation about the widespread reality of colonial dualism. These statements were presented with absolute confidence, based on ostensibly incontrovertible evidence.[10] "The colonial pattern of the twentieth century set African and European urban communities physically apart," Maynard Swanson declared in a classic essay on sanitation and the origins of urban apartheid.[11] In terms of spatial layout and social form, the apartheid city was often depicted as a paradigmatic model of colonial cities elsewhere, structured by rigid oppositions between center and periphery, white metropolis and native location.[12] From an array of specific cases, a cumulative portrait emerged: as David Simon concluded in a conceptual overview in the mid-1980s, "Systematic segregation of the indigenes . . . from colonists was ubiquitous where the former were not exterminated, and one of the dominant structural features of colonial cities."[13]

If the dual city paradigm has been generalized throughout much of the urban scholarship on colonial Africa, it is crucial to note that its locus classicus lay elsewhere. Outside the context of South Africa and a series of coastal enclaves, European colonialism generally came to the continent rather late and drew upon prior experience in other parts of the globe. In the British African sphere, South Asia loomed especially large, providing an accumulated corpus of municipal theory and practice for officials to deploy in new settings. Sanitation and hygiene, segregation and spatial layout, among other forms of emergent biopower, were especially significant in this regard. In the wake of the Indian Rebellion of 1857, the British responded with harsh punitive measures in cities such as Delhi or Lucknow, razing indigenous quarters in revenge and driving through wide streets or open spaces for heightened security and surveillance. At the same time, they drew back more into "civil lines," cantonments, or hill stations, as fears about security were joined by sanitary preoccupations—attempting to reduce high rates of morbidity by isolating military troops or other Europeans in higher, drier, more separate quarters.[14]

It was, however, in the three Presidency cities of the East India Company—Madras, Bombay (Mumbai), and Calcutta—where sociospatial dualism seemed most marked, defining colonial urbanism in the South Asian context. Indeed, research in these sites has led to the formation of what Rebecca Brown calls the "black town/fort paradigm," which became a "central and defining element for all studies of colonial urban areas."[15] This paradigm figures prominently in a host of studies on Indian architecture and urban planning. Most note the division between the European fort and an Indian quarter, or between the white city and a black town, separated by an open *maidan*. And like Abu-Lughod, these accounts highlight the neat symmetry between spatial arrangements and relations of power. In Bombay, writes Miriam Dossal, "the two quarters represented spatially a highly unequal division of power, of dominant-dependent relationships that existed between colonizer and colonized, between the British and the Indians. It was a town divided and the cleavage ran through."[16]

Deconstructing Certainties, Dissolving Boundaries

It is precisely the apparent starkness and clarity of these sociospatial divisions that recent scholars have begun to call into question, subjecting them to increasingly sharp scrutiny. The terms of debate are anything but regional or localized, reflective of much broader trends. In a prescient survey of developments in colonial studies, John Comaroff has discussed how older accounts of colonialism, whether framed by modernization narratives or Marxist critiques, have been displaced by more revisionist views predicated on notions of contingency, indeterminacy, and uncertainty. Even among those not committed to postmodernist perspectives, "dialectics have given way to dialogics, political economy to poetics, class conflict to consumption, the violence of the gun to the violation of the text, world historical material processes to local struggles over signs and styles, European domination to post-Hegelian hybridity."[17] While Comaroff suggests this might be something of an overstatement, a broad range of academic discourse on colonial relations seems to bear out his position. Instead of fixed identities, one increasingly hears of fluid subject positions, negotiated and shifting. Rather than clear oppositions (of race, class, or gender), scholars stress the interstitial and in-between. And in place of the categorical authority of colonial rule, one finds its instabilities, anxieties, and tensions.[18]

These varied critiques carry obvious implications for the study of colonial cities and especially the widespread acceptance of dual city forms. As Ira Bashkow argues, recent work in anthropology, history, and postcolonial studies has greatly complicated our sense of colonial encounters and their consequences. Colonial power relations, he concludes, simply "did not fit the Manichaean image of a morally unambiguous opposition between colonizing master and colonized victim, domination and powerlessness."[19] This stark model of "dominance-dependence" used to provide a crucial underpinning for dualistic urban models in the colonial context. Having the capacity to create separate and divided cities implies that Europeans possessed the ability to command and shape space according to plan. And as Brenda Yeoh points out, this schema largely treats the colonial city as a creation of the colonizers, devaluing or dismissing indigenous agency, spatial practice, and urban contestation.[20] Hence scholars of colonial space have started to draw the lines of dual cities somewhat differently, emphasizing blurred or ambiguous boundaries. While there are numerous examples, Zeynep Çelik's study of Algiers under French rule exemplifies this trend quite well. Behind the "clear message conveyed by the image of dual cities," she asserts, there are "more complicated implications." Looking beneath the surface, she finds that "the architecture of colonialism reveals levels of ambivalence and hybridity while persistently maintaining the overriding theme of difference."[21]

If treatments of the dual colonial city were especially prominent in the Indian context, it should come as little surprise that scholars of South Asia have taken a leading role in formulating a substantial critique. Brown, for instance, notes the pervasiveness of the dual city model in virtually all South Asian studies of the colonial city. While the black town/fort dichotomy might seem correct on the surface, she writes, in actuality it occludes critical features of colonial space. The hegemony of dualistic images lies at the root of the problem, blocking or masking other interpretive possibilities. In her work on Patna, Brown focuses on "ruptures" in the fabric of binary oppositions, such as Europeans who resided in the "black town," the existence of mixed graveyards, and the intrusion of the suburbs. Her intention is not to destroy colonial dichotomies or completely break them down; instead, she seeks in her research "a more nuanced approach, digging within that seemingly rigid and complete structure to find its interruptions, intrusions, and instabilities."[22]

In her analysis of the limits of "white town" in colonial Calcutta, Swati Chattopadhyay echoes and extends many of these arguments. She too starts out by noting the ubiquity of references to dual European and Indian cities, arguing that this perspective has obscured our understanding of colonial space. "By emphasizing the duality of black and white," she observes, "one misses the idea that the critical aspect of colonial cities resided not in the clarity of this duality, but in the tension of blurred boundaries between the two." Calcutta was nothing if not heterogeneous, not only in terms of street layout but even at the level of individual structures. As she remarks, "The landscape of colonial Calcutta was too complex to be usefully described in terms of the duality of black and white towns. The city consisted of overlapping geographies and conceptions of space and territory, both indigenous and foreign, that were constantly negotiated. Not surprisingly, the line of demarcation between the black and white towns shifted depending on the context and the perception of the observer."[23]

If, as Chattopadhyay suggests, colonial cities can no longer be "usefully" described as dual in nature, how can we make sense of the fact that so many previous scholars found this discourse not only useful but insightful and even compelling? What exactly has changed over time, and how do we account for what seems to be on the surface a rather abrupt reversal of interpretation? Did earlier thinkers simply misinterpret the evidence, or were they instead perhaps led astray by ideology? If we assert that they overlooked signs of ambiguity or indeterminacy in the urban landscape, how can we be so sure that we actually see things more clearly now? By remaining silent on these questions, recent analysts run the risk of producing a critique that cannot account for (or even acknowledge) the historical conditions of its own possibility. If we do not attempt to historically situate more recent accounts in terms of their antecedents, assessing both continuities and differences, then crucial questions about epistemological shifts, changing conditions of urban analysis and interpretation, and alterations in research methods will remain beyond our grasp.

More is at stake here than changing currents of academic fashion. Nor is it sufficient to characterize divergent views of the colonial city in terms of a Kuhnian paradigm shift—modernist clarities giving way to more postmodernist concerns. The situation is—perhaps unsurprisingly, given the historical moment in which we live—a bit more "complicated." For her own part, Chattopadhyay suggests one possible way to address these questions when she writes that older dualistic readings of colonial Calcutta "were based on scant evidence," static interpretations of urban plans, and a "lack of critical attention" to changes in urban density over time.[24] Brown, on the other hand, offers a somewhat different approach, raising a number of issues that merit further scrutiny. At "first glance," she writes, even Madras (the "ur" colonial city) seems to confirm the validity of the dual city model. But she then proceeds to cite a range of evidence that ostensibly undermines the solidity of the paradigm. She points out that Europeans as well as Indians resided in the so-called black town (Georgetown), as a careful analysis of period maps can show. Moreover, "garden estate" suburbs sprouted early on in the city's history, showing the desire of Europeans to segregate themselves away from the more intermixed city center. But in her view, none of this counterevidence manages to significantly alter the whole "black town/fort" dichotomy: "The strength and endurance of the paradigm lies in the constitutive role it plays in the designation of colonial city, not its connection to some sort of reality 'on the ground,'" she concludes. Something more than empirical knowledge was at play here: colonizers, after all, were presumably quite familiar with the feel and look of the cityscape; they were historical witnesses to its ambiguous and intermixed character as they went about their daily rounds. These observers could have described the city more accurately, drawing on other terms—for example, characterizing it as a mixed mercantile space. But to Brown, this possibility could never really be actualized: "Given the context of colonialism, however, none of these options could be articulated by the colonizers: The discursive need for stark division dictated the division between the black town and the fort, regardless of the pattern on the ground."[25]

In many respects I find myself in substantial agreement with these critics, altogether sympathetic with the goal of unearthing the complexity and heterogeneity of colonial urban spaces. But by "blurring the boundaries," I'm also concerned that we might be at risk of losing sight of crucial distinctions that are needed for a full and complex understanding of colonial urban landscapes and processes. Brown's account raises a number of questions that remain unaddressed: was the "discursive need" of colonizers really so tenacious and strong that it was able to overwrite reality on the ground, inscribing visions of totalizing dualism where none truly existed? What about the "discursive needs"—or at least the alternative urban visions and practices—of indigenous residents? Did they count for nothing or remain immaterial? And while colonizers might have been prompted by ideological needs or desires to trumpet dualistic visions, subsequent scholars of colonial space certainly were not driven by the same imperatives or impulses. Why then did they find dualism on such a wide scale, evincing little or no doubt about the reality of the phenomenon? How do we make sense of these back and forth shifts between dualism and its opposite, presence and absence, the material and the ideal?

Writing with his usual acuity, Anthony King has praised postcolonial studies for its strong emphasis on the importance of grasping the nuances of cultural forms and processes. At the same time, though, he argues that postcolonial work has been "inadequately interdisciplinary" and "insufficiently conscious of its origins."[26] In assessing the differences between an earlier generation of scholarship on colonialism and more contemporary postcolonial research, he provides important insights into the sociology of knowledge, contextualizing and situating these discourses historically. By and large, he notes, earlier colonial scholarship tended to be located in the social sciences (anthropology, development studies, sociology, political science, and the like). These researchers included mostly Western academics (largely white and male) who either had some experience with the colonies or were concerned with problems confronting the so-called new nations emerging from colonial rule. They wrote for specific (often rather narrow) disciplinary audiences, and questions relating to social, political, and economic development tended to hold sway—whether from the modernization perspective or later Marxian and world-systems critiques. At the time, King notes, "the social sciences were much less interested in culture, and the humanities, as a whole, were much less interested in colonialism."[27] Over a decade later, postcolonial studies began to alter this dynamic, putting the humanities and culture at the forefront, emphasizing linkages between knowledge and power, and bringing more diverse voices to the academic table—people of color, women, scholars with origins in the developing world but now resident in former metropoles, located in between, or moving back and forth (reconfiguring both "centers" and "peripheries," as well as the relations between them).

Implicit in King's account is a series of contrasts or antinomies—between colonial studies and postcolonial accounts, the social sciences and humanities, material relations and discourse, the "real world" of the city and its cultural representation, or structure and symbol. He doesn't set out to champion either side or reify the distinctions between them. By supplying historical context and sociological distinctions, King allows us to pinpoint the strengths and limitations of these successive academic frameworks—realizing, in a sense, how each discourse is reciprocally incomplete without the other. If earlier colonial studies downplayed questions of culture and identity, postcolonial texts have all too often blithely ignored the very real spatial, architectural, and material contexts that shape cultural worlds and social imaginaries. Championing one model over the other does not get us very far; indeterminacy does not stand in for and erase duality. In the wake of colonial studies and the postcolonial response, we cannot be simply satisfied by either/or. The dynamism and complexity of urban sites demand a more imaginative—and integrative—response. The choice here, I want to suggest, is not between an outmoded realist colonial dualism and its more hybrid, inchoate, and postcolonial other. Indeed, these narratives are not so much contradictory or incommensurate as complementary. The challenge is not to set them up as contrasting foils, but to see how they intersect and interact in unexpected ways. By drawing on a detailed specific case—colonial urban Zanzibar—I hope to show how these seemingly divergent visions are in fact two sides of the same coin, informed by different aspects or moments in the same colonial urban landscape. But to do so requires trying to fit the sundered pieces of the puzzle together, questioning the very duality of accounts of colonial dualism.

Historicizing Duality

In attempting to resolve the apparent paradox between modern and postmodern accounts, let us start with an absolutely classic description of the colonial urban sphere:

> The colonial world is a world cut in two. The dividing line, the frontiers are shown by barracks and police stations. . . . The zone where the natives live is not complementary to the zone inhabited by the settlers. The two zones are opposed, but not in the service of a higher unity. . . . No conciliation is possible, for of the two terms, one is superfluous. The settlers' town is a strongly built town, all made of stone and steel. It is a brightly lit town; the streets are covered with asphalt, and the garbage cans swallow all the leavings, unseen, unknown, and hardly thought about. . . . The settlers' town is a well-fed town, an easygoing town; its belly is always full of good things. . . .
>
> The town belonging to the colonized people, or at least the native town, the Negro village, the medina, the reservation, is a place of ill-fame, peopled by men of evil repute. They are born there, it matters little where or how; they die there, it matters not where, nor how. It is a world without spaciousness; men live there on top of each other, and their huts are built one on top of the other. The native town is a hungry town, starved of bread, of meat, of shoes, of coal, of light. The native town is a crouching village, a town on its knees, a town wallowing in the mire.[28]

Within the landscape inscribed by more recent accounts of colonial cities premised on hybridity and indeterminacy, there would seem to be no place for this text. *"No conciliation is possible"*: here, the contrasts could not be more harshly drawn, the oppositions more starkly defined. Intermixture, the fluidity of identity, and the crossing of boundaries seem quite far away, subsumed by all the bristling signs of the militarization of space. This narrative can in no way be construed as the projection of European discursive need. Nor is it the product of a subsequent scholarly misreading. But at the same time, the account cannot be simply taken as a straightforward reflection of material realities on the ground in the colonial city. Something else, something more, is at play here.

The text, of course, comes from Frantz Fanon's *The Wretched of the Earth*, written in the heat of worldwide anticolonial struggles in the 1960s. In his own historical experience, Fanon was intimately familiar with the social forms and spatial dynamics of colonial sites from Martinique to Algiers, and it is hard to believe that he was somehow duped into trumpeting a model of colonial dualism that did not exist (or, alternatively, that he was inventing it out of thin air). Clearly, Fanon is trying here to capture a crucial aspect of colonial experience, something that goes beyond the requirements of memoir, maps, or historical fidelity. His words cannot be readily understood outside of the context of his extensive engagement with anticolonial movements, most closely with regard to the long Algerian war for liberation.

In both his practice and theory, Fanon worked to unveil the deformed and degraded heart of European imperialism, exposing the barbarism at the core of its alleged civilization. He knew well the alterities that colonialism sought to impose, grasped the psychic and material violence involved in these structures of exclusion, and endeavored to find a means of overcoming these divisions. And a crucial part of this effort was to give voice and agency to the colonized, vividly representing their experience and conditions before a global audience. In this sense, the aforementioned passage needs to be read through a different lens. Less a historical description of any specific colonial city whose accuracy can be measured, the passage is a condensed and powerful portrait of what colonialism often looked like from the inside.

It is, in other words, an evocation of colonial experience that viscerally conveys the psychology of the oppressed as they confronted everyday worlds defaced by structures of exclusion and denigration. The text stands as a poetic and compressed distillation that draws from reality even as it does not simply reflect it. It needs to be understood, then, as a particular narrative interpretation, motivated and informed by certain visions and aims, framed by specific experiences and readings, and rooted in the conditions and moment of its own making. Contextualizing Fanon's statement—locating it in time and space—helps us to avoid simply dismissing his claims or reifying them into a general model of truth for the colonial city writ large. We can then begin to grasp how the dual colonial city was formed through the complex interplay of material realities and ideological forms, fixity and fantasy. In this way, a more complex and differentiated reading of the colonial city becomes possible. In order to envision the wider implications of this argument, it is helpful to see what it means in actual practice, delving into the specifics of a particular space.

In the 1960s, very similar Manichaean terms as those deployed by Fanon began to consistently structure representations of colonial urbanism in Zanzibar. Over time, these depictions (which drew on colonial categories, but often reversed their terms and valuations) became solidified through repetition, getting projected far back into the historical past. Nineteenth-century urban forms and relations were reinterpreted according to the ideological categories of what Zanzibaris call the *zama za siasa*, the intensely bitter and contested nationalist politics of the 1950s. If struggles over independence set the stage, the Zanzibar revolution of 1964 served to freeze and set particular views of the city in stone—lasting for well over a generation. As Garth Myers has observed, "most often, the ways in which Zanzibar city's two historic 'sides' are described are synecdoche devices for making comment on the revolution, its causes or its aftermath."[29] The city's past was reworked to legitimate the revolution and its social policies, just as long-term residents were exiled or fled and access to archival sources was tightly restricted. In terms of both popular memory and academic history, the revolution sought to create a rupture or break between the city and its past, and in that gap a hegemonic portrait began to emerge.

Like other accounts of colonial dualism that arose in the 1960s, this revisionist narrative of urban structure in Zanzibar starkly emphasized the divided nature of the city—highlighting the opposition between Stone Town (Mji Mkongwe, literally "old" or "ancient" city) and Ng'ambo, the "other side." As one scholarly text reflected this conventional view in 1965, Zanzibar city "is divided into two parts. Stone Town is the old Arab and Indian city, consisting of tall stone houses separated by narrow streets and alleys: this is the Zanzibar of tourist fame."[30] Building on colonial representations, Stone Town was often depicted as the "city proper," the commercial, ceremonial, and political capital of the islands. It was the symbolic heart of the sultanate, crowned by monumental structures along the seafront, including the Beit el Ajaib (House of Wonders) and Old Fort. This was allegedly the space of the privileged and elite—Arabs, Indians, and Europeans— who occupied stately stone dwellings, rising as high as three and four stories, intricately carved and richly ornamented. Bazaars and central markets, the public baths, parks and gardens, cathedrals and mosques were all located here, concentrating cultural and civic amenities (see Figure 1).

To the east, separated from the urban core by a tidal creek, stood Ng'ambo, which was represented as Stone Town's antithesis: a sprawling "native" quarter, built out rather than up, where the poor, ex-slaves and the working class, lived in single-story, impermanent mud and wattle "huts." Ng'ambo was often glossed as "African" in character as opposed to the more "Eastern" or "Arab" character of Stone Town.[31] It was described as a space of marginalization and deprivation, where the African majority was stigmatized and segregated. This zone (which included by

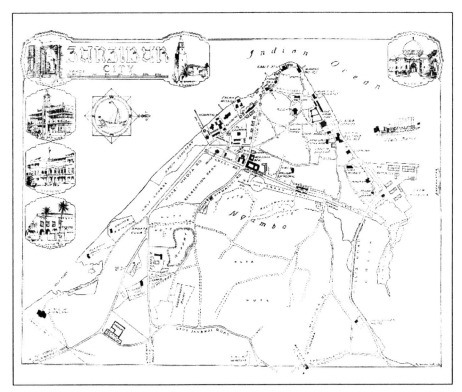

Figure 1. Map of Zanzibar City, contrasting colonial monuments in Stone Town with blankness of Ng'ambo and "huts," drafted by P. C. Harris, 1952
Source: R. H. Crofton, *Zanzibar Affairs, 1914-1933* (London: Francis Edwards, 1953).

far the majority of the city's geographic area and population) was mostly deprived of municipal services and resources under colonialism and branded as a "planless warren of indigency."[32] If Stone Town was depicted as center, Ng'ambo was cast as its quintessential other: peripheral, poor, and unplanned, as a colonial-era guide to the city amply reveals:

> But if the visitor should cross the Creek he steps into a different world or to be more precise, into a different town. Between the water-front and the Creek is the "Stone Town" of two-, three- and four-storeyed houses. Beyond the Creek lies Ngambo—"the Other Side"—a thousand acres of light sandy soil, alternating between narrow open spaces and hectic crowded quarters of African houses. You need a compass and a clear head to penetrate it, for the huts straggle around, conforming to no coherent scheme, a confusing maze of endless twisting alleyways. Here live thirty thousand people, mostly Africans, over half the population of the whole Town. It is by no means all a slum.[33]

Like many stereotypes, this portrayal contains at least a grain of truth, but it also masks and distorts a much more complex and nuanced urban history. Beyond a doubt, by the late colonial period urban Zanzibari society had become deeply polarized by the political strife and violence that marked the run-up to elections for independence. Everyday life—from neighborhood hangouts to local shops and buses—was infused with the antagonism engendered by nationalist political contestation, and many social arenas were reinterpreted as expressing the essential conflict between "Arab" and "African," as if these designated clearly demarcated and opposed groups, each allied with contesting political parties. Entire categories of persons who populated the colonial landscape—especially those identified by Garth Myers as the "colonized middle"—were pushed outside the frame or simply erased from the picture.[34] Interstitial characters, plural or ambiguous identities, and unstable categories had little or no place in the orthodox script. Moreover, the subsequent events of the revolution seemed to both confirm and sharpen these stark oppositions. For ideological reasons, the new regime sought to portray its cause in the sharpest and most righteous light, arguing that the revolt had been sparked by impoverished Africans rising up to cast their wealthy Arab and Indian capitalist oppressors into the sea—Ng'ambo wreaking its revenge on Stone Town, the African countryside taking over the cosmopolitan city.

In the ensuing decades, these crisp oppositions hardened into orthodoxy. The party strictly controlled knowledge production in the islands. History ceased to be a subject offered in Zanzibari schools, and the only authorized accounts of the revolution were Afro Shirazi Party texts that hewed closely to the standard party line (or that interpreted colonial Zanzibar through a reductionist Marxist lens). Many residents of the city left or had their lives severely disrupted; holding on to historical documents, photographs, or objects associated with the *ancien régime* was extremely risky. Possession of such items, if discovered by the security forces during house sweeps, could result in a sentence of hard labor or re-education. And even being seen in contact with foreigners—especially foreigners asking questions—was cause for suspicion, prompting visits from the security police. Neighborhood tales, street histories, and oral accounts of life in the city all languished, as a generation of urbanites grew up with little exposure to or detailed knowledge of the colonial urban past, especially in Stone Town.

This prolonged rupture effectively endowed late colonial accounts with added force and weight. Well into the 1980s, writers on Zanzibar drew on the few published texts to glean some sense of life in the colonial city. One of the last researchers to conduct fieldwork before the revolution, Michael Lofchie, proved particularly influential. Clearly influenced by the social tensions and political struggle he saw around him in the run-up to independence, he represented the city in sharply dualistic terms, emphasizing rigid separation and segregation. Material differences between the two sides of the city, he wrote, "graphically symbolized the basic feature of social stratification in Zanzibar, the impoverishment and subordinate status of the African community."[35] In Lofchie's terms, isomorphic divisions of race and class structured both social and spatial relations—the built environment reflecting political realities in a clear and unambiguous manner.

Following the 1964 revolution, independent research was abruptly curtailed, and late colonial accounts became the only accessible windows onto the city's past. Subsequent studies, drawing on Lofchie and the ideologically tinted narratives sponsored by revolutionary authorities in Zanzibar, all highlighted the same themes of urban division and dualism: Stone Town versus Ng'ambo, elites versus the masses, the wealthy versus workers, Arab versus African.[36] These assertions remained largely unchallenged as later scholars drew on these works as source material, repeating their terms and projecting them back further into the colonial past. Ramachandran Menon, for example, claims that as early as the 1840s, "the poorer sections of the population were gradually edged out of the old stone town. Increasingly, they tended to concentrate at Ngambo, the Swahili and African quarter which grew up to the east of the creek. Zanzibar town had split into two."[37] No substantive evidence was provided to directly support this assertion: like other works of the period, Menon had to rely on secondary sources rather than conducting sustained field or archival research in Zanzibar.[38]

In point of fact, the poor were not edged out of "old" stone town (which in the 1840s was actually quite new) until much later, and this relocation was never complete. In the later nineteenth century, "the homes of the wealthy and the poor continued to be built side by side throughout Zanzibar. . . . Rich and poor, in their stone, mud, and thatch houses co-existed all over the peninsula."[39] Nor was Ng'ambo ever exclusively African or Swahili, much less a unitary "quarter." No question, the terrain of nineteenth-century Zanzibar city was filled with cultural differences and tensions, with relations of subordination and domination, but the terms of opposition were never quite so simple or straightforward as later writers supposed. Binary distinctions, of course, have a long history along the Swahili coast, as elsewhere: master and slave, civilized and savage, urbanized and wild, Muslim and pagan, African and Arab, among many others. But the question is: how do we interpret these contrasts and their social significance? Did they actually structure the rhythms of cultural lives and identities in the city, or were they simply reflective of elite aspirations as to how things should be (but never quite were) ordered?

Take, for instance, the term *ng'ambo*, which serves to express the way that Omani elites sought to mark African slaves brought to the island as subordinate outsiders. Used to describe the "other side" of a creek or river, the Kiswahili term also designates something foreign or alien, such as the lands that lie beyond a border or across the sea, akin to the original Greek root of "barbarian." As a place-name, then, *ng'ambo* functioned to pejoratively mark Africans and others living on the eastern side of the city as somehow "beyond the pale." Zanzibari Kiswahili also makes explicit connections between civilization, culture, urbanity, and Arabness—a legacy of the social prestige and power that the Omani state wielded in the nineteenth century. To be "civilized" was to possess *ustaarabu*, "Arabness" in the sense of wielding all the embodied knowledge, style, and deportment expected of well-born Muslims who could claim prestigious connections across the Indian Ocean; this term was used interchangeably with *utamaduni*, "culture," which in its verb form meant "to become civilized or refined" and was derived from the Arabic root for city, *madina*.[40]

The social existence of these terms, however, tells us little about their actual cultural power or circulation. If Arabicizing elites sought to impose their definitions on others, that does not mean they were successful—or that the terms were socially shared. While all sorts of ideological and embodied differences between various Africans and Arabs existed, this doesn't mean we can grant them hegemonic force, automatically accepting the idea that either colonial elites or authorities wielded the power to make reality conform to their own dictates. Nor can we simply assume that Arabs and Africans were cohesive groups, clearly demarcated and set off against each other. Indeed, a wealth of evidence from Swahili sources clearly indicates the fluid and relational nature of social identities. Coastal elites certainly attempted to mark their social prestige and influence by claiming roots closer to the sources of Islamic piety and learning abroad, adopting Arab fashions and cultural practices, allying themselves with the powerful Omanis. But this terrain was always open to contestation, being negotiated in the context of everyday struggles. Subalterns could (and often did) seize and redeploy the signs and insignia of status, asserting their own claims to citizenship and cultural belonging in coastal society.[41]

Shaping Colonial Spaces: Aspirations, Assertions, and Actualities

As these initial examples indicate, accounts of colonial dualism cannot be simply dismissed: in various times and places, and to different degrees, deep divisions were indeed crucial components of colonial worlds. Rather than deluded by dualism, subsequent scholars were simply echoing the array of evidence that seemed to support widespread segregation and separation in the colonial archive. Instead of dismissing them outright, we need to historicize and locate these sources, interpreting them in context. As Jean and John Comaroff have observed, "Despite the internal complexities of colonial societies, they tended to be perceived and re-presented, from within, in highly dualist, oppositional terms; terms that solidified the singularity of, and distance between, ruler and ruled, white and black, modernity and tradition, law and custom, European and non-European, capitalism and its antitheses, and so on. The objectification of this order of differences was intrinsic to the gesture of colonization itself."[42]

In the face of considerable internal hybridity, in other words, colonialism was widely crafted and articulated through dualistic representations, and objectifying these differences—making them material and meaningful—was perhaps the central challenge that colonial power confronted on an enduring basis. But taking such representations seriously does not necessarily entail accepting them at face value. "'Between European Dakar and native Dakar,'" a French planner named Toussaint vowed in 1931, "'we will establish an immense curtain composed of a great park ... in which we will plant all trees common to the area, a park adorned with fountains of sea water and several basins of drinking water, and done in different motifs recalling native history and customs of long ago.'"[43] On the face of things, this statement seems like a quintessential expression of colonial dualism, coming at the height of what King has called the dual city era in the 1930s and 1940s, "whether in Dakar, Algiers, Cape Town, Delhi, Nairobi, or Singapore."[44] But any initial understanding of the significance of Toussaint's program has to be qualified by the fact that his plan remained just that: a proposal, a scheme, a set of intentions that never went far beyond the drawing board.

Toussaint's Manichaean vision should not be viewed as irrelevant just because it remained unrealized; in fact, quite the contrary. Failed or incomplete schemes were altogether common across colonial urban landscapes, and are all the more intriguing for the fact that these lapses have gone largely ignored.[45] By foregrounding the very real challenges of implementing plans, and moving beyond just considering spatial intentions or ideologies, it becomes possible to open up a quite different perspective on the nature of colonial planning and power. In this respect, postcolonial critics of the dual city model have it exactly right: all too often scholars have treated *assertions* of colonial urban dualism as evidence for its *actual* existence. In making these assumptions, analysts have tended to foreclose precisely the questions that most need to be explored. In many cases, proponents of the dual city paradigm have argued that segregation was pervasive based on slight evidence or implied too direct a correspondence between spatial form and cultural experience. By raising the issue of the relationship between dualistic representations and realities on the ground, a more complicated picture of colonial urbanism emerges as well as a heightened sense of the limits and gaps in colonial power.

In the colonial records on urban Zanzibar, for instance, one can find numerous references to a divided city. As the Zanzibari historian Abdul Sheriff has observed, "conceptions of Zanzibar as a dual town, divided between a patrician Stone Town and a working class 'native quarter,' are fundamentally a product of the colonial and not the pre-colonial period."[46] Indeed, the geographic context of the city seemed ideally suited to a "white" town/"black" town paradigm insofar as a wide tidal creek split the city in two, with the triangular peninsula of original settlement in the west and Ng'ambo across the creek on "the other side" (see Figure 2). Some of the earliest references to a "European quarter" came in the context of public health reports in 1913, when the question of town planning and sanitation was first placed firmly on the local agenda. In that year, the Colonial Office dispatched the foremost sanitary expert of the day, Professor W. J. R. Simpson, on an official mission to assess sanitary conditions throughout urban East Africa. In preparation for Simpson's inspection tour, the public health officer in Zanzibar, Major Dudley Skelton, was told to take up the whole question of public health and planning. As his remarks eventually made clear, much remained to be done. With regard to town improvement, "no very striking work has been put in hand, although a lot of quiet and exceedingly useful work has been done in cleaning up and clearing away ruins."[47]

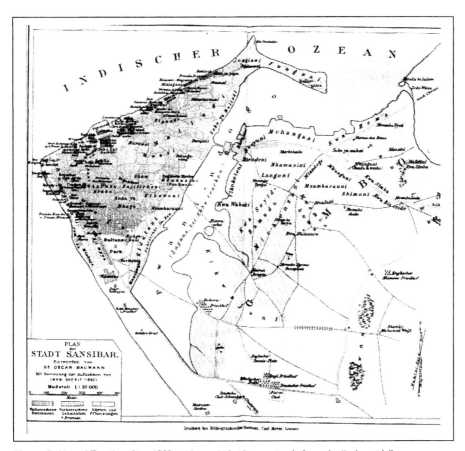

Figure 2. Map of Zanzibar City, 1892, with creek dividing peninsula from the "other side"
Source: Oscar Baumann, *Die Insel Sansibar und Ihre Kleineren Nachbarinseln* (Leipzig: Duncker & Humblot, 1897).

Skelton was writing precisely at a time when the sanitary syndrome was at its height, as fears of contamination and contagion intersected powerfully with European racism and the rise of planning as a sociospatial tool of colonial power. The elaboration of germ theory and the discovery of specific disease vectors (e.g., malaria) had not yet served to supplant earlier discourses that attributed infectious disease to specific places, moral conditions, and practices. But what had earlier been framed as a problem of the tropical environment—the vulnerability of the European body in certain climates or circumstances—was increasingly being reframed as a "native problem," becoming both internalized and interiorized within the bodies of non-Western others. With gradual improvements in empirical tactics, engineering, and particularly sanitation over the course of the nineteenth century, high rates of European morbidity in the tropics began to decline. By the early twentieth century, anxieties about risk had shifted in significant ways from places to people—and especially those seen as less civilized, poorer, or racially other. Indeed, a newly assertive scientific racism only served to intensify colonial desires for exclusivity and superiority, as security fears, sanitary preoccupations, and segregationist planning all came together to stress the importance of isolating and insulating Europeans from native influences.

Hence at the very top of his list of town planning priorities, Skelton emphasized the dangers presented by the house form most closely associated with Africans: the "native hut." All native huts, he insisted, had to be removed from certain areas of the city. The areas he listed were all in close proximity to either the Health offices or the personal residences of European officials, and his ultimate intention was quite clear. He described these huts as "dark houses" that served as hiding places or breeding places for mosquitoes that "sooner or later make their way to the European quarter of town." Teeming biological processes—of breeding, waste, and the spread of disease—were associated with secrecy and darkness and symbolically tied to the figure of the native. This was a colonial discourse par excellence about race and European fears of proximity and pollution: "These native huts, where they exist, as they do, near European and respectable Indian houses must be removed," Skelton flatly concluded. He admitted that all huts could not be cleared out from the heart of the city at once, but insisted that "steady progress" had to be made. The eventual goal of this "progress" was clear: Skelton repeatedly invoked a "European residential quarter" and a "European quarter of town" in his text. The goal of planning, in his view, was to carve out such a quarter, using hut clearances to create zones of order and sanitary separation, "protecting" Europeans from allegedly insidious threats posed by others.[48]

Skelton's proposal received substantial backing when Professor Simpson submitted his official findings to the colonial secretary in 1914. Throughout his colonial career, Simpson had been a staunch advocate of segregation as a pillar of sanitary policy, and his East Africa report amply reflected his racial biases. In the introduction, he attributed the prevalence of disease and disarray in East African cities to two factors: racial intermixture and lack of control over buildings. Putting structures and people in their proper places would restore order. "It is absolutely essential that in every town and trade center the town planning should provide well defined and separate quarters or wards for Europeans, Asiatics, and Africans," with at least three hundred yards of open space as a neutral zone separating Europeans from racial others.[49]

In his specific recommendations for Zanzibar, Simpson sought nothing less than to split the city in two, starkly drawing distinctions between Stone Town and Ng'ambo. To this end, he seized upon the creek as an ideal cordon sanitaire, a line of demarcation that should be strengthened and sharpened. As he phrased it in the report, "The creek which runs through the town from north to south separates the European and business quarters from the native town and in this respect is an advantage."[50] But as was the case with Skelton, the invocation of "European quarters" or a "native town" bore little relationship to the actual landscape of the existing city. There were only a few hundred Europeans (*wazungu*) resident on the island at the time, and they were far too dispersed and few in number to constitute a residential enclave, let alone an entire quarter. The vast majority of *wazungu* lived in indigenous structures in built-up areas surrounded by neighbors of Arab, Indian, and African descent.

Purity of conception and purpose drove Simpson's vision of planning, seeking to compose and cleanse the social order of the city. If a "native" town couldn't quite be located as yet, it would have to be created, and that was precisely the point of sanitary policy: drawing clean lines and keeping things crisply separate. With this in mind, Simpson made sure that many of his recommendations dovetailed together, ultimately seeking to fashion a dual colonial city. He noted that operations had recently commenced to fill in the tidal creek at its southern tip in Mnazi Mmoja. He applauded this initiative, writing that its completion "will secure a dry open space as a recreation ground, on which under no conditions should houses or huts be permitted to be built." Reclaiming this land and using it as a border zone could serve to create precisely the distinctions he sought. The cleared ground, he wrote, "should remain an open space and a neutral zone between the European and the native quarter of the town; and no huts in future should be permitted to be erected on the west side of the creek and neutral zone, and those that now exist should be gradually and systematically removed."[51]

For the next decade, the colonial administration uniformly embraced the desirability of a European quarter—the only question was how to achieve this goal and actually pay for it. Looking back in 1920, the resident at the time, Major F. B. Pearce, touted the planning progress made under his regime. "Zanzibar Town," he pronounced, "is being improved every year." By way of illustration, he proceeded to cite a singular example. "Until quite recently clusters of unsanitary native huts surged up to the very walls of the houses occupied by Europeans. Such areas are being cleared, and open spaces so obtained are laid out as gardens." Hewing closely here to Simpson's logic, cleaning up the city in his view seemed synonymous with clearing out the "natives." Pearce acknowledged that progress might seem slow, but wiping out indigenous disorder couldn't be accomplished overnight. "Matters are improving year by year," Pearce insisted, "and it is hoped that Zanzibar, once the City of Dreadful Night, may in course of time become the City Perfect."[52]

Pearce's text is particularly revealing in light of his private correspondence with the colonial secretary. Earlier, when asked to provide the local administration's response to Simpson's report, Pearce endorsed most of his proposals in the abstract while arguing that it would be very costly and difficult to implement them in practice. "To give effect to the obviously excellent recommendations is not so simple as it might appear; because in the majority of cases the land involved is private property," Pearce wrote to the colonial secretary. Recently, he stated, he had sought "to remove some particularly insanitary native huts which are situated close to certain houses occupied by European officials" but had been prevented from doing so because of the costs of acquisition.[53] By pointing out that the price tag for compensation for removing a few huts in a limited area was around £3,300, he hoped to give the colonial secretary a taste of just how expensive a proposition large-scale urban planning would be. In so doing, he tried to forestall getting saddled with an unfunded mandate—being ordering by London to formulate a plan without any metropolitan funds to pay for it.

The colonial secretary did not accept Pearce's argument that financial limitations foreclosed the need for planning. Indeed, he argued exactly the reverse. To improve the city piecemeal over time as means allowed would not be prudent at all, but instead inefficient and uneconomical. Without a comprehensive scheme in place, there would be no overarching vision to coordinate and order efforts. Urban administration meant taking advantage of the most modern and scientific techniques, and in this sense, planning had to be counted as a means to save money, not just dismissed as an expense. Without "a plan to work up to," the secretary warned, "the Town will remain badly planned and irregularly developed, and a good deal of money will to some extent be wasted."[54] Through this neat reversal of logic, Pearce found himself exactly in the position he most wanted to avoid. From the lofty distance of London, his superiors ordered him to formulate an ambitious plan to rework the city along lines suggested by Simpson while refusing to fund it or provide support to carry it out.

Pearce's concerns about the practical difficulties of imposing Simpson's rationalizing and racializing vision proved all too prescient. Reworking Zanzibar city, with its long established urban fabric, intricate layout, and hybrid population, was a highly complex and costly prospect. Even managing to merely formulate a plan—let alone attempting to implement it—proved an elusive task. By any accounting the war years represented the least auspicious moment for a strapped colonial regime to initiate an ambitious program of sociospatial intervention. By the end of 1916, the chief medical officer, Henry Curwen, was reporting that the colonial secretary's directive remained wholly unfulfilled: "It has been impossible to undertake the detailing of a Town Planning Scheme as required by the Colonial Office," he stated.[55] This inactivity was all the more striking given his bleak assessment of urban affairs: "The insanitary condition of the great majority of town houses and their hopeless lack of light and ventilation owing to narrowness of dividing lanes form a rather stupendous problem. Little can be achieved by attacking individual houses . . . over a term of years money must annually be set aside for the acquisition of whole blocks of buildings to be razed and rebuilt on approved lines."[56]

Despite such findings, little was actually done to carry out this proposal. If Dr. Curwen described 1916 as "abnormal" for his department, by the end of the war matters were much worse. By 1919 the tone of the annual medical report was shot through with frustration: "The year has been disappointedly void of any progress or development. With inadequate staff and the necessity for lending a helping hand to the Public Health Division, it has barely been possible to maintain routine duties."[57] The review of the Public Health Division was even more pessimistic in tone: "This belated report may well be reduced to a minimum as there has been a disappointing lack of any progress on development, proper supervision over important details of established routine has been impossible, reforms of increasing urgency and repeatedly pressed have been further postponed indefinitely, and all educational work has been at a standstill."[58] From the start of discussions about planning in 1913, it took the colonial government almost a full decade simply to locate a planner and engage him to come to Zanzibar. While on leave in London, an assistant chief secretary personally undertook this task. He acknowledged that the colonial secretary had ordered a plan in 1916, but simply noted, "there was no one in Zanzibar fit to prepare such a plan—it was a town planner's job—and nothing more was done."[59]

Visions of the dual city continued to be invoked, but its substance remained far more amorphous—indeed, something altogether illusory, receding into the far horizon. The first master plan for urban Zanzibar, hastily framed by H. V. Lanchester in 1922, made frequent reference to the city as a clearly demarcated and divided space. Despite spending a mere seventeen days in Zanzibar and having little grasp of its social complexities, Lanchester evinced few doubts: his descriptions brim with precise and definitive assertions. He reiterated the colonial fantasy that the city was composed of a series of distinct and homogeneous quarters—the European, the Indian, the Arab, and the Native—mapping these categories onto the physical milieu of the city in stark ways (see Figure 3). Echoing Simpson and Pearce, for example, Lanchester insisted that "the creek separates the European and business quarters from the native town."[60] Overall, his plan sought precisely to impose these differences, offering separate treatments for distinct racialized zones. In this manner he made proposals to deal with "group areas" as a whole, inscribing clear demarcations between residents and claiming to resolve their collective social needs at a single stroke.

But this early inscription of apartheid was merely latent—a projection of how things ideally should be ordered, rather than a description of how they actually stood. Elsewhere, Lanchester revealed just how limited the European presence was on the ground. Without noting the apparent contradiction, he admitted Zanzibar was "exceptional among tropical towns in that hardly any houses have been built for Europeans," most of whom were forced to find lodgings in "Arab" dwellings in already established neighborhoods.[61] In an earlier section, Lanchester cited population statistics from 1921 showing that only 270 Europeans lived on the island. The large urban zone in Stone Town that he marked out as exclusively "European" was in fact one in which they were a distinct minority, far outnumbered by and interspersed among Arab, Indian, and African neighbors.[62]

In a more critical sense, however, one cannot simply read the intentions of plans or interpret their ideological dimensions. Both Myers and Sheriff, among others, have discussed Lanchester's plan, but much of the analysis remains at the level of ideological critique. This is valuable, of course, but never sufficient in and of itself. Myers, for instance, writes: "[Lanchester's] notions of efficiency were deployed in the distribution of police lines and the design of police stations as well as a reorganization of social and economic activities that made markets, shops, houses and neighborhoods more amenable to surveillance."[63] While these design elements are certainly present in the plan, the fact that this wholesale Foucaultian reorganization of space never went far

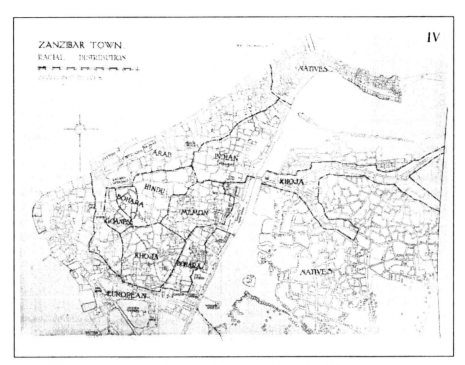

Figure 3. Planning map of Zanzibar City with clear-cut racialized zones, 1923
Source: H. V. Lanchester, *Zanzibar: A Study in Tropical Town Planning* (Cheltenham: E. J. Burrow, 1923).

beyond the drawing board is left unmentioned. By treating the discursive aspects of plans apart from their complex material entanglements with the world (especially implementation), schemes are often endowed with a false presence and power. In analytic terms, texts get rendered as floating signifiers, severed from the vital contexts that shape and support them—diminishing our understanding of the interconnectedness of material worlds and discursive frameworks.

Similarly, Sheriff notes that Lanchester "saw the urban form of *mitaa* [quarters] as natural nuclei for the various ethnic groups in Zanzibari society" and that he sought to split Stone Town from Ng'ambo.[64] True enough—but Lanchester's endorsement of separate European and native quarters takes on an altogether different significance when we realize that his plan, like others, never came close to being realized. It took almost a year for the Zanzibar authorities just to review and "approve" Lanchester's work. Chief Secretary Crofton estimated the total cost of the plan as £466,666, the vast majority of which would be devoted to modernizing the harbor.[65] The resident approved and transmitted the plan to London, where it was endorsed by the Colonial Advisory Medical and Sanitary Committee and enthusiastically supported by the colonial secretary. Once again, however, local officials were presented with an unfunded mandate, as London refused to provide any funds to see the plan through. The colonial secretary suggested that Zanzibar should seek a large loan, while reserving £10,000 annually in the budget to spend on town improvements.[66]

By the end of 1925, however, the colonial secretary was forced to admit, "in view of the financial position it seems unlikely that it will be practicable in the near future to carry out, on any extensive scale, Mr. Lanchester's recommendations with regard to the replanning of the town of Zanzibar."[67] And no loan ever materialized. As late as 1931, the Zanzibar resident was still casting about in search of funds to implement Lanchester's program. He applied for over £500,000 in colonial development loans, citing "urgent" public health concerns as a means to justify the need to support Lanchester's work. In the end, however, only £59,300 was approved, and the Treasury refused to provide even this modest sum without solid guarantees that the money would be paid back—something the colonial secretary declined to provide, given the government's recent string of deficits.[68] In the end, the overwhelming majority of Lanchester's proposals went nowhere, even as his work spawned a burgeoning series of complicated bureaucratic and legal mechanisms that ironically continued to hamper the material implementation of plans. Nor was this an isolated instance. Almost as soon as the Lanchester proposals were officially shelved in the mid-1930s, the colonial government compounded its mistake by embarking on yet another expensive and time-consuming round of planning. This cumbersome process eventually culminated decades later in the 1958 Kendall master plan, which itself was never materially implemented or actualized to any significant degree. Due to the huge expense and complexity involved, the scheme was largely abandoned soon after approval, even as it lingered on in attenuated form, providing an official framework for municipal law and bureaucratic structure even after the revolution. Indeed, the unwieldy Town and Country Planning law fostered by Kendall was eventually resurrected by urban conservationists in the mid-1990s and reauthorized as the legal basis to preserve what they were now calling the "historic" Stone Town.

Conclusion

Even as plans remained incomplete or ineffective, they continued to have a material impact. In this sense, much more was involved in the colonial pursuit of dualistic urban forms than mere fantasy or fiction. Indeed, by taking the *pursuit* of planning seriously—treating it simultaneously as a complex social, discursive, and material process with unanticipated effects—a rather different picture of colonial power results. Without significant infusions of external capital, expertise, and the exercise of authoritarian powers, colonial regimes found it exceedingly difficult to enact their will on urban space—especially in places like Zanzibar where the built environment was already well established. Creating zones of strict separation and segregation was a costly and complicated prospect that presented formidable challenges to regimes that were spread thin on the ground and struggling to locate adequate resources.

As we've seen in Zanzibar, the ideological commitment to shape a dual city was fed by diverse sociocultural sources and widely shared. Yet colonial dualism never remained *purely* textual or phantasmic. Pushed by sanitary experts and superiors in the Colonial Office, local authorities were compelled to formulate urban plans that they could never actually fund or carry out. Rather than just empty exercises, these plans required extensive bureaucratic reorganization, consumed significant time and resources, substituted new policies, and left their imprint on the space of the city itself—if only in the negative. If duality often characterized the forms of appearance of colonial urbanism, its actualization was marked by incompleteness and inconsistency.

In considering the broader implications for urban analysis, three related dimensions come to mind. First, by adopting the approach outlined here, we can better grasp the disjunctive and diffuse nature of colonial rule itself—its extension in space and time and the way it emerged through debates and arguments between different arms or levels of the apparatus of empire. Second, in turn, this draws our attention to the tensions and contradictions that constituted colonialism in different times and places—between the modernizing imperatives of the so-called civilizing mission and the sharp financial constraints experienced by many colonial states; between the metropole and its far-flung colonial satellites; between the Colonial Office, residents, and middle-level officers; between planners, sanitary experts, and municipal authorities; and between plans and their realization. This suggests, of course, that "the" colonial project was neither singular nor unified, but instead often irregular and incomplete. Nowhere was this more evident than in the case of large-scale social engineering or state building exercises. Third, and lastly, by attending to the incompleteness or intangibility of dual city projects, we begin to get a much greater sense of the complexity of the colonial city itself: the way that colonial aspirations to refashion space in a comprehensive manner across a huge swath of territory plunged colonial regimes into conundrums that they often could not comprehend, let alone resolve.

Declaration of Conflicting Interests

The author declared no potential conflicts of interests with respect to the authorship and/or publication of this article.

Funding

Funding for some of the archival research in this article was generously provided by a National Endowment for the Humanities (NEH) Research Fellowship.

Notes

1. Anthony D. King, "Writing Colonial Space," *Comparative Studies in Society and History* 37 (1995): 541-54.
2. For some of the most important comparative accounts, see Anthony D. King, *Urbanism, Colonialism, and the World Economy* (London: Routledge, 1990); Robert K. Home, *Of Planting and Planning: The Making of British Colonial Cities* (London: E & FN Spon, 1997); and Gwendolyn Wright, *The Politics of Design in French Colonial Urbanism* (Chicago: Chicago University Press, 1991).
3. Over a decade earlier, Redfield and Singer's discussion of "heterogenetic" cities had obvious implications for colonial urbanism, but Abu-Lughod seems to have been the first to take up the topic in a sustained way. See Robert Redfield and Milton Singer, "The Cultural Role of Cities," *Economic Development and Cultural Change* 3 (1954): 53-73. R. V. Horvath followed up with an early piece in 1969 ("In Search of a Theory of Urbanization: Notes on the Colonial City," *East Lakes Geographer* 5 [1969]: 68-82), but the field really began to gain focus with Anthony King's work in the mid-1970s, especially his *Colonial Urban Development* (London: Routledge and Kegan Paul, 1976).
4. Janet Abu-Lughod, "Tale of Two Cities: The Origins of Modern Cairo," *Comparative Studies in Society and History* 7 (1965): 429-30. What is especially interesting in Abu-Lughod's account is the way she quickly jumps from material or architectural circumstances to draw sweeping cultural conclusions. Despite physical proximity, the two cities, she asserts, "were miles apart socially and centuries apart technologically" (p. 431).
5. For more on French urban policy in the North African context, see Wright, *The Politics of Design in French Colonial Urbanism*, 79-88; and Janet Abu-Lughod, *Rabat* (Princeton, NJ: Princeton University Press, 1980), 144-45.
6. Raymond F. Betts, "The Problem of the Medina in the Urban Planning of Dakar, Senegal," *African Urban Notes* 4 (1969): 13.
7. "Another striking feature [of Léopoldville] is the pre-Independence layout into two distinct parts: European and Congolese," writes La Fontaine. "The original European quarter of Kalina was separated from the African town, or the *Cité Africaine*, as it is called, by a *cordon sanitaire* of uninhabited ground, consisting of the golf course, the botanical gardens, and the zoo." J. S. La Fontaine, *City Politics: A Study of Léopoldville, 1962-63* (Cambridge: Cambridge University Press, 1970), 19. See also Phyllis Martin, *Leisure and Society in Colonial Brazzaville* (Cambridge: Cambridge University Press, 1995), 70.
8. See, among others, Bill Freund, *The African City: A History* (Cambridge: Cambridge University Press, 2007), 76-82; Garth Andrew Myers, *Verandahs of Power: Colonialism and Space in Urban Africa* (Syracuse, NY: Syracuse University Press, 2003), 5; and Luise White, *The Comforts of Home* (Chicago: Chicago University Press, 1990), 46.

9. Odile Goerg, "From Hill Station (Freetown) to Downtown Conakry (First Ward): Comparing French and British Approaches to Segregation in Colonial Cities at the Beginning of the Twentieth Century," *Canadian Journal of African Studies* 32 (1998): 25-6.
10. Goerg, for example, emphasizes the visual obviousness of dualism. In Conakry, she writes, the French "established a clear visual division in the city, obvious to any visitor. This form of social segregation . . . typified all French colonial cities." See Goerg, "From Hill Station."
11. Maynard W. Swanson, "The Sanitation Syndrome: Bubonic Plague and Urban Native Policy in the Cape Colony, 1900-1909," *Journal of African History* 18 (1977): 388.
12. Achille Mbembe, "Aesthetics of Superfluity," *Public Culture* 16 (2004): 384. For a more extensive discussion of the history of state policies and "native locations" in South Africa, see Jennifer Robinson, "'A Perfect System of Control'? State Power and 'Native Locations' in South Africa," *Society and Space* 8 (1990): 135-62.
13. David Simon, "Third World Colonial Cities in Context: Conceptual and Theoretical Approaches with Particular Reference to Africa," *Progress in Human Geography* 8 (1984): 501.
14. Home, *Of Planting and Planning*, 123ff.
15. Rebecca M. Brown, "The Cemeteries and the Suburbs: Patna's Challenges to the Colonial City in South Asia," *Journal of Urban History* 29 (2003): 151.
16. Miriam Dossal, *Imperial Designs and Indian Realities: The Planning of Bombay City, 1845-1875* (Delhi: Oxford University Press, 1991), 16-17. For other accounts of the black town/fort paradigm, see P. J. Marshall, "The White Town of Calcutta under the Rule of the East India Company," *Modern Asian Studies* 34 (2000): 307-31; Norma Evenson, *The Indian Metropolis: A View Towards the West* (New Haven, CT: Yale University Press, 1989); Thomas R. Metcalf, *An Imperial Vision: Indian Architecture and Britain's Raj* (Berkeley: University of California Press, 1989); and Susan M. Neild, "Colonial Urbanism: The Development of Madras City in the Eighteenth and Nineteenth Centuries," *Modern Asian Studies* 13 (1979): 217-46.
17. John L. Comaroff, "Reflections on the Colonial State, in South Africa and Elsewhere: Factions, Figments, Facts and Fictions," *Social Identities* 4 (1998): 321.
18. For a selection of work developing these themes, see Frederick Cooper and Ann Laura Stoler, eds., *Tensions of Empire* (Berkeley: University of California Press, 1997); Gyan Prakash, ed., *After Colonialism* (Princeton, NJ: Princeton University Press, 1995); Ania Loomba, *Colonialism/Postcolonialism* (New York: Routledge, 1998); Anne McClintock, *Imperial Leather* (New York: Routledge, 1998); and Ann Laura Stoler, *Along the Archival Grain: Epistemic Anxieties and Colonial Common Sense* (Princeton, NJ: Princeton University Press, 2009).
19. Ira Bashkow, *The Meaning of Whitemen* (Chicago: University of Chicago Press, 2006), 4.
20. Brenda S. A. Yeoh, *Contesting Space* (Oxford: Oxford University Press, 1996), 3. This tendency to overemphasize European dominance was a marked feature of some of the earliest colonial city studies. For a classic example, see R. V. Horvath's "In Search of a Theory of Urbanization," *East Lakes Geographer* 5 (1969): 68-82.
21. Zeynep Çelik, *Urban Forms and Colonial Confrontations: Algiers Under French Rule* (Berkeley: University of California Press, 1997), 5-6.
22. Brown, "The Cemeteries and the Suburbs," 158.
23. Swati Chattopadhyay, "Blurring Boundaries: The Limits of 'White Town' in Colonial Calcutta," *Journal of the Society of Architectural Historians* 59 (2000): 154, 157.
24. Chattopadhyay, "Blurring Boundaries," 154.
25. Brown, "The Cemeteries and the Suburbs," 157.
26. Anthony D. King, "(Post)colonial Geographies: Material and Symbolic," *Historical Geography* 27 (1999): 100.
27. King, "(Post)colonial Geographies," 108.

28. Frantz Fanon, *The Wretched of the Earth* (New York: Grove Press, 1968), 38-9.
29. Garth A. Myers, "Narrative Representations of Revolutionary Zanzibar," *Journal of Historical Geography* 26 (2000): 435.
30. John Middleton and Jane Campbell, *Zanzibar: Its Society and Politics* (Oxford: Oxford University Press, 1965), 37.
31. As one European scholar in the 1960s stereotypically formulated the spatial and racial distinction between Stone Town and Ng'ambo: "Rather than calling it [urban Zanzibar] an oriental town, one should speak of an 'Afro-Arabian' town in the sense of a side-by-side existence of districts that are inspired by the 'Orient' and districts that qua housing hardly differ from African villages." Roelof Cornelis Harkema, "The Town of Zanzibar in the Later Half of the 19th Century" (University of Groningen: Ph.D. thesis, 1967), 54.
32. Zanzibar Protectorate, *Report on the Progress of the Development Programme for the Years 1946-1951* (Zanzibar: Government Printer, 1951), 30.
33. *A Guide to Zanzibar*, 4th ed. (Zanzibar: Government Printer, 1952), 30-1. The guide, intended to stimulate tourism, was first compiled by an administrative officer, G. H. Shelswell-White, in 1932, and then revised numerous times in the 1940s and 1950s.
34. Garth Myers, "Colonial Discourse and Africa's Colonized Middle: Ajit Singh's Architecture," *Historical Geography* 27 (1999): 27-55.
35. Michael Lofchie, *Background to Revolution* (Princeton, NJ: Princeton University Press, 1965), 8.
36. For a fuller treatment of discursive representations and the politics of the revolution, see Garth Myers, "Narrative Representations."
37. Ramachandran Menon, "Zanzibar in the Nineteenth Century: Aspects of Urban Development in an East African Coastal Town" (UCLA: M.A. thesis, 1978), 41.
38. For other works of the period, see Esmond Bradley Martin, *Zanzibar: Tradition and Revolution* (London: Hamish Hamilton, 1978); Abdulaziz Lodhi et al., *A Small Book on Zanzibar* (Stockholm: Författares Bokmaskin, 1979); and Anthony Clayton, *The Zanzibari Revolution and Its Aftermath* (London: Archon, 1981). These external treatments need to be seen in tandem with Swahili novels of the period, especially those of Shafi Adam Shafi and Said Ahmed Mohamed. For an English-language analysis of these texts, see Myers, "Narrative Representations," 436-39.
39. Abdul Sheriff, "The Spatial Dichotomy of Swahili Towns: The Case of Zanzibar in the Nineteenth Century," in Andrew Burton, ed., *The Urban Experience in Eastern Africa, c. 1750–2000* (Nairobi: British Institute in Eastern Africa, 2002), 77, 78.
40. James de Vere Allen and Thomas H. Wilson, *Swahili Houses and Tombs of the Coast of Kenya* (London: Art and Archaeology Research Papers, 1979).
41. For more on the shifting and contested nature of social identities on the coast, and especially the struggles of slaves and plebians to be culturally recognized and respected, see Jonathon Glassman, *Feasts and Riot* (London: Heineman, 1995); Laura J. Fair, *Pastimes and Politics* (Athens, OH: Ohio University Press, 2001); and Frederick Cooper, *From Slaves to Squatters* (New Haven, CT: Yale University Press, 1980).
42. Jean Comaroff and John Comaroff, *Of Revelation and Revolution*, vol. 2 (Chicago: University of Chicago Press, 1997), 25.
43. Quoted in Betts, "The Problem of the Medina in the Urban Planning of Dakar, Senegal," 9.
44. King, *Urbanism, Colonialism, and the World Economy*, 42.
45. For more on the sociocultural dynamics of failed bureaucratic schemes, see my "From Iraq to Katrina and Back: Bureaucratic Planning as Strategic Failure, Fiction, and Fantasy," *Sociology Compass* 2 (2008): 1431-461.
46. Sheriff, "The Spatial Dichotomy of Swahili Towns," 80.
47. Dudley Sheridan Skelton, "Public Health Department Report for 1913," Zanzibar National Archives (ZNA): BA 7/1, 24.

48. Skelton, "Public Health Department Report for 1913," 24.
49. "Report on Sanitary Matters in the East Africa Protectorate, Uganda, and Zanzibar by Professor W. J. Simpson, C.M.G., M.D, F.R.C.P," ZNA: AB 2/264, 9-10.
50. Simpson, "Report on Sanitary Matters," 73.
51. Simpson, "Report on Sanitary Matters," 73.
52. Major Francis Barrow Pearce, *Zanzibar: The Island Metropolis of Eastern Africa* (London: T. Fisher Unwin, 1920), 211-12.
53. Resident Pearce to Secretary of State for the Colonies A. Bonar Law, July 15, 1915, ZNA: AB 2/264.
54. Secretary of State for the Colonies to Resident Pearce, June 16, 1916, quoted in Chief Secretary R. H. Crofton, "Secret Memorandum on Town Planning," August 30, 1923, ZNA: AB 39/203.
55. Dr. Henry Curwen, "Annual Report of the Public Health Department," 1916, ZNA: BA 7/40, 2.
56. Curwen, "Annual Report of the Public Health Department," 18.
57. "Annual Report of the Medical Division," 1919, ZNA: BA 7/42, 1.
58. "Annual Report of the Public Health Division," 1919, ZNA: BA 7/42, 21.
59. R. H. Crofton, *Zanzibar Affairs, 1914-1933* (London: Francis Edwards, 1953), 158.
60. H. V. Lanchester, *Zanzibar: A Study in Tropical Town Planning* (Cheltenham: Burrow, 1923), 57.
61. Lanchester, *Zanzibar: A Study in Tropical Town Planning*, 67.
62. Lanchester, *Zanzibar: A Study in Tropical Town Planning*, 11.
63. Garth A. Myers, "From 'Stinkibar' to the 'Island Metropolis': The Geography of British Hegemony in Zanzibar," in Anne Godlewska and Neil Smith, eds., *Geography and Empire* (Oxford: Blackwell, 1994), 220. Myers later notes that "a number" of Lanchester's housing proposals "were not fully enacted" but the substantial failures of the plan and its ambiguous status are never fully addressed.
64. Sheriff, "The Spatial Dichotomy of Swahili Towns," 81.
65. Chief Secretary Crofton, "Secret Memorandum on Town Planning, ZNA: AB 39/203, 23.
66. J.H. Thomas to High Commissioner R.T. Coryndon, July 10, 1924, ZNA: AB 39/203.
67. Secretary of State for the Colonies to High Commissioner, Zanzibar, January 14, 1925, ZNA: AB 39/203.
68. Secretary of State for the Colonies to Acting British Resident, Zanzibar, September 26, 1931, ZNA: AB 39/203.

Bio

William Cunningham Bissell is associate professor in the Department of Anthropology and Sociology, Lafayette College, in Easton, PA. His research interests include cities and space, urban planning and colonialism, modernity, globalization and film, Africa, and the United States. He is the author, most recently, of a book on the contradictions of colonial planning, *Urban Design, Chaos, and Colonial Power in Zanzibar* (2011), issued by Indiana University Press. He is currently engaged in ethnographic research on cities, cinema, and cultural spectacle in the Indian Ocean world, exploring the sociocultural dynamics of an African film festival.

[7]

The Control of "Sacred" Space: Conflicts Over the Chinese Burial Grounds in Colonial Singapore, 1880–1930

BRENDA S.A. YEOH
National University of Singapore

> ... the cemetery stood in a place, valueless when it was chosen, which with the increase of the city's affluence was now worth a great deal of money. It had been suggested that the graves should be moved to another spot and the land sold for building, but the feeling of the community was against it. It gave the taipan a sense of satisfaction to think that their dead rested on the most valuable site on the island. It showed that there were things they cared for more than money....
> *"The Taipan"*, Somerset Maugham[1]

> Singapore should adopt the modern idea of putting all future graveyards well away from the city, where they cannot interfere with free development.
> *W.H. Collyer, Manager of the Singapore Improvement Trust*[2]

The "Sacred" in the Urban Built-Environment

In traditional societies, a sense of the "sacred" is often inherent in the form of the urban built-environment, which, in turn, cannot be understood apart from the "mythical-magical concern with place".[3] According to Mircea Eliade, the act of settlement itself is perceived as a re-enactment of the mythical creation of the world.[4] Ancient Indian cities were designed according to a mandala replicating a cosmic image of the laws governing the universe and, similarly, Chinese cities were conceived as "cosmo-magical symbols" of the universe.[5] These cities were laid out as terrestrial images of the macrocosmos, distinct spaces sacralized for habitation within a continuum of profane space.[6] As Paul Wheatley observes,

> for the ancients the "real" world transcended the pragmatic realm of textures and geometrical space, and was perceived schematically in terms of an extra-mundane,

---

[1] W.S. Maugham, *Collected Short Stories* 2 (London: Pan Books, 1975), p. 310.

[2] "Forwarding Copy of a Letter from the Secretary of Chinese Affairs on the Subject of Acquiring Land Comprised in Grant No. 49 Toah Payoh as a Burial Ground for the Seh Chua Community", Oct. 1924, Singapore Improvement Trust [hereafter, *SIT*] 655/24.

[3] R.D. Sack, *Conceptions of Space in Social Thought: A Geographic Perspective* (London: Macmillan Press, 1980), p. 155.

[4] M. Eliade, *The Myth of the Eternal Return* (Princeton: Princeton University Press, 1954), p. 18.

[5] P. Wheatley, *The Pivot of the Four Quarters; A Preliminary Enquiry into the Origins and Character of the Chinese City* (Chicago: Aldine, 1971), p. 411; Y.F. Tuan, *China* (London: Longman, 1970), p. 106. Cosmogony as a paradigmatic model for the layout of cities and the sacralizing of various urban elements were not only found in India and China but prevalent in a number of other civilizations. For further examples, see M. Eliade, *The Sacred and the Profane: The Nature of Religion*, trans. W.R. Trask (New York: Harvest, 1959), pp. 20–65; A. Rapoport, *House Form and Culture* (Englewood Cliffs, N.J.: Prentice-Hall, 1969), pp. 49–58.

[6] Wheatley, *The Pivot of the Four Quarters*, pp. 450–51.

sacred experience. Only the sacred was "real", and the purely secular — if it could be said to exist at all — could never be more than trivial.[7]

Unlike "pure" geometric space, sacred space, "the space of myth and magic", is non-isotropic because it is structured by rules of inherence.[8] Space and substance are "fused" rather than distinct, and every position and direction in mythical space is endowed as it were with a particular "accent" or "tonality" of its own.[9] As such, in the sacred spaces of traditional cities, geographical locations, geographical directions and other spatial properties are infused with enormous intrinsic significance. With the penetration of a capitalist order, however, space becomes viewed as separate from substances of value, as "empty" land which could be demarcated, parcelled out, commodified and purchased not for its intrinsic but potential value for speculative purposes. Only under profitable circumstances do particular places and substances combine, and "then only until a more profitable arrangement appears to dissociate and recombine them with other places and things".[10] In colonial societies where a capitalistic order was imposed on a traditional one, "sacred" space was often eroded away, giving way to commodified space which was more amenable to measurement, "scientific" planning and commercial development. This process, however, did not occur without conflicts and compromises.

This paper examines the negotiation of power over the urban landscape between the municipal authorities and the Chinese communities in colonial Singapore over a highly contentious question: whether any element of the urban built-environment could be considered "sacred" and hence inalienable and immune to changes demanded by the economic rigours of urban development. By the late nineteenth century, this debate was focused on one particular element of the city's "sacred" geography — the burying places of the Chinese communities. The paper examines the conflicting discourses which developed over the nature and location of Chinese burial grounds, the strategies of negotiation employed by the authorities and the Chinese communities, and the resultant impact on remaking the "sacred" geography of colonial Singapore.

Death and Cemeteries: The Western European Tradition

In western Europe, the late eighteenth century and early nineteenth century marked a profound change in people's attitude to death and their perception of cemeteries. Philippe Aries argues that until the eighteenth century, Latin Christendom was indifferent to "the daily presence of the living among the dead".[11] He attributes the mid-eighteenth century movement to relocate cemeteries outside cities to profound changes in Christian attitudes towards death which engendered a strong desire among the living to detach themselves from the dead. James Riley proposes a modified view that this shift in popular attitudes towards death in Europe was led by public health arguments in the wake of the mid-eighteenth century environmentalist campaign to

---

[7] P. Wheatley, *City as Symbol: an Inaugural Lecture Delivered at University College London, 20 Nov. 1969* (London: H.K. Lewis, 1969), p. 9.

[8] Sack, *Conceptions of Space*, p. 155.

[9] Ibid., pp. 155–56.

[10] Ibid., p. 185.

[11] P. Aries, *In the Hour of Our Death*, trans. H. Weaver (New York: Allen Lane, 1981), pp. 92, 318ff.

modify disease-ridden environments or remove them away from human habitats.[12] In England, the campaign for cemetery reform gathered momentum in the second quarter of the nineteenth century and was inspired both by public health concerns in the wake of the cholera epidemics as well as changes in social behaviour, aesthetic taste and moral outlook. In his 1843 report on internment in towns, the sanitarian Edwin Chadwick advocated the expulsion of the dead from the presence of the living not only on sanitary but also "moral, religious and physical" grounds.[13] Concomitant with the new concern for urban hygiene were new sensibilities which combined to "impart to the cemetery as well as the hospital, the slaughterhouse and the prison the taint of impure institutions that had to be banished to the periphery of the city" in order to "assure the purity of the new Enlightenment urban milieu".[14] In an age where the emphasis upon public hygiene was joined with a concern for moral enlightenment, the image of church graveyards as "horrific spectacles of decomposing corpses, piles of bones and broken coffins"[15] was no longer acceptable, for graveyards not only contaminated the environment and endangered the health of the neighbourhood but also sullied the purity of the church.[16] Instead, cemeteries should present "an ordered arrangement of monuments ... as tokens of a nation's progress in civilization" and act as "'sweet breathing places' for contemplation, the indulgence of sweet melancholy, and the improvement, enlightenment and education of those whose lives had not yet run their course".[17] It was in this mood for reform that inner-city graveyards were closed, and carefully designed and landscaped extramural cemeteries such as Liverpool's St. James Cemetery, the Glasgow Necropolis, London's Kensal Green Cemetery and the South Metropolitan Cemetery in Norwood were established. Just as the living were to live clean and godly lives, the dead were to be buried in pleasant Arcadian surroundings where they would not be disturbed and where they would not harm the living.[18]

Burial Grounds and Urban Development in Colonial Singapore

The campaign for extramural internment and properly managed cemeteries in Britain had little impact on colonial Singapore in the first half of the nineteenth century. In a pluralistic society, the question of cemetery location was complicated by the diversity of death rituals and burial customs prevalent among different ethnic and religious communities. The Government Surveyor, J.T. Thomson, observed that

> in Singapore ... native burial grounds are to be met with in all directions
> The Malays seek out sand ridges or *permatangs* in which to bury their dead. The

---

[12] J.C. Riley, *The Eighteenth-Century Campaign to Avoid Disease* (London: Macmillan, 1987), p. 110.

[13] E. Chadwick, "Report on the Sanitary Condition of the Labouring Population of Great Britain: A Supplementary Report on the Results of a Special Inquiry into the Practice of Internment in Towns", *Parliamentary Papers* 12 (1843), para. 249.

[14] R.A. Etlin, *The Architecture of Death: The Transformation of the Cemetery in Eighteenth-Century Paris* (Cambridge, Massachusetts: MIT Press, 1984), p. x.

[15] P. Coones, "Kensal Green Cemetery: London's First Great Extramural Necropolis", *Transactions of the Ancient Monuments Society* 31 (1987): 48.

[16] Etlin, *The Architecture of Death*, pp. 12–17.

[17] Coones, "Kensal Green Cemetery", p. 50.

[18] J.S. Curl, *A Celebration of Death: An Introduction to Some of the Buildings, Monuments, and Settings of Funerary Architecture in the Western European Tradition* (London: Constable, 1980), p. 207.

Chinese look for round knolls and hillsides. The Hindoos burn their bodies, so that nothing may remain of what was a living soul....[19]

The European and Eurasian Christian communities also had a separate Christian cemetery on Fort Canning Hill from the earliest days of the Settlement.[20] The provision and management of cemeteries were communal responsibilities and prior to 1857, apart from the Christian cemetery, the colonial Government exerted little control over the burying places of the Asian communities. As a result, "native" burial grounds were "met with in unexpected places",[21] proliferating within and close to the town and often presenting spectacles of "fresh human bones and coffins and humus sticking out of the sand by the roadsides".[22] Of the most numerous and extensive were the Chinese burial grounds which were "increas[ing] so fast that Singapore seem[ed] likely to become a vast Chinese cemetery".[23] Although the Indian Conservancy Act [XIV] of 1856 prohibited internment in unregistered and unlicensed grounds, enforcement was slack and the Act a dead letter. Consequently, many Chinese families took full advantage of the *de facto* liberty to lay out family and private burial grounds within and outside municipal limits. Once consecrated as graves, the land was seldom given up and in effect, "locked up in perpetuity".[24]

By the 1880s, however, the physical expansion of the city was increasingly restricted by the scarcity of suitable land for building purposes. Building land was in short supply in the immediate area around the perimeter of the city. The northern edge of the city was surrounded by a wide expanse of low-lying swampy land ineffectively drained by the Kallang and Rochore Rivers (Fig. 1). The swamp extended through the Kallang district as far as the Geylang River and inland to Serangoon Road, with several large Malay, Boyanese, Bugis and Orang Laut *kampungs* forming a ring around the seaward edge of the swamp. The undulating high ground to the west of the city centre, the Claymore-Tanglin district, was already an exclusive residential quarter occupied by the bungalow-compounds and recreational facilities of the Europeans and the wealthy Chinese. Any encroachment by working-class housing or undesirable forms of land-use would have been considered detrimental to the market value and amenity of the area. To the south, between Chinatown and New Harbour, the terrain comprised low ranges of hills interspersed with mangrove swamps and low-lying land in the valleys. Most of the high ground here had been appropriated for Chinese burial grounds, both public and private, whilst the valleys were frequently occupied by squatters. In the eyes of colonial town planners intent on relieving overcrowding in the city proper, the

---

[19] J.T. Thomson, *Some Glimpses into Life in the Far East* (London: Richardson, 1864), pp. 280–81.

[20] The first cemetery was a small plot used between an undetermined date after the founding of the Settlement and late 1822 situated close to the Government Residence on Fort Canning Hill. This was closed and a new cemetery opened lower down the Hill towards the end of 1822 [A. Harfield, *Early Cemeteries in Singapore* (London: British Association for Cemeteries in South Asia, 1988), p. 3]. The second cemetery was closed in 1865 when it became full and a new Christian cemetery, the Bukit Timah Road Cemetery, opened about two miles from the town.

[21] *Report of the Committee Appointed to Make Recommendations Regarding Burial and Burial Grounds in the Colony of Singapore* (Singapore: Government Printing Office, 1952), p. 4.

[22] Thomson, *Some Glimpses*, p. 280.

[23] Ibid., p. 282.

[24] *Straits Times* [hereafter, *ST*], 20 Aug. 1887.

proximity of this area to both the southern congested area and the harbour would have rendered it ideal as an overspill area, but "[where] one would expect ... a network of roads, we find nothing but a space that is barren and waste, because almost all that is not swamp is given over to the dead".[25]

From the perspective of the colonial and municipal authorities, urban building land was scarce not only because swamps around the fringe of the city rendered much of the land unsuitable for building, but also because where there were suitable plots of land, they were alienated by the Chinese who converted them into extensive public and

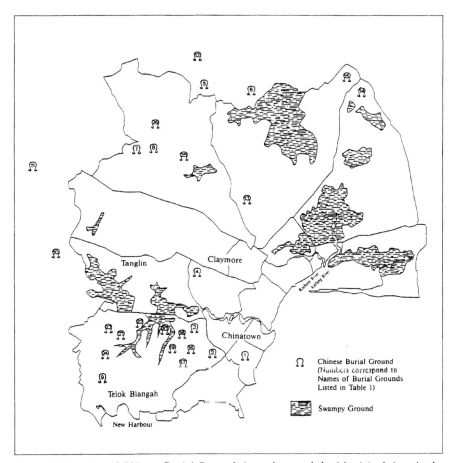

Figure 1: Location of Chinese Burial Grounds in and around the Municipal Area in the Late Nineteenth and Early Twentieth Centuries

---

[25] *Proceedings and Report of the Commission Appointed to Inquire into the Cause of the Present Housing Difficulties in Singapore, and the Steps which should be Taken to Remedy Such Difficulties* [hereafter *RCAICPHD*] 1, 1918, p. A16.

private burial grounds.[26] The Chinese predilection for burying their dead on round knolls and hillsides implied that the same places which would have made ideal residences were "lost to the Colony as far as progress and development [were] concerned, and that in case the land should come into the market, its value [would] have deteriorated".[27] Not only were there fears that it was "a mere question of time before the island of Singapore would become an enormous cemetery",[28] there was also an insistence that selecting "the highest and most beautiful sites" for the dead while "the living [dwelt] on the adjacent low swampy ground" was a misplaced priority among the Chinese.[29] To the western mind, it was an incomprehensible inversion that "[h]aving settled their ancestors ... on the summits of the highest hills in the vicinity, the mourners [should] descend to the swamps and valleys, there to live huddled together in large numbers, [thereby becoming] an easy prey for all infective diseases, especially tuberculosis".[30] The Chinese preference for round knolls and hillsides as burial places was also considered undesirable "from a sanitary point of view" as it was feared that springs at the base of hills from which water for domestic purposes was obtained would become "impregnated with organic matter and thus generate disease among the people in the neighbourhood".[31] By the 1880s, with the emerging pressure for sanitary reform, Chinese burial grounds located within or close to the heart of the city (for example, burial grounds Nos. 1–4 and 16–20 of Table 1; Fig. 1) were increasingly perceived as hazardous to public health, particularly given the persistence of the miasmatic theory of disease which attributed epidemics to pestilential emanations arising from common graves coupled with the popular image of the tropics as a place where "decomposition [was] rapid and where disease assume[d] its acuter forms".[32] The emerging conception of Chinese burial grounds as both insanitary and obstructive to modern urban development soon fuelled a growing contention between the colonial authorities and the Chinese communities over the disposal of the dead, an issue which the *Singapore Free Press* considered "the most vital question that can occupy the attention of any populous community".[33] Just as the relocation of cemeteries in European cities which began a century before implied not simply a modification of urban topography but a general secularization and municipalization of cemetery administration and a reduction of the role of the clergy "to one of supervision and protocol",[34] the debates surrounding the so-called "burials question" in colonial Singapore were complicated by the crucial issue

---

[26] According to the 1905 report of the Burials Committee, there were then in existence 19 Chinese public burial grounds belonging to various dialect and surname organizations, and 59 private burial plots belonging to Chinese families widely distributed within the Municipality ("Report of Committee on the Question of Chinese Burial Grounds", *Proceedings of the Legislative Council of the Straits Settlements* [hereafter, *PLCSS*] 1905, pp. C200-213).

[27] "Report on Chinese Memorial Against the Burial Ordinance [XI] of 1887 by W.A. Pickering, Protector of Chinese, 3 Jan. 1888" (enclosure in Smith to Holland, 1 Feb. 1888, CO 273/151/4517).

[28] *Singapore Free Press* [hereafter *SFP*], 15 Aug. 1887; *ST*, 20 Aug. 1887.

[29] J.D. Vaughan, *The Manners and Customs of the Chinese of the Straits Settlements* (Singapore: Oxford University Press, 1985, first published in 1879), p. 32; *RCAICPHD* 1, 1918, p. A15.

[30] G. Harrower, "Native Medicine and Hygiene in Singapore", *British Medical Journal* 2 (1923): 1175.

[31] *SFP*, 15 Aug. 1887.

[32] Ibid.

[33] Ibid.

[34] Aries, *In the Hour of Our Death*, pp. 484-91.

TABLE 1
CHINESE BURIAL GROUNDS WITHIN MUNICIPAL LIMITS IN
THE LATE NINETEENTH AND EARLY TWENTIETH CENTURIES[1]

No.	Name	Dialect/Surname	Year Opened	Size	Location
1.	Qing Shan Ting	Cantonese/Hakka (public)	1820s	20 acres	Junction of South Bridge Rd and Tanjong Pagar Rd [East of Ann Siang Hill and west of Peck Seah St, on the slopes of Mt Wallich/Scott's Hill]
2.	Heng Shan Ting	Hokkien (public)	1828		Between Silat Rd and Neil Rd
3.	Lu Ye Ting	Cantonese/Hakka (public)	1840	23 acres	Off Outram Rd, between Havelock Rd and Tiong Bahru Rd
4.	Tai Shan Ting	Teochew (public)	1845	70 acres	Bounded by Orchard Rd, Paterson Rd and Grange Rd
5.	Lao Yi Shan	Hainanese (public)	1862	29 acres, 3 roods	Thomson Rd, 5 milestone
6.	Bi Shan Ting	Cantonese (Guang-hui-zhao)	1870		*Kampung* San Teng, off Thomson Rd
7.	Xing Wang Shan/ Tai Yuan Shan	Hokkien *Seh Ong*	1872	221 acres, 2 roods, 34 poles[2]	Near 3½ miles and north of Bukit Timah Rd [Adam Rd, near junction of Kheam Hock Rd]
8.	Lao Shan	Hokkien (public)		98 acres	3½ miles and north of Bukit Timah Rd [off Kheam Hock Rd]
9.	Xie Yuan Shan	Hokkien *Seh Yeo*	1882	128 acres	Silat Gate [4 miles, Telok Blangah Rd]
10.	Yue Shan Ting	Hakka (*Feng-shun, Yong-ding & Da-bu*)	1882	143 acres	Holland Rd, 7½ miles

TABLE 1 (cont'd)

No.	Name	Dialect/Surname	Year Opened	Size	Location
11.	Shuang Long Shan	Hakka (*Jia-ying*)	1887	90 acres	Holland Rd, 5 miles
12.	Xin Yi Shan	Hainanese (public)	1891	33 acres, 2 roods, 31 poles	Thomson Rd, 5½ milestone
13.	Guang En Shan	Teochew (public)			*Kampung* Chia Heng, between Balestier and Thomson Rds
14.	Guang Yi Shan	Teochew (public)		44 acres	Serangoon Rd, 4½ miles
15.		Hokkien *Seh Lee*		66 acres, 1 rood, 7 poles (1952 figure)	Serangoon Rd, 4¾ miles
16.		Hokkien *Seh Choa*			Next to the Lunatic Asylum, between Tiong Bahru and Silat Rds
17.		Hokkien *Seh Khoa* and *Chaw*			*Kampung* Bahru, 2½ miles
18.	Si Jiao Ting	Hokkien (public)			Burial Ground Rd (Tiong Bahru)
19.		Hokkien *Seh Wee*			Off Tiong Bahru Rd
20.		Hokkien *Seh Lim*		44 acres, 3 roods, 61 poles (1952 figure)	Off Tiong Bahru Rd
21.	Lin Ji Shan	Hokkien (public)			Alexandra Rd, 3½ miles
22.		Hokkien (public) Northeast portion set aside for *Seh Gun*			Alexandra Rd, 3 miles

(cont'd overleaf)

TABLE 1 (cont'd)

No.	Name	Dialect/Surname	Year Opened	Size	Location
23.		Hokkien *Seh Ong*			Alexandra Rd, 3rd milestone, about ¾ miles off the road
24.		Hokkien (public)			Alexandra Rd, 4½ miles
25.	Coffee Hill Ka Fei Shan	Hokkien (public)	Licensed 1918	50 acres	Between Mt Pleasant and Whitley Rds
26.	Bukit Brown Chinese Cemetery	Municipal	1922	213 acres	Junction of Kheam Hock Rd and Sime Rd

Notes: [1]This list is confined to burial grounds which were opened to Chinese belonging to particular *seh* or surname groups (such as Nos. 7, 9, 15, 16, 17, 19, 20 and 23), to immigrants from particular districts in China (such as Nos. 6, 10 and 11), or more generally, to particular dialect groups (such as 1–5, 8, 12, 13, 14, 21, 24 and 25). Also included is the Chinese Municipal Cemetery (No. 26) which was opened to all Chinese regardless of affiliations. In colonial sources, these are generally referred to as "public" burial grounds as opposed to "private" ones reserved for family burial.
[2]About 140 acres of this estate was acquired by the Municipality in 1919/20 for the Bukit Brown Municipal Cemetery (*Minutes of General Committee Meeting* [hereafter MGCM], 8 Mar. 1918; *Minutes of Proceedings of Municipal Commissioners at an Ordinary Meeting* [hereafter MPMCOM], 28 Nov. 1919).

Sources: *List of Existing Cemeteries, 1989* (Ministry of Environment, Singapore); *Proceedings of the Legislative Council of the Straits Settlements*, 1905, pp. C202–208; "List of Chinese Burial Grounds within the Municipal Limits of Singapore"; Peng Song Toh, *Directory of Associations in Singapore, 1982/1983* (Singapore: Historical Culture Publishers, 1983), pp. L17–133; *165th Anniversary Commemorative and Souvenir Publication of the Ying Fo Fui Kun, Singapore, 1827–1987* (Singapore, 1989), pp. 26, 30, 90–91; *Historical Account of Fu De Ci and Lu Ye Ting* (Singapore, 1963), pp. 37–38; *Souvenir Magazine of the Opening Ceremony of the Kheng Chiu Building* (Singapore, 1965), p. 173; *The Yang Clan Genealogy* (Singapore, 1965), G16; *118th Anniversary Souvenir Magazine of the Singapore Guang Hui Zhao Bi Shan Ting* (Singapore, 1988), unpaginated; *Souvenir Magazine of the Singapore Kai Min Ong See Benevolent Association* (Singapore, 1977), p. 76; Zhang Qin Yong, "Yang shi jia zu yu xie yuan shan", *Asian Culture* 8 (Oct. 1986): 24–27; *Report of the Committee Appointed to Make Recommendations Regarding Burial and Burial Grounds*, p. 14; and information gathered from the Singapore Hokkien Huay Kuan, the Teo Chew Poit Ip Huay Kuan, the Ying Fo Fui Kun and the Singapore Kiung Chow Hwee Kuan in Sept./Oct. 1989.

The Control of Chinese Burial Grounds:
The Debate Over the 1887 Burials Bill and Subsequent Legislation

In 1887, an attempt was made to bring Chinese burial grounds under some semblance of control through an ordinance authorizing the licensing, regulation and inspection of burial and burying grounds.[35] The *raison d'etre* for the bill appeared to have been two-fold. First, by licensing and controlling the siting of burial grounds, further alienation of land suitable for the construction of buildings and roads could be prevented. Second, by prescribing sanitary regulations governing the depth of graves and proper places for internment, public health would be safeguarded. The introduction of the Burials Bill during the August Legislative Council sessions generated much agitation and concern among the Chinese of all three of the Straits Settlements. Seah Liang Seah, the Chinese member of the Council requested a postponement of the second reading to allow more time for consideration as the Bill "seriously affected the interests of the Chinese community, mostly those of the respectable class".[36] In particular, he perceived that the Bill aimed at "the suppression of private burial grounds", a measure which would "much affect the much-cherished customs of the better class of the Chinese".[37] The Colonial Secretary, in granting the postponement, assured the Council that the Bill had been drawn up "with full regard for the feelings of the Chinese", and that there were no intentions to interfere with their "feelings and religious sentiment".[38] However, he made it clear that Chinese custom could only be tolerated "within reasonable limits and without sacrificing the good of the community":

> it is not right that all other classes of the community should be sacrificed to the desires of one section [the Chinese], to secure, for instance, all the small hills, which are the only places suitable for healthy houses in these countries, and take them for ever, sometimes merely as a monument to the honour of a man's family and his own personal vanity.[39]

From the perspective of the Chinese, the Burials Bill represented an attack on Chinese customary rituals and an erosion of Chinese control over their own sacred spaces. Whilst there were initially rumours of riots and threats of violence, the protest

---

[35] The Burials Bill of 1887 proposed to transfer the control of burial and burning grounds, hitherto vested in the Municipality, to the Government. It directed the Governor-in-Council to issue licences for existing burial grounds on the conditions that application for a licence was made within three months of the Ordinance coming into force and also that the continued use of the burial ground would not endanger "the health and comfort of the public". It further specified that internment was to be allowed only in places licensed for the purpose and that burying or burning corpses in unlicensed grounds incurred a maximum penalty of one hundred dollars. The Governor-in-Council was also authorized to frame rules and regulations to fix the depth of graves, the amount of fees charged for burials, and for the registration, inspection and management of cemeteries and burning grounds (*PLCSS*, 8 Aug. 1887, pp. B91–B92; *ST*, 20 Aug. 1887).
[36] *PLCSS*, 15 Aug. 1887, p. B101.
[37] Ibid.
[38] Ibid., p. B102.
[39] Ibid., p. B103.

against the bill soon resolved itself into constitutional channels.[40] This was mainly because the bill principally affected the wealthier and more prominent members of the Chinese community who could afford private burial grounds and who were chiefly responsible for reserving large parcels of land for use as family graves. Protest against the bill was hence led by leaders of the community who were familiar with the legislative system and conversant with their own rights and privileges under such a system.[41] The means of protest adopted included letters to the press, public meetings to gather support and petitions to the Resident Councillors and the Governor. When the latter failed to arrest the progress of the bill through the Legislative Council,[42] memorials pleading their cause were sent to Sir H.T. Holland, the Secretary of State for the Colonies in London.[43]

In the main, it was argued that among the Chinese, ancestor-worship, and in particular sepulchral veneration, would be incomplete if the liberty to select propitious burial sites according to the principles of geomancy were curtailed by government interference.[44] The concept of control of burial places by an external agency was an alien notion among the Chinese.[45] *Feng-shui*,[46] or Chinese geomancy, was considered

---

[40]Among the Chinese plebeian classes, there were signs of "much alarm", largely because of the rumour that the bill proposed to give magistrates the power to remove bodies which had already been buried ("Report on Ordinance [XI] of 1887 by J.W. Bonser, Attorney-General, 5 Sept. 1887", in Weld to Holland, 10 Sept. 1887, CO 273/146/20985). While widespread "alarm" did not culminate in violence on this occasion, it was probable that ill-feeling against the Government generated by the introduction of the Burials Bill contributed in part to the outbreak of the "verandah riots" in February the following year.

[41]The Penang memorialists, for example, made it clear that not only were they fully aware of the channels of protest open to them, but also from whom they had learnt their strategies:

> We admit that we have not refused to avail ourselves of *constitutional* means to fight our own rights and privileges [sic] when such a vital and important matter as our time-honoured usages were threatened with interference, and probable eventual abolition.... Enlightenment, consequent on liberal education and contact with civilized people, encourages loyal subjects and citizens to act as their brethren in civilized countries, in contending for their rights and privileges when they are deemed to be encroached on, or threatened, by any Legislative measure (*Pinang Gazette and Straits Chronicle*, 14 Oct. 1887).

[42]The Burials Bill was passed as Ordinance [XI] of 1887 on 25 August 1887, merely eighteen days after its first reading (*PLCSS*, 25 Aug. 1887, p. B125).

[43]Each of the Chinese communities in Penang, Malacca and Singapore sent a separate memorial to Holland. See enclosures in Smith to Holland, 1 Feb. 1888, CO 273/151/4517.

[44]To the Chinese, Government control of burial sites was considered oppressive because in China itself, people were not bound, either by law or custom, to bury their dead in special areas. According to de Groot, "everyone had full liberty to inter his dead wherever he [chose], provided he possess[ed] the ground, or [held] it by some legal title acquired from the legal owner". There were also severe laws against the violation of dead bodies and the desecration of graves. See J.J.M. de Groot, *The Religious System of China* 3 (Taipei: Ch'eng-wen, 1969, first published in 1892), pp. 867, 874–75, 939. What often impressed the western observer as unusual about the Chinese landscape in the late nineteenth and early twentieth centuries was "the ubiquity of individual and clan graves among the tilled fields". See R.G. Knapp, "The Changing Landscape of the Chinese Cemetery", *The China Geographer* 8 (1977): 1.

[45]Cf. Knapp, "The Changing Landscape", p. 7.

[46]*Feng-shui* literally means "winds and waters" and is defined by Chatley as "the art of adapting residences of the living and the dead so as to cooperate and harmonise with the local currents of the cosmic breath" inherent in a particular configuration of the landscape. Although translated as "geomancy", it is entirely different from divination methods which passed under that name in the west. See J. Needham, *Science and Civilisation in China* 2 (Cambridge: Cambridge University Press, 1956), p. 359.

central to the Chinese faith because it was believed, so the petitioners claimed, that it was possible to site the grave in relation to the configuration of the landscape and the vicinity of watercourses in such a way that benign influences were drawn from the earth and transmitted to the descendants of the deceased. In general, a favoured burial site was one situated at the conjunction between the "azure dragon" on the left and the "white tiger" on the right, the former signifying boldly rising "male" ground and the latter emblematic of softly undulating "female" ground. The site should ideally contain three-fifths "male" and two-fifths "female" ground and should be open in front to breezes, shut in on the right and left, with a tortuous, winding stream running before it. Such ground contained an abundant supply of beneficial "vital breath" which augured well for descendants. On the other hand, flat, monotonous surfaces or landscapes characterized by bold, straight lines such as the presence of a straight line of ridges, a watershed, railway embankment, road or water running off a straight course tended to concentrate malign influences and were avoided as burial sites.[47] In sum, there was a preference for tortuous or winding structures which fitted with rather than dominated the landscape, and a strong objection to straight lines and geometrical layouts which constrained and imprisoned nature rather than flowed along with it.[48] Once sited according to geomantic principles, both the tomb and its sepulchral boundaries were considered "inviolable"[49] as any interference with them would spoil the efficacy of the *feng-shui* and imperil the welfare and prosperity of the living descendants. In short, burial grounds, by nature of being sacred sites, must be exempt from government control and external interference. The petitioners argued that, as in Roman law, "[t]he ground in which one, who had the right, buried a dead body, became *ipso facto religious*; it ceased to be private property; it would not be bought or sold, or transferred or used; it was for ever dedicated to the dead and reserved from all current usages; and it should be *sacrosanct* to the memory of the departed".[50] In Chinese culture, the burial landscape itself became sacrosanct because landscape formed the basic material of architecture. As Oswald Spengler has argued, for the Chinese, "[i]t is the architecture of the landscape, and only that, which explains the architecture of the buildings.... The temple [or tomb] is not a self-contained building but a layout, in which hills, water, trees, flowers and stones in definite forms and dispositions are just as important as gates, walls, buildings and houses".[51] This view stems from the

---

[47]For more detailed discussions on the use of geomantic principles among the Chinese in Singapore and China in siting burial places see E.J. Eitel, *Feng-Shui* (Singapore: Graham Brash, 1985, first published in 1873); de Groot, *The Religious System in China* 3, pp. 935-55; S. Feuchtwang, *An Anthropological Analysis of Chinese Geomancy* (Vientiane: Vithagna, 1974); E. Lip, *Chinese Geomancy* (Singapore: Times Books International, 1979).

[48]Needham, *Science and Civilisation* 2, p. 361.

[49]"The Humble Memorial from the Undersigned Chinese Merchants, Traders, Planters and other Chinese Inhabitants of Singapore to Sir H.T. Holland, 30 Nov. 1887" (enclosure in Smith to Holland, 1 Feb. 1988, CO 273/151/4517).

[50]Quoted by Koh Seang Tat, one of the Penang leaders in the protest, in his representation to the Governor, dated 25 Aug. 1887 (reproduced in the *Pinang Gazette and Straits Chronicle*, 14 Oct. 1887). The passage appears to be a loose paraphrase of paragraphs 6 and 9 in Book 2 (on "The Law of Things") of *The Institutes of Gaius*, trans. F. de Zulueta (Oxford: Clarendon Press, 1946), Part I, p. 67, which defends the sacro-sanctity and inalienability of burial grounds.

[51]O. Spengler, *The Decline of the West* (London: George Allen and Unwin, English abridged edition 1961, first published 1932), p. 115.

basic conception of space in Chinese culture as a meandering path that wandered through the world, whereby "the individual is conducted to his god or ancestral tomb ... by friendly Nature herself, ... [by] devious ways through doors, over bridges, round hills and walls".[52] Also basic to *feng-shui* was the notion that human intervention in the natural landscape was fraught with risks and generated repercussions on society. The Chinese conception of the universe was one where "men are bonded to the physical environment, working good or ill upon it and being done good or ill to by it".[53] As explained by Maurice Freedman,

> in the Chinese view, ... [t]he physical universe is alive with forces that, on the one side, can be shaped and brought fruitfully to bear on a dwelling and those who live in it, and on the other side, can by oversight or mismanagement be made to react disastrously.... [I]n principle, every act of construction disturbs a complex balance of forces within a system made up of nature and society, and it must be made to produce a new balance of forces lest evil follow.[54]

Feng-shui considerations hence had to be carefully taken into account in siting a grave (or any other building) if harmony between society and the physical landscape were to be maintained. As "a theory of location", it "offers man the opportunity to exercise his 'responsibility' to the cosmos by fixing the limits of 'change' in terms of the visible landscape configuration which represents the cosmos in a living, spatial dimension".[55] Unlike in western science where the "environment" as a concept is often broken down and analyzed in separate categories, *feng-shui* unifies the geological, atmospheric, aesthetic and psychological qualities of the environment in one theory and code of practice which is seen as integral to the lives of the people.

On both sides, arguments were deftly marshalled to press their case home. The Chinese quoted their sages, drew out innumerable examples illustrating how deeply-seated and inviolable the principles of geomancy were among the Chinese, and appealed to the Imperial Charter which provided for due respect of the religious sentiments of all races. The discourse was strategically couched in terms of religious idealism, because religion and sacred places associated with it could claim the privilege of being beyond the purview of a secular government. The Chinese were also quick to counter the charge that hillside burial grounds were insanitary and liable to contaminate the city's water supply. They argued that pollution of hill streams was impossible because unlike those of Malays and Europeans, Chinese graves were of considerable depth and lined with great quantities of quicklime. It was constantly reiterated that the grave of a wealthy Chinese was "substantially built", "planted round at great cost with shrubs" and regularly visited and tended, and that the coffin was made of "the hardest wood that [could] be obtained and well-lacquered" so that it was "perfectly tight and waterproof".[56] The memorial sent to the Colonial Secretary of State summarized these arguments and put forward two main requests. First, notwithstanding the assurances

---

[52]Ibid.

[53]M. Freedman, "Geomancy", in *Proceedings of the Royal Anthropological Institute of Great Britain and Ireland for 1968* (London, Royal Anthropological Institute of Great Britain and Ireland, 1969), p. 7.

[54]Ibid.

[55]B. Boxer, "Space, Change and *Feng-shui* in Tsuen Wan's Urbanization", *Journal of Asian and African Studies* 3 (1968): 235.

[56]*ST*, 19 Aug. 1887; *PLCSS*, 22 Aug. 1887, p. B122, "The Humble Memorial ... 30 Nov. 1887".

given by the local Government that their religious customs would be respected, the memorialists feared that the Burials Ordinance opened up the possibility, and even the likely prospect, that their burial grounds would be "seized and turned to other purposes".[57] Their foremost request was that existing burial grounds would be protected from such "contemplated desecration". Second, they requested the liberty to choose their own burial sites outside a radius of two miles from the town proper in accordance with "their religious faith in ancestor worship" and "as directed in the teachings of their sages Confucius and Mencius".[58]

In their turn, the local Government and the English language press cited the land scarcity, sanitation, the public good, and attempted to counter the Chinese argument by showing that the much-vaunted religious idiosyncrasies of the Chinese were by no means respected by the Mandarins in China who "[did] not scruple to appropriate with little delicacy of feeling burial grounds, shrines, etc. when required for Government purposes".[59] The Colonial Secretary, in defending the Burials Bill, cited evidence demonstrating that in China ancestral temples were summarily demolished to make way for Government projects[60] and claimed that "the Chinese had no real feeling against removing graves". In fact, he had been "reliably informed" by the Consul-General of Shanghai that Chinese people "were in the habit of placing the remains of their ancestors in urns in order that they might at any convenient season remove them from one place to another".[61] In short, the wealthy Chinese had no "real" grievance

---

[57]"The Humble Memorial ... 30 Nov. 1887".

[58]Ibid.

[59]"Report on Chinese Memorial Against the Burial Ordinance [XI] of 1887".

[60]The Colonial Secretary referred to an article published in the *Lat Pau*, the local Chinese newspaper, detailing an actual case in the Nam Hoi district in China wherein an ancestral temple and certain houses in front of the *yamen* were acquired for demolition ("News from China", *Lat Pau*, 28 Aug. 1886, translated by W.A. Pickering, the Protector of Chinese and reproduced in *PLCSS*, 15 Aug. 1887, pp. B102-B103). The *Straits Times* further cited the clearance of graves to facilitate the laying of a railway line from Tientsin to Taku in China. The editor claimed that the incident was clear evidence that "the Chinese Government set little store by any superstitious feelings among the people as regards the disturbance of graves" and urged the Straits Government to "profit from the example given by the Chinese Government" (*ST*, 7 Sept. 1887).

[61]*PLCSS*, 15 Aug. 1887, p. B103. In his representation to the Government, Koh Seang Tat, one of the Penang Chinese leading the protest against the Burials Bill, refuted the view that storage of remains in urns was proof of lack of veneration of the dead among the Chinese. He claimed that this custom, which was only practised by the wealthy Chinese, was not contrary but in fact in accordance with their "well-meaning and pious belief in Geomancy". According to strict geomantic principles, the Chinese were obliged to keep the remains in urns and wait for a propitious time and place for burial (*Pinang Gazette* and *Straits Chronicle*, 14 Oct. 1887). Opposing interpretations of Chinese burial customs were symptomatic of the fact that the ritual repertoire associated with death in Chinese society was extremely complex and also variable among different regions and dialect groups. For example, it has been observed that among the Cantonese, a system of "double burial" was practised whereby the burial of a body in a coffin was followed by exhumation, the temporary storage of the bones in an urn and reburial of the urn in a geomantically suitable tomb [J.L. Watson, "Of Flesh and Bones: The Management of Death Pollution in Cantonese Society", in *Death and the Regeneration of Life*, ed. M. Bloch and J. Parry (Cambridge: Cambridge University Press, 1982), p. 155]. In north China, "double burial" was uncommon and the encoffined body was directly laid to rest in substantial tombs [S. Naquin, "Funerals in North China: Uniformity and Variation", in *Death Ritual in Late and Modern China*, ed. J.L. Watson and E.S. Rawski (Berkeley: University of California Press, 1988), p. 44]. In colonial Singapore, the latter custom was the norm, it being common for wealthy Chinese to prepare elaborate family graves well ahead of time ("Memo. on the Burials Ordinance [XI] of 1887, Straits Settlements by D.F.A. Harvey, 25 Oct. 1887", in Weld to Holland, 10 Sept. 1887, CO 273/146/20985.

and were simply pandering to vested interest under the guise of religious sentiment instead of protecting public health and advancing public good. Their request to be allowed to select their own burial sites outside a two-mile radius of the town was also dismissed by the Governor as tantamount to asking for an "illegal privilege".[62] The Protector of Chinese, W.A. Pickering, further reduced the issue to a question of choosing between two sets of priorities:

> Are [Chinese] customs connected with the burial and worship of the dead compatible with the sanitary welfare of the living general community, and is the practice of buying land and appropriating some of the best sites as private mausolea conducive to the interest of the Government as regards the reasonable development of the Land Revenue, and the progress and prosperity of the Colony?[63]

In his mind, the answer was unassailably clear: the claims of the living must prevail over those of the dead, customs should not be allowed to stand in the way of urban progress and land revenue, and private benefits should be subservient to "that of the superior law, the welfare of the general public".[64] The burials question was hence polarized into choosing between diametrically opposed priorities such as between the living and the dead, the progressive and the customary, and the public and the private.

On receiving the Chinese petitions from each of the three Settlements, Holland, the Secretary of State for the Colonies, felt that the coming into operation of the Burials Ordinance should be postponed[65] and instructed the Governor to repeal the ordinance and re-enact it with modifications to take into account Chinese sentiments. The ordinance was duly repealed but no further legislative action was taken on the burials question during the next eight years. It was not until 1896 when the burials issue was resurrected in relation to the bill to amend the Municipal Ordinance.[66] This time, it was decided to introduce dual legislation. Outside municipal limits, Burial Ordinance [XIX] of 1896 transferred the duty of licensing and controlling burial grounds to the colonial Government. Within municipal limits, however, under sections 232 to 238 of the Municipal Ordinance [XV] of 1896,[67] the control of burial grounds was vested in the Municipal Commission rather than in the colonial Government (as opposed to what was contemplated by the 1887 Burials Bill). The municipal authorities were empowered to license and inspect burial grounds, to close them if they proved "dangerous to the health of persons living in the neighbourhood" and to impose a maximum penalty of five hundred dollars for the disposal of corpses in unlicensed places.

Although the new ordinance signified an important though much delayed victory for the colonial and municipal authorities, certain concessions had to be made to meet

---

[62]Smith to Holland, 1 Feb. 1888, CO 273/151/4517.
[63]"Report on Chinese Memorial Against the Burial Ordinance [XI] of 1887".
[64]Ibid.
[65]*PLCSS*, 29 Nov. 1887, p. B164.
[66]In 1889, when the Indian Act [XIV] of 1856 and the Conservancy Ordinance [II] of 1879 (both containing clauses which hitherto governed burial grounds) were repealed by the Municipal Amendment Ordinance [XVII], no provisions were made to introduce new regulations and hence from 1889 to 1896, no laws existed for the control of burial grounds (*Administrative Report of the Singapore Municipality* [hereafter, *ARSM*] 1900, p. 13).
[67]C.G. Garrad, *The Acts and Ordinances of the Legislative Council of the Straits Settlements from 1st April 1867 to 7th March 1898* 2 (London: Eyre and Spottiswoode, 1898), pp. 1544–46.

Chinese demands. Contrary to the wishes of the municipal authorities, for example, private tombs and family burial grounds were to be licensed but not prohibited.[68] The colonial Government was unable to commit itself to a definite policy aimed at "the final extinction of private burial grounds" as "there were insufficient public burial grounds to provide for the reasonable wants of all communities" and instead preferred to leave "the burning question of private burial grounds" to municipal discretion to be exercised through the granting and refusing of licences.[69] The introduction of licensing fees was, in the opinion of the Municipal President, an "unfortunate one" for "a licence fee [could] not make a burial ground sanitary or reduce the inconvenience caused by it to the general public".[70] Furthermore, the Chinese who could afford the luxury of private burial grounds were unlikely to be deterred by high licence fees but would instead regard licence fees as "another way on the part of Commissioners of squeezing a revenue out of them".[71] That the control of burial grounds was vested in the Municipality rather than the Government was in itself an important concession to the Chinese because Chinese views were far more effectively represented on the Municipal Board than at the level of the colonial Government. Whilst Alex Gentle, the Municipal President in the last decade of the nineteenth century, had consistently opposed the extension of old burial grounds and the multiplication of new ones, he had been frequently outvoted by Commissioners on these issues.[72] Gentle's successor, J.O. Anthonisz, also complained that the perspective of the Commissioners was essentially myopic and far too liberal for they tended to assess what constituted "fit and proper places" for burial purposes on the basis of "the effect on the public health and the avoidance of a nuisance" rather than from the point of view of "the effect on possible town improvements and the future development of the town".[73] A 1897 amendment to the Burials Ordinance [XIX] of 1896 reduced the maximum penalty for unlicensed burials outside municipal limits from five to one hundred dollars, a stroke described by one of the members of the Legislative Council as being tantamount to "an invitation to the Chinese community to bury their dead without any licence at all, wherever they please".[74]

Conflicting Discourses: Chinese Versus Western Conceptions of the Significance of "Sacred" Space

The Chinese burial grounds remained a contentious issue primarily because of diametrically polarized views of the significance and utility of the space they occupied in a congested city. For the Chinese, the significance of raising a grave went beyond the need to commemorate, preserve or identify, and the remains of the dead held more than simply emotional resonance. Instead, a grave was the physical abode of the

---

[68] *ARSM* 1896, p. 16.
[69] *PLCSS*, 23 July 1896, reported in *ST*, 24 July 1896.
[70] *ARSM* 1900, p. 13.
[71] Ibid.
[72] Ibid., p. 12.
[73] Ibid.
[74] The amendment was introduced on the orders of the Secretary of State for the Colonies who objected to the severity of penalties prescribed by the 1896 Burials Ordinance (*PLCSS*, 15 Apr. 1897, p. B29; *PLCSS*, 29 Aug. 1897, pp. B41–42).

soul of the deceased, and an essential component of ancestor-worship.[75] Chinese brick graves were normally horseshoe or omega-shaped, with the word *zu*, meaning "ancestor", and the word *mu*, literally meaning "home of the deceased" inscribed on the top and bottom of gravestones respectively. Space set aside for the dead was sacrosanct; it was not perceived as space which had been alienated from the living, but instead, its preservation was believed to have a propitious and benign effect on the welfare of the deceased's descendants. For the Chinese, the idea of the continuity of kinship beyond death and the notion of exchange between the living and the dead were central to their death rituals.[76] The dead were hence linked to the living by relationships of reciprocity: through the principles of *feng-shui* the living were able to use their ancestors as the media for the attainment of worldly prosperity, and in return, the dead received constant veneration, meticulous attention and offerings of food and joss-paper at the ancestral tomb. It was not clear whether the Chinese believed that the remains of the dead themselves acted as the source of power and beneficence or whether these served as conductors of a power which originated in nature itself[77] but in either case, the ancestral tomb and its "sepulchral boundaries"[78] (that is, the configuration of landscape surrounding the tomb) were considered inviolable because any form of interference could destroy the source of power and lead to a reversal of family fortunes. Geomancy was hence a means through which the Chinese could not so much control as capitalize upon and align themselves to the natural environment in order to appropriate its bounty through the rituals of ancestor-worship.

The classification and spatial organization of Chinese burial grounds were also related to the world of the living in another sense: the burial place and the associated rituals of death were a testimony of the social worth of the dead person as well as his family. For the immigrant Chinese, what was most prestigious was burial in an auspiciously located family-plot back in China, as Low Ngiong Ing, an early twentieth-century Hockchiu immigrant, explained:

> An immigrant, if he could afford it, would return to China every few years. In his perambulations he would keep his eyes open for a desirable burial-plot, a knoll commanding a good view, and auspicious according to the laws of geomancy. For we did not mind being men of *Nanyang*, but that dying, we would hate to be ghost of Nanyang. If we prospered, we would pile up money in China in order to renovate

---

[75] Jan Jakob Mariade de Groot, writing about religious customs in China in the late nineteenth century, observed that for the Chinese, "graves ... are not a means to rid one's self of useless mortal remains in a way considered most decent; nor are they merely rendered sacred to the memory of the dead.... [T]he grave ... is sacred especially as an abode of the soul, not only indispensable for its happiness, but also for its existence, for no disembodied spirit can long escape destruction unless the body co-exists with it to serve it as a natural support. Both the body and the soul require a grave for their preservation. Hence the grave, being the chief shelter of the soul, virtually becomes the principal altar dedicated to it and to its worship." (de Groot, *The Religious System of China* 3, p. 855).

[76] J.L. Watson, "The Structure of Chinese Funerary Rites: Elementary Forms, Ritual Sequence, and the Primacy of Performance", in Watson and Rawski, *Death Ritual*, p.9; Tong Chee Kiong, "Dangerous Blood, Refined Souls: Death Rituals among the Chinese in Singapore" (Ph.D. diss., Cornell University, 1987), pp.340–42.

[77] R.S. Watson, "Remembering the Dead: Graves and Politics in Southeastern China", in Watson and Rawski, *Death Ritual*, pp. 206–207.

[78] "The Humble Memorial ... 30 Nov. 1887".

the ancestral graves and the ancestral homes, to redeem the ancestral fields and add to them ... so that men might know we were somebody.[79]

For Straits-born Chinese and those who could not afford posthumous repartriation, an auspicious burial site in Singapore was the best substitute. In colonial Singapore, Chinese burial grounds were of three classes. First, there were a large number of private burial grounds belonging to wealthy families who had settled in Singapore.[80] Graves were often prepared and reserved for each member of the family well ahead of time on private estates.[81] These family graves were akin to "substantial residences" and were often set in several acres of ground landscaped according to the requirements of *fengshui*.[82] The family name invariably dominated the burial space, and the grave itself represented not only a monument to the family's social standing but also the focus of ancestor-worship, a crucial element in a social system which emphasized filial piety, the sanctity of the family name and the perpetuation of family lineage. The importance of these notions was epitomized in the gravestone on which were inscribed the name of the deceased in green to signify death, as well as the family name in red to signify life and the hope that the family name would never pass away but would be carried on by descendants.[83] A second type of burial grounds were those belonging to separate surname- or district-based associations (Plates 1 and 2). These grounds were set aside as separate burial places for "the better class of Chinese" who in their lifetime belonged to these associations and who were guaranteed a burial place in the communal burial grounds by virtue of membership and financial subscription.[84] They signified both the complex internal divisions of Chinese society in Singapore and the solidarity of those associated by surname or provenance. A third class of burial grounds were those "presented to the Chinese community by wealthy Chinamen and by subscription among Chinamen to give decent burial to the Chinese poor".[85] These were opened to particular dialect groups and contained the graves of the poor who were neither able to afford a private plot nor funeral subscriptions and had to depend on charity to secure a resting place. As in life, the dead were also stratified according to a rigid socio-economic hierarchy and burial places not only symbolized but perpetuated social distinctions which death failed to eradicate. The "social organization of death" not only reflects the social world of the living, but "in the act of reflecting, provides a

---

[79]N.I. Low, *Recollections: Chinese Jetsam on a Tropical Shore [and] When Singapore was Syonan-to* (Singapore: Eastern Universities Press, 1983), p. 112.

[80]According to municipal records, in 1900, there were 162 private burial grounds belonging to all ethnic communities within municipal limits, of which 143 were still in use and 19 disused (*ARSM* 1900, p. 12).

[81]In 1892, Tay Geok Teat, one of the Chinese Commissioners in the latter half of the year, for example, applied for permission from the Municipal Board to make two graves, one for his recently deceased wife and one for himself, on a piece of land in Teluk Blangah where nine family graves were already sited (*MPMCOM*, 26 Oct. 1892). Similarly, in 1893, the wealthy landowner, Cheang Hong Lim, was buried in a grave "already prepared on his property on Alexandra Road" (*MPMCOM*, 15 Mar. 1893). For the Chinese, the procurement of a grave and the preparation of grave clothes and a coffin well before death were considered symbols of longevity and status (de Groot, *The Religious System of China* 3, p. 1031).

[82]Vaughan, *The Manners and Customs of the Chinese*, p. 32; *SFP*, 15 Aug. 1887; "The Humble Memorial ... 30 Nov. 1887".

[83]Tong, "Dangerous Blood, Refined Souls", p. 133.

[84]"The Humble Memorial ... 30 Nov. 1887".

[85]Ibid.

Plate 1 The Hokkien *Seh* Ong burial grounds at Kheam Hock Road, an example of a Chinese burial ground belonging to a surname association. This building houses the Ong family altar and the caretaker's quarters (1990 photograph).

Plate 2 The *Seh* Ong burial grounds, once covering over 220 acres of which less than a quarter remains today, with many omega-shaped tombstones still visible (1990 photograph).

basis and a structure through which the world is sustained and reaffirmed".[86] The principles of unity and lines of cleavage which structured Chinese society in the world of the living were hence equally inscribed and reaffirmed in the sacred spaces of the dead.

The colonial and municipal authorities, however, were unable to appreciate the sanctity of sepulchral veneration and its ramifications, and saw it as an example of the idiosyncratic prejudices of the Chinese. The Attorney-General, J.W. Bonser, for example, dismissed geomantic considerations as "a farrago of superstitious and ignorant nonsense".[87] Thus, as Sack has argued, the irreducible fluidity of meaning inherent in "mythical-magical" space renders it opaque to those in authority who subscribed to the rationality of "scientific" planning, for the transparency of sacred symbols could only be appreciated "through the eyes of the culture" which produced them.[88] From the colonial perspective, progress, development and public welfare could only be advanced by a rational use of space according to the dictates of western planning theory and sanitary science rather than the mysterious workings of geomancy. The Attorney General further urged that while "[r]espect for religious superstition is all very well to a certain extent, ... it must not be allowed to interfere with the interest of the Community" and that it was time the Chinese learnt that the Straits Settlements was "British and not Chinese Territory".[89] Thus, the debate over sacred space in all its well-publicized aspects was not only important in so far as its resolution had landuse and sanitary implications, but was also perceived as symbolic of the more general ideological aspect of the struggle for control over territory.

Less "Visible" Aspects of the Conflict Over Chinese Burial Grounds

The debate provoked by the introduction of burials legislation represented the better publicized, better ventilated aspects of the conflict over the rights of religious practice and the significance of burial grounds. As seen, the main protagonists on both sides employed constitutional measures to advance their claims. The concern for a suitable place of burial was, however, not confined to the wealthy Chinese but shared by a wide spectrum of Chinese immigrant society. Conflicts between the authorities and the Chinese labouring classes over burial grounds were less "visible" but possibly more pervasive. In contrast to their wealthier compatriots, the strategies of the labouring classes in securing places of repose were less public, non-constitutional and often clandestine.

Selecting an ideal burial site in order to procure the benefits of geomancy was to a large extent a privilege of the wealthy Chinese. The bulk of the labouring classes could not afford private sites tailored to meet personal *feng-shui* esoterica but had to be content with common graveyards run by Chinese associations. *Feng-shui* was not entirely disregarded in the siting of clan- or surname-based burial grounds and, as far as possible, associations selected sites in broad conformity with general geomantic principles. The Hokkien "Yeo" clan, for example, claimed that according to the *kan*

---

[86]L. Prior, *The Social Organization of Death: Medical Discourse and Social Practices in Belfast* (Basingstoke: Macmillan Press, 1989), p. 111.

[87]"Copy of a Minute by J.W. Bonser, Attorney-General, 12 Nov. 1887", in Smith to Holland, 16 Nov. 1887, CO 273/148/25479.

[88]Sack, *Conceptions of Space*, pp. 148, 163–64, 189–93.

[89]"Copy of a Minute by J.W. Bonser, Attorney-General, 12 Nov. 1887".

yu jia or professional geomancer, their burial ground at Telok Blangah, *Xie Yuan Shan* (No. 9 in Table 1), had the best *feng-shui* in Singapore.[90] A place of repose after death was highly important to the poorer immigrant Chinese for one of their worst fears was "that they might die overseas, leaving their spirits wandering around without sacrifices".[91] Without the performance of proper burial rites, the deceased would not be ensured of a safe passage through the realms of the underworld, and, unworshipped and unremembered, he would pass into and become indistinct from an undifferentiated mass of anonymous "ghosts" (*gui*) existing in a state of marginality.

In the first century of Indian and later colonial rule, neither the Straits Government nor the municipal authorities established cemeteries to cater to the needs of the Chinese population. Corpses were sometimes dumped on five-foot-ways, back-lanes and other public places in the hope that they would be recovered by the police and given the decency of burial that the relatives themselves could not afford. As Wong Toh, an impoverished cake hawker explained:

> I had no money to bury [my brother] and no one would help me. Also the inmates would not allow the dead body to remain [in the house]. I therefore carried his body on my back to the back-lane. I knew that the police would find the body and bury it, but I did not know it was against the law to put the body there.[92]

Whilst the dumping of bodies was not uncommon among the very poor or where relatives tried to prevent "dangerous infectious diseases" from being traced to particular houses, Chinese society had its own mechanisms to confront the precariousness of life and to prepare for death. Chinese dialect, surname and mutual benefit organizations not only supervised the various practicalities of dying,[93] but through rites and ritual, attenuated the isolation of death and imbued it with social significance. One of their chief functions was the collection of subscriptions during a member's economically productive period as a hedge against funeral expenses. Those who could not afford private burial depended on these organizations to provide a "sacred" place of repose in communal burial grounds. The sanctity of death, the care of the burial site and the welfare of the departed soul were also attended to by these organizations which arranged for proper funeral rites and organized visits to the graveyards to offer sacrifices to the dead during the *Qing Ming* and *Chong Yang* festivals.[94] Chinese public

---

[90] *Yang shi zong pu* [The *Yang Clan Genealogy*] (Singapore, 1965), p. G16. In a different context, David Lai demonstrates retrospectively that geomantic principles were important in the siting of a late nineteenth century burial ground belonging to the Chinese Association in Victoria, British Columbia (C.Y.D. Lai, "A Feng Shui Model as a Location Index", *Annals of the Association of American Geographers* 64, no. 4 (1974): pp. 506-513.

[91] Yen Ching Hwang, *A Social History of the Chinese in Singapore and Malaya, 1800-1911* (Singapore: Oxford University Press, 1986), p. 45.

[92] Cited from *Singapore Coroners' Inquests and Inquiries* No. 229, of Wong Wan, 14 Apr. 1931 by K. Yeo, "Hawkers and the State in Colonial Singapore: Mid-Nineteenth Century to 1939" (M.A. diss., Monash University, 1989), p. 56.

[93] Several clan associations and mutual benefit societies ran so-called "dying houses" where the chronically ill or incapacitated could seek shelter and succour. In 1908, a municipal survey recorded fourteen of these dying houses (*ARSM* 1908, "Health Officer's Report", p. 37).

[94] *Qing Ming Jie* (the Chinese "All Souls' Day") and *Chong Yang Jie* (the "Double Ninth" Festival) are Chinese festive periods devoted to the veneration of deceased ancestors and family members. During these festivals, it is the practice to visit the graves of forebears to make ritual offerings and to sweep the graves (*Hua ren li su jie re shou ce (Chinese Customs and Festivals in Singapore)* (Singapore: Singapore Federation of Chinese Clan Associations, 1989), pp. 45-49, 74-77.

burial grounds ranged in size from a few tens of acres to several hundreds (Table 1), and accommodated not only the resting places of the dead but also joss-houses, temples, the huts of squatters, vegetable gardens and piggeries. It was hence through their own organizations that the Chinese labouring classes were ensured the provision of sacred places for their dead, albeit in close association with the activities of the living.

From the municipal perspective, public Chinese burial grounds were more insanitary than sacred. These grounds were considered unkempt, disorderly, overgrown with brushwood, and a source of contamination to the town's water supply. By the late nineteenth century, existing public burial grounds were also overcrowded and no longer able to cope with the pressing demands of a rapidly burgeoning Chinese population. The municipal authorities passed sanitary regulations to ensure that graves were not overcrowded and were at least five feet deep, brushwood and jungle regularly cleared and burial registers properly kept. Many of the public burial grounds were full and officially closed against further burial by municipal order.

Sanitary regulations were, however, little appreciated by the Chinese, nor were closing orders necessarily complied with. Even when the burial ground was considered full, "it was the habit to dig all over the place till a vacant space was found to bury another body".[95] Given the pressure on space, the Chinese also resorted to clandestine burials in closed or disused burial grounds as well as unused Government land which frequently escaped municipal vigilance at the time of burial. One case of burials in unsanctioned grounds came to light in the early 1880s when the Acting Resident Surgeon of the General Hospital located in Sepoy Lines lodged a "nuisance" complaint that a piece of land adjoining the apothecaries' quarters and reserved as Cantonment practice ground had been "surreptitiously buried upon to a considerable extent" by *Seh* Choa Chinese who owned an adjacent burial ground which was already full.[96] In the period of uncertainty following the postponement of the 1887 burials bill, there was strong suspicion that in the Telok Blangah district, an area already covered by a large number of private and public burial grounds, fresh grounds were continually dug and internments carried out in unregistered and unlicensed grounds. Attempts to prosecute the trustees of various burial grounds had to be withdrawn as the present trustees denied all responsibility for past infringements of the law.[97] In 1889, Major H.E. McCallum, the Colonial Engineer and nominated member of the Municipal Board, pointed out that the question of illegal burials was becoming increasingly serious and moved that the Government be requested to take immediate steps to deal with the burials question "in the cause of sanitation and good order".[98] It was highly desirable, urged Major McCallum, that "all available building sites within easy reach of the town should

---

[95]"Unlawful Burials in the Hokkien Burial Ground, Alexandra Road", 25 Nov. 1924, *SIT* 116/25.
[96]*MPMCOM*, 24 Feb. 1881; *MPMCOM*, 2 June 1882.
[97]*MPMCOM*, 3 July 1889.
[98]The motion was initially opposed by the Chinese Commissioners, Tan Jiak Kim and Tan Beng Wan, who claimed that the fault did not lie with the owners or trustees of burial grounds who were "ignorant of the law" but with the authorities themselves who in former years had neglected to enforce the law. They withdrew their opposition on the assurance that any steps taken to deal with the burials question would only apply to future burial grounds and would not interfere with existing grounds (*MPMCOM*, 3 July 1889; *MPMCOM*, 31 July 1889).

be reserved for houses instead of being occupied ... by private burial grounds" for "sickness was becoming rife in the town and the dangers from overcrowding increasing".[99] He advocated that the Municipality should be given powers to prohibit the digging of fresh graves in anticipation of future internment and the conversion of grounds presently occupied by a few graves into "regular cemeteries".[100] This was the first of several requests on the part of the Municipal Commissioners for greater powers to regulate burial grounds but until the introduction of dual legislation in 1896, no stringent measure could be introduced as "the law [regarding burial] was unsettled as to whether the Municipality or the Government assume[d] responsibility for the supervision of this important custom".[101]

In the meantime, the municipal authorities depended on a system of surveillance to attempt to prevent clandestine burials. An Inspector of Burial Grounds was appointed to make periodic inspections of burial places, and to furnish regular reports and returns of burials but such a system "signally failed" not only because the appointed inspector failed to carry out inspections "regularly and systematically",[102] but also because the "unsystematic" nature of Chinese burial records and the "diffused" layout of the grounds themselves rendered the "inspecting gaze" ineffective. In the first place, the registration, demarcation and mapping of burial grounds were highly imperfect and as a result, encroachment of lands adjoining the boundaries of burial grounds often occurred with impunity.[103] Secondly, Chinese burial records were not systematically kept and appeared highly confusing to municipal inspection as "it was customary among the Chinese to give another name [other than the official name] to a deceased person on the tombstone".[104] Burial records seldom tallied with the monthly death returns for the Municipality. In 1892, an attempt to collate the number of internments from an inspection of twenty burial grounds showed that whilst there had been 423 deaths during the month of May within the Municipality, only 358 burials had been registered, a sign which supported the suspicion that some 15 per cent of burials had been clandestinely carried out.[105] Although the Municipal Ordinance of 1896 strengthened the hand of the authorities by requiring stricter registration and licensing of burial grounds, clandestine burials appeared to have continued unabated for several decades. The assistance of the police or the Detective Branch had to be enlisted to investigate certain suspected cases of illegal burials in closed grounds but even then concrete evidence could only be obtained by reopening graves to ascertain whether they contained fresh bodies, a step unpleasant enough to discourage even Dr P.S. Hunter, the Municipal Health Officer in the 1920s.[106] It was also reported that exhumation of

---

[99]*MPMCOM*, 31 July 1889.
[100]Ibid.
[101]*MPMCOM*, 27 Oct. 1890; *MPMCOM*, 19 Aug. 1891; *MPMCOM*, 6 July 1892; *MPMCOM*, 20 July 1892.
[102]*MPMCOM*, 31 July 1889.
[103]*MPMCOM*, 27 Oct. 1890.
[104]"Tiong Bahru Improvement Scheme, Acquisition of Two Graves from Lot 185 Mukim 1", 28 Oct. 1926, *SIT* 724/26.
[105]*MPMCOM*, 6 July 1892.
[106]"Unlawful Burials in the Hokkien Burial Ground, Alexandra Road". The *Singapore Coroners' Inquests and Inquiries* also contain some evidence that illegal burials were more common than discovered by municipal inspectors (for examples, see Inquests No. 185 of Unknown Female Child, 16 Nov. 1904 and No. 99 of Tan Buan, 1 June 1905).

bodies for repatriation to China were constantly taking place without the knowledge of the authorities.[107]

The Establishment of a Municipal Cemetery for the Chinese

By the early years of the twentieth century, it became patently obvious that not only was there acute pressure for space among the living, existing burial grounds were no longer sufficient to cope with escalating numbers of the dead which inevitably accompanied a rapidly burgeoning population. Many burial grounds belonging to various communities were declared unfit for further use by the municipal authorities and officially closed against burial.[108] The shortage of burial space was further exacerbated by the compulsory acquisition of several old grounds for the purposes of modern urban development. The first of these to be cleared was the disused Cantonese public burial ground at Tanjong Pagar near Chinatown (No. 1 in Table 1) which was acquired in 1907/1908 in order to provide filling material for the Telok Ayer Reclamation Scheme. Although the trustees of the burial ground had to submit to the Legislative Council resolution to compulsorily acquire the site, they managed to secure, through the representations of the Chinese member of Council, Tan Jiak Kim, various concessions. The Government assured the Chinese that due regard would be shown for their "superstitions and feelings", adequate arrangements made for the exhumation and re-internment of remains in other burial grounds according to Chinese rites, and compensation paid based on a "piece-rate" according to the number of sets of bones uncovered.[109] The work of removal was entrusted to the Chinese Advisory Board which undertook to ensure that "everything was done decently and to the satisfaction of the relatives of the deceased".[110] According to the *Free Press*, "the scene at the burial ground was not altogether void of pathos":

> Some of the graves were opened in the presence of well-dressed male and female relatives, whilst, in other cases, two coolies with a solitary broken *changkol* [hoe or shovel] between them took it in turn to unearth all that remained of the unknown dead. The same contrast was seen in the means of transport of the unearthed remains to their new resting-places. The remains of a bygone merchant were carried under a canopy and covered with fine silk and accompanied by relatives and friends and bands of Chinese musicians while the next procession would consist of three coolies, two of whom carried the remains done up in an old "gunny" bag slung on a carrying pole, and the third coolie preceded the procession, holding in one hand a few sprigs of bamboo with a red flag fastened to one of them and piping away on old tin-whistle.[111]

---

[107] *PLCSS*, 23 July 1896, reported in *ST*, 24 July 1896.

[108] *ARSM* 1904, "Health Officer's Department", p. 26; *MPMCOM*, 6 May 1904; *MPMCOM*, 18 Nov. 1904; *ARSM* 1906, "Health Officer's Report", p. 29; *MPMCOM*, 30 Nov. 1906; *ARSM* 1907, "Health Officer's Report", p. 38; *MPMCOM*, 8 May 1908.

[109] Contrary to expectations, a large number of remains were unearthed despite the fact that the burial ground had been closed for forty or fifty years. As a consequence, the initial vote of $10,000 set aside in 1907 for compensation was quickly exhausted and had to be supplemented by two further votes of $10,000 each the following year (*PLCSS*, 17 July 1908, p. B33).

[110] Song Ong Siang, *One Hundred Years' History of the Chinese in Singapore* (Singapore: Oxford University Press, 1984, first published in 1902), p. 421.

[111] *SFP*, quoted in Song, *One Hundred Years' History of the Chinese*, p. 421.

A second extensive clearance of graves was carried out from the mid-1920s when seventy-odd acres of land located in the Tiong Bahru area was acquired by the Singapore Improvement Trust for an Improvement and Housing Scheme. The project involved removing over 280 huts, 2,000 squatters and their pigs as well as a large number of graves, filling in swampy ground, amalgamating irregular holdings and re-allotting them according to a "regular plan", and laying out of roads and drains to provide an overspill area for the southern congested area.[112] The assistance of the Chinese Protector was enlisted to negotiate for the removal of scattered graves and, as compensation, new grave-plots were offered in the municipal cemetery at Bukit Brown with a sum of money sufficient to cover the cost of removal.[113] In general, public burial grounds belonging to various clans or *bangs* were allowed to remain and where acquisition was necessary, the associations were authorized to purchase new burial sites beyond municipal limits.[114]

Not only were several old burial grounds either closed or cleared by the Government and the municipal authorities, conditions for the issue of new licences for private burial grounds were increasingly stringent and after 1 July 1906, the use of any place within the municipal limits was prohibited by law.[115] The Christian cemetery at Bukit Timah Road was closed at the end of 1907 and a new cemetery — the Bidadari Christian Cemetery along Upper Serangoon Road — consecrated and opened on 1 January 1908.[116] A separate section of the Bidadari estate was also purchased from the *Dato Mentri* of Johore by the municipal authorities, laid out as a public Mohammedan Cemetery and opened for internment in 1910.[117] Apart from the Bidadari Mohammedan Cemetery, however, the authorities were extremely reluctant to commit themselves to a policy of providing municipal cemeteries for the various Asian communities.

On several occasions during the first two decades of the twentieth century, a section of the more "progressive" Chinese leaders led by Dr Lim Boon Keng, a Municipal Commissioner in 1906 and an active campaigner for "Straits Chinese reform",[118] petitioned the Municipal Board for the provision of a municipal cemetery for the use of the Chinese communities in view of the severe "overcrowding" in existing burial grounds.[119] In 1906, Dr Lim Boon Keng urged that a Chinese municipal cemetery

---

[112]*ARSM* 1925, "Appendix B: Singapore Improvement Trust [1925]", pp. 23-24; *ARSM* 1926, "Appendix: [Singapore Improvement Trust, 1926]", pp. 16-17; *ARSM* 1927, "Appendix: Singapore Improvement Trust [1927]", pp. 18-19.

[113]"Appendix: [Singapore Improvement Trust, 1926]", p. 17; "Wee Swee Teow and Co. Asks that Some Compensation may be Included in the Award for Acquisition of Lot 15 Mukim I on Account of the Exhumation and Reburial of Their Client's Ancestors"; "Tiong Bahru Improvement Scheme, Acquisition of Two Graves from Lot 185 Mukim 1", 23 Aug. 1926, *SIT* 553/26.

[114]For example, the trustees of the Hokkien Seh Chua burial ground negotiated for a new site in Toah Payoh on the outskirts of the Municipality in place of their old grounds at Silat Road, Telok Blangah, which were acquired by the Singapore Improvement Trust ("Forwarding Copy of a Letter from the Secretary of Chinese Affairs on the Subject of Acquiring Land Comprised in Grant No. 49 Toah Payoh as a Burial Ground for the *Seh* Chua Community").

[115]*Report of the Committee Appointed to Make Recommendations Regarding Burial and Burial Grounds*, p. 4.

[116]*MPMCOM*, 26 July 1907; *ARSM* 1908, "Health Officer's Report", p. 40.

[117]*MPMCOM*, 2 June 1905; *ARSM* 1910, "Health Officer's Report", p. 45.

[118]Lim Boon Keng, "Straits Chinese Reform", *The Straits Chinese Magazine* 3, no. 9 (1899): 22-25.

[119]*MPMCOM*, 2 June 1904; *MPMCOM*, 14 Dec. 1906; *MPMCOM*, 31 Aug. 1911.

should be provided "without delay" and assured the Board that "the educated [Chinese] ... no longer believed in burying according to ideas based on geomancy [and] did not object to burying their dead under municipal regulations [similar to those] in force at the Christian cemeteries".[120] Although geomantic complications were officially not taken into consideration, the search for a suitable piece of land for a public Chinese cemetery proved highly problematic. A minimum of one hundred acres and preferably up to four hundred acres was considered desirable in order for a "reasonable number of full-sized Chinese graves" to be accommodated for a period of ten years but this was either unavailable or too expensive.[121] Although available land could be secured at Bidadari for a Chinese cemetery, the Municipal Commissioners rejected this option as it was felt that the burial customs of the Chinese were incompatible with the general ambience of a site already consecrated to the Christian dead. As the Municipal President explained, since the burial customs of the Chinese were "characterised by noise" and the Christians "by silence", "there might be clashing and inconvenience should burials be taking place in both places at one time".[122] It was ultimately decided to use powers available under the Lands Acquisition Ordinance to compulsorily purchase a 213-acre site at Bukit Brown which formed part of an existing burial ground belonging to the *Seh* Ong *kongsi*. As a result of the opposition of the *kongsi* to the compulsory acquisition of their land and "difficulties in the way of titles and trusteeships", it was not until the end of 1919 that the site passed into municipal hands.[123]

The cemetery at Bukit Brown (Plates 3 and 4) was finally opened for internment on 1 January 1922, eighteen years after the question of a municipal cemetery for the Chinese was first broached. A sub-committee comprising Commissioners See Tiong Wah and Tan Kheam Hock was set up to frame by-laws for the regulation of the cemetery in consultation with the Municipal Health Officer, the Executive Engineer and the Legal Advisor.[124] Initially, the municipal cemetery did not prove popular with the Chinese. Three months elapsed before the first burial after opening took place and up to August 1922, the Municipal President reported that it was "not utilised to the extent which had been anticipated".[125] Part of the reason for the unpopularity of the municipal cemetery was to be found in its spatial layout. Grave-plots were small, laid out in neat rows with one plot in ten left vacant for access, and allotted consecutively. Such a geometrical scheme produced a disciplined spatial order favoured by the municipal authorities but unpopular with those who could afford the individualizing treat-

---

[120]Song, *One Hundred Years' History of the Chinese*, p. 407.

[121]*Minutes of Joint Meeting of Finance and General Purpose and Sanitary Committees* (hereafter, *MJMFGPSYC*), 7 July 1916; *MJMFGPSYC*, 25 May 1917; *MPMCOM*, 26 Oct. 1917.

[122]*MJMFGPSYC*, 25 May 1917.

[123]*MGCM*, 4 Jan. 1918; *MGCM*, 8 Mar. 1918; *MPMCOM*, 25 Oct. 1918; *MPMCOM*, 30 May 1919; *MPMCOM*, 25 July 1919; *MPMCOM*, 31 Oct. 1919; *MPMCOM*, 28 Nov. 1919.

[124]*MCGM*, 12 Mar. 1920; *Minutes of Proceedings of the Municipal Commissioners at a Special Meeting* (hereafter, *MPMCSM*), 29 Apr. 1921.

[125]*ARSM* 1922, "Municipal Health Officer", p. 40D; *MPMCSM*, 25 Aug. 1922. By the end of 1922, there had only been 98 burials in the municipal cemetery for 1922.

Plate 3 The Bukit Brown Municipal Chinese Cemetery at Kheam Hock Road/Sime Road consists of over 200 acres of regularly spaced burial sites on undulating ground. It was closed by the Singapore Government in 1973 (1990 photograph).

Plate 4 One of the better-kept tombs on Bukit Brown contrasted by its neighbour which is almost completely overgrown (1990 photograph).

ment offered by geomantically prescribed burial locations. As Maurice Freedman observed:

> in geomancy there lies the inherent principle that tombs are a means of individualising the fate of the living.... The municipal cemetery which blocks off all opportunity for grand bids for fortune by its discipline of fixed plots is hateful to the Chinese.[126]

In August 1922, after consultation with the Chinese Advisory Board, the Bukit Brown cemetery by-laws were amended to take into account Chinese preferences: plot sizes were increased to twenty by ten feet in the general division and ten by five feet in the paupers' division;[127] plots were oriented facing east and south[128] and space for a path was left after every six rows of graves.[129] A temple, modelled on the Thian Hock Keng Temple in Teluk Ayer, was constructed within the cemetery and farmed out to a Chinese priest who paid an annual sum to the Municipality for the right to sell joss-sticks and other ritual paraphernalia.[130] In subsequent years, municipal burial became increasingly accepted among the Chinese population and by 1929, Bukit Brown accounted for about 40 per cent of all officially registered Chinese burials within municipal limits (Table 2).

Negotiating Control over "Sacred" Space

As already seen, the meaning of "sacred" spaces of death to Chinese communities was different from the significance of extramural "eternal resting places" of western European tradition. Whilst European cemeteries were ordered and organized as park-

---

[126]Freedman, "Geomancy", p. 13.

[127]In Chinese burial grounds, grave-plots measured a minimum of about twenty by ten feet (200 square feet) to provide space not simply for the coffin (the largest taking up about 50 square feet), but also for adequate room in front of the tombstone to provide a platform for ritual. Among the wealthy Chinese, grave-plots were considerably larger. For example, in 1926, in order to re-inter the body of their father from a private site in Tiong Bahru to the Municipal Cemetery, Lim Chan Siew and Lim Chew Chye had to reserve six adjoining plots in the latter in order to accommodate the tombstone (*Report of the Committee Appointed to Make Recommendations Regarding Burial and Burial Grounds*, pp. 8–9; "Tiong Bahru Improvement Scheme, Acquisition of Two Graves from Lot 185 Mukim 1").

[128]For the beneficial power of *feng-shui* to be optimized, grave alignments had to be oriented in particular directions judged auspicious for the deceased's horoscope and birth year. Each birth year is associated with particular auspicious and inauspicious compass directions and as a result, Chinese burial grounds tended to present a helter-skelter appearance with graves oriented in different directions. The provision of plots oriented in two different directions in the municipal cemetery allowed the Chinese a limited degree of geomantic choice. In general terms, a southerly orientation was considered favourable as the south was traditionally considered "the cradle of warmth, light, life and productive summer rains" (Knapp, "The Changing Landscape", p. 7; de Groot, *The Religious System of China*, p. 942).

[129]*Minutes of Meeting of Sub-Committee 2*, 9 Aug. 1922; *MPMCOM*, 25 Aug. 1922; *MPMCSM*, 25 Aug. 1922. It also appears that consecutive burial was not insisted upon, particular in the case of the wealthy. Instead, in certain cases, relatives could request specific plots in accordance with the geomantic requirements of the deceased. In re-intering the remains of two family members from the late Cheang Hong Lim's Alexandra Road estate to Bukit Brown, the Cheang family required a site "well above sea level", supporting their request by reminding the authorities that "Mr Cheang Hong Lim was one of the best known citizens in this Colony during his lifetime" ("Allen and Gledhill to Messrs J.G. Campbell, 14 Oct. 1929" in "Burial Grounds on Lot No. 53 Grant 63 [Tanglin] and Lot No. 4 Grant 2 [Telok Blangah]", 13 Feb. 1928, *SIT* 145/28.

[130]*Minutes of Meeting of Sub-Committee* (Special), 14 Oct. 1921.

TABLE 2
RETURN OF BURIALS IN THE MUNICIPAL CHINESE CEMETERY AT BUKIT BROWN, 1922-29

Year	Annual No. of Burials in Bukit Brown Chinese Cemetery			Cumulative	Total No. of Chinese Burials within Municipal Limits	(a) as a Percentage of (c)
	General Division	Pauper Division	Total (a)	(b)	(c)	(d)
1922			93			
1923			205	298	4,106	5.0
1924			519	817	4,422	11.7
1925			1,005	1,822	4,876	20.6
1926			1,218	3,040	5,632	21.6
1927	797	553	1,350	4,390	5,749	23.5
1928	686	668	1,354	5,744	5,322	25.4
1929	691	1,624	2,315	8,059	5,511	42.0

like expanses for family visits or monuments to illustrious persons serving the purposes of contemplation and commemoration of those who had "passed on" and hence effectively separated from the living, the control and manipulation of the burial places of the dead were perceived by the Chinese as inseparable from the fortunes of the living. Discursive elements such as ritual practices, funerary artifacts and the epistemological precepts underlying *feng-shui* which defined the very nature and meaning of mortality in Chinese society all emphasized the reciprocal and interlocking nature of relationships between the living and the dead through the medium of the landscape. "Sacred" places devoted to the dead were hence not "sterile" sites alienated from the living but instead formed an essential and influential part of the topography of the living. Unlike in the west where the habitations of the living and those of the dead belonged to different worlds, in the Chinese view, "the tomb is the *yin* habitation to match the *yang* habitation of the living" within a single system.[131]

The attempt here is not to examine the rationality or internal consistency of Chinese geomancy as a so-called "science" *vis-à-vis* western conceptions of science,[132] but to

---

[131] Freedman, "Geomancy", p. 13.

[132] Contemporary western observers who had attempted to measure the rudimentary "science" of *feng-shui* against "western views of physics" had often found much to disparage in the Chinese system. Rev. E.J. Eitel of the London Missionary Society, for example, concludes his monograph on *feng-shui* with the following words:

> [W]hat I have hitherto, by a stretch of charity, called Chinese physical science is, from a scientific point of view, but a conglomeration of rough guesses of nature, sublimated by fanciful play with puerile diagrams.... It is simply the blind gropings of the Chinese mind after a system of natural science, which gropings, untutored by practical observation of nature and trusting almost exclusively in the force of abstract reasoning, naturally left the Chinese mind completely in the dark. The system of *feng-shui*, therefore, based as it is on human speculation and superstition and not on [a] careful study of nature, is marked for decay and dissolution (Eitel, *Feng-Shui*, pp. 65, 69).

It was left to later writers in the 1950s such as Joseph Needham in his *Science and Civilisation in China* to re-evaluate the proper role of *feng-shui* within the context of the development of Chinese science for a western readership.

demonstrate the use of *feng-shui* as a strategic discourse in the encounter between the colonial authorities and the Chinese community. Through a discourse which insisted on the "sacred" nature of burial grounds and "mystified" landscape, the Chinese attempted to justify the immunity of certain elements of the environment from colonial or municipal control and as such, challenge western conceptions of urban development and planning priorities. Although the authorities were quick to dismiss geomancy as mere superstition, it is ironic that its very imperviousness to western logic made it much more difficult for the Government or the Municipality to regulate geomantically selected burial grounds.[133]

Whilst the existence of a separate and distinctly different Chinese discourse on death served to prolong the negotiation of control over "sacred" space in the city between the authorities and the communities on a political level, it was the clandestine, everyday strategies of those pressed for burying space in the city which rendered municipal control through surveillance increasingly difficult. In the early twentieth century, the allotment of a municipally sanctified space for Chinese burials, although initially supported only by western-educated Chinese, became an increasingly accepted compromise between the Chinese, who retained some measure of control over their burying places and the municipal authorities, who were able to ensure the gradual removal of already established burial places for the purposes of modern urban development.

---

[133]In a similar vein, Maurice Freedman observes that in the British colony of Hong Kong, the Government experienced difficulty countering "popular resistance by geomancy" largely because it was unable to "talk back [to the people] in their own language". He adds,

> [w]ere the Government ... to share the belief of the people, it would be in a position to resist their consequences, for its officials would then be able to match their own *feng-shui* opinions against those of the objectors, and, if necessary call in professional geomancers to argue with those retained by the people (Freedman, "Geomancy", pp. 8-9).

Part II
Mechanisms of Rule

[8]
Bringing the State Back: The Limits of Ottoman Rule in Jordan, 1840–1910[1]

Eugene L. Rogan

The Ottoman legacy in Jordan is at once over-estimated and under valued. In most histories of Jordan, the Ottoman period is cursorily summarized as four centuries of neglect. Drawn into the Ottoman Empire with the rest of Greater Syria in 1516, Jordan came under Istanbul's authority in name alone until the second half of the nineteenth century.[2] Rather than speaking in terms of four centuries, it is perhaps more relevant to focus on the last seven decades of Ottoman rule. Far from neglect, this period witnessed intense state involvement in what was then the southern frontier lands of the province of Damascus. Istanbul's initiatives to recuperate its Jordanian territories served to overcome certain regional particularisms and make parts of Jordan amenable to direct state rule. Although there were limits to this process, many of the features of Jordanian society and politics attributed to the Mandate period and Hashemite rule may in fact be traced back to this Ottoman legacy.

Jordan was but one of many frontier zones in the Arab provinces to come under the state's centralizing initiatives in the latter half of the nineteenth century. The attrition of Ottoman rule in the Balkans, where between 1820 and 1913 nationalist movements ultimately reduced the

---

1. My research in the Prime Ministry Archives in Istanbul was made possible by the generous support of the Skilliter Library Fund, Newnham College, Cambridge, and by the Hayter Travel Fund, The Oriental Institute, Oxford.
2. Wolf-Dieter Hütteroth and Kamal Abdulfattah's findings suggest that in most of Jordan the Ottoman administrative apparatus was at best incompletely applied in 1595. *Historical Geography of Palestine, Transjordan and Southern Syria in the Late 16th Century* (Erlangen 1977), pp. 17–18.

empire's European domains to Thrace, compelled the government to consolidate and extend its rule in Arabia. A process was initiated during the *Tanzimat* (period of reforms, 1839–76) and accelerated during the reign of Sultan Abdülhamid II (1876–1909), which introduced new instruments of bureaucratic rule in the Syrian and Iraqi hinterlands, the Hijaz and Yemen. At the turn of the century the Ottomans attempted to extend their authority from the *vilayet* (province) of Basra over the Persian Gulf, creating a paper *sancak* (sub-province) of the Najd under Ibn al-Rashid and naming Kuwait and Qatar as *kaza*s (districts), with Mubarak al-Sabah and *Shaykh* Jasim named as their respective *kaymakam*s (district-governors).[3]

Experience was to prove that the Porte's authority could not be extended through paper measures; for Ottoman rule to take root in frontier zones, certain realities had to be changed on the ground. Administrative realities had to be changed, with professional bureaucrats supported by Ottoman troops replacing local leaderships or rule by proxies. In thinly-populated areas, demographic realities had to be changed through village settlement. Agricultural lands had to be put to productive use generating tax revenues for the state. These new settlements needed to be linked to each other and to regional markets by a road network. The Ottoman state thus came to integrate frontier districts through the extension of its bureaucratic network and linkage with regional markets.

In 1840 the Ottomans did not look on what we now call Jordan as a distinct administrative unit. Rather it was the frontier zone which extended from the Hawran to the Hijaz and which was crossed by the pilgrimage caravan to Mecca each year. It was a zone of distinct districts, each perceived as an arena for power struggles between bedouin tribes and/or sedentary communities. It was the tribes, however, which were singled out by the Ottomans as representing the chief obstruction to both regular cultivation and direct administration. Over the following seven decades the Porte would seek to extend its authority over the

---

3. The best treatment of Ottoman rule in the Syrian periphery is Norman Lewis's *Nomads and Settlers in Syria and Jordan, 1800–1980* (Cambridge 1987). Ottoman rule in the Hijaz is the focus of William Ochsenwald's *Religion, Society and the State in Arabia: The Hijaz under Ottoman Control, 1840–1908* (Columbus 1984). On Yemen see Paul Dresch, *Tribes, Government and History in Yemen* (Oxford 1993), pp. 219–24. Ottoman initiatives in Kuwait, the Najd and Qatar remain understudied, though numerous documents in the Prime Ministry Archives in Istanbul attest to Ottoman overtures to local leaders in those regions.

regions of Jordan through both quick paper solutions and political-economic transformation. Not surprisingly the Ottomans were most effective where they invested most time in adapting regions to their order.

Dividing the Frontier into Administrative Units

Irbid and Jabal 'Ajlun
In the first decade of the *Tanzimat*, the Ottoman government in Damascus undertook a number of initiatives to extend its authority over Jordan's northernmost district of Jabal 'Ajlun [Map 2]. The district was of economic importance to Damascus. The northeastern half of 'Ajlun is an extension of the plains of the Hawran and an important grain-producing region, while in the hill lands to the south and west some 80 villages generated enough surplus to be an important source of financing for the annual pilgrimage caravan throughout the Ottoman centuries.[4]

The government's primary concerns in 'Ajlun were thus to assure the security of agricultural production and the collection of tax revenues. The 'Adwan tribe and various branches of the 'Anaza confederation were established in force in Jabal 'Ajlun and so were in a better position to extract surplus from the peasants than was the government. Faced with what amounted to double taxation by tribes and state, peasants were driven to abandon their villages for such areas as were taxed uniquely by one authority. In March 1844, this situation was put before the *Majlis al-Shura* (Consultative Council) in Damascus. In a report to the Council, the *vali* (governor) and *müshir* (commander-in-chief) of the provincial army expressed their concern over bedouin exactions and peasant flight. 'It is now the time for cultivation,' their report continues, 'and it is our duty to examine the means to provide for the safety of the *fallahin* and their speedy resettlement, to assure them in the conduct of their affairs and the preservation of tax revenues.'[5]

The Council adopted a local solution to what they saw as a local problem. It appointed Muhammad Sa'id, one of the Kurdish *aghas* (irregular commanders), to proceed to 'Ajlun with his own troops to assure the district's security. The expenses of the force, which was not to exceed 50 horsemen, were to be levied from the peasants. Muhammad

---

4. Karl K. Barbir, *Ottoman Rule in Damascus, 1708–1758* (Princeton 1980), pp. 122–5.
5. Historic Document Centre, Damascus. *Awamir Sultaniyya* vol. 5, pp. 57–8, report dated 29 *Safar* 1260 (20 March 1844).

Sa'id *Agha*'s tenure in 'Ajlun appears not to have been a success, for within 30 months a new governor in Damascus was petitioning the Grand *Vizier* in Istanbul to appoint a *kaymakam* in the village of 'Il'al to the northeast of Irbid, supported by 600–700 soldiers.[6] While the project was approved by Sultan Abdülmecid in 1846, it appears never to have been executed.

All the histories of Jordan are in agreement that the Ottomans posted their first district governor in Irbid in 1851, though none has provided any details on the initiative. The immediate background involves provincial finances, bedouin troubles and Algerian refugees. According to French consular sources, while the province of Damascus had balanced its budget through 1849, a series of unforeseen expenses had driven the province's accounts to a deficit of some four million piastres by February 1851.[7] When renewed bedouin attacks on settled cultivators in March threatened the harvests in 'Ajlun, the military commander in Damascus pressed for a military solution with attacks on the Sirhan and Bani Kilab tribes, in which some 2200 sheep and 38 camels were confiscated, followed by a raid on the Bani Sakhr in which he claimed to have confiscated 5000 sheep and 400 camels.[8]

While the *serasker* (provincial military commander) pursued military solutions with quick results, the *vali* was working on longer-term administrative solutions. He took his inspiration from the growing community of Algerians seeking refuge in Damascus from General Bugeaud's war against the *Amir* 'Abd al-Qadir. The *vali* was concerned that the impoverished Algerian veterans might turn their military experience to brigandage. He entered into negotiations with the leader of the community to establish an administrative post in Irbid with the military support of his Algerian irregulars. The leader, referred to as Ben Salem in French accounts and Ahmet *Efendi* Salim in Turkish, was not at first interested in the assignment of policing farmlands against

---

6. Engin Akarli, *'Ba'd al-watha'iq al-'uthmaniyya al-muta'alliqa bi-tarikh al-'urdunn, 1846–1851'*, ('Some Ottoman documents related to the history of Jordan, 1846–1851'), paper published by the University of Jordan (Amman 1989).
7. Archives Diplomatiques de Nantes (hereafter ADN), Damascus Consulate Carton 65, de Ségur letters of 5 and 13 February 1851.
8. *Bashbakanlik* (Prime Ministry) Archives, Istanbul (hereafter BBA), I.Dah 13842, report from the *Serasker* to the Porte dated 16 *Jumada al-awwal* 1267 (19 March 1851). ADN, Damascus Consulate Carton 65, de Ségur letter of 31 March 1851.

bedouin; however, as the refugee community swelled with no means of support, the Algerians were left with no alternative.

In October 1851, the Administrative Council in Damascus petitioned Istanbul to find other employment for Muhammad *Agha* the *kaymakam* of the *sancak* of 'Ajlun – quite probably the same Muhammad Sa'id *Agha* appointed in 1844 – and to appoint in his place Ahmet *Efendi* Salim. There was thus no new administrative unit created in 1851, but rather the first attempt to establish a permanent Ottoman mission in the district, to be based in the village of Irbid. The report called for permanent settlement of the Algerians, 'who are in a weakened state [due to] their numbers'. This new community would then 'oversee the desert zone and routes of passage against bedouin and tribes,' enhance the region's security, and encourage settlement and remittance of taxes not just from the district of 'Ajlun but also from the town of al-Salt. The motion passed the *Meclis-i Vâlâ* in Istanbul and ultimately received the sultan's approval in December 1851.[9]

The Algerian colony did not survive. By the time Ben Salem's appointment was approved by the sultan the Algerian colony was already beginning to decamp. In January 1852 the followers of Sidi Ben Amer, former *khalifa* (deputy) of Bousada under 'Abd al-Qadir's administration in Algeria, withdrew from 'Ajlun for Jerusalem and ultimately resettled in Jaffa.[10] Living conditions in Irbid, a village with no source of water except its rain-fed reservoirs, would not have been agreeable. It is unlikely that the Algerians would have enjoyed the cooperation of peasants sceptical of all government interventions or the tribesmen they were assigned to keep under surveillance. If any survived until May, the remainder of the Algerians most probably withdrew when the government's first attempt to introduce conscription in 'Ajlun, among other peripheral districts in Syria, provoked a peasant rebellion.[11] In October of the same year, the administrative council in Damascus sacked the man serving as *kaymakam* of the districts of 'Ajlun, Hawran, Jaydur

---

9. BBA, I.Mec.Vâlâ 7796, *mazbata* of Damascus *Majlis al-Idara* of 20 *Dhu al-Hijja* 1267 (16 October 1851); *mazbata* of *Meclis-i Vâlâ* of 7 *Safar* 1268 (2 December 1851); *irades* of 29 *Safar* and 9 *Rabi' al-awwal* 1268 (24 December and 2 January 1852).
10. ADN, Damascus Consulate Carton 65, de Ségur letter of 2 January 1852.
11. BBA, I.Dah 15570 (May–June 1852); I.Dah 15676 (July 1852); see also C. W. M.Van de Velde, *Narrative of a Journey through Syria and Palestine in 1851 and 1852, Vol. II* (Edinburgh and London 1854), pp. 349, 351, 393, 427.

and Jabal Druze, a certain Faris *Agha*. They recommended the government reapportion his duties and salary to two *mudirs*, one with responsibility for Hawran and Jaydur, the other for Jabal Druze.[12] In 1854, these same districts reverted to the *kaymakam* of Hawran.[13] The experiment of a permanent government presence in 'Ajlun had, for the moment, been abandoned.

For the next 12 years Ottoman administration in Jordan was reduced to a paper structure reproduced in the government yearbooks which grouped the Balqa' and Karak districts under *Liva* (= *sancak*, sub-province) 'Ajlun. In reality, Ottoman rule was reduced to an annual visit by tax collectors, leaving matters of law and security to the more powerful tribes in the plains and to village notables, or *za'ims*, in the hill districts.[14] Two developments reversed this situation definitively: the *Vilayet* Law of 1864, which provided a standard framework of provincial administration to be applied across the empire; and the posting of a strong *vali* in Damascus for an unusually long five-year term to apply the law.

The Vilayet *Law and the Kazas of 'Ajlun and al-Salt*
The *Vilayet* Law established a hierarchy of rule, a pyramid of authority: The empire was divided into *vilayets* or provinces ruled by a *vali*. The *vilayet* was in turn divided into sub-provinces known as *sancaks* governed by a *mutasarrif*. *Sancaks* were composed of a number of *kazas*, or judicial districts, under a *kaymakam*. A *kaza* might include a number

12. BBA, I.Mec.Vâlâ 9073, *mazbata* of 21 *Dhu al-hijja* and *irade* of 25 *Dhu al-hijja* 1268 (6 and 11 October 1852).
13. BBA, I.Dah 18439, *irade* of 8 *Jumada al-akhir* 1270 (8 March 1854), in which Hawran *kaymakam* Faris *Agha* was promoted to *kapici bashi* for having assured security in, and remitted taxes from, the *kazas* of 'Ajlun, Jaydur, Laja and Hawran. If, as seems likely, he was the same official who was sacked in 1852, these documents would serve to underline the pressures under which bureaucrats in the periphery operated to assure security and extract taxes.
14. A survey of the catalogues and documents of the BBA Irade files for the years 1268–83 (1851–67) revealed no direct Ottoman administrative presence in 'Ajlun over those years. See also 'Alayan al-Jaludi and Muhammad 'Adnan al-Bakhit, *Qada' 'Ajlun fi 'ahd al-tanzimat al-'uthmaniyya* (The District of 'Ajlun in the era of Ottoman reforms) (Amman 1992), pp. 14–15. The memoirs of Salih Mustafa Yusif al-Tall (ms in the keeping of Mr Mulhim al-Tell, Amman) preserve fascinating details on 'Ajlun and its *za'ims* in this period, particularly the *za'im* of the Kura district, Yusif al-Shurayda.

of *nahiye*s, the smallest unit of administration, often based around a village of particular importance, headed by a *mudir*. The chain of authority was quite clear: *mudir*s were answerable to *kaymakam*s, who were in turn answerable to *mutasarrif*s, *vali*s, and ultimately the central government in Istanbul. Within this scheme, the *kaza* was the standard unit of administration, bringing together three state functionaries – a district governor, *mufti* and judge – and an administrative council elected from the local population. The law provided a blueprint for bringing the state to the periphery and was to prove one of the most effective pieces of *Tanzimat* legislation.

Good legislation needs implementation, and judging by the record of his actions and the esteem of his contemporaries Mehmet Rashid *Pasha* was unusually capable of applying the law to advance Ottoman administration at the Syrian periphery. Rashid *Pasha* served as *vali* in Damascus for five years (1866–71). Within his first year in office, Mehmet Rashid subdued the 'Alawi community in Jabal Nusayri, reasserted Ottoman authority over the tribes to the east of Hums and Hama, and reorganized the administration of the Hawran.[15] He also laid the foundations for an enduring Ottoman presence in Jordan through the creation of *kaza*s in 'Ajlun and in al-Salt. In applying the administrative structure stipulated by the *Vilayet* Law to these frontier districts Mehmet Rashid moved beyond the paper structures of earlier decades to an actual extension of the administrative grid to 'Ajlun and al-Salt. Perhaps more important, his long tenure of office permitted Rashid *Pasha* the opportunity to reinforce these new administrative units when they were challenged by local forces.

In May 1867 Rashid *Pasha* set about planning an expedition to al-Balqa', the district of Jordan due south of Jabal 'Ajlun extending southwards from the Zarqa' River to the Wadi al-Mujib [Map 3]. Though much of the district consisted of fertile plains, the absence of the state and tribal incursions had reduced permanent settlement to the single village of al-Salt. Built on the hillsides at the convergence of three narrow valleys, crowned by a castle much damaged during the Egyptian occupation in the 1830s, al-Salt provided a secure location for cultivators to negotiate access to farmlands with surrounding tribes. These tribes would ensure the security of cultivation against a share of

---

15. On the governorship of Mehmet Rashid *Pasha* in Damascus, see Max Gross, 'Ottoman Rule in the Province of Damascus, 1860–1909,' (Ph.D. Georgetown University 1979), pp. 116–67.

harvests in a form of taxation known as *khuwa* (lit. 'fraternal' payment). This local order was about to be overturned by the *vali* in Damascus, with his goals of forcing the submission of bedouin tribes to Ottoman rule, the extraction of tax arrears, and the establishment of an apparatus of direct administration to perpetuate Ottoman rule. Rashid *Pasha* expected the tribes to put up a good fight.

The *vali* first secured his position in the Hawran, where he obtained both submission to Ottoman rule and support for his campaign against the Balqa' from the powerful Ruwala, Wuld 'Ali and Bani Hasan tribes, from the Druze, and from the villagers of the Hawran. Rashid *Pasha* then led an expeditionary force of three regular infantry battalions, nine squadrons of regular and irregular cavalry, and light artillery through Jabal 'Ajlun and into al-Balqa'.[16] The leading *shaykh* of al-Balqa' was Dhiyab al-Humud, head of the 'Adwan tribe, who were then in league with the Sirhan, the Sardiyya and the Bani Sakhr. Dhiyab was well aware of the force approaching, but the real source of his concern was that 'a relation of his was with the Turkish army who could act as a guide in all the difficult places, as he knew the country well', which deprived the 'Adwan of the advantage of facing the Ottomans on their home terrain.[17]

Initially, both the residents of al-Salt and the bedouin tribes were intent on resisting the Ottoman force. In the event, Rashid *Pasha* halted his army at a point three hours distant from the village and sent word that the villagers would be pardoned if they abandoned Dhiyab's cause and tendered their submission to the government. Intimidated by the size of the force, the villagers appointed a delegation of Christian and Muslim notables to declare al-Salt's submission to the *vali*. The Ottoman force entered al-Salt without opposition on 17 August 1867, as Dhiyab al-Humud retreated to the south and regrouped his forces near Hisban.

Over the next two weeks Mehmet Rashid consolidated his position in al-Salt. The citadel was repaired and converted into a barracks for the 400 troops to be posted in the town. Al-Salt was endowed with the administrative apparatus of a *kaza*, in accordance with the *Vilayet* Law:

16. ADN, Damascus Consulate Register of Correspondence (hereafter Reg) 26, Rousseau letter of 28 September 1867.
17. Dhiyab al-Humud discussed the approaching army at length with British archaeologist Charles Warren near Amman on 2 August 1867; cf. Warren, 'Expedition to East of Jordan, July and August, 1867,' *Palestine Exploration Fund Quarterly Statement* (hereafter *PEFQS*) 1.6 (1868) p. 297.

Faris *Agha* Kadru, a Damascene Kurd, was appointed *kaymakam* and an administrative council council was elected from the village notables. Massive quantities of grain and livestock were commandeered in the name of tax arrears. According to French consular sources some 6000 purses, or three million piastres, were deposited in the treasury upon the expedition's return.[18] Once Rashid *Pasha* had secured al-Salt, he mobilized his troops and moved south to engage Dhiyab al-Humud's forces. On 30 August the Ottoman column met the bedouin in a four-hour battle in which the 'Adwan suffered some 50 casualties and were forced to abandon their encampment – tents, mounts and livestock. As Dhiyab retreated to al-Karak, his son was captured. After attempting to tender his submission from al-Karak, Dhiyab subsequently presented himself before the *vali* in Damascus and was arrested and imprisoned in Nablus in October 1867.[19]

In all, Mehmet Rashid's campaign represented an unprecedented Ottoman intrusion into Jordan. The permanent administrative posts he created in Irbid and al-Salt were officially recorded in 1868 when the *vali* published the first administrative yearbook (*Salname*) for the province of Damascus. The *Kaza* of 'Ajlun was placed under the *Liva* (or *Sancak*) of Hawran. Significantly, the different *nahiyes* of the district, which were formerly under the authority of *za'im*s, were placed under the authority of the new *kaymakam*. To assist the *kaymakam* were a *naib*, or substitute judge, and a *mufti*. The *kaza* of al-Salt was not attached to the Hawran, but was appended to Nablus as part of a new *sancak* of the Balqa', which comprised Nablus, Janin, Bani Sa'b, al-Salt and al-Karak. As in 'Ajlun, a new *kaymakam*, *naib* and *mufti* represented the Ottoman order in al-Salt.[20]

This new order did not go unchallenged. In the aftermath of the expedition of 1867 the leading tribes of the region sought to challenge Ottoman resolve and resume levying *khuwa*. In the summer of 1869 the Bani Sakhr and 'Adwan overcame past animosities and collaborated in reasserting their claims to *khuwa* from the villages of the Hawran. After a raid on the village of al-Ramtha, Mehmet Rashid mounted a new

---

18. ADN, Damascus Consulate Reg 26, Rousseau letter of 28 September 1867; Constantinople Correspondence avec les Echelles (hereafter CCE), Jerusalem, de Barrère letter of 8 September 1867.
19. Archives des Affaires Etrangeres, Paris. Turquie: Damascus vol. 9, Rousseau letter of 18 October 1867; ADN, CCE Damascus, Roustan letter of 4 July 1869 notes that Dhiyab was still detained in Nablus.
20. *Suriye Vilayeti Salnamesi* 1285 H. (1868/9), pp. 56–9.

expeditionary force for a second Balqa' campaign for fear that, should such an affront to the state's authority not meet with a swift and decisive response, his administrative gains and the district's security would be seriously undermined. Yet such was the *vali*'s confidence of success that he invited the British and French consuls in Damascus to accompany him on the campaign. Using two columns of between 1500 and 2000 men each, the second Balqa' expedition was conducted in a series of pincer attacks on the tribes until the Bani Sakhr and Bani Hamida were arrested in the deep gorges of the Wadi Wala and forced to submit to the state and pay a fine of 225,000 piastres to offset the expense of the campaign.[21] If the first Balqa' expedition introduced direct Ottoman rule to the district, the second campaign confirmed that the Ottomans were in Jordan to stay.

Al-Karak and Ma'an
Ottoman ambitions in Jordan did not stop at al-Salt. Beginning in 1868 the state undertook a number of initiatives to extend direct rule south to Ma'an, a fortified oasis town on the pilgrimage route. Rashid *Pasha* pressed for the establishment of a *kaza* in Ma'an to be attached to the new Balqa' *sancak*.[22] His successor in Damascus, Abdülletif Subhi *Pasha*, attempted to create a new *sancak* in Ma'an in 1872, combining the districts of al-Salt, al-Karak and Jawf. Though the project enjoyed the active support of the Grand *Vezir* (Prime Minister), *Tanzimat* reformer Midhat *Pasha*, the administrative expenses of the new *sancak* proved prohibitive and it was closed the following year.[23] In the aftermath of the British occupation of Egypt the initiative was revived with a proposal to unite the *sancak*s of Jerusalem, al-Balqa' and Ma'an into a single *vilayet* as a buffer against incursions.[24] As nothing came of that grandiose proposal, a new recommendation was made in 1886 to create a *mutasarrifiyya* (= *sancak*) with its center in Ma'an, comprised

21. ADN, CCE Damascus, Roustan letters of 18 June and 4 July 1869 are the French consul's eyewitness reports of the second Balqa' expedition.
22. BBA, I.Shura-yi Devlet 422 includes Mehmed Rashid's proposal of 15 *Muharram* 1285 (8 May 1868) and the sultan's *irade* approving the project of 6 *Rabi' al-akhir* 1285 (27 July 1868).
23. Gross, 'Province of Damascus,' pp. 190–1. According to the French consul in Damascus, the annual expenses for Ma'an totalled 20,000 purses. ADN, CCE Damascus, Robin letter of 28 April 1873.
24. BBA, Y-A.Res 24/38, *vali*'s proposal dated 6 *Sha'ban* 1301 (1 June 1884) and the Prime Ministry's recommendations to adopt the proposal dated 18 *Shawal* 1301 (11 August 1884).

of the *kaza*s of al-Karak and al-Tafila and the *nahiye*s of Amman, Bani Hamida and Wadi Musa.²⁵ The division of the *vilayet* of Syria and creation of *Vilayet* Beirut in 1888 provided yet another opportunity for the *vali* in Damascus to renew the call to establish an administrative centre in Ma'an.²⁶

It is noteworthy that each project targeted Ma'an and showed only secondary interest in al-Karak, in spite of the latter's relative proximity to al-Salt and its links to Hebron and southern Palestine. In this, official thinking appears to have been motivated by strategic concerns: the sedentarization of tribes, the extension of cultivation, linkage with the Hijaz and, after 1882, securing Greater Syria from British incursions following its occupation of Egypt. Experience was to prove that Ma'an was too remote from other administrative centres to be viable. Consequently, it was only when they extended direct administration to al-Karak in 1893 that the Ottomans regained their initiative in Jordan.

In May 1892 the *vali* in Damascus, Osman Nuri *Pasha*, submitted a report to Istanbul detailing yet another plan for the creation of a *mutasarrifiyya* in Ma'an, with *kaza*s in al-Karak and al-Tafila. Abdülhamid II approved the plans in August.²⁷ The founding of the *mutasarrifiyya*, however, was delayed while the authorities assembled the necessary funds for the project. Word of the initiative reached al-Karak by the following spring, prompting the leading *shaykh* of the town, Salih al-Majali, to approach the Ottomans. In April 1893 al-Majali wrote to the *mufti* of Hebron, *shaykh* Muhammad Khalil al-Tamimi, to say that he had heard rumours that the Ottomans were coming to al-Karak but that he was prevented from going to Damascus himself because of hostilities with the Bani Sakhr tribe. He asked the *mufti* to extend his submission to the state and his willingness to perform any service on its behalf. Al-Tamimi conveyed this message to the *vali* in Damascus, who in turn reported this opening to the palace secretariat in Istanbul.²⁸ It

---

25. BBA, Y.Mtv 20/3, proposal from the *vilayet* of Syria to the Palace secretariat dated 3 *Jumada al-awwal* 1303 (7 February 1886).
26. BBA, Y.Mtv 34/51, *vali*'s proposal to the Palace secretariat dated 25 *Dhu al-qa'da* 1305 (3 August 1888).
27. Engin Akarli, 'Establishment of the Ma'an-Karak Mutasarrifiyya, 1891–94,' *Dirasat*, vol. 13, no. 1 (1986), pp. 29–33.
28. It is worth noting that the Majalis and Tamimis were distant relatives. All four letters are preserved in BBA, Y.Mtv 77/86: al-Majali to al-Tamimi dated 6 *Shawal* 1310 (23 April 1893); al-Tamimi to the *vali*, Mehmed Rauf *Pasha*, dated 14 *Shawal* 1310 (1 May 1893) and the *vali*'s reply (n.d.); and the *vali*'s report to Istanbul of 20 *Shawal* 1310 (7 May 1893).

seems likely that al-Majali's overtures convinced the Ottomans to make al-Karak the provisional capital of the new *mutasarrifiyya*. By the end of October 1893, when sufficient resources were raised, the new *mutasarrif*, Hüseyin Helmi *Efendi*, set off with a battalion of infantry and a squadron of cavalry, accompanied by administrative and judiciary personnel, to assume responsibility of the district from his provisional seat in al-Karak.[29]

The troops were needed in spite of al-Majali's assurances. European missionaries residing in al-Karak provide eyewitness accounts, which confirm that the Ottoman force was greeted 'with rifle shots' and by 'huge stones rolled down from above'.[30] From these accounts it appears that the town was in a state of siege for the better part of a week, and that the new administration was only admitted after extensive negotiations and costly presents. Yet there was much to recommend al-Karak over Ma'an as a more important population centre and a regional trade entrepôt linking the desert to southern Palestine and Hebron in particular. Perhaps more significant were the (admittedly shaky) relations between the Majalis and the Ottoman state; since 1867 Muhammad al-Majali had been designated a *kaymakam* over the paper *kaza* of al-Karak. The Ottomans appear to have enjoyed no such relations with notables in Ma'an; as the French consul in Damascus reported, the reality of the situation in 1894 was 'that far from being able to dream of establishing itself at Mâan, the Turkish government can hardly maintain itself in Karak'.[31] Consequently, in mid-1895, Karak was designated officially as the capital of the *mutasarrifiyya*. The *kaza* of al-Salt was detached from the Hawran and appended to al-Karak (March 1894), and *kaymakam*s posted to al-Tafila and Ma'an. From this point onwards, most of modern Jordan, excluding Jabal 'Ajlun (attached to the Hawran) and the port of al-'Aqaba (which in

---

29. ADN, CCE Damascus, Bertrand letter of 9 November 1893.
30. Pierre Médebielle, *Histoire de la mission de Kérak* (Jerusalem 1961), pp. 79–80. Archibald Forder, *'Ventures Among the Arabs* (Boston 1905), pp. 107–8.
31. ADN, CCE Damascus, Guillois letter of 18 March 1894.

September 1892 was designated a *kaza* of the Hijaz *vilayet*), came under a single sub-governor.³²

Over the course of a half century the Ottomans had established permanent administrative and military missions in Jordan stretching from 'Ajlun to al-'Aqaba. These were entrenched through the construction of government offices and barracks. By 1874, a Committee for State Construction in al-Salt had been established which was to build a governor's residence (*konak*) and a government office (*saray*).³³ Similarly in al-Karak a Western visitor wrote in 1896 of 'the continuous construction of extensive Government buildings'.³⁴

Yet the process of drawing a frontier zone into full Ottoman rule required more than a change of administrative realities. The vast expanses between towns in Jordan had to be spanned with new settlements and revived villages. Cultivators had to 'cut the earth', to use the local expression, and plant the plains in grain. New lines of communications were needed linking villages and administrative centres, linking zones of production and markets. And the new administrative districts had to be linked to the regional economy. The changes which the state introduced were imposed from above and reinforced by a military presence. Local society was left to accommodate these changes and, where its interests were advanced by the state's measures, local society would bend to the state's rule. However, where the state failed to cultivate a sufficient constituency, local society could be driven to rebellion against measures deemed too disruptive to the local order. The danger of half-measures was demonstrated in 1910 when attempts to introduce registration, disarmament and conscription

---

32. On the recommendation of the *Shura-yi Devlet* in Istanbul, the Porte ordered the creation of a *kaza* in 'Aqaba because of its 'strategic importance', BBA, Y-A.Res 62/3, report and letter from the prime minister dated 3 *Jumada al-awwal* 1310 (23 September 1892). According to Peake, al-'Aqaba was added to the Karak *mutasarrifiyya* in 1910, though it was returned to the Hijaz on the outbreak of war in 1914. F. G. Peake, *A History of Jordan and its Tribes* (Coral Gables, Florida 1958), p. 93.
33. Victor Lebedev (ed.), *Inventory of the Documents in Arabic Language Kept in the Oriental Department of the 'Cyril and Methodius' National Library in Sofia, XIII–XX C.* (Sofia 1984), p. 224 no. 500, pp. 226–7 no. 507, p. 228 nos 511–12.
34. Theodore Dowling, 'Kerak in 1896', *PEFQS* (1896) p. 329. An extensive listing of public works and government buildings is given by Muhammad Salim al-Tarawna, *Tarikh mantiqa al-Balqa' wa Ma'an wa al-Karak 1864–1918* (The History of the provinces of al-Balqa', Ma'an and al-Karak) (Amman 1992), pp. 352–69.

provoked a full revolt in al-Karak, highlighting the limits of Ottoman rule in Jordan.

Changing Local Realities

Settlement

Settlement as a policy can refer to two different phenomena, both closely interlinked: the basing of a community in a particular site or village, and the award of title to land. The Ottomans' first concern was to populate the lands between administrative centres with cultivators; towards this end they employed title to land strategically.

Three distinct waves of village settlement in Jordan may be distinguished between 1867 and 1910. The first involved local peasants who radiated out from older settlements to establish new villages for reasons of economic gain or intercommunal strife. In the 'Ajlun district, Muslims from al-Husn were resettled in al-Nu'ayma by Ottoman authorities to resolve a dispute with Christian families in June 1869.[35] In the environs of al-Salt, Christians of the Siyagh family established themselves in al-Rumaymin between 1870 and 1879, when they began to register their holdings with the Ottoman land registry.[36] Between 1869 and 1875, the site of al-Fuhays went from an encampment of 16 tents to a village of 25–30 houses inhabited by Christians from al-Salt.[37] And, in 1880, the 'Azayzat led a migration of Christians from al-Karak to Madaba, in the district of al-Salt, with the active support of the Latin Patriarch in Jerusalem and the *vali* in Damascus, *Tanzimat*-reformer Midhat *Pasha*.[38]

---

35. Raouf Sa'd Abujaber, *Pioneers Over Jordan* (London 1989), pp. 167–70.
36. The Christians of al-Rumaymin were visited by Roman Catholic missionaries in 1870 and 1875, who reported a population of 150; cf. Pierre Médebielle, *Salt: Histoire d'une mission* (Jerusalem n.d. (1957)), pp. 59–62. The earliest surviving land register for the *kaza* of al-Salt includes the registration of 52 small properties to 12 residents of al-Rumaymin dating to *Tishrin al-thani* 1295 (September–October 1879). These land registers are kept in the Department of Lands and Survey (hereafter DLS), al-Salt, Jordan.
37. Papers of the Church Missionary Society (hereafter CMS), held in the Library of the University of Birmingham, UK: CMS–CM/O 36/1, al-Jamal report of 7 January 1869; CMS–CM/O 38/9, Johnson letter of 17 December 1875.
38. Sami Salama al-Nahhas, *Tarikh Madaba al-hadith* (The Modern History of Madaba) (Amman 1987) pp. 45–61; Antonin Jaussen, *Coutumes des Arabes au pays de Moab* (Paris 1908), pp. 417–32.

The second wave, spanning the years 1878 and 1906, witnessed the settlement by the state of refugee communities at the frontier of settlement in Jordan as in the rest of Greater Syria. In the 'Ajlun district, Circassians were settled in Jarash (1884). Most of the refugee settlements in Jordan were established in the *kaza* of al-Salt: The Circassian villages of Amman (1878), Wadi al-Sir (1880) and Na'ur (1901); the Türkmen village of al-Ruman (1884) and the mixed Chechen-Circassian villages of al-Zarqa' (1902), Sukhna and al-Rusayfa (both by 1904), and Suwaylih (1906). The only refugee settlement in the district of al-Karak was the Türkmen village of al-Lajjun (*c*.1905).[39]

These settlements in particular were of critical importance to Ottoman expansion in Jordan. All were refugees from Russian wars who were grateful new Ottoman subjects with no loyalty greater than that to their sultan. They built sturdy villages, which they inhabited year-round. As their livelihood was bound to agriculture, they cultivated their lands extensively. Outsiders to the local order, they resisted bedouin claims to a share of their harvests and fought back when attacked. After an initial period of exemption to facilitate settlement, the refugees paid regular taxes to the state. In sum, the Circassians, Türkmen and Chechen were instant constituents of the Ottoman order, subjects bound to the state by the most reliable of loyalties: self-interest.

The third wave resulted to some extent from the second. Bedouin tribes of the region, alarmed by the government's expropriation of their *dira* (tribal domain) to provide land for refugee settlements were driven to settle sharecroppers on their lands in plantation villages. The government's position was made clear by Midhat *Pasha* in 1880 when challenged by one of the *shaykh*s of the Bani Sakhr over land granted to the Christian village of Madaba. When Sattam al-Fayiz went to Nablus to make a formal complaint to the Ottoman authorities, Midhat noted that the *shaykh* had neither registered nor paid taxes on the lands he claimed. While recognizing that Sattam had formerly given the lands of Madaba over to sharecroppers, Midhat claimed that he had created unstable living conditions for the farmers, giving them only one-fifth or one-sixth of their harvest for their labours instead of the standard quarter. He blamed such behaviour by 'bedouin Arab *shaykh*s' for the abandonment of villages in the district. 'Supposing Sattam had usufruct

---

39. On the Circassians and Chechen, see Lewis, Nomads and Settlers, pp. 107–17; on the Türkmen, see Eugene Rogan, 'Turkuman of al-Ruman: An Ottoman Settlement in South-Eastern Syria,' *Arab Historical Review for Ottoman Studies* 1–2 (1990) pp. 91–106.

rights to these lands,' Midhat wrote, 'if they had gone uncultivated and uninhabited for long his rights could not be enforced even if he were found with *tapu* deeds in hand. ... In our opinion, it is regrettable that cultivators do not remain [on the land]. Thus,' he instructed the *mutasarrif* in Nablus, 'you should give as a categorical reply to Sattam al-Fayiz's claims to these and any other lands that he has no right to lands not cultivated.'[40] Here Midhat sought to impress on the tribes that they risked losing lands held by customary rights unless these were registered with the *tapu* (land title) office, placed under cultivation, and their taxes regularly paid.

The result was the bedouin plantation village. Farmed mostly by Palestinian and Egyptian peasants, these were by and large modest hamlets of poor mud huts. Bedouin villages began to appear immediately after the government awarded land grants to the Circassians in Amman and Wadi al-Sir and to the Christians in Madaba. Already by 1883 the government could name nine tax-paying bedouin villages within the *kaza* of al-Salt; by 1908 Jaussen could name 19 villages in the environs of Madaba alone.[41]

Each new village served as a framework for the bureaucratization of land, through the registration of land and settlement of title. This process differed from *kaza* to *kaza* in accordance with local conditions. In Jabal 'Ajlun, where village-based agriculture was the norm, the Ottoman land authorities registered virtually all the lands of the *kaza*, as described by Martha Mundy in her contribution to this volume.[42] In the *kaza* of al-Salt, where until the 1870s only the town of al-Salt was inhabited perennially, villages had to be created. Each newly-created

---

40. The Ottoman Land Law of 1858 authorizes the state to confiscate any lands left fallow for more than three years. Archives of the Latin Patriarchate of Jerusalem, Madaba file, instructions from the *vali* in Damascus, Midhat Pasha, to the *mutasarrif* of al-Balqa' no. 280 dated 20 *Sha'ban* 1297 (28 July 1880).
41. BBA, Y-A.Res 24/38, 9 *Shawal* 1300 (13 August 1883). In addition to the town of al-Salt, the settlement villages of Madaba and Amman, and the Abu Jabir village of Yaduda, the document lists nine tax-paying bedouin plantations within the *kaza* of al-Salt: Jalul, Sahab and Salbud, al-Raqib, Juwayda, al-Dhaban, Manja, Um al-'Amad, al-Ghabya and Barazayn. Jaussen, *Coutumes des Arabes* pp. 243–4.
42. See also Martha Mundy, 'Shareholders and the State: Representing the Village in the Late 19th Century Land Registers of the Southern Hawran', in Thomas Philipp (ed.), *The Syrian Lands in the 18th and 19th Century* (Stuttgart 1992), pp. 217–38.

village was registered by a government official who gave title for specific properties to specific individuals, who were thereafter responsible for paying the designated taxes for the land. Those tribes that feared government expropriation sought out the *tapu* clerk to register their lands and put them under cultivation. The oldest surviving *tapu defters* (registers) for the district of al-Salt, which date back to October 1879 and March 1881, record settlement of title for hundreds of properties to the 'Adwan, 'Abad, and smaller tribes of the *kaza*.[43] Periodic tribal registrations occur in subsequent land registers. For the bedouin, title to land and sharecroppers' yields provided new economic rents to offset the loss in *khuwa* revenues which resulted from direct Ottoman rule. In this way, the tribes of al-Balqa' were given an interest in the Ottoman order. As for the districts of al-Karak and Ma'an, systematic land registration was deferred until 1910 and, when applied, contributed to the tensions that provoked the 1910 revolt.

There were many shortcomings with Ottoman land registration in Jordan. Given the scope of the task and the shortage of resources, surveying was a luxury completely dispensed with. Vague boundaries were the norm: a neighbour's property, a watercourse, a rock. Local estimates of land size were inscribed and converted by a complex formula to give the illusion of science where in fact custom prevailed. The different approaches to land registration in Jordan led to significant regional anomalies between 'Ajlun, which was extensively recorded, and the southern districts, which were approached quite late. However, the land regime was a strategic instrument of Ottoman rule. The areas to which land registration was applied were those most fully integrated into the Ottoman state. And, in spite of all their shortcomings, the Ottoman land registers served as the first reference for land policy in the early years of the Mandate (see chapter by Fischbach).

Communications
With the expansion of settlements, the need arose for a more extensive road network, both for the Ottomans to assure the security of taxpayers and to provide producers access to markets. As is well known, the Circassians are credited with reintroducing wheeled-traffic to Jordan; their villages and fields were soon interconnected by a road network that could accommodate their wicker carts. This network was extended by the southward movement of administrative centres, linking al-Salt,

---

43. DLS, *defters* of *Tishrin al-thani* 1295 and *Mart* 1297.

Amman, Madaba, Dhiban and al-Karak to al-Tafila, Shawbak, Ma'an and the port of al-'Aqaba. Smaller tracks linked administrative centres to their surrounding villages. With troops posted at each of these strategic points, and detachments regularly patrolling the intervening terrain, Western travellers frequently remarked on the greatly-improved security along the roads in Jordan.[44]

The extension of communications westwards to Palestine opened Jordan to regional markets. Ferries were installed on the Jordan River servicing both the Nablus and Jerusalem roads shortly after 1867. A bridge replaced the Nimrin ferry (near the site of the Allenby Bridge) by 1890, though it had to be rebuilt in 1895. Two roads linked al-Salt to Jerusalem, making a 12-hour journey on the 'serious' route and taking 14 hours on the 'moderate'.[45] The government also put a modest fleet of sailing boats into operation on the Dead Sea, running between the shores nearest to Jericho and the closest point to al-Karak, on the north shore of the Lisan peninsula. An English missionary who travelled by these boats in 1895 claimed they reduced the length of the trip from Jerusalem to al-Karak by three days.[46]

From north to south, the most important lines of imperial communications were those linking Damascus to Madina, which crossed the length of Jordan – the telegraph and the Hijaz Railway. Until June 1900, al-Salt had remained the southernmost telegraph station in Syria. The extension of the line southward was prompted by the central government's need for direct communications with its Hijaz and Yemen provinces. Up to this point the Ottomans had been obliged to channel their correspondence through the British Eastern Telegraph Company at a minimum annual expense of some £16,000. To obviate this expense and the irksome reliance on a foreign company, the sultan called for the laying of an Ottoman line, to be paid for by local subscription, linking Madina to Damascus. With 70 telegraph poles per kilometre along the

---

44. Tarawna, *Tarikh mantiqa al-Balqa'*, pp. 178–83. On improved security see Gray Hill, 'A Journey East of the Jordan and the Dead Sea, 1895', *PEFQS* (1896), pp. 24, 38–9; Hill, 'A Journey to Petra – 1896', *PEFQS* (1897), p. 35; Frederick Jones Bliss, 'Narrative of an Expedition to Moab and Gilead in March, 1895', *PEFQS* (1895), p. 203.
45. Islamic Court Registers of al-Salt, Centre for Archives and Manuscripts, the University of Jordan, Amman (hereafter ICR), vol. 11, pp. 55–6, 28 *Rajab* 1321 (21 October 1903).
46. Archibald Forder, *With the Arabs in Tent and Town* (London 1902), pp. 193–5.

1900 km line, a minimum of 133,000 poles were needed to support the wire. To cover the costs of laying the line, the state levied between 170,000 and 200,000 telegraph poles from the residents of the *vilayets* of Beirut and Damascus, to be paid for in kind or, where forests were lacking, in cash. Camels were requisitioned from the bedouin to transport the poles. The line was quickly laid, with telegraph stations opened in Madaba, al-Karak, al-Tafila, Ma'an and al-'Aqaba, whence the line ran inland again to follow the route to Madina. In January 1901, the first telegram was dispatched from Madina to the sultan in Istanbul inaugurating the line.[47] The advent of telegraphic communications not only gave the central government direct access to its outermost territories, but gave the residents of those lands the means to assure the immediate transmission of petitions to both the provincial and imperial capitals.

Like the telegraph line, the Hijaz Railway was conceived out of imperial strategic necessity and paid for by domestic levies and contributions. Built between 1900 and 1908, the railway provided quick transport for administrators, soldiers and pilgrims between Damascus and Madina and, through the spur from Dar'a to Haifa, provided access to Mediterranean markets for Jordanian grain. In balance, the project was more harmful than beneficial to local interests. While still under construction, workers fouled water supplies and provoked a serious outbreak of cholera in Jordan, with deaths reported from 'Ajlun to al-Karak before the epidemic spread through the rest of the *vilayet*, where official figures reported over 4000 deaths.[48] The other major losses suffered by the residents of Jordan as a consequence of the new railway were largely financial. The leading tribes lost revenues formerly obtained for the leasing of camels to the government, merchants and pilgrims. While the government put prominent bedouin on salary to 'guard' the railway line, it seems unlikely that this money was as well distributed among the tribesmen as the camel rentals would have been.[49] The only clear beneficiaries were the merchants who had been

---

47. ADN, CCE Damascus, Savoye letter of 24 June 1901.
48. CMS G3 P/O 1902 no. 130 and 131, Hall's letters from Jerusalem dated 22 and 27 September; 1903 no. 200, Jarvis letter from al-Karak of 28 September. National Archives, Washington, DC, Consular Archives (hereafter NACA), Damascus, Misc. Record Books vol. 1, Mishaqa reports of 5 and 12 December 1902.
49. On the Hijaz Railway, see William Ochsenwald, *The Hijaz Railroad* (Charlottesville, Virginia 1980); on its impact on the bedouin, see Jacob Landau, *The Hejaz Railway and the Muslim Pilgrimage* (Detroit 1971).

making their way to Jordan from neighbouring cities in growing numbers in the years since the advent of direct Ottoman rule.

Urban Merchants

In April 1903, the religious scholar Jamal al-Din al-Qasimi (1866–1914) travelled by train from his native Damascus to Amman. From Amman he visited al-Salt before crossing the bridge over the Jordan to make a pilgrimage to Jerusalem. His description of the *kaza* of al-Salt conveys the state of security and prosperity brought about by Ottoman rule. Yet the greater part of that prosperity fell not to local producers but to the wealthy merchants, primarily from Damascus and Nablus, who were drawn to Jordan by the opportunities for profit which emerged under Ottoman rule.

Both al-Salt and al-Karak had served as trade centres between Palestine and the desert in the years before direct Ottoman rule. Burckhardt, who visited al-Salt in 1812, found 'about twenty shops' operating on a commission basis for merchants from Nablus, Nazareth and Jerusalem, who were attracted to the Jordanian market by prices he estimated were 50 per cent higher than in Damascus. Goods were conveyed in a monthly caravan from Nablus, 'when all who had business in these parts profited by the protection it afforded.'[50] The state could not assure the security of this commerce and did not derive any taxes from it. Exchange was limited to the frequency of caravans, in which merchants sought to reduce their risks by travelling in numbers, with guards.

The establishment of government centres in Jordan, the settlement of new villages, the subsequent extension of land under cultivation, the improved lines of communication and new level of security combined to stimulate commerce tremendously. The primary commodity was grain: in times of surplus, foreign markets for it could be found; in times of shortage, great profits were to be had locally. To the merchants of Palestine and Syria, the plains of Jordan represented a new granary, which they set about appropriating through a three-point strategy of trade, money-lending and land acquisition.[51] Coming to Jordan, urban

---

50. John Lewis Burckhardt, *Travels in Syria and the Holy Land* (London 1822), pp. 350–4.
51. This argument is made more extensively in Eugene Rogan, 'Ottomans, Merchants and Tribes in the Syrian Frontier', forthcoming in the proceedings of The 6th International Conference of the Economic and Social History of the Ottoman Empire and Turkey (Aix-en-Provence, 1–4 July 1992).

merchants would have found themselves competing for suppliers. The advance purchase of grain and other forms of moneylending provided the means to bind suppliers through debt and to obtain produce at favourable prices. Where borrowers could no longer service their loans, merchants could claim the land given as collateral. In time, many urban merchants bought land and farmed it out to sharecroppers. These diversified economic activities are clearly discernible in the inventories of personal property of leading merchants in al-Salt drawn up for the settlement of estates, which reveal extensive property holdings, large stores of grain, and thousands of piastres in loans outstanding.[52] And it was the opportunity for gain that drew leading merchant families such as the Tuqans, the Mihyars, and the Nabulsis to settle in Jordan, where they built extensive shops and opulent homes.[53] This was the Jordan al-Qasimi described in 1903.

Al-Qasimi spent ten days in Amman with 'one of our dearest friends from Damascus' who was working for the Ottoman civil service. He was as impressed by Amman's current vitality as by the remains of its past splendour, noting 'the commerce of the town which is reaching the highest level of activity, as is the construction of buildings, as a result of the numerous people settling there' since the arrival of the Hijaz Railway. On 8 May he moved on to al-Salt, where he spent another ten days, staying this time with his brothers-in-law, who were half-time residents of al-Salt: 'Since their commerce is with the *'arab* there [in al-Salt] they have a home where they reside nearly half the year, after which they return to Damascus.' Not so the merchants of Nablus,

---

52. See, for example, the two inventories drawn up for the estate of Daud *Efendi* Tuqan, ICR vol. 1315–1319, pp. 169–78, 2 *Ramadan* 1318 (25 December 1900); ICR vol. 7, no. 132, pp. 15–24, no. 53, 28 *Dhu al-qa'da* 1319 (9 March 1902). On merchants and moneylending see Eugene Rogan, 'Moneylending and Capital Flows from Nablus, Damascus and Jerusalem to Qada' al-Salt in the Last Decades of Ottoman Rule', in Philipp, *The Syrian Land*, pp. 239–60.
53. Architectural drawings of many of the finest buildings from this period, including the houses of the Abu Jabir, Sukkar, Khatib, Dawud, Mu'ashshar and Tuqan families, and commercial zones such as the Shari'a al-Khadar, are presented in the Royal Scientific Society, *Al-Turath al-mi'mari fi al-mamlaka al-'urduniyya al-hashimiyya: al-Salt* (The Architectural heritage in the Hashemite Kingdom of Jordan: al-Salt) (Amman 1990).

whose impact on the town al-Qasimi described with some consternation:⁵⁴

> The urbanization [*'umran*] of al-Salt is now beginning to get out of control. High-rise houses are beginning to be constructed there in a strange resurgence [*nahda 'ajiba*]. Most of its people are from Nablus, and they still flock to [al-Salt] for trade and construction and government employment so that it could almost be called Nablus the Second or Little Nablus. The reason for their falling one over another to get to al-Salt lies in the delights of its lucrative resources which they have tasted through business dealings with the desert *'arab* of the area. The transactions which [the Nabulsis] conduct with [the bedouin] cover the whole range of commercial dealings.

Though al-Qasimi may have had his reservations, there is no denying the importance of merchants in drawing a frontier zone such as northern Jordan into the region's economy – and by extension, into the empire itself. For in al-Salt, as in the *nahiye*s of the 'Ajlun district, local leaders were displaced by Ottoman officials and wealthy merchants whose interests were closely bound up with those of the state. In districts to the south of al-Salt these changes were viewed with grave concern by local leaders, who would sooner revolt then yield their authority.

The 1910 Revolt and the Limits of Ottoman Rule
With the Young Turk Revolution (1908/9) came a new centralizing initiative, which sought to impose a common rule of law across the empire. For frontier zones this meant an end to tolerance for local particularisms. This was first demonstrated in Syria in the suppression of a Druze revolt (August–November 1910), in which a massive Ottoman force, combining 35 battalions of Anatolian troops with the eight Damascene battalions and three divisions of artillery, effectively conquered the Jabal Druze village by village. Once the army had achieved its objective, the bureaucracy moved in, as all Druze, Christians and Muslims of the Jabal Druze and Hawran were registered with the state. Villagers were disarmed – over 500 rifles were reportedly confiscated

---

54. Zafir al-Qasimi, *Jamal al-Din al-Qasimi wa 'asruhu* (Jamal al-Din al-Qasimi and his age) (Damascus 1965), pp. 103–10.

by the authorities – and some 1000 young men were conscripted into the army. Taxes were collected and arrears extracted in cattle where not available in cash.[55]

Once the Druze had been forced to accept full Ottoman rule, the commander of the Ottoman army, Sami *Pasha* al-Faruqi, sought to apply the same measures in Jordan. The villages of 'Ajlun underwent disarmament and their first conscription. A British missionary in al-Husn described how 400 Ottoman soldiers encircled and disarmed the village and took away 85 conscripts in spite of 'much bribing and lying as to age to rescue the men.'[56] In al-Salt and Madaba, government troops issued identity papers and conducted registration as a prelude to conscription, though they did not actually take conscripts. A British missionary in al-Salt noted significantly that 'there was great weeping and wailing but no insubordination' during registration.[57]

On 6 November 1910, Sami *Pasha* sent a telegram from his base in Jabal Druze to the *mutasarrif* in al-Karak asking for the residents of that district to demonstrate their loyalty to the state by accepting the 'collection of weapons' and 'personal registration'. The measures were understood locally to mean disarmament and conscription.[58] The *mutasarrif* conveyed these instructions to the leading families of the town, who responded the next day:[59]

> We have never questioned the necessity nor withheld obedience in all that the Government orders ... including personal registration or land registration; however, the collection of weapons would depend on [assurance of] security from the harms of the bedouins of the desert who surround our district and attack us continuously. They are our only reason for bearing weapons.

55. NACA, Damascus, Letters Sent 1908–10, Mishaqa report of 12 May 1909; Misc Letters Sent 1910–11, Mishaqa reports of 6 August, 12 August, 6 September, 11 October and 7 December 1910.
56. CMS G3 P/O 1911, Elverson letter from al-Husn dated 28 December 1910.
57. CMS G3 P/O 1911 no. 36, Hicks letter from al-Salt dated 28 December 1910.
58. BBA, DH-SYS 61/3-3, copy of telegram from Sami *Pasha* to the Karak *Mutasarrifiyya* dated 24 *Tishrin al-awwal* 1326 (6 November 1910).
59. BBA, DH-SYS 61/3-3, copy of *mazbata* signed by 27 'foremost *shaykhs*, notables and prominent people of al-Karak' dated 25 *Tishrin al-awwal* 1326 (7 November 1910). Among the signers were Qadar and Rufayfan al-Majali, Husayn al-Tarawna, *Shaykh* Yusif al-Ma'ayta and leading Christians 'Uda and Ibrahim al-Qusus.

The *mutasarrif*, Mehmet Tahir *Pasha*, transmitted the petition with an endorsement and a telegram from the *kaymakam* of al-Tafila, where similar concerns were voiced, to Sami *Pasha*. On 13 November, Sami *Pasha* cabled the *mutasarrif* in Karak to say that 'for now' only registration of persons and lands would be conducted. He reaffirmed that it was the government's chief aim to protect cultivated areas from the desert bedouin, towards which end he would allow people to keep their arms.[60] But in a ciphered appendix to the telegram, Sami *Pasha* asked the *mutasarrif* how many troops would be needed to conduct a general conscription along with registration in the district of al-Karak. The commander of the local military detachment wrote back immediately that great precautions – i.e. large numbers of troops – would be necessary.

What followed was a case of cross and double cross, in which the Ottomans conducted registration as if they had no intention of conscripting, and the Karakis went along with the registration as if they had no intention of rebelling. For 15 days, Ottoman census teams made their way across the district registering names and properties; fatefully, there was no disarmament. All the while, the leading *shaykh* of the town, Qadar al-Majali, went around the countryside agitating for a rebellion against the state. On 4 December, the Ottoman census teams in the countryside around al-Karak were attacked and killed; at dawn on 5 December al-Karak rose up in revolt. The revolt reached al-Tafila and a number of stations along the Hijaz Railway.[61]

In al-Karak, the first victims were the petty merchants from Hebron and Damascus who were readying their shops for the day's commerce. Their cries alerted the Ottomans who, assessing the situation, retreated to the citadel; those who could not reach the safety of the castle perished. Masters of the town, the insurgents first broke into the *saray* and its arsenal, distributing the guns and ammunition they found. All records were burned, and all government buildings set alight – the municipality, the Ottoman Bank, the offices of the Tobacco Régie, the courts and prison, the homes of government officials, even the mosque

---

60. BBA, DH-SYS 61/3-3, copy of telegram from Sami *Pasha* to the Karak *Mutasarrifiyya* dated 31 *Tishrin al-awwal* 1326 (13 November 1910).
61. On the Karak revolt, see BBA, DH-SYS 60/3, 61/3-2, 61/3-3; Peter Gubser, *Politics and Change in al-Karak, Jordan* (London 1973), pp. 106-9; and Eugene Rogan, 'Incorporating the Periphery: The Ottoman Extension of Direct Rule Over Southeastern Syria (Transjordan), 1867-1914', (Ph.D. Harvard University 1991), pp. 178-88.

the Ottomans had built. Without an ideology or a strategy, it was as though the insurgents sought to prevent further state intervention in their lives by obliterating all of its local manifestations. They seemed blind to the fact that behind the local government lay a great empire, which at that moment was reaching out to deal al-Karak's illusions a blow. Ten days after the outbreak of the revolt, Sami *Pasha* arrived at the head of an army to relieve the besieged officials in the citadel of al-Karak and to reassert Ottoman rule with a vengeance.

The 1910 revolt revealed the limits of Ottoman rule in Jordan. Measures of conscription and registration accepted in the districts of 'Ajlun and al-Salt provoked full rebellion in the southern districts. In effect, the state had not changed local realities in al-Karak to the extent it had in the north. To some extent this may be explained by the relative novelty of direct rule in al-Karak. In 1910, 'Ajlun and al-Salt had been Ottoman *kaza*s for 43 years, al-Karak for only 17 years. Life without the Ottomans was not only imaginable, it still figured in the memory of many of the townspeople.

The significance of this difference may be discerned in some of the issues already addressed in this essay. For one, the Ottomans failed to alter the demographic balance in al-Karak. In the *kaza* of al-Salt, numerous refugee settlements created a network of villages loyal to the Ottoman state. In the district of al-Karak, only one Türkmen village was established in al-Lajjun; the Ottomans had no constituents in the district. Where the new settlements drove the tribes in the district of al-Salt to settle their own lands for fear of expropriation, there was no similar threat to motivate the leading tribes of al-Karak to create plantation villages. Further, the tribes in the district of al-Salt who obtained title to their land through registration obtained an interest in the Ottoman state, which the tribes in the Karak district lacked. As there was no notion of title, so there was no fear of confiscation in al-Karak.

The commerce of al-Karak never attracted the same degree of urban participation as that of al-Salt and Irbid. The Damascene and Hebronite merchants killed in the opening moments of the revolt were petty shopkeepers compared to the notables in al-Salt. This may have been due to disparities in relative economic activity in Nablus and Hebron, the respective Palestinian trade partners of al-Salt and al-Karak, or differences in agricultural productivity between the districts of Jordan. The result was that the agriculture of al-Karak never took the same export-orientation as marked the economies of al-Salt and 'Ajlun. More isolated from regional markets, al-Karak was consequently more independent from the regional economy. Revolt did not come with the same price for the district's economy.

Most significantly, the local elites had not been displaced by the Ottoman order. Where Ottoman officials had displaced the *za'im*s of the *nahiye*s of 'Ajlun, and wealthy merchants had emerged as the notability in al-Salt, the state was still too weak and the merchants too poor to displace the Majalis in al-Karak. Yet the initiatives of 1910 threatened the Majalis' power directly: disarmament and conscription would have deprived them of their military strength, and registration would have led to more thorough taxation, diminishing their economic strength. Thus the revolt can be seen as a desperate bid by a local leadership to prevent its displacement by the state.

In the wake of the 1910 revolt, the government reasserted its presence in al-Karak, though for the remaining eight years of Ottoman rule the town remained a frontier town. The districts of 'Ajlun and al-Salt, on the other hand, had become actual Ottoman domains. Here, the experience of Ottoman rule left those districts amenable to centralized governments – an Ottoman legacy of 'stateness' which was to be the inheritance of the British Mandate and the Hashemite state in Jordan.

[9]

State, enterprise and the alcohol monopoly in colonial Vietnam

Gerard Sasges

The state-administered monopoly on the production of distilled rice alcohol instituted in Vietnam after 1897 evolved into one of the colony's most pervasive and unpopular institutions. This article examines the origins and operations of the monopoly, focusing on how much revenue it generated and for whom. It reveals that the monopoly generated little net revenue for the state, and instead functioned to promote the creation of a centralised and ostensibly civilian administration, capable of intervening in the economy to promote the accumulation of capital by local French entrepreneurs, but ultimately dependent on vast, invasive and frequently brutal systems of surveillance and control.

Introduction

From its creation in 1897 to its end in 1945, the alcohol monopoly was one of the most pervasive and unpopular institutions in colonial Vietnam.[1] Together with similar monopolies on opium and salt, the alcohol monopoly was described as one of the three 'beasts of burden' (*bêtes de somme*) of the colonial budget, providing the regime with the tax revenue necessary for its survival. However, unlike opium and salt, which could only be produced in particular areas and thus lent themselves to control and monopolisation, alcohol was produced almost everywhere and consumed by almost everyone whether as part of ritual or everyday socialisation. The creation of the monopoly thus threatened an important part of the indigenous economy, forced

---

Gerard Sasges is Assistant Professor at the Department of Southeast Asian Studies, National University of Singapore. Correspondence in connection with this paper should be addressed to: gerard.sasges@gmail.com. The author would like to thank Scott Cheshier, Phạm Hồng Tung, Nguyễn Thanh Hài, Brad Davis, Chris Goscha, Tuong Vu, Shaun Malarney, Peter Zinoman and the anonymous reviewers of the *Journal of Southeast Asian Studies* for their support and for their critical comments on earlier drafts of the paper.
1 The use of the name Vietnam is anachronistic. During the period of the French presence, Vietnam was divided into three regions: Cochinchina in the South, Annam in the Centre, and Tonkin in the North. Together with Cambodia and Laos, these regions made up French Indochina. Strictly speaking, only Cochinchina was a colony, while the other four were protectorates. In practice, there was little difference, and this article makes general use of the term colony and colonial to describe the French presence in all of Indochina. Similarly, the alcohol monopoly operated differently in time and space across the four regions of Tonkin, Cochinchina, Annam and Cambodia (and in fact never operated in Laos). However, by 1907, the basic features of an effective monopoly of production by the Société des distilleries de l'Indochine (SFDIC), and systems of surveillance and repression operated by the state's Department of Customs and Excise existed across the four regions, justifying the description of the system as a single alcohol monopoly.

consumers to purchase a single, standardised, and, to Vietnamese taste, inferior product, and required the creation of vast and intrusive networks of surveillance and control focused ostensibly on the interdiction of contraband.

Given the opposition it generated and the ways it penetrated into almost every aspect of life in Vietnam, the alcohol monopoly has come to feature prominently in the story of the country's colonisation. For almost 50 years, reformists and revolutionaries alike called for an end to its economic exploitation and intrusive systems of surveillance and repression, and in 1945, the Vietnamese Declaration of Independence highlighted the monopoly as one of the ways in which for more than 80 years, the French had 'acted contrary to the ideals of humanity and justice'.[2] Since 1945, scholars have made the monopoly an important part of their accounts of the colonial period. Ngô Vĩnh Long described the impoverishment, the corrupt and arbitrary enforcement, fines, imprisonment and forced consumption that were all part of an alcohol regime designed to exploit the Vietnamese peasant and underwrite infrastructure projects of benefit only to the French and their collaborators.[3] Trương Bửu Lâm painted a similar picture, adding cultural reasons for opposition to the regime and stressing the ubiquity of clandestine distilling.[4] To date, however, our understanding of the alcohol monopoly has been based on the assumption that it was highly profitable, and that the colonial state's interest in creating and maintaining the monopoly was transparent: that is, the monopoly generated revenue without which the regime itself would be in jeopardy. However, this was not exactly the case.

Since the 1980s, scholars have explored the way that revenue farms in general and opium regimes in particular were part of the development of new forms of state and capital in Asia.[5] In Southeast Asia, revenue farms that taxed products such as opium

---

[2] In their 1918 appeal to the League of Nations for the right to self-determination of the Vietnamese people, Phan Chu Trinh and Nguyễn Ái Quốc (Hồ Chí Minh) described how 'the administration forces even our smallest villages to purchase large quantities of alcohol and opium'. The nationalist Nguyễn An Ninh told his readers, 'You see, our mother country takes really good care of us. We are thirsty for education. She quenches it with alcohol.' *La Cloche Fêlée* [Saigon] 21 Jan. 1924. Even supporters of the French administration such as Bùi Quang Chiêu and Phạm Quỳnh mounted protracted journalistic and political campaigns demanding an end to the monopoly. For the text of the Declaration of Independence, see Hồ Chí Minh, *Toàn Tập* [Complete works], vol. 4, 1945–1946 (Hanoi: Nhà xuất bản sự thật, 2000), p. 10.
[3] Ngô Vĩnh Long, *Before the Revolution: The Vietnamese peasants under the French* (New York: Columbia University Press, 1991), pp. 64–7.
[4] Trương Bửu Lâm, *Colonialism experienced: Vietnamese writings on colonialism, 1900–1931* (Ann Arbor: University of Michigan Press, 2000), p. 48. For a detailed study of the monopoly, see Gerard Sasges, 'Contraband, capital, and the colonial state: The alcohol monopoly in Northern Viet Nam, 1897–1933' (Ph.D. diss., University of California at Berkeley, Department of History, 2006); Erica Peters, 'Negotiating power through everyday practices in French Vietnam, 1880–1924' (Ph.D. diss., University of Chicago Department of History, 2000); Erica Peters, 'Taste, taxes, and technologies: Industrialising rice alcohol in Northern Vietnam, 1902–1913', *French Historical Studies*, 27, 3 (Summer 2004): 569–600; Erica Peters, 'What the taste test showed: Alcohol and politics in French Vietnam', *Social History of Alcohol and Drugs*, 19 (2004): 94–110. See also Hồ Tuấn Dung, *Chế độ thuế của thực dân Pháp ở Bắc Kỳ từ 1897 đến 1945* [The French colonial taxation system in Northern Vietnam from 1897 to 1945] (Hanoi: Nhà xuất bản Chính trị Quốc gia, 2003).
[5] *Opium regimes: China, Britain, and Japan, 1839–1952*, ed. Timothy Brook and Bob Tadashi Wakabayashi (Berkeley: University of California Press, 2000); John M. Jennings, *The opium empire: Japanese imperialism and drug trafficking in Asia, 1895–1945* (Westport: Praeger, 1997); Edward R. Slack Jr, *Opium, state, and society: China's narco-economy and the Guomingdang, 1924–1937*

were a means by which weak colonial states were able to co-opt local Chinese commercial interests, with both benefiting from the revenue the farms generated.[6] However, as time went on, increasingly solvent and extensive colonial states could afford to establish their own systems of control and taxation. At the same time, the capital generated by the revenue farms enabled the Chinese elite to diversify, exploit new opportunities, and enter new markets as their access to the state and to state revenue farms declined. Revenue farming thus 'sowed the seeds of its own destruction' and paved the way for the establishment of state monopolies beginning in the late 1800s.[7]

At first glance, the replacement of alcohol farms and licences with a state monopoly in Vietnam after 1897 would seem to fit nicely within this narrative of the development of a powerful, centralised state able to monopolise sources of revenue that had previously been exploited by Chinese capitalists. However, examining the revenue that flowed from the new monopoly reveals a story with its own particular twists. First, the alcohol monopoly responded less to fiscal realities and more to the need of the central state to find ways of circumventing the Imperial and regional administrative structures that put strict limits on its local authority. Second, the alcohol monopoly generated little net revenue; however, this fact was of little importance as long as high gross revenues allowed the state to justify otherwise unsustainably high levels of debt. Thus, although the alcohol monopoly generated little net revenue, it still played a crucial part in creating the sort of debt-financed budget that has become a feature of the modern state. Third, the bulk of the revenue generated by the monopoly went to its supplier, the Société française des distilleries de l'Indochine (SFDIC) and its founder, A.R. Fontaine. Rather than marking a new phase in the relationship between state and capital, in many ways the alcohol monopoly replicated earlier patterns of tax farming, with the simple substitution of a French capitalist for Chinese. Last, aside from the SFDIC and its shareholders, the other main destination of the monopoly's revenue was the very branch of the administration charged with the monopoly's enforcement: the Department of Customs and Excise (Département des Douanes et Régies). The state's decision to monopolise such a readily available product would necessarily require extensive and costly systems of surveillance and repression that ultimately consumed upwards of one-third of the state's total revenue. Thus, while the monopoly was a remarkably inefficient means of wresting surplus from Vietnamese, it was a somewhat more effective means of enacting their domination.

The way the alcohol monopoly simultaneously justified and funded the creation of invasive and violent systems of control sheds new light on the way that new forms of administration and patterns of capital accumulation coexisted with good old-fashioned practices of domination. Following on the seminal work of Michel Foucault,

---

(Honolulu: University of Hawai'i Press, 2001); *The rise and fall of revenue farming: Business elites and the emergence of the modern state in Southeast Asia*, ed. John Butcher and Howard Dick (New York: St. Martin's Press, 1993).
6 The use of 'Chinese' is shorthand for an extremely diverse population originating from different regions of present-day China, speaking different dialects, and often resident in Southeast Asia for generations.
7 Howard Dick, 'A fresh approach to Southeast Asian history', in Butcher and Dick, *The rise and fall of revenue farming*, p. 9.

many scholars have portrayed imperialism in the nineteenth century as a process involving simultaneously the perfection and exportation of modern forms of disciplinary power to the world.[8] According to Paul Rabinow, 'The colonies constituted a laboratory of experimentation for new arts of government capable of bringing a modern and healthy society into being.'[9] Focusing on such elements as design and discourse, scholars have found ample evidence of the colonial state's deployment of modern forms of symbolic domination.[10] In a less discursive context, Daniel Hémery has described the political project of the colonial state in Vietnam as, 'essentially, to "surveil and punish" by the application of modern means of coercion, those of the twentieth century'.[11] However, we have to wonder how 'modern' these forms of coercion really were. Peter Zinoman's work on the colonial prison revealed an almost complete absence of the practices that for Foucault characterised the operation of the modern state, and Alexander Woodside has observed that 'the French presence in Vietnam was a "modern" one only in the most limited and ambiguous ways'.[12] The example of the alcohol monopoly highlights this ambiguity. While the forms may have been modern, the practices on which they were based — tax monopolies and the draconian systems of surveillance and repression they engendered — evoked a premodern past rather than a modern future.

This article investigates how the alcohol monopoly came to be, how much revenue it generated and for whom, and how that revenue was used. Ultimately, its analysis is based on that most prosaic of criteria: where the money was going. As the following investigation shows, it was not going exactly where it was supposed to, and its ultimate destinations shed a great deal of light on the processes of change that occurred in Vietnam after 1897. These processes transformed the political and economic landscape of the colony, making the alcohol monopoly an integral part

---

8 For Foucault, the modern state was characterised by direct and indirect control of the population in the minutest details of their daily life. Michel Foucault, *Surveiller et punir: naissance de la prison* (Paris: Gallimard, 1975). In English, *Discipline and punish: The birth of the prison*, trans. Alan Sheridan (New York: Pantheon, 1978).
9 Paul Rabinow, *French modern: Norms and forms of the social environment* (Cambridge: MIT Press, 1989), p. 289. See also Gwendolyn Wright, *The politics of design in French colonial urbanism* (Chicago: University of Chicago Press, 1991). Ann Stoler writes that 'under Dutch rule, the plantations located in Sumatra's *cultuurgebied* (or 'plantation belt') were virtual laboratories for technical and social experimentation. They were also microcosms of the colonial capitalist effort, at once compact and enormous ateliers in which racial, class, ethnic, and gender hierarchies were manipulated, contested, and transformed.' Stoler, *Capitalism and confrontation in Sumatra's plantation belt, 1870–1979* (New Haven, Yale University Press, 1985), p. 2.
10 Paul Rabinow, *Symbolic domination: Cultural form and historical change in Morocco* (Chicago: University of Chicago Press, 1975).
11 Daniel Hémery, in the preface to Patrice Morlat, *La répression coloniale au Vietnam (1908–1940)* (Paris: Editions l'Harmattan, 1990), pp. 7–8.
12 Peter Zinoman, *The colonial Bastille: A history of imprisonment in Vietnam, 1862–1940* (Berkeley: University of California Press, 2001); Alexander Woodside, *Community and revolution in modern Vietnam* (Boston: Houghton Mifflin, 1976), p. 3. See also Benedict Anderson's observation that 'centralizing, "absolutizing" tendencies have nothing intrinsically to do with modernization and everything to do with the inherent dynamics of a certain type of state system'. Benedict Anderson, 'Studies of the Thai state: The state of Thai studies', in *The study of Thailand: Analyses of knowledge, approaches, and prospects in anthropology, art history, economics, history and political science*, ed. Eliezer B. Ayal (Athens, OH: Ohio University Center for International Studies: Papers in International Studies, Southeast Asia Series no. 54, 1978), p. 218.

of the new forms of administration, capital accumulation, and surveillance and control that came to characterise French Indochina.

Profits and losses

The first attempts to tax alcohol in Indochina date from the early 1860s, when the new French administration of Cochinchina imposed a sales tax first on 'European' and later on 'indigenous' alcohol.[13] In 1864, with the costs of the military occupation continuing to weigh on the colonial budget, the French instituted a system of licensing for indigenous distillers, and then, in 1871, created a tax 'farm' — sold to a consortium of ethnic Chinese merchants — with control over the production and sale of indigenous alcohol in Cochinchina. In 1874, the Nguyễn government under Emperor Tự Đức adopted the system of licences for its remaining territories in Annam and Tonkin; the only real change after the establishment of the French protectorates in 1884 was a gradual increase in the rate of taxation.[14] However, no attempt was made to force indigenous distillers from the market, and they were in fact taxed at preferential rates compared with their European competitors.[15] These early attempts by the French regime to tax alcohol were pragmatic and limited efforts to raise revenue, rather than ways of trying to alter the colony's economic and social landscape.

There was nothing unique about these early — and rather haphazard — attempts to raise revenue: licences and tax farms were a normal part of revenue generation under the region's colonial regimes. A tax can be defined as any charge imposed by public authority on persons or property for public purposes. Direct taxes are those imposed directly on the payer, such as a property, income or capitation ('head') taxes. Indirect taxes are those that fall mainly and 'indirectly' on consumers, such as import duties or licences for the manufacture, sale or consumption of a commodity. Historically, indirect taxes were often collected through the establishment of monopolies on rare or otherwise easily controlled goods. The Nguyễn dynasty had established monopolies on goods such as peacock feathers and areca nuts, in China there was a tax on alcohol from the Song dynasty until the last days of the Kuomintang, and, even in France, the much hated salt monopoly, the *gabelle*, was only abolished in 1945. In colonial Southeast Asia, the state often auctioned the right to operate monopolies to local entrepreneurs — typically Chinese merchants or consortiums of merchants — in what is aptly called a 'revenue farm'. In exchange for periodic payments, the 'farmers' bore the cost of enforcing the monopoly and kept any excess revenue it generated. First introduced to the region by the Dutch, by the 1800s the practice had become firmly established throughout the region, constituting an economic alliance between Chinese commercial interests and colonial states in Southeast Asia.[16] As relative latecomers to the region, the French

---

13 '*Alcool indigène*' or indigenous alcohol was defined in the legislation as distilled alcohol made from a base of rice using 'indigenous equipment and processes'.
14 Despite the fact that the system of distilling licences adopted by the Nguyễn government in 1874 was modelled on the French system from 1864, the French were happy to use it as proof of the indigenous origins of their later alcohol monopoly.
15 The first indication of the coming shift in alcohol taxation policy was the decree of 3 May 1893, which established the principle of taxation on the basis of real rather than potential production, requiring a higher degree of surveillance and intervention by French authorities.
16 Anthony Reid, 'The origins of revenue farming in Southeast Asia', in Butcher and Dick, *The rise and fall of revenue farming*, p. 79.

almost inevitably made use of this economic alliance, at least initially. Their early tax regime thus was a haphazard mishmash of direct and indirect taxes; some, such as the land tax, were collected by the French administration, and some, such as the alcohol or opium farms, were collected by Chinese entrepreneurs. Taxes were chosen primarily for the ease with which they could be imposed, and show little evidence of an intention to re-engineer the bureaucratic or economic landscape of the colony.

This was to change in 1897, thanks largely to Indochina's new Governor General, Paul Doumer. First elected to parliament in 1893, Doumer quickly made a name for himself as one of the most promising young members of the Radical Party.[17] The immediate context of his appointment as Governor General was the financial crisis that had developed in France's new protectorates of Annam and Tonkin, where costly 'pacification' campaigns and unchecked spending had left the local administrations on the verge of bankruptcy. Doumer had been intimately involved in the project to write off these debts and re-establish the protectorates' financial equilibrium, first serving as the project's parliamentary sponsor, and then as Minister of Finance in the cabinet of Léon Bourgeois, securing the project's passage into law.[18] Doumer thus arrived in Indochina on 13 February 1897 with a plan for the colony's transformation through a combination of fiscal reform, bureaucratic centralisation and large public works projects. Unfortunately, funding for Doumer's projects would have to come from the colony itself. With the liquidation of the colonies' debt in 1896, the government in Paris had signalled clearly that henceforth the colonies were to be financially self-supporting. Doumer thus faced two distinct challenges: not only would he have to put an end to the budget deficits that had characterised the colony's finances before his arrival, but also he would have to find an additional source of revenue sufficient to guarantee large bond issues that would fund the programme of public works. It was a daunting task, but one that Doumer was ready for. As a former mathematics teacher, he was bound to be good with figures.

In 1902, Doumer sketched out his vision of finances in the newly reorganised colony. Key to his transformation of the colony's finances was the use of a hitherto underutilised source of revenue: indirect taxes (see Table 1). Publicly, Doumer made no reference to the fact that opium, alcohol and salt were already subject to indirect taxation, albeit through the medium of Chinese-operated revenue farms. Instead, he focused on how the new state-administered taxes would allow him to double the colony's effective tax burden in the space of just four years, apparently without threatening economic growth or provoking popular unrest. 'Thus it is a revolution that has occurred in the social traditions and fiscal habits of the countries.

---

17 The party had its origins as a political bloc in the 1880s, and was officially constituted as a party at its first national conference in 1901. The party was deeply involved in France's colonial project, resulting in what Jean Martin refers to 'the reign of the Radical high functionaries' at the highest levels of the colonial administrations. Serge Berstein, *Histoire du parti radical: La recherche de l'âge d'or, Vol. 1, 1919–1926* (Paris: Presses de la Fondation nationale des sciences politiques, 1980), p. 29; Jean Martin, *L'Empire triomphant (1871–1936), Vol. 2, Maghreb, Indochine, Madagascar, îles et comptoires* (Paris: Denoël, 1990), p. 230. See also Patrice Morlat, *Les affaires politiques de l'Indochine, 1895–1923: Les grands commis, du savoir au pouvoir* (Paris: l'Harmattan, 1995), p. 118.

18 Doumer's performance as *rapporteur* of the project was such that he was first offered the post of Governor General in October 1895. He declined in order to accept the position of Minister of Finance in the cabinet of Léon Bourgeois on 1 Nov. Amaury Lorin, *Paul Doumer, gouverneur général de l'Indochine* (Paris: l'Harmattan, 2004), p. 36.

Table 1: Indochinese general budgets, 1899–1902 (*piastres*)

	1899	1900	1901	1902
Revenue (Customs)	7,006,000$	5,800,000$	5,940,000$	6,250,000$
Revenue (monopoly products)	10,094,000$	13,500,000$	15,060,000$	17,600,000$
Revenue (diverse)	520,000$	1,503,000$	1,998,000$	3,292,000$
Revenue (total)	**17,620,000$**	**20,803,000$**	**22,998,000$**	**27,142,000$**
Expenses (military)	3,271,000$	4,050,000$	3,891,000$	4,870,000$
Expenses (Customs and Excise)	4,185,000$	4,445,000$	4,572,000$	5,351,000$
Expenses (public works)	3,490,000$	3,386,000$	3,866,000$	4,444,000$
Expenses (diverse)	1,432,250$	1,520,262$	1,312,177$	1,224,000$
Expenses (debt servicing)	0$	2,615,739$	3,482,823$	4,737,000$
Expenses (total)	**17,617,500$**	**20,796,000$**	**22,982,000$**	**20,626,000$**
Surplus	**2,500$**	**7,000$**	**16,000$**	**6,516,000$**

Source: Paul Doumer, *Situation de l'Indochine (1897–1901)* (Hanoi: F.H. Schneider, 1902), p. 166. All figures are in *piastres*, indicated by the use of a '$' in place of the decimal point.

Progress has been accomplished with unexpected rapidity; victory has been won without really having begun to fight.'[19] Figures prepared by the Indochinese Administration for the French Ministry of Finance in 1908 show the three régies together contributing just under half of the total revenue for the general budget (see Table 2). As Doumer put it, 'The present is assured, above all by the grandes régies of opium, alcohol, and salt.'[20]

Needless to say, Doumer's figures are completely fantastical. His plan required doubling the tax burden of an only partially monetised economy where most of the population was engaged in subsistence agriculture, and where much of the country was only just recovering from the French conquest and its aftermath. Moreover, it required price increases that would only exacerbate the problems of smuggling, counterfeiting and contraband.[21] This, in fact, was the crux of the matter: Doumer's figures were projections of gross sales revenue, and they failed to account for the costs of the systems of surveillance and repression that the monopolies required in order to function even to a limited extent. Nevertheless, Doumer presented his thesis so forcefully that, whether true or not, the notion of the three 'beasts of burden' of the general budget has become part of our understanding of Indochina.

---

19 Paul Doumer, *Situation de l'Indochine (1897–1901)* (Hanoi: F.H. Schneider, 1902), p. 135.
20 Ibid., p. 157.
21 Local colonial officials were quick to see the problems involved in the creation of sales and production monopolies. In spring 1897, Customs Director Frézouls circulated to all provincial Residents a draft of the 1897 decree that would establish provincial monopolies of sale and set the stage for the eradication of Vietnamese distilleries. Of 14 Residents who replied, only the Resident-Mayor of Hanoi was willing to endorse the project. Six Residents refused either to endorse or reject the project, while the remaining seven were opposed. For the draft circular, see Director of Douanes Frézouls to Secretary General, Hải Phòng, 5 Apr. 1897. For the Residents' replies, see particularly Adamolle (Resident of Quảng Yên), Miribel (Vice-Resident of Hưng Yên), or Tirant (Resident of Sơn Tây). L'Archives national d'outre-mer, Aix-en-Provence (henceforth ANOM), INDO/GGI//24749.

Table 2: Revenue of three régies as percentage of the general budget's total revenue

Year	Total revenue	Opium (%)	Salt (%)	Alcohol (%)	All régies (%)
1900	21,688,928$32	21.5	9.25	13.9	44.65
1901	23,953,929$54	26.4	9.30	13.6	49.30
1902	28,110,517$95	24.3	6.64	11.6	42.54
1903	29,823,527$77	25.6	8.72	11.7	46.02
1904	30,908,364$33	25.1	9.07	13.7	47.87
1905	28,718,712$73	24.3	10.70	14.1	49.10
1906	27,176,437$10	24.4	10.20	11.6	47.20
1907	33,245,227$63	22.8	9.60	13.9	46.30

Source: ANOM, FM/INDO/NF/460. Total revenue is in *piastres*, indicated by the use of a '$' in place of the decimal point.

Fourteen years later, a French parliamentarian wrote: 'One can say without exaggeration that the entire Indochinese edifice, [an edifice] of considerable importance, rests exclusively on the income from these régies.'[22] Even a century later, the language has changed little: the scholar Charles Fourniau wrote recently that the alcohol monopoly was 'indispensible to the equilibrium of the budget'.[23]

To date, our understanding of colonial monopolies has been shaped by this assumption that they were highly productive, and we have to ask why. Colonial administrators and finance departments, well aware of their audiences in the political and financial capitals of Europe, had a powerful motive to overstate the profitability of the monopolies and understate their costs. For their part, critics and scholars of colonialism have been quick to take up these claims and use them for very different rhetorical ends. For them, the high revenue the colonial state generated through the promotion of the use of drugs such as opium and alcohol was a particularly reprehensible element of a larger project to enslave and exploit. This was the point made so forcefully by the propagandists of the Vietnamese Communist Party, for example, and similar assumptions underlie scholarship such as Chantal Descours-Gatin's *Quand l'opium finançait la colonisation en Indochine* [When opium financed the colonisation of Indochina] or Siddharth Chandra's analysis of the finances of the opium régie in the Netherlands East Indies.[24]

But while many scholars have taken the profitability of the monopolies as a given, others have noted the high operating costs of the monopolies. Analysing the tobacco monopoly in the Philippines, Edilberto C. de Jesus concluded that it probably

---

22 Albert Métin, *L'Indochine et l'opinion* (Paris: Dunod & Pinat, 1916). Métin was a deputy, former minister of labour and social security, and rapporteur of several projects regarding the budget and loans of Indochina.
23 Charles Fourniau, *Vietnam: Domination coloniale et resistance nationale (1858-1914)* (Paris: Les Indes savantes, 2002), p. 742.
24 Chantal Descours-Gatin, *Quand l'opium finançait la colonisation en Indochine: L'élaboration de la régie générale de l'opium, 1860-1914* (Paris: l'Harmattan, 1992); Siddharth Chandra, 'What the numbers really tell us about the decline of the opium regie', *Indonesia*, 70 (Oct. 2000): 101-23.

generated little net revenue.²⁵ F.W. Diehl estimated the operating costs of the opium régie in the Dutch East Indies as 25 per cent of revenue, and Hakiem Nankoe et al. have noted how the establishment of a government opium regime in Cochinchina was accompanied by vastly increased operating costs.²⁶ Even Chandra, who argues that the Dutch opium régie made minimal efforts to interdict smuggling, shows expenses as representing anywhere from a low of 19 per cent to a high of 36 per cent of revenue between 1914–40.²⁷ It seems clear then that the finances of the colonial monopolies could stand a closer examination.

In the case of the alcohol monopoly in Vietnam, that examination is made possible thanks to the reports of French Missions of Inspection (*Inspection des Colonies*), which assumed their final form in 1889 with the creation of an independent Ministry of Colonies. From that date onward, its civilian inspectors were charged with the responsibility for verifying all aspects of the colonial administration. Outranking local administrators and reporting directly to the Minister, inspectors were given wide powers of investigation and control. Particularly in remote colonies such as Indochina, where the Governor General's rule was largely free of ministerial control, Missions of Inspection were an important means for Ministers to get a clearer view of conditions in the colony and exercise some control over their subordinates.²⁸ At least nine missions between 1894 and 1933 investigated aspects of the Department of Customs and Excise, and these missions provide important data on the functioning of the alcohol monopoly.²⁹ Despite the administration's efforts to limit the information available to the missions, inspectors did their best to calculate the real costs of the regimes, factoring in such items as bottling, transport, loan amortisation and salaries, so that they could be deducted from the inflated gross tax figures used in the general budgets.³⁰ Two missions, the Phérivong Mission of 1913 and the le Conte Mission of 1930, undertook detailed investigations of the monopoly that included attempts to calculate its actual net revenue.³¹

---

25 *The tobacco monopoly in the Philippines: Bureaucratic enterprise and social change, 1766–1880*, ed. Edilberto C. de Jesus (Quezon City: Ateneo de Manila University Press, 1980).
26 F.W. Diehl, 'Revenue farming and colonial finances in the Netherlands East Indies, 1816–1925', p. 205; Hakiem Nankoe, Jean-Claude Gerlus and J. Murray Martin, 'The origins of the opium trade and the opium regie in Indochina', p. 192. Both in Butcher and Dick, *The rise and fall of revenue farming*.
27 'Rather than 'plowing some of its millions of guilders of opium profits into the eradication of smuggling, the Regie chose to keep the sizable proceeds as profit, ensuring the perpetuation of the problem and the consequent continuing profitable market for the legal drug'. Chandra, 'What the numbers really tell us', p. 120. For revenue statistics, see ibid., Table 1, p. 104.
28 Arthur Girault, *Principes de colonisation et de législation coloniale: Les colonies françaises avant et depuis 1815, notions historiques, administratives, juridiques, économiques et financières* (Paris: Recueil Sirey, 1943); Pierre Milloz, *Les inspections générales ministérielles dans l'administration française* (Paris: Economica, 1983).
29 Other reports concerning the alcohol regime include that of Inspector General Espeut (1894, ANOM, FM/SG/INDO/AF/143), Inspector Salles (1898, ANOM FM/SG/INDO/AF/146), Inspector General Picquié (1900, ANOM FM/SG/INDO/AF/147) and Inspector Arnaud (1902, ANOM FM/INDO/NF/464).
30 After 1906, the administration only published global figures for all of Indochina, despite the fact that the regime operated differently in each region. See, for example, ANOM INDO/GGI, 'Rapport sur la situation et le fonctionnement du service des Douanes et Régies pendant l'année 1906', or ANOM INDO/GGI/8897.
31 ANOM FM/INDO/NF/464; ANOM FM/INDO/NF/2481.

In 1913, Inspector General Phérivong's subordinate Inspector Berrué made a detailed examination of the alcohol monopoly in Tonkin and North Annam, which by then had been functioning for 10 years. Accepting the administration's argument that sales had increased since the institution of a system of regional wholesalers in 1910, Berrué based his calculations only on figures from the years 1911 and 1912. His purpose was to get a rough idea of two things: the actual net revenue generated by the régie, and the relative distribution of the revenue from the retail price of alcohol. In a calculation that certainly underestimated the cost of enforcing the alcohol monopoly, Berrué concluded that average annual net revenue generated by the alcohol regime in Tonkin and North Annam was about 1,100,000 *piastres*. This meant that annual net revenue generated by the régie in Tonkin and North Annam was only 28 per cent of the gross figure claimed by the Administration and an insignificant 2.7 per cent of the total revenue of the Indochinese budget. He was then able to break down the cost of a litre of alcohol sold to the consumer at 0.81 *piastres* (see Table 3).

Having demonstrated that the monopoly generated less than 3 per cent of the colony's revenue, and served primarily to enrich the alcohol producers and distributors at the expense of the administration, Berrué simply concluded his report.[32] Perhaps he felt that his figures spoke with sufficient eloquence.

By the time of his mission of 1930, Inspector General Le Conte was well aware that his predecessors in 1908, 1913, 1920 and 1927 had all advocated the end of the monopoly, without result. No doubt this contributed to the barely restrained sarcasm that permeates his report on the alcohol régie in Tonkin and North Annam. Apologising for the very rough nature of the figures he was forced to use in his report, he noted with obvious irony, 'however, the real net receipts could be calculated exactly by the Service [of Customs and Excise] with a little patience'. Basing his analysis on figures from 1928, Le Conte found that total revenue from alcohol and associated sources such as fines was 11,940,000 *piastres*. For the same period, the cost of purchasing the alcohol was 7,892,000 *piastres* and expenses associated with bottling

Table 3: Relative share of the price of sale (per litre of pure alcohol)

	Relative share	%
To A.R. Fontaine	0$349	43
To intermediaries (régie, wholesalers and retailers)	0$290	36
To the Treasury	0$171	21
Total	0$810	100

Source: ANOM FM/INDO/NF/464. Relative share is in *piastres*, indicated by the use of a '$' in place of the decimal point.

---

32 For a similar conclusion, see an article that calculated total net receipts from the alcohol regime in Tonkin and North Annam at 2.5 per cent of the 1931 general budget. 'La question de l'alcool', *L'eveil économique*, 707, 11 Oct. 1931.

another 64,000 *piastres*. With alcohol sales in Tonkin and North Annam generating 7 per cent of the Department of Customs' total revenue, Le Conte calculated the proportion of department personnel and resources devoted to the alcohol régie at 7 per cent of its total budget of 5,200,000 *piastres*, or 365,000 *piastres*. Finally, he added in the costs of the régie's building maintenance and amortisation at a total of 55,000 *piastres*. With real expenses now at 8,375,000 *piastres*, real income from the monopoly in Tonkin and North Annam was only 3,565,000 *piastres*, or 4 per cent of the revenue of the general budget. He concluded, 'financially, the monopoly has revealed itself as less advantageous than other regimes. It hinders the proper exploitation of the potential of a tax on consumption. Politically, it is a serious source of discontent among the population. Morally, it cannot be the task of a government to stimulate the sale of alcohol. For my part, I therefore advocate the suppression of the monopoly.'[33]

In fact, real costs were almost certainly higher than those calculated by the two inspectors. When a choice was not clear, both men erred in favour of the administration. As le Conte wrote in his conclusion, 'One can say therefore, that the figure of 3,500,000 *piastres* is certainly the maximum of the real net income of the Régie, but that the figure is possibly considerably lower.' As well, both men underestimated the actual labour costs incurred by the Department in enforcing the monopoly. Whereas a 1927 report found that employees of the Department's Hải Phòng office spent well over half their time on issues related to the alcohol régie, Berrué used a figure of only 12 per cent, and le Conte reported that only 7 per cent of total department resources were devoted to enforcing the monopoly.[34] At the same time, neither inspector attempted to estimate the increased costs incurred by the civilian administration, police, justice and penitentiary systems in their respective roles as enforcers of the unpopular regime. In sum, the alcohol regime almost certainly represented a net fiscal loss for the colony. If the alcohol monopoly did not function to provide net revenue for the central budget, then we have to ask what its real functions were.

New forms of the colonial state

The alcohol monopoly was an important part of creating a centralised colonial state. The legal basis of the French protectorates in Annam and Tonkin and the organisational structures of the colonial state made the collection of taxes a means to project the power of the central government directly into the Vietnamese countryside, bypassing both Imperial officials and local French Residents under the authority of the regional officials in Saigon, Hue and Hanoi. More important, though, the monopolies transformed the financial balance of power in Indochina. Even if the monopolies made little net contribution to Indochina's general budget, their high gross revenue allowed the central government to borrow the funds that gave reality to an administration that had previously been largely fictional, and created the basis for a modern, debt-financed state.

33 Rapport sur la Régie des alcools en Indochine par L'Inspecteur Général des Colonies A. Le Conte, 24 June 1930. ANOM FM/INDO/NF/2481.
34 Report of Inspector of Colonies Gayet, 14 May 1927. Quoted in ibid. Le Conte estimated that the true ratio of Department resources devoted to the régie in Tonkin and North Annam was at least 31 per cent.

Indochina's central government had been created in 1887, imposed with only partial success on the previously semiautonomous colonies and protectorates that France had acquired in the region over the previous three decades. Moreover, its initiative was limited by the terms of its treaty with the Imperial government in Hue and its existing administrative structures. Unlike the colony of Cochinchina, the French administration in the protectorates of Tonkin and Annam was compelled to operate through the intermediary of Imperial Vietnamese authorities. If this was a fiction that wore increasingly thin over the course of the French presence in Indochina, it nonetheless remained the legal basis of French authority in the two protectorates, and served to limit both the number of French administrators outside of the major centres, and their interactions with ordinary Vietnamese. However, while the treaty held that direct taxes were to be collected by Vietnamese officials under French oversight, indirect taxes in the protectorates were the direct responsibility of the French Département des Douanes Maritimes et Frontières (Department of Naval and Frontier Customs). Officials of the Nguyễn government doubtless understood this as applying only to the collection of duties on goods entering or leaving the protectorates. However, the French chose to interpret the clause as applying to all indirect taxes, whether collected inside the territories or at their borders.[35] This is made clear in a seemingly innocuous clause stating that in matters of Customs, the laws of Cochinchina would be extended to the protectorates, and was doubtless part of the motivation for the decision to unify the previously separate Department of Customs with the Department of Excise in 1897. Thus, indirect taxes were to be an important part of circumventing the existing Imperial administrative structures.

Indirect taxes were a similarly effective means of circumventing regional powerbases within the French administration itself. Local French officials answered to their superiors in the regional capitals of Saigon, Hue and Hanoi, and were only indirectly responsible to the Governor General's central administration. By contrast, agents and officials of the Customs Department were responsible to the Department's Director in Hanoi, bypassing Lieutenants Governor and Residents Superior in the regional capitals. Not only did this give the central government in Hanoi direct access to officials in the colony's provinces, but also it created a parallel bureaucracy that the Governor General could use to balance the power of the residential authorities. An expanded Department of Customs became an effective rival to the Residential Administration, allowing the Governor General to play off the two organisations against each other. Archive files are filled with extended exchanges between Residents Superior and the Governor General, on the one hand, and Directors General and the Governor General, on the other, as both sides sought to protect or expand their organisational turf, and to win the favour of the Governor General. One example is the exchange arising out of the murder of a villager by a revenue agent in Hà Đông province in early January 1904. Based on the Resident's report casting doubt on the agent's claim of legitimate defence, the Resident Superior requested that the Governor General arrange for the Department to transfer their employee to a

---

35 Anonymous report prepared for Director of Civil and Political Affairs, Hanoi, 10 Sept. 1885. National Archives One in Hanoi (Cục lưu trữ Quốc gia 1, henceforth CLTQG1), RST 2408.

different post. When the Governor General forwarded the Resident Superior's request to the Department of Customs, Director Crayssac replied angrily, questioning the competence of the local residence and asserting that the Resident Superior had no right to intervene in the internal affairs of his department.[36] It matters little which side the Governor General favoured in this or the hundreds of other similar disputes. What matters is that Doumer and his successors used the Department of Customs to break the exclusive power of the Residents Superior, and to establish the central government as the final arbiter in Indochina.

Nevertheless, the most important limitation on the central government's power was its poverty. The central government's power of taxation was limited to duties on imported or exported goods, and indirect taxes such as excise or customs. More productive direct taxes such as the head tax remained the prerogative of the regional administrations of Tonkin, Annam and Cochinchina. This severely limited the power of the central government while it also encouraged regional independence. Indeed, the problem of regionalism was so acute that in late 1896 Doumer had only just been able to see off an attempt by lobbyists from Cochinchina to have the colony separated from the rest of Indochina, with its own Governor General and control over all of its tax revenue.[37] Winning a share of the revenue from the existing direct taxes would have served to limit the pretensions of Indochina's regions, but would have required difficult negotiations with the regional governments on the one side, and the cabinet in Paris, on the other. Unwilling or unable to devote the time and effort necessary to gain control of the colony's real revenue, Doumer instead chose the expedient of new, and, as time would tell, largely imaginary sources of indirect tax revenue. Whether or not they actually produced any revenue was unimportant: their primary function was to create an apparently sound financial basis for the first issue of government bonds in December 1898. This they did admirably. With one stroke, the resulting infusion of 200 million *francs* fundamentally altered the balance of power in Indochina, giving reality to a central state that had hitherto been largely fictional, and creating the conditions necessary for a subsequent and very particular sort of bureaucratic centralisation.[38]

---

36 In this particular case, the Governor General backed the Resident Superior: in 'a measure that implies no idea of blame', he invited Crayssac to give his subordinate a new assignment. Resident Superior Tonkin to Governor General, Hanoi, 20 Jan. 1904; Resident Superior Tonkin to Governor General, Hanoi, 30 May 1904; Governor General to Resident Superior Tonkin, Hanoi, 18 June 1904. CLTQG1 RST 4206.

37 Edmond Chassigneux, 'L'Indochine', *Histoire des colonies françaises et de l'expansion de la France dans le monde* (vol. 5), ed. Gabriel Hanotaux and Alfred Martineau (Paris: Plon, 1932), p. 493. Doumer was appointed Governor General on 26 Dec. 1896, after the death in office of Governor General Armand Rousseau. The fact that Doumer's intervention with the Minister of Colonies to quash the draft legislation predates his appointment as Governor General would indicate that his appointment had already been decided, if not as early as Oct. 1895 then at least soon after the fall of the Méline cabinet on 29 Apr. 1896.

38 There were four main bond issues associated with the 'Doumer Project'. The first, in 1896, was for 80 million *francs*, and had been made possible by Doumer's project to write off the existing debt of Tonkin and Annam. The 1898 issue for 200 million *francs* was disbursed in three parts: 1898, 1902 and 1905. These were followed by issues of 53 million *francs* in 1909, and 90 million *francs* in 1913. The funds were earmarked for a public works programme defined almost exclusively as the construction of railroads. Charles Robequain, *The economic development of French Indo-China*, trans. Isabel Ward (London: Oxford University Press, 1944).

It also created the conditions necessary for a modern, debt-financed state. Even according to Doumer's own figures, the proportion of the annual budget dedicated to servicing the colony's debt had grown from zero in 1899 to almost 5 million *piastres* in 1902, or 17 per cent of Doumer's highly optimistic total revenue. By January 1910, the total debt of the colony had reached 473,789,205 *francs*. Even with 15 million *francs*, or 18 per cent of the annual budget, devoted to repaying the debt each year, the colony would have to wait for another 74 years to fulfil all of its obligations.[39] In order to attract this kind of capital from the metropole, Doumer needed a general budget with high gross revenue that would give the impression that the administration would be able to meet its obligations. It mattered little that most of the revenue generated by the monopoly would go to administering and enforcing the monopoly itself. Taking, for example, Berrué's finding that net revenue from the alcohol monopoly was only 28 per cent of the figure claimed and applying it to the global figure for the monopolies for 1912, we find that net revenue was probably closer to 5.5 million *piastres*, rather than the 19.9 million claimed.[40] Thus, total net revenue for the year would be 17,943,659 rather than 37,872,579 *piastres*. By this point, the colony was already making annual payments of more than 15 million *francs*, or 6 million *piastres*. Thus, taking the year 1912 as an example, the monopolies played a crucial role in bringing the ratio of debt servicing down from a real 33 per cent of net revenue to the more reassuring figure of 16 per cent of apparent revenue. The latter figure would be acceptable on the Paris bourse, but not the former. Subsequent administrations would find themselves trapped by Doumer's financial sleight-of-hand. Governor General Klobukowski, charged by the Minister with reforming the system of monopolies in 1909, stated publicly that his objective was above all to avoid alarming metropolitan holders of colonial debt, and the issue of debt financing was to prove a powerful argument as the monopoly was renewed essentially unchanged in 1913 and 1923.[41] Raising existing taxes, such as the 'head' tax, by a ratio equal to the real net revenue of the alcohol régie would not have been sufficient: Doumer's commitment to attract and keep metropolitan capital necessitated a form of taxation with high apparent revenue no matter what the real cost.

New forms of capital

This new colonial state was formed in parallel with new forms of capital. As we have seen, much of the centralised bureaucracy's new power flowed from the way the monopolies allowed the state to tap into metropolitan sources of capital. But the alcohol monopoly also facilitated the creation of local — and exclusively French — capital

---

39 Guyho to Minister of Colonies, Hanoi, 1 May 1910. ANOM FM/INDO/NF/926. 'Rapport de l'Inspecteur Général des Colonies Guyho', 1910. Together with 13,650,000 *francs* in annual payments to Paris in return for the military presence, this meant that even by the Administration's own calculations, 34 per cent of the total tax revenue of the general budget was going directly to the metropole. For the same period, Fourniau calculates the total debt of the colony at 499 million *francs*. Fourniau, *Vietnam*, p. 738.
40 The revenue claimed of 19,928,920 *piastres* multiplied by 28 per cent gives 5,580,097 *piastres*. This is necessarily a rough calculation for the purposes of illustration only. All revenue figures from ANOM FM/AGEFOM/215.
41 Fourniau, *Vietnam*, p. 738.

capable of supplanting the Chinese consortiums that had previously benefited from access to Indochina's monopoly profits. After 1902, the primary beneficiary of the profits associated with the alcohol monopoly was the SFDIC and its major shareholder, A.R. Fontaine (see Table 3).

Throughout most of the nineteenth century, commerce and enterprise in Southeast Asia were dominated by Chinese merchants. Chinese controlled both regional and internal trade, with Europeans only able to carve out a position in trade with Europe and North America.

> Chinese were also prominent in most other fields of the capitalist economy where monopoly profits were to be made: revenue farming, moneylending, shipping, urban real estate and production, including rice mills, sugar factories, tin mines and plantations .... Weak states, whether indigenous or colonial, acknowledged their wealth and influence by coopting them as official heads of the Chinese communities, a form of indirect rule with a long history in Southeast Asia.[42]

Revenue farms were one of the major ways the colonial state and Chinese entrepreneurs co-opted each other, providing easy revenue for the state, and generous profits for the Chinese consortiums that administered the farms.[43] Lacking local knowledge, with limited resources, and initially confined to Cochinchina where the Chinese community was numerous and well established, early French administrations had little choice but to adapt themselves to this pattern. Chinese consortiums quickly won the right to administer the opium and alcohol revenue farms, and consolidated their control of the rest of Cochinchina's economy.[44] The few French firms that prospered in this period were limited to import and export between the colony and ports in Europe and the Americas.[45]

By 1884, however, the French had established their protectorates over Annam and Tonkin, and by 1887 had created the General Government for the administration of the entire region. The expanded territory was ruled by an increasingly numerous bureaucracy, with growing knowledge and experience of the territories they administered. At the same time, technological advances such as the steamship and the telegraph served to lessen the physical and notional distance between the colony and the metropole, hardening previously fluid notions of race and hierarchy and placing the interdependence of European administrations and Chinese enterprise in a very different and less favourable light. The latter part of the 1800s thus saw the convergence of a more knowledgeable and capable state apparatus with changing attitudes towards race and a modernist impulse to bring the economy under rational, centralised and exclusively European control.

---

42 Howard Dick, 'A fresh approach to Southeast Asian history', in Butcher and Dick, *The rise and fall of revenue farming*, p. 10.
43 John Butcher, 'Revenue farming and the changing state in Southeast Asia', in Butcher and Dick, *The rise and fall of revenue farming*, pp. 19–44.
44 In the case of the opium farm, for example, a disastrous attempt by two French entrepreneurs to administer the opium farm paved the way for the Chinese to take over after 1864. Hakiem Nankoe, 'The origins of the opium trade', in Butcher and Dick, *The rise and fall of revenue farming*, p. 184.
45 See Gerard Sasges, 'From the consortiums to the colonial conglomerates: Enterprise in Vietnam 1858–1945' (forthcoming).

If that goal were to be achieved, the Chinese consortiums would first have to be deprived of the profits provided by their control of the colonial revenue farms. In Indochina, as in the rest of Southeast Asia, the most obvious targets were the Chinese opium farms. Nankoe et al. write that 'the French attempt to gain control over the opium trade was motivated as much by the aim of increasing colonial revenues as by the official desire to undercut the economic stranglehold which Chinese merchants enjoyed over business activities in the French colony.'[46] In 1883 the administration abolished opium farming and moved to create a direct (state-administered) régie. In theory, French administrators would replace Chinese merchants, and profits that had previously gone to the Chinese would instead go to the colonial treasury. In practice, however, the Chinese not only continued to control storage, distribution and sales, but also engaged in widespread smuggling that undermined the new régie's profits. 'In short, despite the formal introduction of the opium régie, the colonial administration still maintained many features of the farm system.'[47] In the end, the financial repercussions of the change to a 'direct' — but in practice still Chinese-controlled — monopoly were minimal. Perhaps the greatest single change was to shift responsibility for the interdiction of contraband from the Chinese consortiums and their armies of enforcers to the employees of the state's own Department of Customs and Excise.

The attempt to use a state alcohol monopoly to promote French enterprise was somewhat more successful. Like the opium régie before it, the state alcohol monopoly was explicitly conceived as a means of depriving the Chinese consortiums of a source of monopoly profits, and reserving those same profits for French enterprise. In his 1892 paper on the industrialisation of alcohol production in Cochinchina, Albert Calmette wrote, without apparent irony, how scientific production techniques 'will allow our compatriots finally to reclaim for their own profit, a monopoly that it is painful to see remain so long in foreign [i.e. Chinese] hands, in a country that we have paid for so dearly with our gold and our blood.'[48] Fourteen years later, as the SFDIC's production monopoly in Tonkin was being extended to Cochinchina, the Director of Customs justified the change by asking rhetorically, 'Will [Indochina] continue to be a field of commercial exploitation reserved solely for the Chinese?'[49]

The first region of Vietnam to see the production and sale of alcohol monopolised was Tonkin, where Chinese business interests were less well established.[50] Here, Chinese were explicitly barred from bidding for the provincial sales monopolies that the administration created in 1897 as a first step to the creation of Tonkin-wide

---

46 Nankoe et al., 'The origins of the opium trade', p. 189.
47 Ibid., p. 191.
48 Albert Calmette, 'Fabrication des alcohols de riz en Extrême Orient. Étude biologique et physiologique de la levure chinoise et du Koji Japonais par le docteur Calmette', 1892. CLTQG1 RST 14165.
49 Director of Douanes Morel to Minister of Colonies, Hanoi, 1906. ANOM FM/INDO/NF 463.
50 The first regional monopoly officially covered Tonkin and 'Northern Annam'. The decision to append the northern provinces of Annam, which could be supplied from factories in Tonkin thanks to the Hanoi–Vinh railway, reflects how the shape of the monopoly was determined by commercial and logistical concerns rather than administrative rationality. For a discussion of the creation and extension of the monopoly, including Chinese resistance to the monopoly in Cochinchina, see Sasges, 'Contraband, capital, and the colonial state', chapter 4 'Creating the monopoly', pp. 106–38.

monopolies. By 1902, the provincial sales monopolies had been transformed into a single regional monopoly held by the Compagnie Générale, who was supplied by the SFDIC with its monopoly on legal production. However, the attempt to extend the SFDIC's production monopoly to Cochinchina after 1905 ran into concerted resistance from the Chinese consortiums that had previously supplied and administered the state's alcohol farms, and who continued to derive large profits from their commercial activities, both licit and illicit. By 1907 they had forced the alliance of state and capital to come to terms, limiting the SFDIC's share of (legal) alcohol production to 69 per cent and maintaining control of distribution and sales in Cochinchina. In Annam the SFDIC's subsidiaries gradually purchased most of the larger distilleries and proceeded to supply the bulk of the region's legal market with a combination of alcohol produced locally or sourced from its factories in Cochinchina and Tonkin.

If the state was only partially successful in its bid to deprive Chinese entrepreneurs of profits associated with the trade in alcohol, it certainly succeeded in its bid to promote the accumulation of locally based French capital. A.R. Fontaine constructed his first distillery in Tonkin in the early 1890s, and by 1896 had solicited a monopoly of production and sales for Hanoi under Doumer's predecessor, Rousseau. He gained the early support of Customs Director Frézouls, and, by the summer of 1897, that of Doumer.[51] By 1899 he had completed a large modern factory in Hanoi with an annual production capacity of 48 million litres.[52] This factory then formed the core of the SFDIC, incorporated in 1901, and, after the contract of 29 December 1902, the state's exclusive supplier of indigenous alcohol for Tonkin and North Annam.[53] It was a strangely generous contract, giving the SFDIC average profits of 17.15 *piastres* per hectolitre of pure alcohol, more than 800 per cent higher than was the norm in France at the time.[54] Even this probably understates the magnitude of the SFDIC's profits, as it was the SFDIC itself, and not the régie, that was responsible for determining the market price of rice to be used to calculate the sale price of the alcohol: quite literally, the administration paid whatever the SFDIC asked.[55] Using the profits from its monopoly in Tonkin and North Annam, and working closely with the highest levels of the Indochinese administration, the SFDIC proceeded to

---

51 An exchange of letters between Fontaine and Doumer reveals that Doumer may have initially favoured appropriating Fontaine's distilleries and establishing a state monopoly of both production and sales. Fontaine to Governor General, Hanoi, 31 May 1897. CLTQG1 RST 14112. We can only speculate why Doumer subsequently decided to create an alcohol régie that reserved the cost of enforcement for the state, and granted most of the profits to a single private enterprise.
52 Legal consumption for the region at the time was about 52 million litres.
53 A.R. Fontaine was the SFDIC's director and its largest shareholder.
54 Distillers in France producing for the government in the early 1900s made a profit of approximately 5 *francs* per hectolitre, or 2.00 *piastres*. Minister of Finance to Minister of Colonies, Paris, 8 Mar. 1913. ANOM FM/INDO/NF/4040. Also by comparison, the 1897 legislation had granted indigenous distillers a profit of approximately one cent per litre of alcohol at 35 per cent, or 3.0 *piastres* per hectolitre of pure alcohol. Confidential Circular no. 53r, Director of Douanes, Hải Phòng, 10 Feb. 1897. ANOM INDO/GGI//24749. The calculation of the SFDIC's profit is based on an average price of rice in Tonkin in 1902 of 4.57 *piastres* per picul.
55 Report no. 48, 'Régime des alcools en Indo-Chine', Inspector Méray to Minister of Colonies, Hanoi, 29 Apr. 1908, ANOM FM/INDO/NF/880.

establish similar monopolies over alcohol production in Cochinchina and Annam. By 1910, it controlled Indochina's entire legal alcohol market, Laos being the only exception.[56]

Shares in the SFDIC were one of the most profitable investments on the French Bourse: in 1913, for example, the corporation's annual profit was an impressive 50.8 per cent of capital.[57] These profits then provided Fontaine and the SFDIC with the basis for the creation of a vast commercial and financial empire. In 1904, Fontaine was one of the founders of the Société des tabacs Indochinois, later the largest producer of tobacco in Indochina, and an important supplier of the French market. Also in 1904, he entered into a partnership to form the Union Commerciale Indochinoise (UCI). By 1914 the UCI was the largest commercial enterprise in Indochina, with a monopoly on the transport and sale of all régie products (alcohol, opium, salt and tobacco) in Tonkin and import–export operations in almost every colony in the French empire. Fontaine was also an early investor in the rubber industry, in 1907 founding the Société agricole de Suzannah for the exploitation of a large rubber plantation in Cochinchina, and later participating in the foundation of the Société indochinoise de commerce, d'agriculture et de finance (SICAF), which capitalised on the post-war boom by providing expertise and financing for the rubber and plantation industries. In many of these ventures, Fontaine worked in partnership with Indochina's other great monopoly, the Bank of Indochina.[58] Their most important venture was Crédit foncier de l'Indochine, which eventually became the largest landowner in Indochina, and which exists to this day as Crédit Foncier, one of the largest banking and financial services corporations in Europe.[59] The profits that Fontaine derived from the alcohol monopoly were the basis for an extensive and highly diversified business empire that extended into almost every corner of the colonial economy.

Whether or not the capital accumulated through supplying the alcohol monopoly contributed to the long-term development of the Vietnamese economy is debatable. As the above list suggests, Fontaine's investments focused on primary products such as rice, tobacco, rubber and coal. Even more important were his investments

---

56 The SFDIC had factories in Saigon, Phnom Penh, Hanoi, Nam Định and Hải Dương (originally built by the Société des Distilleries du Tonkin, later bought by the SFDIC). Through its subsidiaries, the Société anonyme des distilleries du Centre-Annam (with distilleries in Qui Nhơn, An Thái [Bình Định] and Tuy Hoà), the Société industrielle et commerciale d'Annam (distillery in Đà Nẵng), and the Société anonyme française des distilleries de Battambang (distillery in Battambang, Cambodia), it controlled legal alcohol production for the entire colony except Laos. Laos apparently represented too small a market to warrant the SFDIC's attentions.
57 Marc Meuleau, *Des pionniers en extrême-orient: Histoire de la Banque de l'Indochine (1875–1975)* (Paris: Fayard, 1990), p. 342. Throughout the 1920s, dividends on SFDIC shares were higher than that of the Bank of Indochina itself, which consistently returned some of the highest dividends on the Paris bourse.
58 The relationship between the Bank and the SFDIC began in 1905 when the Bank was granted 500 shares of SFDIC, becoming its second-largest shareholder after A.R. Fontaine. The SFDIC, for its part, became one of the major shareholders in the Bank, for example, in 1920 receiving the bulk of the Bank's issue of 48,000 new shares. Meuleau, *Des pionniers en extrême-orient*, p. 307.
59 Founded by the Bank and the SFDIC on 21 Feb. 1923. Although the institution's subsequent growth was to reduce the Bank's and the SFDIC's share position, the Bank retained the presidency and two seats on the board, while Fontaine retained the vice-presidency (*Annuaire des enterprises 1930*). See Yasuo Gonjo, *Banque coloniale ou banque d'affaires: La Banque de l'Indochine sous la Troisième République* (Paris: Imprimerie nationale, 1993), pp. 315–16.

in import–export, real estate, and, above all, finance. The parallel with the diversification engaged in by earlier Chinese revenue farmers is striking; see, for example, the career of Malaya's Loke Yew, whose control of the Selangor 'general' farm (gambling, pawnbroking and spirits) formed the basis of a vast business empire.[60] In both cases, in the absence of a state willing and able to channel the monopoly's profits into less speculative and more productive enterprises, monopoly capital gravitated towards investment opportunities that offered the quickest and easiest returns possible. This produced a very different developmental outcome than in Japanese-occupied Korea, for example.[61] Whatever the implications for the economic development of Indochina, however, the SFDIC was a key part of the state's attempt to create locally based French capital and dislodge Chinese entrepreneurs from their dominant position in the Vietnamese economy.

New forms of surveillance and control

The final result of the creation of the monopolies was the expansion of the Department of Customs and Excise and the creation of extensive systems of surveillance and control. The state that Doumer envisioned was French and it was civilian. Subcontracting the right to collect taxes — along with the threat of violence that ultimately underpins them — to private Chinese or Vietnamese interests was incompatible with this vision. Similarly, reliance on the military for maintaining Vietnam's tenuous peace belied France's supposed mission as protector and civiliser. And while the state that took shape after 1897 was indeed civilian, centralised, and somewhat capable of collecting its own taxes and enforcing its own laws, the means and the practices it used to achieve these latter goals were not quite as modern and progressive as one might have hoped. For the means it used to enforce its laws was the Department of Customs and Excise, and its practices consisted in the main of coercion, arbitrary fines and arrest, and easy recourse to violence.

Vietnam in 1897 was in many ways still under military occupation. The first three decades of French rule — marked by the invasion of the three southern provinces, invading and 'pacifying' the remainder of Cochinchina, the campaigns in the North and the establishment of the protectorates, the Cần Vương movement, and operations against various 'bandits' — had been anything but pacific. For Doumer's tenure to mark the start of a new and civilising French presence required two things: a quiescent population, and an army that stayed in its barracks. In part, Doumer was assisted by the Vietnamese themselves: the suppression of the Cần Vương movement had ushered in a transitional phase in the history of resistance to French rule as Vietnamese elites searched for new ideologies and techniques of resistance.[62] For the inheritors of older forms of resistance such as the rebel-warlord Đề Thám, Doumer offered

---

60 John Butcher, 'Loke Yew', in Butcher and Dick, *The rise and fall of revenue farming*, pp. 255–61.
61 For a discussion of the legacy of Japanese colonialism for the development of the Korean economy, see Carter Eckert, *Offspring of empire: The Koch'ang Kims and the colonial origins of Korean capitalism, 1876–945* (Seattle: University of Washington Press, 1991); Jung-En Woo, *Race to the swift: State and finance in Korean industrialization* (New York: Columbia University Press, 1991); Atul Kohli, 'Where do high growth political economies come from? The Japanese lineage of Korea's "Developmental State"', *World Development*, 22, 9 (1994): 1269–93. My thanks to Scott Cheshier for familiarising me with this literature.
62 David Marr, *Vietnamese anticolonialism, 1885–1925* (Berkeley: University of California Press, 1971).

generous subventions and local fiefdoms in return for an end to open resistance.[63] But if the military were to stay in their barracks and out of harm's way, then other systems of repression and other ways of enacting French superiority — military and otherwise — would have to be found. Apparently, he found it, for on the eve of his departure from Indochina in 1902, Doumer was able to boast that 'not a single soldier of the Indochinese troops has been killed since 1897. Nothing reveals better than this fact what profound peace has reigned in this colony these past five years.'[64] Conveniently, dead Customs agents did not count.

Some indication of the importance of the Department of Customs for the realisation of Doumer's project can be seen in his order of business: Doumer's first major administrative reform was the decree of 6 October 1897 unifying the previously separate departments of Customs and Excise, and defining the new Department's primary responsibility as the collection of revenue from the three main monopoly products. While Doumer proceeded to grace Indochina with the various administrative apparatuses of a central government such as a treasury, a department of public works, and a unified civil service, these services were to be dwarfed by the Department of Customs and Excise. By 1908, when monopoly regimes had been established in all three regions of Cochinchina, Annam and Tonkin, the Department of Customs was the largest single branch of the Indochinese state, with 1,290 European employees and approximately 2,000 local employees, not including informants, assistants (boys) or local militia (*lính cờ*).[65] These employees were divided among 360 installations covering the entire colony.[66] By comparison, this was more than double the number employed in the next largest department, the Civil Services responsible for the everyday administration of the colony, and more than five times the number of teachers and administrators employed in the Education department (see Table 4).

Although the number of agents of European origin gradually declined as local employees assumed more and more responsibilities, Customs remained the largest single department outside the armed forces and Garde Indigène for the entire period of the French colony. As the largest department, the Customs was also to consume the largest part of Indochina's non-loan revenue. By 1925 an astonishing 20,106,894 *piastres*, or 36 per cent, of the total annual revenue of the Indochinese central government was earmarked for the department's operations and personnel (see Table 5). By comparison, the total budget for sanitary and medical services was 73,362 *piastres*.[67] These sorts of figures would have been unthinkable in a European context: in 1913, the salaries and operating costs of the French Department of Customs and Excise consumed

---

63 See, for example, Nguyễn Duy Hinh, *Đề-Thám: Con hùm Yên-thế* [De Tham: The Tiger of Yên-thế] (Saigon: Khai-Trí, 1961).
64 Doumer, *Situation de l'Indochine*, p. 77.
65 By contrast, 10 years earlier in 1898, the Department had a total of 199 full-time European employees in Tonkin and North Annam. ANOM INDO/GGI//24745.
66 Dominique Niollet, *L'épopée des douaniers en Indochine 1874–1954* (Paris: Editions Kailash, 1998), pp. 232, 242.
67 Total of personnel and materials. From information in Colonie Indochine — Statistique financière, 'Dépenses du Budget Générale de 1899 à 1927', ANOM FM/AGEFOM/215.

Table 4: Administrative personnel of European origin, selected services

Year	Customs and Excise	Civil services	Public works	Education	Justice
1913	1,177	502	360	229	74
1922	848	425	408	229	91
1928	804	474	444	356	103

Sources: From information in the *Annuaire statistique de l'Indochine*, vol. 1: 1913–22 (Hanoi: Imprimerie de l'Extrême-Orient [IDEO], 1927) and *Annuaire statistique de l'Indochine*, vol. 2: 1923–29 (Hanoi: IDEO, 1931).

Table 5: Expenses of the Department of Customs and Excise as a percentage of the Indochinese general budget 1900–25

Year	1900	1905	1910	1915	1920	1925
Percentage of general budget	23	30	29	23	31	36

Sources: 'Dépenses du Budget Générale de 1899 à 1927' and 'Colonie Indochine – Statistique financière. Recettes du budget général de 1899 à 1927', ANOM, FM/AGEFOM/215. Customs and Excise expenses are calculated as the total of salaries for European and indigenous employees, materials, assorted expenses and expenses associated with the operation of the three régies. Revenue generated is the total of all revenue collected by the central government (the general budget's articles 1 and 2).

only 5 per cent of the 800 million *francs* in revenue it generated.[68] Much like the alcohol monopoly it administered, the Department of Customs was a remarkably inefficient means of generating revenue.

It was perhaps a more efficient means of enacting a very particular kind of domination. As with any attempt to control a commonly available product, the alcohol monopoly was characterised by corruption, extortion and abuse. In 1912, the Imperial official Dương Lâm wrote scathingly that 'the customs officers are all dishonest and detestable men who use expedients, perjury, and extortion. We call them customs officers; in reality they are the true bandits.'[69] Stories of extortion, false denunciations and ruin associated with the monopoly became part of village lore, and were eventually taken up in the Socialist realist literature of the 1930s.[70] At times everyday abuse and oppression might turn into incidents of shocking violence, or even murder.[71] Yet such incidents were simply more extreme expressions of a culture of violence intended not just to enforce compliance with the alcohol monopoly, but more generally to symbolise French domination. The instructions of the Resident

---

68 Jean Clinquart, *L'administration des douanes en France de 1914 à 1940* (Paris: Comité pour l'histoire économique et financière de la France, 2000), p. xix.
69 Tổng đốc Dương Lâm to Governor General, Jan. 1912. CLTQG1 RST 74801.
70 See, for example, Nam Cao, *Chi Pheo and other stories* (Hanoi: Foreign Language Publishing House, 1983).
71 It is impossible to list all the incidents in which Vietnamese villagers were murdered by agents of the régie. See, for example, CLTQG1 RST 72188, CLTQG1 RST 4206, CLTQG1 RST 74760, CLTQG1 RST 74647, CLTQG1 RST 46782.

of Hà Tĩnh province to the participants in a series of contraband 'repression raids' reveal the difficulty of distinguishing Douanes operations from the military 'pacification' campaigns that they had supposedly replaced.[72]

> You will approach the villages as closely as possible without being noticed by the inhabitants; and as you approach you will not let yourself be passed by any indigène. As the attack groups will be operating in a concentric movement, it is crucial that not a single piece of evidence be allowed to escape to the outside. To this end, when you are in proximity to the respective villages, you will place the militia under your orders in a semi-circle around the village, at 100 metres from each other, on points of high ground. As much as possible, you will remain in contact with the militia from the other groups, at least by sight. This entire operation must be carried out in complete silence and finished before daybreak. At this moment, you will begin the search .... All the houses without exception, gardens, pens, communal halls, should be carefully searched. The village official will witness the discoveries and will give you the name of the guilty parties. The militia will have instructions from their officers to stop anyone carrying illegal materials who might slip away and attempt to escape to the exterior. All personnel should be equipped with whistles and hand torches if possible. This raid is the first of a series that we shall carry out in various regions of the province. The details of the operations will not vary, and in the future I will simply indicate to you the name of the villages, the composition of the groups, and the direction of their attack.[73]

The raids over the course of the summer and autumn were in fact remarkably ineffective; for example, three raids in September failed to uncover evidence of even a single contraband offence. Yet in the words of a sympathetic chronicler, despite the lack of concrete results 'it must be said that the arrival of a large group of Customs agents in a village could not fail to have the effect of dissuading potential lawbreakers.'[74] These repression raids, with their 'attack groups' of armed soldiers silently encircling villages in the dead of night, were simply a means of demonstrating French domination, and instilling a sense of fear in the Vietnamese population.

Unfortunately for the French, they also instilled a deep sense of injustice and habits of resistance. Much of the resistance stemmed from the way the high price of legal alcohol served as a powerful incentive to distill illegally. Contraband operations could grow to large size and involve sophisticated networks of distribution and sales that reached from the countryside to consumers in urban centres. Incredulous revenue officers reported discovering distilleries with multiple, industrially fabricated stills, thousands of litres of alcohol ageing in caverns dug out of village communal fields, or urban tea-sellers hiding wineskins under their loose-fitting *áo bà ba*, ready to serve thirsty customers at a moment's notice. At times, the abuse and oppression inherent in enforcing the alcohol regime might have been too much

---

72 While the stated objective of the raids was the contraband industry, it should also be noted that just five years earlier the province had been the site of the Xô Viết Nghệ Tĩnh, the first sustained uprising following the founding of the Indochinese Communist Party in 1930.
73 Quoted in Niollet, *L'épopée des douaniers en Indochine*, pp. 482–3. The first raid on 25 July saw 38 Douanes agents and 60 militia from the Garde Indigène divided into six groups, each with different targets.
74 Ibid., p. 484.

for ordinary Vietnamese to bear; revenue agents could find themselves chased out of a village by an angry mob after disturbing the death anniversary of a village notable, for instance, or arrested and beaten after attempting to steal the village taxes during a search for contraband.[75] Few, if any, Vietnamese acknowledged the state's right to monopolise alcohol production, much less the methods used to enforce it. Thus, at the same time that agents of the Department of Customs and Excise enacted French domination, they contributed to the erosion of its legitimacy.

With the chances of meeting a French revenue agent five times greater than meeting a French schoolteacher, the Department of Customs became the primary point of interface between the colonial state and its Vietnamese subjects. As such, it was an important part of the French claim to be a civilian — and civilising — administration. Yet this claim was based on a certain sleight-of-hand. If the days of military operations against 'rebels' and 'bandits' were over, Doumer had replaced them with a system where revenue agents ranged through the countryside in search of illegal distillers, extorting, brutalising, killing, and occasionally, in turn, being killed themselves. Nevertheless, incidents, such as the death of Agent Beaussart, killed after he murdered a woman during a search for contraband alcohol in Hải Dương province in 1899, remained conveniently outside of Doumer's statistics.[76] By far the largest civilian department, with armed agents in every province operating free of the oversight of Imperial officials, the Department of Customs and Excise was to be the primary means by which the central state asserted its rule over its subjects. If this was an important part of the regime's claim to be based on a civil administration rather than a military occupation, we have to ask what, if any, difference this distinction made in the lives of ordinary Vietnamese.

Conclusion

By 1907, the major features of the alcohol monopoly were in place throughout Vietnam: the SFDIC and its subsidiaries enjoyed a monopoly or near-monopoly on the production of alcohol, agents of the Department of Customs and Excise controlled contraband, and millions of ordinary Vietnamese risked arrest and imprisonment in their pursuit of profit and a little drinkable rice alcohol. Cosmetic reforms such as the state's assumption of responsibility for distribution and sale in Tonkin in 1910, or a reduction in the price of sale in 1913 (the 'van Vollenhoven plan') did nothing to alter the political economy of alcohol in Vietnam, or to lessen popular resistance. Opposition to the monopoly was so widespread, in fact, that it provided common ground across the political spectrum. Beginning in 1922, for example, the prominent collaborationist politician Bùi Quang Chiêu orchestrated an unsuccessful press

---

75 See Gerard Sasges, 'The moral economy of oppression and resistance: Towards a deeper contextualisation of resistance to the colonial alcohol regime in Northern Vietnam, 1897–1945'. Paper presented at the third International Conference on Vietnamese Studies, Hanoi, 4–7 Dec. 2008.
76 According to the inquest, the woman was shot at such close range that her forehead was black with powder, and the cardboard cartridge (not just the bullet) was found lodged intact in her skull. Beaussart had attempted to flee but had been captured and beaten unconscious by angry villagers. He died later that day without regaining consciousness, probably from a blow to the head with a staff. 'Meurtre commis sur la personne de l'agent Beaussart de la ferme des alcohols de Nính Giang et mesures administratives prises a l'égard du village de Trịnh Xuyên', 1899. CLTQG1 RST 72188.

campaign to oppose the renewal of the SFDIC's contracts.[77] Chiêu's rhetoric was echoed by the propagandists of the nascent Communist movement: in 1925, Nguyễn Ái Quốc (the future Hồ Chí Minh) noted that in the approximately 1,000 villages of Tonkin, there were 10 state schools, but 1,500 licensed alcohol wholesalers.[78] The first even partial modification to the alcohol monopoly came in 1933, when the journalist, translator and collaborationist politician Phạm Quỳnh led a campaign that saw the SFDIC's share of legal production in Tonkin reduced from 100 per cent to 80 per cent.[79] Yet despite campaigns in the colony's press and consultative assemblies, and resistance in its villages, it was only in 1945 that the basic features of the alcohol regime were finally dismantled.

Given how deeply the alcohol monopoly was imbricated in the colony's economy and society, it should be hardly surprising that the end of the alcohol monopoly would only come with the end of the colonial regime itself. Nevertheless, it is important to clarify exactly how the monopoly functioned within the Vietnamese political economy. The alcohol monopoly is conventionally understood as part of the colonial state's efforts to raise revenue. While scholars have highlighted the exploitative aspects of the monopolies and their intrusive systems of control, they have failed to examine the assumption of profitability bequeathed us by generations of colonial officials and their carefully, if fancifully, balanced budgets. However, a closer look at the revenue flows it generated allows us to understand better how the monopoly functioned and the central role it played in the development of new forms of state, capital and control in colonial Vietnam.

The alcohol monopoly made little, if any, net contribution to the Indochinese budget. However, as an indirect tax, it was a means by which the central government could circumvent Imperial and regional administrative structures and project its authority more directly into the Vietnamese countryside. More important, its high gross revenue underwrote the bond issues that ultimately tipped the economic balance of power from Indochina's regions to its central administration. This is not to say that the monopoly was unprofitable: far from it. The alcohol monopoly was part of a range of policies designed to promote the development of local French capitalist enterprise by diverting monopoly profits away from the Chinese consortiums. While the attempt to deprive the Chinese of an important revenue base was only partially successful, it nonetheless formed the base of a highly profitable business empire centred on the SFDIC and its director, A.R. Fontaine. The other main beneficiary of the monopoly was the Indochinese Department of Customs and Excise. The monopoly transformed the Department into the administration's largest civilian branch, with primary responsibility for the surveillance, repression and 'pacification' previously carried out by soldiers of the colonial army and militia. Customs agents'

---

77 See 'Candidats alcoolistes', *La Tribune Indigène*, 19 Sept. 1922; 'Les monopoles en Indochine', *La Tribune Indigène*, 19 Mar. 1923; 'On aime trop notre pays!', *La Tribune Indigène*, 27 Nov. 1923; 'La logique administrative', *La Tribune Indigène*, 27 Dec. 1923; 'Pas de politique! De Choum-Choum seulement!' *La Tribune Indigène*, 10 May 1924. The story of his campaign against the renewal of the contract is outlined in 'Encore les monopoles: L'intérêt des requins avant celui des masses', *La Tribune Indigène*, 2 Sept. 1924.
78 Nguyễn Ái Quốc, *Bản án chế độ thực dân Pháp*, p. 33.
79 Gerard Sasges, '"Indigenous representation is hostile to all monopolies": Phạm Quỳnh and the end of the alcohol monopoly in colonial Việt Nam', *Journal of Vietnamese Studies*, 5, 1 (2010): 1–36.

enactments of power and domination were far from symbolic and anything but subtle, and they affected ordinary Vietnamese in numbers and in ways that the stunted education system or the monumental architecture of Hanoi and Saigon never would. This sort of success came at considerable cost. For the French, it associated their regime with the corruption, brutality and arbitrary enforcement that were the necessary complement of an unenforceable monopoly. For the Vietnamese, it brought economic dislocation, oppression and familiarity with the forms of negotiation and resistance that allowed them to go on making and drinking their own alcohol. Thus, from its origins in 1897 to its end in 1945, the alcohol monopoly was to play an important role in determining not only the shape of state and enterprise in colonial Vietnam, but also the lived experience of millions of Vietnamese.

[10]
'Martial Races': Ethnicity and Security in Colonial India 1858-1939
David Omissi

> 'Courage goes much by opinion; and many a man behaves as a hero or a coward, according as he considers he is expected to behave.' Henry Lawrence.

The demands of imperial rule ensured that ethnicity and security were closely related. No imperial power could hope to maintain its rule—at a politically acceptable cost—if it treated its subject population as a single, undifferentiated and potentially hostile mass. Successful European rulers identified those indigenous groups who were potential allies, and drew them into the structures of imperial rule. Of these indigenous allies, none were more important than those who joined the ranks of the imperial armies, given that colonial governments relied heavily on armed force to create and extend their political power. But if locally-raised regiments were very often the main guardians of the imperial order they were also a potential menace to it—as the history of dissent and mutiny in such forces shows clearly.[1] Recruiting policy was therefore a matter of acute political importance—particularly after colonial rule had been firmly established, armies under indigenous rulers had been destroyed or disbanded, and a wider range of potential recruits had been opened to the imperial power.

Colonial India offers a most striking example of these problems of selection and incorporation. India was the most populous territory subject to direct imperial rule, and the Indian Army was the largest indigenous force raised under European leadership. Confronted with the remarkable ethnic diversity of the subcontinent, the British elite proved able to identify likely military allies and, for almost a century, bound them to the institutional structure of the Raj.

In the early phase of colonial expansion, however, the European trading companies had little scope for manoeuvre. Confined mainly to coastal enclaves, they were not able to select their recruits with the care that was possible at the apogee of European domination. Indian soldiers had served alongside Company troops from the late seventeenth century but it was not until the 1720s that the French began to raise regular Indian regiments to use against the British on the west coast.[2] Known as 'sepoys'—the term deriving from the Persian *sipahii* or soldier—these regulars proved effective. The British followed the French example from 1748, and by 1765 they commanded 9000 sepoys, this force growing steadily until it reached 82,000 by 1794.[3] The early British sepoy armies were recruited mainly from the same military labour pool that Indian rulers drew upon for their own forces.[4]

The British established three sepoy armies in India, one based on each of the three presidencies (the political units of East India Company rule) at Bengal, Madras and Bombay. These three armies did

not coordinate their recruiting policy, and the Bengal Army came to diverge dramatically in its composition from the forces raised in Madras and Bombay. By the early nineteenth century, the Bengal Army was drawn almost entirely from high-caste Rajputs and Brahmins from Bihar and Awadh.[5] As British rule was consolidated, the opportunities for military employment for the militarised north Indian peasantry grew fewer. The higher castes took advantage of their superior status to dominate posts in the Company regiments at the expense of the lower castes and some traditional military communities.[6] The high caste men were often taller than the average, and hence were considered better fighters hand-to-hand. Many British officers thought them 'the handsomest and cleanest-looking men', and held them to be more 'sightly' on parade;[7] in 1790 Lord Cornwallis remarked that he was very impressed by 'the native black troops' of Bengal—'fine men' who 'would not disgrace even the Prussian ranks'.[8]

Although the Bengal regiments remained mixed, the higher Hindu castes serving alongside Muslim recruits, the caste feelings of Brahmin and Rajput sepoys were respected. Soldiers did not normally have to wield pick and shovel during sieges, as they would lose caste by doing the work of coolies; and they were not required to serve on or across the sea, which would also cost them their status.[9] Low-caste men were rarely promoted, as high-caste sepoys disliked taking orders from them. British officers in Bengal, closer to the centres of power and more conscious of status than those in Madras and Bombay, even developed a certain pride in the identity of their sepoys. This in turn encouraged punctilliousness in matters of caste. 'I have seen a Hindu [sepoy]', recalled one British general, 'who would refuse to drink water out of his own lotah, which he had had filled by his own servant, because it was cooled with ice which had been made in the ice pits, and Europeans had handled it'.[10] Eventually, in deference to Brahmin feeling, the lower-castes were excluded entirely from Bengal regiments—at first only in practice, later by legislation.[11]

Matters were different in the southern presidencies. Denied access by distance and policy to the traditional recruiting grounds of northern India, the Madras and Bombay Armies had to make soldiers of such material as lay to hand.[12] They had to recruit from a broader social base than the Bengal Army—by 1839 'all natives' in Madras were eligible to serve, although in practice the Madras Army maintained a balance between Telugus, Muslims, Tamils and low-caste Hindus.[13] For the most part, little deference was shown to caste feeling in the Madras and Bombay Armies. Recruits were expected to serve and mess together, regardless of whether this would have caused ritual pollution in civilian life.

Some British officers were uneasy about the dependence of the Bengal Army upon a narrow social and geographical range of recruits. 'Our sepoys come too much from the same parts of the country—Oude, the lower Doab, and upper Behar', warned Sir Henry Lawrence in the 1840s. 'There is too much of clanship among them, and the evil should be remedied'.[14] He urged the recruitment of low-caste men, and non-Indians such as Malays, Chinese and Burmese. His warnings went unheeded, but they seemed more perceptive after the events of 1857 had exposed the shortcomings of recruiting policy in Bengal. After the British had annexed Awadh in 1856, most regiments of the Bengal Army rose in revolt in May the following year. The rebellious sepoys joined forces with the discontented peasants, *taluqdars* and *zamindars* of northern India, restored the Mughal Emperor in Delhi, and threatened to sweep the British from the subcontinent. The rebellion was crushed only after a year's hard fighting and much bloodshed.[15]

The rising of 1857-58 discredited the policy of selective high-caste recruitment that had evolved in Bengal. Most regiments of the Bengal Army had mutinied or had been disarmed in anticipation, while the Madras and Bombay Armies—despite some discontent—had remained quiescent, even fighting with distinction against the rebels. Indeed, the civil rebellion was most intense in the very areas of southern Awadh that supplied the best recruits to the Bengal Army.[16] Most British observers attributed the mutiny in Bengal to the excessive recruitment of Brahmins from a restricted geographical area, and to the deference shown to their caste feelings. It was unlikely therefore that the Bengal Army would resume its previous shape after the mutiny.

This article examines the process by which the British identified and tried to incorporate potential military allies after the mutiny. It analyses the changing ethnic composition of the imperial military forces in India, over a period of about 80 years, explaining why the British targeted certain groups as likely recruits and excluded others. By the later nineteenth century, British recruiting strategy had generated its own ideological corpus—the theory of the so-called 'martial races'—whose roots and influence will be examined. But British perceptions and strategies cannot alone explain the evolution of the military relationship between indigenous populations and colonial rulers—not only did the British select their recruits, the recruits selected the British. To understand fully the composition of imperial armies in India it is necessary to explain why certain Indian peoples proved to be willing military allies of the Raj while others rejected the advances of the recruiting officer.

Existing literature has not considered these issues directly.[17] There is a large body of popular writing on the Indian Army, much of which is concerned with the problems of recruiting and the theory of martial races, but this work lacks analytical rigour and is not usually the product of extensive research. The standard history, Philip Mason's *A Matter of Honour* (the title is revealing), makes little effort to achieve a distance from the perceptions and preconceptions of the British officer class.[18] The scholarly literature on the army has focussed mainly on the pre-mutiny period.[19] David Arnold has done most to illuminate British security and recruiting strategies in the later nineteenth and twentieth centuries, but his work is concerned with the Madras Police, rather than the Indian Army itself.[20] There is copious primary evidence, both published and unpublished, but almost all of this emanates from British official sources and must be used with caution—categories defined by the British as 'caste' or 'class' often overlap with regional or linguistic boundaries.[21] The large quantity of official evidence does, however, offer a measure of British concern with recruiting policy—a concern that was evident before the fighting was over in 1858.

MARTIAL RACES AFTER THE MUTINY

In July 1858 a Commission under the Chairmanship of Major-General Peel (the Secretary of State for War) was appointed to inquire into the organisation of the Indian Army.[22] Mainly composed of British army officers and civilians attached to the War Office, the Commission heard evidence from 47 British and Company officers in London between August and December. No Indians sat on the Commission or gave evidence. The Commissioners were invited to discuss a whole range of questions concerning the future composition of the Indian Army; and although they were not asked directly to consider matters of caste and ethnicity, it soon became clear that the process of reconstruction would be deeply concerned with these issues.

The witnesses called before the Commission proposed a variety of schemes for the future garrison of India. One or two suggested that the Indian regiments be entirely disbanded and replaced with an all-British force. The Commissioners had little time for this scheme: there were already many British regiments in India; European manpower was scarce and expensive, and it was more efficiently employed in positions of leadership than in the routine duties of the ranks.[23] A number of witnesses believed the Indian forces could be replaced by troops raised outside the subcontinent—one urged the recruitment of Christians from Burma and southeast Asia; and several others thought a garrison composed of Africans and West Indians would be the safest course.[24] But the Commissioners accepted that a force of outsiders would cause resentment among the Indian population besides displacing Indians who were soldiers by profession. 'The wise policy', observed Lieutenant-Colonel Durand, was not to shoulder such men aside, but 'to feed, use, and control them'.[25]

The vast majority of the witnesses accepted that the future garrison of India would have to be recruited in the subcontinent. But almost all of these were adamant that caste feeling should not be allowed to play any part in the ranks. Typical were the views of Lieutenant-Colonel Robert Master, who 'would not admit the name of caste in any way whatever; that has been the ruin of the army'.[26] Caste should not be tampered with deliberately, argued most witnesses, but equally it could not be permitted to interfere with military duty. 'I would receive a man without enquiring as to his caste', commented one, 'so long as he would do the work which the Europeans would do'.[27]

There was less agreement over exactly which groups should be selected or excluded. Few of the witnesses voiced an opinion, and those opinions were often contradictory. Some believed that a wide range of recruits was the safest policy. One or two held Brahmins to be the best soldiers; others, with the events of 1857 very much in mind, urged they be excluded from the Bengal Army as 'the Brahmin is always at the bottom of every intrigue'.[28] One witness thought 'we should be most guarded and watchful with the Sikhs'; another reckoned there was 'no more dangerous man than a religious Mahomedan'; a third that 'trusting to Ghurkas is to be avoided'—although his view was a maverick one.[29]

Faced with such confusing and contradictory evidence, the Commissioners were understandably cautious; and they made few specific recommendations. 'The Native Army', they advised, 'should be composed of different nationalities and castes, and, as a general rule, mixed promiscuously through each regiment'.[30] They did not suggest which 'different nationalities and castes' were to be recruited and which excluded.

The deliberations of the Peel Commission have been discussed more for the light they shed upon imperial perceptions than for the influence they had on policy, for the reconstruction of the Bengal Army just after the mutiny did not follow the advice of the Commission, but obeyed immediate political and military logic. Bengal regiments which had mutinied were mostly disbanded; regiments raised to fight the mutineers were mostly retained.

During the military crisis of 1857-58 the British had raised fresh battalions wherever they could, mainly in north-central India and the Punjab. Returns for April 1858 show 80,000 men in the Bengal Army: of these, over 18,000 are listed as 'Punjabis'; over 10,000 each as 'Rajputs' and 'Muslims'; nearly 9000 as 'low-caste Hindus' and only 8000 as 'Brahmins'. The total of 80,000 does not include the 52,000 (including police, depots and levies) serving under Sir John Lawrence in the Punjab. Of these, 30,000 are listed as 'Muslims', nearly 15,000 as 'Sikhs', and only 8000 as 'Hindus'.[31]

There are problems with all figures for the Indian Army, but especially with those from the period of confusion immediately after the Mutiny. Figures do not add up, or contradict other available statistics; the categories employed are a bewildering mixture of the linguistic, religious, caste and regional; and it is sometimes unclear whether or not the figures under one head have been included under another. Despite this, the overall trend is clear enough. The process of disbanding and raising regiments had shifted the recruiting ground of the Bengal Army towards the north—above all to the Punjab.

Recruiting policy in the Bengal Army after the mutiny therefore still differed from the strategies employed in Bombay and Madras. The two southern armies accepted a wide range of recruits—Muslims, Mahrattas, Brahmins, Rajputs and other Hindu castes in Bombay; and Muslims, Telingas, Tamils, Mahrattas, Christians and low-caste Hindus in Madras It was deliberate policy to take a wide mix of recruits in Madras: 'it has been an object to maintain a due proportion, so that no one caste should preponderate over another'.[32] The military changes in Bengal in the late 1850s and early 1860s left that army, however, with a distinct bias in its recruiting—a bias that was broadly retained for the remaining life of the Raj. Men from the Punjab and Muslims from elsewhere in the Presidency were the favoured recruits in Bengal after the mutiny, just as the higher castes of Bihar and Awadh had been before it. Given that the dependence of the Bengal Army on a narrow range of recruits was seen by British officers as a major cause of the mutiny, and that the Peel Commission had advised in favour of a wide range of recruits, the continued exclusivity of Bengal recruiting demands explanation.

Late nineteenth and early twentieth century British commentators, particularly popular writers like George MacMunn, liked to argue that only some Indian peoples had the ability to make war. 'It is one of the essential differences between the East and the West', he wrote in 1911, 'that in the East ... only certain clans and classes can bear arms; the others have not the physical courage necessary for the warrior'.[33] The belief that some Indian peoples were warlike by tradition and others were not was the central plank of the 'martial race' theory, which appeared in developed form in the later nineteenth century. Of these so-called 'martial races', Sikhs and Gurkhas were the best known.

Sikh religion and society were undoubtedly informed by martial traditions.[34] In the seventeenth century, under pressure from Mughal rulers, greater Sikh militancy had become evident. The sixth Sikh guru, Hargobind, had taken to arms, fortified the holy city of Amritsar, and worn two swords to symbolise his temporal and spiritual authority. Under the tenth guru, Gobind Singh, there formed the militant Khalsa brotherhood who stressed the martial aspects of the supreme being. But it was the development of the Sikh state under Ranjit Singh and, above all, the disciplined courage demonstrated by its army (trained and equipped in the European fashion) that most persuaded the British that the Sikhs were a martial people.[35] British commentators frequently praised the Sikh armies that had been defeated in the Anglo-

Sikh wars of the 1840s. At first sight, there seems to be some substance to the contention that the British recruited Sikhs simply because they seemed warlike.

The theory of martial races was not a mere figment of the colonial imagination—it would not have been a successful strategy had it been so. Colonial discourse could draw inspiration from the caste system, perceived (not altogether inaccurately) as a systematisation of hereditary occupation.[36] Colonial labelling of certain groups as warlike accorded with some India self-perceptions. 'The duty of a Kshatri is to die on the field of battle ... and ... to kill the enemy' wrote a havildar of the 107th Pioneers to a fellow Indian soldier in August 1915.[37] The self esteem and social status of some castes were dependent upon a perceived warrior tradition; it might seem appropriate for such groups to take service in the colonial army, and a mutually beneficial relationship could develop between them and the colonial state.

But the 'martial races' of colonial discourse cannot be simply equated with Indian self-images; nor was British recruiting policy directed just by the discovery of martial traditions. Policy favoured those groups who had some claim to martial status, and discriminated against those who did not; but this was a tendency, not a fixed rule. Timing is important. The main reconstruction of the Bengal Army was complete by the early 1860s, and the balance of recruits achieved by then remained very roughly the same until the end of the Raj—Sikhs, Punjabi Muslims, Rajputs, Muslims from Hindustan and the Frontier. British observers in the eighteenth century had suggested that warlike qualities were not evenly distributed among the peoples of India, but martial race theory did not achieve its most elaborate form until the last decade of the nineteenth century. Most of the officers consulted by the Peel Commission made no reference to 'martial races', and very few made much of the idea that some Indian social groups were more warlike than others. The martial race theory which emerged in the late nineteenth century was more a symptom than a cause of a restricted recruiting policy.

Selective recruitment was partly an extension of existing colonial strategies of divide and rule. This was part of the instinctive self-defence mechanism of imperialism, an understandable tendency to seek out those groups who might be relied upon by the colonial power and to exclude those who could not.[38] Groups accustomed to political dominance or with a military tradition might be potentially dangerous if they were not coopted to imperial rule. Martial traditions could, after all, become part of an anti-British appeal—during the 1907 agrarian agitation in the Chenab canal colony, for example, the revolutionary Sikh leader Ajit Singh wrote in a widely circulated pamphlet 'Oh! brave soldiers of the Khalsa you are lost to all sense of national honour.

Give up the British service and, if you are brave enough, expel the English from your land'.[39]

Some witnesses before the Peel Commission emphasised the need to exploit divisions in the subject population. '*Divide et impera* was the old Roman motto, and it should be ours', observed Lord Elphinstone. 'The safety of the great iron steamers ... is greatly increased by building them in compartments. I would ensure the security of our Indian Empire by constructing our native army on the same principle.'[40] The example of the Sikhs suggests this principle was followed.

It was during the mutiny that Sikh regiments first became numerous in the Bengal Army. They were recruited in large numbers in 1857 in order to exploit their own grievances against the Bengal sepoys and the restored Mughal emperor.[41] 'It was not because they loved us, but because they hated Hindustan and hated the Bengal Army, that the Sikhs have flocked to our standards', noted Major-General Mansfield.

> They wanted to revenge themselves ... They were not attracted by mere daily pay. It was rather the prospect of ... stamping on the heads of their enemies. We have turned to profit the esprit de corps of the old Khalsa army ... which for a time would most effectively bind the Sikhs to us as long as the active service against their old enemies may last.[42]

Similar comments, somewhat toned down, appear in official publications in the twentieth century. The recruiting handbook for *Rajputana Classes* noted of the Muslim Mers of Merwara that 'they are strongly attached to the British Raj and are proud of the fact that, as a tribe, they never submitted to any other conqueror ... They are inclined to hold themselves aloof from the inhabitants of the surrounding States and to look on themselves as the especial soldiers and retainers of the British Government'. Forty per cent of the male Mer population between the ages of 18 and 30 were enlisted into the Indian Army during the Great War—the highest proportion of any martial race.[43] Garhwalis 'do not regularly mix with other classes of Indians', remarked the Adjutant of the Royal Garhwal Rifles in 1930. 'They mix more easily with British troops owing to their keenness on football.'[44] The handbook for Gurkhas also pointed out that the latter 'despise the natives of India and look up to and fraternise with Europeans'.[45] For religious and historical reasons, Sikhs and Gurkhas were unlikely to combine with Indian Hindus in political dissent—one reason why both groups were targeted by the Bengal Army.[46]

The British selected their recruits not only on the basis of ethnicity, but also of social class. The urban middle classes were excluded from the army, especially so once they had started to become sympathetic to the nationalist movement. The favoured recruits were of independent peasant status, for such men had the most conservative political outlook and the 'right attitude' to soldiering—they were considered less likely than city-dwellers to question or disagree with orders. Muslims of the eastern Punjab, Hyderabad or Rajputana, for example, were not enlisted if they lived in towns: but those who lived in villages were held to make 'very good soldiers'.[47] Jats were highly-prized recruits, partly because 'the Jat is a peasant farmer before anything else ... In spite of the military tenets of his faith, his sayings are all of the plough'.[48] There were exceptions to this tendency. In Madras, the Adi-Dravidan (or Paraiyan) recruits were mostly landless labourers; and Rajputs were everywhere selected partly because of their martial self-image which discouraged them from agriculture.[49]

CHANGING PATTERNS OF RECRUITMENT

But the identity of the martial races was not fixed. Previously 'non-martial' groups could enter colonial discourse as 'martial races'; groups that had long been recruited could suddenly cease to be martial; and others might be put on probation by the British authorities to see if they made the grade. Some examples may illustrate this process of changing martial identity.

The Mappilas (or Moplahs) were the Muslim descendants of Arab traders who had settled in Malabar in large numbers in the eighth century AD.[50] Gradually increasing in relative numbers through conversion from the lower castes, by 1921 they made up about a third of the population. Their vernacular was Malayalam—a Dravidian language closely related to Tamil, with Arabic, Sanskrit, Hindustani, Portuguese and English loanwords. Very few Mappilas owned land, most being cultivating tenants, landless labourers, petty traders and fishermen. Literacy was low, only 6.2 per cent of Mappilas being literate in 1921, compared with 13 per cent of the population of Malabar as a whole. The Mappilas had the makings of a martial tradition—8-10,000 had served as auxiliaries to the forces of Hyder Ali of Mysore during his advance into Malabar in 1766; and Mappila 'outlaws' kept British forces constantly occupied from 1795 to 1805.

The Mappilas seemed to be an ideal 'martial race'. Their low level of literacy, peasant status and martial background promised that they would make fine soldiers; their militant Islam and dislike of Hindus—stemming from the oppression they suffered at the hands of Hindu landlords—suggested that they could be coopted by the Madras government to serve, if need be, against the Hindu majority of the Presidency. But for most of the nineteenth century the Mappilas did not prove to be willing agents of the colonial state. The initially conciliatory attitude of British officials soon turned hostile after a chiefly rebellion broke out in 1800, taking two years to suppress. From then, Mappilas were excluded from subordinate posts in the administration and police. This exclusion fostered an anti-British mentality which traditional intellectuals did much to encourage. Most Mappila contact with the colonial state was through its coercive apparatus, as agrarian discontent led to violence in rural Malabar, 351 separate anti-landlord incidents being recorded between 1836 and 1919. Efforts to recruit Mappilas along with other troops into class-company regiments resulted in failure, and the units were broken up soon after their formation. British observers attributed this failure to the 'clannish propensities' of the Mappilas, no doubt a reflection of their marginal status in Malabar. From 1896, however, Mappilas were enlisted with more success into two all-Mappila class regiments—the 17th and 25th Madras Infantry (later the 77th and 78th Moplah Rifles)—which exploited this strong sense of identity more effectively.

The recruitment of Mappilas illustrates the way the British tried to coopt potentially dangerous social groups. The police authorities in Madras regarded the Mappilas as 'lawless', 'turbulent' and 'criminal' by their very nature; but after the 1896 disturbances, the army was more optimistic, hoping that 'instead of defying lawful authority, the Mappilas may, in future, devote their fighting instincts to some better purpose than fanatically opposing the representatives of Government'. Enlistment was one such 'better purpose' which the army authorities hoped would draw the sting of discontent from their Mappila recruits. Yet, ironically, while the Moplah regiments were becoming successful outside Malabar, the police within the District continued to regard the Mappilas as 'criminal'; they were excluded from police ranks, and were the main object of police surveillance and coercion.[51] The Minas of Jaipur and the Mers of Merwara—both in Rajputana—are two further examples of social groups who were labelled 'criminal' and 'martial' at the same time.[52]

The British tried to turn other groups into military allies, sometimes without success—as in the case of the Coorgs. Coorg is a tiny province in south India, bounded on the north and east by Mysore state. Lying across the mountains of the Western Ghats, nearly one third of the 1593 square miles of Coorg was covered in reserve forest. According to the 1931 census, the population of the province was 163,327—of which 146,007 were Hindus, 13,777 Muslims and 3425 Christians. Hindus by religion, and speaking the Kodagi language, the 41,026 Coorgs were the largest single group.[53] The remoteness and difficult terrain of their home had helped them preserve their distinctive culture. Coorgs had a martial background—they had successfully expelled the Muslim armies of Mysore after a series of rebellions in the 1780s; they served as allies of the British during the wars against Mysore in 1788-99; and they made up the bulk of the armies of the Lingayat Rajas of Coorg before the British annexed the province in 1834. Coorg traditions were steeped in martial references, and competitive fighting featured at every festival. Dominant within Coorg, and regarding themselves as warriors of the

Kshatriya varna, the Coorgs had many of the qualities the British looked for in a martial race.[54]

It was understandable therefore that the British should try to enlist them. The military traditions of the Coorgs had long been recognised by the Raj when the first attempt was made, in 1907, to raise a battalion. This failed, but about 700 Coorgs were persuaded to enlist during the Great War. They were not formed into an all-Coorg battalion, it being considered that the 4000 Coorg males of military age could not sustain the losses likely to be incurred by such a unit in heavy fighting, but served with success in various units of the Madras Army.[55]

A recruiting party from the Indian Signal Corps which visited Coorg in September 1936 had no success, however, the men being unwilling to leave their homes. Although the party made their attempt during the agricultural slack season, they perhaps failed to follow the advice of the Commissioner, who urged that any drive to enlist should be accompanied by a band—Coorg was very isolated, many people would never have heard one, and, he suggested, it would prove 'a first class attraction and [be] appreciated to the full'. There was also no shortage of land in Coorg, and the traditional ties of the *Okka*—the patrilinial joint family with its indivisible parcel of land—remained very strong. The British encouraged the division of *Okka* holdings, a policy which seems to have borne fruit—1500 Coorgs enlisted in the Second World War.

The changing relations between Mappilas, Coorgs and the colonial state indicates that enlistment was not simply the outcome of British attitudes and strategies. Indian self-perceptions, social structures and political strategies must also be invoked to explain the fluctuating relationships between certain social groups, the Indian Army, and the 'martial race' discourse.

The shifts in 'martial race' identity after the mutiny followed a geographical pattern. In 1857-58 the main recruiting areas of the Bengal Army had moved away from Bihar and Awadh towards the Punjab; in the second half of the nineteenth and in the early twentieth centuries this northward movement continued. In 1862, 28 battalions were recruited mainly in the Punjab (including the North-West Frontier); 5 from Nepal; 28 from Hindustan; 30 from the Bombay Presidency and 40 from Madras. By 1897 there were 43 battalions recruited mainly in the Punjab; 15 from Nepal; 24 from Hindustan; 13 from Bombay and 25 from Madras. On the eve of the Great War the shift to the north was even more pronounced: by then there were 58 battalions recruited mainly in the Punjab; 20 in Nepal; 33 in Hindustan; and only 14 and 12 from Bombay and Madras respectively.[56] The general trend was away from Madras and Bombay and towards the north, especially the Punjab. By the outbreak of the Great War, the Punjab (which contained only one-thirteenth of the entire population of the subcontinent) supplied nearly half the recruits to the Indian Army.⁵⁷

As the perceived centres of martial excellence moved northwards, regiments raised in the south of India were progressively disbanded. The Madras Army suffered particularly hard.⁵⁸ It had been at its largest between 1824 and 1861, when 52 battalions of infantry were on the list; 12 of these had been disbanded by 1865 and another eight by 1882. There were 30 battalions on the Madras Army List in 1903; but of these only 15 were recruited from inside the Presidency, the remainder being composed mainly of men from the north.⁵⁹ The exigencies of the Great War ensured that further units had to be raised in Madras, but even this imperial military crisis did not result in any major increase in the proportion of Madrassis in the Army—only 51,223 combatants were recruited from the Presidency during the conflict. Further units were disbanded when the Indian Army was reorganised in 1911, until by 1928 no Madras infantry remained. When the Corps of Pioneers was disbanded in 1933 the only remnant of the old Coast Army was the Madras Sappers and Miners—at least until Field-Marshal Auchinleck revived the Madras infantry in the Second World War. The Bombay Army was also gradually reduced, while more of the recruits for its remaining regiments were drawn from Bengal.

The northward shift in British perceptions of the martial races must be explained. The main architect of the gradual shift towards the northern recruiting grounds was Lord Roberts, who commanded the Madras Army from 1880 and the Bengal Army from 1885 to 1893.⁶⁰ In his memoirs he recalls his first impressions of the southern soldiers: 'long years of peace ... had evidently had upon them ... a softening and deteriorating effect; and I was forced to the conclusion that the ancient military spirit had died in them ... and that they could no longer with safety be pitted against warlike races or employed outside the limits of Southern India'. Looking back, Roberts emphasised his belief in martial race theory, arguing that 'no comparison can be made between ... a regiment recruited amongst ... the warlike races of northern India and of one recruited amongst the effeminate races of the South'.⁶¹ From the mid-1880s, as the Russian Empire expanded to the northern frontier of Afghanistan, Roberts grew anxious that Madras regiments might not stand up to the armies of the Tsar if it came to war for India.

Originally a Bengal Army man, prejudiced against recruits from the south, Roberts and others like him no doubt saw in the Madras sepoys what they wished to find. But there is some evidence that the Madras and Bombay regiments were less efficient than those of Bengal. In 1871 Sir Frederick Haines (the Commander-in-Chief Madras) lamented that the officers and men of his army 'are in danger of falling into the delusion that they have nothing but police duties to perform ... This view of the functions of an army must tend to lower the military spirit in all its members'.[62] Indeed, the 1879 Eden Commission advised reductions in the number of Madras regiments, as that army would not be called upon to perform more than internal security duties. The Madras infantry contained 'very many men whom it is an absurdity to call soldiers' reported one exasperated British general from Burma in 1889, after several Madras regiments had behaved poorly in action.[63]

Furthermore, the British officers of the southern regiments were less efficient than their counterparts in Bengal. As early as 1875 it was noted that the better British officers preferred service in the Bengal Army, as they had more chance of lucrative civil employment there; others avoided the Madras Army in particular as it saw very little active service.[64] The reductions in the Madras Army from the 1880s only exacerbated the problem of quality, since they created a surplus of officers on the Madras List which led in turn to the employment of many who were senior, but old and inefficient.

There was perhaps a correlation between the quality of British officers and the structures of martial race theory. Roberts excepted one southern unit—the Madras Sappers and Miners—from his general critique of the fighting qualities of the Madras Army.[65] He argued that the Sappers were superior to other units in Madras because they selected more intelligent recruits, often those who were shunned by the infantry. But Roberts omitted to point out that their officers also came from a different source—the Royal Engineers, who had the pick of the cadets from the Royal Military Academy. Martial race theory—which focussed on the Indian ranks—was therefore in part at least a means of explaining the geographically varied performance of British officers.

Military reorganisations, undertaken for other ends, also affected recruiting strategy. In 1895 the three Presidency Armies—of Bengal, Madras and Bombay—were amalgamated to form a single Indian Army, divided into four commands. Previously each Presidency Army had enjoyed some independence; but after the amalgamation the officers of the former Bengal Army—by far the majority—were better able to impose their point of view on the remainder. The feelings of the Madras Army officers, who argued for the fighting qualities of southern recruits, could be resisted, and recruiting strategy in Madras could be directed more easily as a matter of general policy.[66]

Many of the southern social groups newly excluded from military service resented their loss of rewards and status.[67] Some distant claim to a military tradition could be mustered by most agrarian castes, and used as an argument against exclusion from the Army List.[68] At the Indian National Congress session of 1891, for example, several representatives of Madrassi social groups presented petitions asking for military service to be opened to them. The Mahars, an untouchable group from Maharashtra, had served in the armies of Shivaji and made up nearly a quarter of the Bombay Army in the early nineteenth century. After army reorganisations reduced, then ended, their service as sepoys, many Mahars grew resentful and anxious. In 1910 a Conference of Deccan Mahars petitioned to be allowed to rejoin the ranks. 'We are making no new demands', observed the petition. 'We do not claim employment in services in which we have not been engaged before ... But the present changes in the Indian Army have been most prejudicial to the interests of our people. We have been excluded from the Military Service entirely, for reasons unknown to us.'[69]

Couched in the most loyal language, the Mahar petition was a conservative reaction to changes in the strategy of the elite. The Mahars, like many other excluded castes, did not at first challenge the prevailing assumption that some Indians were martial and others were not—they merely urged that they be included in the list of 'martial races'. Similar suppositions appeared in the official literature. The 1908 handbook on Mahrattas, written by a sympathetic British officer, ends with a protest at the growing indifference to their martial tradition: 'Whatever they have been called to do, they have done. What other class in India have fought as the Marathas have ... Yet they have been given very little opportunity of showing their worth on active service. It is hard that they should be misjudged without fair trial'.[70]

Some Indian critics went further, and challenged the central assumptions of martial race theory. As early as 1886, at the second session of Congress in Calcutta, Raja Rampal Singh blamed British rule 'for degrading our natures, for systematically crushing out of us all martial spirit, for converting a race of soldiers and heroes into a timid flock of quill driving sheep [prolonged shouts]'.[71] He suggested that the existence of non-martial races was an outcome of British policy; but went on loyally to propose that Indians 'who would be willing to draw sword, and ... lay down our lives' would only do so 'for the support and maintenance of that Government to which we owe so much'. By the early twentieth century, however, some Indian politicians were urging a complete reformation of the army and an abandonment of martial race strategy. G. K. Gokhale argued that the 'mercenary' Indian Army be replaced by a cheaper and more effective citizens' militia, recruited on a wider basis. The astonishing success of the Japanese forces in the war against Russia in 1905 added weight to his contention that all Asians were potentially martial. But the British never seriously considered these proposals, for to broaden recruitment to include all social groups in the subcontinent would have undermined the strategy of *divide et impera* upon which the military security of the Raj was based.

Besides the northward drift of the main recruiting grounds, the martial race strategy showed another main tendency—that fewer and fewer 'martial races' were regularly recruited. Changes in regimental organisation helped to bring this about. In 1863 an Indian infantry battalion had eight companies, and hence in theory could recruit as many different classes, although in practice few class-company regiments used more than four. In 1900 the eight companies were combined into four double companies, formalised into four companies per battalion in 1922. This simplification of regimental organisation, intended to make battalions easier to handle in dispersed fighting, tended to reduce the number of different classes of recruits taken by any individual unit.[72] The number of ethnically homogenous class regiments also increased. The Eden Commission of 1879, although suggesting that class-company regiments would give fuller expression to the political principle of 'divide and rule', recommended on military grounds that existing class regiments in the Bengal Army should be retained, as they proved more efficient in action.[73] As the Russian threat became taken more seriously during the last quarter of the nineteenth century, military efficiency made headway against political safety—in this respect at least. Of the 64 Bengal infantry regiments, 22 were each of one class in 1887; but by 1897 the Bengal Army included 42 class regiments.[74]

The military need for some larger basic grouping than the battalion had long been recognised by the more perceptive Indian Army officers. In the mid-1870s, several officers put forward schemes to group Indian Army battalions in threes, so that drafts from the garrison and reserve battalions in the group might be sent to reinforce the one on active service.[75] For this system to work, all three battalions would have to be of similar ethnic composition, a prospect which aroused some political concern. 'It would be contrary to our policy to promote a union of feeling and a common interest in so large a body as three regiments', wrote the Commander-in-Chief in 1875, 'because disaffection, which is the greatest evil we have to guard against, in any one portion would be certain to pervade the whole'.[76] The Eden Commission agreed in 1879. But the Russian war scare of 1885, which raised the prospect that military efficiency might have to override political security, forced a revision of these views. In 1886 the three-battalion system was introduced; henceforward, individual battalions could not widen their range of recruits, since to do so would be to jeopardise the similarity between battalions of the same group upon which the system relied.[77]

COLONIAL DISCOURSE AND COLONIAL STRATEGY, c.1890-1922

As the pattern of selective recruiting became established, British officers developed a body of ideas to justify and rationalise the strategies employed. Although its origins might be traced further back, this 'martial race' theory first achieved prominence in the later nineteenth century, and reached its most developed and widespread form in the popular literature and military handbooks published just before and just after the First World War. The central assumption of martial race theory—that some Indians were suited by hereditary tradition to bear arms, and others were not—has already been discussed; but the theory had a number of other components which will now be analysed.

British commentators were fond of claiming that the martial races were intellectually backward. George MacMunn talked of 'the stupider martial races' and noted that 'the Jat' was 'proverbially thick in the uptake'.[78] Popular British stereotypes characterised Jats and Sikhs as stolid and unimaginative, yet possessing dogged courage. These patronising generalisations also appear in the official *Handbooks for the Indian Army*, issued to British officers in the early years of this century. That for 'Rajputana classes' noted that the Gujars were 'somewhat quarrelsome by nature and are very thick-headed'; while that for Mappilas seemed to imply that they were best regarded as akin to dogs or horses—'steady, tractable and never troublesome, unless illtreated or abused ... to those who treat them with kindness and consideration they become much attached ... But the hand that controls them must be firm'.[79] These stereotypes demonstrate a different sort of contempt than that shown by the British for the educated 'babu' or the 'sly, scheming Brahmin'.

It is worth noting that such stereotypes were not purely British in origin. Punjabi proverbs suggested the stupidity of Sikhs and Jats; and no British recruiting handbook was complete without its quota of similar Indian popular sayings, included partly to give the fresh officer the illusion of understanding the 'natives'.[80]

These collective stereotypes reflected a political strategy. Most of the martial races were recruited from the less well-educated—and arguably less politically conscious—sections of the Indian population.[81] The suitability of recruits from Garhwal was held to correlate with the altitude, and hence isolation, of their place of residence. Men from the mountainous northeast of the district were preferred—the handbook commenting revealingly that these men lacked 'the educational qualifications of the Lower Garhwali (which perhaps may not be regarded as a failing)'.[82] Literacy rates for the main martial races are one measure of their education; male literacy in British India, according to the 1891 census, averaged 8.8 per cent, but in the British states of the Punjab (one of the main recruiting areas) only 6 per cent of men were literate, despite the greater urbanisation of the region. An average of 13.1 per cent of males aged between 15 and 24 (the main recruiting age) were literate throughout India in 1891, but literacy was lower among the two main martial faiths—only 10.6 per cent of young Sikh men were literate, and only 7.9 per cent of Muslims.[83] British stereotypes reflected the pattern of recruiting, which for political reasons was biased in favour of the less well-educated.

The theory that only some Indian peoples were fit to bear arms later came to have an explicitly racial content. Especially in the popular writings of George MacMunn it was argued that the 'fighting men' of

India—above all Dogras and Punjabis—were the descendants of the Aryans who had invaded the subcontinent 2000 years before. 'The great conquest of India ... by the Aryan race' was at the root of the difference between martial and non-martial peoples, argued MacMunn. 'Only certain races were permitted to bear arms, and in course of time only certain races remained fit to bear arms.'[84] MacMunn stressed, however, that the Aryans had interbred for centuries with the dark-skinned 'lesser' races of India. The theory was a way of coming to terms with the developments during the 1870s in the linguistic theories about the common source of Sanskrit, Latin and Greek. Victorian scholars interpreted this to mean that northern Indians were the racial 'cousins' of the British, but the egalitarian implications of the theory were sidestepped by the notion of gradual degeneracy.[85] A few commentators even saw the British Raj as a latter-day Aryan invasion, this time fulfilling the promise of the first.[86]

The recruiting handbooks gave official sanction to this racial theorising. Several opened by observing that 'the dawn of Indian history discloses two races struggling for the soil. One was a fair complexioned Sanskrit speaking people of Aryan lineage, who entered the country from the north-west; the other a dark skinned race of lower type, the original inhabitants of the land'.[87] They too argued that modern Punjabis and Rajputs were the descendants of the Aryan conquerors.[88] The handbook on Garhwalis took pains to emphasise that the Khasas, the majority population of Garhwal, were 'of pronounced Aryan form and habits ... in physiognomy ... as purely an Aryan race as many in the plains of Northern India'. The handbook linked this theory of racial origins to Khasa traditions, which held that the Khasas were descendants of Rajput warriors who were forced to abandon many of their ceremonial usages by the harsh conditions in their mountain homeland.[89]

Gurkhas, of course, did not fit the Aryan races theory. Usually short in stature, dark-skinned, with sloping eyes and flat faces, they were clearly of Mongolian origin.[90] Their extensive recruitment in the later nineteenth century can only reinforce the notion that the more explicitly racial aspects of martial race theory arose as an *ad hoc* response to recruiting practice; for had MacMunn's notion that the 'fighting races' of India were Aryan remnants been allowed to dictate recruiting policy, then Gurkhas would never have been enlisted.

Arguments about the Aryan races were a symptom of a wider urge to classify and categorise Indians. The mutiny had shown the vital importance of 'knowing the natives', and British administrators were well aware that greater knowledge of Indian society conferred greater power over it. In his 1881 Report on the Census of the Punjab, Denzil Ibbetson remarked that 'ignorance of the customs and beliefs of the people among whom we dwell' was a 'distinct loss of administrative power to ourselves'. British officials collected a vast quantity of information about Indian society, in an attempt to make sense of and to order the bewildering variety of castes, languages, customs and religions of the Indian population. The evolving imperial perceptions did reflect the complexity of Indian society, but also mirrored Western conceptions of the subcontinent.[91]

The urge to measure, codify and classify the Indian population owed much to a post-Darwinian understanding of the natural world. India, it seemed, could be comprehended (and therefore controlled) by the same process of classification and measurement employed by investigators into the evolution of plant and animal life. The collective properties of Indian sects and castes were described in a growing literature, this process of codification reaching its highest military expression in the *Handbooks for the Indian Army*.

The handbooks contained immense detail: that on Garhwalis outlined all 11 *parganas* and 86 *pattis* of British Garhwal, and the six *parganas* and 77 *pattis* of Tehri Garhwal, and listed in 28 pages all the 800 known Garhwali castes—and this, be it noted, for the purpose of recruiting a single regiment, the 39th Garhwal Rifles. Officers were advised on the weight and conformation of the ideal recruit; by 1938 the handbook on Madras Classes even included photographs of fine physical examples of each type. Indians were usually described not as individuals but as specimen representatives of collective entities—'the Pallan is a stout, short, jet black man, sturdy, a meat eater, and not overclean in person or habit'.[92] The skull- and nose-measuring habits of some nineteenth century racial researchers had also left trace elements, such as the remark in the handbook on Mappilas that 'the peculiar height of the cranium observable in many of them would probably strike the ethnologist as remarkable'.[93]

Besides their classificatory tendency, the handbooks displayed great concern with racial hygiene. Having laboured hard to codify and classify, the authors of the handbooks—usually officers from a relevant regiment—showed great distaste for racial mixtures. The 1914 handbook on Hindustani Muslims dismisses almost all of those east of the Jumma—who had formed the bulk of the Company's cavalry and much of its infantry in the early nineteenth century—on the grounds that they now 'live in cities and owing to a life of ease and interbreeding are an effete race'.[94] The Janjuas of the Salt Range, by way of contrast, were held to be among the best Muslim soldiers, and were also 'the only really pure Rajputs in the plains of the Punjab'.[95] The handbooks reflected a widespread belief that racial mixing produced degeneracy; the British preferred their martial races to be as socially exclusive as they were themselves.

The changing composition of the 39th Bengal Native Infantry neatly exemplifies this growing aversion to racial mixtures. Men from the Garhwal district of Kumaon division—a thickly wooded and mountainous area on the southern slopes of the Himalaya to the west of Nepal—were recruited originally into Gurkha regiments.[96] But 'the advance of ethnological knowledge', noted George MacMunn, 'resulted in their being separated very properly from Gurkhas, and gradually eliminated from Gurkha battalions'.[97] Instead, the 39th Bengal Infantry became a class regiment of Garhwalis in 1890, a second battalion being added in 1901.[98] MacMunn's use of the term 'very properly' gives an air of moral rectitude to this administrative decision, as if it were somehow 'improper' for Garhwalis to be confused with and recruited with Gurkhas. The original decision to recruit Garhwalis into Gurkha regiments exposes the shortcomings of British 'martial race' categories, for Garhwal had been under Gurkha domination from 1803 to 1815—when Gurkha brutality became legendary. Families of rank were banished or killed, villages were burned, and many Garhwalis sold as slaves. Indeed, when Garhwalis wished to protest against injustice they would complain, even in the early twentieth century, that 'the rule of the Gurkhas has been restored'.[99]

Martial race theory demanded, once firmly established, that the origins and background of potential recruits be carefully vetted.[100] Since the fighting ability of Asians depended upon 'hereditary instinct', argued the handbooks, it was 'a matter of supreme importance that the men enlisted ... should be the very best of their type'.[101] To ensure this was so, regiments were advised to establish close links with their recruiting areas; men already in the ranks were employed to enlist new recruits who were preferably to be relatives, neighbours or men otherwise known to them.[102] In doubtful cases, the account a recruit gave of his origins could be checked against the information listed in the handbooks—that on Pathans listing all known clans, sections and subsections over 200 pages.[103] Recruiting officers were advised that fairs or festivals were occasions which often produced many recruits, as young men often attended with the express intention of joining up, especially if there was family pressure against such a course; but the handbooks warned that such recruits were almost bound to be strangers and hence verifying their credentials might be difficult. Potential recruits, especially such migrants, sometimes tried to conceal their original caste or religious identity, in the hope of achieving higher status or of enlisting.[104]

The strains of the Great War, however, temporarily reversed this tendency towards more selective recruitment.[105] Between 1914 and 1918 the Indian Army more than trebled in size—from 155,000 to 573,000. Most of the nearly one million men who served at one time or another were drawn from the traditional martial groups—Sikhs, Dogras, Rajputs, Muslims and Gurkhas.[106] But after a serious manpower shortage developed from about March 1916, 75 new classes of recruit were also tried.[107] Many of these (such as Punjabi Brahmins and Christians, south and west Punjabi Muslims, Awadh Rajputs, Saini and Khatri Sikhs, Nandbansi Ahirs, Tamang Gurkhas and Dogra Jats) were from classes closely related—in social, religious or geographical terms—to groups already recruited; others (such as Mahars, Telugus, Bhils and Bengalis) were from groups that had once been recruited but subsequently dropped from the list. Some entirely new sources of recruits were tapped, however, often with success. The conflict showed that even the supposedly non-martial classes could make fine soldiers, provided they were well-trained and well-led, and this rediscovery prompted some criticism of the restrictive martial race policy.[108] 'All men are brave', commented one British officer just after the war. 'The humblest follower is capable of sacrifice and devotion ... These revelations have meant a general levelling and the uplift of classes hitherto undeservedly obscure.'[109]

The First World War had shown the need for a more radical military reorganisation. The Indian Army could not recruit for a prolonged modern war on the basis of a battalion unit less than 1000 strong, even if these were grouped in threes. But the restructuring of the army which was discussed from the end of the war, and enacted in 1922, further confirmed the hold of martial race theory. Demobilisation cut the size of the army dramatically from about 500,000 in 1918 to 120,000 in 1923; the cuts fell most heavily on those classes who had been recruited for the first time in the war, or who had been re-recruited—most of the regiments formed from these classes were disbanded, and the post-war army returned to its pre-war ethnic mix.[110] In 1923 no less than 73 of the battalions in the Indian Army were recruited in the Punjab, 20 in Nepal, 9 in Madras, 6 in Bombay, and 36 from the rest of India.[111] The infantry units (other than Gurkhas) which had survived the wave of disbandments were grouped in regiments of six ethnically similar battalions; each regiment had four active service, one training and a Territorial Force battalion. The training battalion provided recruits to the other battalions in peace and war.[112] The new system carefully preserved the old unit traditions, but also retained the narrow recruiting base which had proved inadequate in the First World War.

CONCLUSION

So paradoxically by the 1920s the martial race strategy had reproduced the very political dangers it was designed originally to avoid. Even just after the mutiny some British officers warned that the Bengal Army should not rely too heavily on Sikhs; and periodically in the nineteenth century—especially after the Second Afghan War—it was suggested that the recruiting base might be too narrow. This fear was also raised by the Nicholson Commission (the last pre-war enquiry into army affairs) in 1912.[113] The political risks of relying so heavily on a narrow range of recruits were exposed after the First World War, when the recruiting grounds were affected by civil unrest—in the Frontier Province during the Afghan *jihad* of 1919 and at the height of the red-shirt movement in 1930; and in the Punjab (partly as a result of excessive wartime recruiting, often accompanied by threats or bribery) in the years just after the war.[114]

Yet despite these warnings, despite the need to broaden recruitment during the military crisis of 1914-18, and despite the civil unrest in the recruiting grounds after it, the martial race strategy was never abandoned—indeed the reorganisation of 1922 deepened and confirmed the British reliance on a few Indian social groups. To understand this, we must not only investigate the conscious aims of policy but also the assumed boundaries within which policy was formulated. Large-scale recruiting in the Punjab was at first an immediate response to the military and political crisis of 1857-58. But once the British had selected their military allies, and these social groups had selected the British by providing recruits, it was difficult to recast the ethnic composition of the army without antagonising important allies of the colonial state. Although it had eighteenth-century precedents, martial race theory took hold only after the British had adopted the strategy of selective recruitment. Drawing on an extensive scientific discourse about the Aryan races, the theory was widely propagated by popular and official writers, eventually itself becoming an ingredient in the making of policy. By the 1920s martial race theory was no longer just a colonial strategy—it was a habit of mind, not simply an instrument of policy but also a constraint upon it.

Notes

An earlier version of this article was presented to the War Discussion Group at the Royal Military Academy, Sandhurst, in November 1990. I am grateful to those taking part for their constructive criticism on that occasion. I learned a great deal from David Arnold, who gave me unpublished work and drew my attention to sources I might have missed. Previous drafts benefited from the scrutiny of Andrew Adonis, Michael Dockrill, Kathryn Jones, John MacKenzie, Peter Marshall, Dominic Omissi, Nicholas Owen, Douglas Peers and Manesh Rangarajan, none of whom is responsible for any errors of fact or expressions of opinion in the final version.

All documentary references are to the Public Record Office and the India Office Library, London.

1. For an Iraqi example see D.E. Omissi, 'Britain, the Assyrians and the Iraq Levies, 1919-1932', *Journal of Imperial and Commonwealth History*, **17** (1989): 301-22. Interestingly, in contemporary Iraq Saddam Hussein's elite

Omissi: 'Martial Races'

 Republican Guard contains a disproportionate number of Turkomans, a national minority of Central Asian origin.
2. S.P. Cohen, *The Indian Army: Its Contribution to the Development of the Indian Nation* (Berkeley 1971), 6-7.
3. Cohen, *Indian Army*, 32. By 1805 the total military strength of the Company was 155,000: C.A. Bayly, *Indian society and the making of the British Empire: The New Cambridge History of India*, II: 1 (Cambridge 1988), 85.
4. I am grateful to Peter Marshall and Douglas Peers for this point.
5. Cmd 2515 (1859 Sess. 1) vol. V, Appendix 58, Evidence of Lord Clyde.
6. D.H.A. Kolff, *Naukar, Rajput and Sepoy: The Ethnohistory of the Military Labour Market in Hindustan, 1450-1850* (Cambridge 1990).
7. Cmd 2515 (1859 Sess. 1) vol. V, Evidence of J. Sinclair, paras 2871-2.
8. T.A. Heathcote, *The Indian Army: The Garrison of British Imperial India, 1822-1922* (London 1974), 83-4.
9. Cmd 2515 (1859 Sess. 1) vol. V, Evidence of Col. Becher, para. 764; and Appendix 4.
10. Cmd 2515 (1859 Sess. 1) vol. V, Evidence of Sir G. Pollock, para. 192.
11. Cmd 2515 (1859 Sess. 1) vol. V, Appendix 61, Evidence of Maj-Gen. Birch; Appendix 65 F, Evidence of Sir P. Grant.
12. Bayly, *Indian society and the making of the British Empire*, 85.
13. D. Arnold, '"Criminal Tribes" and "Martial Races": Crime and Social Control in Colonial India'. Paper presented at the Institute of Commonwealth Studies, 1984, 8-9.
14. Quoted in Cohen, *Indian Army*, 34-5.
15. There is a huge literature on the Mutiny. See especially, E. Stokes, *The Peasant Armed: The Indian Rebellion of 1857* (Oxford 1986) and *The Peasant and the Raj* (Cambridge 1978); R. Mukherjee, *Awadh in Revolt, 1857-58: A Study of Popular Resistance* (Delhi 1984); and S.N. Sen, *Eighteen Fifty-Seven* (Delhi 1958).
16. Bayly, *Indian society and the making of the British Empire*, 181-2.
17. A well-respected textbook of Indian history—S. Sarkar, *Modern India 1885-1947* (second edn, London 1989)—hardly mentions the armed forces. C.H. Enloe, *Ethnic Soldiers: State Security in Divided Societies* (Harmondsworth 1980) is a very general survey of the relationship between ethnicity and security, containing some material on India.
18. P. Mason, *A Matter of Honour: An Account of the Indian Army, Its Officers and Men* (London 1974).
19. This literature is usefully surveyed in D. Peers, 'Contours of the Garrison State: The Army and the Historiography of Early Nineteenth Century India', Paper presented at the International Congress of Asian and North African Studies, Toronto, August 1990. See also P. Burroughs, 'Imperial Defence and the Victorian Army', *Journal of Imperial and Commonwealth History*, 15 (1986): 55-72.

20. D. Arnold, *Police Power and Colonial Rule: Madras, 1859-1947* (Delhi 1986); 'The Armed Police and Colonial rule in South India, 1941-47', *Modern Asian Studies*, 11 (1977): 101-25.
21. See for example the confusion over the precise meaning of the term 'Dogra' in W.B. Cunningham, *Handbooks for the Indian Army: Dogras* (Calcutta 1932), 34-5.
22. Cmd 2515 (1859 Sess. 1) vol. V, Report of the Commissioner Appointed to Enquire into the Organization of the Indian Army (Peel Commission).
23. D. Arnold, 'Bureaucratic Recruitment and Subordination in Colonial India: The Madras Constabulary, 1859-1947' in Ranajit Guha (ed.), *Subaltern Studies IV: Writings on South Asian History and Society* (Delhi 1985).
24. Cmd 2515 (1859 Sess. 1) vol. V, Evidence of Col. Becher, Sir G. Pollock and Lt-Col. Wyllie.
25. Cmd 2515 (1859 Sess. 1) vol. V, Appendix 70, Evidence of Lt-Col. H.M. Durand.
26. Cmd 2515 (1859 Sess. 1) vol. V, para. 1786.
27. Cmd 2515 (1859 Sess. 1) vol. V, para. 1996.
28. Cmd 2515 (1859 Sess. 1) vol. V, paras 761, 1203, 1790.
29. Cmd 2515 (1859 Sess. 1) vol. V, paras 575, 1029-30, 1173, 1792, 2524, 3164, 4764; and Appendices 4 and 74.
30. Cmd 2515 (1859 Sess. 1) vol. V, 14.
31. The figures are taken from Cmd 2515 (1859 Sess. 1) vol. V, Appendix 22; Appendix 61, Evidence of Maj-Gen. Birch; Appendix 70, Evidence of Lt-Col. H.M. Durand; and Appendix 71, Returns for 1 April 1858.
32. Cmd 2515 (1859 Sess. 1) vol. V, Appendices 22 and 64.
33. G. MacMunn, *Armies of India*, (London 1911) 129.
34. A.E. Barstow, *Handbooks for the Indian Army: Sikhs* (Calcutta 1928), 13-15 and ch. 4; R. Kapur, *Sikh Separatism: The Politics of Faith* (Delhi 1986) especially ch. 1. The latter work draws heavily on the former.
35. Bayly, *Indian society and the making of the British Empire*, 126-7.
36. W.B. Cunningham, *Dogras*, 3.
37. Havildar Ramji Lal to Chandra Singh, August 1915, L/MIL/5/825/Pt. 5. Interestingly, the author was a Jat, not normally considered to be of the Kshatriya (or warrior) varna.
38. Arnold, '"Criminal Tribes" and "Martial Races"', 1-2.
39. Kapur, *Sikh Separatism*, 49-50, 57.
40. Cmd 2515 (1859 Sess. 1) vol. V, Appendix 67.
41. Barstow, *Sikhs*, 4, 15-16.
42. Cmd 2515 (1859 Sess. 1) vol. V, Appendix 62.
43. B.L. Cole, *Handbooks for the Indian Army: Rajputana Classes* (Simla 1924) ch. 9.
44. Court of Enquiry, 28 April-7 May 1930, L/MIL/7/7282.

45. C.J. Morris, *Handbooks for the Indian Army: Gurkhas* (Delhi 1933), 51. For anti-Indian sentiments expressed by a Gurkha soldier, see Ram Kishan Thapa to Kishan Sing Kanwar, July 1915, L/MIL/5/825/Pt. 4.
46. Arnold, '"Criminal Tribes" and "Martial Races"', 4.
47. Cole, *Rajputana Classes*, ch. 13. R.M. Betham, *Handbooks for the Indian Army: Marathas and Dekhani Musalmans* (Calcutta 1908), 167; W.F.G. Bourne, *Handbooks for the Indian Army: Hindustani and Musalmans of the Eastern Punjab* (Calcutta 1914), 47.
48. MacMunn, *Armies of India*, 136. Barstow, *Sikhs*, 2.
49. MacMunn, *Armies of India* 144; G.E.D. Mouat, *Handbooks for the Indian Army: Madras Classes* (New Delhi 1938) 59-60; Cunningham, *Dogras*, 39.
50. For the Mappila background see K.N. Panikkar, *Against Lord and State: Religion and Peasant Uprisings in Malabar, 1836-1921* (Delhi 1989) 50-5, 65-7; and P. Holland-Pryor, *Handbooks for the Indian Army: Mappillas or Moplahs* (Calcutta 1904).
51. Arnold, 'Recruitment in the Madras Constabulary', 13-14.
52. Cole, *Rajputana Classes*. Another example are the Awans, a group of Punjabi Muslims. But not all criminals were martial, of course; J.M. Wikeley, *Handbooks for the Indian Army: Punjabi Musalmans* (Calcutta 1915), 50-2, 63-4.
53. M.N. Srinivas, *Religion and Society Among the Coorgs of South India* (Oxford 1952), 1-3.
54. For their martial background see ibid., 13-18, 24, 32, 45-6, 50, 69, 219, 237-8.
55. See Mouat, *Madras Classes*, 70-3 for relations between the Coorgs and the Indian Army.
56. Heathcote, *Indian Army*, 104; Cohen, *Indian Army*, 44. Caste returns for the Indian Army, 1889-1904, L/MIL/7/17081-17084. *Indian Army Lists*, 1897-1914.
57. Barstow, *Sikhs*, 1-2, 5, 19. The military relationship between the Punjab and the Indian Army is also touched upon in I. Ali, 'Malign Growth? Agricultural Colonization and the Roots of Backwardness in the Punjab', *Past and Present*, 114 (1987): 110-32.
58. Mouat, *Madras Classes*, 7-8.
59. *Indian Army Lists*, 1861-1903.
60. Heathcote, *Indian Army*, 87-8.
61. Mason, *Matter of Honour*, 345.
62. Heathcote, *Indian Army*, 91-2.
63. Reports on Operations in Yaw, Upper Burma, Dec 1888-Jan 1889, L/MIL/7/7270.
64. Adjutant-General to Military Department, 3 April 1875, Cmd 1698 (1877) vol. 62. Cohen, *Indian Army*, 47.
65. Heathcote, *Indian Army*, 48-9.
66. MacMunn, *Armies of India*, 170.
67. Betham, *Maratha and Dekhani Musalmans*, 75-6.
68. Arnold, 'Recruitment in the Madras Constabulary', 18.

69. Cohen, *Indian Army*, 59-61.
70. Mason, *Matter of Honour*, 358.
71. Cohen, *Indian Army*, 66-7.
72. Mason, *Matter of Honour*, 344.
73. Cohen, *Indian Army*, 40.
74. P.C.M.S. Braun, *Die Verteidigung Indiens, 1800-1907: Das Problem der Vorwartsstrategie* (Köln 1968); *Indian Army List*, April 1897.
75. Staveley to Bombay Military Department, 26 April 1875, Enclosures A and B, Cmd 1698 (1877) vol. 62.
76. C-in-C to Military Department, 14 August 1875, Cmd 1698 (1877) vol. 62.
77. Cohen, *Indian Army*, 41-2; Heathcote, *Indian Army*, 76. The grouping and the ethnic composition of each regiment are first described in the *Indian Army List* in April 1897.
78. MacMunn, *Armies of India*, 136.
79. Cole, *Rajputana Classes*, 40; Holland-Pryor, *Mappillas or Moplahs*.
80. Cohen, *Indian Army*, 51; Cole, *Rajputana Classes*, 40; Barstow, *Sikhs*, 153; J.C. Christie, *Handbooks for the Indian Army: Jats, Gujars and Ahirs* (Delhi 1937), 10.
81. *The Handbook on Sikhs* noted the political backwardness of the Punjab before the Great War: Barstow, *Sikhs*, 3.
82. J. Evatt, *Handbooks for the Indian Army: Garhwalis* (Calcutta 1904), ch. 6. Illiterate recruits for the 10th Jats were preferred for political reasons; see OC to Dept. Asst AG, Allahabad Bgd, 15 July 1907, L/MIL/7/7156.
83. Census of India, 1891, General Tables, Vol. 1. Recruiting officers were well aware of the educational backwardness of Muslim recruits. See Bourne, *Hindustani Musalmans and Musalmans of the Eastern Punjab*, 25; and Betham, *Mahrathas and Dekhani Musalmans*, 115.
84. MacMunn, *Armies of India*, 129-30, 143.
85. On the scientific background to these racial ideas see N. Stepan, *The Idea of Race in Science: Great Britain, 1800-1960* (London 1982), especially chs 4 and 5.
86. Arnold, '"Criminal Tribes" and "Martial Races"', 6-7.
87. Cunningham, *Dogras*, 1-2; Christie, *Jats, Gujars and Ahirs*, 1-6.
88. Mouat, *Madras Classes*, 63. Similar remarks appear in A. H. Bingley, *Handbooks for the Indian Army: Brahmans* (Calcutta 1918), 50, and in Barstow, *Sikhs*, 57.
89. Evatt, *Garhwalis*, 16-19.
90. Morris, *Gurkhas*, 37.
91. Arnold, '"Criminal Tribes" and "Martial Races"', 2-4
92. Mouat, *Madras Classes*, 40. The word 'specimen' actually appears in Barstow, *Sikhs*, 122.
93. Holland-Pryor, *Mappillas or Moplahs*, 47.
94. Mason, *Matter of Honour*, 357-8.
95. Wikeley, *Punjabi Musalmans*.

Omissi: *'Martial Races'* 27

96. For the regional background see Ramachandra Guha and M. Gadgil, 'State Forestry and Social Conflict in British India', *Past and Present*, 123 (1989): 141-77; Ramachandra Guha, 'Forestry and Social Protest in British Kumaun, c. 1893-1921', in Ranajit Guha (ed.) *Subaltern Studies IV*; and Ramachandra Guha, *The Unquiet Woods: Ecological Change and Peasant Resistance in the Himalaya* (Delhi 1989).
97. MacMunn, *Armies of India*, 164-5.
98. *Indian Army List*, July 1914.
99. Evatt, *Garhwalis*, 14.
100. On this point, and on the gradual formalisation of recruiting, see Morris, *Gurkhas*, 128-30, 145; and Christie, *Jats, Gujars and Ahirs*, 88-90.
101. Holland-Pryor, *Mappillas or Moplahs*, 56.
102. This was urged before the mutiny, but the precautions were not strictly observed. See Cmd 2515 (1859 Sess. 1) vol. V, Appendices 59, 61 and 71.
103. R.T. Ridgeway, *Handbooks for the Indian Army: Pathans* (Calcutta 1910).
104. Newar Gurkhas were not enlisted officially after the First World War, but still enrolled, calling themselves Magars for that purpose. Morris, *Gurkhas*, 123.
105. On the Indian Army in France in the First World War see J. Greenhut, 'The Imperial Reserve: the Indian Corps on the Western Front, 1914-15' *Journal of Imperial and Commonwealth History*, 12 (1983): 54-73.
106. 97,063 Gurkhas and 88,925 Sikhs were enlisted between the outbreak of war and the Armistice. Morris, *Gurkhas*, 175; Barstow, *Sikhs*, 5.
107. Barstow, *Sikhs*, 179.
108. But anti-Bengali prejudice in the Indian Army was confirmed after a shooting affray in the 49th Bengalis in June 1918, less than a year after the regiment had been formed. L/MIL/7/7279.
109. Cohen, *Indian Army*, 69-73.
110. Cohen, *Indian Army*, 76.
111. *Indian Army List*, January 1923.
112. Mason, *Matter of Honour*, 342-3; Heathcote, *Indian Army*, 77-8.
113. Cohen, *Indian Army*, 70
114. Indian Disorders Committee, Conclusions, 6 May 1920, CP 240, CAB 24/105; Foreign Department to SS India, 2 February 1920, CP 575, CAB 24/97.

[11]

'CIRCLE OF IRON': AFRICAN COLONIAL EMPLOYEES AND THE INTERPRETATION OF COLONIAL RULE IN FRENCH WEST AFRICA*

BY EMILY LYNN OSBORN
University of Notre Dame

ABSTRACT: This article investigates the role of African colonial employees in the functioning of the colonial state in French West Africa. Case studies from the 1890s and early 1900s demonstrate that in the transition from conquest to occupation, low-level African colonial intermediaries continually shaped the localized meanings that colonialism acquired in practice. Well-placed African colonial intermediaries in the colonies of Guinée Française and Soudan Français often controlled the dissemination of information and knowledge in the interactions of French colonial officials with local elites and members of the general population. The contributions of these African employees to the daily operations of the French colonial state show that scholars have long overlooked a cadre of men who played a significant role in shaping colonial rule.

KEY WORDS: Guinea-Conakry, Mali, colonial intermediaries.

A 'CIRCLE OF IRON' IN FRENCH WEST AFRICA

IN 1899, the French colonial commander posted to Siguiri, a town located along the Upper Niger River in present day Guinea-Conakry, complained to his superiors that a 'circle of iron' surrounded him.[1] The 'circle of iron' consisted of a wall of deceptions and lies built by the local interpreter and the local chief. The commander explained his vulnerability: '[I am] almost always alone as the head of my district and cannot, as a result, travel'.[2] The commander confessed that he had come to rely totally on the interpreter, Lassana Oularé, and the chief of Siguiri, Mamoussa Makassouba, for implementing policy, for communicating with the population and for gathering news of the district. Certain 'irregularities' finally prompted the French commander to launch an investigation into the actions of his trusted associates.[3]

---

* The research on which this article is based was funded by a Fulbright IIE fellowship and the Department of History, Stanford University. I am indebted to the many men and women of Upper Guinée whom I interviewed for the larger project, and the archivists of the Archives Nationales de la Guinée, Guinea-Conakry (ANG), and the Archives Nationales du Sénégal in Dakar, Sénégal (ANS). I thank two anonymous readers for their comments. I also appreciate suggestions made by Walter Hawthorne, Richard Roberts and Thomas Spear. This paper was presented in a previous form at the African Studies Association in Houston, 2000; it has also benefited from insights made by participants in the History Seminar, the Johns Hopkins University and the Africa Workshop at the University of Michigan.

[1] Correspondance, Siguiri, 15 oct. 1899. Archives Nationales du Sénégal, Section Afrique Occidentale Française-AOF 7 G 30.   [2] *Ibid.*   [3] *Ibid.*

The French commander discovered that not only had he fallen victim to a massive campaign of misinformation, but that the interpreter and chief had used their positions to levy fines, imprison opponents, confiscate cattle and sheep and take women as wives without making requisite bridewealth payments.[4] That these events took place without the commander's knowledge – yet were carried out 'in the name of the French commander' – exposes some of the challenges French officials faced in their efforts to establish colonial authority over the interior of West Africa.[5] When the French arrived in Siguiri in 1889, a gulf of language and knowledge separated the general population from the French conquerors. As Siguiri's commander discovered, Oularé and Makassouba exploited this chasm by controlling the transmission of information within the district.

The 'circle of iron' constructed by Oularé and Makassouba exposes a dynamic that was often overlooked by colonial administrators and has subsequently been overlooked by scholars. Oularé's conduct demonstrates the capacity of African colonial employees to influence the knowledge, interpretations and actions of their French superiors. The unofficial corridors of power that sprouted out of the nascent colonial bureaucracy in the early colonial period point to the significance of those low-level colonial employees who possessed the linguistic capabilities, symbolic trappings and cultural know-how to mediate colonial rule. Investigating the role of these African employees provides a fresh perspective on colonialism by opening up a new set of questions: how did African 'middle figures' broker and shape the relationships of local elites and French colonial officials? How did the actions of African interpreters, clerks and scribes affect local social and political hierarchies? And how did the place of these low-level employees change from conquest to occupation, as the colonial state established itself and knowledge of the French language and the French colonial project spread among the general population?

This article uses three case studies from French West Africa to explore the contributions of African colonial employees to the functioning of the colonial state from the 1880s to 1910. Two cases from the 1890s, one from Siguiri and another from Medine, illustrate that the first decade of colonial rule consisted of a period during which the peoples of the Soudan learned about a state that was itself coming to terms with the meaning and purpose of colonial rule. The French occupation forced African colonial employees as well as local chiefs to embark on a process of discovery that uncovered the assumptions, vulnerabilities and capacities of the colonial regime.

By 1910, the French colonial state had solidified its presence in the interior of West Africa and standardized the administration of its French West African territories. But letters written by a prisoner in the city of Kankan, Guinée Française, reveal that the outward appearance of the French state – its regularized bureaucracy, its clear-cut chain of command – obscures

---

[4] Rapport 'au sujet des exactions commises par l'interprète auxiliaire Lassana Oularé de [en?] complicité avec le chef de village de Siguiri Moumoussa Makassouba', cercle de Siguiri, 14 oct. 1899. ANS 7 G 30.

[5] Bulletin politique, cercle de Kankan, Soudan français, jan. 1894. ANS 7 G 46; Besançon à M. le lieutenant-colonel commandant supérieur du Soudan. Siguiri, 1 août 1890. Archives Nationales du Mali (ANM) 2 M 348.

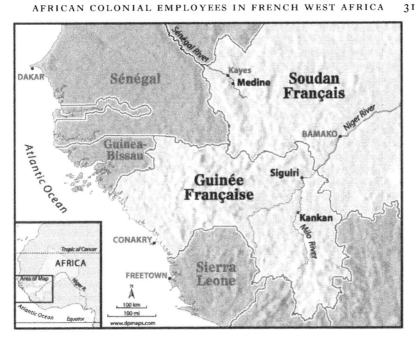

Map 1. Guinée Française and Soudan Française, c. 1900.

the malleable underbelly of colonial rule. At the local level, key Africans had come to understand the priorities and peculiarities of the colonial state. African colonial employees and local elites adapted to the French presence by filtering colonial policy and procedures and building unofficial networks that linked the colonial bureaucracy to indigenous hierarchies. Colonialism in practice thus developed highly localized permutations and cadences that shaped the interactions of the majority of the population with the French colonial state.

INTERPRETING COLONIAL RULE

The process of colonial conquest and the nature of the colonial occupation have sparked considerable scholarly debate.[6] Writing in the 1960s, Ronald Robinson remarked on the strategies that European powers used to build their empires, noting that colonial conquest and occupation could not have taken place without the 'collaboration' of local elites.[7] While the term 'collaborator' has fallen out of favor, Robinson raises a critical point about colonialism that echoes in Karen Fields's pointed question, 'How did a

---

[6] Thomas Spear reviews the historiography on colonial rule in 'Neo-traditionalism and the limits of invention in British colonial Africa', *Journal of African History* (*JAH*), in this issue. This paper owes much to the insights of Spear's paper.

[7] Ronald Robinson, 'Non-European foundations of European imperialism: sketch for a theory of collaboration', in Roger Owen and Bob Sutcliffe (eds.), *Studies in the Theory of Imperialism* (London, 1972), 117–42.

notoriously small handful of white men rule gigantic territories?'[8] To explain this imbalanced ratio of colonial officials to African populations, scholars have emphasized that colonization was a dynamic process that involved negotiations and concessions by European colonial officials, African elites and subject populations.[9] Scholars have explored 'indirect rule', by which local power structures were incorporated into the colonial state, as well as the forces that motivated and compelled African chiefs to carry out the demands of colonial authorities.[10]

These investigations have reached a range of conclusions about the nature and legacies of colonial rule. Mahmood Mamdani argues that colonialism exploited the 'authoritarian possibilities' in African societies to create 'decentralized despots', chiefs whose power over their subjects went unchecked as a result of the backing of colonial authorities.[11] Mamdani's interpretation of colonial rule as a period that brought about utter transformation in relations of power and authority in Africa parallels the explanation offered by Crawford Young, who invokes 'bula matari', or the 'stone crusher', to describe the 'vocation of domination' of European colonialism.[12] Other scholars, however, emphasize the limits that operated on the colonial state: Fields points out that the colonial state became a 'consumer of power' produced by African systems and institutions.[13] Jeffrey Herbst argues that European rule did not necessarily represent 'a fundamental break in the way power was exercised on the African continent'.[14] Richard Roberts likewise questions the transformative capacity of the colonial state in his study of cotton production and colonial rule in the French Soudan. He points to the strength of 'local processes ... to withstand empire and ultimately to shape the experience of colonialism'.[15] Pointing to the dismal failure of French policies aimed at increasing cotton yields, Roberts shows that the colonial period must be viewed from the vantage point of local power relations and indigenous epistemologies. Similarly, Bruce Berman and John Lonsdale view the colonial state as essentially weak, stretched thin by limited resources and contradictory agendas.[16]

---

[8] In Zambia, African colonial officials outnumbered British ones 6:1. Karen Fields, *Revival and Rebellion in Colonial Central Africa* (Princeton, 1985), 30–1. The term 'collaborator' is problematic in part because it is premised on a pan-Africanist identity that flattens out the complexities of Africa's histories.

[9] Bruce Berman and John Lonsdale, 'Coping with the contradictions: the development of the colonial state, 1895–1914', in Berman and Lonsdale (eds.), *Unhappy Valley: Conflict in Kenya and Africa*, 1 (London, 1992), 77–95; Martin Chanock, *Law, Custom and Social Order: The Colonial Experience in Malawi and Zambia* (Cambridge, 1985); Terence Ranger and Eric Hobsbawm (eds.), *The Invention of Tradition* (Cambridge, 1983).

[10] A. E. Afigbo, *The Warrant Chiefs: Indirect Rule in Southeastern Nigeria, 1891–1929* (London, 1972); Sara S. Berry, *No Condition is Permanent* (Madison, 1993), 22–42; Adu Boahen, *African Perspectives on Colonialism* (Baltimore, 1987), 27–57; Shula Marks, *The Ambiguities of Dependence in South Africa* (Baltimore, 1986).

[11] Mahmood Mamdani, *Citizen and Subject: Contemporary Africa and the Legacy of Late Colonialism* (Princeton, 1996), 21–3, 37–61.

[12] Crawford Young, *The African Colonial State in Comparative Perspective* (New Haven, 1994), 2.   [13] Fields, *Revival*, 31.

[14] Jeffrey Herbst, *States and Power in Africa* (Princeton, 2000), 61.

[15] Richard Roberts, *Two Worlds of Cotton* (Stanford, 1996), 16–17.

[16] Berman and Lonsdale, 'Coping', 77–95.

AFRICAN COLONIAL EMPLOYEES IN FRENCH WEST AFRICA 33

But these and other investigations of colonialism, be they inquiries into ethnicity, colonial policies and systems, or colonial laws and courtrooms, almost uniformly overlook a group of men who made critical contributions to colonial rule.[17] Scholars have explored the role of 'collaborators', 'intermediaries' and 'middle figures' – African chiefs, missionaries and soldiers – in the colonial order, and studies of colonial chieftaincies have proliferated in recent years.[18] But little of that work has focused on African colonial employees.[19] This is an oversight that Pierre Alexandre, a former French colonial official and scholar, warned against in a volume on chiefs published in 1970. Alexandre argued that studies of chieftaincy and colonialism must consider the cadre of African colonial employees with whom local elites came into most frequent contact.[20] Though Alexandre's own experience of colonialism is based on the last years of colonial rule in Africa, his insights nevertheless resonate with an earlier period. The interpreter of Siguiri – who built a bridge to the local chief while barricading his French superior into isolation in the 1890s – confirms that African colonial employees should not be excluded from analyses of colonialism. Especially in the first years of occupation, when very few people spoke French and most of them worked for the colonizers, African interpreters and clerks helped to transform colonial posts, courtrooms, and palavers into sites of struggles, debates, communication – and miscommunication. Interpreters were critical to the construction of this 'middle ground' that brought together elites, commoners, and French officials and in doing so they did more than act as mere 'translating machines'.[21] They negotiated different worldviews and

[17] James Merrell notes a similar gap in Americanist colonial historiography. Referring to the go-betweens who negotiated settler–Indian relations, Merrell remarks: 'Given their importance, it is astonishing how far these figures remain cloaked in obscurity'. He comments that the 'alchemy of interpretation ... has been all but forgotten'. James Merrell, *Into the American Woods* (New York, 1999), 28, 32.

[18] 'Middle figure' is a term used by Nancy Rose Hunt, *A Colonial Lexicon of Birth Ritual, Medicalization and Mobility in the Congo* (Duke, 1999). On chiefs: Sara Berry, *Chiefs Know Their Boundaries: Essays on Property, Power and the Past in Asante, 1896–1996* (Portsmouth NH, 2001); Michael Crowder and Obaro Ikime (eds.), *West African Chiefs: Their Changing Status under Colonial Rule and Independence* (New York, 1970); Mamdani, *Citizen*. On the role of African catechists in the extension of African Christianity: Thomas Spear and Isaria Kimambo (eds.), *East African Expressions of Christianity* (Oxford, 1999); Marcia Wright, *Strategies of Slaves and Women* (New York, 1993), 77–9. On African soldiers: Myron Echenberg, *Colonial Conscripts: The Tirailleurs Sénégalais in French West Africa, 1857–1960* (Portsmouth NH, 1991).

[19] Exceptions include Hunt, *Colonial Lexicon*; David Robinson, *Paths of Accommodation: Muslim Societies and French Colonial Authorities in Senegal and Mauritania, 1880–1920* (Athens OH, 2000), 4, 49–54; Mahir Saul and Patrick Royer, *West African Challenge to Empire: Culture and History in the Volta-Bani Anticolonial War* (Athens OH, 2001). Jean Allman discusses the impact of 'cultural translators' on scholarly, ethnographic interpretations in T. E. Kyei, *Our Days Dwindle: Memories of My Childhood Days in Asante*, ed. Jean Allman (Portsmouth NH, 2001), xiv–xv.

[20] Pierre Alexandre, 'Chiefs, *commandants* and clerks: their relationship from conquest to decolonisation in French West Africa', in Crowder and Ikime (eds.), *West African Chiefs*, 7, 9.

[21] Richard White defines the term 'middle ground' as 'the place in between: in between cultures, peoples ... On the middle ground diverse peoples adjust their differences through what amounts to a process of creative, and often expedient, misunderstandings. People try to persuade others who are different from themselves by appealing

beliefs, and often incompatible notions of causality, governance, authority and responsibility.

Perhaps counter intuitively, the significance of African colonial employees to the functioning of the colonial state did not decline as the French occupation stretched into its second decade. On the contrary, local employees used their formal authority to institutionalize their influence, accumulate wealth and build stability amidst the uncertainties of shifting colonial policy and personnel. In recognizing the strength of the localized networks in which African employees held key positions, Alexandre asserted that the 'ideal' French officer at the district level was one who recognized his own limitations: a 'well-behaved *commandant* ... filled in his forms regularly, buried himself under a mound of papers, and left local problems to look after themselves as best they could'.[22] Alexandre's counsel serves as a reminder that French officials did not fully control or understand the conflicts and contests that took place within their colonial empires. Moreover, the actions of low-level African colonial employees expose the contingencies of colonial rule. These colonial employees demonstrate that efforts by the colonial state to transform African societies into colonial ones did not proceed unhampered in the aftermath of occupation. Focusing on the lowest rank of the colonial state opens a new perspective on the period of colonial rule while also showing that Europeans failed to develop a monopoly on knowledge or interpretation in their colonies.

COLONIAL EMPLOYEES

In occupying a continent with more languages and ethnicities than any other, European powers faced formidable challenges in establishing colonial rule in Africa. At the end of the nineteenth century, French conquerors learned that the linguistic landscape of West Africa could change from one city to the next and from one hamlet, river valley or village to the next. Not only were the language barriers significant, but newly arrived European conquerors frequently knew little about the social and political configurations of the regions that they occupied. In what became Guinée Française, Europeans had very limited previous contact with states of the Upper Niger and Milo River valleys. For example, only two Europeans – Rene Caillié and Etienne Peroz – visited the major Maninka trading metropolis of Kankan prior to the arrival of Colonel Archinard and the French marines in 1891.

The marginal influence of Europe in the Soudan differed sharply from pockets along the Senegambia and Guinean coasts that hosted a complement of European-oriented communities. In Sierra Leone, Guinea-Bissau, Nigeria

---

to what they perceive to be the values and practices of those others. They often misinterpret and distort both the values and the practices of those they deal with, but from these misunderstandings arise new meanings'. Wyatt MacGaffey notes that in the Kongo 'a special colonial vocabulary' came into use 'in which the colonized and the colonizer could appear to converse while in fact understanding the conversation in quite different ways'. Richard White, *The Middle Ground: Indians, Empires, and the Republics in the Great Lakes Region, 1650–1815* (Cambridge, 1991), x; Wyatt MacGaffey, *Religion and Society in Central Africa: The BaKongo of Lower Zaire* (Chicago, 1986), 200.

[22] Alexandre, 'Chiefs', 9.

and Senegal, strong African communities well-versed in European languages, norms and values cropped up and thrived through the nineteenth century. But in the heart of the Soudan, no cultural equivalent to Krios, LusoAfricans, the Saros and their descendants, and the citizens of the Four Communes, existed before the colonial conquest of the late nineteenth century.[23]

Unlike those communities along the coast oriented towards Europe and the Americas, populations living in the commercial towns and cities along the Milo and Niger River valleys inhabited a world animated by the cultural and intellectual influences of Islam. Kankan's scholars, clerics and traders participated in an Islamic diaspora that stretched through the Soudan, North Africa, and the Arabian Peninsula. Traders from the Milo and Niger River valleys certainly traveled to Europeanized port cities along the Atlantic coast and these *dyulas*, or Muslim traders, imported European goods that they procured there to the Soudan. But *dyula* trade routes provided no entry point to Christian missionaries or European commercial interests. And while news of French military forays into the Soudan traveled interior trade routes, military confrontations did little to inculcate a deep familiarity with European institutions or practices among the bulk of the population of the Soudan.[24] The French occupation of the Soudan thus opened a new chapter in the relations of Soudanese peoples with Europe and with European peoples, ideas, and conventions.

The French arrived in the Milo and Upper Niger River valleys with great speed and force in the late 1880s.[25] The French military marched in pursuit of Samori Turé, the Maninka empire builder and colonial resistor. The French marines occupied the city of Siguiri in 1889, delineated an administrative district, and did the same in the city of Kankan two years later.

---

[23] On Creoles of Sierra Leone: Christopher Fyfe, *A History of Sierra Leone* (Oxford, 1962); Fyfe, 'Four Sierra Leone recaptives', *JAH*, 1 (1961), 77–85; Hollis R. Lynch, 'Edward W. Blyden: pioneer West African nationalist', *JAH*, 6 (1965), 373–88; Martin Lynn, 'Technology, trade and "a race of native capitalists": the Krio diaspora of West Africa and the steamship, 1852–95', *JAH*, 33 (1992), 421–40. On Nigeria: Philip Zachernuk, *Colonial Subjects: An African Intelligentsia and Atlantic Ideas* (Charlottesville, 2000). On Senegal: George Brooks, 'The *Signares* of Saint-Louis and Gorée: women entrepreneurs in eighteenth-century Senegal', in Nancy Hafkin and Edna Bay (eds.), *Women in Africa* (Stanford, 1976); H. O. Idowu, 'The establishment of elective institutions in Senegal, 1869–1880', *JAH*, 9 (1968), 261–77; G. W. Johnson, *The Emergence of Black Politics in Senegal: The Struggle for Power in the Four Communes, 1900–1920* (Stanford, 1971); Hilary Jones, 'The Métis of Saint Louis, Senegal: marriage, wealth and politics in the colonial period (1871–1914)' (unpublished paper, 2001).

[24] In the early 1870s, the French figured only peripherally in Samori's range of vision. Samori thought of the French as a 'not very populous' group devoted to commerce. Yves Person, *Samori: une revolution dyula* (3 vols.) (Dakar, 1968–75), II. On Islam and *dyula* trade networks, Jean-Loup Amselle, *Les negociants de la savanne: histoire et organisation sociale des Kooroko (Mali)* (Paris, 1977); Abner Cohen 'Cultural strategies in the organization of trading diasporas', in Claude Meillassoux (ed.), *Development of Indigenous Trade Markets in West Africa* (London, 1971); Yves Person, 'Samori and Islam', in John Willis (ed.), *Studies in West African Islamic History: The Cultivators of Islam* (London, 1979).

[25] On the military conquest of the Soudan: A. S. Kanya-Forstner, *The Conquest of the Western Soudan* (London, 1969); Etienne Peroz, *Au Soudan français: souvenirs de guerre et de mission* (Paris, 1889).

These two districts were incorporated into the military territory of the Southern Soudan. By 1892 the French succeeded in driving Samori out of the region, although Samori evaded capture until 1898.

In the early colonial period, Africans, and not Frenchmen, wore most of the French military and 'fonctionnaire' uniforms in the Soudan. In conquest and occupation, Africans outnumbered their French counterparts: Africans formed the bulk of the military and civilian corps. During the military offensives of the 1880s and early 1890s, French officers accepted and promoted certain actions on the part of their African subordinates in the interest of instilling terror, suppressing opposition and sustaining their armies. Looting, taking captives and confiscating foodstuffs and livestock were strategies considered necessary to the sustenance and success of campaigns led by French officers and carried out by African troops. One African soldier, or *tirailleur*, for example, earned praise from his French superior for 'the liveliness with which he opened huts and shot the inhabitants found inside' during his six years of service.[26] The French conquest of the Soudan resulted in new territories for France's colonial empire; it also provided the peoples of the Soudan with a rapid introduction to the violence and coercion implied by French symbols, institutions and uniforms. The terms of this initial encounter helped to determine the meaning that French affiliation and French symbols acquired and carried through the early colonial period.

In the aftermath of the conquests of the 1880s and 1890s, the French military and its civilian successors settled down, built posts and tried to regularize relations with local populations. This process of occupation forced French officials to confront their deficits of language and information. To overcome barriers of communication and contact, the colonial administration charged low-level African employees with carrying out the daily requirements of rule and gathering information on local political, economic and social situations.[27] But the premises of the *mission civilisatrice* dictated that little official authority could be conferred on the lowest echelon of the French bureaucracy. These mouthpieces, bean-counters and paper-pushers were supposed to convey colonial policy and collect African resources.[28] The colonial hierarchy operated on the assumption that its African employees would act as transparent, unthinking conduits who would link white colonial authorities to black African colonial subjects. But the low status of African employees within the colonial hierarchy camouflages the influence these men could wield on the day-to-day functioning of the colonial state. African

---

[26] Colonel Archinard, Campagne de 1888–9. ANS I D 95.

[27] Colonel Gallieni commented on the reliance of French commanders on their African employees in 1857, noting that French commanders 'never visited the surrounding villages. They limited themselves to accepting, without verification, the information of their interpreters'. As quoted by William B. Cohen, *Rulers of Empire: The French Colonial Service in Africa, 1880–1960* (Stanford, 1968), 16.

[28] An exception to the typically low status of African employees of the colonial state is Mademba, a telegraphist in the French military who was crowned king of Sinsani. He reigned for over nearly three decades, despite official investigations into accusations of corruption and excesses. Félix Dubois, *Tombouctou la mysterieuse* (Paris, 1897), 86–94; Pierre Chandoné, 'Mademba, roi de Sansanding', *Revue indigène*, 7 (1906), 189–92; Abd-el-Kader Mademba, *Au Sénégal et au Soudan français: le fama Mademba* (Paris, 1931).

colonial agents served as the filter through which information and funds passed, and they controlled the flow of knowledge in the encounters and palavers of French authorities with African elites and members of the general population. When African interpreters and clerks exercised a linguistic monopoly, these supposedly obeisant, invisible lackeys could profoundly shape their superior's construction of knowledge.[29]

The actions of an interpreter in Medine, Ousmane Fall, and those of Makassouba and Oularé in Siguiri demonstrate the possibilities that presented themselves to nimble employees who managed the contact of French officials with local peoples. These colonial employees exploited the chasms of language and information of the early colonial period, when French officials knew almost nothing about the areas and populations among whom they found themselves, and when the general population knew little about these new foreign invaders except for their military prowess.

In reflecting on the role of African intermediaries in colonization, Alexandre argues that this group was still in its 'embryonic' stage in the initial phase of conquest. As will be shown below, however, evidence indicates that the early years of colonialism opened opportunities to those who could capitalize on the legibility of French symbols and the mutual ignorance of French officials and local populations.[30]

OUSMANE FALL IN MEDINE

The case of Ousmane Fall, an interpreter who worked in the French Soudan, reveals the capacity of African employees to create new circuits of power that owed their origins to – but operated independently of – the colonial state.[31] Fall joined the military as a *tirailleur* in 1880. In 1886, he was nominated to the position of interpreter. In the letter of nomination recommending him for the post, Colonel Gallieni praised Fall's ability to procure laborers who worked without compensation on the railroad being built to Kayes. Fall spoke a handful of languages – Wolof, FulFulde, Sarakole, Kassonke – and could read and write in French and Arabic. He dealt easily with the 'little questions', that is, the complaints, demands and requests of 'natives of diverse nationality'.[32] Throughout the late 1880s, Fall received a string of awards and honors for his distinguished service to the colonial state. At times, however, the commendation letters written about Fall sound an ominous note, for they indicate that French officials knew they did not fully grasp the extent of Fall's influence. In 1888, Colonel Gallieni warned that Fall should be awarded the Chevalier medal, in part because Fall might grow resentful if he did not receive the honor. Gallieni wrote, 'I fear that this compensation, if it is not accorded, could diminish the zealousness of this interpreter who, I repeat, has considerable influence'.[33]

Fall received the Chevalier medal in 1888 and was subsequently posted to Medine, near Kayes, in the French Soudan. In 1890, rumors alerted the local

---

[29] David Robinson makes a similar point, *Paths*, 49–50.   [30] Alexandre, 'Chiefs', 6.
[31] There was a similar case in Upper Volta. Saul and Royer, *West African Challenge*, 115.
[32] Cmdt. de cercle, Medine, 11 mai 1888, Archives Nationales de la France, Outre-Mer, Aix-en-Provence (ANFOM) Soud/XVI/14.   [33] *Ibid.*

French commander to certain 'irregularities' in the district. The commander launched an investigation that revealed that the roots of Fall's loyalty to the colonial state lay quite apart from his official duties of district interpreter. As it turned out, Fall had designed and supervised an elaborate 'colonial' justice system that employed four other Africans who traveled through the district, hearing cases, and passing down judgments – all in the name of the colonial state. These judges settled disputes, collected fines and occasionally demanded presents or tribute from members of the local population. To confer legitimacy on these circuit justices, two of these 'officials' carried letters that Fall had written in Arabic and to which he had signed the French commander's name. Other actions demonstrate that Fall used his position within the French colonial bureaucracy to achieve distinctly 'traditional' markers of status and wealth: he captured a woman who had recently acquired a liberty certificate, burned the certificate and held her captive. In another instance, he kidnapped and sold a woman after the death of her husband.[34]

During his investigation of Fall, the French commander came across a letter in which a local chief requested that Fall send a judge to settle a local dispute. The chief explained that he 'wanted the justice of the whites', but trusted Fall's ability 'to settle the affair without it arriving in the hands of the whites'.[35] This fine distinction indicates that the chief hoped to capitalize on the recognition and allusions of French symbols and institutions. But the chief also sought to exploit the elasticity of those symbols and institutions in the hands of a secure ally. As the letter implies, weak or newly appointed chiefs could use Fall's judges to fortify their position without risking the unpredictable intervention of a French official. Fall's circuit court mirrored that of the French state, but it offered flexible, predetermined outcomes responsive to local political conditions, social mores and to the payments and influence of interested parties.

Accused of 'substituting his power for that of the commander', the French commander convicted Fall in 1890 of 'disloyalty, extortions, and abuse of power', sent him back to his home in Senegal, and forbade him to ever return. The French commander also stripped Fall of the numerous medals he had earned during his service, not only because they were unmerited, but because Fall might use his medals 'to mislead the natives who may believe him to still [be] in office'.[36] The confiscation of Fall's medals reveals a central paradox of French rule in the Soudan. The French succeeded in establishing the colonial state as a force to be reckoned with in the Soudan. Yet colonial symbols, personnel and instruments could be used for purposes that diverged significantly from official goals and policies. The ambiguity that surrounded French trappings of rule undermined efforts by the colonial state to organize a smooth running bureaucracy and to assert French authority consistently and reliably.

In personifying the French state, African employees such as Ousmane Fall often did more than simply exploit barriers of language and knowledge for personal gain. They also threw African social hierarchies into disarray. Many

[34] *Ibid.* [35] *Ibid.*
[36] *Ibid.*; Lettre, gouverneur du Sénégal et dependances, 5 nov. 1890. ANFOM Soud/XVI/6.

of the men who accompanied the French as soldiers and who later worked as clerks, scribes and interpreters were slaves or descendants of slaves; the dependence of the colonial state on these local hires reshuffled the social and political hierarchies of the Soudan. Thus, with the French occupation of the 1880s, Soudanese elites found themselves in the uncomfortable position of relying on – and falling prey to – men who they perceived as their social inferiors. Chiefs came to terms with this jumbling of rank in a variety of ways. Some chiefs cultivated the favor of African colonial employees by showering them with gifts and even wives. Other chiefs practiced avoidance, not only of African employees, but of the whole apparatus of colonial rule.[37] Deliberate avoidance, however, became increasingly untenable as the French presence proved to be neither ephemeral nor transient. Tracing the evolving relationship of local elites with the colonial state also shows that some African colonial employees successfully parlayed their liminal positions at the base of the colonial bureaucracy and at the bottom of local social hierarchies into a major intersection of power and authority.

MAKASSOUBA AND OULARE IN SIGUIRI

Because of their reliance on a handful of key local figures, French officials sometimes became the object of campaigns of propaganda and misinformation coordinated by their 'most reliable' interpreter and 'most loyal' chief, as in the case that opened this paper. That case involved the local colonial interpreter, Oularé, and the chief of Siguiri, Makassouba.

By 1899, Oularé had served as the official interpreter of Siguiri for over four years. Personnel records indicate that his service had consistently earned praise from his French superiors. When Oularé's conduct fell into doubt, the French commander was taken aback:

Lassana Oularé [the interpreter], whom I have known since 1895 ... has never known ... any reproach, and as an interpreter under the orders of my predecessors or under mine seems sworn to regular conduct and seemed worthy of the confidence that he knew he inspired in me. Nothing, until this recent time, warned me that he could, like all others, abuse this confidence and commit the faults of which he is accused.[38]

The interpreter cast doubt upon himself when he asked the French commander for permission to marry a former wife of Samori Turé. The French commander denied the request of marriage, noting the gap between the status of the interpreter and his proposed partner. The woman was of noble birth, whereas Oularé, like most African colonial employees, was of 'lowly', probably slave, birth.[39] The documentary record fails to indicate why Oularé asked the French commander for permission to marry one of Samori's wives; it was not common for African employees to request that their French supervisors approve their marital choices. Probably Oularé

---

[37] The first chief of Kankan to hold office during the colonial occupation became increasingly withdrawn and distant as the permanence of French rule became evident in the late 1890s. Emily Lynn Osborn, 'Gender, power, and authority in Kankan-Baté' (Ph.D. dissertation, Stanford, 2000), ch. 3.
[38] Correspondance et renseignements, région sud, cercle de Siguiri, 15 oct. 1899. ANS 7 G 30.   [39] Ibid.

hoped that the commander's blessing would confer legitimacy on his designs for Samori's former wife and help to override the force of local norms. The commander implied as much when he remarked that Oularé 'believed himself sufficiently noble' to deserve the same privileges as local elites.[40] The unsuccessful attempts of the interpreter to co-opt French officialdom into sanctioning his union show that while the colonial state enabled certain men to exceed the restrictions of their birth, affiliation with the French alone was not enough to overcome the entrenched hierarchies of the Soudan.

After forbidding the union of the interpreter and the former wife of Samori, the commander discovered that Oularé had married the woman anyway.[41] This disregard for orders prompted the commander to launch an official inquiry and the subsequent investigation revealed that Oularé was not the devoted interpreter he appeared to be. It became clear that Oularé worked in close concert with Siguiri's chief, Makassouba, long an indispensable aide to local French administrators. Like Oularé, Makassouba had garnered the approbation of local commanders for years. In personnel reports, French officials described Makassouba as an 'intelligent [chief], having great qualities and good will'.[42] In remarks that later proved ironic: Makassouba 'makes himself heard by the administrator ... [He is] always very devoted to the French, [and] puts himself completely at the disposition of the Commander of the District for the least information asked'.[43] And on the eve of the investigation: 'A good servant for our cause, [Makassouba] does all possible to make himself useful'.[44]

Siguiri's French commander discovered that over the previous five years, Oularé and Makassouba had committed a litany of abuses. Oularé used his position to fine a local man 250 francs and four slaves in an attempt to settle an old family quarrel that dated from 'well before [the French] occupation'.[45] Oularé held one of his rivals hostage and confined him to irons, probably in the local prison. Makassouba and Oularé eventually released the prisoner upon the payment of four horns of gold and another slave. In collaboration with Makassouba, Oularé sent another man to prison on trumped up charges, for which they both received remuneration from an unnamed source. The two repeatedly intervened in the affairs of surrounding villages, for which they demanded payments of cows and sheep. Oularé threatened prison sentences to local men that could only be avoided through the payment of 'fines' that he personally levied. Several men gave female relations to Oularé in marriage, but they complained that the promised bridewealth payments never materialized. Makassouba and Oularé also demanded 'presents' from chiefs and commoners alike to arrange audiences with the French commander.[46] Oularé's success at exploiting his affiliation with the colonial state showed itself in the wealth the commander discovered

---

[40] Ibid.   [41] Ibid.

[42] Fiche de renseignement des notables, région sud, 1897–9. Date unclear, probably 1896. ANS 7 G 34.   [43] Ibid. 1ière sem., 1897. ANS 7 G 34.

[44] Ibid. 1ière sem., 1898. ANS 7 G 34.

[45] Correspondance et renseignements, région sud, cercle de Siguiri, 15 oct. 1899. ANS 7 G 30.

[46] Rapport 'au sujet des exactions commises par l'interprète auxiliaire Lassana Oularé de [en] complicité avec le chef de village de Siguiri Moumoussa Makassouba', cercle de Siguiri, 14 oct. 1899. ANS 7 G 30.

at his home. Oularé had married six women and owned seven slaves; the commander realized that an interpreter's salary alone could not provide the resources for such a level of accumulation.[47]

In their willingness to cooperate with French officials and to act as 'indispensable' sources of information on the district, Makassouba and Oularé fed the mistaken perception on the part of a succession of colonial commanders that French supremacy had introduced a reign of colonial order to the district. But in carrying out duties commissioned by French officials, Makassouba and Oularé complicated colonial rule, for they interspersed their own agendas and ambitions with those of the French. To the French commander, Makassouba's and Oularé's manipulations of their affiliation with the colonial state smacked of corruption and 'abuse'. But this nuanced interpretation of Makassouba's and Oularé's actions was probably lost on Siguiri's general population. At their core, the demands made by the interpreter and the chief were not much different from the demands made by the French. Like the French, Makassouba and Oularé sought to extract wealth and labor from the district. That the pair had engaged in 'abuses' may have been difficult for the average colonial subject to ascertain in a district where the channels of communication were tightly controlled and where the precise functions and purpose of the colonial post remained unexplained. Perhaps it was Oularé's class-defying marriage – which constituted an assault on local social norms – that unleashed the currents of discontent running through the district.

The 'circle of iron' built by Makassouba and Oularé show the capacity of a local interpreter to influence the functioning of the colonial state. In a coalition that unified the local chieftaincy and the colonial bureaucracy, the chief and the interpreter manipulated the local French official and acted as his gatekeepers. They created an institutional barrier that distilled news of the district and checked the commander's contact with the population. Oularé's and Makassouba's actions – obscured for years from French officials – indicate that the newly laid French hierarchy of rule was not as straightforward and orderly as it appeared from above.

Swift judgments followed the investigation into Oularé's and Makassouba's 'abuse of power'. Oularé received a ten-year prison sentence, his goods and slaves were confiscated and his family expelled from Siguiri. Makassouba received a five-year sentence and his personal belongings were confiscated as well.[48] That the interpreter received a more severe punishment than the chief transmits a clear message, one that was repeatedly broadcast by French officials through the 1890s. French officials held their own employees to a higher standard than the rest of the population, even chiefs. Prison sentences were passed down to discipline individual African employees; sentences also articulated the boundaries within which colonial

---

[47] *Ibid.* More research needs to be done on the various and changing pay scales and positions of the colonial bureaucracy; in French West Africa, the wages and hierarchies of low-level African employees changed from colony to colony. Jean-Hervé Jezequel discusses the nuances of status and salary in French West Africa in '"Collecting customary law": *les évolués africains* and the making of colonial justice in French West Africa' (Unpublished proceedings from 'Interpreters, letter writers and clerks: mediating law and authority in colonial Africa', 8th annual Stanford–Berkeley Law and Colonialism symposium, Stanford University, 2002).   [48] *Ibid.*

employees were expected to operate. That these boundaries changed over the course of the 1890s reveal the shifting interests that drove French policy, as the colonial state underwent the transition from conquest to occupation. But not all local employees picked up on or adhered to the erratically evolving code of conduct, and Oularé and Makassouba were certainly not alone in overstepping mutating French standards. Nearly one third of Siguiri's prisoners in the 1890s were former employees – *tirailleurs*, clerks, interpreters – of the colonial state, imprisoned for 'abuses of power'.[49]

By 1910, however, the number of colonial employees imprisoned for 'abuse of power' declined dramatically.[50] This drop is telling, because it indicates that employees and other key figures on the local stage had learned the language, rules and concerns of the French colonial state, as well as the loci of colonial ignorance, indifference and disregard. And while more members of the general population uncovered the language and priorities of French colonial rule, the chasm that separated French officials from the general population did not disappear as colonial rule hardened in the early 1900s. While French officials transferred in and out of 'far flung' posts throughout the colonial empire, African employees and chiefs continued to develop new uses of and meanings for the bureaucracy of colonial rule. By the early 1900s, low-ranking African colonial employees posted to the Soudan lost the monopoly of language and knowledge that they had enjoyed during the first decade and half of the colonial occupation. Local populations, particularly the first generation of men and boys who had attended local colonial schools, came better to understand the alien institution in their midst. But the dispersal of knowledge and language did not necessarily diminish the influence of African interpreters and clerks. Throughout the early colonial period, low-ranking African employees maintained a key position that shaped the access of their French superiors to local populations. Local African employees with strong ties to local elites and with a good 'read' on colonial policy proved indispensable to French officials who were often more interested in advancing up the colonial hierarchy than in the drudgery of administering a district.

KAMISSOKO AND THE COLONIAL OCCUPATION IN KANKAN

As conquest hardened into occupation, the French folded their West African colonial possessions into a centralized bureaucracy based in Dakar, Senegal. The military territory of the Southern Soudan was incorporated into the colony of Guinée Française in 1900, and the cities along the Milo and Niger River valleys were included in a region now referred to as Upper Guinée. In the hopes of achieving uniformity in their imperial domains, the French opened a training school in Paris for French colonial officials and imple-

---

[49] Correspondance et renseignements, région sud, cercle de Siguiri, 1899. ANS 7 G 30; Etat nomatif des indigènes détenus à Siguiri ou en residence obligatoire, cercle de Siguiri, 1899. ANM I F 108.

[50] By 1910 colonial court cases rarely involved colonial employees as is indicated by trial and sentencing records in 'Tribunale de cercle de Kankan', 1 juillet, ANG 2 D 139; 'Prisons et penitencier de Fotoba, 1910', Rapports d'ensemble, 1910, ANS 2 G 10 18; 'Etat des arrestations, 1904', ANS K 28.

mented a policy of transferring mid- and high-level officers from colony to colony on regular rotations.[51] This policy did little to encourage French colonial employees to learn the languages of the colonized or familiarize themselves with the regions in which they were posted; in effect, fixed tours of duty decreased the incentive for French administrators to learn local languages or develop extensive knowledge of their districts. The transition to a more bureaucratic regime indicates the generational shift that took place as the French confronted the demands of administering their freshly acquired territories. The 'men on the spot' who fought enemies and forged coalitions with sympathetic elites were replaced by colonial administrators trained to contend with the demands of day-to-day administration. The colonial hierarchy expanded to include new offices and administrative branches while professional responsibilities were regularized, legal codes created and processes of review and inspection established.[52] In this process, African employees emerged as the official record keepers. Colonial officials charged clerks, secretaries and interpreters with taking censuses, collecting taxes, transcribing court proceedings and recording the flow of funds in and out of colonial coffers.

At the same time, the bureaucratization of the French colonial state focused the ambitions of its employees in divergent directions. French employees sought to climb a colonial hierarchy that stretched from rural districts and command posts up the administrative ladder to Dakar and Paris. The implementation of the 'turn table' principle, intended to prevent French colonial officials from developing strong ties to any particular area, turned colonial officers into 'nomadic administrators' as they were transferred from post to post and colony to colony.[53] In the district of Kankan, for example, 16 men filled the position of commander from 1905 to 1914, 8 of whom passed through from 1911 to 1913. By contrast, African colonial employees led much more sedentary careers and were rarely transferred outside the colony in which they were employed. The rootedness of African colonial officials gave them the opportunity to develop strong ties to the

---

[51] Cohen, *Rulers of Empire*, 48–9; Alice L. Conklin, *A Mission to Civilize: The Republican Idea of Empire in France and West Africa, 1895–1930* (Stanford, 1997), 82.

[52] On the creation of the government-general, C. W. Newbury, 'The formation of the government general of French West Africa', *JAH*, 1 (1960), 111–28. In 1903, Governor-General Roume sought to create a uniform education system and to organize and systematize French West Africa's justice system. Routinizing law and judicial proceedings figured prominently in efforts by the French to standardize colonial rule. Roume and his successors also relied on regular colonial inspections to ensure that various branches of the colonial administration adhered to their purposes and procedures. Conklin, *Mission to Civilize*, 47; inspection reports, ANFOM. On colonialism and efforts to promote the rule of law, see Richard Roberts and Kristin Mann (eds.), *Law in Colonial Africa* (Portsmouth NH, 1991). Efforts to organize the colonial bureaucracy coincided with another major administrative challenge that the French faced, that of slavery. Martin Klein investigates French labor ideologies and efforts to eliminate slavery in Klein, *Slavery and Colonial Rule in French West Africa* (Cambridge, 1998), 126–40, 178–96.

[53] Alexandre, 'Chiefs', 5. One inspector commented on the 'extreme frequency' of transfers in French West Africa and in Guinée Française in particular. Ministère des colonies à M. le gouverneur-général de l'AOF. No. 111, 15 avril 1909. Mission Saurin, 1909, ANFOM contr/908. Alexandre notes that he served in a district in Cameroon in which he was the 26th commander in 23 years. Alexandre, 'Chiefs', 7.

districts in which they worked while French employees became increasingly dependent on African colonial employees for knowledge and information.[54]

The consequence of the constant rotations of French personnel was not lost on African employees or on chiefs. As Alexandre explains, 'Officials always moved on, while the chiefs stayed behind and both chiefs and *commandants* were aware of this: The *commandant* tended therefore to be in a hurry and the chief to be patient to the point of inertia'.[55] Now intimately acquainted with the idiosyncrasies of colonial rule, African employees and local elites constructed mutually beneficial relationships and were generally more subtle and circumspect than the first generation of local figures living with colonial rule. Local elites and colonial employees recognized the importance of the appearance of French hegemony. Moreover, these men recognized the criteria that the French used to assess colonial hegemony: the collection of taxes and labor for colonial projects, the compilation of written records and the regular, public displays of the local French commander's authority. While the frequency and degree to which chiefs and African employees harmonized their accounts and coordinated their actions certainly varied greatly from district to district and colony to colony, the bargains struck by African colonial agents and chiefs conferred clear advantages on their authors. The networks and narratives constructed by chiefs and employees not only reaped profits of power and wealth, but helped to mitigate the volatility of colonial policy and personnel.

Reflecting on the final days of colonial rule, Alexandre made an observation that applies to earlier periods as well. In the typical French post in West Africa, he writes, 'there are three players in the game: The chief, the administrator, and the interpreter. Every possible combination of three factors occurred and the most important thing to note is that in most cases, the interpreter represented the decisive element'.[56] French officers may have privately resigned themselves to the expertise of their employees, too ashamed to admit to knowing less than an African subordinate.[57] Conversely, some French officials understood their limits and came to rely on the knowledge, contacts and subterranean networks of their employees; they simply neglected to mention the source of their insight to their superiors.[58]

[54] Alexandre, 'Chiefs', 7.   [55] Ibid. 9.

[56] Ibid. 7. John Smith makes a similar point about the functioning of the colonial state in northern Nigeria. John Smith, 'The relationship of the British political officer to his chief in Northern Nigeria', in Crowder and Ikime (eds.), *West African Chiefs*, 19.

[57] A colonial inspector discovered in 1920 that the French warden of the prison on the island of Fotoba off the coast of Conakry depended entirely on one of his wards to fulfill his administrative responsibilities. The French warden, as it turned out, was not only a drunk, but totally illiterate; one of the prisoners maintained all of the correspondence and records of the prison. Mission Kair, 1920–1, ANFOM affpol/3052.

[58] Oral interviews and a number of African novels and memoirs also shed light on the influence of African interpreters and clerks on the day-to-day functioning of the colonial state. An example of how French officials accessed their subordinate's networks figures into Amadou Hampâté Bâ's memoirs. In this case, a worried French colonial official asks his clerk to use his contacts to find out how one of his reports was received by the governor. Amadou Hampâté Bâ, *Oui, mon commandant* (Paris, 1994), 345–6. See also Hampâté Bâ, *Amkoullel, L'enfant Peul* (Paris, 1994); *The Fortunes of Wangrin*, trans. Aina Pavolini Taylor (Bloomington, 1999; orig. 1973). Elders in and around Kankan sometimes described colonial interpreters and clerks as 'more powerful' than their

AFRICAN COLONIAL EMPLOYEES IN FRENCH WEST AFRICA 45

Letters written by a prisoner in Kankan shed light on the subterranean colonial networks that operated in that district in the early 1900s. Revealing the degree to which knowledge of colonial rule had been disseminated to at least a small sector of the general population, Kamissoko's letters also reveal a clear comprehension of the hierarchies of race and gender that the French used to justify their *mission civilisatrice*. Kamissoko 'nicknamed Charles' wrote regularly to Guinée's high French officials, including the governor, over the course of two years. Imprisoned for child molestation in 1907, Kamissoko claimed that the local French commander had framed him, and that he was actually a 'political prisoner', a victim of the local commander's personal vendetta.[59] In writing to high-level officials, Kamissoko stated that his purpose was to expose the true functioning of Kankan's French post.[60] In so doing, Kamissoko made no effort to mask his own agenda. Familiar with the principles of colonial rule, driven by intense passions and a powerful ambition, and fed by a series of remarkable delusions, Kamissoko sought to destroy the local French commander while promoting his own candidature for a position within the colonial bureaucracy. Although Kamissoko's letters are steeped in personal biases, they nevertheless bring substance and detail to complaints about colonial officials who extended their influence far beyond the formal capacities of their positions.[61] Kamissoko's letters thus vividly illustrate the patterns and possibilities that emerged in the early colonial period in the interior of French West Africa; they also provide an alternative narrative and interpretation of colonial rule than that presented by official French reports and documents.

Throughout his correspondence, Kamissoko contended that the loyalty of Kankan's head interpreter, Fodé, lay with the local chieftaincy, not with the French. Referring to Fodé as one of the 'Muslim prophets of Kankan', Kamissoko enumerated the flow of gifts and information that sealed the bond between Fodé and Kankan's Muslim elders.[62] Kamissoko posited that Fodé and the elders of Kankan engaged in the slave trade, and that the interpreter 'falsified interpretations' during trials and palavers. 'Being a Muslim, [Fodé] protects the Muslims and hides their politics from the French and drives the pagans to prison'.[63] Because of Fodé's close ties to

---

French superiors. Soumayela Kané in a group interview with Kaba Sidibe, Numke Camara and Kaba Keita (Yalafarini, 1 Aug. 1997); Bilinan Nankouma Doumbouya made a similar point in a joint interview with Fodé Amadou Doumbouya (Narassouba, 24 July 1997).

[59] Jugement de l'affaire Kamisoko Gabry and Bintou Kaba, cercle de Kankan, 30 août 1907. ANG 2 D 136. On being a political prisoner: Kamissoko à M. l'administrateur Tallerie, stamped 15 mars 1909. Kamissoko's correspondence is located in ANG 2 D 139.

[60] Kamissoko à M. l'administrateur, doc. #13, 1 avril 1909; Kamissoko à M. l'administrateur, doc. #14, 2 avril 1909.

[61] See, for example, Rapport concernant la verification de M. Drouin, administrateur adjoint, cercle de Kouroussa, 10 jan. 1921, Mission Kair, 1920–1, ANFOM; Rapport politique, cercle de Kankan, oct. 1909, ANG 2 D. 139.

[62] Fodé, the same interpreter who raised Kamissoko's ire, was described by Thoreau-Levaré in a 1909 report as 'one of our most indispensable auxiliaries'. But in October of that year Thoreau-Levaré reprimanded Fodé for becoming personally involved in a dispute with a chief. Rapport politique, cercle de Kankan, oct. 1909, ANG 2 D 139.

[63] Kamissoko à M. Tallerie, doc. #5, 11 mars 1905.

Kankan's chief, asserted Kamissoko, no correspondence, order or decree that crossed the French commander's desk remained confidential for long. 'As soon as the administrator wants to enter into political intrigues', the interpreter 'reveals all of the administrator's secrets [to the chief]'.[64] Proof of Fodé's wealth could be found at his compound: 'Here is why Fodé is very rich today in Kankan: six women, three horses, [and] a house'.[65] Kamissoko claimed that Fodé collected grain for his horses from outlying villages 'without the knowledge of the commander', in addition to honey, butter and chickens for his own consumption. Fodé, Kamissoko declared, 'is the king of Kankan'.[66]

Other agents employed by Kankan's post did not escape Kamissoko's scrutiny. One of the scribes in the Native Tribunal 'does not pronounce Koranic sentences ... until he has met with Fodé in a corner'.[67] Kamissoko further described the system developed by clerks to manipulate local transport systems to their own profit. He claimed that these agents doctored records and evaded taxes, bilking the colonial state of thousands of francs.[68] Kamissoko announced that the local head-sergeant confiscated rice intended for prisoners, and that a soldier imprisoned a local woman until she agreed to marry him.[69] According to Kamissoko, the enthusiasm of Kankan's soldiers for imprisoning local women until they succumbed was well known throughout the district.[70] All of these machinations, Kamissoko contended, remained hidden from the commander.[71]

While ignorant of the conduct of his employees, Kamissoko argued that the local French commander was hardly innocent of wrong doing. On the contrary, Kamissoko reserved his most vitriolic attacks for Abdel Thoreau-Levaré, asserting that the commander 'writes monstrosities and vomits rubbish about me' and that 'he is a fraud and everything that he does in Kankan is fraudulent'.[72] Kamissoko's discussion of the actions of the French commander – who was Algerian in origin, not French – shows Kamissoko's keen awareness of the standards to which a high-ranking colonial officer was expected to adhere. Kamissoko knew that a district commander was not supposed to extort from members of the population or make arbitrary requisitions, nor was he supposed to consort with local women or fraternize with his African employees. Kamissoko sought systematically to expose the incompatibility of Thoreau-Levaré's behavior with the premises and goals of the French *mission civilisatrice*. He did so by detailing the manner in which Thoreau-Levaré exploited local resources and people, in particular the women of the district.

Characterizing Thoreau-Levaré's stewardship of Kankan's prison as 'abuse in oppression', Kamissoko pointed out that the residents of the district were forced to supply more than 10,000 bundles of wood per year for the local employees' kitchens. 'All of the villages of the district of Kankan bring bundles ..., I did not see the same thing even in Conakry ... If the [Governor] buys wood on the market, why does Levaré and his consort

---

[64] *Ibid.*; Kamissoko à M. l'administrateur, doc. #13, 1 avril 1909.
[65] Doc. #13, 1 avril 1909.   [66] Doc. #12, 31 mar. 1909.   [67] *Ibid.*
[68] Kamissoko au ministère, doc. #13, 1 avril 1909; doc. #1, 15 fev. 1909.
[69] Kamissoko à M. l'administrateur, doc. #8, 15 mars 1909.   [70] *Ibid.*
[71] Kamissoko, doc. #1, 15 fev. 1909.
[72] Kamissoko à M. Tallérie, doc. #5, 11 mar. 1909.

demand ... wood ... without paying one cent to the villagers!'.[73] Thoreau-Levaré allegedly justified these requisitions by saying that they were 'included in local regulations'.[74]

Kamissoko's discussion of race and sex underscores his cognizance of the racial hierarchies that informed the colonial project. Besides accusing Thoreau-Levaré of framing him, 'How do you expect me not to keep all of my grief against [hold a grudge against] this Algerian!', Kamissoko repeatedly objected to Thoreau-Levaré's Algerian origins.[75] In a stunning display of logic, Kamissoko reasoned: 'Thoreau-Levaré is capable of anything. He does not have the soul of a Frenchman. In philology this word "français" comes from the word "franc" [frank]. This means to approach without submission, without deceit'.[76] Because of his Algerian roots, Kamissoko implied, Thoreau-Levaré could not possibly live up to the definition of the word 'français' and was not worthy of his post within the colonial administration.[77] Kamissoko painted a wildly different portrait of himself, a true black colonial subject schooled in the nuances of the French language and enlightened by French values. Kamissoko implied that he was infinitely better positioned than 'this Arab' for carrying out France's mission in Africa.[78]

To solidify his case against Thoreau-Levaré, Kamissoko composed a list of all the women with whom the commander had 'relations'. Kamissoko contended that 'this Arab has married six young women in Kankan, without paying the bridewealth to their families'.[79] Not that 'this Arab' was the only one to take up with local women; Kamissoko carefully noted all of the women on the list who had had 'relations' with previous French commanders, adding that 'all the commanders who come to Kankan have numerous, beautiful women'.[80] According to Kamissoko, French commanders often ordered their employees to help them identify potential partners, such as one previous official who directed Fodé the interpreter to help him 'look for women'.[81] When this commander, rich with gold from the Siguiri mines, went on leave back to France, he left Fodé responsible for looking after his seven wives. The rare French official who eschewed sexual relations with local women earned Kamissoko's admiration, such as one official, whose uninterest in Kankan's women revealed that 'he is serious, he does not want black women ... not him'.[82]

Kamissoko's reactions to the relationships between French men and African women highlight an important dimension of colonial rule. 'Local marriages' between French men and African women were not uncommon in French West Africa, but these relationships were frowned upon and almost

[73] Doc. #14, 2 avr. 1909.   [74] Ibid.   [75] Doc. #8, 15 mar. 1909.   [76] Ibid.

[77] Unlike most French administrators, Thoreau-Levaré remained stationed in Guinée for almost his entire career; he was posted to Kankan twice, once in 1906 during Kamissoko's initial prison term, and again from 1909 to 1910. Kamissoko's allegations seem to have had little impact on Thoreau-Levaré's career. Personnel records confirm that Thoreau-Levaré was of Algerian origin. ANFOM, dossier personnel, 1279.

[78] Kamissoko à M. Vienne, doc. #4, 9 mar. 1909.

[79] Kamissoko entitled his letter to M. Vienne, 'L'offensé Kamissoko contre l'offenseur Thoreau-Levaré', Kamissoko à M. Vienne, doc. #4, 9 mar. 1909.

[80] Kamissoko au gouvernement de la Guinée française, chef lieu Conakry, doc. #2, 6 mars 1909.   [81] Kamissoko à M. l'administrateur, doc. #11, 27 mars 1909.

[82] Doc. #2, 6 mar. 1909.

never openly acknowledged by colonial institutions and administrators.[83] The unions of white men and black women posed a threat to the colonial 'civilizing mission' because they blurred the line between white and black, 'civilized' and 'uncivilized'. French officials entered into local marriages for personal reasons, reasons that were incompatible with colonial institutions and ideals. French officials did not take up with local women to serve a larger purpose: to build coalitions with local elites, to signify domination or to bear children invested in the continued supremacy of French rule. When administrators transferred to a different post they typically dissolved their 'local marriages' and left behind their African wives and *métis* children. In marrying local women, French administrators thus cordoned off their private lives, and the documents they produced ignore the domestic relations and sexual exploits that contributed to the daily routines of colonial rule. But memories of these marriages remain alive in and around Kankan. In oral interviews, the elders in and around Baté readily acknowledged the frequency with which 'local marriages' occurred. They discussed the temporary nature of these unions and point to certain families whose ancestors include a French official.[84] Evidence that the French did not always practice sexual restraint is further corroborated by the intimate details for which some French officials became known, such as the commander who earned the nickname 'Uncircumcised Man'.[85]

In this context, Kamissoko's frank discussion of French officials' female partners tells much about the inner workings of colonialism in Kankan, as well as Kamissoko's own clear understanding of French colonial rule. Kamissoko provided particulars on the personal relationships of French commanders because he knew they could provoke embarrassment and official disapproval; he also knew that these relations operated outside the purview of official bureaucratic channels and reports.

Kamissoko's letters shed light on the underbelly of Kankan's colonial post in the early colonial era, from the plottings of its agents and the ties that linked chiefs and intermediaries, to the sexual exploits of its French officials. The letters that Kamissoko wrote are erratic, gossipy, outraged, bitter and erudite; he quotes Latin, draws parallels between himself and Michel de Montaigne and excuses his lack of formality by declaring his intention to communicate in a 'transcendental' style.[86] Kamissoko never questioned his own importance or insight; he justified his policy recommendations to the governor by pointing to his 'qualities as a man of politics', even noting that he 'personified politics' in Kankan.[87]

But Kamissoko's motives in writing to Guinée's high officialdom were hardly altruistic. Kamissoko's personal ambitions demonstrate a sharp

---

[83] Local African bureaucrats did not overlook these 'local wives' in mediating relations with French commanders, although little evidence of this process can be sifted from the documentary record. For some indication of how these relations unfolded, see Hampâté Bâ, *Fortunes of Wangrin*, 30–5.

[84] Interviews with Al hajja Kaba (Kankan, 26 May 1997) and Jenné Kaba (Kolonin, Kankan-Baté, 9 Oct. 1997).

[85] Interview with Fodé Amadou Doumbouya (Narassoba, 24 July 1997).

[86] Kamissoko wrote: 'Monsieur l'administrateur, je suis comme Michel de Montaigne à qui tout le mot était bon pour exprimer la pensée', doc. #8, 15 Mar. 1909.

[87] Kamissoko à M. l'administrateur, doc. #9, 19 mar. 1909.

awareness of the opportunities that lay within the colonial apparatus for a black colonial subject who could read and write French. In almost all of his letters, Kamissoko did not hesitate to offer a personal resolution to the challenges faced by Guinée's administration. Kamissoko suggested that it was in France's best interest immediately to release him from prison. He further proposed that he be appointed to a position within the colonial bureaucracy. Pointing to his linguistic skills and local knowledge, Kamissoko argued that he was best qualified to serve the French cause as – what else? – an interpreter.[88]

CONCLUSION

Many obstacles hinder analysis of the roles of interpreters, clerks and secretaries who were so critical to the daily functioning of the French colonial state in the Soudan. Most significantly, these employees did not, by and large, leave behind a paper trail that gives voice or understanding to their actions, thoughts and goals. African employees may have copied and even authored reports in the name of their French superiors, but generally their positions were not vested with authority to make recommendations, write evaluations or critique policy. The fleeting presence of employees in the written records is compounded by the limited and infrequent comments of their French superiors. Except for the increasingly rare 'scandal' and outcry over 'abuses of power', the potential of African employees to expand on their official duties went largely unremarked by European officials in the early colonial period.

In 1931, a French colonial official, H. Labouret, made a rare comment about the role of African employees in the colonial state. 'The interpreter or the secretary, who is always correct, considerate, discreet and devoted, [acts as] the obliging intermediary between the administrator, who does not speak the native language, and the natives, who do not understand French'. Labouret continued, 'district police, interpreters or secretaries are nearly always the true chiefs of the country'.[89] While Labouret omits mention of African chiefs and their role in the negotiations produced by the colonial occupation, he nevertheless draws attention to the importance of African colonial employees to the form and shape of the colonial occupation. African clerks, interpreters and agents who worked for the French state illuminate the new alliances and networks of power produced in the aftermath of French conquest. African colonial employees thus provide a fresh view point on the continuities and ruptures that shaped the transition to French rule; they also expose the gaps that opened between colonialism in practice and colonialism as envisioned by its architects in the colonial capital cities of Bamako, Conakry, Dakar and Paris.

But as the cases involving Fall, Oularé and Kamissoko indicate, the bureaucratic apparatus of French colonial rule blurred at its lowest ranks, demonstrating that European pathways of power did not produce wholly European results. At those ranks where the mass of the population encountered colonial rule, unofficial and highly localized corridors of power

[88] Kamissoko, docs. #1, 4, 5, 8, 21.
[89] H. Labouret, *A la recherche d'une politique indigène dans l'ouest Africaine* (Paris: Comité de l'Afrique française, 1931), 40.

entangled the French colonial bureaucracy. The intersections of local relations of power with colonial ones – and the place of African colonial employees in the construction of those intersections – show that the colonial state functioned quite differently day to day than French officials often knew or wished to acknowledge. African colonial employees and their place in the equation of colonial rule reveal that French attempts to reshape African societies into French colonial ones were constantly challenged by the force and resilience of local processes and local relationships.

[12]

Negotiated Spaces and Contested Terrain: Men, Women, and the Law in Colonial Zimbabwe, 1890–1939

ELIZABETH SCHMIDT
(Department of History, Loyola College, Baltimore, Maryland)

During the early years of European occupation in Southern Rhodesia, people on the margins of African society took advantage of the erosion of indigenous authority structures. Women, in particular, challenged male control over their mobility, sexuality, and productive and reproductive capacities. Initially, a degree of female 'emancipation' was encouraged by European missionaries and the colonial state, who considered such customs as child-pledging, forced marriage, and polygamy to be 'repugnant' to European concepts of morality. During the first three decades of colonial rule, legislation was enacted that outlawed child marriages, set limitations on bridewealth, and prohibited the marriage of women without their consent.

The resulting crisis of authority in the rural areas, foreshadowing the possibility of a total breakdown in law and order, forced state officials to reconsider their earlier policies. By the 1920s, a backlash against female emancipation was well under way, intensifying under the pressures of the Great Depression. By the 1930s, the colonial state and rural African patriarchs were engaged in full-scale collaboration, determined to reassert control over the mobility and sexuality of African women.

This article explores the dynamics of the struggle over female 'emancipation', as it was waged between generations of Africans, between African women and men, and between missionaries, who generally welcomed female refugees, and the colonial state, intent upon upholding the authority of senior African men, and by extension, the entire system of indirect rule. One of the primary terrains of contest, the power to create and implement 'customary' law, is a central focus of this investigation.

Introduction

During the early years of European occupation in Southern Rhodesia, alternative ways of living emerged for people at the margins of Shona and Ndebele society.[1]

---

[1] I would like to thank Martin Chanock, Carol Dickerman, Norma Kriger, and Luise White, as well as anonymous *JSAS* reviewers, for their helpful comments on earlier drafts of this

Human pawns transferred between lineages in payment of a debt, reparation for a crime, or tribute to a chief, hostages taken to avenge a wrong or as captives of war, young women forced to marry against their will, and dissatisfied co-wives found a variety of new options open to them.[2] Women, in particular, took advantage of these opportunities, fleeing to mission stations, mining compounds, European farms, and urban locations.

Initially, a degree of female 'emancipation' was encouraged by European missionaries and the colonial state, who considered such customs as child-pledging (the betrothal of young girls to older men), forced marriage, and polygamy to be 'repugnant' to European concepts of morality. Therefore, during the first three decades of colonial rule (1890–1920), legislation was enacted that outlawed child marriages, set limitations on bridewealth (marriage payments from the husband's to the wife's kin), and prohibited the marriage of women without their consent. Such measures also undermined indigenous authority structures, serving the interests of European mining and agricultural capital bent upon obtaining large supplies of African male labour, which seemed possible only if African social, economic, and political institutions were weakened or destroyed.[3]

Chronic shortages of male labour, particularly marked in 1908–1911, 1914–1920 and 1925–1929, as well as the post-war recession of the early 1920s, forced state

---

article. Unless otherwise indicated, all documents cited in the footnotes are housed at the National Archives of Zimbabwe in Harare, Zimbabwe. Some references are made to documents held in the Jesuit Archives in Harare, and in the Wesleyan Methodist Missionary Society Archives (WMMS) in London. Interviews were conducted by the author in Zimbabwe between August 1985 and March 1986. When discussing the colonial period, Zimbabwe will be referred to by its colonial name, 'Southern Rhodesia'.

[2] In the early decades of colonial occupation, Shona men and women whose family members were or who were themselves hostages and pawns took advantage of new legal channels in an attempt to obtain their freedom. Civil cases heard by the Native Commissioner, Goromonzi District, provide ample evidence of this trend. See, for instance, NSL 1/1/1: Tshivu versus Manyinga, 17 October 1899; Tshirawu versus Meyaniwa, 26 April 1900; Tshitswatsa versus Tshikaje, 29 April 1900; Paramount Shipolilo versus Tshifamba, 29 October 1900; Jowo versus Tshigwediri, 22 February 1901; Ooni versus Tshingor, 20 July 1901; Bigwanya versus M'Juru, 9 October 1901; Gonomwe versus Gwebera, 23 July 1903.

For evidence of bonded women elsewhere in the region fleeing to mission stations and seeking their freedom in colonial courts, see Marcia Wright, 'Women in Peril: A Commentary on the Life Stories of Captives in Nineteenth-century East-central Africa, *African Social Research* 20 (December 1975), pp. 800–819; *Women in Peril: Life Stories of Four Captives* (Lusaka: National Educational Company of Zambia for the Institute for African Studies, 1984); 'Bwanikwa: Consciousness and Protest Among Slave Women in Central Africa, 1886–1911', in *Women and Slavery in Africa*, eds. Claire C. Robertson and Martin A. Klein (Madison, 1983), pp. 246–267.

[3] Ian Phimister, *An Economic and Social History of Zimbabwe, 1890–1948; Capital Accumulation and Class Struggle* (New York, 1988), pp. 146–147. A forthright statement of administration policy during this period is quoted in Phimister (p. 147). Advocating the gradual destruction chiefly power, the chief native commissioner of Mashonaland wrote in 1912:

Contact with civilisation is the cause of this, and though chiefs and others complain, no steps should be taken to prevent this gradual evolution. The increased powers granted to Native Commissioners have materially assisted in breaking up these tribal methods of control, and I am glad to say the results so far have been satisfactory.

officials to reassess their African policy.[4] Having encouraged a break down in local authority structures, the state had provided no viable substitute. Social forces beyond state control were being rapidly unleashed, and the maintenance of law and order seriously jeopardised. Within the Native Department, 'advocates of reconstituted "traditionalism" and "tribalism"' carried the day, promoting policies that 'bolstered the waning authority of African chiefs and headmen'.[5] By the late 1920s, African chiefs, headmen and other male elders, whose duties and powers were assigned and manipulated by the colonial state, were the backbone of the administrative system of indirect rule.

In order to appease African patriarchs, thus preserving law and order in the colonial system, the state moved to undo the 'damage' it had done to local authority structures.[6] Even as it continued to enact new emancipatory legislation in the late 1910s, the state began to close many of the loopholes it earlier had opened. By the 1930s, the colonial state and rural African patriarchs were engaged in full-scale collaboration, determined to control the mobility and sexuality of African women.

This article explores the dynamics of the struggle over female 'emancipation', as it was waged between generations of Africans, between African women and men, and between missionaries, who generally welcomed female refugees, and the colonial state, intent upon upholding the authority of senior African men, and by extension, the entire system of indirect rule. One of the primary terrains of contest, the power to create and implement 'customary' law, is a central focus of this investigation.

The Creation of 'Customary' Law

In March 1896, six years after the occupation of Southern Rhodesia by the British South Africa Company, the Shona and Ndebele people rose up against their foreign rulers. There were a number of stimuli for the rebellion. Among the most serious were forcible evictions from ancestral land, forced labour and brutal recruitment methods, onerous tax obligations, and the outlawing of various African customs by

---

[4] For data concerning the labour shortages, see Paul Mosley, *The Settler Economies; Studies In the Economic History of Kenya and Southern Rhodesia, 1900–1963* (New York, 1983), pp. 125, 141.

[5] Phimister, *Economic and Social History*, pp. 147–148. Also see Murray Cairns Steele, 'The Foundations of a 'Native' Policy: Southern Rhodesia, 1923–1933,' Ph.D., Simon Fraser University, 1972, pp. 74–75.

[6] The term 'patriarchy' is employed according to the usage of Heidi Hartmann. Thus patriarchy is defined as 'a set of social relations between men, which have a material base, and which, though hierarchical, establish or create interdependence and solidarity among men that enable them to dominate women.' While men of different ranks, classes, ages, races, and ethnic groups occupy positions of varying status within the structure, all men 'are united in their shared relationship of dominance over their women; they are dependent upon each other to maintain that domination.' Heidi Hartmann, 'The Unhappy Marriage of Marxism and Feminism: Towards a More Progressive Union', in *Women and Revolution; A Discussion of the Unhappy Marriage of Marxism and Feminism*, ed. Lydia Sargent (Boston, 1981), pp. 14–15.

European missionaries. The revolt was finally put down in 1897, primarily as a result of the superior weaponry of the European forces.

In the post-rising period, the primary objectives of the newly created Native Department were the generation of tax revenue and the recruitment of African labour, while employing methods that forestalled another uprising. For the first time, serious attention was paid to the methods of African administration. In order to mollify African discontent, African customs were to be respected, insofar as they did not interfere with European concepts of a just and civilised society. Toward this end, the Order in Council of 1898 stipulated that in civil cases between Africans, the courts 'shall be guided by native law so far as that law is not repugnant to natural justice or morality'.[7] It was up to European administrators to judge what was 'repugnant', according to their own views of justice and morality, and it was their job to determine precisely what constituted African law and custom.

Seeking versions of Shona and Ndebele customs that would promote their own agenda, state officials consulted an array of 'legal experts', invariably chiefs, headmen, and male elders. While such prominent constituents were given the benefit of the doubt in most areas concerning family law, the administration opposed them where customs were deemed 'repugnant' to European values. Foremost among the disparaged customs were child pledging and the forced marriage of older girls and women. During the first three decades of colonial rule, African women and girls were able to take advantage of these small openings, challenging fathers, husbands, and guardians in the colonial courts.[8] From the mid-1910s, however, the state, fearing the consequences of female emancipation, increasingly sought to legitimate 'customs' that would justify continued female subordination. From this period onward, it became ever more difficult for African women to manipulate the colonial legal system to their advantage.

By the 1940s, anthropologists employed by government agencies were contributing their expertise to the retrieval — and creation — of 'customary' law. In his attempt to record and codify Shona 'customary' law, J.F. Holleman, a staff anthropologist at the state-run Rhodes-Livingstone Institute in Northern Rhodesia, collected case material from:

---

[7] Steele, 'Foundations', pp. 137–138.

[8] Women took advantage of similar changes in the law during the early colonial period in Northern Rhodesia and Nyasaland. See Martin Chanock, 'Making Customary Law: Men, Women, and Courts in Colonial Northern Rhodesia', in *African Women and the Law: Historical Perspectives*, eds. Margaret Jean Hay and Marcia Wright, Boston University Papers on Africa, no. 7 (Boston, 1982), pp. 57–60, 66; *Law, Custom and Social Order: The Colonial Experience in Malawi and Zambia* (London, 1985), pp. 145–159, 186–216; Marcia Wright, 'Justice, Women, and the Social Order in Abercorn Northeastern Rhodesia, 1897–1903', in *African Women and the Law*, pp. 33–50; 'Bwanikwa', pp. 248, 261–266; Jane L. Parpart, 'Sexuality and Power on the Zambian Copperbelt, 1926–1964', in *Patriarchy and Class: African Women in the Home and the Workforce*, eds. Sharon B. Stichter and Jane L. Parpart (Boulder, 1988), pp. 117–119; Sally Engle Merry, 'The Articulation of Legal Spheres', in *African Women and the Law*, pp. 86–89; Megan Vaughan, *The Story of An African Famine: Gender and Famine in Twentieth-Century Malawi*, Cambridge, 1987, pp. 139–144.

... teams of carefully selected informants, practically all of them people who were taking an active part in the tribal administration of justice as assessors to a chief's or headman's court, and who could therefore quote from personal experience.

Holleman also attended numerous sessions of the 'tribal courts', making 'extensive use of the services of Native interpreters', that is, elite male members of the local colonial administration.[9]

Holleman's informants, primarily older men of relatively high social position, clearly had a vested interest in what passed as custom. Their influence was particularly marked in the rendition of family law, which governed gender relations in the context of marriage, divorce, inheritance, and child custody and property rights within marriage. As the emergence of towns, farms, mining centres, and mission stations presented opportunities for women to escape patriarchal control in the countryside, older men sought new ways to reassert their waning authority. As legal advisers to the colonial state, male elders were presented with countless opportunities to bolster old bases of power and to establish new ones. Having based their assessment of African custom on the accounts of such interested parties, state officials generally deemed women's counterclaims contrary to tradition and dismissed them from the colonial courts.[10]

According to Martin Chanock, who has pioneered recent investigations into the creation of 'customary' law in colonial Africa, the collection of information from such sources 'must be seen ... not as part of the process of discovering the rules of customary law but as a vital part of the rule-making process'. So-called customary laws were established when the concerns of the informants 'coincided with the moral predilections and administrative purposes of the officials'. Fluid and flexible practices were turned into hard and fast rules.[11] While custom had been both adaptable and sensitive to extenuating circumstances, 'customary' law was not. African 'customary' law, heavily biased toward the male elite, was now written in stone.[12]

From the mid-1910s, colonial officials frequently argued against legislative measures designed to promote female emancipation, claiming that such actions

---

[9] J.F. Holleman, *Shona Customary Law; With Reference to Kinship, Marriage, the Family and the Estate* (Manchester, 1952), p. x.

[10] Chanock, 'Making Customary Law', pp. 66–67. The claim by senior African men that it was their right to assert control over women of all ages found a sympathetic ear among state officials. Arguing that elevating the legal status of African women would constitute undue interference in African custom, the native commissioner of Gokwe contended in 1924:

It is always a dangerous matter to tamper with the vital principles governing the internal economy of a tribe or a nation under our tutelage and more especially when this is not contrary to our laws.

(CNC S138/150, NC, Gokwe to Superintendent of Natives, Gwelo, 5 March 1924. No.86.)

[11] Chanock, 'Making Customary Law', pp. 65, 66–67. Also see Chanock, *Law, Custom and Social Order*, pp. 4, 8, 146, 149; Terence Ranger, 'The Invention of Tradition in Colonial Africa', in *The Invention of Tradition*, eds. Eric Hobsbawm and Terence Ranger (New York, 1983), pp. 212, 247–258.

[12] For a similar critique of 'customary' law as it was applied to the Shona, see M.F.C. Bourdillon, 'Is 'Customary Law' Customary?' *NADA* 11, 2 (1975), pp. 142–143, 147.

interfered with 'native custom'. Writing in 1924, the native commissioner of Chipinga was one of those who opposed such changes, contending that ' ... dangerous ground would be trodden unless we have the support of the native'.[13] The 'native', of course, was presumed to be male, and 'native custom' was what male elders claimed it to be.

Advocating the retention of laws that condemned African women to perpetual minority status, a colleague writing at the same time stressed that African women should remain under the firm control of their fathers, guardians, or husbands for the duration of their lives. 'It is very doubtful whether any further violent breach with native custom would not do far more harm than good until the native woman has learnt to adapt herself to her new-found liberty however limited it may be', he declared.[14] Another official reasoned that if European women had only recently acquired the ability to conduct their own affairs, then African women were certainly in need of male guidance for generations to come. 'Indeed', he wrote:

> ... until quite recent years, this was the condition among our own race. The native woman of today has not the brain power or civilisation of the mothers and grandmothers of the present white generation; her brain is not sufficiently balanced to allow her to think and act in all matters for herself, and I consider the male should be encouraged and assisted to exercise tutelage, within all reasonable bounds, over his womenfolk.[15]

Throughout the period under consideration, state attitudes towards women's rights were highly ambiguous and contradictory. Having based their system of colonial administration on the manipulation of indigenous authority structures, using local leaders to implement state policies, colonial officials could not afford to let those structures be undermined by agents outside their control. Thus, the administration was fundamentally concerned with safeguarding the domestic authority of African male guardians. The refusal of women to marry their appointed partners, their desertion of unwanted husbands, and their flight to missions, mines, farms, and urban areas posed a serious threat to African male authority, and consequently, to the entire system of indirect rule.[16]

---

[13] CNC S138/150, NC Chipinga to Superintendent of Natives, Umtali, 5 March 1924, No. 34/237/24.

[14] CNC S138/150, NC Inyanga, 7 March 1924.

[15] CNC S138/150, NC, Hartley to Superintendent of Natives, Salisbury, 28 February 1924. Also see CNC S138/150, NC, Bikita to Superintendent of Natives, Fort Victoria, 12 March 1924, No.26/24.

[16] For elaboration on this theme see Nancy Folbre, 'Patriarchal Social Formations in Zimbabwe', in *Patriarchy and Class*, p. 67; Terence Ranger, 'Women in the Politics of Makoni District, Zimbabwe, 1890–1980', unpublished paper, Manchester University, 1981, pp. 10–11.
Colonial officials in Northern Rhodesia and Tanganyika expressed a similar understanding of the relationship between patriarchal control over female mobility and sexuality and the survival of the system of indirect rule. See Kenneth Little, *African Women in Towns: An Aspect of Africa's Social Revolution* (New York, 1973), pp. 18–19; George Chauncey Jr., 'The Locus of Reproduction: Women's Labour in the Zambian Copperbelt, 1927–1953', *Journal of Southern African Studies* 7, 2 (April 1981), pp. 136, 153; Parpart, 'Sexuality and Power', pp. 115, 119–120; Jane L. Parpart, 'Class and Gender on the Copperbelt: Women in Northern Rhodesian

Child Pledging and Forced Marriage

In the interests of bolstering male authority, the state chose to ignore certain customs otherwise considered 'repugnant' to the European sense of morality. While colonial officials were highly critical of bridewealth transfers and polygamy, these practices were not considered so offensive that they warranted intervention and the provocation of the older men's ire. In 1910–1911, the Native Affairs Committee of Enquiry recommended that 'polygamy should not be interfered with but should be left to die out'.[17] A decade later, the native commissioner of the Marandellas District acknowledged that 'any legislation to improve the legal status of the woman' within marriage 'must necessarily cut at the very root of Native institutions', particularly that of bridewealth. For this reason, bridewealth could not be abolished outright, as such an action 'would seriously upset the equilibrium of tribal and family life'.[18]

In other instances, state officials felt compelled to take more immediate action. Despite the general tendency of the administration to support the claims of African male elders, there were some instances in which women gained from state intervention in the legal sphere. From the early days of European occupation, child pledging and forced marriages were deemed 'repugnant' to European standards of justice and morality.[19] As such, they provided a terrain for struggle between older African men, young African women, and the colonial state.

The Native Marriages Ordinance of 1901, which governed all non-Christian marriages between Africans — and thus, the majority of African marriages — outlawed child pledging and required that the woman's consent be obtained before a marriage could take place.[20] In its 1911 report, the Native Affairs Committee of Enquiry urged that the pledging of children be made criminally punishable. The following year, this recommendation was incorporated into the amended marriage law.[21] A further amendment in 1917 stipulated that any man who entered into a marriage agreement concerning a girl who was not of marriageable age (twelve

---

Copper Mining Communities, 1926–1964', in *Women and Class in Africa*, eds. Claire Robertson and Iris Berger (New York, 1986), p. 143; Chanock, *Law, Custom and Social Order*, pp. 111 124, 207 208; Marjorie Mhilinyi, 'Runaway Wives in Colonial Tanganyika: Forced Labour and Forced Marriage in Rungwe District, 1919–1961', *International Journal of the Sociology of Law* 16 (1988), pp. 3, 11–12, 25.

[17] Jesuit Archives, Box 317, Southern Rhodesia, *Report of the Native Affairs Committee of Enquiry, 1910–11* (Salisbury: Government Printer, 1911), Appendix, p. 68.

[18] CNC S138/150, NC, Marandellas to Superintendent of Natives, Salisbury, 30 November 1923, No. 21/331.

[19] See Steele, 'Foundations', p. 143; CNC S235/432, Assistant NC Bindura to NC Mazoe, 30 September 1946, No. 523/46.

[20] CNC S235/432, ANC Inyati (Matabeleland) to NC Inyati, 4 October 1946; W.R. Peaden, *Missionary Attitudes to Shona Culture, 1890–1923*, Local Series, no. 27 (Salisbury, 1970), p. 22; Phimister, *Economic and Social History*, p. 147.

[21] Jesuit Archives, Box 317, Native Affairs Committee of Enquiry, p. 68; Joan May, *Zimbabwean Women in Colonial and Customary Law* (Gweru, 1983), p. 46.

years or older), was liable to a fine of up to fifty pounds or to imprisonment with or without hard labour for up to one year.[22]

In order to enforce the ban on child pledging and to ensure that the bride had consented to her marriage, the Native Marriages Ordinance of 1901 stipulated that all African marriages were to be solemnised before a registering officer, usually the native commissioner, before cohabitation occurred.[23] Amendments in 1917 carried the restrictions even further. African marriages were henceforth considered invalid if they were not registered. It was the husband's responsibility to register the marriage before his bride left her guardian to live with him. If he failed to accomplish this task in a timely manner, he was liable to a fine of up to ten pounds or imprisonment with or without hard labour for up to three months. If the guardian was aware that the marriage was not registered, but did not intervene to ensure that the matter was properly resolved, he, too, was considered guilty of an offence and liable to the same penalties.[24]

Amendments to the Ordinance in 1929 retained the criminal sanction for non-registration of a marriage. However, henceforth non-registration would not invalidate the marriage. Thus, a man would be liable to pay the annual tax of ten shillings for every wife after the first on unregistered as well as registered wives.[25] State officials perceived the new law as a great boon to colonial tax revenues.[26] Moreover, men married according to Christian rites, who were legally bound to remain monogamous, could now be prosecuted for bigamy if they married further wives under the Native Marriages Ordinance, whether they registered them or not.[27] Not surprisingly, this amendment was widely supported by missionaries, who constantly complained about the bigamous practices of their back-sliding converts.[28]

Despite these advances, legal contradictions continued to hamper African women's ability to fully exercise their new rights. Even as the marriage law opened

---

[22] N3/17/4/2, 'Native Marriages Ordinance, no. 15 of 1917', Promulgated 1 February 1918; CNC S138/47, NC Umtali to CNC Salisbury, 30 January 1928, No. 20/28/95/38; Steele, 'Foundations', p. 143.

[23] Peaden, *Missionary Attitudes*, p. 22; Jesuit Archives, Box 317, Native Affairs Committee of Enquiry, p. 68.

[24] N3/17/4/2, 'Native Marriages Ordinance, no. 15 of 1917', Promulgated 1 February 1918.

[25] CNC S235/432, ANC Bindura to NC Mazoe, 30 September 1946, No. 523/46.

[26] N3/17/4/1, NC Victoria to Superintendent of Natives, Victoria, 19 March 1908, No. D 626/08; CNC S138/47, NC Mazoe, to CNC Salisbury, 17 January 1928, No. 7/76/2; N3/17/4/1, 8 February 1915, 'Memorandum by His Honour the Administrator' to Executive Council and CNC, re Native Christian Marriages; CNC S138/47, NC Umtali to CNC Salisbury, 30 January 1928, No. 20/28/95/38; CNC S1542/A1/11, Assistant NC, Goromonzi to NC, Salisbury, 19 February 1935, No. 105/64/35; CNC S235/432, Acting NC Wankie to Provincial NC, Bulawayo, 17 September 1946, No. 235/232/46; CNC S235/432, Provincial NC Salisbury to CNC Salisbury, 1 November 1946, No. Z.9001.

[27] CNC S138/47, CNC Salisbury to Secretary, Law Dept., 31 May 1932, No. 2106/2703; CNC S138/47, CNC to Staff Officer, B.S.A. Police, 4 July 1930, No. Q 2844/3430/M; CNC S235/432, ANC Inyati (Matabeleland) to NC Inyati, 4 October 1946.

[28] CNC S138/150, NC, Marandellas to Superintendent of Natives, Salisbury, 30 November 1923, No. 21/331; CNC S138/47, CNC Salisbury to Secretary, Law Dept., 31 May 1932, No. 2106/2703.

avenues of opportunity for African women, their options were sharply limited by other measures. In the interests of maintaining law and order, state officials accepted the premise that African females were perpetual minors under the tutelage of a male guardian – whether it be father, uncle, husband, or son.[29] Thus, while the 1901 ordinance stipulated that a woman's consent was now required for marriage, her guardian's approval remained a prerequisite.[30] A 1917 amendment permitted a woman to appeal her guardian's decision if she believed that he had unreasonably withheld his consent. However, she was permitted to marry without his authorisation only if the administrator of the territory of Southern Rhodesia gave *his* approval.[31] In other words, her tutelage was transferred from an African guardian, deemed incompetent by the state, to a substitute European patriarch. Independent action by women was not considered a desirable alternative.

Prior to the codification of 'customary' law, a Shona woman could circumvent her guardian's objections to her marriage by eloping with her suitor. The elopement custom (*kutizira* or *Kutizisa mukumbo*) was a socially acceptable way for a young woman to marry the man of her choice, against her guardian's wishes.[32] The state, however, held rigidly to the view that Shona custom *always* required the guardian's consent in order for a marriage to be valid. Native commissioners, therefore, attempted to prevent elopement. 'I hesitate to advise [young people] to follow this custom', wrote the Salisbury native commissioner in 1930, 'as it may be considered to conflict with the spirit of [the Native Marriages Ordinance], if not the letter.'[33] African custom, as interpreted by male elders and state officials, was inviolable only so long as it did not interfere with other objectives of the colonial state.

Despite more than three decades of legislative activity, the custom of child pledging was still prevalent in the 1930s.[34] Forced marriages, while perhaps more covert, continued to be widely practiced. The emancipatory mission of the state was clearly frustrated by its contradictory goal of bolstering African male authority.

---

[29] CNC S138/47, CNC to Secretary, Law Dept., 4 July 1928, No. 4. 3108/3054; CNC S138/150, NC, Marandellas to Superintendent of Natives, Salisbury, 30 November 1923, No. 21/331.

[30] Peaden, *Missionary Attitudes*, p. 22. More than four decades after the passage of the 1901 Native Marriages Ordinance, state officials were still preoccupied with shoring up African male authority – even as that authority was being rapidly undermined by social and economic transformations. Writing in 1946, the acting native commissioner of the Shangani Reserve held that the state should give an African woman's guardian 'every support in his attempts to restrain his ward from leaving his home without his permission'. Noting African women's widespread resistance to patriarchal authority, the official decried the fact that '... at present most daughters decide who they will live with and when they will leave their parents' home'. CNC S235/432, Acting NC, Shangani Reserve to Provincial NC, Bulawayo, 9 November 1946.

[31] N3/17/4/2, 'Native Marriages Ordinance, no. 15 of 1917', Promulgated 1 February 1918; Peaden, *Missionary Attitudes*, p. 22.

[32] Interview with Miriam Zhakata, Epworth Mission, Harare, 27 January 1990, conducted by Martin Makururu.

[33] CNC 138/47, NC Salisbury to CNC Salisbury, 10 March 1930, Ref. 19/1603/30.

[34] CNC S138/47, Acting CNC, Salisbury, to All Native Department Stations in Southern Rhodesia, 'Pledging of Children: Native Marriage Ordinance', 25 January 1933, No. N.14/49/33.

State officials were well aware of the inadequacy of their legislative measures. Native commissioners' reports of the period are replete with references to girls who agreed to arranged marriages out of respect for their fathers' authority and to others who were physically coerced into accepting unwanted husbands.[35]

The public nature of the marriage ceremony, in the presence of the registering officer, was not sufficient to ensure that compulsion was not used. Writing in 1920, one native commissioner indicated that he had personal knowledge of cases 'where the woman has been threatened with violence or even death on the way to the Native Commissioner's Office'. Afraid to disobey their fathers, such women frequently told the registering officers that they had given their consent to the marriages.[36] The chief native commissioner of Mashonaland concluded that while girls often agreed to marry old men to whom they had been pledged in infancy, many did so as a result of threats by their parents. 'It is no uncommon occurrence for parents to inflict torture on their daughters to compel them to marry against their will', he wrote. 'Cases are always coming to light of native girls running away to Missions, or drifting on to Mines, rather than submit to the hardships inflicted at home to compel them to marry.'[37]

> Born near Salisbury in 1902, Elijah Marwodzi described one of the methods used when he was a young man to 'persuade' a girl to accede to a marriage. Marwodzi recalled that the girl's father would ... take a very big branch of a tree, and split it into two and tie it on her head, and screw it, clamp it ... knocking so that it increased the pain ... until the daughter says, 'Leave me alone. Release me. I plead to go.'

Under such duress the girl usually agreed to marry her appointed husband.[38]

---

[35] N3/17/4/1, Acting NC Chilimanzi to Superintendent of Natives, Victoria, 6 July 1912, No. 389/12; N3/17/4/2, vol. 2, CNC Salisbury to Secretary, Dept. of the Administrator, 18 January 1917, NMO, No. N.194/1917; N3/17/4/2, vol. 1, ANC Hartley to Acting NC Hartley, 31 December 1919, NMO, No. 304/19; CNC S138/47, NC Fort Rixon to Superintendent of Natives, Matabeleland, 17 April 1929, No. 146/199/29; N3/17/4/2, vol. 1, Acting NC Hartley to Superintendent of Natives, Salisbury, 3 January 1920, NMO, No. 2/1/20; N3/17/4/2, Acting NC Hartley to Superintendent of Natives, Salisbury, 12 January 1920, NMO, No. 3/226; N3/17/4/2, CNC Salisbury to Secretary, Dept. of the Administrator, 19 January 1920, NMO, No. A.4315/5315; CNC S138/47, NC Mazoe to CNC Salisbury, 8 December 1924, No. 116/1413/24; Jesuit Archives, Box 65/1, 'Minutes of Missionary Conference Held at St. George's, Bulawayo', June 22–27, 1920; Interview with Elijah Marwodzi, Epworth Mission, 27 January 1986, 4 February 1986.

[36] N3/17/4/2, vol. 1, Acting NC Hartley to Superintendent of Natives, Salisbury, 3 January 1920, NMO, No. 2/1/20.

[37] N3/17/4/2, vol. 2, CNC, Salisbury to Secretary, Dept. of the Administrator, 18 January 1917, NMO, No. N.194/1917; N9/1/14, Report of the Chief Native Commissioner, Mashonaland, for the Year 1911.

[38] Interview with Elijah Marwodzi, Epworth Mission, 4 February 1986.

Natives Adultery Punishment Ordinance of 1916

Having made a few tentative steps toward the emancipation of African women, in the mid-1910s the state balked. With the encouragement of native commissioners and missionaries, African women and girls were asserting new found rights and freeing themselves from the control of senior African men. Refusing to marry men to whom they had been pledged as children and running away from husbands they had married under pressure, often with a lover of their own choice, women and girls were causing a crisis of authority in the rural areas. Colonial officials accused women of taking advantage of the 'freedom of choice bestowed on them by the Native Marriage Ordinance', showing fickleness and irresponsibility and 'chang[ing] their husbands as often as they please[d]'.[39] Blaming the colonial state for having 'done away with the restraints' of indigenous laws and customs, without substituting an alternative means of control, government officials and older African men were determined to block some of the outlets created by earlier legislation.[40]

As the self-appointed trustees of African patriarchal authority, as well as the primary detractors from it, state officials considered it their duty to bring African women back under male control.[41] Wives who absconded to other men were a major focus of male discontent. Claiming that if adultery continued unchecked, African men would soon resent 'the inability of the white government to deal properly with adulterers', one colonial official concluded that the problem 'threatens to upset the peace of the native races under our control'. Unless the government supports African men in exercising 'their rights over the wives', he warned, not only the family, 'but the whole existence of a nation' may be placed in jeopardy.[42]

In an attempt to bolster the husbands' authority, the state suggested the criminalisation of adultery, with heavy penalties for both the male and female offenders. According to Attorney General C.H. Tredgold, the criminalisation of adultery was recommended almost unanimously by officials and 'natives' who had testified before the Southern Rhodesia Native Affairs Committee of Enquiry in

---

[39] N3/17/2, Assistant NC, Umtali, to Superintendent of Natives, Umtali, 12 May 1914, No. J960. Also see N3/17/2, NC, The Range, Charter, to Superintendent of Natives, Salisbury, 14 March 1923, No. 88/23.

[40] N3/17/2, Superintendent of Natives, Victoria to CNC Salisbury, 20 June 1914, No. V.611-14; For similar views see: N3/17/2, NC, Gutu to Superintendent of Natives, Victoria, 12 May 1914, No. D.G. 7/150/14; N3/17/2, Attorney General Tredgold to the Administrator, 16 August 1918, No. 0.16; N3/17/2, CNC, Salisbury to Secretary, Law Department, 15 May 1915, No. F.1228/1915; N3/17/2, NC, Mrewa to Superintendent of Natives, Salisbury 11 May 1914, No. 353/14; N9/1/13, Annual Report of the Chief Native Commissioner, Salisbury, for the year 1910, p. 1. For discussion of similar periods of leniency and backlash in Northern Rhodesia, see Chanock, 'Making Customary Law', pp. 53-67; *Law, Custom and Social Order*, pp. 145-159, 186- 216; Wright, 'Justice, Women', pp. 33-50; 'Bwanikwa', pp. 248, 261-266; Parpart, 'Sexuality and Power', pp. 115-138.

[41] N3/17/2, Acting NC, Wankie, to Superintendent of Natives, Bulawayo, 7 May 1914, No. N174/14.

[42] N3/17/2, Assistant NC, Umtali, to Superintendent of Natives, Umtali, 12 May 1914, No. J960. Also see CNC S138/150, NC, Gwanda, 27 February 1924.

1910–1911.[43] 'Natives', of course, referred only to African men, specifically older men of the highest social and political strata.[44]

In an attempt to justify the impending crackdown on African women, state officials referred to a 'mandate' bestowed upon them by African men. Writing in 1913, the chief native commissioner in Salisbury noted that throughout Mashonaland:

> At almost every meeting of Chiefs held by me the chief topic of conversation is in regard to their wives and the way they run off with other men (chiefly aliens on mines) with impunity. The Chiefs are very bitter on the subject and would welcome an amendment to the [Native Marriages] Ordinance placing some restraint on their wives running away as they do.[45]

Another official referred to the 'continual outcry' for the criminalisation of adultery from 'the more influential portion of the community'. He maintained that the present law 'does not meet the most urgent claims of the older and middle aged men' — the primary constituents of the Native Department and those whose discontent was to be most assiduously avoided.[46]

As a 'result of continuous representations made by Chiefs, Headmen, Heads of Kraals and responsible natives throughout the country', the Natives Adultery Punishment Ordinance was enacted in 1916.[47] The new law rendered adultery between an African man and a married African woman a criminal offence punishable by a fine of £100 — several times the annual wage of African male workers — or one year's imprisonment with hard labour. Both partners were subject to the penalty.[48] A double standard remained. Married African men could continue to have sexual intercourse with as many unmarried African women as they

---

[43] N3/17/2, C.H. Tredgold, Attorney General. 'Minute by Mr. Tredgold, Attorney General of Southern Rhodesia', 27 August 1914.

[44] Peter Nielson, the assistant native commissioner of Shabani, held a view of female emancipation that differed markedly from that of the majority of his colleagues. While the Superintendent of Natives at Gwelo claimed that the Natives Adultery Punishment Ordinance 'was enacted at the unanimous request of the Natives of this country', Nielson wrote, '... he overlooks the fact that the women, who form, perhaps, more than half of the population, were not directly consulted.' Nielson anticipated the objection 'that Native women have no say in the shaping of their own destiny; that they have always been forced to obey the law laid down by the strong sex', but he felt it was his duty 'to see that the woman's interests are also taken into account.' N3/17/2, Peter Nielson, ANC Shabani, to CNC Salisbury 9 May 1923.

[45] N/17/4/1, CNC to Secretary, Department of the Administrator, 9 May 1913, No. 25/1121/13.

[46] N3/17/2, NC, Gutu, to Superintendent of Natives, Fort Victoria, 12 May 1914, No. D.G.7/150/14. Also see: N3/17/2, Assistant NC, Umtali, to Superintendent of Natives, Umtali, 12 May 1914, No. J960; N3/17/2, NC, Chilimanzi to Superintendent of Natives, Victoria, 8 May 1914, No. 2/331/14.

[47] N3/17/2, NC, Mtoko, to Superintendent of Natives, Salisbury, 12 March 1923, No. 26/23.

[48] N3/17/2, NC, Hartley to Superintendent of Natives, Salisbury, 13 March 1923; CNC S235/429–31, Alfred Drew, 'The Black and White Cohabitation Problem', in *Drew's Articles on Native Affairs, Southern Rhodesia*, Part II, no. 26, ca. 1921, pp. 10, 13.

chose, without fear of criminal penalty.[49] European men could have sex with African woman of any marital status without being liable to charges of adultery, despite the pleas of African elders that European males be included within the law.[50]

Signing the bill into law at the height of a labour crisis on European farms and mines, state advocates of the bill exposed an interesting intersection of gender ideology and economic objectives. In the course of the debate preceding enactment, the native commissioner of Mtoko wrote:

> Adultery is becoming more and more frequent amongst Natives, and in almost all cases the women concerned are the wives of absentees at work.[51]

Rather than attributing the increase in adultery to the migratory labour system and the consequent disruption in family life, the official asserted that the problem lay in the fact that too few men were going out to work. The 'more vicious and debauched characters' who spent 'their lives in idleness in their kraals' were committing adultery with the wives left behind by the migrant labourers. The fear that they would lose their wives made African men hesitant to seek wage employment. However, if adultery were made a criminal offence, and men could be assured of their wives' fidelity in their absence, the official concluded, 'there would be a marked improvement in the number of males turning out to work'.[52] In the interests of economic development and the financial well-being of the territory, the sexual practices of African women had to be brought firmly under control.[53]

---

[49] N3/17/2, Peter Nielson, ANC Shabani, to CNC Salisbury 9 May 1923.

[50] R. Kent Rasmussen, *Historical Dictionary of Rhodesia/Zimbabwe*, African Historical Dictionaries, no. 18 (Metuchen, N.J., 1979), p. 350; Dane Kennedy, *Islands of White: Settler Society and Culture in Kenya and Southern Rhodesia, 1890–1939* (Durham: Duke University Press, 1987), pp. 177, 242 n. 39; Philip Mason, *The Birth of a Dilemma: The Conquest and Settlement of Rhodesia* (London: Oxford University Press, 1958), pp. 240–242, 246–247, 251; Steele, 'Foundations', pp. 124–125, 499; CNC S235/429-31, Drew, 'Black and White', pp. 10–13.

[51] N3/17/2, Acting NC, Mtoko, to Superintendent of Natives, Salisbury, 12 May 1914, No. C68/14.

[52] N3/17/2, Acting NC, Mtoko to Superintendent of Natives, Salisbury, 12 May 1914, No. C 68/14. For similar statements in support of criminalisation see: N3/17/2, NC, Marandellas, to Superintendent of Natives, Salisbury, 4 May 1914, No. 1/266/14; N3/17/2, NC, Goromonzi, to Superintendent of Natives, Salisbury, 8 May 1914, No. S.N.354/14; N3/17/2, C.H.Tredgold Attorney General, 'Minute by Mr. Tredgold, Attorney General of Southern Rhodesia', 27 August 1914; N3/17/4/1, CNC, Salisbury, to Secretary, Department of the Administrator, 9 May 1913, No. 25/1121/13; N3/17/2, Acting NC, Wankie, to Superintendent of Natives, Bulawayo, 7 May 1914, No. N174/14; N3/17/2, NC, Gutu, to Superintendent of Natives, Fort Victoria, 12 May 1914, No. D.G.7/150/14.

[53] The 'immorality' of African women, rather than the migratory labour system, was frequently blamed for the fragility of African families. In 1914, the acting native commissioner of Wankie noted that:

> Even to the casual observer it must be evident that the family life of the Natives is rapidly being undermined. No lasting progress or development is therefore possible until we secure a healthier family and social life for the Natives.

He recommended the criminalisation of adultery for 'moral persuasion has no effect in this instance, last of all on a defiant and obstinate Native woman, often a slave to gross passion,

Debate Over Bridewealth

The state's ambivalent attitude toward African marriage customs and its periodic need to support the interests of older men, on the one hand, and younger men, on the other, is reflected in the contradictory legislation concerning bridewealth transactions. During the pre-colonial period, the transfer of bridewealth or marriage payments (*lobola*, *rovoro*, or *roora*) from the kin of the husband to the kin of the wife represented the creation of a social bond between two lineages, and the transfer of the woman's productive and reproductive capacities from her kin to that of her husband and his kin. As a result of the bridewealth transaction, the woman was expected to labour for her husband and his relatives rather than her own; all children produced from the union belonged to her husband's rather than her patrilineage. The transfer of marriage gifts, which could include blankets, baskets of grain, hoes, goats, or cattle, constituted a symbolic social act. Yet it was also a means of petty accumulation in which subordinate women and material goods changed hands.[54]

After the onset of European occupation and the introduction of a cash economy, bridewealth became increasingly commoditised. As cattle gained in productive value and young men entered wage employment, older men began to demand dramatically inflated bridewealth payments, composed primarily of cattle and cash.[55] Gradually, bridewealth degenerated into a fundamentally commercial transaction in which wealth was transferred between generations of males, and women were the bartered goods.[56] Bridewealth had become an important means of redistributing societal

---

deaf to all reason.' NAZ, N3/17/2, Acting Native Commissioner, Wankie to Superintendent of Natives, Bulawayo, 7 May 1914, No. N174/14. For a similar view, see N3/17/2, Assistant Native Commissioner, Umtali to Superintendent of Natives, Umtali, 12 May 1914, No. J 960.

[54] For evidence of early colonial bridewealth offerings in the Goromonzi District, see Native Commissioner's Civil Cases, NSL 1/1/1, 7 June 1900, Masanaweduno versus Tshibekeshwa; 10 September 1900, Kuremba versus Tshigitshi; 31 August 1900, Vatayemura versus Subani; 9 June 1900, Mwidza versus Maziya; 7 May 1900, Madzima versus Shikwana; 1 June 1901, Tshirunga versus Kaseke; 4 May 1900, Kaduku versus Zewere. For a discussion of the social, symbolic, and material significance of bridewealth, see Holleman, *Shona Customary Law*, pp. 33, 148–156; Claude Levi-Strauss, *The Elementary Structures of Kinship* (Boston, 1969), p. 115; Gayle Rubin, 'The Traffic in Women; Notes on the 'Political Economy' of Sex', in *Toward an Anthropology of Women*, ed. Rayna Rapp Reiter (New York, 1975), pp. 171–177.

[55] For evidence of inflating bridewealth demands in the Goromonzi District, see Native Commissioner's Civil Cases, NSL 1/1/1, 7 June 1900, Masanaweduno versus Tshibekeshwa; 10 September 1900, Kuremba versus Tshigitshi; 31 August 1900, Vatayemura versus Subani; 9 June 1900, Mwidza versus Maziya; 7 May 1900, Madzima versus Shikwana; 1 June 1901, Tshirunga versus Kaseke; 4 May 1900, Kaduku versus Zewere; Case No. 313, ca. January 1904, N'Gwendere versus Gave; 17 October 1904, M'swera versus M'dghariwa; 22 October 1903, Gompi versus Mynyenga; 12 November 1903, Chahoonza versus Gwebera. Also see: CNC S138/47, Acting Assistant NC, Goromonzi to NC, Salisbury, 5 September 1929, No. 347/502/29; S1542/N2 (E–G), 'Minutes of the Native Board Meeting, Goromonzi District', 4 February 1932, p. 9; S1542/A1/11, Assistant NC, Goromonzi to NC, Salisbury, 19 February 1935, No. 105/64/35; Holleman, *Shona Customary Law*, pp. 161–165.

[56] For a discussion of the degeneration of bridewealth into a commercial transaction, see CNC S138/150, NC, Mrewa to Superintendent of Natives, Salisbury, 10 March 1924; CNC S138/47, NC, Mrewa to CNC, Salisbury, 14 April 1932, No. 3/106/32 M; CNC S138/150, NC, Marandellas to Superintendent of Natives, Salisbury, 30 November 1923, No. 21/331; CNC

resources, and one of the few ways in which older men could gain access to the cash wages of younger ones.[57] The practice which European observers described as bride buying, was the product of both African custom and European intervention in African society.

Colonial officials and missionaries manifested a distinctly equivocal attitude toward bridewealth. They frequently decried the practice as a savage one that needed to be stamped out, if only gradually. They worried that the greed of older men had caused bride 'prices' to inflate far beyond the means of most young men, creating a potential for social unrest. Yet, they were unwilling to undermine the authority and economic well-being of senior men, and they welcomed the supposed restraining influence of bridewealth on the sexual practices and mobility of African women. One colonial official described bridewealth as 'the only corrective to a woman's tendency to go wrong'. If a woman deserted her husband, he explained, her guardian would have to return the substantial bridewealth, causing severe financial distress to the woman's relations. Since a loyal daughter would want to avoid such a situation at all costs, she would undoubtedly remain with her husband and refrain from extra-marital affairs.[58]

S235/514, Annual Report, Goromonzi District, 1935, pp. 27–28; S1542/A1/11, Assistant NC, Goromonzi to NC, Salisbury, 19 February 1935, No. 105/64/35; S1542/A1/11. CNC, Salisbury to NC, Salisbury, 28 February 1935, No. E.736/A1/4; Jesuit Archives, Box 32, Henry Quin, S.J., St. Joseph's Mission, Umvuma, 'Letters and Documents', 27 October 1924; R. Sykes, S.J., 'Hindrances to Native Conversions in South Africa', *Zambesi Mission Record* 2, 16 (April 1902), p. 55.

[57] For evidence that bridewealth became a means by which elderly men consciously acquired cash from younger wage earners, see CNC S138/47, ANC, Goromonzi to NC, Salisbury, 10 February 1932, No. 14/10/32; CNC S138/47, Assistant NC, Buhera to NC, The Range, Enkeldoorn, 3 March 1932, No. 25/32; CNC S138/47, NC, The Range, Enkeldoorn to CNC, Salisbury, 20 April 1932; CNC S138/47, NC, Salisbury to CNC, Salisbury, 19 March 1923, No. 88/90/32; S1542/A1/11, NC, Salisbury to CNC, Salisbury, 26 February 1935, No. 151/31/35. For an in-depth analysis of this process in neighbouring Lesotho, see Colin Murray, 'Marital Strategy in Lesotho: The Redistribution of Migrant Earnings', *African Studies* 35, 2 (1976), pp. 99–121; 'High Bridewealth, Migrant Labour and the Position of Women in Lesotho', *Journal of African Law* 21, 1 (1977), pp. 79–96.

[58] CNC S235/475, Federation of Women's Institutes of Southern Rhodesia, 'Report of the Standing Committee on Domestic Service, July 1930', Testimony of E.R. Morkel, p. 48; Also see: CNC S138/47, NC, Salisbury to CNC, Salisbury, 19 March 1932, No. 8118/90/32; CNC S138/47, NC, Wankie to Superintendent of Natives, Bulawayo, 10 September 1930, No. 630/30; CNC S138/150, Assistant NC, Melsetter to Superintendent of Natives, Umtali, 7 March 1924, No. 70/225/24.

Interestingly, other officials claimed that inflated bridewealth demands had precisely the opposite effect. 'Because of the prohibitive number of cattle demanded', young men could not afford to marry, claimed the chief native commissioner of Mashonaland. As a result, young men and women were entering into sexual relationships outside of marriage, leading to an increase in immorality.

While acknowledging the impoverished state of the young men, state officials tended to blame women for the immoral state of affairs. Thus, the native commissioner of Zaka complained about 'the alarmingly increasing habit of young girls flouting parental authority and going to some lover who is unable to pay large sums, due to his youth and poverty.' Similarly, the native commissioner of Belingwe noted that the proposal to place a legal limitation on *lobola* 'is put forward as a remedy for the laxity of the morals of native females.'

Older men, who had long since paid their own bridewealth and now looked forward to receiving an even greater amount for their daughters, tended to concur with this opinion. The Native Department was careful to seek their advice. In the 1930s, advisory committees consisting of chiefs, headmen, and elders were instituted in each of the Southern Rhodesian rural districts. Intended as state-controlled safety valves for African discontent, countering the influence of independent African political organisations, the native boards served as forums for complaints concerning bridewealth transactions, marital disputes, and women who were increasingly escaping the control of older African men.[59]

In 1932, the assistant native commissioner of the Goromonzi District met with the local native board to discuss the possibility of placing a ceiling on *lobola* payments. Reporting to his superior in Salisbury, the official indicated that senior African men in Goromonzi felt that:

> ... nowadays women were fickle enough anyhow, but ... if *lobola* was reduced to a small amount there would be even less hold on them, as there was no doubt that the average girl, if tempted to leave her husband for no real cause, was at the moment influenced to a certain extent by the fact that her father had received a large amount of *lobola* for her which he would find difficult to refund.[60]

Muzonde, an elder present at the meeting, remarked that high bridewealth payments made women stay with their husbands, even if the husbands were elderly men. 'Most girls do not feel like giving much trouble to their fathers in refunding the *lobola*, [and] therefore will stick on to their husbands', he claimed. He also warned, 'A native woman [could] easily leave her husband if *lobola* paid for her is only one goat. We believe our daughters stick to their husband on account of much *lobola* paid for them.'[61] The assistant native commissioner heartily endorsed this view. 'Native women are daily becoming more intractable and running away to lovers in Salisbury and on the farms', he complained. 'If a larger amount of *lobola* than used to be customary has some effect in checking the growing laxity of morals it is doing some good.'[62]

CNC S235/432, CNC, Salisbury to Secretary to the Premier (Native Affairs), 6 August 1930, No. R.3258/30; CNC S138/47, NC, Zaka to CNC, Salisbury, 9 February 1932, No. Za.50/32; CNC S138/47, NC, Belingwe to Superintendent of Natives, Bulawayo, 17 December 1930, No. 555/30. Also see S1542/A1/11, Assistant NC, Goromonzi to NC, Salisbury, 19 February 1935, No. 105/64/35; Jesuit Archives, Box 100/4, F.J. Richartz, S.J. to R. Sykes, S.J., 28 June 1913.

[59] Steele, 'Foundations', pp. 178–179; Phimister, *Economic and Social History*, p. 149.

[60] CNC S138/47, Assistant NC, Goromonzi, to NC, Salisbury, 10 February 1932, No. 14/10/32. African elders in Northern Rhodesia embarked upon a similar pattern of inflating bridewealth payments in order to keep dissatisfied women from leaving their husbands. See Parpart, 'Sexuality and Power', p. 120; 'Class and Gender', p. 144; Chanock, *Law, Custom and Social Order*, pp. 178–181.

[61] CNC S1542/N2–G, Minutes of the Meeting of the Native Board, Goromonzi District, 4 February 1932, pp. 7–8.

[62] CNC S138/47, Assistant NC, Goromonzi, to NC, Salisbury, 10 February 1932, No. 14/10/32.

New consumer and cash needs resulting from European intervention in African society had further stimulated bridewealth demands. Muzonde explained that:

> Most people in the reserves do not want *lobola* to be limited, because there is a lot of trouble in bringing up a girl to a marriageable age. The parents of the girls spent a lot of money in clothes, and other things, therefore they expect to get something in return ... .People in [the] reserves depend on *lobola* paid for their daughters to pay taxes, debts, etc. and to take more wives.[63]

Another elder added that, 'In old days children wore skins. But today they wear expensive clothes. Parents also spend money on their education.' It was therefore not unreasonable that the 'parents want something in return for bringing up these girls'.[64]

Ironically, while missionaries were the most vocal detractors of the bridewealth custom, their practices were partly responsible for bridewealth inflation.[65] Graduates of mission schools, who had learned to read and write and had acquired such skills as carpentry, shoemaking, masonry, and building, tended to earn higher wages than other men. Their high wages resulted in inflated bridewealth demands by business-minded fathers. Christian families had also generated new material and financial needs to match their 'civilised' life style: clothing, school fees, different standards of accommodations, European-made agricultural equipment, and a variety of consumer goods. Thus, rather than helping to stamp out the bridewealth custom, mission stations had indirectly encouraged its perpetuation.[66]

While older African men opposed legislation imposing limits on the amount of *lobola* that could be transferred, younger men naturally favoured such laws.[67] The

---

[63] CNC S1542/N2-G, Minutes of the Native Board, 4 February 1932, pp. 4-5.

[64] CNC S1542/N2-G, Minutes of the Native Board, 4 February 1932, pp. 7. Also see CNC S138/47, Assistant NC, Goromonzi to NC, Salisbury, 10 February 1932, No. 14/10/32.

[65] For missionaries' criticisms, see: Jesuit Archives, Box 100/4, F.J. Richartz, S.J. to R. Sykes, S.J., 28 June 1913; CNC S235/432, Southern Rhodesia Missionary Conference, 1930, Resolution Two; H. Cripps, 'Should *Lobola* Be Restricted by Legislation?' *NADA*, 24 (1947), pp. 41-47; Steele, 'Foundations', pp. 143-144.

[66] Describing the origin of bridewealth inflation, one native commissioner wrote in 1932 that:

> the increased payments had their origin at Epworth Mission and Chishawasha, the former in particular. In those [areas] the natives were earning good wages and were affluent. It was the non-indigenous element such as Zambezia and northern natives who courted the Mission girls. Parents objected to them as being strangers but on being offered up to 20 [pounds] as *Rutsambo* (seek consent) they were tempted and agreed. As girls became scarcer the suitors went further afield and eventually penetrated into remoter districts.

(CNC S138/47, NC, The Range, Enkeldoorn to CNC, Salisbury, 20 April 1932.) Also see CNC S138/47, NC, The Range, Enkeldoorn to CNC, Salisbury, 7 October 1930, No. 88/347/30.

[67] See, for instance, CNC S138/47, NC, Marandellas to CNC, Salisbury, 2 March 1932, No. 160/32; CNC S138/47, NC, Umtali to CNC, Salisbury, 27 February 1932, No. D.9/32; CNC S1542/N2-G, Minutes of the Native Board, 4 February 1932, p. 4. Describing the cyclical nature of male opinion on bridewealth prices, one official commented that in the Chiweshe Reserve, 'the young men, at present of marriageable age, are in favour of a reduction of *lobola* whereas their elders are strongly opposed to any such reduction. No doubt the former will be of the same opinion as their elders now are when they reach their age and are responsible for

state vacillated on the issue. The Native Marriages Ordinance of 1901 limited the amount of *lobola* to four head of cattle for the daughter of a commoner and five head for that of a chief, or cash at the rate of five pounds per head of cattle.[68] Ten years later, the Native Affairs Committee of Enquiry claimed that this legislation was intended to prevent a rich suitor from currying favour with a woman's guardian, thus interfering with her freedom of choice. However, because the law was frequently evaded and virtually impossible to enforce, the Committee recommended that the limitation should be abrogated.[69] The perpetuation of unenforceable legislation would not only promote social disorder, it would undermine African respect for the law.

Under pressure from senior African men, and upon the recommendation of the Native Affairs Committee of Enquiry, the legal limitation on *lobola* was abolished in the amended Native Marriages Ordinance of 1912.[70] Debate on the issue, however, continued throughout the colonial period.

Women's Resistance to Patriarchal Authority

As restrictive as their choices may have been, women took advantage of openings created by legislation promulgated during the first three decades of colonial rule. Native commissioners frequently commented on African women's awareness of their new found rights and their tendency to act upon them. 'The status of native women has advanced very considerably since the occupation', wrote one colonial official in 1924. 'Most native women are well aware that they cannot legally be forced into marriage against their will and refusals are far from uncommon.'[71] Another official wrote that girls often appeared before the registering officer, supposedly to give their consent to a union, but instead, 'stating they are being forced into an undesirable marriage'.[72]

---

lobola for their own sons.' CNC S138/47, NC, Amanders to CNC, Salisbury, 13 April 1932, No. 809/32.

[68] Jesuit Archives, Box 317, Native Affairs Committee of Enquiry, p. 68; CNC S235/432, ANC Inyati (Matabeleland) to NC Inyati, 4 October 1946; Henri Rolin, *Rolin's Rhodesia*, trans. Deborah Kirkwood (Bulawayo, 1978), p. 134.

[69] Jesuit Archives, Box 317, Native Affairs Committee of Enquiry, p. 68. For non-observance of the legal limits see CNC S138/47, NC, The Range, Enkeldoorn to CNC, Salisbury, 20 April 1932. In a similar vein, the native commissioner of Mrewa wrote in 1924 that the number of cattle demanded for *lobola* was continually increasing, and that 'in many cases the girl is "sold" to the highest bidder'. He explained that while the girl was not literally purchased, 'the number of cattle offered and the amount of cash accompanying them carries a great deal of weight with the parents of the girl.' CNC S138/150, NC, Mrewa to Superintendent of Natives, Salisbury, 10 March 1924. Also see Jesuit Archives, Box 100/4, F.J. Richartz, S.J. to R. Sykes, S.J., 28 June 1913.

[70] N3/17/4/1, NC Mazoe to CNC Salisbury 24 February 1913; CNC S138/150, NC Chipinga to Superintendent of Natives, Umtali, 5 March 1924, No. 34/237/24; Rolin, *Rolin's Rhodesia*, p. 134.

[71] CNC S138/150, NC Inyanga, 7 March 1924.

[72] CNC S138/150, NC Chipinga to Superintendent of Natives, Umtali, 5 March 1924, No. 34/237/24. Also see: NC S138/47, NC Mazoe, to CNC Salisbury, 5 April 1929, No.

The extent of women's rebellion against patriarchal authority was particularly notable in the Goromonzi district on the eastern edge of Salisbury. Between October 1899 and February 1905, the native commissioner heard 345 civil cases. Of this total, 95 cases pertained to girls who refused to marry men who had paid bridewealth for them, while 65 concerned wives who had actually runaway. Thus, nearly half the civil cases heard by the state during this period involved men attempting to obtain the return of their recalcitrant wives.[73]

Prior to the colonial period, if a woman ran away, her husband was much more likely to petition for her return — even over the course of several years — than attempt to get his bridewealth back. Generally, he had no interest in severing the ties between his wife's lineage and his own, which the return of bridewealth was bound to do.[74] European officials frowned upon the custom of accepting errant wives back into the fold, considering the practice morally offensive, and encouraged African men to divorce wives who had been unfaithful to them.

European intervention had a major impact on the type of domestic litigation that occurred once colonial rule was firmly established. Whereas in the early years of European occupation African men were primarily concerned with the return of their wives, by the 1930s they were seeking dissolution of their marriages, along with damage payments, return of bridewealth, and child custody. Thus, the vast majority of cases heard by the Goromonzi native commissioner during the 1930s involved divorce petitions by abandoned husbands. Of the 171 cases heard between July 1931 and July 1939, 128, or 75 per cent, were petitions for divorce, most brought by husbands who accused their wives of refusing to have sex with them, prostitution, and adultery. In only fourteen cases did husbands plead for the return of their runaway wives.[75]

Vehemently opposed to child pledging and forced marriages, missionaries encouraged young girls to seek refuge at the missions where they were able to work and go to school. Many even built hostels to accommodate the numerous runaways.[76] Girls and women frequently requested that missionaries intervene on

---

145/436/29; CNC S138/47, CNC, Gwelo to Superintendent of Natives Bulawayo, 13 August 1929; CNC S138/47, Acting NC Inyanga to CNC Salisbury, 4 April 1929, No. 17/181/29; 'Pledging of Children, Section 11(2), NM Ordinance 15 of 1917'; CNC S138/47, NC the Range, to CNC Salisbury, 9 April 1929, No. 222/152/29; CNC S138/47, ANC, Mtetengwe, to NC Gwanda, 18 April 1929, No. 21C29.

[73] NSL 1/1/1, Civil Cases, Goromonzi District, October 1899– February 1905.

[74] Chanock, 'Making Customary Law', pp. 56–58, 64–65.

[75] S370, Civil Cases, Goromonzi District, July 1931–July 1939. Also see: N3/17/2, NC, Rusapi to Superintendent of Natives, Umtali, 13 March 1923, No. 218/21/23. Chanock and Mbilinyi found similar trends in Northern Rhodesia and Tanganyika. Chanock, 'Making Customary Law', pp. 64–65; Mbilinyi, 'Runaway Wives', pp. 8, 15.

[76] Peaden, *Missionary Attitudes*, p. 22; Ranger, 'Women in Politics', pp. 7–9; Kersten England, 'A Political Economy of Black Female Labour in Zimbabwe, 1900–1980', B.A. thesis, University of Manchester, 1982, pp. 32–33; Interview with Emelda Madamombe, Seke Communal Lands, 26 January 1986; Interview with Elijah Marwodzi, Epworth Mission, 27 January and 4 February 1986; CNC S138/47, NC the Range, to CNC Salisbury, 9 April 1929, No. 222/152/29.

their behalf, with both their fathers and colonial officials.[77] 'Girls had more choice ... as more and more European influence permeated into these areas', asserted Lawrence Vambe, who was born at the Jesuit-run Chishawasha Mission in 1918. 'If they were forced to marry somebody they didn't want', he said,

> ... they ran to the mission, or appealed to the Native Commissioner or went into the towns, simply because they didn't want to [be] forced to get married to anybody they didn't love.[78]

Elijah Marwodzi, who grew up on a Wesleyan Methodist mission near Salisbury, recalled that the Jesuit fathers and Dominican sisters at Chishawasha were particularly anxious to receive runaways, hoping they could recruit them as nuns.[79] The Wesleyan Methodist Church also opened its doors to female runaways. According to Marwodzi, Wesleyan Methodist missionaries appealed to native commissioners on behalf of girls who were being forced into unwanted marriages, resulting in their fathers' arrest. Marwodzi remembered many men who were punished for violating the Native Marriages Ordinance. 'The government sent the police investigating in the villages, and they would find a lot of them ... .And those fathers and the son-in-laws were put in jail for about five or six months.'[80]

African teachers also assisted girls intent upon avoiding arranged marriages. Chief Seki refused to allow Wesleyan Methodist missionaries to establish a school near his village because, as he explained to one missionary, 'When I beat my wives they will run to the teacher for protection'.[81] Elijah Marwodzi's father, one of the first African evangelists in the Southern Rhodesian Wesleyan Methodist Church, taught near Salisbury during the first two decades of the twentieth century. Marwodzi recalled that his father was frequently called upon to help girls escape unwanted marriages:

> There were girls coming to school ... Some of them had been pledged as babies ... I know of Mathilda, Adelene, Agita, Mapumarodza, whose fathers had tried to force them [into arranged marriages]. My father had to help them, and to advise them where to go so that they may be released. My father consulted Reverend John White about it. And the fathers were counselled by the [native] commissioner not to force any daughter ... to be married. I can tell you many girls I knew.[82]

---

[77] CNC S138/47, Acting NC Inyanga to CNC Salisbury, 4 April 1929. No. 17/181/29: 'Pledging of Children, Section 11(2), NM Ordinance 15 of 1917'; A Dominican Sister, *In God's White-Robed Army; The Chronicle of the Dominican Sisters in Rhodesia, 1890– 1934* (Cape Town: Maskew Miller, Ltd., ca. 1947), p. 255; Interview with Elijah Marwodzi, Epworth Mission, 27 January and 4 February 1986.

[78] Interview with Lawrence Vambe, Harare, August 20, 1985.

[79] Interview with Elijah Marwodzi, Epworth Mission, 27 January 1986.

[80] Interview with Elijah Marwodzi, Epworth Mission, 27 January and 4 February 1986.

[81] As quoted in Wesleyan Methodist Missionary Society (WMMS), Box 828, Rev. Latimer P. Hardaker, Epworth to Miss Bradford, 4 March 1924; Rev. Latimer P. Hardaker, 'Epworth Circuit Report', 1923, p. 7.

[82] Interview with Elijah Marwodzi, Epworth Mission, 27 January 1986.

The missionaries gave the girls letters explaining their situation to present to the native commissioner, 'And of course, the [native] commissioner took drastic steps against the father', Marwodzi recalled.[83]

Reflecting on her own experience as a runaway, Emelda Madamombe gave the following account. Born in Chief Seki's reserve on the outskirts of Salisbury in 1918, Madamombe and her three sisters were raised by an elder brother who pledged them all in marriage. Madamombe's prospective husband was 'a very old man who already had two wives'. Anxious to make good his pledge and collect the bridewealth, Madamombe's brother put an end to her schooling and told her to prepare for marriage. Having learned from local villagers that the government had outlawed the pledging of young girls, Madamombe's sisters ran away and married other men, while she absconded to Chishawasha Mission where she enrolled in school. At the mission station she could both free herself from an unwanted marriage, particularly hateful to her because it was polygamous, and continue her education. 'That is the reason I ran away to Chishawasha and refused to marry the man he had chosen for me', she explained.[84]

While missionaries encouraged female rebellion against forced marriages and polygamy, like state officials they feared the consequences of free-thinking economically independent African women unfettered by patriarchal controls. Thus, they aimed to transfer authority over women from African male guardians, particularly non-Christians, to European missionaries. Unencumbered by the responsibility of maintaining the system of indirect rule, missionaries were more willing to risk antagonising senior African men than were state officials.

Throughout Southern Rhodesia, mission stations offered refuge to African women and girls fleeing forced and polygamous marriages or other forms of ill treatment.[85] From the early years of colonial occupation through the 1930s, women and girls took advantage of this new opening. In growing numbers they chose to submit to the strict disciplinary codes of puritanical Christians, rather than remain in even less tolerable circumstances at home.[86]

---

[83] Interview with Elijah Marwodzi, Epworth Mission, 4 February 1986.

[84] Interview with Emelda Madamombe, Seke Communal Lands, 26 January 1986.

[85] Jesuit Archives, Box 100/1, 'African Visitors etc. at Chishawasha, 1892–3', from Father Rea's manuscript notes; Box 98, Letter Book, Father F.J. Richartz to Native Commissioner Campbell, 1 November 1897.

[86] Missionary and colonial records are replete with cases of girls seeking refuge at missions to avoid forced marriages, and occasionally, to further their education. At St. Paul's Mission, Musami, 45 miles northwest of Salisbury, a Dominican Sister recalled that by 1926, the convent had become 'a place of refuge for girls whose pagan parents insisted on their marrying a pagan youth, and in some places even an old man.' Dominican, *White-Robed Army*, pp. 232, 215, 233. Also see: Ranger, 'Women in Politics', pp. 7–9; 'Chishawasha Notes', *Zambesi Mission Record* 1, 4 (May 1899), p. 118; Jesuit Archives, Box 305, Southern Rhodesia, *Report of the Commission Appointed to Enquire into the Matter of Native Education in all its Bearings on the Colony of Southern Rhodesia* (Salisbury: Government Printer, 1925), p. 68; CNC S138/47, NC, Rusapi to CNC, Salisbury, 5 February 1927, No. 317; Interviews with: Elizabeth Sande, Chishawasha Mission, 18 December 1985; Elijah Marwodzi, Epworth Mission, 27 January 1986; Hamundidi Mhindurwa and Emelda Madamombe, Seke Communal Lands, 26 January 1986; Lawrence Vambe, Harare, August 20, 1985.

Life at the mission stations did not mean female emancipation, but the exchange of African for European patriarchal authority. Missionaries intervened into the most intimate aspects of the refugees' daily lives, monitoring their sexual and marital practices and forcing them to leave the mission if they failed to comply with regulations. Jesuit and Wesleyan Methodist missionaries, for instance, required that newcomers agree to marry monogamously and only according to Christian rites. They banned premarital sex and the custom of elopement, which would have entailed sexual relations before a church wedding. Any woman who became pregnant out of wedlock, who married according to local custom rather than Christian rites, or who ran away with a man who was not her husband was summarily expelled from the mission.[87]

Mission women were required to work hard. At Chishawasha, women and girls made and maintained mission roads. They weeded and harvested crops on the mission farm, as well as taking care of their own fields.[88] Nonetheless, for many, such a life was preferable to the one they had abandoned. They could go to school; they would not be forced to marry against their will, and they could marry without the consent of their guardians.[89]

The free spaces provided by the missions became an early source of tension between missionaries and colonial officials.[90] In an attempt to shore up African male authority, the Native Affairs Committee of Enquiry (1910–1911) advised that mission stations be prohibited from giving refuge to any woman or girl who did not have her guardian's permission to be there, a recommendation that later became state law.[91] Throughout the colonial period, missionaries challenged this law through their actions, continuing to give sanctuary to female refugees.[92]

---

[87] Lawrence Vambe, *An Ill-Fated People: Zimbabwe Before and After Rhodes* (Pittsburgh, 1972), pp. 3–14; Interviews at Chishawasha Mission (Jesuit) on 12 December 1985: Sophia Chitia; Peter Gotora; Evangelista Mazhindu; Theresa and Anthony Tapfumanei; on 14 December 1985: Angela Munemo; Alfonsi Mashonganyika; on 18 December 1985: Mutota Muzanenhamo; Joseph and Stanislaus Ngandu; Anastasi Nyamayaro and Elizabeth Mahungo; Elizabeth Sande; on 21 December 1985: Veronica Chigomo; on 29 December 1985: Juliana Dzangare; Mariana Pedzi Inyanga; on 4 January 1986: Nicholas Mbofana. Interviews at Epworth Mission (Wesleyan Methodist): Elijah Marwodzi and Rhoda Maruva, 27 January 1986; AOH/72, Interview with Isaac Chiremba, Epworth Mission, Harare, 29 October 1981, p. 41.

[88] Interviews at Chishawasha: Mission Elizabeth Mbofana, 4 January 1986; Eve Dembetembe, 23 November 1985.

[89] Peaden, *Missionary Attitudes*, p. 22; Ranger, 'Women in Politics', p. 15; Jesuit Archives, Box 317, Native Affairs Committee of Enquiry, par.6.42.

[90] Peaden, *Missionary Attitudes*, p. 24; England, 'Political Economy', p. 35.

[91] Jesuit Archives, Box 317, Native Affairs Committee of Enquiry, p. 68; Francis C. Barr, S.J., *Archbishop Aston Chichester, 1879–1962. A Memoir* (Gwelo, 1978), p. 23; Ranger, 'Women in Politics', p. 16; Dominican, *White-Robed Army*, p. 243.

[92] Jesuit Archives, Box 100/1, 'African Visitors at Chishawasha, 1892-3'; Jesuit Archives, Box 98, Letter Book, Father F.J. Richartz to NC Campbell, 1 November 1897; Jesuit Archives, Box 317, Native Affairs Committee of Enquiry, par. 6.42; Jesuit Archives, Box 305, Native Education Commission, p. 68; WMMS, Box 828, Rev. Latimer P. Hardaker, Epworth to Miss Bradford, 4 March 1924; Rev. Latimer P. Hardaker, 'Epworth Circuit Report', 1923, p. 7; Ranger, 'Women in Politics', pp. 7–9; England, 'Political Economy', 32; Peaden, *Missionary Attitudes*, pp. 24–27; Barr, *Archbishop*, pp. 23–29; Dominican, *White-Robed*, pp. 189, 232–233; Interviews with: Father Francis Barr, S.J., Harare, 5 February 1986; Anastasi Nyamayaro,

Control Over Women's Mobility

In spite of the passage of laws aimed at reasserting patriarchal control over African women's sexuality, the situation did not improve — insofar as African men were concerned. Nearly two decades after the passage of the act, African men in the rural areas were still complaining to the government that their women had broken the bonds of male authority. They were running away to farms, towns, mining compounds, and mission stations, taking husbands of their own choosing, even becoming prostitutes. According to the interpretation of one native commissioner:

> ... the women are out of domestic control, and this is due, without question, to the fact that the women, finding themselves 'free' do not know what to do with their freedom.[93]

The facility with which African girls and women gained access to 'motor lorries' and trains was the object of criticism from numerous sources. In 1927, it was reported that several chiefs were calling for a pass system for women, in an effort to limit the number who 'escaped' by taking trains to the urban centres. According to one native commissioner, it was far too easy for women to abscond:

> If a woman has a grievance against anybody — if she has been smacked by her husband for not cooking properly — she is off by the next train.[94]

A few years later a chief in the Goromonzi District complained that girls and women 'go out to farms and townships and mines' as prostitutes:

> Our daughters go about everywhere because they are helped to travel by motor lorries. Also whenever a man punishes his daughter by beating for going away without the father's permission they complain to the police and the father is prosecuted.[95]

A frequent refrain among colonial officials at this time was that the state itself was largely responsible for the breakdown in male authority. Writing in 1930, the native commissioner of Belingwe lamented,

> Under our administration tribal and parental control has been broken down and is practically non-existent. A native female, married or single, can wander where she wishes. No restrictions are placed on her movements and the lure of the town and compounds attract her.

Elizabeth Mahungo, Elizabeth Sande, Chishawasha Mission, 18 December 1985; Hamundidi Mhindurwa, Seke Communal Lands, 26 January 1986.

[93] CNC S235/514, Annual Report, Goromonzi District, 1935, p. 28.

[94] Quoted in England, 'Political Economy', p. 53.

[95] S1542/N2 (E–G), 'Minutes of the Fourth Session of the Native Advisory Board of Salisbury District', Goromonzi, 12 October 1933, p. 5.

The official claimed that African men often came to his office, protesting that a wife or daughter had 'absconded to one of the many compounds in this part of the Colony'. The offending woman was usually located and sent home, but shortly thereafter, she was bound to run away again. 'It is difficult, if not impossible, to punish this woman', he concluded.[96]

The complaints of senior African men took on a special urgency during the 1930s. The agricultural crisis in the rural areas and the town-ward exodus of junior African men resulted in an intensification of female labour, sparking an upsurge in female migration to the cities.[97] Recognising the importance of rural women's productive and reproductive labour to the national as well as domestic economy, state officials advocated increasingly stronger legal measures for the control of African women's mobility. Writing to his superior in 1930, the native commissioner of Wankie claimed that 'to re-establish parental control the indiscriminate movements of females must be checked', adding,

> This can only be done by a Pass Law applicable to them — the precedent having been given by the Juvenile Employment Act 10/1926 ... This will curtail their wander lust and prevent flouting of the consent of the parent, guardian or husband.[98]

The same year, the all-white Federation of Women's Institutes of Southern Rhodesia suggested that the pass law, Ordinance 16 of 1901, be amended so that women and girls who sought domestic employment in the towns would be required to obtain permits from senior administration officials. Such permits would be granted only 'at the request of the guardian ... of the native female in question'.[99]

In 1932, following the advice of the Federation of Women's Institutes and numerous witnesses of its own, the administration's Departmental Committee on Native Female Domestic Service suggested that:

---

[96] CNC S138/47, NC, Belingwe to Superintendent of Natives, Bulawayo, 17 December 1930, No. 555/30.

[97] Mosley, *Settler Economies*, p. 168; England, 'Political Economy', p. 52; Phimister, *Economic and Social History*, pp. 204–205. For further elaboration on this point see Elizabeth Schmidt, 'Farmers, Hunters, and Gold–Washers: A Reevaluation of Women's Roles in Precolonial and Colonial Zimbabwe', *African Economic History* 17 (1988), pp. 66–70; 'Keeping Hearth and Home Together: African Women, Peasant Production, and Resistance to Proletarianisation in Southern Rhodesia, 1890–1939', forthcoming.

[98] CNC S138/47, NC, Wankie to Superintendent of Natives, Bulawayo, 10 September 1930, No. 630/30.

[99] CNC S235/475, Federation of Women's Institutes of Southern Rhodesia, *Report of the Standing Committee on Domestic Service*, July 1930, pp. 9–10. Missionaries in South Africa devised similar proposals. In 1908, for instance, Anglican deaconess, Julia Gilpin, recommended that African women and girls be brought under the pass regulations, thereby ensuring that only those with proper permission could seek work in the towns. Such measures, together with the provision of decent accommodations, ought to convince African parents to release their daughters for domestic service, she wrote. See Deborah Gaitskell, '"Christian Compounds for Girls": Church Hostels for African Women in Johannesburg, 1907–1970', *Journal of Southern African Studies* 6, 1 (October 1979), p. 46.

Native girls entering towns should be required to present themselves at the office of the local official of the Native Department for registration, and that they should be required to bring with them evidence to show that their coming to town to seek work has the approval of their parents or guardians.[100]

Blaming the state for having encouraged female disobedience, senior African men continued to call upon the state to rectify the situation. A member of the native board in the Goromonzi District spoke for many of his colleagues when he urged the administration to 'arrest unmarried women in locations ... also on farms and mining compounds', forcing them to return to their fathers and guardians.[101] Members of the Goromonzi native board proposed that marriage registration certificates serve as a form of pass document for African women; no woman should be allowed to stay on European farms, in mining compounds or in town locations unless she could produce a marriage registration certificate.[102] In this way, the marital status and guardianship of every woman could easily be established. Unmarried women, or at least those whose unions were not recognised under the Native Marriages Ordinance, could thus be identified and forced to return to the rural areas.[103] Presumably married women who were living alone, or with someone other than their legal spouse, would also have been forced to leave the urban locations. Thus, the Native Marriages Ordinance, which initially provided African women and girls with a degree of protection, ultimately served as one of the primary instruments of male control.

By the late 1930s, legal restrictions on African women's mobility had been tightened considerably, although enforcement was erratic.[104] The 1936 Native Registration Act, as implemented in 1938, stipulated that in order to enter an urban area, all 'unmarried' women (that is, women without marriage registration

---

[100] S1561, Native Female Domestic Labour Committee, Salisbury, to the Colonial Secretary, October 1932, pp. 10–11. Also see S1561/48, Southern Rhodesia, *Report of the Departmental Committee on Native Female Domestic Service*, 1932, p. 12.

[101] S1542/N2 (E–G), Minutes of the Native Board, 12 October 1933, p. 71. Also see S1542/N2 (E–G), 'Resolutions Passed at Meeting of Native Board of Salisbury Native District', Goromonzi, 5 May 1933; NC, Salisbury to CNC, Salisbury, 16 May 1933, No. 12/246/33, p. 2, concerning Resolution No. 3, passed at the Native Board meeting on 5 May 1933.

[102] S1542/N2 (E–G), Resolutions of the Native Board, 5 May 1933.

[103] Similar demands were made by male elders in other parts of Africa. In the interest of guaranteeing the success of indirect rule, colonial authorities responded to their appeals in like fashion. See, for instance: Jeanne K. Henn, 'The Material Basis of Sexism: A Mode of Production Analysis', in *Patriarchy and Class*, p. 50; Little, *African Women in Towns*, pp. 16–19; Chanock, *Law, Custom and Social Order*, pp. 111–124, 207–208; Parpart, 'Sexuality and Power', pp. 115, 119–120; 'Class and Gender', pp. 143–144; Chauncey, 'Locus of Reproduction ', pp. 155–157, 159–160; Mbilinyi, 'Runaway Wives', pp. 3, 9, 11–12, 14, 25; Margaret Strobel, *Muslim Women in Mombasa, 1890–1975* (New Haven: Yale University Press, 1979), pp. 146–147; Regina Smith Oboler, *Women, Power, and Economic Change: the Nandi of Kenya* (Stanford: Stanford University Press, 1985), pp. 173–174; Sharon Stichter, 'Women and the Labour Force in Kenya, 1895–1964', *Rural Africana* 29 (Winter 1975–76), p. 56.

[104] See Teresa Barnes, '"To Raise a Hornet's Nest" The Effect of Early Resistance to Passes for Women in South Africa on the Pass Laws in Colonial Zimbabwe', *Agenda: A Journal About Women and Gender* 5 (1989), pp. 40–52; Teresa Barnes, personal communication, 4 January 1990.

certificates), as well as married women who did not meet exemption criteria, were required to obtain passes from an authorised state official. A pass could be refused if the official determined the applicant was

> ... a person of loose or immoral character ... (or) is seeking to visit the township for an unlawful purpose or for the purpose of gambling or sexual immorality ... (or) is a minor according to native law and is seeking to visit the township for the purpose of evading parental authority.[105]

In 1939, the native commissioner of Salisbury ruled that female visitors to that city would 'receive no pass unless the consent of their husbands or guardians has been obtained'.[106] By the end of the decade, women and girls who had come to town in defiance of male authority, and who remained in the urban areas after having been ordered to leave, were fingerprinted and fined or imprisoned.[107]

In practice, older women, those who were legally married, were longstanding residents of the urban areas, or in paid employment were treated with more leniency. Such women were considered stabilising influences rather than threats to the maintenance of law and order. Contributing to the European economy through their own employment or through the provision of domestic and sexual services to male workers, these women helped to reproduce the African labour force in the urban areas.[108] Newcomers to the locations, particularly unmarried girls and younger women without formal sector employment, were the most vulnerable targets of administrative action. Such women were most likely to be evicted from the town locations.[109] They were castigated as the source of immoral behaviour and of violence between men. They were derided as transmitters of venereal disease that weakened male workers. Their most serious offence, however, was that they were rebels who undermined patriarchal authority and flouted the laws of the colonial state.

Conclusion

As the Southern Rhodesian state moved to undermine indigenous authority structures during the first three decades of colonial rule, people on the margins of African society were able to eke out some benefits. Taking advantage of the erosion of African patriarchal power and playing upon the contradictions of colonial

---

[105] As quoted in Barnes, 'Hornet's Nest', pp. 49–50.

[106] S235/517, Annual Report for the Salisbury District, 1939, p. 11.

[107] Teresa Barnes, Review of Ian Phimister's, *An Economic and Social History of Zimbabwe, 1890–1948: Capital Accumulation and Class Struggle*, in *Southern African Review of Books* 2, 3 (February/March 1989), p. 6.

[108] For an extensive analysis of the reproduction of the urban labour force in colonial Kenya, see Luise White, *The Comforts of Home; Prostitution in Colonial Nairobi* (Chicago: University of Chicago Press, 1990); 'Prostitution, Identity, and Class Consciousness in Nairobi During World War II', *Signs* 11, 2 (Winter 1986): 255–273; Idem., 'Domestic Labour in a Colonial City: Prostitution in Nairobi, 1900–1952', in *Patriarchy and Class*, pp. 139–160.

[109] Barnes, 'Hornet's Nest', pp. 48, 50; Barnes, personal communication, 4 January 1990.

policies, African women, in particular, challenged male control over their mobility, sexuality, and productive and reproductive capacities. The reconstitution of African 'customary' law by the colonial state, in collaboration with African chiefs, headmen, and other senior men, provided fertile terrain for contests between African women and men, as well as between men of different generations.

The crisis of authority in the rural areas, foreshadowing the possibility of a total break down in law and order, as well as the need to maintain female agricultural production in the reserves, forced state officials to reconsider their earlier policies. By the 1920s, a backlash against female emancipation was well under way, intensifying under the pressures of the Great Depression. While an increasing number of laws regulated African women's mobility after 1930, neither the colonial state nor senior African men could stem the town-ward flow. Choosing between heavily circumscribed options, African women left the rural reserves in increasing numbers, moving to European mission stations, farms, and mining compounds, and African locations in the urban areas. The rural to urban migration had begun in earnest, and African women were an integral part of it — with or without the permission of their male guardians.

[13]
The Colonial Development of Concentration Camps (1868–1902)

Iain R. Smith and Andreas Stucki

The forced labour and extermination camps established in Europe during the Second World War gave the meaning to the term 'concentration camp' which it has for the general public today. But the practice of concentrating civilians in guarded camps or centres, specifically as part of a counter-guerrilla military strategy during wartime, long predated and outlasted the Second World War. In the light of fresh research, this article looks comparatively at the function of the camps in three different colonial arenas between 1868 and 1902. It emphasises the different purposes between these exercises in civilian concentration and the 'camp culture' of the Nazi era in Europe and challenges the linkage between the two asserted by Hannah Arendt half a century ago and by many others since.

It has long been argued that the origins of concentration camps lie in the colonial arenas of imperial powers at the turn of the nineteenth and twentieth centuries.[1] It was in the context of the British camps in South Africa (1900–2) that the term 'concentration camp' was first put into general currency in English—as Goering pointed out to the British ambassador to Berlin in 1938.[2] But the phenomenon has usually been traced back to the Spanish–Cuban War of 1895–98. Reference to *(re)concentrados*, however, occurred earlier in Cuba, during the Ten Years' War (1868–78) and the *Guerra chiquita* (1879–80), though the term 'concentration *camp*' is rarely found in the Cuban case, where civilians were concentrated in towns and villages under surveillance by Spanish regulars and irregulars. The internment of civilians in guarded camps, under conditions which regularly resulted in high mortality, was also a feature of strife-torn Europe long before the Second World War.[3] Yet it is the forced labour and extermination camps in Europe, between 1939 and 1945, which gave the common meaning to the term 'concentration camp' which it has today.[4] Since the later Nazi associations of the term 'concentration camp' have been deliberately

---

Correspondence to: Dr Iain R. Smith, Department of History, University of Warwick, Coventry CV4 7AL, UK. Email: iain.leamington@googlemail.com; Dr Andreas Stucki, Oberassistent für Neueste Geschichte und Zeitgeschichte, Universität Bern, Historisches Institut, Länggassstrasse 49, CH-3000 Bern 9. Email: andreas.stucki@hist.unibe.ch

exploited in South Africa and Cuba, it is important to acknowledge distinctions when the same term is used to describe widely differing phenomena in different contexts and eras. Historians tend to look for continuities, links and precedents and historians of modern Germany have had particular reasons for doing so. There is now a sizeable literature, in the German case, linking what took place in colonial contexts in Africa, between 1904 and 1908, and what occurred later in Europe.[5] The camps established by the German military in South West Africa, during the suppression of the rebellion by the Herero and Nama, were not essentially part of an anti-guerrilla strategy but were rather 'punishment' and 'pacification' camps for an enemy who had already been defeated. They are, therefore, functionally different from the three cases considered here.[6]

In this article, we focus on the establishment of concentration camps in colonial contexts as part of a military strategy against guerrilla warfare during colonial rebellions, and we argue that this differs, in fundamental respects, from the camps established in Europe by, for example, Italy, Germany and the Soviet Union before and during the Second World War as part of wider systems of terror and political repression. In the camps established by the Spanish in Cuba, the British in South Africa and the Americans in the Philippines, there was no intention of the physical extermination of those interned in them. In this article, we show that the main purpose of civilian concentration lay in 'clearing' the countryside of possible civilian support for an evasive enemy who had resorted to guerrilla warfare.[7] While our focus is on the two cases where we have done fresh research—the Spanish *concentrados* in Cuba (1895–98) and the British camps in South Africa (1900–2)—we also try, in the limited space of an article, to bring the American camps in the Philippines (1899–1902) into comparative view.

Civilians in Colonial Warfare

The resort to 'civilian concentration' by colonial powers struggling to contain rebellions in situations of guerrilla warfare illuminates the fragility of colonial regimes which often found it difficult to occupy effectively the territory over which they claimed sovereignty during the 'high noon' of imperialism. There were many further colonial contexts in which this forced concentration of civilians was to occur, as a military measure sometimes accompanied by enforced 'modernisation', during the course of the twentieth century and especially during the armed struggles which accompanied the process of decolonisation after 1945.[8] In the period under discussion (1868–1902), the Spanish in Cuba, the British in South Africa and the Americans in the Philippines were compelled to involve far more troops than had originally been envisaged in protracted conflicts with usually smaller numbers of guerrilla fighters. The rebellions in Cuba and the Philippines resulted in external (American) intervention and the end of Spanish colonial rule. In South Africa, the terms of the peace agreed with the Boers by the Treaty of Vereeniging in May 1902 replaced the earlier British insistence on 'unconditional surrender' in order to bring the war to an end.

In all these cases, a blurring of the distinction between combatant and non-combatant civilians occurred, as is usually the case when there is a resort to guerrilla warfare. In these cases, civilian concentration has to be regarded as essentially a military measure, the purpose of which was to separate the guerrilla fighters from any support from the civilian population among whom they could merge so easily. As a counter-guerrilla strategy, this has a long history and a clear military rationale, even if, in our cases, humanitarian claims were also made in terms of enabling these civilians or refugees to be concentrated in places where—amidst an accompanying 'scorched earth' policy—they allegedly could be accommodated and fed. Preoccupied with fighting the war, the organisation and administration of civilian concentration camps were never a priority for the military authorities. It takes a strong, developed, adequately funded administration to organise and run a concentration camp *system*—the contrast between the British and Spanish cases is most striking here—and the presence of a civilian government capable of taking over this task was, in the South African case, critical to reducing the mortality rate and improving the conditions within the camps. In all these cases, the ability of the metropolitan government to intervene, check and control the military authorities in time of war was of crucial importance, as was the role of public opinion in exercising its influence on the metropolitan government and compelling it to intervene in ways which it might otherwise not have done.

Both political and military decision-makers were influenced by contemporary racial ideology and its accompanying Social Darwinist ideas and by the concept of a 'civilising mission' which was a recurrent feature of European colonial involvement with the non-European world at that time. For all the European colonial powers, fighting an enemy categorised as 'uncivilised' lowered the barrier against the resort to more extreme measures of warfare. The Spanish regarded the Cuban rebels—consisting predominantly of Afro-Cubans—as 'savages' beyond the pale of civilisation. In South Africa, the black population was not the enemy. Tens of thousands of native Africans were employed by the British army and many looked to a British victory to improve their lot. In areas under temporary Boer control, some paid with their lives for their British loyalty.[9] Meanwhile, Kitchener, exasperated by the failure of the Middelburg peace negotiations in early 1901, described the Boers as 'uncivilized Africander savages with only a thin white veneer' and proposed 'getting rid of' those still fighting and their families by deporting them to Fiji or getting the French or Dutch to take them in Madagascar or Java.[10] In the Philippines, the paternalist gloss given to the American takeover there by President McKinley was accompanied, after his re-election in November 1900, by the declaration of martial law and authorisation, by the Secretary of State for War, for use of the tough 'methods which have proved successful in our Indian campaigns in the West'. US Officers regarded Filipinos as 'by no means civilized' and in 'identically the same position as the Indians of our country have been for many years'. Therefore, in their opinion, the Filipino insurgency 'must be subdued in much the same way'.[11]

CUBA (1868–98)

Spanish colonial rule in Cuba had been repeatedly threatened during the second half of the nineteenth century. Frustrated political and organisational reforms for the once 'ever faithful island' led, in October 1868, to a general uprising in eastern Cuba. Rebellions usually began in the poorer, less developed and more turbulent *Oriente*. In 1868, property owners there 'freed' their slaves—to encourage them to join the rebellion—and fought together with the cattle farmers from Puerto Príncipe against Spanish rule. The Spanish army and voluntary units managed to keep the insurgency more or less out of the rich, western provinces. Heavily dependent on slave labour, western planters feared not only economic loss but also that this revolt against Spanish rule would result in social revolution and a 'race war'. Panic at the prospect of a 'second Haiti' was eagerly nurtured by Spanish propaganda. However, while inhabitants in the east suffered from ruthless guerrilla and anti-guerrilla warfare, the destruction of livestock, expropriation and forced resettlement—until the peace settlement of February 1878—in western Cuba sugar production increased.[12]

During the Ten Years' War, a lively discussion had developed about how to deal with the insurrection, in general, and on concentration policies, in particular—even beyond military circles. Most of the operational plans (many published in the early 1870s) had in common prompt pacification, closely connected with the intense concentration of the rural population along military communication lines. In 1872, the medical officer Echauz y Guinart, for example, recommended a master plan which included the forced resettlement and 'clearing' of half the island. Although continuous changes in the high command in Havana and political transformations in Madrid prevented a unified and concerted military strategy, tens of thousands of deportees had merged with refugees in crowded cities such as Puerto Príncipe and Ciego de Ávila, along the fortified military line between Júcaro and Morón. Mortality soared and internees begged for authorisation to leave the points of reconcentration that lacked potable water and to escape disease. In eastern Cuba, this early experience of regrouping the rural population in wartime left deep memories.[13]

In the following years of peace, Spain proved to be unable to tackle her 'last chance in Cuba'. When new uprisings occurred, in February 1895, these benefited from a broader social base and a party system which was well-organised, both on the island and from exile: the *Partido Revolucionario Cubano* headed by José Martí. Socio-political preconditions seemed to favour not only an anti-colonial uprising but also a social revolution. Furthermore, Cuban exiles provided the Liberation Army *Ejército Libertador Cubano* (ELC) with the much needed supplies from the Florida Keys and other Caribbean islands. Charismatic veterans from the Ten Years' War (Antonio Maceo, Máximo Gómez and Calixto García) returned to Cuba. Superiority in numbers, equipment and funding seemed to give a big advantage to the Spanish army. But the ELC balanced some of these asymmetries with greater mobility, better knowledge of the terrain and adaptation to the island's climate together with widespread civilian support in Oriente. Spanish military power proved to be literally helpless in the face of tropical diseases: of 44,389 fatalities during the war of 1895–98, only 3,996 died in combat; over 40,000 (of the more than 200,000 Spanish forces in Cuba) died from diseases, with yellow fever being the biggest single killer of the Spanish troops.[14] Spanish military performance, therefore, depended on the support given by Cuban and Spanish-born irregulars whose anti-guerrilla units accompanied regular troops as flying columns and operated as local anti-guerrilla forces around towns and cities. With up to 60–80,000 such irregulars on Spain's payroll (as volunteers, town militias and fire units), they clearly outnumbered the ELC, which never recruited much more than 40,000 men. But this high number of irregulars should not be mistaken for widespread support for Spain. Only a minority took part in actual fighting, and joining the local anti-guerrilla units and working on Spanish fortifications were among the few ways to earn a living during wartime and get the family on the official ration list. Nevertheless, Cubans fighting in Spanish lines are an important indication of the degree of civil strife involved in this war, an aspect which has often been ignored in the nationalist historiography.[15]

By January 1896, Spanish Captain-General Arsenio Martínez Campos had suffered serious setbacks and the ELC had managed to penetrate the rich sugar districts of Santa Clara, Matanzas and Havana. The ELC developed a policy of economic warfare involving the deliberate destruction of crops and sugar mills and attacks on towns and villages, with the purpose being to make Cuba economically unrewarding to Spain. This triggered a massive refugee displacement and migration in the western provinces. Some Spanish historians have interpreted this movement as a first concentration of country folk in fortified centres. Historian W. Millis argued that the ELC's 'scorched earth' policy and 'deconcentration'—forcing farmers either to work in the 'liberated territory' or to move to the cities—began the radicalisation of warfare which has usually been associated with Captain-General Valeriano Weyler. This view—that it was the insurgents who initiated 'civilian concentration'—has been strongly denied by P. S. Foner and Cuban scholars.[16]

Amidst this controversy, there is no doubt that the plight of civilians came low on the list of imperial Spain's priorities. Facing the impending collapse of Spanish rule in Cuba, powerful pressure groups on the island and large parts of the metropolitan press demanded a tougher war effort. Unsurprisingly, in January 1896, Spain's liberal–conservative government, under Antonio Cánovas del Castillo, decided upon the intensification and radicalisation of warfare, sending General Weyler to Cuba. Already in 1891, Cánovas had told Congress that, in a future war in Cuba, those 'who were willing to shed more rivers of blood' would win.[17] With the outbreak of the war in 1895, a broad consensus had developed—between Spanish liberals and conservatives—that the island of Cuba, 'the pearl of the Antilles', should be defended to the 'last man and the last peso'.[18] Cuba was considered as a matter of 'national integrity', especially among politicians and the armed forces. There was a long-standing fear that losing control of Cuba would lead to the breakdown of the metropolitan Restoration government of 1874 and of Spain's artificially implemented two-party system which had lasted since 1885.

Weyler was regarded as the man to do a 'dirty job'. He was widely experienced in colonial anti-guerrilla warfare (Santo Domingo, Cuba and the Philippines) and ready to 'defend Spain's honour in Cuba'. As anticipated, one of his first decrees, in February 1896, ordered the concentration of the rural population of the eastern part of the island in Spanish-held, fortified towns. In October 1896 and January 1897, the decree was extended to both the island's western and the central provinces. With this measure—in combination with a 'scorched earth' strategy—civilian support for the insurgents was to be prevented and no intelligence, weapons, ammunition, clothing, medicine or new recruits should reach the Cuban guerrilla forces. Civilian concentration was an important part of Spain's response to the insurgents' irregular warfare. The physical separation of rebels and civilians seemed the only way to defeat an agile and often invisible opponent. In contrast to the US policy of counter-insurgency in the Philippines, however, there was hardly any 'offer of development' in Cuba to win the civilians' 'hearts and minds'. On the contrary, many local civil governments were simply overwhelmed by the arrival of tens of thousands of *concentrados*. Meanwhile, Weyler was preoccupied with fighting the guerrillas and was reluctant to devote resources or organise rations for the destitute civilians. Many in the military regarded refugees and *concentrados* as disguised insurgents or sympathisers of the 'Republic in Arms'. The local town elites considered *concentrados* as bearers of potential epidemics and diseases such as smallpox as well as unwanted additional mouths to feed.[19] Neglect contributed to the high mortality among the *concentrados* caused by inadequate housing and sanitary conditions, food shortages and subsequent epidemics. The ELC also contributed to this civilian catastrophe by blockading cities and towns from the much needed supplies and by raids on the so-called cultivation zones. After a few weeks on rations, *concentrados* were expected to grow their own food for subsistence. The concentration policy in Cuba during 1896–97 was 'unprecedented at the time for its scale, intensity and efficiency'. Recent research concludes that at least 170,000 civilian internees, about one-tenth of the total population, lost their lives in these concentration centres.[20] The forced resettlement in towns and cities had a lasting social impact on the island. Families were torn apart, and women and girls were forced into prostitution. The balance between the urban and rural populations altered substantially.

Contemporaries estimated that some 400,000–600,000 people were assembled in over 80 concentration points, located predominantly in the western part of the island, during the war. Some villages accommodated only a small number of *concentrados*, but in cities such as Artemisa (Pinar del Río), with a normal population of about 2,000 inhabitants, civilian internees amounted to 6,364 by the end of November 1897; among them, 3,244 were children and 1,239 were women. High numbers of *concentrados* and escalating mortality were reported from Matanzas and Santa Clara. Numbers given by provincial civil governors between November 1897 and February 1898, although incomplete, enable us to reach an approximation for the total civilian deaths during the Cuban war of independence: data show that 50 per cent of 47,800 *concentrados* died in Pinar del Río; of the 88,000 internees in Matanzas, 25,977 died. Santa Clara province reported 140,000 concentrated civilians and 52,997 deaths, whereas there are no exact figures for Havana, Puerto Príncipe and Santiago. The figures given above, therefore, represent only single 'snapshots' at a particular time.

Data from Santiago, Matanzas and Santa Clara, for example, show that civilian concentration was not a static phenomenon. For these provinces, we can detect important migration movements in and out of the main cities, sometimes over a few weeks. The number of *concentrados* was not only closely related to specific military actions. Even the announcement of forthcoming military operations was followed in Puerto Príncipe by a civilian influx into fortified towns. But people also left Trinidad (Santa Clara) in the spring of 1897, violating Weyler's orders, in order to flee from a smallpox epidemic. At Jovellanos (Matanzas), we know that many people left the town to work in the countryside during the months of the sugar harvest. In Matanzas province, a large exodus occurred when concentration was eased in November 1897 by the new decrees of Captain-General Ramón Blanco, who had replaced Weyler in October 1897.[21]

In strictly military terms, Weyler's concentration policy achieved considerable success. By autumn 1897, the ELC was mainly confined to Cuba's eastern provinces. In addition, General Camilo García Polavieja—who had replaced General Blanco in the Philippines in December 1896—asked Madrid whether he might resort to similar strategies as Weyler to subdue the Katipuna's uprising after resistance to Spanish rule had broken out on Luzon in August 1896. But the Pact of Biak-na-bato, which brought the uprising to an end in mid-December 1897, was more the result of divisions in the Filipino revolutionary front than of successful Spanish anti-guerrilla strategies. In Cuba, however, Weyler's methods of extreme warfare, regardless of civilian losses, made him unacceptable to the newly constituted liberal government in Spain. In the USA, the massive number of civilian deaths which occurred under Weyler's regime was regarded as a demonstration of Spain's 'uncivilised warfare' and formed a major justification for the US Army's 'humanitarian intervention' in April 1898. The fragility of Spanish imperial rule was clearly revealed when Spain was seriously challenged by the combination of liberation movements in Cuba and the Philippines with the readiness of the USA, as the emerging world power, to intervene and bring about the end of the Spanish Empire in both the Caribbean and the Pacific.

Philippines (1899–1902)

After the American takeover of the Philippines in December 1898, war broke out again in early February 1899. The insurrection was limited to a few areas in the scattered archipelago where the extreme geographical, social and ethnic divisions led US imperialists to question the idea that the Tagalog and Ilocano forces led by Emilio Aguinaldo on Luzon constituted a 'national' movement. After his capture in 1901 and the fall of Miguel Malvar's guerrillas in Batangas the following year, the war was, at least rhetorically, brought to an end in July 1902 with the presence of around 70,000 American troops and a ruthlessness which dismissed further insurrectional activity as banditry.[22]

At the beginning of the uprising in 1899, Filipino revolutionary leaders tried to wage conventional warfare and were reluctant to resort to guerrilla strategies. On the one hand, this restriction was nurtured by the hope for acceptance among the 'civilised' nations; on the other hand, there was the elite's fear of loosing control, both over territory and over the majority of their forces which might slip from an independence movement into social revolution. In the wake of the first defeats against the US troops, Aguinaldo had to take these risks and organise local guerrilla units all over the country.[23] As the war continued, US officers and soldiers demanded a tightening of military measures. Anti-guerrilla strategies included not only the confiscation of property, summary executions, massacres, deportations and crop destruction but also civilian concentration in designated areas. J. Franklin Bell's concentration order on 8 December 1901 for Batangas province illustrates how extreme measures in anti-guerrilla warfare, targeting especially the civilian population, were gradually implemented.[24] At the same time, in the 'pacified' towns and villages, American civil administrators tried to implement allegedly social 'uplifting' programmes and economic development: new roads, schools, medical infrastructure, sanitation and 'protection' from the guerrilla forces. In Julian Go's words, the occupying power's efforts in social engineering predated 'modernisation theories of democratisation later proposed in the 1950s'. Officers were convinced 'that economic development stimulated by American capital would undo the putatively medieval social condition in the two colonies and stimulate socio-political development'. However, G. A. May has pointed to the early 'hearts and minds' campaign's 'relative failure'. Indeed, many civilians cooperated with the US authorities during the day, but at night, they regularly served the guerrillas. Furthermore, the success of public instruction campaigns existed in many locations only on paper: schoolbooks were lacking in Batangas, school buildings were inadequate and teachers were unqualified—to name only a few of the many problems.[25]

When Americans resorted to civilian concentration in the Philippines, officers were influenced not only by the contemporary examples of the British in South Africa and the Spanish in Cuba but also by previous American experience of establishing 'reservations' for native Americans during the 'Indian Wars' in North America earlier in the nineteenth century. In the 'concentration zones' in the Philippines, tens of thousands of people died in the space of a few months from malnutrition and disease. In all our cases, 'the war of numbers' has been politically exploited and the problem of statistics has challenged several generations of historians. Due to unreliable or fragmentary evidence, it is doubtful if the precise number of deaths, as a result of civilian internment in each of our cases at the turn of the nineteenth and twentieth centuries, will ever be established. This is especially true for the Philippines, where it is difficult to separate deaths in the 'concentration zones' from the even greater number which followed as a result of epidemics of cholera and other diseases.[26]

In the light of the concentration order for Batangas province and the accounts which followed from the abuse and torture committed by the US troops, American anti-imperialists sensed a link between 'butcher' Weyler's way of warfare in Cuba and the methods being resorted to by the American forces in the Philippines. If the Spanish army's similar anti-guerrilla strategy had brought about the recent American 'humanitarian intervention' in Cuba, was the US army in the Philippines acting according to the laws of 'civilised warfare' recently embodied in the Hague Convention of 1899?[27] Sustained by the idea of a 'civilising mission', American public opinion was persuaded that analogies were not necessarily parallels and took comfort from the contemporary British example in South Africa where extensive imperial experience and military necessity, it was argued, had justified their actions. In 1902, the *Boston Journal* argued that how civilian dislocation and internment were implemented determined 'whether it is a harsh method or not'.[28]

Moreover, the Filipinos were regarded as an 'inferior race', superstitious, fragmented, politically immature and incapable of self-rule. 'Filipino independence', declared Theodore Roosevelt, would be 'like granting self-government to an Apache reservation under some local chief'.[29] Through policies of 'chastisement' and social engineering, the Americans embarked on a 'civilising mission' in the Philippines to bring about a cultural transformation in which colonialism was claimed as a benevolent form of nation-building. Thus, both in Cuba and in the Philippines, the occupying powers resorted to civilian concentration in order to defeat the insurgents and, as Emily Hobhouse put it in her book about the contemporary situation in South Africa, *The Brunt of the War and Where It Fell* (1902), it was the non-combatant civilians who suffered most.

South Africa (1900–2)

The concentration camps established by the British military in South Africa (1900–2) have remained the most controversial and highly mythologised aspect of the South African War (1899–1902).[30] Small wars are big wars to those that lose them and this war was more important than either the First or Second World War in the making of twentieth-century South Africa and in firing the furnace of Afrikaner nationalism which blazed its way to political dominance in its aftermath. For Britain, this was the most extensive, costly and humiliating war fought between 1815 and 1914 and the greatest of the wars accompanying the European 'scramble for Africa'. By March 1900, over 200,000 British and Empire troops (30,000 volunteers came from Canada, Australia and New Zealand) were fighting Boer forces numbering no more than 45,000. By 1902, this war was costing £1.5 million a week. What began as a colonial war, a Boer–British conflict over the Transvaal republic, soon developed into a regional war, with civil war dimensions to it, involving the whole population—black as well as white. This was not just a 'white man's war' and historians have spent the past 30 years exploring the involvement of the black population in it. They have revealed how war went on at many different levels in South Africa between 1899 and 1902 apart from the battlefields which have so preoccupied military historians. Many of the conflicts which then erupted into open warfare were home-grown, internally generated out of the recent South African past. The arrival of the British army enabled some of the conflicts endemic within South African society to become part of the Boer–British struggle.[31]

The South African camps were first established by the British military as 'protection camps' for Boers who had surrendered (*Hendsoppers*) and their families to prevent them from being re-commandeered by Boers who were still fighting on commando

(*Bitterenders*). After the British annexed the two republics in mid-1900, without effectively occupying them, this was a real danger. Soon, however, other refugees, mostly women and children (some of them the families of Boers who were still fighting), who had been displaced from their homes were forced to join them, and already by late 1900, a blurring had occurred between 'protection camps' for surrendered Boers and 'concentration camps' for other civilian refugees. Many surrendered Boers initially supported the policy of concentrating the women and children in camps in their home districts, where they allegedly could be protected and fed by the British. Before the high mortality in the camps became generally known, some Boers still fighting on commando and unable to look after their families encouraged them to go there. The British hoped that the existence of the camps might bring a speedy end to the war since they announced that burghers on commando who laid down their arms and took an oath of neutrality could join their families in the camps, whereas they risked losing everything and having their farms confiscated or burnt if they continued to fight. 'They love their property more than they hate the British', declared Milner, the British High Commissioner.[32] Those caught on the battlefield were treated as prisoners of war (POW) and sent overseas to POW camps. The earliest refugee/concentration camps were already in existence by September 1900, but the number of their inmates was small until the beginning of 1901. Then, the harsh 'scorched earth' and 'clearance' policy, initiated by Lord Roberts and systematically adopted and extended as an anti-guerrilla measure by Lord Kitchener (after he had succeeded Lord Roberts as the Commander-in-Chief of the British army at the end of November 1900), swept tens of thousands of civilians—black and white—off the veld and into hastily improvised tented camps, established along the railway lines for military monitoring and supply purposes, in an operation for which there had been no adequate planning. Assuming that the war would soon be brought to an end, these camps were expected to be a short-lived, temporary measure; but as the guerrilla war dragged on, they became part of a much wider counter-guerrilla military strategy which included a guerrilla-catching network of thousands of blockhouses connected by barbed wire and manned by over 50,000 soldiers and African auxiliaries.[33]

The South African camps reconsidered

The general picture of the British concentration camps in South Africa was established by Afrikaner nationalists in the decades after the war. They developed a powerful mythology of victimhood and suffering which fed into the emerging Afrikaner nationalist movement for which the deaths of 27,927 Boer civilians in these camps (the suspiciously precise figure calculated by the Transvaal archivist P. L. A. Goldman in 1906 by a suspect methodology) became a key reference point for the rest of the twentieth century.[34] After the political transition in South Africa in the 1990s, African nationalists re-worked these camps as sites of common African and Afrikaner victimhood and 'shared suffering' at the hands of British imperialists. What is extraordinary is not these efforts at quarrying the past for present purposes of nation-building—all nationalists do this—but the lack, until very recently, of any substantial, empirical and dispassionate research into these camps for which the surviving evidence is far richer, more detailed and extensive than that for any of the other cases of concentration camps considered here. Our recent research, in British and South African archives, has led to conclusions which are very revisionist of the established picture.

The counter-guerrilla purpose of these camps during the protracted, guerrilla phase of the war (1900–2) needs to be emphasised. These were not 'punishment' camps for a defeated enemy, as was the case for the Herero and Nama in German South West Africa (Namibia) during the war of 1904–8. As Lord Roberts made it clear, the Boer camp inmates were regarded as British subjects who were expected to become part of a self-governing, white minority-ruled dominion within the British Empire. Although these were called 'concentration camps', the terms 'refugee camps' and 'burgher refugee camps' were also used to denote what were essentially internment camps for civilians. These were clearly distinguished from the POW camps to which captured Boer combatants were dispatched, both in South Africa and overseas. A further distinction was made between the system of about 40 'white' camps, established mainly in the Transvaal and Orange River Colony and administered by the Department of Burgher Refugees from the headquarters in Pretoria and Bloemfontein, and the quite separate system of about 60 'black' camps ('native refugee camps') which were organised by the Department of Native Refugees. These two systems of camps need to be considered separately since their differences are so marked.

Understandably, it is the numbers of deaths in these camps which have preoccupied all who have written about them. The 'white' camps had about 150,000 inmates, mostly women and children, along with a small number of their 'black' domestic servants. Utilising the surviving camp registers, death certificates and lists of camp deaths published in the Government Gazettes, we have established a database of over 100,000 Boer camp inmates and estimated the total Boer camp deaths at around 25,000. This is less than Goldman's figure but a good deal more than the official British total of 20,139. The thousands of deaths in the 'black' camps were omitted from the picture until S. B. Spies and P. Warwick established that there were 14,154 recorded deaths, a figure which is certainly an underestimate of the total deaths which occurred.[35] In 2001, S. Kessler made an estimate of 20,000, but too much of the evidence about the 'black' camps has been destroyed for the precise total to be known.[36] Our research has led us to conclude that the total number of deaths in these camps for whites and blacks was at least 40,000.

The system of 'white' camps was administered from two headquarters, in Bloemfontein and Pretoria, with weekly statistical 'returns' and monthly reports from each camp along with reports from medical officers and inspectors, most of which were forwarded to London and some of which were published in government Blue Books.[37] This reflects the highly developed administrative systems of the British War Office and Colonial Office and the existence in South Africa of an effective civil government under the hawk-eyed British High Commissioner, Sir Alfred Milner. It was he who, in April 1901, insisted that individual details of the deaths of Boer civilians in the 'white' camps be published weekly in the Government Gazettes. 'We owe it to their relatives', he said.[38] As the mortality increased, reaching a peak in October 1901, these entries occupied many pages of the publications and, together with the revelations in the Blue Books, fuelled the public outcry. The paper trail left by the administrative system for these camps reveals not only facts and figures but also how these were queried and checked at each stage of their collection.

It has long been known that the majority of these deaths (three-quarters of them were of children under 16 years of age) were due to epidemics of measles and its accompanying complications. Measles is a highly infectious and deadly disease now, as then, especially among children in undeveloped countries, though the development of inoculation has greatly reduced its mortality record since the 1960s. What had been feared were typhoid epidemics. Typhoid also occurred in some of the camps and caused the deaths of around 8,000 British soldiers in what the British army came to regard as 'the last of the typhoid campaigns'; but there were only four recorded British deaths from measles.[39] Unlike the British troops, the Boers came from a thinly scattered, rural 'frontier' population which had little previous contact with measles and thus an extremely low immunity to the disease. Swept from their homes into hastily improvised, overcrowded, tented camps by the British army, with inadequate food, shelter, sanitation and medical supervision in the early months, they succumbed to the epidemics which spread from camp to camp during 1901—when extensive measles epidemics and mortality also occurred outside the camps for which we have no comparable record. The camp records reveal the desperate situation in many of the camps during the early months with some camp superintendents being described by visiting inspectors as 'at their wits' end trying to meet their responsibilities and begging the British forces not to send more people into camps where there was a raging measles epidemic and where facilities were already stretched beyond their limit. Their pleas were usually ignored by a military only too ready to hand over responsibility for civilians to the civilian authorities. Contingents of several hundred Boer civilians, mostly women and children, were regularly 'dropped off', often without any advance notice, in a state of weakness and exhaustion after many days on the march. The mortality rates reached a peak of over 400 per 1,000 per annum for brief periods in some camps.

These shocking mortality rates caused a public outcry in Britain when they were first revealed in mid-1901 by Emily Hobhouse, who had visited some of the camps. Her role is a striking example of the working of a free press in wartime and the nineteenth-century non-conformist conscience in action.[40] The British government was pushed into dispatching the first ever all women's Commission of Enquiry to investigate the situation under the redoubtable leadership of Millicent Garrett Fawcett. The reforms which this Ladies Committee recommended were promptly enacted.[41] The administration of the camps, having been transferred from military to civilian control, came under the sustained scrutiny of the Colonial Office and its officials rather than under that of the otherwise preoccupied War Office. The accommodation, funding, food rations and sanitation in the camps were improved. Doctors, teachers and nurses were hastily recruited in Britain and dispatched to the camps. What Milner called some 'Indian geniuses' arrived in South Africa to bring Indian experience to bear on the administration of the camps in South Africa.[42] The large influx of new camp inmates ceased. Historians have assumed that these developments, and especially what T. Pakenham called 'the magical effect' of the rapid implementation of the Fawcett committee's recommendations, brought about the dramatic improvement in the camps and the fall in mortality by the end of 1901.[43] Yet our research shows that incremental reforms in the camps were already underway, that the measles epidemics were already over and that mortality in many of the camps had markedly declined before these reforms came into effect. The epidemiological dynamics of measles (including epidemic 'fade out' with the end of large new influxes of susceptible people) need to be integrated into the analysis.

A quite separate system of 'black' camps was organised by the Native Refugee Department under the leadership of the capable and well-intentioned Canadian, Captain de Lotbinière, whose reports form our most important source of information since most of such detailed data as were ever collected about individual 'black' camps were later destroyed. There were an even larger number of 'black' camps, though many of these were short-lived holding centres.[44] The 'black' camps in this war were 'farm and labour' camps in which African families, who had been displaced by 'clearing', were settled on unoccupied land close to the railway system guarded by British forces. There they were dumped and largely left to themselves to construct temporary huts or shanties. These 'black' camps were regarded by the British as a labour reservoir from which men were dispersed for long periods all over South Africa to meet the huge labouring needs not only of the British army but of private employers as well. For this, they were paid at the rate of a shilling a day. Meanwhile, the women and children—who, as in the 'white' camps, formed the bulk of the population in the 'black' camps—were expected to cultivate their own subsistence and sell any surplus. Some of the 'black' camps acted as satellites from which labour was drawn for menial tasks in the 'white' camps. Captain de Lotbinière was expected to keep start-up costs to a minimum and to move rapidly towards making the 'black' camps self-supporting. Certainly, they had far fewer staff and resources than the 'white' camps and experienced some of the same epidemics, though disease-specific data are largely absent. Particularly in relation to the expectation that these camps would cultivate their own subsistence and cost little, the 'black' camps were very different from the 'white' camps and would seem to have more in common with the concentration centres in Cuba. In the organisation of concentration camps in South Africa, racial categorisation played a crucial role.

The ideas and ideology which the British brought to bear on the camps they established in South Africa were influenced by previous experience in Ireland (during the Famine in the 1840s) and India (where cholera and famine camps had been set up during the 1870s and 1880s) and by administering workhouses, the Poor Law and social welfare in England itself.[45] Wherever possible, the important thing, as the camps administration put it, was 'not to pauperise the people' and reduce them to dependence on hand-outs. Creating schools and employment—within or without the camps—was regarded as good for morale and would enable the inmates to 'earn their rations' and even to become self-supporting, to be taken off the rations list and, in many such cases, to leave the camps. The South African camps were not prisons—many of them were not even fenced in until late in the war—and Brodrick (Secretary of State for War) made it clear that they were not penal and any of their inmates who could support themselves should be allowed to go to the towns.[46] The camp registers reveal how many of the inmates moved about, in and out of the camps: to join relatives in other camps or to find employment and reside in nearby towns. But this was wartime, many had witnessed the destruction of their homes by the British army (30,000 farmhouses were burnt down), permits were needed for travel and most had nowhere else to go.

The presence of Boer men of working age in the camps has been largely air-brushed out of the picture by Afrikaner nationalists who thought that they should have been out fighting the British not living in camps and earning wages from them. So far, we have found over 13,000 and practically all of them were in some form of paid employment: either within the camps as guards, police, inspection teams, builders, carpenters, brick-makers, shoe-makers, etc., or in the nearby towns. The camp registers also reveal the considerable number of Boer men in the camps who took the oath of allegiance and left the camps to take up active military service with the British in the Burgher Corps, formed for the purpose, where their pay was twice as much as they received in camp employment. Their importance to the British was as scouts and guides with an intimate knowledge of the terrain and the likely hideouts of the commandos among whom some of them had once lived. They were hated by the Boers still fighting and, if caught, were court-martialled and shot. A. Grundlingh's research reveals that about a quarter of the Boers still fighting at the end of this war were fighting on the British side.[47] Their wages could markedly improve the situation for their families. How do we know this? Because we have found records of the Transvaal camp shops, run by Poynton Brothers, some with takings of over £1,000 per month from camp inmates. Money was earned and spent in these camps on a scale that has been totally left out of the picture. The British camps in South Africa cost about £2.5 million to run. And what was the second highest item of expenditure—after food and camp supplies? The surprising answer is wages to camp inmates. More was spent on this than on the total wage bill for the official camp staff. Wages were paid not only to the men but also to many of the young women who became probationer nurses in the camp hospitals, assisted in camp inspections or taught in the camp schools—where, by the beginning of 1902, more Boer children were attending school than had ever been the case in the pre-war republics.[48] The opportunity the camps offered for social engineering and the acquisition of training and skills which would be of benefit to those who acquired them after the war was over were all part of the imperial mind-set of the British in South Africa as in many later colonial situations.[49]

When a peace settlement was finally reached by the Treaty of Vereeniging on 31 May 1902, the British hoped that post-war policies of reconstruction, reconciliation and the move towards self-government (accelerated by the new Liberal government in Britain during 1906–7) would result in a united, transformed, white minority-ruled South African dominion in which the British influence would prevail. Having won the war, they lost the peace to a mobilised Afrikaner nationalist movement which swept into power as soon as elections were held. The Union of South Africa, which came into being in 1910, was Boer-led and Boer-dominated and skilfully achieved under the leadership of Botha and Smuts. The deaths of all those Boer civilians in British camps, especially of women and children, were unintended but they were deaths all the same, and they have cast a long shadow over Boer–British relations ever since.

Conclusions

In all our cases, ideological concepts, the exclusion of the enemy from 'civilisation' or blunt racial attitudes of superiority were used to justify the intensification of warfare. The resort to civilian internment, involving a blurring of the fragile border between combatants and non-combatants, became acceptable. In a rapid process of racialising the 'enemy', US soldiers increasingly envisaged the whole Filipino population as hostile, and racial categorisation thus played a key role in sanctioning extreme measures of warfare and in condoning high civilian losses.[50] In Cuba, civilian concentration was accompanied by the rural districts being declared as 'free fire zones': everybody outside the fortified towns was considered as an insurgent and treated as such. Inside the fortified towns, neglect, incompetence and lack of resources resulted in mortality on a scale that shocked the world and fuelled the American intervention. But in Spain, people were too preoccupied with the miserable health and supply situation of their own army overseas and the terrible state of its returnees from Cuba—skeleton-like men, shaken by tropical disease—to really care about the Cuban civilian population. Indignation about the Cuban situation reached Spain's liberal opposition party through the American and liberal press, and it used this to challenge the government. In the case of the Philippines, the high civilian death rate among the Filipino population and the atrocities committed by American forces during the anti-guerrilla war there aroused few demonstrations of public concern in the USA apart from that of a few academics and the steadfast members of the Anti-Imperialist League. In Britain, by contrast, the press and public opinion were far more exercised about the situation in the South African camps than about the typhoid epidemics among British troops. The scale of mortality in those camps led the Liberal Party leader, Campbell-Bannerman, to accuse the government of fighting the war in South Africa by 'methods of barbarism' and did much to prick the bubble of jingoistic imperialism which had accompanied the war.

At first sight, there might seem to be more differences between the camps examined in this article than aspects in common. Fortified and sometimes fenced towns in Cuba, with internees herded together in old warehouses, barracks or improvised huts, had little in common with British tented camps, though many of the British camps for the wartime refugees who flocked to the towns also began in already existing buildings. *Concentrados* in Cuba, like the inmates of the 'black' camps in South Africa but unlike those in the 'white' camps, were also expected to cultivate their own subsistence and serve as a labour reservoir, building fortifications for the Spanish and maintaining the island's infrastructure, for which they were sometimes paid. Here, too, the idea behind these work schemes was to enable men to maintain their families, although in practice they contributed little to defusing the critical humanitarian situation. Neither the Cuban nor the South African cases can be compared with the degree of forced labour in the German military's camps in Namibia (1904–8) which, in contrast with the three other cases examined here, were not established essentially as part of an anti-guerrilla strategy. They also differed in terms of organisation and administration. Whereas the British developed centralised camp administrations for both the 'white' and the 'black' camps in South Africa, in Cuba, local committees (mayor, military commander, church and local elite) were left to care independently for the destitute and compete for scant resources from the Captain-General. A distinguishing feature in Cuba was the element of class warfare inherent in civilian concentration where wealthy property owners (who had paid their taxes and could afford volunteer forces to protect their estates) were excluded. In this respect, civilian concentration acknowledged and strengthened unequal property and land-owning structures by sweeping 'unlawful residents' away. In South Africa, after the war, the British reinstated the pre-war social order, assisted the Boer landowners to return to their farms and did nothing to change the position of the African population. Just as the British in South Africa liked to refer to their 'protection' and 'refugee' camps, Spanish Generals also claimed in Cuba to 'protect' refugees from abuse and interference by the insurgents. Furthermore, it was argued that the rural population ('savages') would benefit from the 'civilising' influences of concentration and urbanisation. Ideas of social engineering were—as we have shown—much more explicit in South Africa and were well developed by the USA in the Philippines. But the rhetoric of the 'civilising' or 'modernising mission' should not blind us to the fact that, in all these cases, the rationale for the camps was essentially military.

The military purpose of the camps, as a counter-guerrilla strategy in wartime—of separating insurgents from any support by civilian non-combatants—is the common denominator of the camps in Cuba, South Africa and the Philippines. As part of an anti-guerrilla strategy, this was not new. The attempt to 'isolate' the civilian population from insurgent guerrilla fighters emerges as a characteristic feature of anti-guerrilla warfare. Referring to the well-known work of C. E. Callwell,[51] the British military historian, I. Beckett, emphasises that the resort to civilian concentration emerged 'entirely independently in different armies faced with the same kind of difficulties'.[52] He makes a strong case for a structural understanding of anti-guerrilla policies. Recent research also indicates that in areas such as southern Africa, where British and German colonial powers were neighbours, they were ready, in a limited way, to assist each other during the first decade of the twentieth century at a time when there was a mounting antagonism between them in Europe.[53] Indeed, the different colonial powers were well informed about the 'small wars' of their contemporaries and could be said to have learned from each other's counter-guerrilla measures, during the suppression of colonial rebellions, as well as from previous guerrilla wars. In some cases, individual soldiers drew on experience in several of these conflicts. Therefore, we argue that the colonial development of concentration camps can be understood at best as a combination of structural factors and situational decisions that were influenced by both the personal experience of the decision-makers and the example of other colonial powers.

The colonial development of concentration camps, examined in this article, was part of a process which continued during the twentieth century with the later appearance of the 'new villages' in Malaya, the 'camps de regroupement' in Algeria, the camps during the Mau Mau revolt in Kenya and the 'strategic hamlet' system in Vietnam. We argue that none of these have much in common—either in purpose or in organisation—with the Nazi camps in Germany (from 1933) or in occupied Europe (1939–45). Our goal is to point the way ahead for future work on the diverse phenomena of forced civilian concentration which, in the twentieth century, was by no means limited to Europe or to European colonial arenas.

Acknowledgements

This article has been developed out of a presentation given by us at a conference on 'Helpless Imperialists: Imperial Failure, Radicalization, and Violence' at the Institute for Advanced Study, Freiburg University, in January 2010. We wish to record our thanks to Gregor Thum and Maurus Reinkowski for their invitation to participate in that conference. Iain Smith also thanks Elizabeth van Heyningen (University of Cape Town), his co-researcher on the South African camps, and the Wellcome Trust for their generous funding of that project.

Notes

[1] Arendt, *The Origins of Totalitarianism*, 440. For Arendt's work, see King and Stone, eds, *Hannah Arendt and the Uses of History*. See also Madley, 'From Africa to Auschwitz', and Olusoga and Erichsen, *The Kaiser's Holocaust*.
[2] Henderson, *Failure of a Mission*, 29.
[3] This is currently the subject of research by members of A. Kramer's team based at Trinity College, Dublin: http://www.tcd.ie/warstudies/projects.php#concentration. The camps in Nazi Germany (1933–39) are the subject of a recently completed research project led by N. Wachsmann at Birkbeck College, London: www.camps.bbk.ac.uk. See also Caplan and Wachsmann, eds, *Concentration Camps in Nazi Germany*.
[4] Scholars of the Nazi camp-system long ago discarded the overall heading 'concentration camp' and refer, for example, to 'early camps' to indicate the functional changes over the years after 1933. Furthermore, a clear distinction is drawn between concentration and extermination camps. See Orth, *System*, 25–26, 337.
[5] For a recent critical assessment of this literature, see Gerwarth and Malinowski, 'Hannah Arendt's Ghosts', 279–300.
[6] For the fullest recent study of this case, see Olusoga and Erichsen, *The Kaiser's Holocaust*. See also Kreienbaum, 'Guerrilla Wars and Colonial Concentration Camps'.
[7] For an overview of different camps and their functions, see Kotek and Rigoulot, *Le siècle des camps*.
[8] Gerlach, 'Sustainable Violence', 361–93.
[9] Nasson, *Black Participation* and *Abraham Esau's War*.
[10] Kitchener to Brodrick (War Office), 21 June 1901. Kitchener Papers, 30/57/20/2, National Archives, Kew.
[11] Linn, *The US army and counter-insurgency*, 23. Brig. Gen. Theodore Schwan is cited in May, *Batangas*, 95.
[12] For an overview, see Pérez Jr., *Cuba*, 77–96.

[13] Echauz, *Lo que se ha hecho*, 5, 24–30. 'Instancia dirigida al Comandante General de Sancti Spíritus por varios vecinos del Cuartón de Jobosí solicitando se les permita trasladarse a sus respectivas fincas para erradicar el brote de la epidemia extendida con la reconcentración de familias', 6 Feb. 1870, Archivo General Militar de Madrid (AGMM), Ultramar/Cuba (U/C) 5841.40; Pérez Guzmán, *Herida profunda*, 41, 45.

[14] For 1896, official statistics ascribed 9,052 deaths out of 17,897 to this tropical illness which the Spanish medical service did not know how to control. Larra, *Datos para la historia*, 5–7, 22, 28–29, 39, 41–42; Tone, 'How the Mosquito (Man) Liberated Cuba', 283–84. Spanish combatants deaths from 'Bajas de oficiales y tropa durante toda la campaña', 22 Oct. 1898; AGMM, U/C 5791.2.

[15] See both orders and lists on rations in AGMM, U/C 4921. Tone, *War and Genocide*, 9, 93, 142; Foner, *Antonio Maceo*, 172. For a nationalist interpretation, see Roig, *La guerra libertadora*, 135–44.

[16] Cardona and Losada, *Weyler*, 206; Diego, *Weyler*, 24; Millis, *Martial Spirit*, 59–60; Foner, *Spanish-Cuban-American War*, 77, 106–7, 110.

[17] Cited in Elorza and Hernández Sandoica, *Guerra de Cub*, 157–58.

[18] One of the few exceptions were the republicans of Francisco Pi i Margall and his newspaper *El Nuevo Régimen* that advocated independence for Cuba.

[19] For disinfection stations implemented at the city's entry of Pinar del Río, see Archivo Provincial Pinar del Río, Gobierno Civil de la Colonia, Actas Capitulares, libro 10, entry of 27 October 1897, 54.

[20] See Tone, *War and Genocide*, 209–17, quote: 223.

[21] AGMM, U/C 5741.2 & 5809, 3441 & 3444.

[22] A good start on the published literature is provided by Linn, *US Army and Counter-Insurgency*.

[23] Kramer, 'Race-Making', 172, 194–200; Gates, 'Philippine Guerrillas', 56.

[24] See Linn, 'Provincial Pacification', 62–66; May, 'Total War?', 437–57.

[25] Go, 'Imperial Power', 208–9; May, *Batangas*, 158–60.

[26] On the difficulties regarding civilian deaths, see Gates, 'War-related Deaths in the Philippines', and May, '150,000 Missing Filipinos'.

[27] For the difficulties with irregular warfare in the international treaties, see Nurick and Barrett, 'Legality of Guerrilla Forces', 563–83.

[28] Welch, 'American Atrocities', 246. On the conflicting interconnections with the British, see Kramer, 'Empires, Exceptions, and Anglo-Saxons', 1335–44.

[29] Schumacher, *Wars for Empire*, 170.

[30] See van Heyningen, 'The Concentration Camps', 24–43, and F. Pretorius' Introduction in *Scorched Earth*, 9.

[31] In an extensive literature, the best short account of this war is Nasson, *South African War* (1999) and especially the expanded version: *The War for South Africa* (2010).

[32] Milner to Kitchener, 31 October 1900; Milner Papers, 45, Bodleian Library, Oxford.

[33] Maurice and Grant, *Official History*, Vol. IV, 568–76; Pakenham, *The Boer War*, 536–37.

[34] van Heyningen, 'Costly Mythologies', 495–513. For details on the camps, visit the recently established website http://www.lib.uct.ac.za/mss/bccd/index.php.

[35] Spies, *Methods of Barbarism?* 250–51, 288; Warwick, *Black People*, 150–51.

[36] Kessler, 'Black and Coloured Concentration Camps', 147–48.

[37] *Reports etc. on the Working of the Refugee Camps.* Covering over a thousand pages, these include (for 1901–2) Cd. 608, 694, 789, 793, 819, 853, 893, 939, 942, 902, 934, 936, 1161.

[38] Milner to Sir Hamilton Goold-Adams, 4 April 1901; Goold-Adams Papers, file 1, Rhodes House Library, Oxford.

[39] Low-Beer, Smallman-Raynor and Cliff, 'Disease and Death in the South African War', 223–45.

[40] Emily Hobhouse has generated an extensive literature. See Fisher, *That Miss Hobhouse*, and especially her own publications and the volume of her letters edited by van Reenen, *Emily Hobhouse* and Hobhouse Balme, *To Love One's Enemies*.

[41] *Report on the Concentration Camps in South Africa of the Committee of Ladies*, Cd. 893.
[42] Milner to Sir H. Goold-Adams, 14 Jan. 1902. Milner Ms. 173. Bodleian Library, Oxford.
[43] Pakenham, *The Boer War*, 518.
[44] Warwick, *Black People*, 154; Mohlamme, 'African Refugee Camps', 110–31.
[45] Kessler, 'Black and Coloured Concentration Camps', 144–45; Arnold, 'Social Crisis', 385–404.
[46] Brodrick to Kitchener, 21 June 1901. Kitchener Papers 30/57/22/(2), National Archives, Kew.
[47] Grundlingh, *The Dynamics of Treason*.
[48] Zietsman, 'The Concentration Camp Schools', 89; Riedi, 'Teaching Empire', 1316–47.
[49] See van Heyningen, 'A Tool for Modernisation?'.
[50] Kramer, 'Race-Making', 201.
[51] Callwell, *Small Wars*.
[52] Beckett, *Modern Insurgencies and Counter-Insurgencies*, 36. H. Strachan makes a similar point regarding the emergence of British counter-insurgency strategies in the second half of the twentieth century: Strachan, 'Introduction', 8.
[53] Lindner, 'Imperialism and Globalization', 4–28.

References

Arendt, Hannah. *The Origins of Totalitarianism*. New York: Harcourt Brace & Co., 1973.
Arnold, D. 'Social Crisis and Epidemic Disease in the Famines of Nineteenth Century India'. *Social History of Medicine* 6, no. 3 (1993): 385–404.
Beckett, Ian F. W. *Modern Insurgencies and Counter-Insurgencies. Guerrillas and Their Opponents since 1750*. London: Routledge, 2001.
Callwell, C. E. *Small Wars: Their Principles and Practice*. London: HMSO, 1st ed., 1896, 3rd ed., 1906.
Caplan, Jane, and Nikolaus Wachsmann, eds. *Concentration Camps in Nazi Germany: The New Histories*. London: Routledge, 2010.
Cardona, Gabriel, and Juan Carlos Losada. *Weyler, nuestro hombre en La Habana*. Barcelona: Planeta, 1997.
Diego García, Emilio. *Weyler, de la leyenda a la historia*. Madrid: Fundación Cánovas del Castillo, 1998.
Echauz y Guinart, Félix de. *Lo que se ha hecho y lo que hay que hacer en Cuba. Breves indicaciones sobre la campaña*. 2nd ed. Havana: Viuda de Soler y Compañía, 1873.
Elorza, Antonio, and Elena Hernández Sandoica. *La Guerra de Cuba (1895–1898). Historia política de una derrota colonial*. Madrid: Alianza, 1998.
Emily Hobhouse. Boer War Letters, edited by Rykie van Reenen. Cape Town: Human & Rousseau, 1984.
Fisher, John. *That Miss Hobhouse*. London: Secker & Warburg, 1971.
Foner, Philip S. *The Spanish-Cuban-American War and the Birth of American Imperialism*, 2 vols. New York: Monthly Review Press, 1972.
———. *Antonio Maceo. The 'Bronze Titan' of Cuba's Struggle for Independence*. New York: Monthly Review Press, 1977.
Gates, John M. 'Philippine Guerrillas, American Anti-Imperialists, and the Election of 1900'. *Pacific Historical Review* 46, no. 1 (1977): 51–64.
———. 'War-Related Deaths in the Philippines, 1899–1902'. *The Pacific Historical Review* 53, no. 3 (1984): 367–78.
Gerlach, Christian. 'Sustainable Violence: Mass Resettlement, Strategic Villages, and Militias in Anti-Guerilla Warfare'. In *Removing Peoples. Forced Removal in the Modern World*, edited by R. Bessel and C. B. Haake. Oxford: Oxford University Press, 2009.
Gerwarth, Robert, and Stephan Malinowski. 'Hannah Arendt's Ghosts: Reflections on the Disputable Path from Windhoek to Auschwitz'. *Central European History* 42, no. 2 (2009): 279–300.

Go, Julian. 'Imperial Power and Its Limits: America's Colonial Empire in the Early Twentieth Century'. In *Lessons of Empire. Imperial Histories and American Power*, edited by C. Calhoun, F. Cooper, and K. W. Moore. New York: The New Press, 2006: 201–14.

Grundlingh, Albert. *The Dynamics of Treason: Boer Collaboration in the South African War of 1899–1902*. Pretoria: Protea Book House, 2006.

Henderson, Nevile. *Failure of a Mission. Berlin 1937–1939*. London: Hodder and Stoughton, 1940.

Heyningen, Elizabeth van. 'A Tool for Modernisation? The Boer Concentration Camps of the South African War, 1900–1902'. *South African Journal of Science* 106, no. 5–6 (2010): 1–10. Available from http://www.sajs.co.za/index.php/SAJS/article/view/242/290.

———. 'Costly Mythologies: The Concentration Camps of the South African War in Afrikaner Historiography'. *Journal of Southern African Studies* 34, no. 3 (2008): 495–513.

———. 'The Concentration Camps of the South African (Anglo-Boer) War, 1900–1902'. *History Compass* 7, no. 1 (2009): 22–43.

Hobhouse Balme, Jennifer. *To Love One's Enemies: The Work and Life of Emily Hobhouse*. Cobble Hill, BC: Hobhouse Trust, 1994.

Kessler, Stowell V. 'The Black and Coloured Concentration Camps'. In *Scorched Earth*, edited by F. Pretorius. Cape Town: Human & Rousseau, 2001.

King, Richard H., and Dane Stone, eds. *Hannah Arendt and the Uses of History. Imperialism, Nation, Race, and Genocide*. New York: Berghahn Books, 2007.

Kotek, Joël, and Pierre Rigoulot, eds. *Le siècle des camps. Détention, concentration, extermination. Cent ans de mal radicale*. Paris: JC Lattès, 2000.

Kramer, Paul A. 'Empires, Exceptions, and Anglo-Saxons: Race and Rule Between the British and United States Empires, 1880–1910'. *The Journal of American History* 88, no. 4 (2002): 1315–53.

———. 'Race-Making and Colonial Violence in the US Empire: The Philippine-American War as Race War'. *Diplomatic History* 30, no. 2 (2006): 169–210.

Kreienbaum, Jonas. 'Guerrilla Wars and Colonial Concentration Camps: The Exceptional Case of German South West Africa (1904–1907)'. Paper presented at the conference 'Waterloo to Desert Storm: New Thinking on International Conflict, 1815–1991', Glasgow, 24–25 June 2010.

Larra y Cerezo, Ángel. *Datos para la historia de la campaña sanitaria en la guerra de Cuba. Apuntes estadísticos relativos al año 1896*. Madrid: Impr. de R. Rojas, 1896.

Lindner, Ulrike. 'Imperialism and Globalization: Entanglements and Interactions Between the British and German Colonial Empires in Africa before the First World War'. *Bulletin. German Historical Institute London* 32, no. 1 (2010): 4–28.

Linn, Brian McAllister. 'Provincial Pacification in the Philippines, 1900–1901: The First District Department of Northern Luzon'. *Military Affairs* 51, no. 2 (1987): 62–66.

———. *The US Army and Counter-Insurgency in the Philippine War 1899–1902*. Chapel Hill, NC: University of North Carolina Press, 1989.

Low-Beer, Daniel, Matthew Smallman-Raynor, and Andrew David Cliff. 'Disease and Death in the South African War: Changing Disease Patterns from Soldiers to Refugees'. *Social History of Medicine* 17, no. 2 (2004): 223–45.

Madley, Benjamin. 'From Africa to Auschwitz: How German South West Africa Incubated Ideas and Methods Adopted and Developed by the Nazis in Eastern Europe'. *European History Quarterly* 35, no. 3 (2005): 429–64.

Maurice, Frederick, and M.H. Grant. *Official History of the War in South Africa*. London: Hurst & Blackett, 1906–10.

May, Glenn Anthony. '150,000 Missing Filipinos. A Demographic Crisis in Batangas, 1887–1903'. *Annales de Démographie Historique* 21 (1985): 215–43.

———. *Battle for Batangas. A Philippine Province at War*. New Haven, London: Yale University Press, 1991.

———. 'Was the Philippine-American-War a "Total War"?'. In *Anticipating Total War. The German and American Experiences, 1871–1914*, edited by M. F. Boemeke, R. Chickering, and S. Förster. Cambridge: Cambridge University Press, 1999.

Millis, Walter. *The Martial Spirit. A Study of Our War with Spain*. Cambridge: The Riverside Press, 1931.
Mohlamme, J. S. 'African Refugee Camps in the Boer Republics'. In *Scorched Earth*, edited by F. Pretorius. Cape Town: Human & Rousseau, 2001.
Nasson, Bill. *Abraham Esau's War: A Black South African War in the Cape, 1899–1902*. Cambridge: Cambridge University Press, 1991.
———. *Black Participation in the Anglo-Boer War 1899–1902*. Randburg: Ravan Press, 1999.
———. *The South African War 1899–1902*. London: Arnold, 1999.
———. *The War for South Africa*. Cape Town: Tafelberg, 2010.
Nurick, Lester, and Roger W. Barrett. 'Legality of Guerrilla Forces under the Laws of War'. *The American Journal of International Law* 40, no. 3 (1946): 563–83.
Olusoga, David, and Casper W. Erichsen. *The Kaiser's Holocaust. Germany's Forgotten Genocide and the Colonial Roots of Nazism*. London: Faber and Faber, 2010.
Orth, Karin. *Das System der nationalsozialistischen Konzentrationslager. Eine politische Organisationsgeschichte*. Zurich: Pendo, 2002.
Pakenham, Thomas. *The Boer War*. London: Weidenfeld & Nicolson, 1979.
Pérez Guzmán, Francisco. *Herida profunda*. Havana: Ediciones Unión, 1998.
Pérez Jr, Louis A. *Cuba. Between Reform and Revolution*. 4th ed. New York: Oxford University Press, 2011.
Pretorius, Fransjohan, ed. *Scorched Earth*. Cape Town: Human & Rousseau, 2001.
Report on the Concentration Camps in South Africa of the Committee of Ladies. London: HMSO, 1902.
Reports etc. on the Working of the Refugee Camps. London: HMSO, 1901–2.
Riedi, E. 'Teaching Empire: British and Dominions Women Teachers in the South African War Concentration Camps'. *English Historical Review* 120, no. 489 (2005): 1316–47.
Roig de Leuchsenring, Emilio. *La guerra libertadora cubana de los treinta años, 1868–1898. Razón de su victoria*. 2nd ed. Havana: Oficina del Historiador de la Ciudad, 1958.
Schumacher, Frank. 'Wars for Empire. The United States and the Conquest of the Philippine Islands, 1899–1913'. In *The American Experience of War*, edited by G. Schild. Paderborn: Ferdinand Schöningh, 2010.
Spies, Stephanus Burridge. *Methods of Barbarism? Roberts and Kitchener and Civilians in the Boer Republics: January 1900–May 1902*. Cape Town: Human & Rousseau, 1977.
Strachan, Hew. 'Introduction'. In *Big Wars and Small Wars. The British Army and the Lessons of War in the Twentieth Century*, edited by H. Strachan. London/New York: Routledge, 2006.
Tone, John L. 'How the Mosquito (Man) Liberated Cuba'. *History and Technology* 18, no. 4 (2002): 277–308.
———. *War and Genocide in Cuba 1895–1898*. Chapel Hill, NC: University of North Carolina Press, 2006.
Warwick, Peter. *Black People and the South African War 1899–1902*. Cambridge: Cambridge University Press, 1983.
Welch Jr, Richard E. 'American Atrocities in the Philippines: The Indictment and the Response'. *Pacific Historical Review* 43, no. 2 (1974): 233–53.
Zietsman, Paul. 'The Concentration Camp Schools'. In *Scorched Earth*, edited by F. Pretorius. Cape Town: Human & Rousseau, 2001.

Internet resources

www.camps.bbk.ac.uk
http://www.lib.uct.ac.za/mss/bccd/index.php
http://www.tcd.ie/warstudies/projects.php#concentration

[14]

Sleeping sickness epidemics and public health in the Belgian Congo

Maryinez Lyons

Colonial powers commonly regarded their medical and public health programmes as a form of compensation for the hardships caused by their colonisation of African peoples.[1] By the early 1940s the Belgians were proud of their colonial medical services in the Congo which they considered to be an outstanding feature of their 'civilising mission'. The history of medical services in the Congo is intimately linked to the special campaign to fight epidemic sleeping sickness early this century. That campaign formed the basis both for a public health programme and for the creation of a medical service, since it was, as in many African colonies, the first real effort made by the Europeans to deal with the health of Africans.

Following the British discovery in 1901 of a major sleeping sickness epidemic in Uganda, King Leopold of Belgium invited the recently established Liverpool School of Tropical Medicine to examine his Congo Free State. Alarmed at the high mortality rate in neighbouring Uganda, Leopold feared a demographic collapse in the Congo Free State which would frustrate its economic exploitation. By 1902, the year of his invitation to the Liverpool School, the violent practices of Congo Free State agents had aroused international indignation and condemnation. Leopold was much concerned about his tarnished image and he realised that prompt response to a possible epidemic of sleeping sickness in the territory might help to improve his reputation. From the outset, medical provision for the Congolese was related to economic and political considerations. While the Belgian government, which subsequently took over the running of the Congo from Leopold, tried to avoid further administrative mismanagement, medical provision remained closely related to economic and political objectives.

Declaring the disease to be epidemic in some regions of the State, the Liverpool researchers advised Leopold to take urgent measures to

IMPERIAL MEDICINE

protect areas which they considered to be as yet uninfected – such as the vast northeast, later known as Province Orientale. The 'medicalisation' of the Congolese began soon after this with the sleeping sickness campaign, through which the population was systematically introduced to the idea that European doctors and their medications were the solution to problems of ill health. The Belgian campaign was elaborated and refined over time until by the 1930s it formed the core of the colonial public health programme. However, as one specialist has noted, 'The various colonial sleeping sickness campaigns became a kind of conditioned reflex . . . routine, even a fixation of ideas with the result that all epidemics were fought in stereotyped manner without asking if methods were best from region to region.'[13]

La lutte: the campaign against sleeping sickness

The sleeping sickness campaign operated on two fronts which the Belgians referred to as the *médicamenteuse* and the *biologique*. The former included all the more purely medical aspects such as development and training of staff, European and African; the creation of the annual, itinerant medical missions which by 1930 were examining nearly three million people; the gradual evolution of a network of hospitals and rural clinics, especially in Province Orientale; and research into the disease and possible cures. The second front, *biologique*, was primarily administrative and involved public health measures intended to control the incidence and spread of the disease. The measures within this front were often early attempts at 'social engineering' through the reorganisation, restructuring and control of African societies. Features of this front were the identification and mapping of infected and non-infected zones and the creation of a *cordon sanitaire* to protect mainly non-infected regions such as large portions of the northeast; isolation of infected individuals in one of the special lazarets, or isolation camps, located on the fringes of uninfected zones; the regrouping and re-siting of African populations as part of the overall programme with which the Belgians hoped simultaneously to solve public health, political and economic problems; and, finally, a score of administrative measures designed to regulate various African activities in order to control the incidence and spread of sleeping sickness.

Disease was regarded as an enemy agent against which the Belgian colonial administration fought on these two fronts. The predominantly military administration of the Congo Free State, which was only gradually altered after Leopold's state became a Belgian colony in 1908, quite naturally conceptualised the battle against sleeping sickness as a

SLEEPING SICKNESS EPIDEMICS

military campaign, *la lutte*. Sleeping sickness, the foe, had to be isolated, cordoned off, contained and eliminated. After 1903–4 when the aetiology of the disease was discovered, those factors believed by the Europeans to cause the disease – trypanosomes and tsetse-flies – could be targeted for the attack. Supported by the assumption that European science with its superior technology and medicine would succeed where primitive African societies simply floundered, the colonial authorities had no doubts about their methods. After all, said a medical administrator in 1943, 'we know how primitive and futile was the knowledge of the natives in matters of hygiene'.[4]

Diseases, like recalcitrant Africans, were to be forced into submission. In protecting from infection their future labourers and tax-payers, the new colonial authorities felt fully justified in attempting to assert total control. The major feature of the early campaign against sleeping sickness, the *cordon sanitaire*, reflected the paternalistic nature of Belgian colonial policy in which health priorities formed a part of the justification for the methods of the social engineer. African societies, like the labouring classes in Europe, had, it was felt, to be controlled for their own protection. There was a crucial difference, however, in the scope of measures possible in a colonial setting, where social control could sometimes be exercised to a degree unimaginable in the metropole. A growing profusion of legislation from both Brussels and Boma, the capital of the Congo, was sanctioned by the judiciary and enforced by the military and the police. At the same time, an evolving medical infrastructure of personnel, facilities and procedures was directed at locating, isolating and dealing with all those infected with the trypanosome.

Cordon sanitaire and isolation: 1903–9

The sleeping sickness campaign began officially on 5 May 1903 when the Vice Governor-General announced that isolation of victims was the 'principal precaution to take in order to check the spread of the disease'. One doctor raised the 'delicate question' of what to do about victims' families. Should they also be isolated? But, he added, considering the 'insouciance and negligence of hygiene of the Africans', how could effective surveillance be achieved? Reminding the Governor-General that during the recent cholera and plague epidemics in Asia Minor and Arabia more than one port in the Mediterranean had become infected in spite of the *cordon sanitaire*, the doctor explained that he feared the Congolese manifested the same 'hatred of all hygiene measures conceived of by Western civilisation' as did the oriental popu-

IMPERIAL MEDICINE

lations, and that would prevent a successful *cordon* being established.[5]

Local officials as well as all religious and philanthropic organisations in the state were instructed to investigate villages in their localities and alert the chiefs of the measures they were to take. These included, naturally, the isolation of victims at a distance from the village and the burning of their huts, as well as the destruction of all the clothing and daily utensils of those who had died of the disease. There were no instructions on how these aims were to be achieved (even when suitable language translators were available), and there was no discussion of the possible relevance of cultural differences between African societies, especially how these affected indigenous ideas of disease management.

In December 1905 the campaign was futher systematised when formal directions were issued to all colonial agents. Infected individuals were strictly forbidden to travel *except* to lazarets on the instructions of a doctor. Anyone, it was believed, could easily recognise the enlarged glands, particularly the cervical glands at the back of the neck, which were considered to be the main symptom of infection. Agents were accordingly instructed to send suspected victims immediately to the nearest medical post where lymph fluid and blood could be examined under a microscope for evidence of infection. However, under *no* circumstances was a suspect to be sent to an uncontaminated region. If victims had to use river transport, to reach a lazaret, 'they were [to be] placed in movable cages surrounded on all sides by fine wire net' in order to prevent tsetse-flies biting them and spreading the disease.[16]

There were no significant policy changes between 1903 and mid-1906 because there was no available cure and, as sleeping sickness was always fatal, the only feasible measure was the total isolation of all suspected victims. But the situation was greatly changed in December 1906 when new sleeping sickness regulations were issued as a result of the development of the arsenical compound, atoxyl. This drug was valuable for victims in the first stage of the disease while parasites were present in the peripheral circulatory system. It was mistakenly believed that it could effect a cure in four to six weeks, thus regular screening was undertaken to identify suspect cases. Some doctors, however, were reluctant to use atoxyl which they considered to be dangerous even in the hands of specialists.[7]

SLEEPING SICKNESS EPIDEMICS

Surveillance and search

From 1906 the emphasis accordingly shifted to use of the new drug. 'Incessant surveillance' with the full co-operation of all Europeans was henceforth the battle cry of the campaign. Identifying victims in the advanced stages of the disease was not as difficult as the new priority of finding those in the early stages of infection. The latter were both more contagious and, it was believed, more easily curable. Efforts were made to teach African authorities how to look for suspect glands and they were told to report suspected cases immediately. It was deemed imperative that Africans understood the role of the tsetse-fly in spreading the infection and administrators were directed to identify the flies and to convince the chiefs of the importance of clearing away from their villages all tsetse-sheltering bush.[8]

Some state doctors questioned the utility of the policy of isolation as a blanket measure. As one doctor in 1905 explained, there were so many Africans with enlarged glands that isolation of all of them would not only be impossible because of the lack of personnel, it would also paralyse commerce. In his view, 'one could not sequester people without clinical symptoms' other than enlarged glands. He had further doubts about the ethic of infringing upon individual liberty by such a sweeping policy. After all, he pointed out, in Europe, individuals with infectious tuberculosis were allowed to retain their liberty even when the public at large was at risk from infection.[9]

Other doctors were also concerned about the legality of treating patients against their wills. Responding to the queries of a state doctor in 1907, the Director of Justice put the state firmly behind forced treatment, though with some reservations. He declared that the state had not only the right, but even the obligation, to take measures necessary to prevent the spread of contagious and infectious disease. He argued that it was desirable to respect individual liberty as much as possible, but it was the state, not private individuals, which had to take decisions on the best means of fighting an epidemic. This was true even in countries that guaranteed constitutional rights where the individual was sacrificed to the requirements of public security or public hygiene. However, on the question of the right of the state to impose a treatment which sometimes resulted in blindness, the Director of Justice believed that such a therapy would be inhumane and its administration to unwilling victims would be contrary to elementary principles of 'natural law'. If it were proved that such blinding resulted to all those who received it, then it could be used only with the consent of

IMPERIAL MEDICINE

the victim who would have to be forewarned of its danger.[10]

The cordoned 'triangle'

Perhaps the most significant feature of the act of 5 December 1906 was the *cordon sanitaire* it placed around Uele District in the northern Congo, a territory some 300,000 square kilometres in extent. This was achieved by means of a series of lazarets located on the periphery of the district. Between 1907 and 1910 the key lazarets and observation posts were established at the state posts of Ibembo, Barumbu, Stanleyville, Aba and Yakoma. By 1912, there were fourteen observation posts throughout the whole colony, with the major epidemic areas designated as the Semliki basin, Kivu, the Kwilu basin, and Kwango, all lying to the south and west of Province Orientale.[11]

The main principles of the lazaret system were described by Inge Heiberg, the first director of the principal lazaret for the north, located at Ibembo. He advised that isolation camps should be located at the limits of contaminated areas, rather than inside them, and stressed that the traffic caused by labour recruitment from infected areas was highly instrumental in the spread of the disease. All recruitment should be accompanied by thorough medical examinations which should be repeated along the transit routes, and, in effect, constitute a 'sieve' to catch sleeping sickness victims. Heiberg also described how a search tour should be conducted to trap all suspects. The doctor should begin at a point furthest from the centre of the area and in that way 'brush ahead of him like the hunter' all suspects and expel them through the observation post, or 'key' to the district.

Once inside the lazaret, victims would receive atoxyl injections and periodic examinations which were to be carefully recorded in registers. Isolation would vary from complete 'lock-up' to relatively unrestrained surveillance. Heiberg felt that prison-style confinement was administratively preferable for both Europeans and Africans. The boundaries and tasks were clear and public order was not disrupted, 'except, perhaps, at the moment of internment of a sleeping sickness victim'. No meeting could occur between victim and African soldiers or natives and more significantly, no arms would find their way inside the lazaret. 'After all,' the doctor added, 'it is isolation which makes a lazaret.' He saw, however, some disadvantages to the prison-style system, which required, 'energetic and firm surveillance' and other stringent measures. The major problem was the ever-present threat of rebellion, and Heiberg consequently favoured more liberal and open lazarets, keeping strict isolation for the really obstinate or advanced cases.

SLEEPING SICKNESS EPIDEMICS

Patients' families were not officially allowed to visit them in the lazarets, but kin often accompanied victims and tried to remain with them. The conflict which arose from the Belgians' failure to understand the importance of this social aspect of African responses to sickness and disease management provides a rich area of enquiry for the historian.[12] In the early Congo, administrators all too frequently revealed their ignorance of African social and medical practices. But sometimes humanitarian concern broke through, as in 1907 when an unusually sensitive zone administrator addressed the Governor-General: 'I want to know if the families of the patients can live at the post and if they can be rationed by the State, as often, if one member is hospitalized, the others in the family do not want to leave. It would be cruel to send them away.'[13]

The problem of accompanying kin also illuminates the Belgians' extremely legalistic approach to 'native affairs'. For instance, the doctor at Stanleyville lazaret in 1907 asked if he should return the *legitimate* wives of victims to their home villages, pointing out that this would be done only after ascertaining the legality of the marriages, and only one wife would be considered as having legal status.

Heiberg warned that it was of paramount importance to treat the patients with kindness, goodwill and indulgence. They must be carefully fed. He advised that it was best to allow people to live in culturally similar, small groups – 'village style' – with a former sergeant or corporal of the *Force Publique* appointed as the headman. Doctors and administrators should interfere as little as possible in the people's internal disputes.[14]

Lazarets in trouble

By 1910 the prison-style, total isolation system was clearly in difficulties although serious problems had arisen almost immediately with the policy of 1905–6. Lazaret doctors very soon realised that, contrary to earlier hopes, atoxyl cured very few patients in the early stages of the disease, with some relapses, while it had no effect on those in the advanced stages. Africans were very quick to observe the poor results. The mortality rates were appalling – at Ibembo lazaret, nearly one-third of those admitted had died by 1911. Furthermore, there was a dreadful side effect of atoxyl injections – up to thirty per cent of those treated became blind as the drug atrophied the optic nerve. Africans were terrified of *la lutte* and the lazarets became popularly known as 'death camps'. Wild rumours circulated that the colonial officials were not only causing the disease, but were rounding up people in order to eat

IMPERIAL MEDICINE

them. A missionary's advice of 1902 that the state should establish 'colonies of incurables' had been made a reality.[15]

Heiberg's professional experience in European insane asylums makes it most relevant to note his views on the difference between an insane European and an African sleeping sickness patient. According to him, nearly all European patients in an asylum would have their own particular delusions. That made a co-ordinated riot in a hospital an unknown, even impossible event. But in the Congo, thought Heiberg, sleeping sickness victims had a different kind of 'insanity'. Their disease reduced, but did not destroy, their power to reason. Sleeping sickness victims were obsessed with such ideas as 'the injustice of their imprisonment', and a hundred sleeping sickness victims with an identical 'obsession' comprised a formidable threat. When the local administrator visited the lazaret in September 1910, he was repeatedly approached by patients with the same complaint that they were being prevented from 'seeing home'.

Heiberg's views on insane and 'irrational' behaviour are of interest in that they reveal contemporary European attitudes about the insane as obsessive people who have fixed ideas and who act individually, not in groups. Among Africans, however, Heiberg proposed a different kind of insanity, that of a group of people sharing an obsessive and irrational idea. Perhaps more importantly, he could only view the Africans' desire to escape western biomedicine in order to return to their own people and their ways of dealing with misfortune as totally irrational – or insane – behaviour. Like many colonialists, he believed that Africans were acting irrationally in rejecting the benefits of western civilisation.[16]

All along, some lazaret inmates had managed to escape into the surrounding areas, but the growing frustration and hostility of the victims isolated at Ibembo found expression in two serious riots in 1909 and 1910, thus confirming Heiberg's concerns. The Ibembo riots signalled the need for reform. As Heiberg said of the lazaret in 1910, 'Strictly speaking, it was a permanent prison and should bear the inscription, "Abandon all hope, ye who enter here."'[17]

The sleeping sickness campaign, like other Belgian colonial policies, was highly centralised with most instructions issued directly from Brussels. There was no separate colonial medical department until December 1922. A medical service had functioned from Brussels since December 1909, but doctors in the colony remained strictly subordinated to the authority of their local territorial administrators. Before December 1910 and the first medical department for the Congo, there was no true 'medical authority which made sanitation regulations'. All such regulations were issued by civil and military authorities. Thus

SLEEPING SICKNESS EPIDEMICS

measures such as medical passports and the epidemiological maps upon which the *cordon sanitaire* was based emanated from non-medical administrators. Ordinances controlling African life – village siting, fishing, salt-production, travel, kin relations – were all drafted by non-medical staff.

At the same time, doctors who were instructed to carry out the sleeping sickness measures frequently found themselves in the impossible situation of having to request assistance from the local territorial administrator. And, very often, the administrator was reluctant to support the doctors' requests. The main reason for the lack of co-operation was the political necessity of maintaining African tolerance for Belgian rule. Implementing public health measures made the local administrator more unpopular that he already was among the people. Pressed to achieve certain political and economic goals, namely labour recruitment and tax collection, the local administrators chose to ignore medical and public health measures as much as they could.

In 1909 the major features of *la lutte* were the *cordon sanitaire* and isolation in lazarets, considered by one doctor as being together 'the great panacea for public health in the Congo'. But, as he acknowledged, combined with the ineffective, even dangerous, chemotherapy, the campaign evoked intense distrust from the people. Furthermore, he said, the sporadic surveys for victims in African villages were viewed as 'little more than man hunts' and the result was that 'people fled [from] the doctors more quickly than they did the tax collectors!'[18] Often the army was required to assist doctors to examine Africans and then to effect their isolation. Clearly, the combination of a complicated and blundering bureaucracy with an isolation system from which the only exit was escape or death and in which one third of those treated became blind was a failure.

African responses to the early period of *la lutte* made it apparent to the colonial administration that no public health programme could be really effective unless everyone involved, African and European, co-operated. Slowly, the realisation dawned that medical and administrative staff would have to co-operate in order to implement sleeping sickness measures. There had been calls previously for the understanding and support of African authorities in the campaign to examine all of the people and to isolate infected individuals, but by late 1909 it had become clear that the understanding and support of all Africans affected by the campaign would be necessary if it were to stand any chance of success. The responses of the people to the Belgian sleeping sickness campaign were indeed a significant factor which shaped the future development of public health in the colony.

IMPERIAL MEDICINE

The pre-war period: 1910–1914

There were significant reforms in both health policy and the colonial medical service in the years immediately preceding the First World War. The shift began in 1910 with a series of reforms. The major change in policy was that lazarets were to be more open, becoming 'village-lazarets' in which only very advanced or troublesome patients would stay. Unlike the prison-like atmosphere of the earlier lazarets, the new institutions would accommodate members of the victims' immediate families. All other victims of the disease would be treated as outpatients and attend injection clinics which would be conveniently located near their own homes. Thus victims, while still able to do so, could continue labouring or being involved in food production.[19]

The reforms reflected administrative concerns beyond purely medical ones, and several issues were involved. First, there was the serious matter of the notorious reputation of the Leopoldian administration of the Congo Free State which the Belgian government wished to dispel after it took over in 1908. Then, too, the Belgians were still greatly involved in the process of establishing state control in several parts of the Congo including the northeast. Thus, while still engaged in the process of conquest and consolidating, the administration of the new colony had to appear to be more humane than Leopold's regime in order to avoid further condemnation by the 'Great Powers'.

While it is important to see events during this period in the context of the broader political policy of improving the administration's image, it must be pointed out that medical personnel in the Congo had been lobbying for some time for the creation of a separate medical department which would permit the rationalisation of the health service and enable the development of a more systematic public health policy. Following a tour of a district much infected with sleeping sickness, the Governor-General in 1910 proposed a major new campaign to combat the disease throughout the colony. The combination of pressure from colonial doctors for a medical department and the apparently increasing epidemicity of sleeping sickness resulted in the creation of such a department at the end of 1909, although a comprehensive sleeping sickness programme was not put into effect until 1918. The new medical department, like other branches of the colonial administration, was still based in Belgium where it remained so firmly centralised that one contemporary commented that the sleeping sickness campaign was being fought from offices in Brussels, not Africa.[20]

SLEEPING SICKNESS EPIDEMICS

Sleeping sickness and administrative control

Sleeping sickness policy was intertwined with broader issues of territorial administration, and this linkage began to emerge clearly after 1910. For instance, there was the problem of controlling the movements of people both within the colony and across its international frontiers. French Congo, Sudan and Uganda, all bordering the northeast, each contained areas of seriously epidemic sleeping sickness by 1910. The movements of people in and out of the Congo was therefore a primary concern for the administration. There was significant interplay between sleeping sickness measures, particularly those concerning the *cordon sanitaire*, and the broader economic and social concerns of territorial administration. Northern Congo was an important source of labour for economic projects such as the Kilo-Moto Gold Mines, the army and road construction. Those responsible for labour recruitment for these activities pressured the colonial authorities to allow easy access to African labour in the northern Congo while at the same time the medical experts pressed for stricter controls over population movements in order to protect the northern Congo from sleeping sickness. Ironically, one colonial sector, the economic, pushed for policies which could adversely affect the health of Africans while another colonial sector, the medical, strove to protect Africans from the spread of disease. Colonial policy was not monolithic but was instead a combination of interests which sometimes conflicted. It would be farfetched to impute Machiavellian motives to those who made public health policy and to the local administrators who implemented measures. Nevertheless, sleeping sickness measures formed part of the system of control used by the Belgian rulers.

The crucial element in the reform of sleeping sickness policy was the introduction on 30 April 1910 of mandatory medical passports.[21] Formerly, all Africans travelling beyond the immediate confines of their home regions had been required to obtain a travel pass on which doctors recorded details of all medical examinations. From April 1910 the new medical passports superseded the less-specific travel documents in the increasing attempt to control every movement of Africans.

An important element in the revision of public health policy was the standardisation of observation posts. These were strategically located surveillance and screening stations at which a medical helper, ideally a European *agent sanitaire*, or medical assistant, but very often a lone African *infirmier*, or dresser, was based with a microscope. It

IMPERIAL MEDICINE

was his duty to screen all travellers, being especially alert to those coming from regions known to be infected with the disease. A major function of the observation post was issuing medical passports in an attempt to further restrict movements of people.

It had been said that considering the large numbers of victims and restricted resources and personnel, that much of the voluminous legislation was 'of academic interest' only, a mere 'paper war'. While it is true that many of the instructions could not be successfully implemented because of the lack of resources, especially personnel, it would be a mistake to dismiss the early sleeping sickness policy as simply a 'paper war'. Many state officials ignored the regulations, but others made considerable effort to enforce them.[23]

Another significant feature of the campaign in this early period was the emergence of a discernible policy regarding the organisation and shape of African societies. Re-structuring African societies would remain for decades an important and troublesome issue for the colonial authorities. It became a particular problem when the public health authorities came into conflict with the local administrators, for the two departments had quite different motives for wishing to reorganise African society. When the two were in agreement over the reorganisation and re-siting of a group of people, there was less conflict, although increasingly, territorial administrators were loathe to involve themselves in a form of administrative interference which was so unpopular with the people.

From very early in the campaign against sleeping sickness, the regrouping and relocation of African populations had been a much used tactic. Ostensibly to protect people from the danger of infection through proximity to the infected tsetse-flies, the regrouping and relocation of entire populations also conveniently served other requirements of the local administration, especially during the early colonial period when state control was still precarious. Local administrators preferred their subjects to be sited for ease of administrative access even though many agents actually on the scene were extremely reluctant to tamper with this aspect of African life for fear of increased hostility and resistance. This tactic was important in labour recruitment and tax collection. It was simply easier to deal with groups of people conveniently located near communication routes or administrative centres than it was to 'chase up' scattered individuals far from the main sites of colonial power. With some people like the Azande, whose normal settlement pattern was one of dispersed family clusters separated by stretches of forest or savannah, the policy of regrouping was especially controversial. The topography of most of the northern Congo made it impractical to attempt to relocate Africans away from tsetse

SLEEPING SICKNESS EPIDEMICS

areas, and when such moves were carried out, people simply returned to their rivers to fish and to their fields to cultivate. During this early period of the campaign it was quite unrealistic for the colonial authorities to think of a grand restructuring of African socieities, if for no other reason than the lack of staff and resources to enforce such policy. Nevertheless, it was often discussed, and it was an important underlying consideration behind sleeping sickness policy.[25]

By 1910, doctors had been delegated considerable powers by the central administration in Belgium to request the reorganisation and relocation of Africans within their districts. Also by 1910, doctors had the right to request assistance from the army – the *force publique* – as well as the co-operation of the territorial administration, in their attempts to implement the public health policy. Thus it was not uncommon for the doctor to arrive in an area accompanied by armed soldiers and an administrator, and then to begin a systematic examination of the people, who were obliged by this show of force to present themselves regardless of the activities they may have been engaged in at the time. The doctor was also entitled to the co-operation of the local *capitas*, or village headmen appointed by the state, as well as that of the *chef médaille*, or officially recognised chief, also a colonial appointment. But these were not the only authority figures available to implement the programme. From 1912 most posts had, in addition to their contingent of the *force publique*, other law enforcement agents in the form of police who might be territorial or local. Finally, by 1912, the central government had made it quite clear that every European in the district – whether in government employment or not – was obliged to participate in the campaign against sleeping sickness.[26]

The First World War

The exigencies of war revealed not only the coercive nature of European medical intervention in the Belgian Congo, they also brought about changes in the nature of that intervention. An outstanding feature of the sleeping sickness campaign during the First World War was the manner in which the colonial administration contradicted its own public health policy and, in fact, in so doing aggravated the problem of human sleeping sickness in the northern Congo. The war meant that the Belgian government needed the labour and resources available in its colony more than ever before. Evacuated to England because of the German occupation of Belgium, the Belgian government looked to its African colony for material assistance in the war effort and the northern Congo was suddenly of great importance as the pro-

IMPERIAL MEDICINE

vider of three vital resources – gold, rubber and men.

But the increasing demands for gold, rubber and labour forced the colonial administration to violate much of its own recent public health policy in the northeast. The escalating labour requirements resulted in an intensification of the movement of population throughout the northeast, and thus the recently imposed *cordon sanitaire* became a hindrance to the war effort. Until the early 1920s both rubber and gold production remained particularly labour-intensive activities which required substantial investment of production forces.[27]

It is clear from the evidence that, at the local and provincial levels, administrators in the northern Congo were anxious to continue the campaign against sleeping sickness during the war. In spite of growing evidence that there were areas of epidemic sleeping sickness in north-central Uele, the Belgian administration remained unwilling to acknowledge the local government's claims that such regions were epidemic because it wished to avoid the restrictions of an effective *cordon sanitaire*. The war further exacerbated such differences of opinion. Unfortunately for the inhabitants, it was precisely the north-central regions of Uele district that were richest in wild rubber and Africans were continually pressured by the state to collect rubber to meet their tax demands. The rubber was most prolific in tsetse-infested gallery forests where trees and brush grew fringe-like along the waterways. It was quite clear, complained the District Commissioner, that the central government simply refused to declare an epidemic in north-central Uele district and such official recognition was required before a *cordon sanitaire* could be legally enforced. As a result, during the First World War there was a slow-down, virtually a cessation, of the campaign to control sleeping sickness in the northern Congo.

A major consequence of the war for Uelians was the increase and spread of epidemic sleeping sickness.[28] In some north-central territories like Gwane, Bili and Dakwa where the disease was already serious, sleeping sickness now became intensely epidemic with entire *chefferies* afflicted. The region would have to await the end of the war before the first really effective steps were taken to cope with the increase and spread of the disease – the first effective steps, that is, from the point of view of the 'medicalisation' of the region.

Missions maladie du sommeil: 1920–30

The most highly organised attempts to deal with the problems of endemic disease were the mobile services set up in Africa to combat human trypanosomiasis and on to these were later grafted field units with wider terms of reference, whose diagnostic and treatment facilities

SLEEPING SICKNESS EPIDEMICS

were directed at a number of different endemic disease problems.[29]

During the decade 1920–30 special sleeping sickness missions were launched and developed. For many Congolese, these teams were their first intimate contact with the new colonial state. It was a contact not always comprehensible or pleasant. *Missions maladie du sommeil* were special teams which were systematically to survey certain regions of the colony in order to identify and treat victims in their own villages. The cardinal features of the teams were their mobility and their attempt to examine the entire African population of the colony. New staff was recruited specifically for this campaign, and the hope of the Governor-General who first ennunciated the programme in August 1917 was that the colonial medical service would be able to recruit medical staff in Europe when military corps began demobilising following the end of the war.[30]

The first sleeping sickness team in the Belgian Congo began functioning in Kwango District in 1919, followed by a second team in Uele in 1920. Within four years three more sleeping sickness teams were established in Bangala, Stanleyville and Mayumbe districts. So well did this policy take hold that by 1932 there were at least five such teams operating in the northeast alone: Uele, Semliki, Stanleyville-Basoko, Kivu, and Maniema. But difficulties soon emerged. The divergent goals of different colonial departments resulted in *impasses* over the implementation of the public health measures. Doctors found themselves confronted with local administrators who were unwilling to enforce public health policies and recommendations. In addition, increasingly through the 1920s, the work and responsibilities of the special sleeping sickness teams overlapped with the colonial medical service until it became very difficult to perceive separate and distinctive roles for the two services.

The surveys continued almost annually between 1920 and 1930. Basically, the aim was the identification and treatment of every single victim in the colony, an ambitious goal indeed. It was not always easy to gain the co-operation of the people, and thus the colonial doctors often found it useful to be accompanied by the local headman who was familiar with the territory and who could locate the isolated settlements. It was also found useful to take along police agents who could assist with 'recalcitrants' and those who attempted to flee.

All adult males in the *chefferies* were given identity cards which displayed the names of their wives and children, and the sleeping sickness team issued dated medical visas with details of their examinations. The most important individual who helped with the survey,

IMPERIAL MEDICINE

according to one survey director, was the chief, and if he happened to be co-operative the number of daily examinations was greatly increased. For instance, people working in the fields were most reluctant to break off to attend medical examinations and were only brought in with difficulty. Here the chief's persuasion could be vital. Some groups, like the Azande, always hid their women from the teams. Although ambulatory patients were supposed to present themselves for fortnightly injections, it was 'extremely rare' for patients to appear voluntarily fortnightly or even monthly. One doctor voiced the ceaseless complaint of the coloniser, 'We do not know how to change African thinking.'[31]

Settlement patterns: social engineering and medical missions

By 1931 the sleeping sickness campaign reflected both major strands of Belgian public health policy – *prophylaxie médicale* and *prophylaxie biologique*. It was in the latter, the realm of 'social engineering', that colonial doctors were most often frustrated, especially as they found themselves in the awkward situation of making demands which conflicted with the goals of other sectors of the colonial administration.

There was a serious lack of co-ordination, and even conflict, between various administrative departments in the colony according to Marone, the doctor in charge of the 1931 survey. He urged that doctors be granted sanctions to arm them in their attempts to effect reorganisation of African societies for the purposes of public health as this remained the greatest problem facing the sleeping sickness campaign. He devoted fifteen pages of his 1931 report to a discussion of the one issue of regrouping and re-siting of Africans. Since clearing all of the tsetse-infested brush along major rivers was impossible, it was particularly important, he felt, to reorganise people into villages which should be placed at locations 'chosen by the medical service' in accord with the territorial administration. As things were, he said, doctors could only attempt medical prophylaxis: biological prophylaxis, the 'social engineering', was up to the territorial administration. Clearly severe tensions had developed between medical staff, who pressed for further preventive measures, and local administrators, who saw medicine as limited to a curative function.

Marone's lengthy articulation of the frustration experienced by doctors in their attempts to advise and implement public health measures designed to prevent the spread of the disease, reveals the

SLEEPING SICKNESS EPIDEMICS

extent of this problem by 1930. From 1920, doctors had implored territorial administrators to heed certain measures which, they believed, would decrease the incidence of sleeping sickness. The measures focused on several critical areas of African life including population movements due to their own travel, labour recruitment, kin ties and trade. Doctors were concerned about the movements of Africans induced by their search for rubber, and the medical authorities expressed reservations about the epidemiologically deleterious effects of state taxation policies. They offered advice on matters concerning African economic activities such as fishing and trade. They advised the 'sealing off' of certain badly afflicted regions, asking that outsiders be prevented entry even when seeking to fulfil their mandatory rubber tax. Medical advice related to sleeping sickness touched upon state policies concerning the growing of cash crops such as cotton, and those concerning porterage and road construction were directly affected by the acceptance of such medical advice. By 1930 the issue of regrouping people into larger villages and resiting villages in areas considered safer from infection of sleeping sickness had become a major problem for the medical staff and for the local administration alike.

From the mid-1920s, demands by some doctors for greater autonomy for the special sleeping sickness teams conflicted with the demands of others who recommended unification of the two services. Discrete sleeping sickness teams functioned alongside an evolving colonial medical service, but there was considerable confusion as the two services tended to compete for the same limited funds and personnel. Resources were shunted between the two services, producing uncertainty over which staff or facilities belonged to which service and which functions were the responsibility of each.

The relation of the sleeping sickness missions to the medical service became more, rather than less, unclear over time. In 1924 Dr Van Campenhout, the director of the *Service de l'Hygiène* at the Colonial Ministry in Brussels and a man who just two years earlier had solidly supported the special sleeping sickness team concept, suggested that the autonomous sleeping sickness teams be discontinued. He felt that one single, unified colonial medical service could better manage the sleeping sickness campaign.[32] By 1928 the chief medical officer felt that the sleeping sickness mission had 'lost sight of its principal aim', which was the survey of the district for all victims of the disease; instead it had become 'bogged down' in the treatment of victims. The head of the provincial medical service in Province Orientale thought that the same goals could be attained with half the staff if redundancies were

IMPERIAL MEDICINE

eliminated: 'I have not been able to find a clear line of demarcation between the work of the regular Medical Service and the Sleeping Sickness Mission of Uele. The latter spends a great deal of its effort on "general medicine".'

Some doctors were 'too busy with private patients'. Dispensaries directed by the district medical service were next door to dispensaries, and in one case, to a hospital, directed by the chief of the sleeping sickness team. Throughout the decade the confusion increased between the roles of the sleeping sickness missions and those of the medical service until by the end of the 1920s the medical tactics, too, were being challenged with explicit complaints about the system's 'creaking bureaucracy'.[33]

By 1930, *la lutte* reached into every area of life for both coloniser and colonised in the northern Congo, and had become inextricably entangled with other sectors of the colonial administration. Measures advised by medical authorities to curb the spread of sleeping sickness unavoidably affected areas of colonial policy such as transport, road construction and villagisation. African life, too, was markedly affected by the public health measures that had been instituted.

Summary

Events in the northern Congo between 1903 and 1930 are illustrative of the ways in which disease, especially when epidemic, can both illuminate social relations and itself affect the course of history. Medicine clearly helped to shape the political and administrative character of imperialism in the early Belgian Congo. Government responses to epidemic sleeping sickness in the Congo were at first predominantly legislative while the colonial medical service and a sleeping sickness campaign only gradually took shape. The pervasive, bureaucratic nature of Belgian colonial policy was exemplified in public health and medicine too, with local administrators being inundated with instructions, ordinances and decrees concerning sleeping sickness policies. These also touched upon myriad aspects of African life and by their very complexity led to confusion in the actual implementation of medical policy, while administrative neglect of medical requirements led to conflict with the political and economic ambitions of colonial officialdom.

SLEEPING SICKNESS EPIDEMICS

Notes

1. Ministère des Affaires Etrangères, Archives Africaines, Brussels. [Hereafter MAEAA] MAEAA 4389.1090, 19 November 1943, Dr A. Duren to Leemans, des Distributions d'Eau, Brussels, 'Etat sanitaire des populations du Congo avant sa colonisation par la Belgique.'
2. D. J. Bradley, 'The situation and the response', in E. E. Sabben-Clare, K. Kirkwood and D. J. Bradley, *Health in Tropical Africa During the Colonial Period*. Oxford, 1980, p. 9.
3. F. M. J. C. Nevens, 'Projet de plan général de l'organisation de la lutte contre les trypanosomiases en Afrique', *Bulletin de la Académie Royale des Sciences d'Outre-Mer*, Classes des Sciences Naturelles et Médicales, XVII, 1965, pp. 12-13.
4. MAEAA 4389.1090, 19 November 1943, Duren to Leemans.
5. MAEAA 846.18, 22 February 1903, Secretary of State to Governor-General; MAEAA 846.19, 4 April 1903, Broden to Governor-General.
6. Musée Royal de l'Afrique Centrale, Section Historique, Archives, Tervuren, Belgium. [Hereafter MRAC] Fuchs papers 114, 7 December 1905, Vice-Governor Lantonnois to all administrators, camp commanders, doctors, missionaries and companies.
7. J. Rodhain, 'Documents pour servir à l'histoire de la maladie du sommeil au Congo Belge, III. La période 1907 à 1911. Les premiers lazarets et les débuts de l'expérimentation de l'atoxyl et de l'émétique', *Bulletin de l'Institut Royal Colonial Belge*, XIX, 1948, pp. 943-55; F. M. J. C. Nevens, 'Projet de plan général de l'organisation de la lutte contre les trypanosomiases en Afrique', p. 11. MAEAA 847.372, 25 January 1908, Dr Zerbini; MAEAA 838.3, 19 June 1908, Vice Governor-General to Secretary of State.
8. MRAC 50.30.221, 16 October 1912, Chef de Zone André Landeghem to all Administrateurs Territoriales.
9. MAEAA 847.112, 28 November 1905, Dr Zerbini, Boma to Governor-General.
10. MAEAA 845.6, 24 October 1907, Director of Justice, de Meulemeester to Director of the Medical Service; 4 September 1907, Note for Governor-General.
11. MAEAA 4420.20, 25 September 1912, Notes for the 1913 Annual Report.
12. J. M. Janzen with Dr Arkinstall, *The Quest for Therapy in Lower Zaire*, Berkeley, 1978, pp. 3-11.
13. MAEAA 843.1, 19 July 1907, Landeghem to Governor-General.
14. MAEAA 843.20, 14 February 1910, Dr Heiberg, Report on Ibembo Lazaret; MRAC Fuchs Papers 114, Dr Trolli 1907; MAEAA 843.35, 29 September 1910, Landeghem to Governor-General.
15. J. Rodhain, 'Documents pour servir à l'histoire de la maladie du sommeil au Congo Belge, III. La période 1907 à 1911. Les premiers lazarets et les débuts de l'expérimentation de l'atoxyl et de l'émétique', *Bulletin de l'Institut Royal Colonial Belge*, XIX, 1948, p. 950; J. Schwetz, *L'Evolution de la Médecine au Congo Belge*, p. 100. Schwetz reported the rumour widespread among Africans that the sick were inoculated with the illness by the Europeans who then placed them inside lazarets to await their deaths. The bodies, it was believed, were then 'cut into bits and put into containers sold in the shops under the names "corned beef", "carbonnade flammands", etc.' MAEAA 846.1, 24 October 1902, Dr Rossignon to Governor-General.
16. MAEAA 843.20, 14 February 1910, Heiberg Report; MAEAA 843.35, 29 September 1910, Chef de Zone Landeghem to Governor-General; MAEAA 843.20, 14 February 1910.
17. MAEAA 843.20, 14 February 1910, Heiberg Report.
18. MAEAA 4419.4, c. 1909; J. Rodhain, 'Notes et propositions'; Schwetz: 'l'Evolution de la Médecine au Congo Belge, p. 90.
19. MAEAA 4419.602, 25 June 1909, A. Broden to Minister enclosing 'La lutte contre la trypanose humaine,' by Doctors Broden and Rodhain; MAEAA 843.20, 14 February 1910, Heiberg Report; MAEAA 847.143, 23 April 1906, J. Todd to Van Campenhout.

IMPERIAL MEDICINE

20 MAEAA 850.9, 10 May 1918, Governor-General to all Vice Governor-Generals and District Commissioners; F. O. Stohr in *Bulletin of the Sleeping Sickness Bureau*, 4, 1912, p. 302.
21 MAEAA 850.260, 30 April 1910, Vice Governor-General Fuchs' circular.
22 MAEAA 847.143, 23 April 1906, J. L. Todd to Van Campenhout; MAEAA 831, 10 June 1910, *Mesures complementaires prises en 1910 pour enrayer le developpement de la maladie du sommeil;* MAEAA 848.114, 17 January 1910; MAEAA 848.115, 17 January 1910; MAEAA 849.206, 30 April 1910, Fuchs' instruction on medical passports; 8 September 1910, *Receuil Mensuel*, 9 (new sleeping sickness regulations which replaced those of 5 December 1906).
23 On Paper War, see J. Burke, 'Historique de la lutte contre la maladie du sommeil au Congo'. *Annales de la Société Belge de Médecine*, 51, 1971, p. 468. For instance in 1911, the doctor at Buta complained that issuing medical passports took up half of each day. MAEAA 849.291, 18 May 1911.
24 MAEAA Affaires Indigènes, 1422.3, 27 August 1929, Gregoire, 'Rapport politique, 1929, District de l'Uele-Nepoko.' MAEAA Rapports Congo Belge 151.1, 21 May 1932, Dr L. Fontana.
25 MAEAA 4429.20, 25 September 1912, Note for 1913 annual report of the medical service.
26 MAEAA 848.118, 29 October 1909. For instance, Dr Heiberg suggested to the Governor-General that special 'sanitary police' should be based at Aba and frequently patrol the frontier.
27 MRAC 50.30.16, Landeghem, 'Rapport Annuel, Bas-Uele, 1915'. MRAC 50.30.156, 23 July 1915, Vice Governor-General Malfeyt. Circular to administrators in Province Orientale.
28 MRAC 50.30.91, 19 September 1915, Dr Dubois, Buta to District Commissioner, Buta.
29 A. J. Duggan, 'Tropical medicine: a submerging art?', *Transactions of the Royal Society of Tropical Hygiene and Medicine*, 76, 1982, p. 569.
30 MAEAA 850.9, 10 May 1918, Governor-General to Vice Governor-General and District Commissioners. These ideas parallel those implemented in neighbouring French territories a year earlier. In 1916, the French Colonel Jamot had created the first *equipes mobiles* to survey and treat sleeping sickness in the Oubangui-Chari region of French Congo. It was a new idea of 'mobile-prevention'. Marcel Beby Eyidi, *Le Vainqueur de la Maladie du Sommeil: le Docteur Eugène Jamot, 1879–1937*, Paris, 1950, p. 45.
31 MAEAA 855.63, 18 November 1921, Dr S'Heeren Report of Sleeping Sickness Mission in Uele District.
32 MAEAA 4461.56, 3 September 1924, Emile Van Campenhout, London, 'Report to the Société des Nations, Re: Campagne contre la maladie du sommeil en Afrique équatoriale.'
33 MAEAA Rapports Congo Belge 150.1, 12 April 1929, J. Schwetz, Report on Sleeping Sickness in Province Orientale.

[15]

Sanitation and Security
The Imperial Powers and the Nineteenth Century Ḥajj
William R. Roff

In the course of the nineteenth century the pilgrimage to Mecca – and more especially the maritime pilgrimage – came to be of increasing interest and concern to non-Muslim, European powers. The reasons were numerous. European state rivalries at the turn of the century, notably between Britain and France, took as one of their many arenas the outlying parts of the enfeebled Ottoman Empire, not least peninsular Arabia. Concomitantly renewed interest in maritime transit from India to Europe – and in Jidda and Suez as termini in relation to this – led to a fresh emphasis on the control of the Red Sea and of the southern and western Arabian coast. The resulting increase in trade and shipping, hesitant initially but dramatically impelled by the advent of steam and in due course the opening of the Suez Canal, was accompanied by a marked rise in sea-borne pilgrim traffic from India and the East. And the pilgrim traffic in turn brought to Arabia from the 1820s – increasingly for further transmission to Europe – Asiatic cholera.

For the European powers, a kind of twin infection came to be implied, against which defences has to be devised.[1] Arabia – Nejd and the Hijaz – was the source of the zealotry known (if little understood) as Wahhâbism, and later 'pan-Islam', credited with introducing widespread unrest into India and the Malay peninsula and archipelago, to the unsettlement of British and Dutch rule there. India – the Ganges plain – was the source of *cholera morbus*, which not only ravaged the pilgrim (and settled) populations of peninsular Arabia, when brought by sea from Calcutta or Bombay, but spread onwards into Europe and even to the Americas. So it was, that alongside the other political imperatives of the century, there developed around the *hajj* a growing imperial concern to control the sanitary and subversive threats of which was seen as the vehicle. Because too direct an interference in performance of the *hajj* was recognized to carry its own political dangers, this was seldom resorted to. Instead, surveillance, regulation, and (eventually) organizational participation became the principal means of expressing this concern, so that, by the early twentieth century, non-Muslim European powers were directly involved in the management of pilgrimage visitation to the Holy Cities. Whilst that involvement may not have affected the meaning, or perhaps even the nature, of the *hajj* for its participants, it had a considerable effect on its dimensions, its conditions, and its conduct. It is this process that the present article seeks in some measure to describe and discuss.

Arabian Studies VI

Though it was stated in the latter part of the nineteenth century that the East India Company had maintained commercial agents in the lower Red Sea – specifically in Jidda and Mocha – more or less from the outset of the Company's history,[2] and there is probably some truth in this, all were resident merchants and their functions seem to have been concerned entirely with trade. Many, indeed, were not even Muslims (Indian or Armenians) but Banians, a generic term for Hindu merchants from the sub-continent. It is probable that Muslim Indian merchants, Company servants or no, became involved in pilgrimage affairs, but largely by way of business – in relation to shipping and lodging, and possibly by arranging advances on return passages in return for local employment. Many Indian pilgrims on leaving Jidda after completing the *hajj* are known to have taken country ships to the Yemen or Hadramawt, there to await Indian vessels. After the British seizure of Aden, no fewer than two-thirds of the substantial Indian Muslim community there were pilgrims *en route* to or from Mecca.[3] Earlier European visitors to Red Sea Arabia at the end of the eighteenth and begining of the nineteenth century refer repeatedly to the size, distinctiveness and diversity of Indian settlement, comprising the wealthiest as well as the poorest inhabitants of Mecca, Jidda, Mocha and elsewhere, their presence due entirely to the combination of trade and pilgrimage.[4]

The evolution that took place during the first three decades or so of the nineteenth century from irregular East India Company commercial agents in the lower Red Sea ports to more institutionalized, more political and more generally imperial forms of representation, is in detail obscure, though its character is clear enough. Its inherent ambivalence – that of the non-Muslim power trying to understand and influence affairs in an area the heartland of which, the inner Hijaz and the Holy Places, was forbidden to it – was early reflected in Sir Home Popham's recourse in 1803 to an Indian Muslim emissary to treat with Amīr Ghālib of Mecca.[5] Its imperial proclivity to dictate was demonstrated (though not, indeed, for the first time) by the bombardment of Mocha in 1820 in order to obtain the right to establish a British Resident there, with extra-territorial powers.[6] Though it is not certain that such an official was appointed, there was a 'British Agent' in Mocha – a Bohrah named Tayeb Ibramji – by 1833, and by 1840 a 'British consular agent' (or 'British vice-consul'), also Indian, Abd-er-Rasoul.[7] In Jidda, the first appointment under the new dispensation, was of Muhammad 'Alī Pasha's own commercial agent, Husayn Aghā, employed by the British from 1826 or earlier, and succeeded in 1831 by an Armenian Muslim merchant, Abim (or Malim, or Yacoub) Yûsuf, described by 1835 as 'unpaid British Vice-Consul'.[8] As these terminologies suggest, the role of agent, and its responsibilities, were changing, though those filling the office remained for the time being much as in the past. Confusion exists concerning remuneration – whether as fixed salary, allowances, or in the form of presents – and about the nature of the commission or patent (some or all appear to have been granted letters patent by the British Consul General in Egypt, as well as a commission by the Company and, on occasion, by the Porte), but it is evident that what was being sought was more reliable intelligence concerning passage through the Red Sea, and more direct protection of British interests on the littoral. Such protection and intelligence was made the more pressing with the increase in the use of steam vessels, affecting both the volume and the nature of trade.

In 1778, the Ottoman Sultan, at the instance of the Sharif of Mecca, had instructed his Viceroy in Egypt that 'The sea of Suez is destined for the noble pilgrimage to Meccah. To suffer Frankish ships to navigate therein, or to neglect opposing it, is betraying your Sovereign, your religion, and every Mahometan ...'[9] Sixty years later in October 1837 the Directors of the East India Company resolved without contest to appoint 'English' (i.e. 'non-Native' and non-Muslim) Package Agents at Suez, Qusayr (temporarily stationed at Mocha), and Jidda, 'with a view to facilitate Steam communication' between India and Egypt,[10] and, in August 1838, the British Foreign Office authorized the appointment of these agents as British Vice-Consuls at their respective posts.[11] Alexander Ogilvie, the first to go to Jidda, took up his duties there towards the end of the year, and the Frenchman Fulgence Fresnel, in the Hijaz with Muhammad 'Alī's troops (and later himself to become French Consul there) wrote: 'Jidda, that old concierge of the Holy City, received within its walls, stupefied, a European consul arrayed in the European fashion, and the cannon of the Muslim fortress saluted with 21 guns the English flag as it was hoisted over the consular residence'.[12]

Though it was to be another twenty years before European consuls in the Hijaz became caught up in any important way in pilgrimage affairs, the process had been set in train. It is as well, therefore, to look at the maritime pilgrimage itself, as it appears to have functioned towards the mid-century. There is little reliable information about the size of the pilgrimage to Mecca from the East at this time, though the Muslim populations of the Indian sub-continent and the Malay peninsula and archipelago were already among the largest in the world and had been sending sizeable contingents of *hajjis* for centuries. Around the mid-nineteenth century there appear to have been about 2,000 pilgrims annually from the archipelago, several hundred from the Malay peninsula, and perhaps 5-7,000 from the sub-continent[13] – possibly close to 10,000 in all, though perhaps also considerably fewer. They came from areas which, though increasingly subject to colonial rule were, in many cases, not yet under either British or Dutch jurisdiction. Most pilgrim voyages were made in small sailing vessels of 100 to 300 tons burthen, under a variety of kinds of ownership and flag. Though ports of embarkation were very various, there was a growing tendency (that became more marked with the coming of steam) to concentrate departures at the central collection points of Singapore, Calcutta and Bombay, with substantial subsidiary traffic from ports such as Batavia, Palembang and Acheh, Madras and Surat, and a host of smaller harbours. Though most pilgrims took ship to Jidda, some disembarked on the south Arabian coast, at ports such as al-Mukallā, and made the rest of the journey by land, through the Yemen. Conditions of passage were often poor, and overcrowding was common. In an exchange of correspondence between Singapore and Bengal in 1849, in which *inter alia* there is reference to 83 deaths *en voyage* in a vessel of 290 tons that had embarked 520 pilgrims in Jidda for Singapore, it is proposed that 'representations be made to the Jedda authorities', though the consensus was that not much would result and that more might be achieved by local regulation, such as had been attempted in Madras in 1846.[14]

145

Arabian Studies VI

Little restraint was, in fact, placed upon intending pilgrims or their carriers in the British-controlled areas of India and Malaya, though the Dutch had long since established to their own satisfaction a relationship between returned *hajjīs* and rebelliousness against colonial authority and attempted to restrict numbers by making obligatory the acquisition of a heavily taxed pilgrim passport.[15] Pilgrims from British territories seem to have required no travel documents in the first half of the century, though the institution of Turkish passport and visa regulations in the late 1840s prompted proposals for British Indian passport rules which appear, however, to have been shelved when the Turks were persuaded to exempt all British subjects.[16] A great many Indian pilgrims undertook the *hajj* without possessing sufficient funds to return, resulting in significant numbers of destitute Indians in Mecca and Jidda (remarked upon, for example, by Burckhardt in 1814).[17] Referring to this problem in 1853, the Vice-Consul in Jidda noted that by his consular instructions 'I am directed to afford relief to all destitute British subjects and to enable them to return to their own country', but added that he supposed this to apply only to natives of the United Kingdom, and that with respect to Indians any charges should be laid to the Government of India. The latter replied simply that it was of the opinion 'that the Government have no right to prevent any person who desires to do so, from proceeding on pilgrimage,'[18] and the question was postponed, though it was to recur with increasing force in later years. The Dutch, in 1859, introduced regulations requiring all departing pilgrims to be in possession of sufficient funds to make the journey in both directions,[19] and intervention of this kind was to be increasingly insisted upon by imperial authorities.

Prior to the mid-century there is little reference to health with respect to the *hajj*, apart from concern about overcrowding of vessels and Indian destitution, and recognition of the nature of the epidemiological questions that were to loom so large by the end of the century seems to have been slow. Cholera, which came to assume the principal role in these discussions, was first recorded in Arabia, in Nejd, in 1821, and again in 1828-29,[20] having arrived from India by way of the Gulf (though this was not clearly understood at the time). In 1831 it appeared in the Hijaz for the first time, with a very intense epidemic that caused the deaths of up to 20,000 pilgrims.[21] But the Arabian outbreak was just one episode in the first of the great cholera pandemics of the nineteenth century, and the spread of the disease into Europe took place to the north, through Astrakhan, Russia and Germany. The Hijaz suffered further outbreaks, of varying intensity, always in association with the pilgrimage season, in 1841, 1847, 1851, 1856/57, and 1859.[22] Not until 1865, however, was it implicated in the spread of the disease to Europe, by way of Egypt. Once this was established, however, and because of the great severity of the 1865 epidemic in Europe and America, the role of the *hajj* in spreading the disease became an obsession. Dr. Achille Proust, Professor of Hygiene at the Faculty of Medicine of the University of Paris, and one of the chief protagonists in what became known as *'la politique sanitaire'*, wrote shortly after the 1865 epidemic, 'The peoples of the Midi were terrified. Europe realized that it could not remain like this, every year, at the mercy of the pilgrimage to Mecca.'[23]

What Europe did was to embark on a series of international sanitary conferences, directed principally towards restricting the movement of maritime-borne cholera carriers, by inspection and quarantine of ships and their passengers. Among other things this was to lead in due course to the establishment of lazarets, or quarantine stations, at the northern and southern ends of the Red Sea. The anxiety felt in some quarters in Europe in the late sixties, however, was not reflected among European officials directly responsible for Red Sea matters. On the contrary, for some years from 1869 the British Consulate in Jidda was occupied only in an acting capacity by its Dragoman, and then by one Hafizoodin, a Mahomedan merchant and a broker who has a personal interest in the pilgrim trade,' and in 1873 the Foreign Office proposed abolishing it altogether.[24] That it did not do so arose from concern on the part of the Government of India, a concern which related, apart from its commercial interests, more to political subversion than sanitation. The strong religious element in local political movements, one official urged, 'cannot be safely disregarded either in Aden or in India. The Hedjar [sic] is the natural asylum for fanatical moslem exiles from India, [who] may there pass their lives in a congenial atmosphere of fanaticism.'[25] If these remarks were, necessarily, based largely on hearsay, so were the observations and actions of successive British consuls charged with protecting the interests not merely of British residents in the Hijaz (who numbered at this time some 5,000, mainly Indian) but annually of the thousands of pilgrims who arrived from British India and the Straits Settlements, for no non-Muslim was permitted to stir outside the walls of Jidda town. As early as 1864, the then British Consul, complaining about problems of recovering the property of deceased pilgrims, invariably attached by the Sharif's *Bayt al-Māl*, had suggested the appointment of 'Muslim Consuls in the holy cities'.[26] Though this suggestion was not immediately pursued, it was the next logical step.

In 1878, the Indian Government detailed Assistant Surgeon Abdur Razzack, of the Bengal Medical Service, to accompany that year's Indian pilgrimage to Mecca. The appointment was made in the context of growing official concern not simply about epidemic cholera but about general questions of welfare associated with overcrowded shipping (much of it emanating from the Straits Settlements), indigent pilgrims (mainly Indian), and the absence of anything like adequate health facilities in the Hijaz.[27] Dr. Abdur Razzack's responsibilities were solely to report on the sanitary conditions surrounding the *hajj*, which he did in March 1879 with a variety of practical recommendations.[28] A few months later the newly appointed British Consul in Jidda, J.N.E. Zohrab, addressing somewhat larger issues, wrote that 'in order to thoroughly sift the questions of aid and protection to pilgrims' their condition throughout must be fully understood, and 'to do this effectively it is in my opinion necessary that a Confidential Agent of the Consulate be sent to watch and follow this year's pilgrimage.'[29] In a further report, written in September 1879, Zohrab listed the duties of the Consulate, beginning with 'the political', under which head he wrote:

The province of Hedjaz is the centre to which the ideas, opinions, sentiments and aspirations of the Mussulman world are brought for discussion. The annual meeting at a fixed time ostensibly for the purposes of the Pilgrimage of Representatives from every Mussulman Community affords a means without creating suspicion to exchange opinions, to discuss plans, to criticize the actions of the European Governments and form combinations to resist the supremacy of the Christian Powers. For the discussion in secret of Political Questions there is no country offering such security and facilities as the Hedjaz. Meetings of Delegates from Mohammaden Countries at any other point could not fail of attracting Public attention but in the Hedjaz such meeting can and it is stated annually do take place and at them discussion is free without fear of betrayal.[30]

It appears to have been Lord Dufferin, British Ambassador to Constantinople, who first suggested that surveillance of sanitation and security could usefully be combined. Having proposed in September 1881 the appointment of 'a secret paid agent residing at Mecca,'[31] he saw at once, when informed from India that the government had in contemplation the appointment of a Muslim Vice-Consul at Jidda with medical qualifications, that the same man might perform both cleansing tasks.[32] In August 1882, Dr. Abdur Razzack, who had made the original sanitary report and was said to be 'an excellent man for your purpose and altogether *separated* from the Delhi and Wahabi schools ... clever and ambitious,'[33] was appointed Vice-Consul in Jidda. His duties were first and foremost 'to render all possible assistance to the large number of Her Majesty's subjects of the Muhammadan faith who resort annually to the Hejjaz.... to promote the comfort of the pilgrims and to assist them in their dealings with the officials of the Ottoman Empire.' In addition, however, he was informed, the Consul 'may wish to avail himself of your assistance in obtaining trustworthy information regarding the course of affairs, and of public opinion, in Mecca and neighbouring places. If so, I am to say that you should make use of the advantages which your position may give you in order to afford all the assistance in your power.'[34]

Abdur Razzack's appointment as Vice-Consul, and the institution a year or two earlier of record keeping at the Dutch Consulate,[35] mark (among other things) the appearance of a somewhat better numerical accounting of pilgrims from the East. It is clear that by the 1880s there had been a substantial increase from under 10,000 annually hazarded for the mid-century. In 1874, 45 ships had been recorded as touching at Aden 'containing upwards of 13,640 natives of India and the Straits Settlements' en route to Jidda,[36] and in the same year there may have been close to another 5,000 from the Netherlands East Indies.[37] In 1879, Zohrab (engaged in making the best possible case for the Jidda Consulate) had estimated the settled 'British Indian' population in the Hijaz at 15,000[38] (compared with the 3,000 given for 1861), and spoke of between 30,000 and 60,000 'British subjects' (from all parts, presumably) landing annually at Jidda, though the latter figure is undoubtedly much too high, even for a *Hajj Akbar* year (in which the 'standing' at 'Arafat was thought likely to fall on a Friday).[39] In 1884 (the first year for which he gives complete figures) Abdur Razzack put total arrivals in the Hijaz by sea (from north and south) at 31,157, of whom 16,978 (54 per cent) were from India and Southeast Asia - 9,262 'Indian' (including Afghans and Turcomans coming via Bombay) and 7,716 *Jāwah* ('Javanese') from the Malay peninsula and archipelago, 3,391 of them in ships coming from Singapore.[40]

Table 1 gives what statistics are available from this time forward until the turn of the century, from which it may be noted that, while the *Jāwah*

Sanitation and Security and the Ḥajj

pilgrimage grew fairly steadily throughout, the Indian fell away sharply in the late 1890s, for reasons that will become clear.

From about 1880, performance of the *Hajj* from India and even more from south-east Asia was increasingly affected by external regulation – imposed by, or in some instances upon, the colonial governments, and administered by their consular officials in the Hijaz – relating to passports and visas, shipping conditions, possession of adequate funds, provision for return passage, and matters of health. In several of these respects the Dutch authorities in the Indies had long been active – for political rather than humanitarian reasons as has been noticed. Acquisition of passports had been compulsory since 1825, and from 1859 intending pilgrims had been required in addition to give evidence of possession of sufficient funds to make the return journey. These regulations had, however, been administered from (or evaded in) the Indies themselves. The establishment of the Dutch Consulate in Jidda in 1872 made it possible to regulate pilgrims there as well, and by the late 1870s they were being required on arrival to register themselves at the Consulate, and to deposit there sufficient money to ensure their return passage. This system commended itself to the then British Consul, concerned about the large numbers of indigent Indian pilgrims left behind after every *hajj*, and he proposed that the British do likewise. Voluntary registration was introduced in 1878[41] but relatively few pilgrims responded, and attempts to require the deposit of return passage money were even less successful.[42] What the Consul's representations did result in, however, was action by the Straits Settlements Government, which, from 1881, required of all pilgrims under its own and related British jurisdictions the deposit on departure of Straits dollars $150-200 in the form of a bond or promissory note.[43] On the basis of this, the Consul in Jidda was requested to collect from pilgrims the cost of a return ticket, giving the ship's captain a certificate that would procure him payment on arrival back in Singapore. This cumbersome system does not seem to have worked well, and may indeed have been rescinded. The Indian Government, by contrast, did not even attempt it, either in the form of the payment of Rs. 40 on arrival in Jidda or in terms of a requirement that pilgrims give proof of possession of a minimum of Rs. 200 on departure from India.[44] In consequence, 'paupers' continued to form a significant proportion – between 20 and 50 per cent. – of all pilgrims from the sub-continent, and to present problems of destitution in the Hijaz.[45]

The passport question of the 1880s, though one that related to the consular desideratum that pilgrims register themselves, was prompted more by Turkish than by European colonial authority. Direct Turkish involvement in the administration of the Hijaz, although it had remained throughout a vilayet of the Ottoman Empire, garrisoned as such and with a succession of provincial Valis, had always been latent but its actuality had fluctuated a good deal. A marked revival of the display of Turkish authority seems to have followed upon the opening of the Suez Canal, rendering the Hijaz more directly governable by Turkish troops, and considerably altering the relationship between Sultan and Sharif, to the latter's detriment.[46] This was reflected in the imposition of Turkish forms of municipal government in Mecca, and by increasing Turkish regulation of internal affairs, including those relating to

149

Arabian Studies VI

the *hajj*. In 1880, Sharif Husayn of Mecca was assassinated (for reasons that were never determined) by a foreigner, a Baluchi from the borders of India.[47] This prompted the Ottoman Government to announce that henceforth all entry to Turkish possessions, including the Hijaz, must be controlled by the issue of passports and provision of visas – though the British professed to see in this simply the devising of a new source of revenue. Calling the renewed requirement 'useless and troublesome' ('we know nothing whatever of ninety-nine hundredths of the annual ten thousand')[48], the Indian Government sought and was again successful in obtaining exemption for British Indian subjects. The Straits Settlements Government, sharing something of the Netherlands East Indies view of the *hajj*, and considering it unwise 'to facilitate pilgrimages to any great extent, as they cannot be said to promote the interests of the families of the pilgrims, and too often lead to the demoralization of the pilgrims themselves,'[49] issued regulations in 1881 requiring all pilgrims embarking in the Straits Settlements to obtain passports.[50]

Table 1: Statistics of the Eastern Pilgrimage

	(1) India	(2) N.E.I.	(3) S.S.	(2+3) *Jāwah*	(1+2+3) Total Eastern	Total O'seas	Percent. Eastern
1882	9,800	4,302	n.a.	–	–	25,580	–
1883	10,146	5,269	n.a.	–	–	27,263	–
1884	9,262	4,540	3,176	7,716	16,978	31.157	54.5
1885	8,318	4,692	3,685	8,377	16,695	53,010	31.5
1886	9,479	2,523	2,889	5,412	14,891	42,374	35.1
1887	10,324	2,426	2,524	4,950	15,274	42,185	36.2
1888	10,566	4,328	2,659	6,987	17,553	50,221	35.0
1889	10,912	3,146	2,361	5,507	16,419	44,686	36.7
1890	9,346	5,149	3,532	8,951	18,297	39,186	46.7
1891	11,212	6,044	4,120	10,164	21,376	45,475	47.0
1892	n.a.	6,841	3,160	10,001	–	54,419	–
1893	20,937	8,092	5,764	13,856	34,793	90,173	38.6
1894	n.a.	6,874	2,209	9,083	–	49,628	–
1895	n.a.	7,128	2,678	9,806	–	57,503	–
1896	n.a.	9,110	2,837	11,947	–	62,726	–
1897	n.a.	7,075	4,635	11,710	–	41,133	–
1898	1,432	7,895	2,528	10,423	11,855	38,247	31.0
1899	1,712	7,694	3,090	10,784	12,496	36,380	34.3
1900	2,162	5,068	2,107	7,175	9,337	35,861	26.0

Comments: It should be emphasized that the figures are approximate, and are included for the sense they give of proportion and change. Principal sources are Vredenbregt, *op. cit.*, Appendix II (from the *Koloniaal Verslag*), and the British Consular and Kamaran reports in the Indian National Archives and the Public Record Office, London.

Column 1 gives pilgrims from Indian ports. Column 2 gives pilgrims from 'Indonesia', based largely on passport applications. Column 3 represents the difference between the figure given in Consular and other reports for the *Jāwah* (variously described) and that given by Vredenbregt for 'Indonesians', and thus provides a hypothesized figure for pilgrims from Straits Settlements ports; though this figure cannot be regarded as the peninsular Malay component of the *Jāwah* (many 'Indonesians' travelled by way of the Straits Settlements), it clearly includes Malays and there is some evidence that towards the end of the century it comes close to the true Malay figure.

Sanitation and Security and the Hajj

The figure for total overseas pilgrims (an ambiguous phrase that may sometimes have meant pilgrims arriving by sea) is derived from Vredenbregt and various Consular and Kamaran reports, with Vredenbregt prevailing where there is conflict.
1893, the year of the great cholera epidemic, was also a *Hajj Akbar* year.

At much the same time, actual shipping conditions for pilgrims were being brought to public attention. In August, 1880, the steamship *Jeddah*, eighteen days out of Penang with nearly a thousand pilgrims on board, came close to foundering off Cape Guardafui, at the entrance to the Gulf of Aden, and was abandoned in panic by her British officers, who took to one of the few ship's boats.[51] Picked up by a passing steamer, to whom they described the *Jeddah* as lost with all hands, they were taken to Aden, where they were discomfited twenty-four hours later by the arrival of the *Jeddah* herself, under tow to a third vessel. The incident became an international *cause célèbre* and a matter of great embarrassment to British authority—and, in 1898, provided the basis for Joseph Conrad's novel *Lord Jim*. Conrad gives a vivid picture of the embarkation of the pilgrims aboard the shabby little steamer:

> They streamed aboard over three gangways, they streamed in urged by faith and the hope of paradise, they streamed in with a continuous tramp and shuffle of bare feet, without a murmur, or a look back; and when clear of confining rails spread on all sides over the deck, flowed fore and aft, overflowed down the yawning hatchways, filled the inner recesses of the ship—like water filling a cistern, like water flowing into crevices and crannies, like water rising silently even with the rim.[52]

Conrad's *Patna*—the *Jeddah*—was like most pilgrim ships of the time: small, overcrowded, completely inadequately served by lifeboats or other safety equipment, offering no amenities beyond two or three cabins for the well-to-do, carrying no provisions for the deck passengers beyond an emergency store of rice, and with barely enough fresh water for drinking. With a ratio of one passenger per ton deadweight (the *Jeddah*, at 993 tons, carried 992 pilgrims) space was minimal (even the regulations specified only nine superficial feet per adult), sanitation poor, and medical attention non-existent. Pilgrims carried their own provisions and did their own cooking, often with makeshift apparatus—at least one vessel burning to the waterline off Jidda as a result. Steamship conditions were in some respects no worse than those in the sailing vessels that had preceded them, and the voyage was shorter and on the whole safer. Increasingly, however, steamships, with their higher capital costs, were owned by European firms and came under the surveillance of European governments, with pressure from officialdom to provide acceptable standards of passage and contrary pressure from shipping interests to maximize numbers and restrict amenities to hold down costs and compete with vessels sailing under other flags. To increase space requirements from nine to sixteen superficial feet per pilgrim (as new Ottoman regulations sought) would have been to reduce to 337 the number of pilgrims that could be carried by a ship now licensed to carry 600. Fares would rise, as they would if, in addition, ships were required to carry provisions, and the competitive position of British shipping would decline.[53] Already, by 1884, Dutch companies, which had entered the business only in the late 1870s, were carrying 40 per cent of pilgrims for the Netherlands Indies.[54]

151

Arabian Studies VI

The repercussions of the *Jeddah* incident, however, together with the introduction of a new Indian Native Passenger Ship Act in 1887 (replacing earlier and more limited legislation of the late 1850s), and the promulgation in 1888 of proposed new Ottoman Pilgrim Traffic Regulations based on the Indian Act, together forced the Straits Government to follow suit and establish more rigorous control of shipboard conditions.[55] The institutionalization of pilgrim transport that this process represents found its ultimate expression in a brief experiment conducted by the Government of India from 1886. Some years earlier, following his first pilgrimage, Assistant Surgeon Abdur Razzack had proposed that consideration be given to the establishment of a 'pilgrimage agency' to administer the *hajj* 'if the Muslim community could find the funds.'[56] Nothing came of this, but in 1881, and again in 1885, the Government approached T. M. Cook of the travel firm of Thomas Cook & Son, with a proposal that the firm cooperate 'in devising plans for better treatment and safer travel' of those making the *hajj* from India.[57] By a resolution of the 21 January, 1886, the Government of India appointed Cook's as sole pilgrimage agents for the whole of India, with a central Pilgrimage Office in Bombay, and responsibility for arranging rail transport to the ports, shipping, and issuing tickets covering all necessary fees and costs.[58] Though in fact the system did not work (from the point of view of the Government, largely, it would seem, because Cook's confined themselves to ship chartering, with no resulting improvement in conditions), and was terminated in 1893,[59] it heralded perception of the pilgrimage as, organizationally, that segment of the travel industry which it seems in many respects to have now become.

Underlying much of the official concern over management of the *hajj* was persistent anxiety about public health and international hygiene. Cholera continued to attack the Hijaz during the pilgrimage season, with outbreaks almost yearly and major epidemics in 1883, 1889, 1891 and 1893.[60] A Muslim doctor in the Ottoman service, describing the ravages of the disease in Mecca in the last of there years, wrote:

> No-one came to bury the dead, they were left in the streets. Many streets were blocked with corpses. Cholera was not just cholera; it was not just a sickness, it was something more terrible than a sickness! Cholera had transfigured itself; it had become "death". One no longer saw the ill, one found corpses everywhere. It was death that accomplished its work of destruction. The gravity of the situation was such that one spoke only of death; instead of saying "cholera" one said "death".[61]

Deaths in Mecca were estimated at 13,436, with a further 16,900 lives lost in the surrounding areas and among departing caravans—a total of 30,336, from a *hajj* that had seen 90,713 pilgrims from overseas, and at least 150,000 at 'Arafat.[62] The disease threatened, as usual, to spread, and the words uttered by Achille Proust before the Académie de Médecine in Paris in 1890 seemed again to have been prophetic: 'The pilgrimage to Mecca is a constant menace to Europe.'[63]

The first of the international sanitary conferences to address itself solely and directly to cholera (it was in fact known as the Cholera Conference) was held, as been seen, in 1886, in Constantinople, setting in train a thirty year process during which, as a later French writer put it, the European powers with a

Sanitation and Security and the Ḥajj

direct interest in the pilgrimage from territories controlled by them, exercised 'their right to meddle a little in the question of the purification of Jidda.'[64] The principal results of the Conference in this connection, though delayed in their application, were the determination of obligatory quarantine procedures for vessels from affected areas, and a proposal that lazarets, or quarantine stations, be constructed in the Gulf of Suez and at the entrance to the Red Sea.[65] These measures were to be carried out under an International Sanitary Board, but British objections to international enforcement, repeated at ensuing conferences in 1874 and 1885, led to nominal Turkish and Egyptian direction of Red Sea sanitary facilities even as they were operated 'under the control and with the assistance of Europe.'[66]

Two commissions, one designated by the 1866 Conference and one by the Ottoman Government, deliberated on possible sites for the lazarets. That eventually chosen for the southern station was the small, sandy island of Kamarān, off the coast of Turkish Yemen. Largely unoccupied, Kamarān enjoyed a good water supply (said to be 'the best for 300 miles around'), and a safe inner anchorage that had made it a frequent place of call in the past for vessels travelling between Jidda and the south. Construction of the Kamarān lazaret was long delayed, but it finally came into operation in 1881 (effectively, for the 1882 season) under Turkish regulations that required all ships proceeding to Jidda to stop there for observational or strict quarantine of from 10 to 5 days, depending on the reported state of health on board and the duration of the prior voyage.[67] Notwithstanding formal British objections to obligatory quarantine and international control, the Government of India and the Foreign Office appointed to the lazaret in 1884 an Indian Muslim doctor, who became Vice-Consul for Hodeida and Kamarān[68] and thereby the third British consular official to be directly associated with the *hajj*. From the outset Kamarān lazaret was involved in controversy, both medical and administrative. Though it was indeed, as one proponent said, open to 'the cleansing sun' and possessed of a plentiful natural water supply, these alone were insufficient to control cholera while observing quarantined vessels. Understanding of the mode of propagation of the disease was still in its infancy, despite Robert Koch's identification of the bacillus *vibrio cholera* in 1883, and wide agreement that human carriers, and their excreta, were its principal agents. There were disputes about etiology, about the incubation period, about what was called 'latent microbism', and much else, which led to a situation in which the very facility set up to stop the entry of cholera into the Hijaz was suspected of being or becoming one of its principal vehicles. The progressive introduction of fumigant devices, new disinfectant techniques, and distilled water machines in the course of the next twenty years, contrived, however, to alter the balance of opinion, and probably to justify the lazaret's existence.[69] But for the pilgrims involved, Kamarān meant a long period of detention in a sweltering climate, either on board their ships or in rudimentary and closely guarded quarters ashore, more fees to pay, and frequent subjection to unpleasant procedures, often to no apparent good end.

In the Hijaz itself the sanitary position was not much improved. Abdur Razzack, making his first official pilgrimage in 1882, had referred to his 'indignation as a Muslim as well as disapproval as a doctor' at the state of the Holy Places.[70] One of his first tasks was to report on the feasibility of establishing a hospital for Indian pilgrims, but he saw in this 'a few drawbacks', notably the problem of getting permission not only from the local Turkish and Sharifan authority but from the Sultan (in the form of a *Firmān*), and the probability that if established, use of the hospital could not be confined to Indians, a suggestion 'not proper in a country where all are of one caste and creed.'[71] In the result, he was permitted to set up a 'home dispensary', with medicines supplied by the Indian Government. Aside from cholera, which attracted the greatest amount of European attention, there was a good deal of other endemic illness in the Hijaz cities, notably smallpox from time to time, some malaria and dengue fever, and a great deal of dysentery. Though Mecca especially (and certainly more than Jidda) was described at this time by a sympathetic observer as essentially hygienic in construction, with much more open space, the overcrowding that took place during the *hajj* made what public health measures there were often ineffective, and there was little medical attention available to the sick, especially among the poor who constituted such a high proportion of pilgrims.[72]

In the course of the 1880s, at the cost of alienating the Sharīf of Mecca by contesting both his powers and his revenues, a somewhat more vigorous Ottoman local administration seems to have done a certain amount to improve public hygiene, though it was to take the appalling epidemic of 1893 to produce radical change, as well as to direct international attention not just to the quelling of cholera in the Hijaz but to regulating more strictly its exodus from India. In the years immediately prior to this, international sanitary conferences had continued to concern themselves primarily with *post facto* defence of Europe. That at Venice, in 1892, produced an international convention which, in addition to strengthening maritime quarantine (against renewed British protests on behalf of freedom of trade and movement), acted additionally to 'protect Egypt', recreating *de novo* the Conseil Sanitaire Maritime et Quarantenaire d'Egypte by giving it a large preponderance of European over Egyptian members and adding to its powers.[73] The conference at Dresden, early in 1883, though mainly concerned about the Danube area, moved further towards substituting for the principle of of prophylaxis after arrival that of control of departure.[74] The Paris Conference, called in 1894 after the preceding year's epidemic, moved decisively to control the maritime pilgrimage, by requiring medical inspection of all pilgrims and pilgrim ships prior to departure and by devising new and stringent regulations concerning the provision of doctors and hospitals on board, increasing space and water allowances, and by setting in motion a complete reorganization of the quarantine stations at Kamarān and El Tor (al-Tawr).[75] Accepting, finally, the need for such controls, the British declined to accede to the further requirement that pilgrims must give evidence of possession of adequate return funds, before departure.[76] Nonetheless, after the embodiment of the bulk of the Paris provisions in new Indian Government regulations the number of pilgrims travelling from the sub-continent fell very markedly in the last years of the century.[77]

In the Hijaz itself, a renewed effort was made by the Ottomans to improve public health facilities. At the opening of the Paris Conference in 1894, Turkey had announced the introduction of urgent measures involving reorganisation of the lazaret at Jidda, improvement of sanitary conditions in

Sanitation and Security and the Ḥajj

Mecca, provision of a refuge capable of sheltering up to 1,400 poor pilgrims at a time, construction of new hospitals at Mecca and Munā and improvement of the existing hospitals in Mecca and Jidda.[78] In April, 1895, an imperial *Firmān* made provision for additional doctors during the pilgrimage, a pharmacy, and a corps of sanitary police.[79] Not all these measures were equally welcome or equally well understood. On 31 May, 1895, a party of 'supposed Beduins' attacked members of the foreign community in Jidda walking outside the walls of the town, killing Dr. Abdur Razzack and wounding the British, French and Russian consuls. The Bedu were reported to have declared that it was the sanitary authorities who had brought cholera to the Hijaz, and that they wanted in addition to destroy the hospital.[80] Cholera deaths in 1895, after the reorganization of the *Service Sanitaire* in Mecca, amounted to only 306, the lowest for many years, though whether as a direct result of the improvements is open to some question. At any rate, no epidemic was ever again as severe as that of 1893 and after 1912 epidemic cholera disappeared altogether from the Hijaz. Its career, however, had brought non-Muslim European powers into direct involvement with management of the Meccan pilgrimage, and set up machinery for surveillance that ensured that the Holy Places were never again to go without some form of international supervision.

The remaining issue that continued to draw the imperial powers into a somewhat more covert intervention in the affairs of the Hijaz was that of feared subversion. This had a number of focuses, but related mainly to real or supposed plotting within the inaccessible Holy Cities, and to certain aspects of the organization of pilgrims from overseas. As early as 1881, when Abdur Razzack was first appointed Muslim Vice-Consul in Jidda, it was stated (wholly unrealistically) that one of his duties would be to appoint, 'in concert with the Grand Sheriff', the Indian pilgrimage *shaykhs*, all of whom should be British subjects.[81] The *shaykh* (or *mutawwif*) system was one of great antiquity which, despite its vested interests and abuses, served to provide pilgrims with cicerones conversant with their own tongue and customs, and its organization was an integral part of Meccan administration and government.[82] The British and Dutch objected to it in the late nineteenth century in part because increasing bureaucratization of the system (with licensed monopolies and a good deal of corruption) was thought to be exploitative,[83] and in part because they could not readily control the activities of recruiting agents appointed in but operating outside the Hijaz. The unsuccessful Indian attempt to ensure that all such agents at least be British subjects was paralleled by a Dutch regulation in 1897, which required that no foreigner from the Hijaz be permitted to enter the Netherlands East Indies unless provided with a passport stamped by the consul in Jidda.[84] An even greater nervousness was displayed in relation to other Hijazis travelling to the East, assumedly for dubious political purposes, as with the mission to south-east Asia in 1881 of three prominent Meccans, said to be 'suspicious persons', who occupied 'so important a position in the Mohamedan world that their movements seldom fail to have a political effect.'[85] Their movements on this occasion, reported first by the British Consul in Jidda and then by the police in Singapore (they were not permitted to enter the Netherlands Indies), were closely watched, and after three months, with nothing substantiated, they were returned to the

Arabian Studies VI

Hijaz, still assumed to have been engaged in 'pan-Islamic' propaganda.[86]

It was in this latter realm that the greatest anxiety was always felt. The role played by Christian Snouck Hurgronje, following his surreptitious stay in Mecca in 1884-85, in changing Dutch policies towards the *hajj*, by distinguishing between the general run of pilgrims and the *muqim* who stayed longer and became politicized, is well known, but did not take effect before the end of the century.[87] British and Dutch alike continued (with reason) to suspect the Holy Places of harbouring dissidents of all kinds, and of infecting *hajjis* with anti-colonial ideas. Means of learning about this had been discussed, as has been seen, since at least the 1870s, when the British 'pilgrim' J.F. Keane wrote, 'Who can know what alarming projects or conspiracies may not at this moment be on foot in Meccah, that centre and hotbed of Mohammedan intrigue? For my part I regard the Christians in Jeddah as sitting on the safety-valve of the Hejaz, and sooner or later an explosion inevitable.'[88] The proposal made in 1882 that the Muslim Vice-Consul combine intelligence with medical duties was revived again in 1888, when the Indian Government wrote to the Consul in Jidda saying that it had been suggested that the Vice-Consul might collect information on 'politico-religious movements' which, originating in the Hijaz, influenced India, and asked whether Dr. Abdur Razzack could perhaps submit a quarterly report on these matters. In reply the Consul agreed, but said that the Vice-Consul has pointed out that he would have to visit Mecca frequently in order to obtain such information, and that in order to avoid arousing Turkish suspicions it would be necessary for him to take a house there, and to have an allowance that would permit him 'to give some small presents to some of the religious heads.' These arrangements were approved, though there is no clear evidence of reports resulting.[89]

Perhaps because the Muslim Vice-Consuls did not provide sufficient intelligence, the question came up again in 1897, in the context of a larger proposal to establish 'an Indian Muhammadan Detective Agency at Constantinople, Mecca, Jeddah and Baghdad', though some felt that the object might be better achieved by occasional despatch of secret agents from India, because of the difficulty of finding 'the right class of men' for permanent employment. In addition, it was noted, the Government of India 'find it difficult to believe that any respectable Muhammadan would consent to work as a secret agent at Mecca, Jeddah or Baghdad.' In the result, it was suggested that, in order to get information from Jidda and Mecca, one could scarcely do better than continue to rely on Her Majesty's Consul in the Hijaz, 'who might perhaps be given a secret service grant.'[90] Again, there seems to have been no explicit consequence, and the focus of attention in the new century tended to move away somewhat from the Hijaz proper, towards questions associated with the excitements attendant upon inauguration of the Damascus-Medina railway scheme after 1900, the revival of Sa'ūdī power in Nejd after 1902, and the repercussions of political events in Turkey in 1908.

By the end of the nineteenth century, however, the European imperial powers had established more than a foothold in the Arabia of the Holy Places, had succeeded in institutionalizing their relationship with the *hajj*, and were in a position to ensure a substantial measure of surveillance over imperial interests in the religion - from the sanitary to the political - for any foreseeable future.

Sanitation and Security and the Ḥajj

Notes

I am grateful to the John Simon Guggenheim Memorial Foundation for a Fellowship which, during 1973, made possible the research in New Delhi and London reflected in much of this paper.

1. The terminology was often consciously military, as witness the title of such works as A.A. Proust, *La défense de l'Europe contre le choléra*, Paris, 1892; A. Durasnel, *La défense de l'Europe contre l'invasion des épidémies indiennes par voie maritime*, Lille, 1899; and, not least, Dr. Torel, 'Défense de la Mediterranée contre le pélerinage de la Mecque. Organisations sanitaires du Maroc', *Archives de médecin navale*, Paris, LXXVIII, Sept. 1902, 195-209.
2. Sir B.H. Frere to Foreign Office, 28 May, 1873, (in Indian National Archives) For. Dept. Proc., Pol.A., Mar. 1874, no. 302. Frere had been Governor of Bombay and was a member of the Council of India.
3. R.L. Playfair, *A history of Arabia Felix and Yemen*, Bombay, 1859, 14.
4. See e.g., C. Niebuhr, *Travels through Arabia*, Edinburgh, 1792, I, 317, 400-401, 408; and esp. J.L. Burckhardt, *Travels in Arabia*, London, 1829, 16, 190-191 and *passim*.
5. See e.g., M. Abir, 'The "Arab rebellion" of Amīr Ghālib of Mecca (1788-1813)', *Middle Eastern Studies*, London, 1971, VII, 195f.
6. Playfair, *op.cit.*, 139.
7. *Ibid.*, 144 and 147.
8. Memorandum by Sir A. Ryan, 'British representation in Jeddah up to 1930', 22 Mar. 1936, Encl. 10 and associated correspondence in FO 905/37.
9. Quoted in D. Kimche, 'The opening of the Red Sea to European ships in the late eigtheenth century', *Middle Eastern Studies*, 1972, VIII, 71, note 26.
10. Bombay Political Despatch to Court of Directors, no. 4 of 1838, 15 Feb. 1838.
11. Memorandum by Sir A. Ryan, *op.cit.*
12. F. Fresnel, 'L' Arabie', *Revue des Deux Mondes*, Paris, 1839, IV, XVII, 256.
13. The estimate for the archipelago appears in J. Vredenbregt, 'The haddj, some of its features and functions in Indonesia', *Bijdragen tot de Taal-, Land- en Volkenkunde*, Gravenhage, CXVIII, 1962, 93; that for the sub-continent derives from various consular despatches (e.g., Consul, Jidda, to FO, 8 Jan. 1861, in G.E. Stanley's Letter Book, 1859-63, FO 685/1).
14. Encls. to Sec. to Govt. of Bengal to Sec. to Govt. of India, 19 April 1851, For. Dept. Proc., Pol., 9 May 1851, no. 2.
15. Vredenbregt, *op. cit.*, 98-99.
16. Polit. Agent, Baghdad, to Sec. to Govt. of India, 26 April 1847, For. Dept. Proc., Pol., for 1847, nos. 1220-1233; Resident, Lahore, to Asst. Res., 16 Aug. 1848, For. Dept. Proc., Pol., for 1848, 2 Sept. 1848, no. 27; For. Dept., Ft. William, to Resident, Lahore, 2 Sept. 1848, *ibid.*, no. 28.
17. Burckhardt, *op.cit.*, 259.
18. Vice-Consul, Jidda, to Chief Sec. to Govt. of Bombay, 7 Dec. 1853, and Sec. to Govt. of India to Chief Sec. to Govt. of Bombay, 5 May 1854, For. Dept. Proc., Pol., for 1854, nos. 16-18.
19. Vredenbregt, *op.cit.*, 100.
20. R. Bayley-Winder, *Saudi Arabia in the nineteenth century*, New York, 1965, 56-57 and 90.
21. *Ibid.*, 90, and cf. C. Izzedine, *Le choléra et l'hygiène à la Mecque*, Paris, 1909, 28.
22. Izzedine, *op.cit.*, 28-29.
23. A.A. Proust, *Essai sur l'hygiène international...Avec une carte indiquent la marche des épidémies de choléra par les routes de terre et la voie maritime*, Paris, 1873, 45. Proust speaks of the 1865 epidemic as 'inaugurating' the maritime route (p. 258), and he concludes, 'It is established, without question, that every time cholera has shown itself in the Hejaz it has been in consequence of the pilgrimage to Mecca and that it has always been preceded by the arrival of Indian pilgrims' (285-286).
24. Correspondence and Papers relative to the Consulate, Jiddah, in For. Dept. Proc., Pol. A, Jan. 1872, nos. 132-145; June 1872, Cons. no. 533; Jan. 1873, no. 299; Feb. 1874, no. 296.
25. Sir B.H. Frere to FO, 28 May 1873, cited in footnote 2, above.
26. Quoted in G. de Gaury, *Rulers of Mecca*, New York, n.d., 252.
27. Consul, Jidda, to FO, 10 March 1879 (Sanitary no. 1), in J.N.E. Zohrab's Letter Book, 1879, FO 685/1, refers.
28. Copy encl. in *ibid.*
29. Consul, Jidda, to FO, 3 July 1879 (Consular no. 43), in Zohrab's Letter Book, FO 685/1.
30. 'Report on the Establishment required to carry on the duties of Her Majesty's Consulate at Jeddah', undated (mid-September 1879), in Zohrab's Letter Book, 442f, FO 685/1.
31. Ambassador, Constantinople, to FO, 20 Sept. 1881, copy encl. in For. Dept. Proc., A. Polit. E, Oct. 1882, no. 329.

Arabian Studies VI

32 Ambassador, Constantinople, to FO, 10 Dec. 1881, copy in *ibid.*, no. 331.
33 Minute (emphasis in original) by J. O'Kinealy, 2 June, 1882, in the papers concerning Abdur Razzack's appointment, cited in footnote 34, below.
34 Sec. to Govt. of India to Abdur Razzack, Conf., 25 Aug. 1882, For. Dept. Proc., A. Polit. E, Oct. 1882. no. 347 (another copy in FO 685/1, Pt. II)
35 A Dutch Consul had been appointed at Jidda in 1872, solely for the purpose of overseeing the pilgrimage from the Netherlands East Indies, and resident there only during the *hajj* season.
36 Polit. Resident, Aden, to Sec. of State for India, 8 Aug. 1874, For. Dept. Proc., Polit. A, no. 189.
37 Vredenbregt, *op.cit.*, Appendix I, 140. The figure given, 4,801, represents pilgrim passports applied for, and, as Vredenbregt explains, bears an uncertain relationship to pilgrims actually travelling. It is also possible that some or all of the NEI passport holders are included in the Straits Settlements figure.
38 Consul, Jidda, to FO, 24 March 1879, (Consular no. 12), in Zohrab's Letter Book, FO 685/1. Six years later Abdur Razzack estimated that there were nearly 10,000 Indian *muqīm* (residents) in Mecca, and about 1,500 in Jidda, with periods of residence of from 2 to 30 years. Vice-Consul, Jidda, to Consul, 10 Jan. 1885, For. Dept. Proc., Extl. A, June 1885, no. 152.
39 A year later, Zohrab stated, more modestly, that there were from 10,000 to 15,000 'British Indian' pilgrims annually. Consul, Jidda, to FO, 10 Sept. 1880, For. Dept. Proc., A. Polit. E, Oct. 1882, no. 256.
40 Vice-Consul, Jidda, to Consul, 10 Jan. 1885, For. Dept. Proc., Extl. A, June 1885, no. 152. The term *Jāwah* was in common use in the Hijaz for all south-east Asian pilgrims, irrespective of place of origin (cf. C. Snouck Hurgronje, *Mekka in the latter part of the 19th century*, Leiden, 1931, 215) and appears as 'Javanese' in the non-Dutch sources. It will be used in this sense in the remainder of the present article.
41 Consul, Jidda, to FO, 20 July 1879, (Consular no. 5), in Zohrab's Letter Book, FO 685/1.
42 Hurgronje suggests (*op.cit.*, 7) that the European consulates, especially the British, were for most pilgrims a problem rather than a protection, from the fear that association would lead them to be 'mocked and insulted by the inhabitants and unceremoniously expelled by the Government' if they went near them.
43 FO to Govt. of India, 29 Sept. 1881, For. Dept. Proc., A. Polit. E, Oct. 1882, no. 147 (quoting from corresp. between Jidda Consul and FO).
44 *Ibid.* These amounts had been proposed by the Consul. Abdur Razzack suggested that the minimum cash requirement be Rs. 300. In a later communication, Abdur Razzack gives a detailed cost analysis of the pilgrimage, itemizing 26 separate fees and other heads. Including return (but not outward) deck passage, it amounted to Rs. 236.14, to which he added a further Rs.63.2 for contingencies. Vice-Consul to Consul, 14 Dec. 1884, For. Dept. Proc., Extl. A, March 1885, no. 45.
45 F. Borel, *Etude statistique et épidémiologique sur le lazaret de Camaran et les pèlerins qu'il a reçu de 1887 à 1902*, Constantinople, 1902, 9, Table 5, gives a figure of 20.88 per cent. for Indian 'poor', compared with 0.85 per cent. for the *Jāwah*. In 1887, the consular report on the *hajj* gives a figure 47.9 per cent. for Indian 'paupers' (compared with 6.3 for the *Jāwah*), and says that it was much higher in earlier years. Vice-Consul, Jidda, to Consul, 15 Feb. 1888, encl. in Consul to Sec. to Govt. of India, no. 3 of 29 Feb. 1888, FO 685/2 (Pt.V). No definition is given of 'poor' or 'pauper'.
46 See, e.g., de Gaury, *op.cit.*, 253. Resumption of Turkish control may be said to have dated from 1858, when the British and French Consuls in Jidda and about twenty other Christians, were attacked and killed, followed by a British naval bombardment of the town, punitive indemnities, and the stationing there of a Turkish garrison. Details in 'Papers relating to the Outbreak at Jeddah in June 1858', FO Confid. Print. FO 424/18.
47 Minute, For. Dept. to Sec. to Govt. of India, 6 Sept. 1880, in 'Notes on Pilgrim Traffic Question forwarded by Home Department', For. Dept. Proc., A. Polit. E, Oct. 1882, no. 234. Cf. also de Gaury, *loc. cit.*
48 Govt. of India to Sec. of State for India, 27 Oct. 1884, For. Dept. Proc., Extl. A, Nov. 1884, no. 146.
49 FO to Govt. of India (quoting Governor of Straits Settlements), 11 Aug. 1881, in *ibid*, no. 123.
50 Consul, Jidda, to Resident, Aden, 20 May 1881, For. Dept. Proc., A. Polit. E, Oct. 1882, no. 261. Ten years later the Ottoman authorities rejected a British request to re-extend the Indian exemption to the Straits Settlements, on the ground that if it were granted a similar privilege would be sought for pilgrims from the Netherlands East Indies, 'many of whom obtain their passports at Singapore: the number of these pilgrims was already considerable and would certainly increase largely if the passport regulations were not enforced'. Ambassador,

Constantinople, to FO, Commercial no. 189, 24 Nov. 1902, For. Dept. Proc., March 1903, no. 92
51 The event and its aftermath are described in detail in J. Allen, *The sea years of Joseph Conrad*, Garden City, N.Y., 1965, 120-150.
52 Joseph Conrad, *Lord Jim*, London, 1961, 17.
53 Governor, Straits Settlements, to CO, 22 Nov. 1888, no. 17 in 'Selection of Papers respecting the Regulations for Ships Carrying Pilgrims to or from the Mahommedan Holy Places, 1888-90', Confid. Print, FO 424/170. The Papers contain much additional material on shipping regulation.
54 Vredenbregt, *op. cit.*, 130.
55 The relevant legislation is Ordinance XIII of 1888, amending Ordinance VI of 1874.
56 Minute, For. Dept. to Gov.-Gen., 16 July 1881, in 'Notes on Pilgrim Traffic Question etc.', *op.cit.*
57 W.F. Rae, *The business of travel: a fifty years' record of progress*, London: Thos. Cook & Son, 1891, 209.
58 Home Dept. Proc. (Sanitary), Calcutta, nos. 1-21-33.
59 Draft, For. Dept. to Netherlands Consul, Calcutta, 25 May 1894, For. Dept. Proc., Extl. B., June 1894, no. 15. Cook's had, however, been instrumental in exposing a long-standing ticket racket operated by the British and Dutch consuls and their staffs in conjunction with Hijaz authorities. See Thos. Cook & Son to Govt. of India, 27 Dec. 1886, FO 685/2 (Pt.V), and, for further detail, W.R. Roff, 'The conduct of the *haj* from Malaya, and the first Malay pilgrimage officer', *Sari Terbitan tak Berkala*, Occasional papers, no. 1, Kuala Lumpur: National University of Malaya, Institute of Malay Language, Literature & Culture, 1975, 82, note 12.
60 Izzedine, op.cit., 30-36.
61 Ibid., 67.
62 Ibid., 71-73. Dr. Oslchanjetzki of the Kamaràn staff, who was sent to Jidda to assist, gives a figure of 40,000 dead out of 200,000, in a memoir apparently written forty years later, 'Souvenirs de l'épidémie de choléra au Hedjaz en 1893', in F. Duguet, *Le pèlerinage de la Mecque*, Paris, 1932, 297.
63 Quoted in Durasnel, op.cit., 24.
64 Duguet, op.cit., 173.
65 On the Conference, which produced no official report, see, e.g., British Cholera Commission to FO, 3 Oct. 1866, Annex II to *Despatch from Her Majesty's Ambassador at Constantinople...regarding the conclusions arrived at by the Cholera Conference*. Great Britain Parliamentary Papers, and separately printed.
66 See, e.g., *Conférence Internationale Sanitaire, Vienne, 1874. Procès-verbaux*, Vienna: Imprim. Impériale et Royale, 1874, 419. Cf. *Conférence Internationale Sanitaire, Rome, 1885. Protocoles et procès-verbeaux*, Rome: Imprim. de Ministère des Affaires Etrangères, 1885, Resolution 59. In 1831, after the first cholera pandemic, Muhammad 'Ali Pasha 'to calm the fears of Europe, judged it useful to engage the participation of the Consular Corps in the sanitary control of Egypt', and created an Intendance de Santé Publique, to be divided in 1881 into an internal body and the Conseil Sanitaire Maritime et Quarantenaire d'Egypte. Separately, the Ottoman Conseil Supérieur de Santé had been formed in 1838, 'administered largely by the foreign consulates in Constantinople'.
67 Turkey. Conseil Supérieur de Santé. *Règlement applicable aux provenances de choléra*, Constantinople: Imprim. Osmanie, 1883. The regulation was first approved by the Council in January 1867, following the Constantinople Conference.
68 Sec. to Govt. of India to Asst. Surgeon Shaikh Atta Muhammad, 22 Aug. 1884, FO 685/2 (Pt.IV).
69 Borel, *op.cit.*, passim. Hurgronje in 1884 (*op.cit.*, 218) was among those who saw in Kamarān 'no other genuine purpose than exploitation' and thought it a dangerous imposition upon pilgrims
70 'Report on the Haj, 1882', Part I, FO 685/1 (Pt.III).
71 Vice-Consul, Jidda, to Ag. Consul, 7 May 1883, FO 685/2 (Pt.IV).
72 Izzedine, *op.cit.*, 9-11.
73 A.K. Nazare-Aga, *Contribution à l'étude des conférences sanitaire internationales dans leur rapports avec le prophylaxie des maladies pestilentielles en Perse*, Paris, 1903, 10. Duguet later remarked (*op.cit.*, 165), 'Will the pilgrimage to Mecca find its gendarme in the Conseil Quarantenaire of Alexandria?'
74 Durasnel, *op.cit.*, 43.
75 Ibid., 44-45. The official proceedings are in *Conférence Internationale Sanitaire, Paris, 1894. Procès-verbaux*, Paris: Imprim. Nationale, 1894.
76 Extract from Procs. of the Govt. of India, Home Dept., Sanitary, 28 June 1895, For. Dept.

Proc., Extl. A, Aug. 1895, nos. 4-5. The Straits Settlement Government, by contrast, did introduce compulsory return tickets, by a regulation that came into force on 15 Nov. 1898. Consul, Jidda, to Sec. to Govt. of India, 20 Feb. 1900, enclosing report on the *hajj* for 1897-98, For. Dept. Proc., Extl. A, April 1900, no. 32.

77 The total number of pilgrims from India fell by 74.5 per cent., and those coming by sea by 46.5 per cent. The reduction was to some extent due to a concurrent outbreak of plague. Borel, *op.cit.*, 10-11 and Table 7.

78 Duguet, *op.cit.*, 169.

79 Izzedine, *op.cit.*, 97-98. Izzedine was the senior Ottoman doctor in Mecca in 1895, and responsible for many of the improvements.

80 Telegram, FO to Viceroy, Simla, 31 May 1895, For. Dept. Proc., Secr. E., Sept 1895, no. 44. A full account appears in Consul, Jidda, to FO, 17 June 1895, *ibid.*, no. 63.

81 Minute, 1 Sept. 1881, in 'Notes on Pilgrim Traffic Question etc.', *op.cit.*

82 For a description of the system as it was in 1884-85, see Hurgronje, *op.cit.*, 23-29 & 78-79. There were 180 *mutawwifin* catering to the *Jāwah*, organized in a guild with its own chief (*Shaykh al-Mashāyikh*), who controlled purchase of licences and was answerable to the Sharif's government. A similar system operated for the Indian and other groups.

83 Repeated representations were made to the Hijaz authorities to provide pilgrims with greater freedom of choice as to *shaykhs*, and to limit the fees due to them. See, e.g., Ag. Consul, Jidda, to Turkish Vali, 11 July, 1894, and ensuing correspondence. FO 685/3 (Pt.VI); and cf. *Vredenbregt, op.cit.*, 126.

84 Vredenbregt, *op.cit.*, 127, note 109.

85 Governor, Straits Settlements, to CO, May 18 and 28, 1881, CO 273/108, quoted in A. Reid, 'Nineteenth century pan-Islam in Indonesia and Malaysia', *Journal of Asian studies*, London, 1967, XXVII, 279.

86 Consul, Jidda, to Polit. Resident, Aden, 27 April, 1881, and Supt. of Police, Singapore, to Inspector-General of Police, 5 May 1881, For. Dept. Proc., Secret, July 1881, nos. 193 and 196. A few years later concern was expressed about the intention of an English convert, 'Hadjee A. Browne', to make a lecture tour of India 'advocating an Anglo-Muslim alliance'. Asked for information about him, a Special Branch official minuted, 'I have looked through the C.S.B. Abstracts, the Pan Islamic file, and the Muhammadan Perverts file, but can find nothing.' For. Dept. Proc., Secr. E, Sept. 1894, nos. 45-55.

87 For Hurgronje's views see, e.g., Der Hadji-politiek der Indische Regering, in his *Verspreide Geschriften*, Bonn & Leipzig, 1924, 173-198 (first publ. in 1909) and succinctly expressed in his *Politique Musulmane de la Hollande*, Paris, 1911, 80-81: for discussion of his views and their influence see H.J. Benda, 'Christian Snouck Hurgronje and the foundations of Dutch Islamic policy in Indonesia', *Journal of Modern History*, Chicago, 1958, XXX, 338-47.

88 J.F. Keane, *Six months in the Hejaz: an account of the Muhammadan pilgrimages to Meccah and Medinah*, London, 1887, 286-87. Keane made the *hajj* in 1877-78.

89 Sec. to Govt. of India to Consul, Jidda, 27 July 1888, and resulting corresp., For. Dept. Proc., Secr. I, June 1889, nos. 1-8. Cf. also For. Dept. Proc., Secr. 1, Oct. 1889, nos. 39-42.

90 Corresp. in For. Dept. Proc., Secr. E, Jan. 1897, nos. 138-142.

Part III
The Social World of Empire

[16]

The Making of Race in Colonial Malaya: Political Economy and Racial Ideology

Charles Hirschman
Cornell University

The conventional interpretation of the "race problem" in Peninsular Malaysia (Malaya) is founded upon the supposedly inevitable frictions between ethnic communities with sharply divergent cultural traditions. In this view, assimilation between the indigenous Malay population and the descendants of immigrants from China and India was always a remote possibility. In this paper I argue that modern "race relations" in Peninsular Malaysia, in the sense of impenetrable group boundaries, were a byproduct of British colonialism of the late nineteenth and early twentieth centuries. Prior to 1850, inter-ethnic relations among Asian populations were marked by cultural stereotypes and occasional hostility, but there were also possibilities for inter-ethnic alliances and acculturation. Direct colonial rule brought European racial theory and constructed a social and economic order structured by "race." A review of the writing of observers of colonial society provides a crude test of this hypothesis.*

> "The idea of race is a situational imperative; if it is not there to begin with, it tends to develop in a plantation society because it is a useful, maybe even necessary, principle of control. In Virginia, the plantation took two peoples originally differentiated as Christian and heathen, and before the first century was over it had made two races."
> —Thompson, 1975:117

Ethnic inequality and conflict appear to be widespread, if not ubiquitous phenomena in plural societies around the globe (Helsler, 1977; Horowitz, 1985; van den Berghe, 1981). Ethnic frictions and antagonism are recurrent problems in developing societies in Asia, Africa, and Latin America as well as in the industrialized countries of Europe and North

---

* A revised version of a paper presented at the Malaysia Society Colloquium on "Malaysian Social and Economic History" at the Australian National University, Canberra, Australia, June 8–10, 1985. I am grateful to Milton Esman, William Lambert, Victor Nee, Norman Parmer, Frank Young, and especially to John Butcher for critical comments on an earlier draft of this paper. I also thank Adriene Dawkins for help in tracking down key sources.

America. Nor are modern socialist societies free of the strains of the "national question" (Connor, 1984). Given this seemingly universal pattern, the thesis of ethnicity as a primordial force—waiting just beneath the surface of social relations—has a strong appeal in popular thinking as well as in social science theory.

Yet at best, the hypothesis of ethnicity as a universal primordial bond or extended kinship feeling among a people can not be more than a partial explanation for the state of ethnic relations across societies. The problem is that there is tremendous variation in the patterns of ethnic antagonism, segregation, intermarriage, and even of ethnic identity across societies. This variation is even evident for a single ethnic-origin population, e.g., the differential status and assimilation of Afro-Americans in South and North America (Harris, 1964; van den Berghe, 1976), and the wide variety in the cultural and socioeconomic adaption of Chinese populations in the new nations of Southeast Asia (Skinner, 1960; Somers-Heidhues, 1974). A constant—the primordial bond of ethnicity—can not serve to explain a variable.

An alternative approach to the ethnic question is to begin with sociological theories of stratification, conflict, and social change. The dynamics of class formation and conflict, imperialism, and long distance labor migration are often linked with ethnic and racial boundaries (Bonacich, 1980; Hechter, 1975; Lieberson, 1961). When these processes are examined, especially within an historical perspective, it is often possible to discover how ethnic divisions are socially created, institutionalized, and modified (Bonacich and Modell, 1980; Lieberson, 1980; van den Berghe, 1967). From this perspective, I begin my study of the social bases of the origins of ethnicity in Malaysia. In this article—a preliminary version of a larger work—I propose and evaluate the hypothesis that the twentieth century structure of "race-relations" of Peninsular Malaysia is largely a product of social forces engendered by the expansion of British colonialism of the late nineteenth century.

Almost every writer who addresses the "race problem" or the "plural society" of Peninsular Malaysia[1] suggests that roots of contemporary ethnic divisions and antagonisms were formed during the colonial era. Beyond the point that the past has an important influence upon the present there is, however, little agreement on what it was about the colonial era that contributed to the troubled relations between Malays, Chinese

---

[1] Although Peninsular Malaysia is the presently appropriate name for the area under study, historical references can become confusing. Malaya, Colonial Malaya, British Malaya are used interchangeably as historical references to the area, even though political boundaries varied considerably over time. At present, Peninsular Malaysia consists of the eleven states of Malaysia on the mainland of Southeast Asia. The other states of contemporary Malaysia are Sabah and Sarawak on the island of Borneo, more than five hundred miles across the South China Sea from the peninsula.

331

Sociological Forum

and Indians in the post-independence period. Was it that British colonialism created an unstable demographic balance among widely divergent cultural populations by an unrestricted immigration policy (Comber, 1983; Freedman, 1960)? Or did the British practice "divide and rule" policies that sowed fear and mistrust among the Malays, Chinese and Indian populations (Abraham, 1977, 1983; Cham, 1977; Loh, 1975; Stenson, 1980)? My analysis acknowledges both these elements and links them to broader interpretation of the spread of racial theory from Europe and the development of the colonial political economy.

In a nutshell, I argue that there was a qualitative shift in ethnic relations and ideology in late nineteenth century Malaya. Beyond question there were ethnic divisions and widespread ethnic stereotypes prior to this time—both between Europeans and Asians and within the many Asian populations of the region. On the other hand, there is also considerable evidence in these earlier times of patterns of acculturation, shifting ethnic coalitions, and the possibility of ethnic boundaries being bridged or shifted as opportunities arose. But from the middle of the nineteenth century, these possibilities were diminished as European "racism" was imported and as direct colonial dominance was widened geographically and deepened institutionally. It is important to note at the outset that I do not claim that every instance of inter-ethnic hostility is of European origin. But I do argue that the problematic inter-ethnic relationships of the pre-1850 era, which contained the potential of acculturation and even assimilation, were transformed into "racial relations" by the colonial experience.

Although the empirical content of this article is confined to one relatively small Southeast Asian society, I believe the theoretical implications are far broader. In part, my effort is inspired by the work of Edgar Thompson (1975) who suggests that racial categories (and racial ideology) in the United States were a cultural byproduct of the coercive labor system of early American plantations. This interpretation, which is linked to a broader body of scholarship on the development of slavery in the United States (Fredrickson, 1981; Cox, 1948), presents a reversal of much conventional thinking about "race relations" in the United States and elsewhere. The point is that differences in skin pigmentation, initial cultural differences, and existing belief structures were of lesser importance than the exploitative institutional framework which required ideological justification. Slavery as it developed in the Americas was one of the most dehumanizing institutions ever created and required a powerful form of racist ideology to justify it. The development of multiethnic societies in Southeast Asia and accompanying social construction of "race relations" followed, of course, quite a different historical trajectory from the settler and slave societies of the New World. But the basic idea that the institutional framework—particularly political and economic structures—may be the central influence on the definition and character of "racial" ideology and ethnic relationships guides my inquiry.

HISTORICAL SETTING

By the time European powers arrived in Southeast Asia in the sixteenth century, the ebb and flow of regional empires and extensive trading networks had already created multiethnic communities. Port cities in Sumatra and the Malay peninsula contained not only peoples from throughout the Indonesian archipelago, but also from China and India (Lamb, 1964; Reid, 1980; Wheatley, 1961). Over the course of the next four centuries, patterns of regional migration accelerated, as Western powers disrupted local economies but also stimulated the expansion of other areas by setting up new trading centers and increasing the demand for local products. After several centuries of oscillation, the Southeast Asian world was transformed in the nineteenth century as the industrial revolution in Europe took hold and as its reverberations shook the world. The demand for raw materials outpaced the capacity of traditional systems to produce them. Competition for control of the supply of raw materials (or potential raw materials) stimulated a burst of European imperialist expansion in Southeast Asia (and elsewhere). Responding to the growth of world markets, capital, labor, and new organizational forms were mobilized and deployed in a variety of ways throughout Southeast Asia. Nowhere were these events more spectacular than on the Malay peninsula.

The British, who had staked their colonial claim to this part of the region, had occupied three port cities (with a bit of hinterland), known collectively as the Straits Settlements. Penang and Singapore were acquired through concessions by local rulers in 1786 and 1819, respectively, as trading stations. Malacca was added permanently in 1824 (having been temporarily occupied earlier), with the Dutch-British division of spheres of influence in Southeast Asia. Although the Straits Settlements administration intervened occasionally in the adjacent Malay states during the first half of the nineteenth century, the primary imperial interest was in the maintenance of their trading position, both regionally and on the route to China.[2] The relative independence of the Malay

---

[2] In spite of the general policy of noninterference in the Malay states during this period, this does not mean that British actions were without significant consequences. As Emerson observes "the conflicts within the Malay courts were utilized by the Europeans for their own purposes, with the result that the natural development of the Malay polity was checked and perverted. The history of Malaya since the 16th century is the confused chronicle of petty potentates, more or less closely linked with the intrigues of the European invaders" (Emerson, 1964:15).

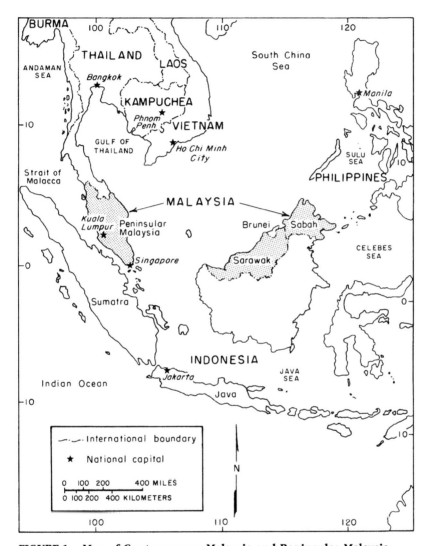

FIGURE 1. Map of Contemporary Malaysia and Peninsular Malaysia

Source: Bunge, Frederica M., ed. *Malaysia: A Country Study.* Area Handbook Series. Foreign Area Studies, The American University. Washington, DC: U.S. Government Printing Office, 1984:xxii,34.

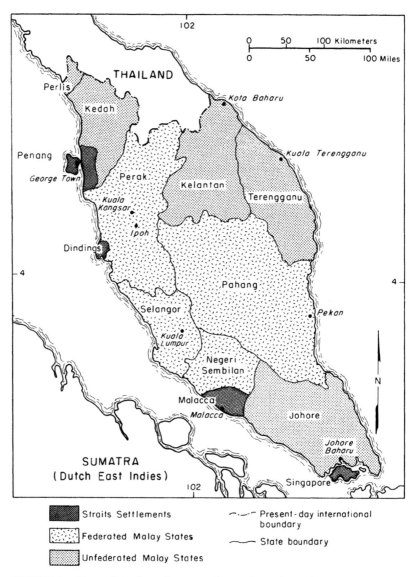

FIGURE 2. Map of Malaya (Peninsular Malaysia) under British Colonialism

Sociological Forum

states was finally ended by the British "forward movement," beginning in the 1870s (Khoo, 1966).

By the middle of the nineteenth century, there was clear evidence of enormous wealth to be made with the expansion of the tin mining industry in the west coast states of the peninsula, and there was also a strong belief in the potential for agricultural development. Malay rulers, often working with commercial interests in the Straits Settlements, had begun to develop this potential by bringing in Chinese labor to expand tin production. Traditional rivalries among Malay chiefs and disputes among the various Chinese groups were exacerbated by competition for the immense economic gains to be had by control of tin production (Khoo, 1972). Sporadic fighting, usually between one Malay-Chinese coalition against another Malay-Chinese faction, led to frequent disruptions in tin production. With heavy investments in the Malay states, merchants in the Straits Settlements continually pressed for British intervention to provide "stable government." Finally, in a complex series of political and military moves, beginning with the Pangkor Agreement in 1874, the British took effective control of three west coast states in the mid-1870s (Cowan, 1961; Parkinson, 1960). Under the fiction of assigning British advisors to the Malay Sultans, the colonial government established direct administration over virtually all aspects of government. The process was not as smooth as retrospective accounts make it appear. There was armed Malay resistance in Perak, Selangor, and Sungei Ujong in 1875, and later in Pahang (Gullick, 1954; Parkinson, 1960:Chs. 10–11; Clifford, 1929:3–75). But with a disunited Malay aristocracy and the force of superior arms, the British were able to consolidate their colonial administration in a fairly brief time. Subsequently, pensions for the Malay aristocracy (made possible by taxes on the Chinese expansion of the tin industry; see Butcher, 1979a) and conciliatory diplomacy by some of the early colonial administrators established a generally harmonious relationship with the Malay rulers (who continued in their symbolic roles, but without any real power).

As the British colonial system expanded its grip over the entire peninsula, Chinese and European capitalists directed the creation of an export economy built on tin and later on rubber (Wong, 1965; J. Jackson, 1968). Chinese, Indian, and Indonesian laborers were imported in such large numbers as to soon outnumber the Malay population in the west coast states (J. Jackson, 1964). The years following 1874 were not only a period of total political and economic transformation of the Malay states, but also a watershed era of change in the development of Malaysian ethnic relations (Khoo, 1981).

The plural society of contemporary Peninsular Malaysia (Malaya) is largely a product of this period of colonial expansion and the waves of immigration that accompanied it (Saw, 1963). Certainly, the balance of numbers—with the twentieth century Malay population only slightly larger than the combined total of Chinese, Indians, and others—is a result of immigration from 1850 to 1930. But the significance of the colonial period was more far-reaching than just the effects of the search for cheap Asian labor. If Thompson's insight is to be taken seriously, we must look to the institutional framework of colonial society—in the economy, the polity, and social structure—and in the construction of a colonial vision of "race." These features will allow a more adequate basis for assessing the effects of the legacy of the colonial experience on ethnic relations. I begin with some general observations on ethnic relations for the period prior to the late nineteenth century.

ETHNIC RELATIONS AMONG ASIANS PRIOR TO THE LATE NINETEENTH CENTURY

The development and protection of trade, both regional and long-distance, were the economic bases of political expansion in the pre-colonial Malay world (Meilink-Roelofsz, 1962; Wolters, 1970). In these conditions, the desirability of maintaining amicable relationships among the culturally diverse peoples involved in distant trading networks was certainly obvious. Military conquest by ascendant powers was a frequent mechanism for regional dominance, but long term inter-regional hostility was probably not conducive to the maintenance of trade. With an enormous land frontier and easy mobility by sea and river, it was difficult to maintain exploitative economic structures. Conquered areas were frequently brought into formal or informal federations that shared some of the economic rewards of trade. Dependencies could most easily be made allies by creating kinship ties through marriage alliances. In such an environment, it seems that bridging the ethnic diversity of Southeast Asia (and the Malay world within it) was a common interest. *Ethnocentrism,* the belief in the superiority of one's own people and culture, was probably ubiquitous, but a *racial ideology of inherent differences* seems less likely. The former permits the absorption of subject peoples; the latter creates caste lines.

This general picture gains some support from the history of political alliances in the Malay world after European intervention. With the move of the Malacca sultanate to Johor in the early sixteenth century, there was a series of military campaigns against the Portuguese, against the Dutch, and against rival Malay powers (L. Andaya, 1975; Hall, 1981:366–379; Lewis, 1982). Shifting coalitions between Southeast Asian peoples and European forces seem to be based not upon cultural background or even religion, but on political expediency. Another example was the absorption of the Bugis population into the Malay aristocracy (in spite of the wars between Malays and Bugis; see Andaya and Andaya,

Sociological Forum

1982:Ch. 2). Barbara Andaya (1979:273) notes that Bugis rulers in Selangor were aware of their *parvenu* status in the Malay world and sought to increase their standing by marriages into prestigious families and by the adoption of royal symbols which had meaning in Malay society.

It was into this complex and diverse Southeast Asian world that early visitors, missionaries, and merchants from India and China also arrived. From South Asia came religious traditions, forms of state organization, and a wide variety of cultural expressions (Sandhu, 1969:Ch. 1). Trade links to China were important for traditional Southeast Asian polities in the Malay world. Malacca's dominant position in the fifteenth century was recognized, in part, through the acceptance of its offer of tribute to China (Sandhu, 1961; Wang, 1981:81–96). Although there already were Chinese populations in Malacca and other towns along the Malay peninsula, it seems that the opening of British settlements in Penang in 1786 and in Singapore in 1819 triggered a significant increase of Chinese migration to the Malay peninsula (Purcell, 1948:Ch. 1–3).

The record indicates that early contacts between Chinese, Indians, and Malays may not have been entirely harmonious and free of mutual suspicion, but it does not seem that racial divisions (in the sense of impenetrable barriers) were present. One measure of the relative openness of ethnic relations is the evidence of intermarriage. The Baba or Straits Chinese communities of Penang and Malacca retained their Chinese identity, but they adopted many aspects of Malay culture (Clammer, 1980; Gosling, 1964; Tan, 1983).[3] On the nearby island of Java in the early years of the seventeenth century, prior to Dutch control, "Resident Chinese were free to adopt the Indonesian cultural attributes or marry into the local indigenous society and become 'Indonesian' " (Kemasang, 1982:61).

The assimilation of many Indian Muslims with Malays seems to have progressed even further. The Jawi Peranakan (identified as Jawi Pekans in the nineteenth century censuses of the Straits Settlements) community is a product of Indian-Malay intermarriages in the eighteenth and nineteenth centuries. Often speaking Malay as their mother tongue, Jawi Peranakans were employed by the British as clerks and interpreters (Roff, 1967:48–49). An early British administrator in the Malay states, describing his experiences in his journal, observes "a dark girl of about eighteen, certainly not a pure Malay" (Sadka, 1954:97). Even at present, there are fairly loose boundaries between Indian Muslims and Malays (Nagata, 1974) and few barriers to intermarriage.

---

[3] Clammer (1983:157) questions Purcell's statement (1951:132) that the Baba Chinese community is a product of Malay-Chinese intermarriage. Even if there was little Malay-Chinese intermarriage, the Baba Chinese community is clearly a long resident population with a high degree of acculturation to the Malay world.

The Making of Race in Colonial Malaya

In terms of economic relationships, it seems that in spite of wide cultural and linguistic differences, traditional Malay elites and Chinese interests worked together for mutual gain. The problem faced by Malay rulers interested in responding to the growth of demand for primary products was the shortage of labor. Chinese laborers first worked for Malays on gambier plantations in the Riau islands in the late eighteenth century (Trocki, 1976; Begbie, 1967:315). Quite apart from any European influence, the rulers of Johor successfully encouraged Chinese entrepreneurship and settlement in the mid-nineteenth century (Trocki, 1979:Ch. 4). In fact, in the 1860s, the Johor government appointed Chinese members to the advisory council of the state and also employed a Malay administrator who spoke and wrote Chinese (Andaya and Andaya, 1982:139–143). The same model did not work so well in the tin mining areas of the west coast states, but when disputes and fighting broke out over control of the wealth, the parties did not always split along ethnic lines. More often it was coalitions of Malays and Chinese fighting other Malay-Chinese groupings (Khoo, 1972).

A claim frequently heard is that racism was indigenous in the attitudes and behavior of Malays toward the Orang Asli—the aboriginal peoples of the interior of the peninsula. It is difficult to sort out changes in attitudes over the past century, but recent studies (Dodge, 1981; Couillard, 1984) suggest a complex set of economic and social relationships between Malays and the Orang Asli in the period prior to British interventions. Malays were involved as middlemen in the economic exchange of forest products gathered by the Orang Asli. With the disappearance of this trade, the functional ties between Malays and the Orang Asli were broken. As the Malay population was increasingly seen as the "backward people" of colonial society, the image of an even more backward population in the jungle may have filled an ideological niche in Malay culture.

CHANGES IN EUROPEAN THINKING ABOUT RACE AND ETHNIC DIVERSITY

European images of Asian peoples during the nineteenth century had significant consequences for the practice of colonialism and for subsequent inter-ethnic relationships among Asians. To begin the study of this question, we first must examine the conceptions of race and ethnicity which Europeans brought with them to Asia.

With the European expansion of the fifteenth and sixteenth centuries, Europeans encountered a world of Asian, African, and Amerindian peoples of immense physical, cultural and technological diversity. There was no universally accepted explanation to give conceptual order to such diversity. Perhaps the dominant paradigm in Europe to explain dif-

339

ferences between groups of people was provided by the Old Testament (Banton, 1983:39). While the biblical explanation of descent via genealogies suggested different origins, there was no divine interpretation of inherent capacities of different peoples. Beliefs about the relative influences of geography, climate, and moral development could all coexist without any standards to evaluate them, save for personal experience and the position of the person expressing the statement. One reading of European intellectual history suggests that, "A substantial, perhaps dominant, body of scientific opinion in the eighteenth century was . . . committed to the belief that racial differences were rather evanescent and subject to the control of both natural and cultural aspects of the environment" (Harris, 1968:265).

The lack of orthodoxy of belief about racial differences did not prevent the capture and enslavement of millions of Africans nor a wide variety of "inhuman" practices against nonEuropean peoples by the European powers (Curtin, 1964). Rationalizations based upon religious or cultural superiority initially may have been sufficient. There appears to have been a flexible and pragmatic exercise of white superiority. For example, Dutch colonial behavior in Indonesia is said to have revealed "that innate conviction of white superiority" (Boxer, 1965:233), but the Dutch were much more respectful in their dealings with China and Japan. It seems that the relative degree of power was the key determinant of inter-group relations, and race was a frequent correlate in the equation.

During the nineteenth century, European thought about race underwent a radical shift, partly as a response to developments in "scientific" theories of human diversity and to the widening gap in technological progress between European and nonEuropean societies (Banton, 1983:Ch. 3; Harris, 1968; Jones, 1980:Ch. 8). European intellectuals were attempting to extend the Linnean classificatory system of zoological types of the phenotypical variation of humankind. The meaning of "race" began to shift from a relatively general term that distinguished peoples on almost any criteria to a more narrow classification of biologically defined subspecies, with specific assumptions about the inheritability of cultural predispositions and the potential for progress. These ideas were given a significant scientific standing (later discredited) with the application of evolutionary theory to the origins of the different races. As opposed to the earlier era of multiple explanations of human diversity, the racial theory of innate differences encountered little dissent in the Western world: "Darwin, Wallace, Huxley, Haeckel, Spencer, and every other evolutionist of the late nineteenth century, as well as almost every major social scientist from Marx to Morgan, regarded racial differences as essential to the understanding of human behavior" (Harris, 1968:265; also see Gould, 1981).

The Making of Race in Colonial Malaya

Not only did science give racial theory the aura of legitimacy in the late nineteenth century, but such beliefs also fitted well with the larger body of social Darwinist thought in the wake of the rapid technological and economic advances of European societies. Conquest and dominance of the world by European peoples could be given a moral purpose—it was natural, inevitable, ordered by differential endowments granted by a Creator, and beneficial to the progress of all mankind. It was this shift in European thinking about racial differences that accompanied the last burst of imperialist enthusiasm of the nineteenth century and rationalized colonial empires until racist ideology was finally exposed by its logical extension in the gas chambers of the Third Reich.

EUROPEAN CONCEPTIONS OF RACE AND ETHNICITY IN SOUTHEAST ASIA

Based upon the summary of accounts in the two preceding sections, I suggest that the late nineteenth century witnessed a significant change in the ideology of Europeans about themselves and their relations with Asian communities in Malaya. The expectation of attitudinal change is based upon two factors: (1) the increasing legitimacy of racial theory with the maturation of social Darwinist thought in Europe and the unquestioned worldwide political, economic and technological dominance of white (especially British) societies, and (2) the need for a justification for the spread and maintenance of direct colonial rule in the Malay states.

The idea of change in colonial ideology in the late nineteenth century is a hypothesis that can be tested, at least in an approximate fashion, by an examination of the writings of Europeans in Malaya during this period.[4] Several problems arise in the course of such a "test," not the least of which is that I have only surveyed a small fraction of the vast body of literature for this time period (for a model of a comprehensive survey, see Curtin's (1964) account of the European image of Africa from 1780 to 1850).

A fundamental methodological problem in this inquiry is that most authors rarely give an unambiguous expression of their views—they often mix environmental, cultural, and genetic interpretations of ethnic differences. Moreover, it is difficult to evaluate the statements of a few individual writers as representing a larger climate of opinion. Drawing upon their own experiences and insights, individuals can and do differ from the prevailing ideology of an era. Some individuals may be ahead or behind their times in expressing their views. And many writers find

---

[4] In another paper, I test this hypothesis with an examination of changes in the ethnic classification used in the censuses of colonial Malaya (Hirschman, 1985).

Sociological Forum

it unnecessary to spill much ink on "common opinion" or widely shared assumptions. What is left unsaid is often as important as what is said. Even with these qualifications, I think it is possible to present some empirical support for the thesis of change in colonial ideology, although I must admit that much more evidence will be necessary to convince the skeptic.

The first priority is to provide some conceptual order of topics under the rubric of "racial and ethnic ideology." As a preliminary guide, I separately review Europeans' attitudes toward Malays and nonMalays, and then consider Europeans' attitudes about themselves. Under the section on European attitudes toward Malays, three somewhat separate, though obviously interrelated, dimensions are considered: paternalism, Malay capacities, and Malay "laziness."

European Attitude Toward Malays

Paternalism. Paternalism is the belief that the management of the affairs of the country or of individuals should be done in the manner of a father dealing with his children. The social base of such attitudes must be the relative powerlessness of the subject population. This base was not always present prior to the late nineteenth century. Although the Portuguese and Dutch had achieved military supremacy in overall terms in the sixteenth and seventeenth centuries, they were constantly facing problems in exercising their influence. Non-cooperation is evident by the frequent European expressions concerning native treachery and disloyalty—to say nothing of piracy. An eighteenth century Dutch Governor of Malacca expressed this attitude: "The people of Rombouw must also be well watched for they are of a murderous and rapacious disposition, deceitful and treacherous" (Harrison, 1954:33). In a fine study of eighteenth century Perak, Barbara Andaya notes that the Malay kingdom always "dealt [with the Dutch in Malacca] from a position of strength; [Sultan Iskandar] did not beg, he demanded . . . the Dutch were always on the defensive" (1979:250).

It seems that the independence of the Malay states (in spite of European intervention) and their willingness to defend their interests created some fear, and perhaps a bit of respect, in European hearts. The frequent paternalistic vision of Malay docility, loyalty, and dependence that was the staple of later British colonial attitudes is conspicuously absent from these earlier writings. Begbie, a British military officer who served in Malacca in the 1830s, provides a detailed account of the Nanning War, in which the British eventually attained military dominance in the hinterland of Malacca, but only after considerable Malay resistance (1967:Ch. 4–6). Begbie shows few signs of European paternalism for Asian peoples, in fact, one of his major concerns is that unwise colonial land policies have made the Malay peasantry restless and hostile (1967:384–386).

In the years after 1874, the Malays were literally and figuratively disarmed.[5] Malay dependence (especially of the elite class) was bought by pensions and recognition as the nominal rulers of the country. In the early twentieth century a glowing account of imperial progress reports that earlier European commentators' references to Malay laziness and treachery were, in light of recent history, shown to be unjust—indeed the Malays were "nature's gentlemen" (Wright and Reid, 1912:313–315). This vision of Malays as happy underlings is also reflected in Swettenham's comment that: "you will wish for no better servant, no more pleasant or cheery companion" (1955:139).

Malay Capacities. The evidence on changes in European conceptions of Malay inherent potential is mixed. There are several examples of quite racist judgments prior to the late nineteenth century (noted below), but other writings raise doubts as to whether this was the dominant ideology among Europeans at the time. After the turn of the century, there are again contradictory expressions, but there seem to be many signs that most Europeans doubted that Malays were as able as other "races."

The earlier critical expressions of Malay capacities can be found in some of the major "scholarly" writings of the early and mid-nineteenth century. John Crawfurd, a colonial administrator who worked with Raffles in Java and was one of the early governors of Singapore, was one of the most prolific of scholarly writers on Southeast Asia in the early to mid-nineteenth century. His two-volume *History of the Indian Archipelago* (published in 1820) gives an ethnographic account of the region. On one hand he defends the "natives" against charges of indolence: "The islanders are found to be industrious like other peoples . . . they have no constitutional listlessness nor apathy, and whenever there exists a reasonable prospect of advantage, they are found to labour with vigour and perseverance" (pp. 42–43). However, in other respects, Crawfurd finds Southeast Asians wanting: "With respect to their intellectual faculties, the Indian islanders may be pronounced slow of comprehension, but of sound, though narrow judgment . . . it must be confessed that an Indian islander of the best capacity is unequal, in most respects, to an individual not above mediocrity in a civilized community" (pp. 45–46).

Although A. R. Wallace, the great nineteenth century naturalist and contributor to evolutionary theory, would later disavow any biological

---

[5] Swettenham (1955:135) reports, "In 1874 every Malay had as many weapons as he could carry . . . two daggers in his belt, two spears in his hand, a gun over his shoulder, and a long sword under his arm."

Sociological Forum

basis of racial differences, his *The Malay Archipelago* (first published in 1869) gave a quite different account: "The intellect of the Malay race seems rather deficient. They are incapable of anything beyond the simplest combinations of ideas and have little taste or energy for the acquirement of knowledge" (Wallace, 1983:448–449).

These expressions of belief in racial differences confirm the tendency in some nineteenth century European thinking about non-European peoples. Yet it would be premature to suggest that this was the dominant component of European attitudes toward Malays.

Another nineteenth century observer of British rule in the Straits Settlements, Cameron (1965, original publication in 1865) gives a generally positive account of the Malay population, although he refers to their lack of industriousness (pp. 133–134). In fact, Cameron pays Malays the highest possible compliment by comparing them with the English; he says the Malays are "adventurous, and, in many respects, [a] noble race, that like English colonists in more modern instances, have laid the foundation of a great empire on but a very small beginning" (pp. 8–9).

The journals (written in the 1870s) of Swettenham (Burns and Cowan, 1975) and Low (Sadka, 1954), two of the earliest pioneers of the British forward movement, are notable for the absence of any broad claims about Malay capacities or abilities. Low brought a good opinion of Malay abilities with him from his prior years in Borneo: "He [Low] describes Malays as 'a people so naturally sagacious and clever [and] whose abilities are probably not inferior to any of the nations of Europe'" (quoted in Loh, 1969:4). However, J. W. W. Birch, the first Resident appointed to Perak and who was murdered by Malay leaders who resented both British intervention and Birch's arrogant manner, was full of disdain for Asian capacities for self-government (Burns, 1976).

After the "watershed" period when British control was complete, new ideological justifications were given for the British running the country on behalf of the Malay population, or at least on behalf of the Malay sultans. Since the British did not claim to be administering as conquerors or even to further their own financial interests, their paternalistic attitudes must rest upon a judgment that Malays do not have the ability to run their own country. For example, in addresses to the Royal Colonial Institute in London, Hugh Clifford, a sensitive colonial administrator observes, "unless a people is possessed of considerable intellectual energy, such as the Malays can lay no claim to" (Kratoska, 1983:241) and later, "anyone who is acquainted with the two races will at once acknowledge that the Siamese are the intellectual superiors of the Malays" (Kratoska, 1983:279).

It is interesting to note that Swettenham, who was one of the most outspoken imperialists of his age (Allen, 1964), was at pains to state that Malays have no lack of intellectual capacities (Swettenham, 1900:207, and 1955:284). I suspect that his defense of Malay intelligence was partially a reaction against the growing body of colonial opinion to the contrary. Perhaps the level of general European opinion is illustrated by Emerson's perception in the 1930s of the "common European and Chinese complaint that the Malays are a lazy and shiftless people who are wantonly refusing to accept the benefits which are offered to them" (Emerson, 1964:18). Or as Stockwell put it: "Dismissive generalizations about the Oriental were part of the mental furniture of even the most experienced Europeans" (Stockwell, 1982:54).

Malay Laziness. One of the most frequent stereotypes of Southeast Asians, especially of Malays, was of indolence or laziness. In his excellent book, *The Myth of the Lazy Native,* Hussein Alatas (1977) finds such expressions about Malays, Javanese, and Filipinos throughout the colonial period. Hussein Alatas concludes that this stereotype was founded on the unwillingness of Southeast Asians to work for Europeans. Given the terms of employment—in wages and working conditions—offered by Europeans relative to traditional fishing and agriculture, Malays made the economically rational choice.

As opposed to subsequent twentieth century colonial officials who compared the lack of Malay interest in working in the rubber plantations and tin mines with the hard working Chinese and Indians, many of the early European writers explain Malay characteristics as a consequence of environmental or social factors. The environmental explanation is that Malays find it unnecessary to work hard because nature is so bountiful. With abundant fresh fish and productive padi fields, the environment has not disciplined Malays to work hard or plan for the long term. The social explanation says that any economic gains will simply be confiscated by local elites: "It is no advantage to a man to cultivate a goodly piece of land, and raise crops that were not for his own eating, to grow fruits that were absorbed by the Sultan or chief and their numerous followings; or to become the possessor of buffaloes that might be seized any day to draw the properties of his lord" (McNair, 1972:293–294). Both of these arguments were offered by Swettenham in his description of Malay character (1955:137).

Butcher (1971:Ch. 7) observes that early British Residents saw Malay lack of economic activity as a problem for colonial administration. If the proper motivation could be instilled by government policy or supervision, Malays might then respond accordingly. To a greater extent than would be true later, government projects (irrigation, etc.) were dependent on Malay participation. After the rubber boom began and Indian immigrants were available for the plantation sector and for public works projects, British officials no longer had to worry about the problem of getting Malay labor or cooperation (Butcher, 1971:62–63). In this context, Malay laziness could become a permanent piece in the "mental furniture" of the colonial mind. Disdain for manual labor was perhaps a bit quaint—and a not wholly unattractive feature for "nature's gentlemen"—and also served as a ready-made excuse for the plight of the poor Malays in the richest of all British colonies. As late as 1969, an old Malaya hand could still write, "Depending on one's point of view, the Malays could be described as carefree or indolent, contented or unambitious, pleasure-loving or idle. To some extent all of this would be true" (Slimming, 1969:7).

European Attitudes towards Chinese and Indians

Europeans were decidedly ambivalent in their attitudes toward the Chinese in Malaya. On one hand, the British colonial establishment, both in the Straits Settlements and for the early decades of their rule in the Malay states, was almost completely dependent upon Chinese entrepreneurial activity for their economic base. Taxes on opium and gambling—the pastimes of the Chinese working class—and on tin—a field dominated by Chinese interests until the first decade of the twentieth century—were the chief sources of revenue for the colonial administration. Nor could any observer deny the extraordinary determination and perseverance shown by most Chinese—workers and entrepreneurs alike.

Most Europeans felt a grudging admiration for the Chinese. For example, a Singapore merchant commented that, "[the Chinese] are, as a race, capable of civilization of the highest kind. They are at once laborers and statesmen. They can work in any climate, hot or cold, and they have great mercantile capacity . . . we are pleased to see them flocking [to Malaya] as they do in thousands" (Walter Adamson, quoted in Kratoska, 1983:76–77). Yet these same qualities were also the source of European derisive comment: "In short, whenever there is money to be made, you can be sure that the Chinaman is not far away" (Wright and Reid, 1912:323). An earlier statement shows the strength of this European resentment of Chinese economic gain: "Whenever money is to be acquired by the peaceful exercise of agriculture, by handicrafts, by the opening of mines of tin, iron ore or gold, amidst savage hordes and wild forests, there will be found the greedy Chinese" (Newbold, 1839:Vol. 1:10).

Since the condescension and paternalism which the colonial mind applied to the Malays did not fit the Chinese population, Europeans developed a sense of resentment and hostile admiration for most Chinese. This ambivalence is expressed by Swettenham: "The Chinese have, under direction, made the Protected States what they are. They are the bees who suck the honey from every profitable undertaking. A thorough experience of Malays will not qualify an official to deal with Chinese—

a separate education is necessary for that, but it is a lesson more easy to learn. It is almost hopeless to expect to make friends with a Chinaman, and it is, for a Government officer an object that is not very desirable to attain. The Chinese, at least that class of them met with in Malaya, do not understand being treated as equals; they only realize two positions—the giving and receiving of orders; they are the easiest people to govern in the East for a man of determination, but they must know their master, and he must know them" (Swettenham, 1900:38–39).

For most Europeans, the dominant view of Indians was as a source of cheap and docile labor—especially in comparison with Chinese who were thought to be too independent. In an 1885 speech discussing the development of North Borneo, a British official stated, "There are many who prefer the Indian coolie, and consider [them relative to Chinese labor] better suited to the peculiar wants of the locality. . . . They regard the Indian, moreover, as a creature far more amenable to discipline and management than the sturdy and independent Chinese" (Walter H. Medhurst, quoted in Kratoska, 1983:105). In summarizing Swettenham's attitudes, Allen says that he (Swettenham) expresses physical, but not economic contempt for Indians (Allen, 1964:46).

Europeans' Attitudes About Themselves

It is impossible to understand colonial ideology and its impact upon development of ethnic relations in Malaya without seeing the vision the British held of themselves. Like Europeans generally, they saw themselves as superior to Asians, not only in economic terms, but also in their unique capabilities to bring progress—politically, economically and ethically—to the world. Looking back with hindsight, it is easy to penetrate the double standards of colonial thinking, but this was not so at the time. The heyday of imperialism around the turn of the century presented an almost unquestioned orthodoxy. In his review of Swettenham and Clifford's writings, Allen notes that the "missionary impulse of British imperialism . . . had a wide appeal to men of high mental calibre" (1964:46). The intellectual appeal did not rest on material interests, but rather represented a call to bring civilization and leadership to the backward races of the world. The imperial ideology contrasted the incapable "natives" and the capable Englishman. Frederick Weld, an influential colonial administrator at the time of expansion and consolidation of colonial administration of the Malay states observes; "I doubt if Asiatic(s) can ever really be taught to govern themselves" [quoted in Allen, 1964:45], and "I think that capacity for governing a characteristic of our race [British]" (quoted in Kratoska, 1983:46).

An important element of this attitude is that it provides a theory of *entitlement*. In every society rewards, whether in terms of social sta-

Sociological Forum

tus or material benefits, are legitimated in terms of the dominant ideology. Colonial society has a particular form of ideological justification about the distribution of rewards—individuals are entitled to rewards on the basis of membership in a particular race.

COLONIAL INSTITUTIONS AND THE SELF-FULFILLING PROPHECIES OF RACIAL DISTINCTIONS

"Race" was constructed in colonial Malaya, not only with the ideological baggage brought by Europeans but also by the political and economic framework sponsored by imperialism. This is not to say that the initial differences between Malays, Chinese, and Indians were unimportant or that ethnic frictions would have been absent if European colonialism had not touched Southeast Asia. Rather the question is whether the structure of constraints and opportunities shaped by colonial rule widened the initial differences even further, and then created an ideology to explain ethnic inequality as an inevitable reflection of inherent "racial" differences. In this section, I will only explore several of the potential topics that could be considered, namely: the lack of Malay participation in wage labor, the lack of Malay entrepreneurship, and the question of Malay-Chinese antagonism. The hypothesis is that these features were, in part, byproducts of the institutional framework of the colonial period, and not simply inevitable outcomes of differences in cultural predispositions.

Malays and Wage Labor

Popular thinking suggests that Malays are uninterested in economic gain. This idea has been given academic respectability (in Malaysia and in other colonial societies) by reference to the lack of "the need for achievement" and the "backward bending supply curve for labor." The evidence given for this attribute is that Malays rarely participated in wage employment, and when they did, employers frequently found them to be unsatisfactory employees. These facts are not in dispute; the question is whether Malays displayed "laziness" or "economic rationality" in their economic endeavors.

The feudal structure of the Malay states prior to British intervention did not appear to have much of a niche for wage labor. The Malay sultans and chiefs were the major entrepreneurs who controlled tin mining production and taxed the traffic on rivers. Peasants were compelled to provide labor (*kerah*) for the chiefs and also to provide for their own sustenance by agriculture and fishing. Collection of forest products, perhaps via exchange relationships with the Orang Asli, was another potential avenue of economic gain. Although the degree of peasant oppression by the aristocracy was limited by the possibility of flight to the frontier (the Malay peninsula was sparsely settled), peasants probably had few incentives to maximize production. The observation by early colonial administrators that Malay elites frequently confiscated any surplus peasant production is probably true (this was common practice in other feudal societies, including Europe). Given the evident barriers to social mobility in a feudal society and the futility of material acquisition, productive work beyond what was necessary for survival made little sense.

Among the major changes of the late nineteenth century were the end of the traditional means of peasant exploitation by the Malay aristocracy, and the expansion of wage employment in the mining and plantation industries. After some hesitation, the colonial system terminated debt slavery and compulsory labor service for Malay peasants. The Malay aristocracy, who now received pensions far above their traditional levels of income, were no longer economically dependent upon the Malay peasantry. For peasants, especially in the west coast states, the ability to pursue their traditional livelihood without the threat of warfare and confiscation probably offered them, at least by the standards of the day, a fairly positive situation. Again the description by colonial observers of a bountiful environment for fishing, hunting, and rice production should not be entirely discounted. How did this way of life compare with the employment and wages offered for work in the early mines and plantations?

Even if all Malays had opted for wage labor in the early mines and plantations, there would still have been a labor shortage. But most of the early entrepreneurs, largely Chinese, thought in terms of immigrant labor. Although there may have been some cultural preference by employers for Chinese workers, their primary interest was probably in plentiful and cheap labor. Malay peasants were neither.

To draw Malay peasants out of their traditional pursuits, employers would have had to offer a wage that was superior to the "real wage" of peasant agriculture. This was not necessary as immigrant labor was readily available—on terms that were undoubtedly much cheaper. The accounts of Jackson (1961), Blythe (1947), and Sandhu (1969) on the living conditions and compensation of Chinese and Indians on the early estates and mines paints a dreadful picture. Mortality rates were very high, and employers faced a recurring problem of workers running away before completing their contracts. Most workers were tied to their places of employment by cycles of debt. The passage from the home country had to be repaid; then there were a variety of mechanisms used by employers to keep a captive labor force. For Malay villagers to give up their autonomy and relatively positive socioeconomic standards for the conditions of work of wage employment in the late nineteenth century,

349

they would have to be considered economically irrational (for similar observations, see C. Y. Lim, 1967:115 and 122).

There is other evidence, however, that Malay peasants did respond to economic incentives when it was in their economic interest to do so. In the early decades of the twentieth century, as the economy became synonymous with the rubber plantation industry, Malay villagers were engaged in widespread planting of rubber on their smallholdings. This "peasant innovation" (Rudner, 1970; T. G. Lim, 1977) was undertaken in the face of official disapproval from the colonial government and the Malay aristocracy. Laws were passed to prevent rice lands from being planted with rubber and the "restriction schemes" of the 1920s and 1930s discriminated against smallholders in favor of the estate sector. This peasant innovation is all the more impressive because it required a new technology of production, a wait of six to seven years until rubber trees come into production, and the entry of peasants into the market with a crop that had no local use. But there was no disguising the fact that rubber produced a much higher income than rice or any other rural occupation. Peasants recognized the opportunity and pursued it.

After the problem of labor shortage for the export sector had been solved (with Indian workers), the official colonial policy was to preserve traditional Malay society. Most notably, education was seen as a mechanism of social maintenance rather than social mobility (Stevenson, 1975; Loh, 1975). This fitted well with the interest of the Malay aristocracy in preserving a subject population that would respect and be loyal to feudal sovereigns. The British could acknowledge their responsibilities to the Malay population by promoting the welfare of the aristocracy. In turn, the Malay aristocracy would support the colonial administration as being in the interest of the Malays. The British reinforced class distinctions within the Malay community by building an elite school for the children of noble birth (Roff, 1967:Ch.4). For the Malay masses, the English language was thought to be an undesirable ingredient in their education. It might lead to discontent and natives who did not know their rightful place (Roff, 1967:136).

As colonial society matured, there was only a slow growth of opportunities in wage employment for Malays. The estate and mining sectors, where wage levels gradually rose, were linked to a steady supply of immigrant labor. Urban areas were primarily centers of government administration and trade. The former was in the hands of the British with the assistance of a few Malays in the lower ranks (Roff, 1967:98–109). Trade, in both its retail and wholesale components, became the preserve of Chinese and Indian merchants. They tended to hire kinsmen who shared a common language and a feeling of mutual dependence as a "middleman minority" (Bonacich, 1973). The possibilities for Malay social mobility were minimal.

Malay Entrepreneurship

One of the first casualties of European intervention in Southeast Asia was the local trading class (Hussein Alatas, 1977:Ch. 12). The Dutch, through their control of the sea, eliminated the indigenous trading class in order to achieve a monopoly over trade. This was achieved by the seventeenth century. Chinese merchants, who served to maintain the trade with China—vital for Southeast Asia throughout this period—were able to continue in their positions.

The British fostered an open-system of trade in their freemarket ports of Penang and Singapore. This allowed a fair degree of smaller-scale trade in Malay hands, but nothing similar to the pre-European era. In the pre-colonial Malay world, trade and state power were usually in the same hands. Control over trade, or the tax on trade, was the major source of wealth for Malay chiefs and sultans. Given the looseness of rules of royal succession in Malay courts, wealth might provide a pretext or a means to secure political power (Milner, 1982:Ch.2). It is no surprise that the Malay aristocracy closely guarded access to trade and were likely to confiscate the property of anyone who might be considered a threat.

With the end of the traditional Malay polity in the late nineteenth century, the Malay aristocracy shifted from a trading and warrior class to a dependent rentier class. There was a small segment of independent Malay entrepreneurs who remained active in local and long distance trade (Gullick, 1985), but the political and economic transformation in the late nineteenth century narrowed their scope of social mobility. To get a firm footing in the growing capitalist economy in the late nineteenth century required capital, control over land, and labor. Such resources were generally in the hands of a few European and Chinese capitalists who were aided by the colonial government. As the export economy began to boom and capital costs for production rose, access to participation in the higher levels of the economy became even more remote from the world of most Malays.

Why did not urban Malays take to commerce? In his review of Singapore society in the mid-nineteenth century, Cameron (1965:135) notes the varied occupations of Malays: they worked as sailors, grooms, coachmen, servants, and they hawked poultry, fish, and other products. Cameron expresses surprise that none of the Malays in trade rise from hawkers to merchants. This is not due to lack of education, he says, as most Malays are able to read and write. In a significant comment, Cameron notes that Malays rarely hire labor (pp.163–164). I think this provides a clue to the problem of Malay entrepreneurial success. For any business to rise above the minimal level, there must be a source of available labor. Moreover, given the very competitive nature of urban commerce, an employer must be able to find cheap labor. Chinese merchants had no problem as there was a ready supply of recent immigrants plus the already sizeable population of urban laborers. With only a small urban Malay population, Malay entrepreneurs would necessarily have to seek workers from the rural peasantry. Here the aspiring Malay merchant encountered the familiar problem—the lack of cheap Malay labor. To offer a wage sufficient to draw labor from the rural sector, the potential Malay employer would have found it difficult to be cost-competitive in the urban economy. Newbold, describing conditions in the 1830s, reports the wages of Malay laborers to be significantly below those of Chinese workers (1839, vol. 1:14–15). Although employers may have believed that lower wages were a product of relative productivity, the lower compensation to Malay labor may have reinforced the difficulties of recruiting Malay labor.

Another structural problem that probably confronted an aspiring Malay entrepreneur was the control over various spheres of the urban economy by Chinese kinship (or clan) networks. Almost every business must depend upon the cooperation of other businesses for sources of supply, credit, transport, and market access. Without a strong base of kinship networks to provide these supporting services, entry into the entrepreneurial world was probably quite precarious. Neither the colonial government nor the Malay aristocracy were motivated to intervene. As the colonial administration developed in the twentieth century, the few educated Malays could find alternative employment in the junior ranks of the civil service or in the teaching profession. These positions offered low pay, but did give job security and high status in the highly status-oriented colonial society.

Malay—Chinese Antagonism

Hostility between Chinese immigrants and Malays certainly predates British colonial intervention. Begbie reports the case of Malay slaughter of Chinese workers in Linggi in 1830 (1967:408) and similar incidents occurred later (Cheah, 1981). However, these events do not mean there was universal distrust or hostility between Malays and Chinese. Recall the earlier description of an effective working relationship between the Johor state and Chinese entrepreneurs in the late nineteenth century. For the present study, the important question is whether colonial rule narrowed or increased the social and cultural distance between Malays and other ethnic communities as the growing tide of immigrants arrived in the Malay states in the late nineteenth and early twentieth centuries. The historical record is fairly clear that the colonial administration provided few meaningful opportunities for inter-ethnic interaction. Moreover, by refusing to recognize Chinese (and Indian) residents as permanent members of the Malayan community with local loyalties, the colonial administration reinforced Malay xenophobic attitudes.

During the colonial era, ethnic communities were physically and socially segregated. Mines and plantations were almost completely populated by Chinese and Indian labour. Land policies tended to discourage Chinese and Indians from entering subsistence agriculture (T. G. Lim, 1984; for an alternative interpretation, see Kratoska, 1982). Malays were encouraged to remain in their rural villages. Even in towns where there was the potential for inter-ethnic contact, residential areas, market places, and recreational space were typically segregated along ethnic lines. Although there may have been traditional preferences for socializing within one's own community, colonial policies did nothing to encourage movement toward an integrated society.

It was only in schools and in some professional occupations that there was a possibility for structured inter-ethnic interaction. Except for the English language schools in urban areas, the overwhelming majority of children attended vernacular schools that were ethnically homogenous. Schooling was seen as a welfare expenditure in colonial society— and a possible source of social discontent. Education was not meant to be a national institution that fostered common knowledge, a common language, or even acquaintance of the different communities of society. Not until Independence approached would such goals be made policy.

More directly the British fostered the belief that Chinese really did not belong to local society—regardless of length of residence—and only Malay aristocrats and their colonial advisors should be allowed full participation in political or administrative roles. The origin of the British color bar against non-Malay Asians is critically reported by George Maxwell (a former high ranking colonial civil servant): "With thirty-five years service in Malaya, and with intimate friendship with Rulers over two generations, I can say that I never heard one of them say anything that would tend to support such an idea [exclusion of non-Malays from administrative appointments]. From the very earliest days of British protection, the Rulers have welcomed the leaders of the Chinese communities as members of their State Councils, and have paid the greatest deference to their opinions and advice. Other non-Malayans [non-Malays] are now members of the State Councils. The policy of keeping non-Malayans out of the administration owes its inception to British officials, and not to the Rulers" (Maxwell, 1943:118).

Perhaps most telling is the comment by one of the most distinguished of the colonial administrator/scholars on the contradiction in colonial practice towards Chinese: "In race and sympathy they might be Chinese; politically they regard themselves as Malayans . . . [but] the Malayan Government . . . gave no encouragement at all to the Malayan-born Chinese to regard themselves as citizens of Malaya" (Purcell, 1965:156).

Given the hostility toward Chinese expressed by many colonial officials and the lack of physical and social integration, it is not surprising that most Malays formed the opinion that Chinese were only transients in Malaya with no real attachments to the country.

THE COLONIAL OBSESSION WITH STATUS AND RACE AND ITS LEGACY FOR THE MULTIETHNIC MALAYSIAN SOCIETY

In an age when democratic principles were becoming accepted to some extent in European societies, the social organization of colonial societies moved in the opposite direction. Wertheim's characterization of Southeast Asia as a whole aptly fits the Malayan case: "Nineteenth century colonial society was molded on racial principles: belonging to the dominant white upper caste provided one with prestige and power largely independent of one's personal capabilities. A strict ritual was introduced and maintained, by force when necessary, to preserve the white caste from contacts with Asiatics on the basis of equality and to maintain the former's prestige as the dominant group" (1968:432). This obsession with the maintenance of the symbols as well as the structure of white superiority continued for most of the first half of the twentieth century. An account of the pre-World War II era notes, "The British colonial code . . . draws the most rigid color line of all. . . . The entire social ritual of the colonies symbolizes the separateness of rulers and ruled. Nowhere in the colonial world are the lines of caste drawn more rigidly: in clubs, residential areas, places of public accommodation, and informal cliques" (Kennedy, 1945:320).

These color bars served several purposes. Most basically, they reinforced the role of racial distinctiveness as the ideological basis of colonial society. All the usual criteria for social achievement in the late nineteenth and twentieth century—such as ability, educational attainment, and personal qualities—had to be denied, and skin color was taken as the only acceptable criterion for advancement to the highest realms of the colonial administrative service and the European business world. As the decades passed, there grew to be a larger social base of acculturated, English-speaking Asians whose credentials were no less than those of most Europeans (Butcher, 1979b). The social distance created by exclusive white clubs, informal cliques, and the disdain for Europeans who married Asians, allowed most Europeans to avoid thinking about the contradictions between modernization and the racial ideology of colonial society.

Racial ideology also legitimated the vast inequality in economic terms between Europeans and Asians. Butcher (1979b:130–131) records the remarkable assumption of a five to one ratio in income needed to maintain European and Asian standards of living in colonial Malaya. The gaps in economic standards between Europeans and Asians in the civil service also served to maintain the social distance that froze relationships in a vertical plane between superiors and inferiors. Racism—the ideology of inherent differences—provided a theory of entitlement for unequal rewards which could not otherwise be justified.

Colonial ideology had a number of consequences for Asians. For many, especially intellectuals, there was deep resentment and hostility toward colonial rule and its economic system (see Roff, 1967: Ch.5 on the origins of the Malay nationalism among vernacular school teachers). For the Malay aristocracy, however, colonialism had a number of beneficial elements. The sultans and their families received fabulous allowances and were given appropriate status deference by colonial officials anxious to maintain the fiction of Malay sovereignty. The children of the Malay aristocracy were allowed to join the junior ranks of the elite colonial service. Even if they were not paid equally with Europeans and encountered cultural snobbery, Malay aristocrats could identify with the Europeans as their allies in the political struggle with the immigrant populations, especially the Chinese. Since the colonial government never accepted the Chinese as permanent residents of the country and frequently questioned their loyalties, it is not surprising that Malay elites (and masses) also believed the Chinese should not be considered as having equal political rights.

For the Chinese elite (and to a lesser extent the Indian community), colonial rule was both a blessing and a curse. On one hand, many Chinese benefitted economically from the freedoms of the private economy (within limits), but they also resented their marginal position in the political life. For the Chinese working class and their representatives, the only solution was a struggle to end colonial rule and its exploitative economic system. For both Chinese elites and workers, relationships with the Malay community were often distant and strained. Since Malay elites possessed no power, Chinese acculturation and intermarriage into the Malay world (even if Islam were not a barrier) was not an attractive path for social mobility (Hirschman, 1984). Rather it was the English speaking world that offered channels for prestige, status, and possible wealth. One of the cultural features of the English speaking world was racial thinking, including the idea of Malay inferiority. Prejudice and snobbery were not marks of ignorance, but could be acquired

355

with higher education and mixing in the right circles.[6] These ideas probably reinforced the latent feelings of many Chinese about the potential of the Malay population. Given the close links between the colonial system and the recognition of the traditional Malay aristocracy as the nominal rulers of the country, British colonialism was often seen as a prop for a "backward" and feudal Malay society.

CONCLUSIONS

In this paper, I offer the interpretation that the "racial divisions" among the multiethnic population of Peninsular Malaysia are largely a product of colonial practices and European ideology in the decades following the "forward movement" in the 1870s. Cultural barriers and hostility between Asian populations in the region predate European imperialism. But there were also mechanisms whereby these differences were bridged or accommodated in pursuit of other goals. Over time, perhaps over the course of generations, there appears to have been a gradual process of inter-marriage or at least acculturation among Asian peoples in the region. This cycle was broken with the quantum leap in colonial intervention and the creation of an export economy built upon immigrant labor in the late nineteenth century.

These changes stimulated a wave of Chinese and Indian immigrants, on an historically unprecedented scale, to the states on the Malay peninsula. This phenomenon alone certainly created a new demographic situation that would have required a long period of ethnic accommodation and adjustment. The new immigrants, however, were not thrown into contact with Malays but were segregated geographically, economically, and socially from the local population. The colonial government "managed" the plural society by trying to maintain the Malay feudal social structure in the countryside and a "temporary" immigrant population working in the mines, plantations, and cities.

On top of this unbalanced structure perched the European elites who ruled and reaped enormous economic gains. By their actions and words, the colonial establishment expressed an ideology of racial differences. Although it might never be said so crudely in official reports, the basic philosophy is well-stated by an early European gold and tin miner in Malaya: "From a labour point of view, there are practically

---

[6] The skeptical reader will undoubtedly like to see more evidence to support this assertion. I assume that if most Europeans held racial stereotypes, their ideology was communicated in European dominated institutions such as English language schools. This argument parallels the role of elite schools and universities in the creation and maintenance of a caste ideology in Western societies (Baltzell, 1964). At this point, I can not yet offer the detailed historical evidence that is necessary to confirm my interpretation.

three races, the Malays (including Javanese), the Chinese, and the Tamils (who are generally known as Klings). By nature the Malay is an idler, the Chinaman is a thief, and the Kling is a drunkard, yet each in his own class of work is both cheap and efficient, when properly supervised" (Warnford-Lock, 1907:31–32).

This ideology, spread through acculturation to the English speaking world and by the social organization of colonial society, permeated deeply into the consciousness of most Asians. Even if Asians rejected the colonial assumptions of white superiority and the stereotypes of their own ethnic community, they tended to accept the unfounded generalizations of innate racial differences about other communities. Once established, ideas have a life of their own. Moreover, racial ideologies tended to legitimate actions by Malay and nonMalay leaders in both colonial and postcolonial society. More than rubber and tin, the legacy of colonialism was racial ideology.

REFERENCES

Abraham, Collin E. R.
1977 Race Relations in West Malaysia with Special Reference to Modern Political Economic Development. Unpublished Ph.D. thesis, Oxford University.
1983 "Racial and ethnic manipulation in colonial Malaya." Ethnic and Racial Studies 6 (January):18–32.

Allen, J. de V.
1964 "Two Imperialists: A study of Sir Frank Swettenham and Sir Hugh Clifford." Journal of the Malayan Branch of the Royal Asiatic Society 37(1):41–73.

Andaya, Barbara Watson.
1979 Perak, the Abode of Grace: A Study of an Eighteenth Century Malay State. Kuala Lumpur: Oxford University Press.

Andaya, Barbara Watson and Leonard Y. Andaya
1982 A History of Malaysia. London: Macmillan Press.

Andaya, Leonard Y.
1975 The Kingdom of Johor, 1641–1728. Kuala Lumpur: Oxford University Press.

Baltzell, E. Digby
1964 The Protestant Establishment: Aristocracy and Caste in America. New York: Vintage Books.

Banton, Michael
1983 Racial and Ethnic Competition. Cambridge: Cambridge University Press.

Begbie, P. J.
1967 The Malayan Peninsula. (1834*) Kuala Lumpur: Oxford University Press.

Blythe, W. L.
1947 "Historical sketch of Chinese labour in Malaya." Journal of the Malayan Branch of the Royal Asiatic Society 20:64–114.

Bonacich, Edna
1973 "A theory of middleman minorities." American Sociological Review 38:503–594.
1980 "Class approaches to ethnicity and race." Insurgent Sociologist 10(Fall):9–23.

Bonacich, Edna and John Modell
1980 The Economic Basis of Ethnic Solidarity: Small Business with Japanese American Community. Berkeley: University of California Press.

Boxer, C. R.
1965 The Dutch Seabourne Empire. London: Hutchinson and Co.

Burns, P. L., ed.
1976 The Journals of J. W. W. Birch: First British Resident to Perak 1874–1875. Kuala Lumpur: Oxford University Press.

357

Burns, P. L. and C. D. Cowan, eds.
1975 Sir Frank Swettenham's Malayan Journals, 1874–1876. Kuala Lumpur: Oxford University Press.

Butcher, John G.
1971 Attitudes of British Colonial Officials Toward Malays. Unpublished masters thesis, University of Wisconsin.
1979a "Toward the history of Malayan society: Kuala Lumpur District, 1885–1912." Journal of Southeast Asian Studies 10(March):104–118.
1979b The British in Malaya 1880–1941: The Social History of a European Community in Colonial Southeast Asia. Kuala Lumpur: Oxford University Press.

Cameron, John.
1965 Our Tropical Possessions in Malayan India. Oxford in Asia Historical Reprint. (1865*) Kuala Lumpur: Oxford University Press.

Cham, B. N.
1977 "Colonialism and communalism in Malaysia." Journal of Contemporary Asia 7:178–199.

Cheah, Boon Kheng
1981 "Sino-Malay conflicts in Malaya, 1945–46: Vendetta and Islamic resistance." Journal of Southeast Asian Studies 12 (March):108–117.

Clammer, John R.
1980 Straits Chinese Society: Studies in the Sociology of the Baba Communities of Malaysia and Singapore. Singapore: Singapore University Press.
1983 "The Straits Chinese in Melaka." In Kernial Singh Sandhu and Paul Wheatley (eds.), Melaka: The Transformation of a Malay Capital, c. 1400–1980. Vol. 2. 156–173. Kuala Lumpur: Oxford University Press.

Comber, Leon
1983 13 May 1969: A Historical Survey of Sino-Malay Relations. Kuala Lumpur: Heinemann Asia.

Connor, Walker
1984 The National Question in Marxist-Leninist Theory and Strategy. Princeton: Princeton University Press.

Clifford, Hugh
1929 Bushwacking and Other Asiatic Tales and Memories. New York: Harper and Brothers.

Couillard, Marie-Andre
1984 "The Malays and the 'Sakai': Some comments on their social relations in the Malay Peninsula." Kajian Malaysia (Penang, Malaysia) 2(June):81–108.

Cowan, C. D.
1961 Nineteenth-Century Malaya: The Origins of British Political Control. London: Oxford University Press.

Cox, Oliver C.
1948 Caste, Class, and Race. New York: Doubleday.

Crawfurd, John
1820 History of the Indian Archipelago, 2 Vols. Edinburgh: Archibald Constable.

Curtin, Philip D.
1964 The Image of Africa. Madison: University of Wisconsin Press.

Dodge, N. H.
1981 "The Malay-Aborigine nexus under Malay rule." Bijdragen tot de Taal-, Land-en Volkenkunde, deel 137, alevering 1–16.

Emerson, Rupert
1964 Malaysia: A Study in Direct and Indirect Rule. (1937*) Kuala Lumpur: University of Malaya Press.

Fredrickson, George M.
1981 White Supremacy: A Comparative Study of American and South African History. New York: Oxford University Press.

Freedman, Maurice
1960 "The growth of the plural society in Malaya." Pacific Affairs 33:158–168.

Gosling, L. A. P.
1964 "Migration and assimilation of rural Chinese in Trengganu." In John Bastin (ed.), Malayan and Indonesian Studies: Essays Presented to Sir Richard Winstedt: 201–221. Oxford: Clarendon Press.

Gould, Stephen Jay
1981 The Mismeasure of Man. New York: W. W. Norton.

Gullick, J. M.
1954 "The war with Yam Tuan Antah."

Journal of the Malayan Branch of the Royal Asiatic Society 27(May):123.
1985 "The entrepreneur in late nineteenth century Malay peasant society." Journal of the Malayan Branch of the Royal Asiatic Society 58(1):59–70.

Hall, D. G. E.
1981 A History of South-East Asia, 4th ed. New York: St. Martins Press.

Harris, Marvin
1964 Patterns of Race in the Americas. New York: Walker.
1968 "Race." In David L. Sills (ed.) International Encyclopedia of the Social Sciences, Vol. 13:263–268. New York: The Macmillan Company and the Free Press.

Harrison, Brian, translator
1954 "Malacca in the eighteenth century: Two Dutch governors' reports." Journal of the Malayan Branch of the Royal Asiatic Society 37(1):24–34.

Hechter, Michael.
1975 Internal Colonialism: The Celtic Fringe in British National Development. Berkeley: University of California Press.

Heisler, Martin, O., ed.
1977 Ethnic Conflict in the World Today. The Annals 443 (September): 1–160.

Hirschman, Charles
1984 "Ethnic diversity and social change in Southeast Asia: Some preliminary thoughts." In Ronald Morse (ed.), Southeast Asian Studies: Proceedings of a Conference at the Wilson Center, March 26, 1984:106–122. Washington, DC: University Press of America.
1985 "The meaning and measurement of ethnicity in Malaysia: An analysis of census classifications." Unpublished manuscript, Department of Sociology, Cornell University.

Horowitz, Donald
1985 Ethnic Groups in Conflict. Berkeley: University of California Press.

Hussein Alatas, Syed
1977 The Myth of the Lazy Native: A Study of the Image of the Malays, Filipinos, and Javanese From the 16th to the 20th Century and its Function in the Ideology of Colonial Capitalism. London: Frank Cass.

Jackson, James
1964 "Population changes in Selangor state, 1850–1891." Journal of Tropical Geography 19(December):42–57.
1968 Planters and Speculators, Chinese and European Agricultural Enterprise in Malaya 1786–1921. Singapore: University of Malaya Press.

Jackson, R. N.
1961 Immigrant Labour and the Development of Malaya: 1786–1920. Kuala Lumpur: Government Press.

Jones, Greta
1980 Social Darwinism and English Thought: The Interaction Between Biological and Social Theory. Sussex: The Harvester Press.

Kemasang, A. R. T.
1982 "The 1740 massacre of Chinese in Java: Curtain raiser for the Dutch plantation econony." Bulletin of Concerned Asian Scholars 14 (January-March):61–71.

Kennedy, Raymond
1945 "The colonial crisis and the future." In Ralph Linton (ed.), The Science of Man in the World Crisis. New York: Columbia University Press.

Khoo, Kay Kim
1966 "The origins of British administration in Malaya." Journal of the Malayan Branch of the Royal Asiatic Society 39(1):52–91.
1972 The Western Malay States 1850–1873. Kuala Lumpur: Oxford University Press.
1981 "Sino-Malay relations in Peninsular Malaysia before 1942." Journal of Southeast Asia Studies 12(March): 93–107.

Kratoska, Paul. H.
1982 "Rice cultivation and the ethnic division of labor in British Malaya." Comparative Studies in Society and History 24(April):280–314.

Kratoska, Paul H., ed.
1983 Honorable Intentions: Talks on the

British Empire in Southeast Asia Delivered at the Royal Colonial Institute 1874–1928. Singapore: Oxford University Press.

Lamb, Alastair
1964 "Early history." In Wang Gungwu (ed.), Malaysia: A Survey: 99–112. New York: Praeger.

Lewis, Dianne
1982 "The last Malay Raja Muda of Johor." Journal of Southeast Asian Studies 13(September):221–235.

Lieberson, Stanley
1961 "A societal theory of race and ethnic relations." American Sociological Review 26:902–910.
1980 A Piece of the Pie: Blacks and White Immigrants Since 1880. Berkeley: University of California Press.

Lim, Chong Yah
1967 Economic Development of Modern Malaya. Kuala Lumpur: Oxford University Press.

Lim, Teck Ghee
1977 Peasants and their Agricultural Economy in Colonial Malaya, 1874–1941. Kuala Lumpur: Oxford University Press.
1984 "British colonial administration and the 'ethnic division of labour' in Malaya." Kajian Malaysia 2(December):28–66.

Loh, Philip Fook Seng
1969 The Malay States, 1877–1895: Political Change and Social Policy. Singapore: Oxford University Press.
1975 Seeds of Separation: Educational Policy in Malaya 1874–1940. Kuala Lumpur: Oxford University Press.

McNair, J. F.
1972 Perak and the Malays. (1878*) Kuala Lumpur: Oxford University Press.

Maxwell, George
1943 "The mixed communities of Malaya." British Malaya (February):115–121.

Meilink-Roelofsz, M. A. P.
1962 Asian Trade and European Influence in the Indonesian Archipelago Between 1500 and About 1630. The Hague: Martinus Nijhoff.

Milner, A. C.
1982 Kerajaan: Malay Political Culture on the Even of Colonial Rule. Tucson, AZ: University of Arizona Press.

Nagata, Judith
1974 "What is a Malay?: Situational selection of ethnic identity in a plural society." American Ethnologist 1:331–50.

Newbold, T. J.
1839 Political and Statistical Account of the British Settlements in the Straits of Malacca. London: Albemarle.

Parkinson, C. Northcote
1960 British Intervention in Malaya 1867–1877. Singapore: University of Malaya Press.

Purcell, Victor
1948 Chinese in Malaya. London: Oxford University Press.
1951 The Chinese in Southeast Asia. London: Oxford University Press.
1965 The Memoirs of a Malayan Official. London: Cassell.

Reid, Anthony
1980 "The structure of cities in Southeast Asia, fifteenth to seventeenth centuries." Journal of Southeast Asian Studies 11(September):235–250.

Roff, William
1967 The Origins of Malay Nationalism. New Haven, CT: Yale University Press.

Rudner, Martin
1970 "The state of peasant innovation in rural development: The case of Malaysian rubber." Asian and African Studies 6:75–96.

Sadka, Emily
1954 "The journal of Sir Hugh Low, Perak 1877." Journal of the Malayan Branch of the Royal Asiatic Society 27(4):1–108.

Sandhu, Kernial Singh
1961 "Chinese colonization in Melaka." Journal of Tropical Geography 15:1–26.
1969 Indians in Malaya: Some Aspects of Their Immigration and Settlement (1786–1957). Cambridge: Cambridge University Press.

Saw, Swee Hock
1963 "Trends and differentials in inter-

national migration in Malaya." Ekonomi 4(December):87–113.

Skinner, G. William
1960 "Change and persistance in Chinese culture overseas: A comparison of Thailand and Java." Journal of the South Seas Society 16(1/2):86–100.

Slimming, John
1969 Malaysia: Death of a Democracy. London: John Murray.

Somers-Heidhues, Mary F.
1974 Southeast Asia's Chinese Minorities. Hawthorne, Victoria, Australia: Longman Australia Pty. Limited.

Thompson, Edgar T.
1975 "The plantation as a race making situation." In Plantation Societies, Race Relations, and the South: The Regimentation of Populations/Selected Papers of Edgar T. Thompson: 115–117. Durham, NC: Duke University Press.

Trocki, Carl A.
1976 "The origin of the Krangchu System." Journal of the Malayan Branch of the Royal Asiatic Society 59(2):132–155.
1979 Prince of Pirates: The Temanggongs and the Development of Johore and Singapore. Singapore: Singapore University Press.

van den Berghe, Pierre L.
1967 Race and Racism: A Comparative Perspective. New York: Wiley.
1976 "The African diaspora in Mexico, Brazil, and the United States." Social Forces 54(March):530–545.
1981 The Ethnic Phenomenon. New York: Elsevier.

Wallace, Alfred Russel
1983 The Malay Archipelago. (1869*) Singapore: Graham Brash (Pte) Ltd.

Stenson, Michael
1980 Class, Race, and Colonialism in West Malaysia: The Indian Case. Vancouver: University of British Columbia.

Stevenson, Rex
1975 Cultivators and Administrators: British Educational Policy Toward the Malays, 1875–1906. Kuala Lumpur: Oxford University Press.

Stockwell, A. J.
1982 "The white man's burden and brown humanity: Colonialism and ethnicity in British Malaya." Southeast Asian Journal of Social Science 10(1):44–68.

Swettenham, Frank
1900 The Real Malay. London: John Lane.
1955 British Malaya: An Account of the Origin and Process of British Influence in Malaya. (1906*) London: George Allen.

Tan, Chee Beng
1983 "Acculturation and the Chinese in Melaka: The expression of Baba identity today." In L. A. Peter Gosling and Linda Y. C. Lim (eds.), The Chinese in Southeast Asia, Vol. 2. Singapore: Maruzen Asia.

Warnford-Lock, C. G.
1907 Mining in Malaya for Gold and Tin. London: Carwither and Goodman.

Wang, Gungwu
1981 Community and Nation: Essays on Southeast Asia and the Chinese. Singapore: Heinemann.

Wertheim, W. F.
1968 "Southeast Asia." In David L. Sills (ed.), International Encyclopedia of the Social Sciences, Vol 1:423–434. New York: Macmillan and the Free Press.

Wheatley, Paul
1961 The Golden Khersonese: Studies in the Historical Geography of the Malay Peninsula Before A.D. 1500. Kuala Lumpur: University of Malaya Press.

Wolters, O. W.
1970 The Fall of Srivijaya in Malay History. Ithaca, NY: Cornell University Press.

Wong Lin Ken
1965 The Malayan Tin Industry to 1914. Tucson, AZ: Association for Asian Studies.

Wright, Arnold and Thomas H. Reid
1912 The Malay Peninsula: A Record of British Progress in the Middle East. London: T. Fisher Unwin.

* For reprinted publications, the date in parenthesis is the original publication date.

[17]

making empire respectable: the politics of race and sexual morality in 20th-century colonial cultures

ANN L. STOLER—*University of Michigan*

The shift away from viewing colonial elites as homogeneous communities of common interest marks an important trajectory in the anthropology of empire, signaling a major rethinking of gender relations within it. More recent attention to the internal tensions of colonial enterprises has placed new emphasis on the quotidian assertion of European dominance in the colonies, on imperial interventions in domestic life, and thus on the cultural prescriptions by which European women and men lived (Callan and Ardener 1984; Knibiehler and Goutalier 1985; Reijs, et. al 1986; Callaway 1987; Strobel 1987). Having focused on how colonizers have viewed the indigenous Other, we are beginning to sort out how Europeans in the colonies imagined themselves and constructed communities built on asymmetries of race, class and gender—entities significantly at odds with the European models on which they were drawn.

These feminist attempts to engage the gender politics of Dutch, French and British imperial cultures converge on some strikingly similar observations; namely that European women in these colonies experienced the cleavages of racial dominance and internal social distinctions very differently than men precisely because of their ambiguous positions, as both subordinates in colonial hierarchies and as active agents of imperial culture in their own right. Concomitantly, the majority of European women who left for the colonies in the late 19th and early 20th centuries confronted profoundly rigid restrictions on their domestic, economic and political options, more limiting than those of metropolitan Europe at the time and sharply contrasting the opportunities open to colonial men.

In one form or another these studies raise a basic question: in what ways were gender inequalities essential to the structure of colonial racism and imperial authority? Was the strident misogyny of imperial thinkers and colonial agents a byproduct of received metropolitan values ("they just brought it with them"), a reaction to contemporary feminist demands in Europe ("women need to be put back in their breeding place"), or a novel and pragmatic response to the conditions of conquest? Was the assertion of European supremacy in terms of patriotic manhood and racial virility an expression of imperial domination or a defining feature of it?

With sustained challenges to European rule in African and Asian colonies in the early 20th century, sexual prescriptions by class, race and gender became increasingly central to the politics of rule and subject to new forms of scrutiny by colonial states. Focusing on the Netherlands Indies and French Indochina, but drawing on other contexts, this article examines how the very categories of "colonizer" and "colonized" were increasingly secured through forms of sexual control which defined the common political interests of European colonials and the cultural investments by which they identified themselves. The metropolitan and colonial discourses on health, "racial degeneracy," and social reform from this period reveal how sexual sanctions demarcated positions of power by enforcing middle-class conventions of respectability and thus the personal and public boundaries of race. [sexuality, race-thinking, hygiene, colonial cultures, Southeast Asia]

In this paper I examine some of the ways in which colonial authority and racial distinctions were fundamentally structured in gendered terms. I look specifically at the administrative and medical discourse and management of European sexual activity, reproduction and marriage as it articulated with the racial politics of colonial rule. Focusing on French Indochina and the Dutch East Indies in the early 20th century, but drawing on other contexts, I suggest that the very categories of "colonizer" and "colonized" were secured through forms of sexual control which defined the domestic arrangements of Europeans and the cultural investments by which they identified themselves.[1] Gender specific sexual sanctions demarcated positions of power by refashioning middle-class conventions of respectability, which, in turn, prescribed the personal and public boundaries of race.

Colonial authority was constructed on two powerful, but false, premises. The first was the notion that Europeans in the colonies made up an easily identifiable and discrete biological and social entity; a "natural" community of common class interests, racial attributes, political affinities and superior culture. The second was the related notion that the boundaries separating colonizer from colonized were thus self-evident and easily drawn (Stoler 1989). Neither premise reflected colonial realities (see for example, Cooper 1980; Drooglever 1980; Ridley 1983; Prochaska 1989; Comaroff (this volume)). Internal divisions developed out of conflicting economic and political agendas, frictions over appropriate methods for safeguarding European privilege and power, competing criteria for reproducing a colonial elite and for restricting its membership.

This latter, the colonial politics of exclusion, was contingent on constructing categories, legal and social classifications designating who was "white," who was "native," who could become a citizen rather than a subject, which children were legitimate progeny and which were not. What mattered were not only one's physical properties but who counted as "European" and by what measure.[2] Skin shade was too ambiguous; bank accounts were mercurial; religious belief and education were crucial but never enough. Social and legal standing derived not only from color, but from the silences, acknowledgments, and denials of the social circumstances in which one's parents had sex (Martinez-Alier 1974; Ming 1983; Taylor 1983). Sexual unions in the context of concubinage, domestic service, prostitution or church marriage derived from the hierarchies of rule; but these were negotiated and contested arrangements, bearing on individual fates and the very structure of colonial society. Ultimately inclusion or exclusion required regulating the sexual, conjugal and domestic life of *both* Europeans in the colonies and their colonized subjects.

Colonial observers and participants in the imperial enterprise appear to have had unlimited interest in the sexual interface of the colonial encounter (Malleret 1934:216; Pujarniscle 1931:106; Loutfi 1970:36). Probably no subject is discussed more than sex in colonial literature and no subject more frequently invoked to foster the racist stereotypes of European society. The tropics provided a site of European pornographic fantasies long before conquest was underway, but with a sustained European presence in colonized territories, sexual prescriptions by class, race and gender became increasingly central to the politics of rule and subject to new forms of scrutiny by colonial states (Loutfi 1971; Gilman 1985:79).[3]

While anthropologists have attended to how European, and particularly Victorian, sexual more affected *indigenous* gendered patterns of economic activity, political participation and social knowledge, less attention has been paid to the ways in which sexual control affected the very nature of colonial relations themselves (Tiffany and Adams 1985). In colonial scholarship more generally, sexual domination has figured as a social metaphor of European supremacy. Thus, in Edward Said's treatment of orientalist discourse, the sexual submission and possession of Oriental women by European men "*stands for* the pattern of relative strength between East and West" (1979:6). In this "male power-fantasy," the Orient is penetrated, silenced and possessed (ibid:207). Sexuality illustrates the iconography of rule, not its pragmatics; sexual assymetries are tropes to depict other centers of power.

Such a treatment begs some basic questions. Was sexuality merely a graphic substantiation of who was, so to speak, on the top? Was the medium the message, or did sexual relations always "mean" something else, stand in for other relations, evoke the sense of *other* (pecuniary, political, or some possibly more subliminal) desires? This analytic slippage between the sexual symbols of power and the politics of sex runs throughout the colonial record and contemporary commentaries upon it. Certainly some of this is due to the polyvalent quality of sexuality; symbolically rich and socially salient at the same time. But sexual control was more than a "social enactment"—much less a convenient metaphor—for colonial domination (Jordan 1968:141); it was, as I argue here, a fundamental class and racial marker implicated in a wider set of relations of power (Ballhatchet 1980).

The relationship between gender prescriptions and racial boundaries still remains unevenly unexplored. While we know that European women of different classes experienced the colonial venture very differently from one another and from men, we still know relatively little about the distinct investments they had in a racism they shared (Van Helten and Williams 1983; Knibielher and Goutalier 1985; Callaway 1987). New feminist scholarship has begun to sort out the unique colonial experience of European women as they were incorporated into, resisted and affected the politics of their men. But the emphasis has tended to be on the broader issue of gender subordination and colonial authority, not more specifically on how sexual control figured in the construction of racial boundaries per se.[4]

The linkage between sexual control and racial tensions is both obvious and elusive at the same time. While sexual fear may at base be a racial anxiety, we are still left to understand why it is through sexuality that such anxieties are expressed (Takaki 1977). If, as Sander Gilman (1985) claims, sexuality is the most salient marker of Otherness, organically representing racial difference, then we should not be surprised that colonial agents and colonized subjects expressed their contests—and vulnerabilities—in these terms (see Chatterjee this volume).

An overlapping set of discourses has provided the psychological and economic underpinnings for colonial distinctions of difference, linking fears of sexual contamination, physical danger, climatic incompatability, and moral breakdown to a European colonial identity with a racist and class-specific core. Colonial scientific reports and the popular press are laced with statements and queries varying on a common theme: "native women bear contagions"; "white women become sterile in the tropics"; "colonial men are susceptible to physical, mental and moral degeneration when they remain in their colonial posts too long." To what degree are these statements medically or politically grounded? We need to unpack what is metaphor, what is perceived as dangerous (is it disease, culture, climate, or sex?) and what is not.

In the sections that follow I look at the relationship between the domestic arrangements of colonial communities and their wider political structures. Part I examines the colonial debates over European family formation, over the relationship between subversion and sex in an effort to trace how evaluations of concubinage, morality and white prestige more generally were altered by new tensions within colonial cultures and by new challenges to imperial rule.

Part II examines what I call the "cultural hygiene" of colonialism. Focusing on the early 20th century as a break point, I take up the convergent metropolitan and colonial discourses on health hazards in the tropics, race-thinking and social reform as they related to shifts in the rationalization of colonial management. In tracing how fears of "racial degeneracy" were grounded in class-specific sexual norms, I return to how and why biological and cultural distinctions were defined in gender terms.

the domestic politics of colonialism: concubinage and the restricted entry of European women

The regulation of sexual relations was central to the development of particular kinds of colonial settlements and to the allocation of economic activity within them. Who bedded and wedded with whom in the colonies of France, England, Holland and Iberia was never left to chance. Unions between Annamite women and French men, between Javanese women and Dutch men, between Spanish men and Inca women produced offspring with claims to privilege, whose rights and status had to be determined and prescribed. From the early 1600s through the 20th century the sexual sanctions and conjugal prohibitions of colonial agents were rigorously debated and carefully codified. In these debates over matrimony and morality, trading and plantation company officials, missionaries, investment bankers, military high commands and agents of the colonial state confronted one another's visions of empire, and the settlement patterns on which it would rest.

In 1622 the Dutch East Indies Company (VOC) arranged for the transport of six poor but marriageable young Dutch women to Java, providing them with clothing, a dowry upon marriage and a contract binding them to five years in the Indies (Taylor 1983:12). Aside from this and one other short-lived experiment, immigration of European women to the East Indies was consciously restricted for the next 200 years. Enforcing the restriction by selecting bachelors as their European recruits, the VOC legally and financially made concubinage the most attractive domestic option for its employees (Blussé 1986:173; Ming 1983:69; Taylor 1983:16).

It was not only the VOC which had profited from such arrangements. In the 19th and early 20th centuries, salaries of European recruits to the colonial armies, bureaucracies, plantation companies and trading enterprises were kept artificially low because local women provided domestic services for which new European recruits would otherwise have had to pay. In the mid-1800s, such arrangements were *de rigueur* for young civil servants intent on setting up households on their own (Ritter 1856:21). Despite some clerical opposition, at the end of the century concubinage was the most prevalent living arrangement for European colonials in the Indies (Ming 1983:70; Taylor 1983:16; van Marle 1952:486).

Referred to as *nyai* in Java and Sumatra, *congai* in Indochina, and *petite épouse* throughout the French empire, the colonized woman living as a concubine to a European man formed the dominant domestic arrangement in colonial cultures through the early 20th century. Unlike prostitution, which could and often did result in a population of syphilitic and therefore nonproductive European men, concubinage was considered to have a stabilizing effect on political order and colonial health—a relationship that kept men in their barracks and bungalows, out of brothels and less inclined to perverse liaisons with one another.

In Asia and Africa corporate and government decision makers invoked the social services which local women supplied as "useful guides to the language and other mysteries of the local societies" (Malleret 1934:216; Cohen 1971:122). Handbooks for incoming plantation employees bound for Tonkin, Sumatra and Malaya urged men to find local "companions" as a prerequisite for quick acclimatization, as insulation from the ill-health that sexual abstinence, isolation and boredom were thought to bring (Butcher 1979:200, 202; Hesselink 1987:208; Braconier 1933:922; Dixon 1913:77). Although British and Dutch colonial governments officially banned concubinage in the early 20th century, such measures were only selectively enforced. It remained tacitly condoned and practiced long after (Hyam 1986; Callaway 1987:49). In Sumatra's plantation belt newly opened in the late 19th century, for example, Javanese and Japanese *huishoudsters* (householders) remained the rule rather than the exception through the 1920s (Clerkx 1961:87–93; Stoler 1985a:31–34; Lucas 1986:84).

Concubinage was a contemporary term which referred to the cohabitation outside of marriage between European men and Asian women; in fact, it glossed a wide range of arrangements which included sexual access to a non-European woman as well as demands on her labor and legal rights to the children she bore (Pollman 1986:100; Lucas 1986:86).[5] Native women (like European women in a later period) were to keep men physically and psychologically fit for work, marginally content, not distracting or urging them out of line, imposing neither the time consuming nor financial responsibilities that European family life was thought to demand (Chivas-Baron 1929:103).[6]

To say that concubinage reinforced the hierarchies on which colonial societies were based is not to say that it did not make those distinctions more problematic at the same time. Grossly uneven sex ratios on North Sumatran estates made for intense competition among male workers and their European supervisors, with *vrouwen perkara* (disputes over women) resulting in assaults on whites, new labor tensions and dangerous incursions into the standards deemed essential for white prestige (Stoler 1985a:33; Lucas 1986:90–91). In the Netherlands Indies more generally an unaccounted number of impoverished Indo-European women moving between prostitution and concubinage further disturbed the racial sensibilities of the Dutch-born elite (Hesselink 1987:216). Metropolitan critics were particularly disdainful of such domestic arrangements on moral grounds—all the more so when these unions *were* sustained and personally significant relationships, thereby contradicting the racial premise of concubinage as an emotionally unfettered convenience.[7] But perhaps most important, the tension between concubinage as a confirmation and compromise of racial hierarchy was realized in the progeny that it produced, "mixed-bloods," poor "indos," and abandoned *"métis"* children who straddled the divisions of ruler and ruled threatened to blur the colonial divide.

Nevertheless, colonial governments and private business tolerated concubinage and actively encouraged it—principally by restricting the emigration of European women to the colonies and by refusing employment to married male European recruits. Although many accounts suggest that European women chose to avoid early pioneering ventures, and this must have been true in some cases, the choice was more often not their own (cf. Fredrickson 1981:109). Nor were the restrictions on marriage and women's emigration lifted as each colony became politically stable, medically upgraded and economically secure, as it is often claimed. Conjugal constraints lasted well into the 20th century, long after rough living and a scarcity of amenities had become conditions of the past. In the Indies army, marriage was a privilege of the officer corps while barrack concubinage was instituted and regulated for the rank and file. In the 20th century, formal and informal prohibitions set by banks, estates and government services operating in Africa, India, and Southeast Asia, restricted marriage during the first three to five years of service, while some prohibited it altogether (Moore-Gilbert 1986:48; Woodcock 1969:164; Tirefort 1979:134; Gann and Duignan 1978:240).

European demographics in the colonies were shaped by these economic and political exigencies and thus were sharply skewed by sex. Among the laboring immigrant and native populations as well as among Europeans, the number of men exceeded that of women by 2 to 25 times. While in the Netherlands Indies, the overall ratio of European women to men rose from 47:100 to 88:100 between 1900 and 1930, on Sumatra's plantation belt in 1920 there were still only 61 European women per 100 European men (Taylor 1983:128; *Koloniale Verslag* quoted in Lucas 1986:82). In Tonkin, European men (totaling more than 14,000) sharply outnumbered European women (just over 3000) as late as 1931 (Gantes 1981:138). What is important here is that by controlling the availability of European women and the sorts of sexual access condoned, state and corporate authorities controlled the very social geography of the colonies, fixing the conditions under which European populations and privileges could be reproduced.

The marriage prohibition was both a political and economic issue, defining the social contours of colonial communities and the standards of living within them. But, as significantly, it revealed how deeply the conduct of private life, and the sexual proclivities which individuals expressed were tied to corporate profits and to the security of the colonial state. Nowhere were the incursions on domestic life more openly contested than in North Sumatra in the early 1900s. Unseemly domestic arrangements were thought to encourage subversion as strongly as acceptable unions could avert it. Family stability and sexual "normalcy" were thus linked to political agitation or quiescence in very concrete ways.

Since the late 19th century, the major North Sumatran tobacco and rubber companies had neither accepted married applicants nor allowed them to take wives while in service (Schoevers

1913:38; Clerkx 1961:31–34). Company authorities argued that new employees with families in tow would be a financial burden, risking the emergence of a "European proletariat" and thus a major threat to white prestige (Kroniek 1917:50; *Sumatra Post* 1913). Low-ranking plantation employees protested against these company marriage restrictions, an issue which mobilized their ranks behind a broad set of demands (Stoler 1989:144). Under employee pressure, the prohibition was relaxed to a marriage ban for the first five years of service. This restriction, however, was never placed on everyone; it was pegged to salaries and dependent on the services of local women which kept the living costs and wages of subordinate and incoming staff artificially low.

Domestic arrangements thus varied as government officials and private businesses weighed the economic versus political costs of one arrangement over another, but such calculations were invariably meshed. Europeans in high office saw white prestige and profits as inextricably linked and attitudes toward concubinage reflected that concern (Brownfoot 1984:191). Thus in Malaya through the 1920s, concubinage was tolerated precisely because "poor whites" were not. Government and estate administrators argued that white prestige would be imperiled if European men became impoverished in attempting to maintain middle-class lifestyles and European wives (Butcher 1979:26). In late 19th century Java, in contrast, concubinage itself was considered to be a major source of white pauperism; in the early 1900s it was vigorously condemned at precisely the same time that a new colonial morality passively condoned illegal brothels (Het Pauperisme Commissie 1901; Nieuwenhuys 1959:20–23; Hesselink 1987:208).

What explains such a difference? At least part of the answer must be sought in the effects concubinage was seen to have on European cultural identity and on the concerns for the community consensus on which it rests. Concubinage "worked" as long as the supremacy of *Homo Europeaus* was clear. When it was thought to be in jeopardy, vulnerable, or less than convincing, as in the 1920s in Sumatra, colonial elites responded by clarifying the cultural criteria of privilege and the moral premises of their unity. Concubinage was replaced by more restricted sexual access in the politically safe (but medically unsatisfactory) context of prostitution, and, where possible, in the more desirable setting of marriage between "full-blooded" Europeans (Taylor 1977:29). As we shall see in other colonial contexts, such shifts in policy and practice often coincided with an affirmation of social hierarchies and racial divisions in less ambiguous terms.[8] Thus, it was not only morality which vacillated but the very definition of white prestige—and what its defense should entail. What upheld that prestige was not a constant; concubinage was socially lauded at one time and seen as a political menace at another. Appeals to white prestige were a gloss for different intensities of racist practice, gender-specific and culturally coded.

Thus far I have treated colonial communities as a generic category despite the sharp demographic, social and political distinctions among them. North Sumatra's European-oriented, overwhelmingly male colonial population, for example, contrasted sharply with the more sexually balanced mestizo culture which emerged in 17th- and 18th-century colonial Java.[9] Such demographic variation, however, was not the "bedrock" of social relations (Jordan 1968:141); sex ratios derived from specific strategies of social engineering, and were thus political responses in themselves. While recognizing that these demographic differences and the social configurations to which they gave rise still need to be explained, I have chosen here to trace some of the common politically gendered issues which a range of colonial societies shared; that is, some of the similar—and counter-intuitive—ways in which the positioning of European women facilitated racial distinctions and new efforts to modernize colonial control.[10]

racist but moral women: innocent but immoral men

Perhaps nothing is as striking in the sociological accounts of colonial communities as the extraordinary changes which are said to accompany the entry of European-born women. These adjustments shifted in one direction; toward European lifestyles accentuating the refinements of privilege and the etiquettes of racial difference. Most accounts agree that the presence of these women put new demands on the white communities to tighten their ranks, clarify their boundaries, and mark out their social space. The material culture of French settlements in Saigon, outposts in New Guinea, and estate complexes in Sumatra were retailored to accommodate the physical and moral requirements of a middle-class and respectable feminine contingent (Malleret 1934; Gordon and Meggitt 1985; Stoler 1989). Housing structures in Indochina were partitioned, residential compounds in the Solomon Islands enclosed, servant relations in Hawaii formalized, dress codes in Java altered, food and social taboos in Rhodesia and the Ivory Coast became more strict. Taken together, the changes encouraged new kinds of consumption and new social services catering to these new demands (Boutilier 1982; Spear 1963; Woodcock 1969; Cohen 1971).

The arrival of large numbers of European women thus coincided with an embourgeoisment of colonial communities and with a significant sharpening of racial lines. European women supposedly required more metropolitan amenities than men and more spacious surroundings to allow it; their more delicate sensibilities required more servants and thus suitable quarters—discrete and enclosed. In short, white women needed to be maintained at elevated standards of living, in insulated social spaces cushioned with the cultural artifacts of "being European." Whether women or men set these new standards is left unclear. Who exhibited "overconcern" and a "need for" segregation (Beidelman 1982:13)? Male doctors advised French women in Indochina to have their homes built with separate domestic and kitchen quarters (Grall 1908:74). Segregrationist standards were what women "deserved," and more importantly what white male prestige required that they maintain.

Colonial rhetoric on white women was riddled with contradictions. At the same time that new female immigrants were chided for not respecting the racial distance of local convention, an equal number of colonial observers accused these women of being more avid racists in their own right (Spear 1963; Nora 1961). Allegedly insecure and jealous of the sexual liaisons of European men with native women, bound to their provincial visions and cultural norms, European women in Algeria, the Indies, Madagscar, India, and West Africa were uniformly charged with constructing the major cleavages on which colonial stratification rested (Spear 1963:140; Nora 1961:174; Mannoni 1964[1950]:115: Gann and Duignan 1978:242; Kennedy 1947:164; Nandy 1983:9).

What is most startling here is that women, otherwise marginal actors on the colonial stage, are charged with dramatically reshaping the face of colonial society, imposing their racial will on African and Asian colonies where "an iron curtain of ignorance" replaced "relatively unrestrained social intermingling" in earlier years (Vere Allen 1970:169; Cohen 1971:122). European women were not only the bearers of racist beliefs, but hardline operatives who put them into practice, encouraging class distinctions among whites while fostering new racial antagonisms, no longer muted by sexual access (Vere Allen 1970:168).[11] Are we to believe that sexual intimacy with European men yielded social mobility and political rights for colonized women? Or, even less likely, that because British civil servants bedded with Indian women, somehow Indian men had more "in common" with British men and enjoyed more parity? Colonized women could sometimes parlay their positions into personal profit and small rewards, but these were *individual* negotiations with no social, legal, or cumulative claims.

Male colonizers positioned European women as the bearers of a redefined colonial morality. But to suggest that women fashioned this racism out of whole cloth is to miss the political chronology in which new intensities of racist practice arose. In the African and Asian contexts already mentioned, the arrival of large numbers of European wives, and particularly the fear for their protection, followed from new terms and tensions in the colonial encounter. The presence and protection of European women was repeatedly invoked to clarify racial lines. It coincided with perceived threats to European prestige (Brownfoot 1984:191), increased racial conflict

(Strobel 1987:378), covert challenges to the colonial order, outright expressions of nationalist resistance, and internal dissension among whites themselves (Stoler 1989:147).

If white women were the primary force behind the decline of concubinage as is often claimed, they did so as participants in a broader racial realignment and political plan (Knibiehler and Goutalier 1985:76). This is not to suggest that European women were passive in this process, as the dominant themes in their novels attest (Taylor 1977:27). Many European women did oppose concubinage not because of their inherent jealousy of native women, but, as they argued, because of the double standard it condoned for European men (Clerkx 1961; Lucas 1986:94–95).[12] The voices of European women, however, had little resonance until their objections coincided with a realignment in racial and class politics.

dealing with transgressions: policing the peril

The gender-specific requirements for colonial living, referred to above, were constructed on heavily racist evaluations which pivoted on the heightened sexuality of colonized men (Tiffany and Adams 1985). Although European women were absent from men's sexual reveries in colonial literature, men of color were considered to see them as desired and seductive figures. European women needed protection because men of color had "primitive" sexual urges and uncontrollable lust, aroused by the sight of white women (Strobel 1987:379; Schmidt 1987:411). In some colonies, that sexual threat was latent; in others it was given a specific name.

In southern Rhodesia and Kenya in the 1920s and 1930s, preoccupations with the "Black Peril" (referring to the professed dangers of sexual assault on white women by black men) gave rise to the creation of citizens' militias, ladies' riflery clubs and investigations as to whether African female domestic servants would not be safer to employ than men (Kirkwood 1984:158; Schmidt 1987:412; Kennedy 1987:128–147). In New Guinea the White Women's Protection Ordinance of 1926 provided "the death penalty for any person convicted for the crime of rape or attempted rape upon a European woman or girl" (Inglis 1975:vi). And as late as 1934, Solomon Islands authorities introduced public flogging as punishment for "criminal assaults on [white] females" (Boutilier 1984:197).

What do these cases have in common? The rhetoric of sexual assault and the measures used to prevent it had virtually no correlation with the incidence of rape of European women by men of color. Just the contrary: there was often no evidence, *ex post facto* or at the time, that rapes were committed or that rape attempts were made (Schmidt 1987; Inglis 1975; Kirkwood 1984; Kennedy 1987; Boutilier 1984). This is not to suggest that sexual assaults never occurred, but that their incidence had little to do with the fluctuations in anxiety about them. Secondly, the rape laws were race-specific; sexual abuse of black women was not classified as rape and therefore was not legally actionable, nor did rapes committed by white men lead to prosecution (Mason 1958:246–247). If these accusations of sexual threat were not prompted by the fact of rape, what did they signal and to what were they tied?

Allusions to political and sexual subversion of the colonial system went hand in hand. Concern over protection of white women intensified during real and perceived crises of control—provoked by threats to the internal cohesion of the European communities or by infringements on their borders. While the chronologies differ, we can identify a patterned *sequence* of events in which Papuan, Algerian, and South African men heightened their demands for civil rights and refused the constraints imposed upon their education, movements, or dress (Inglis 1975:8,11; Sivan 1983:178). Rape charges were thus based on perceived transgressions of political and social space. "Attempted rapes" turned out to be "incidents" of a Papuan man "discovered" in the vicinity of a white residence, a Fijian man who entered a European patient's room, a male servant poised at the bedroom door of a European woman asleep or in half-dress

(Boutilier 1984:197; Inglis 1975:11; Schmidt 1987:413). With such a broad definition of danger, all colonized men of color were potential aggressors.

Accusations of sexual assault frequently followed upon heightened tensions within European communities—and renewed efforts to find consensus within them. In South Africa and Rhodesia, the relationship between reports of sexual assault and strikes among white miners and railway workers is well documented (van Onselen 1982:51; Kennedy 1987:138). Similarly, in the late 1920s when labor protests by Indonesian workers and European employees were most intense, Sumatra's corporate elite expanded their vigilante organizations, intelligence networks and demands for police protection to ensure their women were safe and their workers "in hand" (Stoler 1985b). In this particular context where the European community had been blatantly divided between low-ranking estate employees and the company elite, common interests were emphasized and domestic situations were rearranged.

In Sumatra's plantation belt, subsidized sponsorship of married couples replaced the recruitment of single Indonesian workers and European staff, with new incentives provided for family formation in both groups. This recomposed labor force of family men in "stable households" explicitly weeded out the politically malcontent. With the marriage restriction finally lifted for European staff in the 1920s, young men sought marriages with Dutch women. Higher salaries, upgraded housing, elevated bonuses, and a more mediated chain of command between colonized fieldworker and colonial managers clarified economic and political interests. With this shift, the vocal opposition to corporate and government directives, sustained by an independent union of European subordinates for nearly two decades, was effectively dissolved (Stoler 1989:152–153).

The remedies intended to alleviate sexual danger embraced a common set of prescriptions for securing white control: increased surveillance of native men, new laws stipulating severe corporal punishment for the transgression of sexual and social boundaries, and the creation of areas made racially off limits. This moral rearmament of the European community and reassertion of its cultural identity charged European women with guarding new norms. While instrumental in promoting while solidarity, it was partly at their own expense. As we shall see, they were nearly as closely surveilled as colonized men (Strobel 1987).

While native men were legally punished for alleged sexual assaults, European women were frequently blamed for provoking those desires. New arrivals from Europe were accused of being too familiar with their servants, lax in their commands, indecorous in speech and dress (Vellut 1982:100; Kennedy 1987:141; Schmidt 1987:413). The Rhodesian immorality act of 1916 "made it an offence for a white woman to make an indecent suggestion to a male native" (Mason 1958:247). In Papua New Guinea "everyone" in the Australian community agreed that rape assaults were caused by a "younger generation of white women" who simply did not know how to treat servants (Inglis 1975:80). In Rhodesia as in Uganda, women were restricted to activities within the European enclaves and dissuaded from taking up farming on their own (Gartrell 1984:169; Kennedy 1987:141). As in the American South, "etiquettes of chivalry controlled white women's behavior even as [it] guarded caste lines" (Dowd Hall 1984:64). A defense of community, morality and white male power affirmed the vulnerability of white women and the sexual threat posed by native men, and created new sanctions to limit the liberties of both.

Although European colonial communities in the early 20th century assiduously monitored the movements of European women, some European women did work. French women in the settler communities of Algeria and Senegal ran farms, rooming houses, and shops along with their men (Baroli 1967:159; O'Brien 1972). Elsewhere, married European women "supplemented" their husbands' incomes, helping to maintain the "white standard" (Tirefort 1979; Mercier 1965:292). Women were posted throughout the colonial empires as missionaries, nurses, and teachers; while some women openly questioned the sexist policies of their male superiors, by and large their tasks buttressed rather than contested the established cultural order (Knibiehler and Goutalier 1985; Callaway 1987:111).

French feminists urged women with skills (and a desire for marriage) to settle in Indochina at the turn of the century, but colonial administrators were adamantly against their immigration. Not only was there a surfeit of widows without resources, but European seamstresses, florists and children's outfitters could not compete with the cheap and skilled labor provided by well established Chinese firms (Corneau 1900:10, 12). In Tonkin in the 1930s there was still "little room for single women, be they unmarried, widowed or divorced"; most were shipped out of the colony at the government's charge (Gantes 1981:45).[13] Firmly rejecting expansion based on "poor white" *(petit blanc)* settlement as in Algeria, French officials in Indochina dissuaded *colons* with insufficient capital from entry and promptly repatriated those who tried to remain.[14] Single women were seen as the quintessential *petit blanc*, with limited resources and shopkeeper aspirations. Moreover, they presented the dangerous possibility that straitened circumstances would lead them to prostitution, thereby degrading European prestige at large.

In the Dutch East Indies, state officials identified European widows as one of the most economically vulnerable and impoverished segments of the European community (Het Pauperisme onder de Europeanen 1901:28). Professional competence did not leave European women immune from marginalization. Single professional women were held in contempt as were European prostitutes, with surprisingly similar objections.[15] The important point is that numerous categories of women fell outside the social space to which European colonial women were assigned; namely, as custodians of family welfare and respectability, and as dedicated and willing subordinates to, and supporters of, colonial men. The rigor with which these norms were applied becomes more comprehensible when we see how a European family life and bourgeois respectability became increasingly tied to notions of racial survival, imperial patriotism and the political strategies of the colonial state.

white degeneracy, motherhood and the eugenics of empire

de-gen-er-ate (adj.) [L. *degeneratus*, pp. of *degenerare*, to become unlike one's race, degenerate < *degener*, not genuine, base < *de-*, from + *genus*, race, kind: see genus]. 1. having sunk below a former or normal condition, character, etc.; deteriorated. 2. morally corrupt; depraved-n. a degenerate person, esp. one who is morally depraved or sexually perverted- vi -at'ed, -at'ing 1. to decline or become debased morally, culturally, etc. 3. Biol. to undergo degeneration; deteriorate
[Webster's New World Dictionary 1972:371].

European women were essential to the colonial enterprise and the solidification of racial boundaries in ways that repeatedly tied their supportive and subordinate posture to community cohesion and colonial peace. These features of their positioning within imperial politics were powerfully reinforced at the turn of the century by a metropolitan bourgeois discourse (and an eminently anthropological one) intensely concerned with notions of "degeneracy" (Le Bras 1981:77). Middle-class morality, manliness and motherhood were seen as endangered by the intimately linked fears of "degeneration" and miscegenation in scientifically construed racist beliefs (Mosse 1978:82).[16] Due to environmental and/or inherited factors, degeneracy could be averted positively by eugenic selection, or negatively by eliminating the "unfit" (Mosse 1978:87; Kevles 1985:70–84). Eugenic arguments used to explain the social malaise of industrialization, immigration and urbanization in the early 20th century derived from the notion that acquired characteristics were inheritable and thus that poverty, vagrancy and promiscuity were class-linked biological traits, tied to genetic material as directly as nightblindness and blonde hair.

Appealing to a broad political and scientific constituency at the turn of the century, eugenic societies included advocates of infant welfare programs, liberal intellectuals, conservative businessmen, Fabians, and physicians with social concerns. By the 1920s, however, it contained an increasingly vocal number of those who called for and put into law, if not practice, the sterilization of significant numbers in the British, German and American working-class populations (Mosse 1978:87; 1982:122).[17] Negative eugenics never gained the same currency in Holland as it did elsewhere, nevertheless, it seems clear from the Dutch and Dutch Indies scientific and popular press that concerns with hereditary endowment and with "Indo degeneracy" were grounded in a cultural racism that rivaled its French variant, if in a somewhat more muted form.[18]

Feminists attempted to appropriate this rhetoric for their own birth control programs, but eugenics was essentially elitist, racist and misogynist in principle and practice (Gordon 1976:395; Davin 1978; Hammerton 1979). Its proponents advocated a pronatalist policy toward the white middle and upper classes, a rejection of work roles for women that might compete with motherhood, and "an assumption that reproduction was not just a function but the purpose . . . of a woman's life" (Gordon 1976:134). In France, England, Germany, and the United States, positive eugenics placed European women of "good stock" as "the fountainhead of racial strength" (Ridley 1983:91), exalting the cult of motherhood while subjecting it to more thorough scientific scrutiny (Davin 1978:12).

As part of metropolitan class politics, eugenics reverberated in the colonies in predictable as well as unexpected forms. The moral, biological and sexual referents of the notion of degeneracy (distinct in the dictionary citation above) came together in how the concept was actually deployed. The "colonial branch" of eugenics embraced a theory and practice concerned with the vulnerabilities of white rule and new measures to safeguard European superiority. Designed to control the procreation of the "unfit" lower orders, eugenics targeted "the poor, the colonized, or unpopular strangers" (Hobsbawm 1987:253). It was, however, also used by metropolitan observers against colonials, and by colonial elites against "degenerate" members among themselves (Koks 1931:179–189). While studies in Europe and the U.S. focused on the inherent propensity of the poor for criminality, in the Indies delinquency among "European" children was biologically linked to the amount of *"native blood"* among children of poor Indo-Europeans (Braconier 1918:11). Eugenics provided not so much a new vocabulary as it did a medical and moral basis for anxiety over white prestige which reopened debates over segregated residence and education, new standards of morality, sexual vigilance and the rights of certain Europeans to rule.

Eugenic influence manifested itself, not in the direct importation of metropolitan practices such as sterilization, but in a translation of the political *principles* and the social values which eugenics implied. In defining what was unacceptable, eugenics also identified what constituted a "valuable life": "a gender-specific work and productivity, described in social, medical and psychiatric terms" (Bock 1984:274). Applied to Europe colonials, eugenic statements pronounced what kind of people should represent Dutch or French rule, how they should bring up their children and with whom they should socialize. Those concerned with issues of racial survival and racial purity invoked moral arguments about the national duty of French, Dutch, British, and Belgian colonial women to stay at home.

If in Britain racial deterioration was conceived to be a result of the moral turpitude and the ignorance of working-class mothers, in the colonies, the dangers were more pervasive, the possibilities of contamination worse. Formulations to secure European rule pushed in two directions: on the one hand, away from ambiguous racial genres and open domestic arrangements, and on the other hand, toward an upgrading, homogenization, and a clearer delineation of European standards; away from miscegenation toward white endogamy, away from concubinage toward family formation and legal marriage; away from, as in the case of the Indies, mestizo customs and toward metropolitan norms (Taylor 1983; van Doorn 1985). As stated in the bulletin of the Netherlands Indies' Eugenic Society, "eugenics is nothing other than belief in the possibility of preventing degenerative symptoms in the body of our beloved *moedervolken*, or in cases where they may already be present, of counteracting them" (Rodenwaldt 1928:1).

Like the modernization of colonialism itself, with its scientific management and educated technocrats with limited local knowledge, colonial communities of the early 20th century were rethinking the ways in which their authority should be expressed. This rethinking took the form of asserting a distinct colonial morality, explicit in its reorientation toward the racial and class markers of "Europeanness," emphasizing transnational racial commonalities despite national differences—distilling a *homo europeaus* of superior health, wealth and intelligence as a white man's norm. As one celebrated commentator on France's colonial venture wrote: "one might be surprised that my pen always returns to the words *blanc* [white] or "European" and never to "*Français*" . . . in effect colonial solidarity and the obligations that it entails allies all the peoples of the white races" (Pujarniscle 1931:72; also see Delavignette 1946:41).

Such sensibilities colored imperial policy in nearly all domains with fears of physical contamination merging with those of political vulnerability. To guard their ranks, whites had to increase their numbers and to ensure that their members neither blurred the biological nor political boundaries on which their power rested.[19] In the metropole the socially and physically "unfit," the poor, the indigent and the insane were either to be sterilized or prevented from marriage. In the British and Belgian colonies, among others, it was these very groups among Europeans who were either excluded from entry or institutionalized while they were there and when possible were sent home (Arnold 1979; see also Vellut 1987:97).

Thus, whites in the colonies adhered to a politics of exclusion that policed their members as well as the colonized. Such concerns were not new to the 1920s (Taylor 1983; Sutherland 1982). As early as the mid-18th century, the Dutch East Indies Company had already taken "draconian measures" to control pauperism among "Dutchmen of mixed blood" *(Encyclopedie van Nederland-Indie 1919:367)*. In the same period, the British East Indies Company legally and administratively dissuaded lower-class European migration and settlement, with the argument that it might destroy Indian respect for "the superiority of the European character" (quoted in Arnold 1983:139). Patriotic calls to populate Java in the mid-1800s with poor Dutch farmers were also condemned, but it was with new urgency that these possibilities were rejected in the following century as challenges to European rule were more profoundly felt.

Measures were taken both to avoid poor white migration and to produce a colonial profile that highlighted the vitality, colonial patriotism, and racial superiority of European men (Loutfi 1971:112–113; Ridley 1983:104).[20] Thus, British colonial administrators were retired by the age of 55, ensuring that "no Oriental was ever allowed to see a Westerner as he aged and degenerated, just as no Westerner needed ever to see himself . . . as anything but a vigorous, rational, ever-alert young Raj" (Said 1978:42). In the 20th century, these "men of class" and "men of character" embodied a modernized and renovated colonial rule; they were to safeguard the colonies against physical weakness, moral decay and the inevitable degeneration that long residence in the colonies encouraged and the temptations that interracial domestic situations had allowed.

Given this ideal, it is not surprising that colonial communities strongly discouraged the presence of nonproductive men. Dutch and French colonial administrators expressed a constant concern with the dangers of unemployed or impoverished Europeans. During the succession of economic crises in the early 20th century, relief agencies in Sumatra, for example, organized fund raisers, hill station retreats and small-scale agricultural schemes to keep "unfit" Europeans "from roaming around" (Kroniek 1917:49). The colonies were neither open for retirement nor tolerant of the public presence of poor whites. During the 1930s depression when tens of thousands of Europeans in the Indies found themselves without jobs, government and private resources were quickly mobilized to ensure that they were not "reduced" to native living standards (Veerde 1931; Kantoor van Arbeid 1935). Subsidized health care, housing and education complemented a rigorous affirmation of European cultural standards in which European womanhood played a central role in keeping men *civilisé*.

on cultural hygiene: the dynamics of degeneration

The shift in imperial thinking that we can identify in the early 20th century focuses not only on the Otherness of the colonized, but on the Otherness of colonials themselves. In metropolitan France a profusion of medical and sociological tracts pinpointed the colonial as a distinct and degenerate social type, with specific psychological and even physical characteristics (Maunier 1932; Pujarniscle 1931).[21] Some of that difference was attributed to the debilitating results of climate and social milieu, "such that after a certain time, he [the colonial] has become both physically and morally a completely different man" (Maunier 1932:169).

Medical manuals warned that people who stayed "too long" were in grave danger of overfatigue, of individual and racial degeneration, of physical breakdown (not just illness), of cultural contamination and neglect of the conventions of supremacy, and *agreement* about what they were (Dupuy 1955:184–185). What were identified as the degraded and unique characteristics of French colonials—"ostentation," "speculation," "inaction," and a general "demoralisation"—where "faults" contracted from native culture, which now marked them as *décivilisé* (Maunier 1932:174; Jaurequiberry 1924:25).

Colonial medicine reflected and affirmed this slippage between physical, moral and cultural degeneracy in numerous ways. The climatic, social and work conditions of colonial life gave rise to a specific set of psychotic disorders affecting *l'equilibre cerebral*, predisposing Europeans in the tropics to mental breakdown (Hartenberg 1910; Abatucci 1910). Neurasthenia was a major problem in the French empire and supposedly accounted for more than half the Dutch repatriations from the Indies to Holland (Winckel 1938:352). In Europe and America, it was "the phantom disease . . . the classic illness of the late 19th century," intimately linked to sexual deviation and to the destruction of the social order itself (Gilman 1985:199,202).

While in Europe neurasthenia was considered to signal a decadent overload of "modern civilization" and its high-pitched pace, in the colonies its etiology took the *reverse* form. Colonial neurasthenia was allegedly caused by a *distance* from civilization and European community, and by proximity to the colonized. The susceptibility of a colonial male was increased by an existence "outside of the social framework to which he was adapted in France, isolation in outposts, physical and moral fatigue, and modified food regimes" (Joyeux 1937:335).[22]

The proliferation of hill stations in the 20th century reflected these political and physical concerns. Invented in the early 19th century as sites for military posts and sanatoria, hill stations provided "European-like environments" in which colonials could recoup their physical and mental well-being by simulating the conditions "at home" (King 1976:165). Isolated at relatively high altitudes, they took on new importance with increasing numbers of European women and children, considered particularly susceptible to anemia, depression and illhealth.[23] Vacation bungalows and schools built in these "naturally" segregated surroundings provided cultural refuge and regeneration (Price 1939).

Some doctors considered the only treatment to be "le retour en Europe" (Joyeux 1937:335; Pujarniscle 1931:28). Others encouraged a local set of remedies, prescribing a bourgeois ethic of morality and work. This included sexual moderation, a "regularity and regimentation" of work, abstemious diet, physical exercise and *European* comradery, buttressed by a solid family life with European children, raised and nurtured by a European wife (Grall 1908:51; Price 1939: also see Kennedy 1987:123). Guides to colonial living in the 1920s and 1930s reveal this marked shift in outlook; Dutch, French and British doctors now denounced the unhealthy, indolent life styles of "old colonials," extolling the active, engaged and ever-busy activities of the new breed of colonial husband and wife (Raptchinsky 1941:46). Women were exhorted to actively participate in household management and childcare, and otherwise to divert themselves with botanical collections and "good works" (Chivas-Baron 1929; Favre 1938).

cultural contamination, children and the dangers of metissage

[Young colonial men] are often driven to seek a temporary companion among women of color; this is the path by which, as I shall presently show, contagion travels back and forth, contagion in all senses of the word [Maunier 1932:171].

Racial degeneracy was thought to have social causes and political consequences, both tied to the domestic arrangements of colonialism in specific ways. Metissage (interracial unions) generally, and concubinage in particular, represented the paramount danger to racial purity and cultural identity in all its forms. It was through sexual contact with women of color that French men "contracted" not only disease but debased sentiments, immoral proclivities and extreme susceptibility to decivilized states (Dupuy 1955:198).

By the early 20th century, concubinage was denounced for undermining precisely those things that it was charged with fortifying decades earlier. Local women who had been considered protectors of men's well-being, were now seen as the bearers of ill health and sinister influences; adaptation to local food, language, and dress, once prescribed as healthy signs of acclimatization, were now sources of contagion and loss of (white) self. The benefits of local knowledge and sexual release gave way to the more pressing demands of respectability, the community's solidarity and its mental health. Increasingly French men in Indochina who kept native women were viewed as passing into "the enemy camp" (Pujarniscle 1931:107). Concubinage became the source not only of individual breakdown and ill-health, but the biological and social root of racial degeneration and political unrest. Children born of these unions were "the fruits of a regrettable weakness" (Mazet 1932:8), physically marked and morally marred with "the defaults and mediocre qualities of their [native] mothers" (Douchet 1928:10).

Concubinage was not as economically tidy and politically neat as colonial policy makers had hoped. It concerned more than sexual exploitation and unpaid domestic work; it was about children—many more than official statistics often revealed—and who was to be acknowledged as a European and who was not. Concubine children posed a classificatory problem, impinging on political security and white prestige. The majority of such children were not recognized by their fathers, nor were they reabsorbed into local communities as authorities often claimed. Although some European men legally acknowledged their progeny, many repatriated to Holland, Britain or France and cut off ties and support to mother and children (Brou 1907; Ming 1983:75). Native women had responsibility for, but attenuated rights over, their own offspring. They could neither prevent their children from being taken from them nor contest paternal suitability for custody. While the legal system favored a European upbringing, it made no demands on European men to provide it; many children became wards of the state, subject to the scrutiny and imposed charity of the European-born community at large.

Concubine children were invariably counted among the ranks of the European colonial poor, but European paupers in the late 19th century Netherlands Indies came from a far wider strata of colonial society than that of concubines alone (Rapport der Pauperisme-Commissie 1903). Many Indo-Europeans had become increasingly marginalized from strategic political and economic positions in the early 20th century despite new educational opportunities encouraged at the turn of the century. In the 1920s and 1930s Indies-born and educated youth were uncomfortably squeezed between an influx of new colonial recruits from Holland and the educated *inlander* ("native") population with whom they were in direct competition for jobs (Mansvelt 1932:295).[24] At the turn of the century, volumes of official reports were devoted to documenting and alleviating the proliferation on Java of a "rough" and "dangerous pauper element" among (Indo) European clerks, low-level officials and vagrants (Encyclopedie van Nederland-Indie 1919:367).

European pauperism in the Indies reflected broad inequalities in colonial society, underscoring the social heterogeneity of the category "European" itself. Nonetheless, as late as 1917, concubinage was still seen by some as its major cause and as the principal source of *"blankenhaters"* (white-haters) (Braconier 1917:298). Concubinage became equated with a progeny of "malcontents," of "parasitic" whites, idle and therefore dangerous. The fear of concubinage was carried yet a step further and tied to the political fear that such Eurasians would demand economic access, political rights and express their own interests through alliance with (and leadership of) organized opposition to Dutch rule (Mansvelt 1932; Blumberger 1939).[25]

Racial prejudice against *métis* was often, as in the Belgian Congo, "camouflaged under protestations of 'pity' for their fate, as if they were *'malheureux'* [unhappy] beings by definition" (Vellut 1982:103). As objects of charity, their protection in Indochina was a cause célèbre of European women—feminists and staunch colonial supporters—at home and abroad (Knibiehler and Goutalier 1985:37). European colonial women were urged to oversee their "moral protection," to develop their "natural" inclination toward French society, to turn them into "partisans of French ideas and influence" instead of revolutionaries (Chenet 1936:8; Sambuc 1931:261). The gender breakdown is clear: moral instruction reflected fears of sexual promiscuity in *métisse* girls and the political threat of *métis* boys turned militant men.

Orphanages for abandoned European and Indo-European children were not new features of 20th century colonial cultures; however, their importance increased vastly as an ever larger number of illegitimate children of mixed parentage populated grey zones along colonial divides. In the Netherlands Indies by the mid-18th century, state orphanages for Europeans were established to prevent "neglect and degeneracy of the many free-roaming poor bastards and orphans of Europeans" (quoted in Braconier 1917:293). By the 19th century, church, state and private organizations had become zealous backers of orphanages, providing some education but stronger doses of moral instruction. In India, civil asylums and charity schools cared for European and Anglo-Indian children in "almost every town, cantonment and hill-station" (Arnold 1979:108). In French Indochina in the 1930s virtually every colonial city had a home and society for the protection of abandoned *métis* youth (Chenet 1936; Sambuc 1931:256–272; Malleret 1934:220).

Whether these children were in fact "abandoned" by their Asian mothers is difficult to establish; the fact that *métis* children living in native homes were often *sought out* by state and private organizations and placed in these institutions to protect them against the "demoralised and sinister" influences of native kampung life suggests another interpretation (Taylor 1983). Public assistance in India, Indochina and the Netherlands Indies was designed not only to keep fair skinned children from running barefooted in native villages but to ensure that the proliferation of European pauper settlements was curtailed and controlled.[26] The preoccupation with creating a patriotic loyalty to French and Dutch culture among children was symptomatic of a more general fear; namely, that there were *already* patricides of the colonial fatherland in the making; that as adult women these children would fall into prostitution; that as adult men with emotional ties to native women and indigenous society they would join the enemies of the state, *verbasterd* (degenerate) and *décivilisé* (Braconier 1917:293; Pouvourville 1926; Sambuc 1931:261; Malleret 1934).

European motherhood and middle-class morality

"A man remains a man as long as he is under the watch of a woman of his race" [George Hardy quoted in Chivas-Baron 1929:103].

Rationalization of imperial rule and safeguards against racial degeneracy in European colonies merged in the emphasis on particular moral themes. Both entailed a reassertion of European conventions, middle-class respectability, more frequent ties with the metropole and a restatement of what was culturally distinct and superior about how colonials ruled and lived. For those women who came to join their spouses or to find husbands, the prescriptions were clear. Just as new plantation employees were taught to manage the natives, women were schooled in colonial propriety and domestic management. French manuals, such as those on colonial hygiene in Indochina, outlined the duties of colonial wives in no uncertain terms. As "auxiliary forces" in the imperial effort they were to "conserve the fitness and sometimes the life of all around them" by ensuring that "the home be happy and gay and that all take pleasure in clustering there" (Grall 1908:66; Chailley-Bert 1897). Practical guides to life in the Belgian Congo instructed (and indeed warned) *la femme blanche* that she was to keep "order, peace, hygiene and economy" (Favre 1938:217), "perpetuate a vigorous race," while preventing any "laxity in our administrative mores" (Favre 1938:256; Travaux du Groupe d'Etudes coloniales 1910:10).

This "division of labor" contained obvious asymmetries. Men were considered more susceptible to moral turpitude than women who were thus held responsible for the immoral states of men. European women were to create and protect colonial prestige, insulating their men from cultural and sexual contact with the colonized (Travaux . . . coloniales 1910:7). Racial degeneracy would be curtailed by European women charged with regenerating the physical health, the metropolitan affinities and the imperial purpose of their men (Hardy 1929:78).

At its heart was a reassertion of racial difference which harnessed nationalistic rhetoric and markers of middle-class morality to its cause (Delavignette 1946:47, Loutfi 1971:112; Mosse 1978:86). George Mosse describes European racism in the early 20th century as a "scavenger ideology," annexing nationalism and bourgeois respectability such that control over sexuality was central to all three (1985:10, 133–152). If the European middle class sought respectability "to maintain their status and self-respect against the lower-classes, and the aristocracy," in the colonies respectability was a defense against the colonized, and a way of more clearly defining themselves (Mosse 1985:5). Good colonial living now meant hard work, no sloth, and physical exercise rather than sexual release, which had been one rationale for condoning concubinage and prostitution in an earlier period. The debilitating influences of climate could be surmounted by regular diet and meticulous personal hygiene over which European women were to take full charge. Manuals on how to run a European household in the tropics provided detailed instructions in domestic science, moral upbringing and employer-servant relations. Adherence to strict conventions of cleanliness and cooking occupied an inordinate amount of women's time (Hermans 1925; Ridley 1983:77). Both activities entailed a constant surveillance of native nursemaids, laundrymen and live-in servants, while reinforcing the domestication of European women themselves (Brink 1920:43).

Leisure, good spirit, and creature comforts became the obligation of women to provide, the racial duty of women to maintain. Sexual temptations with women of color would be curtailed by a happy family life, much as "extremist agitation" on Sumatra's estates was to be averted by selecting married recruits and by providing family housing to permanent workers (Stoler 1985a). Moral laxity would be eliminated through the example and vigilance of women whose status was defined by their sexual restraint, and dedication to their homes and to their men.

The perceptions and practice that bound women's domesticity to national welfare and racial purity were not applied to colonial women alone. Childrearing in late 19th century Britain was hailed as a national, imperial, and racial duty, as it was in Holland, the U.S. and Germany at the same time (Davin 1978:13; Smith-Rosenberg 1973:35], Bock 1984:274; Stuurman 1985). In France, where declining birth rates were of grave concern, popular colonial authors such as Pierre Mille pushed mothering as women's "essential contribution to the imperial mission of France" (Ridley 1983:90). With motherhood at the center of empire building, pronatalist policies in Europe forced some improvement in colonial medical facilities, the addition of maternity wards, increased information and control over the reproductive conditions of European and colonized women alike. Maternal and infant health programs instructed European women in the use of milk substitutes, wet nurses and breastfeeding practices in an effort to encourage more women to stay in the colonies and in response to the many more that came (Hunt 1988). But the belief that the colonies were medically hazardous for white women meant that motherhood in the tropics was not only a precarious but a conflicted endeavor. French women bound for Indochina were warned that they would only be able to fulfill their maternal duty "with great hardship and damage to [their] health" (Grall 1908:65)

Real and imagined concern over individual reproduction and racial survival contained and compromised white colonial women in a number of ways. Tropical climates were said to cause low fertility, prolonged amenorrhea and permanent sterility (Rodenwalt 1928:3; Hermans 1925:123). Belgian doctors confirmed that "the woman who goes to live in a tropical climate is often lost for the reproduction of the race" (Knibiehler and Goutalier 1985:92; Vellut 1982:100). The climatic and medical conditions of colonial life were associated with high infant mortality, such that "the life of a European child was nearly condemned in advance" (Grall 1908:65; Price 1939:204).

These perceived medical perils called into question whether white women and thus "white races" could actually reproduce if they remained in the tropics for extended periods of time. An international colonial medical community cross-referenced one another in citing evidence of racial sterility by the second or third generation (Harwood 1938:132; Cranworth quoted in Kennedy 1987:115). While such a dark view of climate was not prevalent in the Indies, psychological and physical adaptation was never a given. Dutch doctors repeatedly quoted German physicians, if not to affirm the inevitable infertility among whites in the tropics, at least to support their contention that European-born women and men *(totoks)* should never stay in the colonies too long (Hermans 1925:123). Medical studies in the 1930s, such as that supported by the Netherlands Indies Eugenic Society, were designed to test whether fertility rates differed by "racial type" between Indo-European and European-born women, and whether children of certain Europeans born in the Indies displayed different "racial markers" than their parents (Rodenwalt 1928:4).

Like the discourse on degeneracy, the fear of sterility was less about the biological survival of whites than about their political viability and cultural reproduction. These concerns were evident in the early 1900s, coming to a crescendo in the 1930s when white unemployment hit the colonies and the metropole at the same time. The depression made repatriation of impoverished French and Dutch colonial agents unrealistic, prompting speculation as to whether European working classes could be relocated in the tropics without causing further racial degeneration (Winckel 1938; Price 1939). Although white migration to the tropics was reconsidered, poor white settlements were rejected on economic, medical and psychological grounds (Feuilletau de Bruyn 1938:27). Whatever the solution, such issues hinged on the reproductive potential of European women, invasive questionnaires (which many women refused to answer) concerning their "acclimatization," and detailed descriptions of their sexual lives.

Imperial perceptions and policies fixed European women in the colonies as "instruments of race-culture" in what proved to be personally difficult and contradictory ways (Hammerton 1979). Childrearing manuals faithfully followed the sorts of racist principles that constrained the activities of women charged with childcare (Grimshaw 1983:507). Medical experts and women's organizations recommended strict surveillance of children's activities (Mackinnon 1920:944) and careful attention to those with whom they played. Virtually every medical and household handbook in the Dutch, French and British colonies in the early 20th century warned against leaving small children in the unsupervised care of local servants. In the Netherlands Indies, it was the "duty" of the *hedendaagsche blanke moeder* (modern white mother) to take the physical and spiritual upbringing of her offspring away from the *babu* (native nursemaid) and into her own hands (Wanderken 1943:173). Precautions had to be taken against "sexual danger," uncleanly habits of domestics, against a "stupid negress" who might leave a child exposed to the sun (Bauduin 1941; Bérenger-Féraud 1875:491). Even in colonies where the climate was not considered unhealthy, European children supposedly thrived well "only up to the age of six" when native cultural influences came into stronger play (Price 1939:204; Grimshaw 1983:507). In the Dutch East Indies, where educational facilities for European children were considered excellent, some still deemed it imperative to send them back to Holland to avoid the "precocity" associated with the tropics and the "danger" of contact with *Indische* youths not from "full-blooded European elements" (Baudin 1941:63).

> We Dutch in the Indies live in a country which is not our own . . . we feel instinctively that our blonde, white children belong to the blonde, white dunes, the forests, the moors, the lakes, the snow. . . . A Dutch child should grow up in Holland. There they will acquire the characteristics of their race, not only from mother's milk but also from the influence of the light, sun and water, of playmates, of life, in a word, in the sphere of the fatherland. This is not racism. . . [Baudin 1941:63–4]

But even in the absence of such firm convictions, how to assure the "moral upbringing" of European children in the colonies remained a primary focus of women's organizations in the Indies and elsewhere right through decolonization.[27] In many colonial communities, school age children were packed off to Europe for education and socialization. In those cases European women were confronted with a difficult set of choices which entailed separation either from their children or husbands. Frequent trips between colony and metropole not only separated families, but also broke up marriages and homes (Malleret 1934:164; Grimshaw 1983:507; Callaway 1987:183–184). The important point is that the imperial duty of women to closely surveil husbands, servants and children profoundly affected the social space they occupied and the economic activities in which they could feasibly engage.

shifting strategies of rule and sexual morality

> Though sex cannot of itself enable men to transcend racial barriers, it generates some admiration and affection across them, which is healthy, and which cannot always be dismissed as merely self-interested and prudential. On the whole, sexual interaction between Europeans and non-Europeans probably did more good than harm to race relations; at any rate, I cannot accept the feminist contention that it was fundamentally undesirable [Hyam 1986a:75].

The political etymology of colonizer and colonized was gender and class specific. The exclusionary politics of colonialism demarcated not just external boundaries but interior frontiers, specifying internal conformity and order among Europeans themselves. I have tried to show that the categories of colonizer and colonized were secured through notions of racial difference constructed in gender terms. Redefinitions of sexual protocol and morality emerged during crises of colonial control precisely because they called into question the tenuous artifices of rule *within* European communities and what marked their borders. Even from the limited cases we have reviewed, several patterns emerge. First and most obviously, colonial sexual prohibitions were racially asymmetric and gender specific. Thus racial attributes were rarely discussed in nongendered terms; one was always a black *man*, an Asian *woman*. Secondly, interdictions against interracial unions were rarely a primary impulse in the strategies of rule. Interracial unions (as opposed to marriage) between European men and colonized women aided the long-term settlement of European men in the colonies while ensuring that colonial patrimony stayed in limited and selective hands. In India, Indochina and South Africa in the early centuries—colonial contexts usually associated with sharp social sanctions against interracial unions—"mixing" was systematically tolerated and even condoned.[28]

Changes in sexual access and domestic arrangements have invariably accompanied major efforts to reassert the internal coherence of European communities and to redefine the boundaries of privilege between the colonizer and the colonized. Sexual union in itself, however, did not automatically produce a larger population legally classified as "European." On the contrary, miscegenation signaled neither the absence nor presence of racial prejudice in itself; hierarchies of privilege and power were written into the *condoning* of interracial unions, as well as into their condemnation.

While the chronologies vary from one colonial context to another, we can identify some parallel shifts in the strategies of rule and in sexual morality. Concubinage fell into moral disfavor at the same time that new emphasis was placed on the standardization of European administration. While this occurred in some colonies by the early 20th century and in others later on, the correspondence between rationalized rule, bourgeois respectability and the custodial power of European women to protect their men seems strongest during the interwar years when Western scientific and technological achievements were then in question, and native nationalist and labor movements were hard pressing their demands.[29] Debates concerning the need to systematize colonial management and dissolve the provincial and personalized satraps of "the old-time *colon*" in the French empire invariably targeted and condemned the unseemly domestic arrangements in which they lived. British high colonial officials in Africa imposed new "character" requirements on their subordinates, designating specific class attributes and conjugal ties that such a selection implied (Kuklick 1979). Critical to this restructuring was a new disdain for colonials too adapted to local custom, too removed from the local European community, and too encumbered with intimate native ties. As in Sumatra, this hands-off policy distanced Europeans in more than one sense: it forbade European staff both from personal confrontations with their Asian fieldhands and from the limited local knowledge they gained through sexual ties.

At the same time, medical expertise confirmed the salubrious benefits of European comradery and frequent home leaves, of a *cordon sanitaire*, not only around European enclaves, but around each home. White prestige became defined by this rationalized management and by the moral respectability and physical well-being of its agents, with which European women were charged. Colonial politics locked European men and women into a routinized protection of their physical health and social space in ways which bound gender prescriptions to class conventions, thereby fixing the racial cleavages between "us" and "them."

I have focused here on the multiple levels at which sexual control figured in the substance, as well as the iconography, of racial policy and imperial rule. But colonial politics was obviously not just about sex; nor did sexual relations reduce to colonial politics. On the contrary, sex in the colonies was about sexual access and reproduction, class distinctions and racial privileges, nationalism and European identity in different measure and not all at the same time. These major shifts in the positioning of women were not signaled by the penetration of capitalism per se but by more subtle changes in class politics, imperial morality and as responses to the vulnerabilities of colonial control. As we attempt broader ethnographies of empire, we may begin to capture how European culture and class politics resonated in colonial settings, how class and gender discriminations not only were translated into racial attitudes, but themselves reverberated in the metropole as they were fortified on colonial ground. Such investigations should help show that sexual control was both an instrumental image for the body politic, a salient part standing for the whole, and itself fundamental to how racial policies were secured and how colonial projects were carried out.

notes

[1] Here I focus primarily on the dominant male discourse (and less on women's perceptions of social and legal constraints) since it was the structural positioning of European women in colonial society and how their needs were defined for, not by, them which most directly accounted for specific policies.

[2] See Verena Martinez-Alier (1974) on the subtle and changing criteria by which color was assigned in 19th century Cuba. Also see A. van Marle (1952) on shifting cultural markers of European membership in the 19th and early 20th century Netherlands Indies.

[3] See Malleret (1934:216–241). See also Tiffany and Adams who argue that "the Romance of the Wild Woman" expressed critical distinctions between civilization and the primitive, culture and nature, and the class differences between repressed middle-class women and "her regressively primitive antithesis, the working-class girl" (Tiffany and Adams 1985:13).

[4] Many of these studies focus on South Africa and tend to provide more insight into the composition of the black labor force than into the restrictions on European women themselves (Cock 1980; Gaitskell 1983; Hansen 1986). Important exceptions are those which have traced historical changes in colonial prostitution and domestic service where restrictions were explicitly class specific and directly tied racial policy to sexual control (Ming 1983; Van Heyningen 1984; Hesselink 1987; Schmidt 1987).

⁵As Tessel Pollman suggests, the term *nyai* glossed several functions: household manager, servant, housewife, wife and prostitute. Which of these was most prominent depended on the character of both partners and on the prosperity of the European man (1986:100). Most colonized women, however, combining sexual and domestic service within the abjectly subordinate contexts of slave or "coolie," lived in separate quarters, and exercised very few legal rights; they could be dismissed without reason or notice, were exchanged among European employers and most significantly, as stipulated in the Indies Civil Code of 1848, "had no rights over children recognized by a white man" (Taylor 1977:30). On Java, however, some *nyai* achieved some degree of limited authority, managing the businesses as well as the servants and household affairs of better-off European men (Nieuwenhuys 1959:17; Lucas 1986:86; Taylor 1983).

⁶While prostitution served some of the colonies for some of the time, it was economically costly, medically unwieldy and socially problematic. Veneral disease was difficult to check even with the elaborate system of lock hospitals and contagious disease acts of the British empire and was of little interest to those administrations bent on promoting permanent settlement (Ballhatchet 1980; Ming 1983). When concubinage was condemned in the 1920s in India, Malaya and Indonesia, venereal disease spread rapidly, giving rise to new efforts to reorder the domestic arrangements of European men (Butcher 1979:217; Ming 1983; Braconier 1933; Ballhatchet 1980).

⁷See Ritter who describes these arrangements in the mid-19th century as a "necessary evil" with no emotional attachments, because for the native woman, "the meaning of our word 'love' is entirely unknown" (1856:21).

⁸In the case of the Indies, interracial marriages increased at the same time that concubinage fell into sharp decline (van Marle 1952). This rise was undoubtedly restricted to *Indisch* Europeans (those born in the Indies) who may have been eager to legalize preexisting unions in response to the moral shifts accompanying a more European cultural climate of the 1920s (van Doorn 1985). It undoubtedly should not be taken as an indication of less closure among the highly endogamous European-born population of that period (I owe this distinction in conjugal patterns to Wim Hendrik).

⁹On the differences between Java's European community which was sharply divided between the *totoks* (full-blooded Dutch born in Holland) and the *Indisch* majority (Europeans of mixed parentage and/or those Dutch born in the Indies), and Sumatra's European-oriented and non-*Indisch* colonial community see Muller (1912), Wertheim (1959), van Doorn (1985), Stoler (1985b).

¹⁰Similarly, one might draw the conventional contrast between the different racial policies in French, British and Dutch colonies. However, despite French assimilationist rhetoric, Dutch tolerance of intermarriage, and Britain's overtly segregationist stance, the similarities in the actual maintenance of racial distinctions through sexual control in these varied contexts is perhaps more striking than the differences. For the moment, it is there similarities with which I am concerned. See, for example, Simon (1981:46–48) who argues that although French colonial rule was generally thought to be more racially tolerant than that of Britain's, racial distinctions in French Indochina were *in practice* vigorously maintained.

¹¹Cf. Degler who also attributes the tenor of race relations to the attitudes of European women; not, however, because they were inherently more racist, but because in some colonial contexts they were able to exert more influence over the extramarital affairs of their men (1986[1971]:238).

¹²Although some Dutch women in fact championed the cause of the wronged *nyai*, urging improved protection for nonprovisioned women and children, they rarely went so far as to advocate for the legitimation of these unions in legal marriage (Taylor 1977:31–32, Lucas 1986:95).

¹³Archive d'Outre Mer "Emigration des femmes aux colonies" 1897–1904:GG9903, 1893–4:GG7663.

¹⁴See the French Archive d'Outre Mer, Series S.65 "Free Passage accorded to Europeans," including dossiers on "free passage for impoverished Europeans," for example GG 9925, 1897; GG 2269, 1899–1903).

¹⁵Cf. Van Onselen (1982:103–162) who argues that the presence of European prostitutes and domestics-turned-prostitutes in South Africa was secured by a large, white working-class population, and a highly unstable labor market for white working-class women (1982:103–162). Also see Van Heyningen who ties changes in the history of prostitution among continental women in the Cape Colony to new notions of racial purity and the large-scale urbanization of blacks after the turn of the century (1984:192–195).

¹⁶As George Mosse notes, the concept of racial degeneration had been tied to miscegenation by Gobineau and others in the early 1800s but gained common currency in the decades that followed, entering European medical and popular vocabulary at the turn of the century (1978:82–88).

¹⁷British eugenicists petitioned to refuse marriage licenses to the mentally ill, vagrants and the chronically unemployed (Davin 1978:16; Stepan 1982:123). In the U.S. a model eugenic sterilization law from 1922 targeted among others "orphans, homeless and paupers," while in Germany during the same period "sterilization was widely and passionately recommended as a solution to shiftlessness . . . illegitimate birth. . . , poverty; and the rising costs of social services" (Bajema 1976:138; Bock 1984:274).

¹⁸The active interest of French anthropologists in the relationship between eugenics and immigration (and therefore in the U.S. sterilization laws, in particular) was not shared in the Netherlands (see Schneider [1982] on the particularities of eugenics in France). On the other hand, for some examples of eugenically informed race studies in the Dutch colonial context see *Ons Nageslacht*, the *Geneeskundig Tijdschrift voor Nederlandsh-Indie*, as well as the numerous articles relating to "the Indo problem" which appeared in the Indies popular and scientific press during the 1920s and 1930s.

[19] The topics covered in the bulletin of the Netherlands Indies Eugenics society gives some sense of the range of themes included in these concerns: articles appearing in the 1920s and 30s discussed, among other things, "biogenealogical" investigations, the complementarity between Christian thought and eugenic principles, ethnographic studies of mestizo populations, and not least importantly, the role of Indo-Europeans in the anti-Dutch rebellions (*Ons Nageslacht* 1928–32).

[20] See Mosse (1985) for an examination of the relationship between manliness, racism and nationalism in the European context.

[21] The relationship between physical appearance and moral depravity was not confined to evaluations of European colonials alone. Eugenic studies abounded in speculations on the specific physical traits signaling immorality in the European lower orders, while detailed descriptions of African and Asian indigenous populations paired their physical attributes with immoral and debased tendencies.

[22] Adherence to the idea that "tropical neurasthenia" was a specific malady was not shared by all medical practitioners. Among those who suggested that the use of the term be discontinued did so on the belief that neurasthenia in the tropics was a pyschopathology caused by social, not physiological, maladjustment (Culpin [1926] cited in Price 1939:211).

[23] On the social geography of hill stations in British India and on the predominance of women and children in them, see King 1976:156–179.

[24] European pauperism in the Indies at the turn of the century referred primarily to a class of Indo-Europeans marginalized from the educated and "developed" elements in European society (Blumberger 1939:19). However, pauperism was by no means synonymous with Eurasian status since nearly 80 percent of the "Dutch" community were of mixed descent, some with powerful political and economic standing (Braconier 1917:291). As Jacques van Doorn notes "it was not the Eurasian as such, but the "Kleine Indo" [poor Indo] who was the object of ridicule and scorn in European circles" (1983:8). One could argue that it was as much Eurasian power as pauperism that had to be checked.

[25] French government investigations, accordingly, exhibited a concern for "the *métis* problem" which was out of proportion with the numbers of those who fell in that category. While the number of "Indos" in the Indies was far greater, there was never any indication that this social group would constitute the vanguard of an anticolonial movement.

[26] In colonial India, "orphanages were the starting-point for a lifetime's cycle of institutions" in which "unseemly whites" were secluded from Asian sight and placed under European control (Arnold 1979:113). In Indonesia, *Pro Juventate* branches supported and housed together "neglected and criminal" youth with special centers for Eurasian children.

[27] See, for example, the contents of women's magazines such as the *Huisvrouw in Deli* for which the question of education in Holland or the Indies was a central issue. The rise of specific programs (such as the *Clerkx-methode voor Huisonderwijs*) designed to guide European mothers in the home instruction of their children may have been a response to this new push for women to oversee directly the moral upbringing of their children.

[28] I have focused on late colonialism in Asia, but colonial elite intervention in the sexual life of their agents and subjects was by no means confined to this place or period. See Nash (1980:141) on changes in mixed marriage restrictions in 16th-century Mexico and Martinez-Alier on interracial marriage prohibitions in relationship to slave labor supplies in 18th- and early 19th-century Cuba (1974:39).

[29] See Adas (1989) for a discussion of major shifts in colonial thinking during this period.

references

Abatucci
    1910   Le milieu africain consideré au point de vue de ses effets sur le système nerveux de l'européen. Annales d'Hygiène et de Médecine Coloniale 13, 328–335.
Adas, Michael
    1989   Machines as the Measure of Men: Scientific and Technological Superiority and Ideologies of Western Dominance. Ithaca: Cornell University Press.
Arnold, David
    1979   European Orphans and Vagrants in India In the Nineteenth Century. The Journal of Imperial and Commonwealth History 7:2, 104–27.
    1983   White Colonization and Labour in Nineteenth-Century India. Journal of Imperial and Commonwealth History 11:2, 133–158.
Bajema, Carl, ed.
    1976   Eugenics Then and Now. Stroudsburg, PA: Dowden, Hutchinson & Ross.
Ballhatchet, Kenneth
    1980   Race, Sex and Class under the Raj: Imperial Attitudes and Policies and Their Critics, 1793–1905. New York: St. Martin's Press.
Baroli, Marc
    1967   La vie quotidienne des Français en Algérie. Paris: Hachette.

Bauduin, D. C. M.
  1941(1927) Het Indische Leven. 'S-Gravenhage: H. P. Leopolds.
Beidelman, Thomas
  1982 Colonial Evangelism. Bloomington: Indiana University Press.
Bérenger-Féraud, L.
  1875 Traité Clinique des Maladies des Européens au Sénégal. Paris: Adrien Delahaye.
Blumberger, J. Th. Petrus
  1939 De Indo-Europeesche Beweging in Nederlandsch-Indie. Haarlem: Tjeenk Willink.
Blussé, Leonard
  1986 Strange Company: Chinese Settlers, Mestizo Women and the Dutch in VOC Batavia. Dordrecht: Foris.
Bock, Gisela
  1984 Racism and Sexism in Nazi Germany: Motherhood, Compulsory Sterilization, and the State. In When Biology Became Destiny: Women in Weimar and Nazi Germany. New York: Monthly Review Press, 271–296.
Boutilier, James
  1984 European Women in the Solomon Islands, 1900–1942. In Rethinking Women's Roles: Perspectives from the Pacific. O'Brien, Denise and Sharon Tiffany, eds. Pp. 173–199. Berkeley: University of California Press.
Braconier, A. de
  1913 Het Kazerne-Concubinaat in Ned-Indie. Vragen van den Dag 28, 974–95.
  1917 Het Pauperisme onder de in Ned. Oost-Indie levende Europeanen. In Nederlandsch-Indie (1st yr.), 291–300.
  1918 Kindercriminaliteit en de verzorging van misdadiq aangelegde en verwaarloosde minderjarigen in Nederlansch Indie. Baarn: Hollandia-Drukkerij.
  1933 Het Prostitutie-vraagstuk in Nederlandsch-Indie Indisch Gids 55:2, 906–928.
Brink, K.B.M. Ten
  1920 Indische Gezondheid. Batavia: Nillmij.
Brou, A. M. N.
  1907 Le Métis Franco-Annamite. Revue Indochinois. (July 1907):897–908.
Brownfoot, Janice N.
  1984 Memsahibs in Colonial Malaya: A Study of European Wives in a British Colony and Protectorate 1900–1940. The Incorporated Wife. Hilary Callan and Shirley Ardener, eds. London: Croom Helm.
Butcher, John
  1979 The British in Malaya, 1880–1941: The Social History of a European Community in Colonial Southeast Asia. Kuala Lumpur: Oxford UP.
Callan, Hilary and Shirley Ardener
  1984 The Incorporated Wife. London: Croom Helm.
Callaway, Helen
  1987 Gender, Culture and Empire: European Women in Colonial Nigeria. London: Macmillan Press.
Chailley-Bert, M. J.
  1897 L'Emigration des femmes aux colonies. Union Coloniale Francaise-conférence, 12 January 1897. Paris: Armand Colin.
Chenet, Ch.
  1936 Le role de la femme française aux Colonies: Protection des enfants métis abandonnés. Le Devoir des Femmes, 15 February 1936, p. 8.
Clerkx, Lily
  1961 Mensen in Deli. Amsterdam: Sociologisch-Historisch Seminarium voor Zuidoost-Azie. Publication no. 2.
Chivas-Baron, Clotide
  1929 La femme française aux colonies. Paris: Larose.
Cock, J.
  1980 Maids and Madams. Johannesburg: Ravan Press.
Cohen, William
  1971 Rulers of Empire: The French Colonial Service in Africa. Stanford: Hoover Institution Press.
  1980 The French Encounter with Africans. White Response to Blacks, 1530–1880. Bloomington: Indiana University Press.
Cool, F.
  1938 De Bestrijding der Werkloosheidsgevolgen in Nederlandsch-Indie gedurende 1930–1936. De Economist, 135–47; 217–243.
Cooper, Frederick
  1980 From Slaves to Squatters. New Haven: Yale University Press.
Corneau, Grace
  1900 La femme aux colonies. Paris: Librairie Nilsson.
Courtois, E.
  1900 Des Règles Hygiéniques que doit suivre l'Européen au Tonkin. Revue Indo-chinoise 83, 539–541; 564–566; 598–601.

Davin, Anna
    1978   Imperialism and Motherhood. History Workshop 5, 9–57.
Degler, Carl
    1971   Neither Black nor White. New York: Macmillan.
Delavignette, Robert
    1946   Service Africain. Paris: Gallimard.
Dixon, C. J.
    1913   De Assistent in Deli. Amsterdam: J.H. de Bussy.
Douchet
    1928   Métis et congaies d'Indochine. Hanoi.
Dowd Hall, Jacquelyn
    1984   "The Mind that Burns in Each Body": Women, Rape, and Racial Violence. Southern Exposure 12:6, 61–71.
Drooglever, P.
    1980   De Vaderlandse Club, 1929–42. Franeker: T. Wever.
Dupuy, Aimé
    1955   La personnalité du colon. Revue d'Histoire Economique et Sociale 33:1, 77–103.
Encylopedie van Nederland-Indie.
    1919   S'Gravenhage: Nijhoff and Brill.
Etienne, Mona and Eleanor Leacock
    1980   Women and Colonization. N.Y.: Praeger.
Fanon, Franz
    1967[1952]   Black Skin, White Masks. New York: Grove Press.
Favre, J. L.
    1938   La Vie aux Colonies. Paris: Larose.
Feuilletau de Bruyn, W.
    1938   Over de Economische Mogelijkheid van een Kolonisatie van Blanken op Nederlandsch Nieuw-Guinea. In Comptes Rendus du Congrès International de Géographie, Amsterdam. Leiden: Brill, 21–29.
Fredrickson, George
    1981   White Supremacy. New York: Oxford University Press.
Gaitskell, Deborah
    1983   Housewives, Maids or Mothers: Some Contradictions of Domesticity for Christian Women in Johannesburg, 1903–39. Journal of African History 24, 241–256.
Gann, L. H. and Peter Duignan
    1978   The Rulers of British Africa, 1870–1914. Stanford: Stanford University Press.
Gantes, Gilles de
    1981   La population française au Tonkin entre 1931 et 1938. Memoire. Aix-en-Provence: Institut d'Histoire des Pays d'Outre Mer.
Gartrell, Beverley
    1984   Colonial Wives: Villains or Victims? The Incorporated Wife. H. Callan, and S. Ardener. London: Croom Helm, 165–185.
Gilman, Sander L.
    1985   Difference and Pathology. Ithaca: Cornell University Press.
Gordon, Linda
    1976   Woman's Body, Woman's Right. New York: Grossman.
Gordon, R. and M. Meggitt
    1985   Law and Order in the New Guinea Highlands. Hanover: University Press of New England.
Grall, Ch.
    1908   Hygiène Coloniale appliquée. Paris: Baillière.
Grimshaw, Patricia
    1983   Christian Woman, Pious Wife, Faithful Mother, Devoted Missionary: Conflicts in Roles of American Missionary Women in Nineteenth-Century Hawaii. Feminist Studies, 9:3, 489–521.
Hammerton, James
    1979   Emigrant Gentlewomen. London: Croom Helm.
Hansen, Karen Tranberg
    1986   Household Work as a Man's Job. Sex and Gender in Domestic Service in Zambia. Anthropology Today 2:3, 18–23.
Hardy, George
    1929   Ergaste ou la Vocation Coloniale. Paris: Armand Colin.
Hartenberg
    1910   Les Troubles Nerveux et Mentaux chez les coloniaux. Paris.
Harwood, Dorothy
    1938   The Possibility of White Colonization in the Tropics. Comptes Rendu du Congrès Int'l de Géographie. Leiden: Brill, 131–140.
Hermans, E. H.
    1925   Gezondscheidsleer voor Nederlandsch-Indie. Amsterdam: Meulenhoff.

Hesselink, Liesbeth
  1987 Prostitution: A Necessary Evil, Particularly in the Colonies: Views on Prostitution in the Netherlands Indies. *In* Indonesian Women in Focus. Locher-Scholten, E. and A. Niehof. Dordrecht: Foris, 205–224.
Het Pauperisme Commissie
  1901 Het Pauperisme onder de Europeanen. Batavia: Landsdrukkerij.
  1903 Rapport der Pauperisme-Commissie. Batavia: Landsdrukkerij.
Hobsbawn, Eric
  1987 The Age of Empire, 1875–1914. London: Weidenfeld and Nicholson.
Hunt, Nancy
  1988 Le bébé en brousse: European Women, African Birth Spacing and Colonial Intervention in Breast Feeding in the Belgian Congo. International Journal of African Historical Studies 21:3.
Hyam, Ronald
  1986a Empire and Sexual Opportunity. The Journal of Imperial and Commonwealth History 14:2, 34–90.
  1986b Concubinage and the Colonial Service: The Crewe Circular (1909). The Journal of Imperial and Commonwealth History 14:3, 170–186.
Inglis, Amirah
  1975 The White Women's Protection Ordinance: Sexual Anxiety and Politics in Papua. London: Sussex University Press.
Jaurequiberry
  1924 Les Blancs en Pays Chauds. Paris: Maloine.
Jordan, Winthrop
  1968 White over Black: American Attitudes Toward the Negro, 1550–1812. Chapel Hill: University of North Carolina Press.
Joyeux, Ch. and A. Sice
  1937 Affections exotiques du système nerveux. Précis de Médecine Coloniale. Paris: Masson.
Kantoor van Arbeid
  1935 Werkloosheid in Nederlandsch-Indie. Batavia: Landsdrukkerij.
Kennedy, Dane
  1987 Islands of White. Durham: Duke University Press.
Kennedy, Raymond
  1947 The Ageless Indies. New York: John Day.
Kevles, Daniel
  1985 In the Name of Eugenics. Berkeley: University of California Press.
King, Anthony
  1976 Colonial Urban Development. London: Routledge & Kegan Paul.
Kirkwood, Deborah
  1984 Settler Wives in Southern Rhodesia: A Case Study. *In* The Incorporated Wife. Callan, H. and Ardener, S., eds. London: Croom Helm.
Knibiehler, Y. and R. Goutalier
  1985 La femme au temps des colonies. Paris: Stock.
  1987 Femmes et Colonisation: Rapport Terminal au Ministère des Relations Extérieures et de la Co-opération. Aix en-Provence: Institut d'Histoire des Pays d'Outre-Mer.
Koks, Dr. J. Th.
  1931 De Indo. Amsterdam: H.J. Paris.
Kroniek
  1917 Oostkust van Sumatra-Instituut. Amsterdam: J.H. de Bussy.
Kuklick, Henrika
  1979 The Imperial Bureaucrat: The Colonial Administrative Service in the Gold Coast, 1920–1939. Stanford: Hoover Institution Press.
Le Bras, Hervé
  1981 Histoire secrète de la fécondité Le Débat 8:76–100.
Loutfi, Martine Astier
  1971 Littérature et Colonialisme. Paris: Mouton.
Lucas, Nicole
  1986 Trouwverbod, inlandse huishousdsters en Europese vrouwen. *In* Vrouwen in de Nederlandse Kolonien. Reijs, J. et al. Nijmegen: SUN, 78–97.
Mackinnon, Murdoch
  1920 European Children in the Tropical Highlands. Lancet 199, 944–945.
Malleret, Louis
  1934 L'Exotisme Indochinois dans la Littérature Française depuis 1860. Paris: Larose.
Mannoni, Octavio
  1964 Prospero and Caliban. New York: Praeger.
Mansvelt, W.
  1932 De Positie der Indo-Europeanen. Kolonial Studien, 290–311.

Martinez-Alier, Verena
  1974 Marriage, Class and Colour in Nineteenth Century Cuba. Cambridge: Cambridge University Press.
Mason, Philip
  1958 The Birth of a Dilemma: The Conquest and Settlement of Rhodesia. New York: Oxford University Press.
Maunier, M. René
  1932 Sociologie Coloniale. Paris: Domat-Montchrestien.
Mazet, Jacques
  1932 La Condition Juridique des Métis. Paris: Domat Montchrestien.
Mercier, Paul
  1965 The European Community of Dakar. *In* Africa: Social Problems of Change and Conflict. Berghe, Pierre van den, ed. San Francisco: Chandler, 284–304.
Ming, Hanneke
  1983 Barracks-Concubinage in the Indies, 1887–1920. Indonesia 35 (April), 65–93.
Moore-Gilbert, B.J.
  1986 Kipling and "Orientalism." New York: St. Martin's.
Mosse, George
  1978 Toward the Final Solution. New York: Fertig.
  1985 Nationalism and Sexuality. Madison: University of Wisconsin Press.
Muller, Hendrik
  1912 De Europeesche Samenleving. Neerlands Indie. Amsterdam: Elsevier:371–384.
Nandy, Ashis
  1983 The Intimate Enemy: Loss and Recovery of Self under Colonialism. Delhi: Oxford University Press.
Nash, June
  1980 Aztec Women: The Transition from Status to Class in Empire and Colony. *In* Woman and Colonization: Anthropological Perspectives. Mona Etienne and Eleanor Leacock, eds. New York: Praeger, 134–148.
Nieuwenhuys, Roger
  1959 Tussen Twee Vaderlanden. Amsterdam: Van Oorschot.
Nora, Pierre
  1961 Les Français d'Algerie. Paris: Julliard.
O'Brien, Rita Cruise
  1972 White Society in Black Africa: The French in Senegal. London: Faber & Faber.
Pollmann, Tessel
  1986 Bruidstraantjes: De Koloniale roman, de njai en de apartheid. *In* Vrouwen in de Nederlandse Kolonien. Reijs, J. et. al. eds. Nijmegen: SUN, 98–125.
Pourvourville, Albert de
  1926 Le Métis. Le Mal d'Argent. Paris: Monde Moderne, 97–114.
Price, Grenfell A.
  1939 White Settlers in the Tropics. New York: American Geographical Society.
Prochaska, David
  1989 Making Algeria French: Colonialism in Bone, 1870–1920. Cambridge: Cambridge University Press.
Pujarniscle, E.
  1931 Philoxène ou de la litterature coloniale. Paris.
Raptschinsky, B.
  1941 Kolonisatie van blanken in de tropen. Den Haag: Bibliotheek van weten en denken.
Reijs, J., E. Kloek, U. Jansz, A. de Wildt, S. van Norden, M. de Baar
  1986 Vrouwen in de Nederlandse Kolonien. Nijmegen:SUN.
Ridley, Hugh
  1983 Images of Imperial Rule. New York: Croom & Helm.
Ritter, W.L.
  1856 De Europeaan in Nederlandsch Indie. Leyden: Sythoff.
Rodenwalt, Ernest
  1928 Eugenetische Problemen in Nederlandsch Indie. Ons Nageslacht 1–8
Said, Edward W.
  1978 Orientalism. New York: Vintage.
Sambuc
  1931 Les Métis Franco-Annamites en Indochine. Revue du Pacifique, 256–272.
Schneider, William
  1972 Toward the Improvement of the Human Race: The History of Eugenics in France. Journal of Modern History 54:269–291.
Schoevers, T.
  1913 Het leven en werken van den assistent bij de Tabakscultuur in Deli. Jaarboek der Vereeniging "Studiebelangen." Wageningen: Zomer, 3–43.

Schmidt, Elizabeth
  1987   Ideology, Economics and the Role of Shona Women in Southern Rhodesia, 1850–1939. Ph.D. dissertation, University of Wisconsin.
Simon, Jean-Pierre
  1981   Rapatriés d'Indochine. Paris: Harmattan.
Sivan, Emmanuel
  1983   Interpretations of Islam. Princeton: Darwin Press.
Smith-Rosenberg, Carroll and Charles Rosenberg
  1973   The Female Animal: Medical and Biological Views of Woman and Her Role in Nineteenth-Century America. Journal of American History 60(2):332–356.
Spear, Percival
  1963   The Nabobs. London: Oxford University Press.
Stepan, Nancy
  1982   The Idea of Race in Science. London: Macmillan.
Stoler, Ann
  1985a   Capitalism and Confrontation in Sumatra's Plantation Belt, 1870–1979. New Haven: Yale University Press.
  1985b   Perceptions of Protest. American Ethnologist 12:4, 642–658.
  1989   Rethinking Colonial Categories: European Communities and the Boundaries of Rule. Comp. Studies in Society and History 13(1):134–161.
Strobel, Margaret
  1987   Gender and Race in the 19th and 20th Century British Empire. In Becoming Visible: Women in European History. R. Bridenthal et al., eds. Boston: Houghton Mifflin, 375–396.
Stuurman, Siep
  1985   Verzuiling, Kapitalisme en Patriarchaat. Nijmegen:SUN.
Sutherland, Heather
  1982   Ethnicity and Access in Colonial Macassar. In Papers of the Dutch-Indonesian Historical Conference. Leiden: Bureau of Indonesian Studies, 250–277.
Takaki, Ronald
  1977   Iron Cages. Berkeley: University of California Press.
Taylor, Jean
  1977   The World of Women in the Colonial Dutch Novel. Kabar Seberang 2, 26–41.
  1983   The Social World of Batavia. Madison: University of Wisconsin Press.
Tiffany, Sharon and Kathleen Adams
  1985   The Wild Woman: An Inquiry into the Anthropology of an Idea. Cambridge, MA: Schenkman Publishing Co.
Tirefort, A.
  1979   'Le Bon Temps': La Communauté Francaise en Basse Cote d'Ivoire pendant l'Entre-Deux Guerres, 1920–1940. Troisème Cycle, Centre d'Etudes Africaines, Paris.
Travaux du Groupe d'Etudes Coloniales
  1910   La Femme Blanche au Congo. Brussels: Misch & Thron.
Van Doorn, Jacques
  1983   A Divided Society: Segmentation and Mediation in Late-Colonial Indonesia. Rotterdam: CASPA.
  1985   Indie als Koloniale Maatschappy. In De Nederlandse samenleving sinds 1815. Holthoon, F.L. van, ed. Assen: Maastricht.
Van Helten, J. and K. Williams
  1983   'The Crying Need of South Africa': The Emigration of Single British Women in the Transvaal, 1901–1910. Journal of South African Studies 10:1, 11–38.
Van Heyningen, Elizabeth B.
  1984   The Social Evil in the Cape Colony 1868–1902: Prostitution and the Contagious Disease Acts. Journal of Southern African Studies 10;2:170–197.
Van Marle, A.
  1952   De group der Europeanen in Nederlands-Indie. Indonesie, 5:2, 77–121; 5:3, 314–341; 5:5, 481–507.
Van Onselen, Charles
  1982   Studies in the Social and Economic History of the Witwatersrand 1886–1914. Vol. I. New York: Longman.
Veerde, A.G.
  1931   Onderzoek naar den omvang der werkloosheid op Java, November 1930–Juni 1931). Koloniale Studien 242–273; 503–533.
Vellut, Jean-Luc
  1982   Materiaux pour une image du Blanc dans la société coloniale du Congo Belge. In Stéréotypes Nationaux et Préjuqés Raciaux aux XIXe et XXe Siècles. Jean Pirotte ed. Leuven: Editions Nauwelaerts.
Vere Allen, J. de
  1970   Malayan Civil Service, 1874–1941: Colonial Bureaucracy Malayan Elite. Comparative Studies in Society and History. 12,149–178.
Wanderken, P.
  1943   Zoo leven onze kinderen. In Zoo Leven Wij in Indonesia. Deventer: Van Hoever: 172–187.

Wertheim, Willem
    1959 Indonesian Society in Transition. The Hague: Van Hoeve.
Winckel, Ch. W. F.
    1938 The Feasibility of White Settlements in the Tropics: a Medical Point of View. Comptes Rendus du Congrès International de Géographie Amsterdam. Leiden: Brill, 345–56.
Woodcock, George
    1969 The British in the Far East. New York: Atheneum.

submitted 6 April 1989
accepted 6 July 1989
final version received 27 July 1989

[18]

CULTURAL MISSIONARIES, MATERNAL IMPERIALISTS, FEMINIST ALLIES: BRITISH WOMEN ACTIVISTS IN INDIA, 1865-1945

BARBARA N. RAMUSACK
Department of History, University of Cincinnati, Cincinnati, OH 45221, U.S.A.

Synopsis—Beyond memsahibs and religious missionaries, there were British women outside the formal imperial establishment who went to India because of their concern for the condition of Indian women. Five such women whose careers in India paralleled the development of British imperial power from firm self-confidence to approaching demise are Mary Carpenter (1807-1877), Annette Akroyd Beveridge (1842-1929), Margaret Noble-Sister Nivedita (1867-1911), Margaret Gillespie Cousins (1878-1954), and Eleanor Rathbone (1872-1946). An examination of their careers reflects how the categories of race and gender influence efforts to promote social reforms within an imperial relationship. Once in India these women functioned as cultural missionaries preaching a gospel of women's uplift based largely on models adapted from their experience in Britain. At least three of them became maternal imperialists who treated Indian women as daughters whom they were preparing for adult responsibilities as modern women. All five women were most able to cross the boundary of race as feminist allies when their skills most suited the needs of Indian women.

The dominant images of British women in India are either memsahibs, the wives of British officials and businessmen, or missionaries, either single women or the wives of male missionaries. They have often been characterized as arrogant exponents of British culture or Christianity as practiced in a western context and individuals with almost no interest in India, its culture or its people. More recent scholarship has began to depict a more sympathetic and complex view of memsahibs (Barr, 1976; Lind, 1988). Although much smaller in number, there were

I would like to acknowledge with appreciation fellowships from the American Institute of Indian Studies (1976-77), the Fulbright Faculty Research Abroad Program of the U.S. Department of Education (1981-82), and the Smithsonian Institution (1985) that supported my research in India, and a Summer Fellowship from the National Endowment for the Humanities (1979) for research in England.
An early version of this essay was presented at the annual meeting of the American Historical Association in December 1979. Since then I have benefitted greatly from the helpful comments of Geraldine Forbes, Allen Greenberger, a group of Indian scholars at a Fulbright-sponsored seminar in Calcutta in January 1981, and from a seminar on the Other at the National Humanities Center. Any errors of fact and interpretation are my responsibility.

British women outside the formal imperial establishment who came to India because of their declared concern about the condition of Indian women. Five such women whose careers in India parallel the development of British imperial power from firm self-confidence to approaching demise are Mary Carpenter, Annette Akroyd Beveridge, Margaret Noble-Sister Nivedita, Margaret Gillespie Cousins, and Eleanor Rathbone. An examination of their activities will provide one avenue of exploring how the categories of race and gender influence efforts to promote social reforms within an imperial relationship. An analysis of the initial attraction of these women to India, their network of contacts within the British imperial establishment and among Indians, and their endeavors on behalf of Indian women will provide the basis for an assessment of the shifts in their orientation and activities over the eight decades from 1865 to 1945. The changes delineated reflect much about the British women as individuals, about the evolution of the imperial relationship, and about developments in Indian society, especially in the situation of Indian women.

Larger questions that then will be addressed relate to the nature of the boundaries of race and gender within an imperial structure. Is it possible for women from one race or ethnic group to promote effectively reforms or institutions designed to modify or improve the conditions of women of another race or ethnic group? How far can women cooperate or collaborate across racial or ethnic categories? How does the shared category of gender affect the development of movements and institutions designed for the benefit of women in a colonial setting? Finally, should these British women be labelled cultural missionaries who preached the gospel of women's uplift based on models evolved in Britain, maternal imperialists who wanted to socialize immature daughters to their adult rights and responsibilities, or feminist allies whose effectiveness depended on their own personalities and skills, the institutional and personal alliances they formed, and the state of the women's movement in India when they were active? Perhaps individual women might embody all three roles in varying combinations.

MARY CARPENTER

Daughter of a prominent Unitarian minister in Bristol who was the most significant influence on her life, Mary Carpenter (1807–1877) was a notable example of the 19th-century English spinster who dedicated her life to philanthropy and social reform (Banks, 1985, pp. 46–48; Carpenter, 1974; Manton, 1976; Prochaska, 1980; Schupf, 1974). She was unusual in that she had received a rigorous, classical education with her brothers so that she might assist in a family-operated school. While teaching, the angular, frail Miss Carpenter had her first contact with India when Raja Rammuhan Roy, the founder of the Brahmo Samaj, a rationalist Hindu reform group in Bengal, came to visit her father in 1833. Her admiration for Roy and her view of England's mission of salvation in India are expressed in some sentimental sonnets, which she wrote after Roy's unexpected death in Bristol that same year. According to Carpenter, England was

> Far from thy [Roy's] native clime a sea-girt land/Sit thron'd among the nations; in the breasts/Of all her sons immortal freedom rests;/And of her patriots many a holy band/Have sought to rouse the world from the command/Of that debasing Tyrant who detests/The reign of truth and love. At their behests/The slave is free! and Superstition's hand/Sinks powerless. (Carpenter, 1974, p. 33)

India was to remain a shadowy concern for three decades while Carpenter pursued a career as a social reformer that focussed on the needs of destitute children who crowded urban streets in England as industrial development created social problems beyond the capacity of older social institutions to solve. She became noted for ragged schools for underclass children, reformatories for delinquent children, and a crusade for reforms in the penal system. During the 1860s renewed contacts with Indian male social reformers, most notably a Christmas in 1865 shared with three Hindu students, including Monomohan Ghose, a member of the Brahmo Samaj then in England to compete for the entrance examination of the Indian Civil Service (ICS), revived her interest in India (Carpenter, 1868, Vol. 1, pp. 3–4). Krishna Lahiri has also argued that Carpenter was experiencing personal despondency and was looking for new fields of endeavor during these years (1979, pp. 20–22). On January 8, 1866, the 59-year-old reformer confided to her diary:

> Heavenly Father! by tokens drawn from the marvellous workings of Thy providence, I believe that Thou has destined for me the unspeakable privilege before leaving this world, of going to our distant India, and there working with the spirits of my beloved father and the noble Raja for the elevation of woman, and perhaps also for the planting of a pure Christianity. (Carpenter, 1974, p. 245)

Her emphases are significant: On guidance from her father and Rammuhan Roy and on women first and Christianity second. The Englishwoman wanted to assist Indian men such as her recent guests who sought to change some social conditions for the women in their own class, but she also implicitly accepted the ethnocentric views of British officials and Christian missionaries that the "degraded" position of Indian women was a major indication that Indian civilization ranked below that of the enlightened British.

She joined the movement to "uplift" Indian women.

After her arrival in Bombay in late 1866, Mary Carpenter first considered spending all her time in Bombay Presidency where she was impressed by the commitment to female education (Carpenter, 1868, Vol. 1, pp. 102–103). Ultimately she decided to go to Bengal via Madras since she wanted support from the British colonial government whose capital was at Calcutta. Her primary goal was to promote female education although she also toured penal institutions and subsequently was particularly critical of the lack of concern for the rehabilitation of women prisoners.

Throughout her six-month tour, Carpenter displayed ambivalent attitudes toward Indian culture and Indian women. A devout Christian, she was disdainful of what she labelled the superstitious religious practices of Hindus, Muslims, and Parsis. Still she was aware that much opposition to female education among Indians was from fear that it was a preface to conversion, and so she respected Indian concerns and carefully avoided any appearance of proselytization. At the same time she clearly desired to socialize Indian girls into Victorian domesticity. Education was to enable Indian girls to be gracious hostesses presiding over simple, neat homes in which children and husbands would find their moral center.

Carpenter was critical of the elderly male pundits who taught young girls in schools since that practice meant that girls would be withdrawn from schools as they approached puberty to avoid contact with the opposite sex. *Zenana* education provided by female missionaries in Indian homes was at best a transitional step since it was "obviously far preferable for young girls to have their minds expanded by seeing something beyond the walls in which they are afterwards to be immured" (Carpenter, 1868, Vol. 1, p. 188). For Carpenter the key to any expansion of female education was an increase in the supply of female teachers. In her visits to Ahmedabad, Surat, Bombay, Madras, and Calcutta, she met untiringly with Indian male reformers anxious to secure education for their wives and daughters. She lobbied with British officials and presented memorials that urged the Government of India to give grants to support female normal schools to provide secular female teachers for Indian girls as they already did to train male teachers for boys (Carpenter, 1868, Vol. 2, pp. 142–145). Carpenter sought government patronage of this institution for three reasons: First, "as a guarantee to the natives that it is *not* a proselytising institution," (Carpenter, 1868, Vol. 1, p. 123, emphasis in the original); second, because the Englishwomen who were needed as principals required the protection of the British government before they exposed "themselves to the difficulties and dangers they would have to encounter in a distant and tropical country"; and third, only the government could ensure the permanency of such an institution (Carpenter, 1868, Vol. 2, p. 157).

Her efforts were thwarted by cautious British officials who were more willing to support education that would provide inexpensive male clerks than a more altruistic venture for women who could not be so employed (Carpenter, 1868, Vol. 2, pp. 154–155; Lahiri, 1979). Carpenter's authoritative personality was also a factor that offended white males who might have been allies. In February 1869 Lord Napier, Governor of Madras, advised Carpenter that he was "of the opinion that you could do more for the cause of female education by *staying at home and supporting* those who are interested in it" (emphasis in the original, Manton, 1976, p. 209). Charles Dall, an American Unitarian missionary in Calcutta, who was upset that Carpenter financially supported some Indian Unitarian establishments but not his, bluntly commented to the American Unitarian Association on December 14, 1869, that:

> Miss Carpenter has been very cooly [sic] received on her return to Bombay, the mischief being, in the one hand, that she walks roughshod over everybody and meets her best advisers with rebuke, saying, "she knows better." This style of hers has become so inveterate that the old lady has hardly a friend left. If she could but begin to see how little she knows of India. (Lavan, 1977, p. 116)

On her return to England Mary Carpenter used her celebrity status to awaken public opinion to conditions in India and to English responsibilities to promote social reform in their colony. Besides her memoirs (1868), she published a collection of her speeches in India, spoke before the Social Science Association on both female education and penal reform in India, and had interviews with Queen Victoria, Florence Nightingale, and the Secretary of State for India. This propaganda activity became her dominant focus after her effort to assume a direct leadership role in India during three other visits in 1868, 1869, 1875 failed. In September 1870 in response to a request from Keshub Chandra Sen, the charismatic leader of Brahmo Samaj, Carpenter founded the National Indian Association to spread knowledge of India in England and understanding of English culture among Indian visitors to the "sea-girt land" (Carpenter, 1974, p. 257). The Bengal branch of this Association served as a prototype for reform associations among Bengali women (Borthwick, 1984, p. 280).

ANNETTE AKROYD BEVERIDGE

The daughter of a successful business man, public figure and Unitarian of Stourbridge, and his first wife (who died in 1849), Annette Akroyd Beveridge (1842-1929) was educated at Bedford College in London during the early 1860s (Beveridge, 1947). From age 22 to 27, her life in Stourbridge was a rather dull routine as reflected in her diary entries.

> 22 Feb 1865. Bachelors Ball. Very great fun in some things. Not very lively (mentally). Good Dancing.
>
> 22 Mar 1865. Read Max Muller & Cicero.
>
> 9 Jul 1865. To church to hear a mission sermon, more brains in the parson than usual but very slow still.
>
> 16 Jul 1865. To church. Very slow indeed. Won't waste my time again. (Beveridge Collections, 176/41)

The death of her father in 1869 provided the opportunity for new directions. Without any particular career commitment and no financial constraints, Annette Akroyd was ready to follow when Keshub Chandra Sen, the Bengali reformer, proclaimed at the Victoria Discussion Society in London on August 1, 1870, that:

> I now have the honour to make an urgent yet humble appeal to you Englishwomen—I may say English sisters. I sincerely and earnestly call upon you to do all in your power to effect the elevation of the Hindu women. . . . The best way in which that help can be given is for some of you to embark on the grand and noble enterprises of going over personally to that great country. . . . And what sort of education do we expect and wish from you? An unsectarian, liberal, sound, useful education. (Cheers.) . . . an education calculated to make Indian women good wives, mothers, sisters and daughters. (Beveridge, 1947, pp. 84-85)

When Akroyd arrived in Calcutta in December 1872, she lacked the support of missionary colleagues and introductions to government officials, the latter of which Carpenter enjoyed. She had to confront Indian male attitudes of blank wonder toward her status as an independent woman and then Sen's complex, and to her mind, ambivalent attitudes toward women and female education. Sen had wanted her to teach at his Native Ladies' Normal School, which emphasized the domestic arts, since he argued for gradualism in female emancipation and against Anglicized curriculum and personal habits for Bengali girls. Akroyd aspired to teach arithmetic, geography, physical science, reading, writing, and history as well as needlework and household management and to reform the domestic habits of her students (Beveridge, 1947, pp. 89-93; Borthwick, 1984, pp. 88-90; Kopf, 1979, pp. 34-41).

Akroyd did not favor overt westernization, but she was offended by the dress of the *bhadramahila* or middle-class, respectable Bengali women, which she considered vulgar at best and immodest at worst. Their heavy jewelry, their transparent muslin saris, and their lack of undergarments that were suitable for purdah she found out of place in the public spheres into which she tried to draw Indian women (Diary entry for December 26, 1872, Beveridge Collection, 176/104). Annette did not favor the English gowns proposed by some dress reformers, but was particularly concerned to put Bengali women in shoes and stockings. In writing to her sister in 1873 on the dress of Indian women she reflected on her cultural bias that, "I am thrown back on radical questions of modesty and delicacy often, and have to ask myself why are such sights so shocking to me" (Borthwick, 1984, p. 252, pp. 243-256). Her acceptance of Victorian ideals of womanhood influenced not only her concern over the immodest dress of Bengali women but also led her, as it did Mary Carpenter, to want Bengali girls to establish households in which Victorian domesticity would prevail.

Akroyd quickly broke with Sen but continued for a while to receive support from other liberal members of the Brahmo Samaj and some English officials. In 1873 she opened a boarding school, the Hindu Mahila Bidyalaya, with five students, so that she could assume overall direction of the lives of her students. Her disheartening struggle to maintain an adequate enrollment, staff, and building reflected the relevance of Mary Carpenter's judgment on the need for government support for female education if such institutions were to be permanent. Annette ended her career as an educational entrepreneur by accepting a proposal of marriage from Henry Beveridge, an independent-minded Indian Civil Service officer, who had been a steady subscriber to her school. She bore four children, including Lord William Beveridge, and translated memoirs of Mughal emperors and a Mughal princess.

MARGARET NOBLE-SISTER NIVEDITA

Conflict within the Brahmo Samaj over the most appropriate curriculum for girls and the proper pace of female emancipation reflected a growing reaction among Hindu social reformers against following western models. The effort to reconcile Hindu social customs and western ideals in programs to improve the situation of Indian women emerges in the work of two extraordinary Irish Protestant social and political activists. The first to arrive in India was Margaret Noble (1867-1911) who had taught in various English schools before opening an experimental school for children and adults in Wimbledon. In 1895 she met Swami Vivekananda, a Bengali Hindu reformer who preached a mystical devotion to Siva, the Hindu god who destroys evil, and to Kali, the black goddess who slays demons and reconciles her Bengali devotees to the inevitability of death, and the need to manifest this commitment in social service. Powerfully attracted to Vivekananda's charismatic personality and his appeal to help Indian women, Noble began to study Hindu scriptures, especially the Bhagavad Gita, and the life of the Buddha. After much debate within herself and with Vivekananda, Noble left for India in 1897 (Atmaprana, 1967; Foxe, 1975; Noble, 1982; Reymond 1953).

After her arrival in Calcutta, Margaret Noble pursued initiation into the neo-traditional, Hindu monastic community founded by Ramakrishna and then led by Vivekananda. She also moved from being a stout defender of the British empire to a sympathetic popularizer of Indian culture and the Indian demand for greater political autonomy (Noble, 1982, Vol. 1, p. 11). At the same time she accepted the social discipline of an orthodox Hindu woman so that she might become a more effective educator of Hindu women (Noble 1967, Vol. 2, p. 505). She received the name of Sister Nivedita (she who has been dedicated) and began to observe *zenana* restrictions in her Calcutta home, in a lower class quarter near that of Sarada Devi, the widow of Ramakrishna (Noble, 1967, Vol. 2, pp. 293-303).

In 1898 on the feast of the goddess Kali, November 13th, Margaret Noble opened her school for Hindu girls. A firm advocate of the kindergarten, her educational goals were only gradually and vaguely defined. At one point she declared that, "first and foremost, we must root them in their own past" and then give Indian women the three characteristics of a modern mind, "Scientific standards, geographical conception, historical prepossessions . . . " (Atmaprana, 1975, pp. 28-30). Like Akroyd, Noble wanted key elements of a western education, but unlike her predecessor, she sought a synthesis with Indian culture. Her curriculum usually included both English and Bengali, arithmetic, geography, history, art, sewing, and needlework. Because of her simple life-style and her respect for Hindu customs, Nivedita was able to secure the cooperation of some orthodox Hindu parents of young girls in her neighborhood. When students were irregular in attendance, Nivedita would personally visit their homes to encourage more regular attendance (Atmaprana, 1967, pp. 233-234). Thus she was able to work among a class and a religious category that were inimical to the appeal of the rationalist Brahmo Samaj reformers. In 1903 Nivedita opened a women's section designed to provide education for married women in her neighborhood, and this effort at informal education for young women was far in advance of its time (Atmaprana, 1967, pp. 156–161).

Sister Nivedita, however, channeled her abundant energies and talents into many different spheres. She lectured in India, England, and the United States on topics ranging from modern Indian art to devotion to the Mother Goddess and wrote articles and books in an effort to interpret Indian culture sympathetically to wider audiences and to raise money for her school (Ramusack, 1987). In Calcutta she did personally dangerous relief work during plague epidemics; she served as an intermediary between the more rationalist Brahmo reformers and the more revivalist Ramakrishna Mission; and she became a close friend of and editor for J. C. Bose, a major Bengali botanist. After the death of Vivekananda in 1902, she decided to live independently of the Ramakrishna group in order to become active in Indian nationalist politics. She soon emerged as an inspirational figure to the more radical segment of Bengali nationalists. In 1907 she returned to England to escape arrest in India, to visit her family, and to found a pro-Indian information center in London. When she returned to India in 1909, she concentrated on her writing and personal spiritual life until her death in 1911.

MARGARET GILLESPIE COUSINS

During this same era another red-haired Irish woman, the first one of this quintet who was a self-declared feminist, became interested in India first through the Bhagavad Gita and then the Theosophical Society headed by Annie Besant and headquartered in India. Margaret Gillespie (1878–1954) had received a degree from the Royal Irish Academy of Music in Dublin where she met James Cousins, an Irish poet active in the Irish literary revival dominated by W. B. Yeats (Cousins & Cousins, 1950; Denson, 1967). They were married in 1903 and Margaret inaugurated their possibly celibate life together by joining her husband in his commitment to vegetarianism at their wedding banquet (Cousins & Cousins, 1950, pp. 88–91). During the first decade of her married life she experienced both deepening receptivity to communication with the world of spirits and imprisonment for her work on behalf of the suffragist movement in England.

In 1915 her husband sought and accepted an invitation from Annie Besant to work as a journalist in Madras. The Cousinses soon shifted to teaching at a Theosophical college. After entertaining local Indian women and becoming bored with grading essays from English classes at the college, Margaret formed the Abala Abhivardini Samaj or Weaker Sex Improvement Society in 1916 (Cousins & Cousins, 1950, p. 299). It provided the model for the Women's Indian Association (WIA) that she and Dorothy Jinarajadasa, another Theosophist, helped to found in 1917 to involve Indian women in public life.

Throughout the remainder of her life in India, Cousins worked in many arenas for feminist causes (Ramusack, 1981a). In 1917 she formed a deputation of Indian women to petition for the franchise. In 1926 when women first became eligible to run for provincial legislatures, she organized the election campaign for Kamaladevi Chattopadhyay, a former student of hers and a radical social and cultural activist (Chattopadhyay, 1986, pp. 81–82; Kamaladevi Chattopadhyay, personal interview, New Delhi, March, 1977). Later that year she helped to establish the All India Women's Conference (AIWC) that debated the expansion of educational opportunities and the most appropriate curriculum for women (Report for First AIWC, 1927, p. 48, AIWC Archives). The AIWC soon decided to widen its scope since education was so inextricably related to political and social conditions, and Indian women officers were appreciative of Cousins' role as an intermediary among various Indian, regional groups (Hilla Rustomji Faridoonji to Kamaladevi Chattopadhyay, November 3, 1927; Sushama Sen to Cousins, April 22, 1928, AIWC Archives, Series 1, File No. 6). In 1936 Margaret was elected president of the AIWC, partly to honor her but also because contending factions preferred the neutral figure of a sympathetic Irishwoman (Rajkumari Amrit Kaur to Hansa Mehta, October 17, 1936, Hansa Mehta Collection, No. 5). By 1943 Cousins was withdrawing from active participation in Indian political and feminist organizations since, as she wrote:

I longed to be in the struggle against such foreign [British] imbecility; but I had the feeling that direct participation by me was no longer required, or even desired, by the leaders of Indian womanhood who were now coming to the front, and, as we saw it, were being marshalled by what Tagore in "Jana gana mana" called the "Dispenser of India's destiny" for some national service that was not far below the horizon. (Cousins & Cousins, 1950, p. 740)

Shortly thereafter she suffered a stroke that physically disabled her until her death in 1954.

ELEANOR RATHBONE

Eleanor Rathbone (1872–1946), probably the most well-known British woman politician who campaigned for social reform measures related to Indian women, was born in London where her father was serving in Parliament as a Liberal member from Liverpool. Educated at Somerville College during the early 1890s, Rathbone remained single and continued her father's social and parliamentary service. Eleanor was committed to the constitutional wing of the suffragist movement, becoming the president of the National Union of Societies for Equal Citizenship in 1919 and being elected to Parliament in 1929. In the public mind she was the principal proponent of family allowances paid directly to mothers. Like Carpenter, Rathbone's Unitarian-Quaker family had also hosted the peripatetic Rammohan Roy, but Eleanor herself did not become involved with Indian women's issues until she was a mature woman of 55 (Banks, 1985, pp. 166–169; Stocks, 1949).

During her summer holiday in 1927 Rathbone read Katherine Mayo's *Mother India*, a highly popular polemical work that opened with a graphic critique of the impact of child marriage and other Hindu social customs on the mortality of Indian women (Ramusack, 1987). Rathbone's first concern was to determine the accuracy of Mayo's data. She organized a small conference in London to discuss the issues described in *Mother India* and initiated a survey on women in India. Her efforts evoked mixed responses from Indian women and organizations, since Rathbone was trying to study her subject from London without any Indian associates. The AIWC refused to cooperate with Rathbone for several reasons, arguing "that such a Survey cannot adequately and surely be made by women who do not know India by long residence and by sympathetic co-operation in the life of its women" (Rameshwari Nehru to Rathbone, AIWC, Bombay Report, 1930, p. 32, AIWC Archives). Dhanvanthi Rama Rau, the wife of an Indian official stationed in London, attended the conference at Caxton Hall in October 1929 and heatedly "disputed the right of British women to arrange a conference on Indian social evils in London, where all the speakers were British and many had never even visited India" (Rama Rau, 1977, pp. 170–171; Dhanvanthi Rama Rau, personal interview, Bombay, March 16, 1977).

In 1929 Eleanor Rathbone was elected to Parliament and launched a double pronged campaign related to Indian women. First, she lobbied stubbornly to raise the minimum age for Indian women at marriage. This goal meant pressing for more energetic implementation by the colonial government of existing legislation (Rathbone to W. Wedgwood Benn, Sec. of State for India, Rathbone Collection, Fawcett Library, Box 92, Folder 2), educating public opinion in both England and India (Rathbone, 1934), and supporting the passage of more stringent legislation in India (Ramusack, 1981b). Second, she worked for greater involvement of Indian women in the constitutional governance of India. She sought to have Indian women appointed as delegates to the numerous conferences and commissions that were formulating constitutional reforms for India from 1927 to 1935 (Letter to *The Times*, December 12, 1927; Rathbone to Wedgwood Benn, April 16, 1931, Rathbone Collection, Fawcett Library, B92, F2); she maneuvered for a wider extension of the franchise among Indian women (Rathbone to Sarala Ray, March 13, 1933, Rathbone Collection, Fawcett Library, B93, F9, No. 2; Rathbone to Lord Lytton, February 15, 1934, Rathbone Collection, Fawcett Library, B93, F13, No. 26; Rathbone to R. A. Butler, February 15, 1934, Rathbone Collection, Fawcett Library, B93, F6); and she sought mechanisms to ensure that Indian women would be members of the reformed central and provincial legislatures (Ramusack, 1981a). Her only visit to India came in January 1932 when she went to influence testimony being given to the Indian Franchise Committee then collecting evidence (Rathbone, Circular Letters, 1932, Rathbone Collection, Sydney Jones Library). Rathbone faced indifference and some hostility among British officials in London and New Delhi who placed female suffrage and legislative seats in the category of minor minorities (religious communities such as Muslims and Sikhs and caste groups such as the so-called "untouchables" were considered the major minorities) in their correspondence (Nevile Butler to Rathbone, Rathbone Collection, Fawcett Library, B93, F4; S. Hoare, Sec of State for India to Lord Willingdon, Governor-General of India, March 2, 1934, and Willingdon to Hoare, April 3, 1934, Templewood Collection, 240/12 (b)). On the other side, her achievements that were incorporated into the Government of India Act of 1935 seemed insignificant to members of the AIWC who wanted adult suffrage or nothing. Rajkumari Amrit Kaur, then president of the AIWC, advised Rathbone:

> I am sorry I do not *quite* agree with your theory of "get what you can & make it a basis for getting more." In a free country like yours—yes—but in a subject country—no—because a start on the wrong basis means disaster ab initio and can never lead to the ultimate true goal. (Kaur to Rathbone, February 11, 1935, Rathbone Collection, Fawcett Library, B93, F12, I24)

PATTERNS OF ASSOCIATION

What do these five diverse individuals reveal about the involvement of British women activists in India? Personal characteristics, which several of them shared, were one factor leading them to India and would later influence their effectiveness. Four were single, and none had the social responsibilities linked with biological motherhood when they came to India. All were from families with a deep commitment to forms of Protestant Christianity that these women gradually found did not fulfil their spiritual or emotional needs (Carpenter, 1974, pp. 220–221, 294; Cousins & Cousins, 1950, p. 87; Foxe, 1975, pp. 15–17). Most of them were close to their fathers, whose relatively early deaths allowed the daughters to pursue independent careers. All had more formal education than did most other women of their generation and had assertive personalities. After working in the public sphere in England as educators, social reformers, and suffragists, these women extended their purview to include other women within the British Empire. At a particular point in their lives India offered them an escape from unpleasant personal circumstances or institutional settings that restricted their capacity for social experiments as well as opportunities for professional achievements or spiritual satisfaction (Borthwick, 1984, p. 58; Cousins & Cousins, 1950, pp. 240–242; Schupf, 1974, p. 17). In some ways India served as an environment of alternatives for these women as it did for British men who joined the ICS. Excluded from the ICS, these women went to India as independent activists; they were unlikely *memsahibs* because of their high level of education and public experience, and unlikely religious missionaries because of their declining enthusiasm for mainstream Christianity.

All of these women viewed their work for Indian women within an imperial political context. All lobbied extensively with British officials, although these men tended to regard these female reformers as busybodies who did not understand the broader political imperatives of maintaining imperial power or local law and order. In order to counter this indifference from British men who did not have reforms for Indian women as a major goal, these women sought to influence British public opinion through their publications, speaking tours, and London-based organizations. As might be expected, Eleanor Rathbone, a member of Parliament, was the most assiduous in cultivating British public and political opinion; but even Noble and Cousins, who saw India as their home, continued to write and lecture in Britain. Although Noble, Cousins, and Rathbone were active supporters of Indian nationalists and their demand for self-government, all five women continued to think of the colonial government as a considerable factor in achieving improvements in the condition of Indian women. By appealing to the imperial power, these women re-enforced its authority in determining the legal context of male-female relationships among Indians. At the same time many Indian political and social leaders were denying the validity of any imperial legislation that affected their personal relationships (Engels, 1983, 1987; Liddle and Joshi, 1986, pp. 19-38; Sinha, 1989).

Initially, personal ties based on shared gender were not a key factor in the formulation of programs for the colonized women by these women from the colonizing power. The desire of these British women to help Indian women did not arise from any immediate contact with Indian women. In the 19th century, Indian men sought the assistance of British women: Rammohan Roy, Monomohan Ghose, and Keshub Chandra Sen from Mary Carpenter; Keshub Chandra Sen from Annette Akroyd; Swami Vivekananda from Margaret Noble. These men were all from Bengal where British cultural ideas about ideals of womanhood were first introduced but also were elite, western-educated Indian men were led to argue for reform because of concern for the life situations of their wives, daughters, and sisters (Mukherjee, 1982). In the 20th century, foreign women stimulated the interest of these British activists: Annie Besant for Margaret Cousins and Katherine Mayo for Eleanor Rathbone. Finally, only Margaret Noble had more than the most minimal contact with Indian men and women who were not of the educated elite.

Barriers of differing experiences, languages, and cultural attitudes had to be overcome before British women could collaborate effectively with elite Indian women. Carpenter does not give evidence of really knowing Indian women as individuals. Although she refers to Indian men by name in her writing, Carpenter describes Indian women as the wife of Tagore or Banerjea or a group of underdressed women at a purdah party (Carpenter, 1974, pp. 260-261). She had spent much of her life working with dependent children and she seemed to consider Indian women in the same category. In 1866 Mary hosted the first tea party in Calcutta at which both Indian men and women were present. Since she spoke no Bengali, she "explained a portfolio of prints and drawings to a circle of gentlemen, and then requested them to do the same to the ladies" (Carpenter, 1868, Vol. 1, pp. 183-184). Akroyd learned Bengali but still did not communicate with Indian women on an equal basis nor mention the personal names of the wives of Keshub Chandra Sen or of her Brahmo supporters. Margaret Noble is a transitional figure. In her religious life Noble had close ties with Sarada Devi and her orthodox companions, and in her educational ventures she was assisted by Indian women, most notably the sister and the wife of J. C. Bose, as well as foreign women, such as the American Christine Greenstidel. Margaret Cousins is the first to cooperate almost exclusively with Indian women in her organizational and political activities on their behalf and to serve as a mentor to younger Indian women such as Kamaladevi Chattopadhyay and Muthulakshmi Reddy, the first woman legislator in India (Reddy, 1956). After her minimal consultation with Indian women in London, Eleanor Rathbone maintained an extensive correspondence with Indian women, including some who opposed her views, such as Rajkumari Amrit Kaur (also Lakshmi Menon, Rathbone Collection, Fawcett Library, B93, F14, No. 30; Rameshwari Nehru, Rathbone Collection, Fawcett Library, B93, F13, No. 29).

Thus British women activists gradually learned to collaborate with Indian women and work across racial barriers. They became potential allies as they lived for extended periods in India, developed intellectual and personal respect for Indian culture, and were willing to contribute the skills needed at a particular historical moment in reform programs initiated by Indian women. Although Carpenter, Akroyd, and Noble worked mainly in Bengal and Cousins spent most of her Indian career in Madras, the regional setting was less important than the time period in which they were active. When Carpenter and Akroyd were in India, Indian women had begun to form local groups to discuss and promote change in their social conditions, but their meetings were sporadic and conducted in Indian languages in which these two Englishwomen were not comfortable. Margaret Noble knew Bengali but she remained relatively aloof from the Bengali women's organizations in which women from the

Brahmo Samaj were dominant. When Cousins and Rathbone were active in the 1920s and 1930s, elite Indian women activists were using English and so the foreign women had a common means of communication. Cousins was more effective than Rathbone in entering an Indian network since she could utilize the Theosophical Lodges in which both European and Indian women had significant leadership roles.

The projects that these British women initiated on behalf of or in cooperation with Indian women reveal how changes in Indian society determined the most effective role for British feminists. None of these women could create the networks necessary to sustain permanent institutions. At first, Carpenter, Akroyd, and Noble sought to establish schools that would produce women who would be suitable wives for western-educated Indian men or for Indian nationalist leaders. Their schools had very limited enrollments and precarious existences since they lacked the continuity afforded by either governmental grants-in-aid or missionary contributions. They were only stabilized when Indian groups took them over, retaining at most a name and a vague commitment to the ideals of the founder. The spiritual descendant of the efforts of Carpenter and Akroyd was the Banga Mahila Bidyalaya, the first women's liberal arts college in India, founded in June 1876. It soon merged with the Bethune School founded in 1849 to become the Bethune College, which named its main hall after Mary Carpenter (Borthwick, 1984, pp. 90–96). Noble's school, which was heavily dependent on her fundraising tours in the west and donations from western devotees of Vivekananda, also experienced personal problems in 1911 when Christine Greenstidel and Sudhira Devi left to join the rival, more western-oriented Brahmo Samaj School for Girls (Atmaprana, 1967, pp. 286–287). Although the written record is silent, it seems that both the American and the Indian woman found it difficult to work with Nivedita, who was increasingly removed from the daily operation of the school but anxious to retain control of its policies. Eventually some of Noble's students opened an institution known as the Sister Nivedita School that was associated with the Ramakrishna Sarada Mission.

Carpenter, Akroyd, and Noble soon realized that education for women was only one aspect of a complex of social factors that needed modification. Thus they all became involved in other Indian organizations: Carpenter in her National Indian Association; Akroyd in the Brahmo Samaj; and Noble in the Ramakrishna Mission and then nationalist, political groups in Bengal. Carpenter and Akroyd cooperated in these associations with Indian men whose western education made them more similar in intellectual orientation and organizational style with these British women than were Indian women's groups then emerging. Margaret Noble, living in a slum area of north Calcutta, was the first of these British activists to try to cross class lines as well as to work with orthodox Hindu women, but after the death of Vivekananda she became more involved with Indian male political leaders such as Aurobindo Ghose who were committed to Hindu revivalism and political radicalism.

Margaret Cousins was the transitional figure in collaborating with Indian women across racial lines. By the late 1910s she saw the need for regional and national feminist organizations led by Indian women. Her efforts capitalized on the growing organizational sophistication among Indian women who had been working in local groups since the 1860s. The spread of western education among elite Indian women also meant that they now shared a cultural vocabulary with British women who were sympathetic to Indian culture. Cousins' 40 years of residence in India were extraordinary, and her personal sensitivity meant that she was an able ally. Her ability to communicate across racial boundaries is reflected in an address of welcome from members of a small branch of the Women's Indian Association in Tanjore, south India:

> Born in Ireland, a land that is suffering untold miseries for some centuries past, and a member of the Theosophical Society, you have atonce [sic] a natural sympathy for any suffering cause.
>
> This sympathy, rare from one of your own colour, except from a Theosophist, you have shown in abundance by your work for the women of India in general and Madras in particular. (Address from WIA, Tirumiyachur, Peralam P. G., August 27, 1921, Reddy Collection, File No. 2)

Kamaladevi has also reminisced about how Cousins could present plans so tactfully that the other party accepted them as her own (Chattopadhyay, 1986, pp. 83–84).

By the 1930s Eleanor Rathbone's well-intentioned, wide-ranging efforts were both too late and too early. Her campaign for an extension of legal and political rights demonstrates the increasing difficulty for British women to work from within Indian organizations as had Noble and Cousins. Indian women now demanded the right to formulate their own objectives and tactics and to disagree with western feminists over the likely consequences of their strategies. Rathbone's attempt to start an organization focussed on eradicating child marriages was hampered by her London base, but it was also premature. Single issue organizations were not politically popular when the dominant emphasis was on a united front to achieve independence. They would become more feasible after independence when hard decisions had to be made to establish priorities on legislation and the distribution of scarce resources.

CULTURAL MISSIONARIES, MATERNAL IMPERIALISTS, OR FEMINIST ALLIES?

In some ways these women might be viewed as cultural missionaries preaching a gospel of women's uplift. Like religious missionaries, they started with the goals of promoting female education, raising the minimum age of marriage for women, and improving the situation of Hindu widows. Although they were not overtly working to convert Indian women to Christianity, Carpenter and Akroyd sought to mold the lifestyle of Indian women according to Victorian ideals that reflected Christian influence such as their campaign for modest dress. Furthermore, all of these women thought that Indian women would profit from models, principles, and techniques derived from European experience. Carpenter had few qualms about giving advice after a six-month tour of India, deeming her principles universal in application, although based on decades of work in England (Carpenter, 1974, pp. 266–267). Akroyd wanted to establish an Indian school based on advanced British models that were not yet accepted in England itself. Noble sought to apply the theories of Pestalozzi and Frobel even though she recognized the need for the integration of Indian myths and art. Cousins used her earlier experiences in the Irish home rule movement and the English suffragist campaign as guides for her activity in India. Rathbone applied the techniques of social science research developed in England that made the subject into an object. In such ways, these women functioned as secular missionaries for western cultural forms.

Some might label these women cultural imperialists, but perhaps the term "maternal imperialists" is more accurate. In India British political imperialism became paternalistic autocracy. During much of its existence, it was justified as preparation of child-like Indians for self-government and the ICS officer was described as the *ma-bap*, or mother and father, for the people of his district. In various ways these British women activists embodied a benevolent maternal imperialism. They were frequently referred to as mothers or saw themselves as mothering India and Indians. Carpenter remarked, "In India I am regarded as 'the old Mother,' and I am proud of the title" (Carpenter, 1974, p. 310). Sister Nivedita considered herself the daughter of Vivekananda and the mother of her students, but prized the title of Sister most since " . . . We were all 'Mother' to them — now, I am 'Sister,' and funny as that sounds, the latter title indicates a more genuine and individual relationship than the former" (Noble, 1982, Vol. 1, p. 14). Margaret Cousins was not referred to as a mother, although Kamaladevi has spoken of her with daughter-like affection. Eleanor Rathbone assumed a "mother knows best" tone when she lectured Indian women on the lessons to be learned from the British suffragist movement.

The use of terms of fictive kinship could have been one way of integrating these women into Indian culture. In India, as elsewhere, mothers can be sources of great affection for their children, and so mother can be a title of honor. Still the mother-daughter relationship involves elements of inequality, and the fact that the mother figures were British and the daughters were Indian heightened the aspects of inequality and suspicions about the motivations of the mothers. The possibility for resentment became acute when Indian women had extensive education and greater political experience. Like maturing daughters or Indian men who organised politically to seek more government positions or greater representation in legislatures, Indian women wanted to be treated as equals. They were increasingly sensitive to unintentional as well as overt gestures of inequality or condescension. Thus the women who were most successful in collaborating with Indian women were those like Noble and Cousins who could enter relationships on a basis of equality and respect. Their Irish background and their extended residence in India probably helped them to span the gap between colonizer and colonized.

Although this quintet carried political and cultural baggage, they functioned as feminist allies when Indian women had particular need of their organizational and communications skills. Therefore, they provided examples of ways in which the boundaries of race but not class may be crossed in the imperial context. These activists kept the issue of women's rights and opportunities to the forefront when Indian women had limited access to public arenas or were concentrating on the goal of self-government. They contributed plans and prototypes that Indian men and women could either adapt wholly or partially or discard as they deemed most appropriate. They were articulate and publicized the condition of Indian women through lectures, polemical tracts, newspaper articles, monographs, surveys, and personal memoirs to publics in India and in English-speaking countries. They secured statistical data to buttress pleas for reform; they raised funds for institutions and organizations when Indian women possessed limited control over discretionary funds; they organized deputations and political campaigns with Indian women when Indian men were preoccupied with their own political future. Thus these British women activists provided useful skills at crucial stages of organizational development and were most effective when they worked to achieve the goals set by Indian women.

REFERENCES

[All India Women's Conference (AIWC) Archives]. Margaret Cousins Library, New Delhi.

Atmaprana, Pravrajika. (1967). *Sister Nivedita* (2nd ed). Calcutta: Sister Nivedita Girls' School.

Atmaprana, Pravrajika. (Ed.). (1975). *Sister Nivedita's lectures and writings: Hitherto unpublished collection of lectures and writings of Sister Nivedita on education, Hindu life and thought and so on.* Calcutta: Ramakrishna Sarada Mission, Sister Nivedita Girls' School.

Banks, Olive. (1985). *The biographical dictionary of British feminists: Vol I. 1800-1930.* New York: New York University Press.

Barr, Pat. (1976). *The memshahibs: The women of Victorian India.* London: Secker and Warburg.

[Beveridge Collections]. MSS Eur C 176. India Office Library and Records, London.

Beveridge, William H. (1947). *India called them.* London: George Allen & Unwin.

Borthwick, Meredith. (1984). *The changing role of women in Bengal, 1849-1905.* Princeton: Princeton University Press.

Carpenter, J. Estlin. (1974). *The life and work of Mary Carpenter.* Montclair, New Jersey: Patterson Smith. (First published in 1879.)

Carpenter, Mary. (1868). *Six months in India* (2 vols.). London: Longmans, Green.

Chattopadhyay, Kamaladevi. (1986). *Inner recess outer spaces: Memoirs.* New Delhi: Navrang.

Cousins, James H., & Cousins, Margaret. (1950). *We two together.* Madras: Ganesh.

Denson, Alan. (1967). *James H. Cousins (1873-1956) and Margaret Cousins (1878-1954): A bio-bibliographical survey.* Kendal, Westmoreland: Author.

Engels, Dagmar. (1983). Age of consent act of 1891: Colonial ideology in Bengal. *South Asia Research, 3*(2), 107-134.

Engels, Dagmar. (1987). *The changing role of women in Bengal, c.1890-c.1930: With special reference to British and Bengali discourse on gender.* Unpublished doctoral dissertation, School of Oriental and African Studies, University of London, London.

Foxe, Barbara. (1975). *Long journey home: A biography of Margaret Noble (Nivedita).* London: Rider and Company.

Kopf, David. (1979). *The Brahmo Samaj and the shaping of the modern Indian mind.* Princeton: Princeton University Press.

Lahiri, Krishna. (1979). Mary Carpenter and the early crisis in teacher training for women in Calcutta. In Richard L. Park (Ed.), *Patterns of change in modern Bengal* (pp. 19-47). East Lansing MI: Asian Studies Center, Michigan State University.

Lavan, Spencer. (1977). *Unitarians and India: A study in encounter and response.* Boston: Beacon Press.

Liddle, Joanne, & Joshi, Rama. (1986). *Daughters of independence: Gender, caste and class in India.* London: Zed Books.

Lind, Mary Ann. (1988). *The compassionate memsahibs: Welfare activities of British women in India, 1900-1947.* Westport, CT: Greenwood Press.

Manton, Jo. (1976). *Mary Carpenter and the children of the streets.* London: Heinemann.

[Hansa Mehta Collection]. Nehru Memorial Museum and Library, New Delhi.

Mukherjee, S. N. (1982). Raja Rammohun Roy and the Debate on the Status of Women in Bengal. In Michael Allen & S. N. Mukherjee (Eds.), *Women in India and Nepal* (pp. 155-178). Canberra: Australian National University.

Noble, Margaret. (Sister Nivedita). (1967). *The complete works of Sister Nivedita: Birth centenary publi-*

cation (4 vols.). Calcutta: Ramakrishna Sarada Mission, Sister Nivedita Girls' School.

Noble, Margaret. (Sister Nivedita). (1982). In Sankari Prasad Basu (Ed.), *Letters of Sister Nivedita* (2 vols.). Calcutta: Nababharat Publishers.

Prochaska, Frank K. (1980). *Women and philanthropy in nineteenth-century England*. Oxford: Clarendon Press.

Rama Rau, Dhanvanthi. (1977). *An inheritance: The memoirs of Dhanvanthi Rama Rau*. New York: Harper & Row.

Ramusack, Barbara N. (1981a) Catalysts or helpers? British feminists, Indian women's rights, and Indian independence. In Gail Minault (Ed.), *The extended family: Women and political participation in India and Pakistan* (pp. 109-150). Columbia, MO: South Asia Books.

Ramusack, Barbara N. (1981b). Women's organizations and social change: The age-of-marriage issue in India. In Naomi Black & Ann Baker Cottrell (Eds.), *Women and world change: Equity issues in development* (pp. 198-216). Beverly Hills, CA: Sage Publications.

Ramusack, Barbara N. (1987, June). *Sister India or mother India: Margaret Noble and Katherine Mayo as interpreters of the gender roles of Indian women*. Paper presented at 7th Berkshire Conference on the History of Women, Wellesley College, Wellesley, MA.

Rathbone, Eleanor. (1934). *Child marriage: The Indian Minotaur*. London: George Allen & Unwin.

[Eleanor Rathbone Collection]. Fawcett Library, London.

[Eleanor Rathbone Collection]. Sydney Jones Library, University of Liverpool, Liverpool.

[Muthulakshmi Reddy Collection]. Nehru Memorial Museum and Library, New Delhi.

[Reddy, Muthulakshmi]. (1956). *Mrs. Margaret Cousins and her work in India* (Compiled by One Who Knows). Madras: Women's Indian Association.

Reymond, Lizelle. (1953). *The dedicated: A biography of Nivedita* [Translated from the 1945 French edition]. New York: John Day.

Schupf, Harriet Warm. (1974). Single women and social reform in mid-nineteenth century England: The case of Mary Carpenter. *Victorian Studies, 17*(3), 301-317.

Sinha, Mrinalini. (1989). The age of consent act: The ideal of masculinity and colonial ideology in nineteenth century Bengal. In Tony K. Stewart (Ed.), *Shaping Bengali worlds, public and private* (pp. 99-111). East Lansing, MI: Asian Studies Center, Michigan State University.

Stocks, Mary D. (1949). *Eleanor Rathbone: A biography*. London: Victor Gollancs.

[Templewood Collection]. MSS Eur E 240. India Office Library and Records, London.

[19]

Empire and the Confessional State: Islam and Religious Politics in Nineteenth-Century Russia

ROBERT CREWS

> The various modes of worship, which prevailed in the Roman World, were all considered by the people, as equally true; by the philosopher, as equally false; and by the magistrate, as equally useful.
>
> Edward Gibbon, *Decline and Fall of the Roman Empire* (1776).

AT THE END OF THE NINETEENTH CENTURY, a "Muslim question" confronted the tsarist regime. Islam provoked intense anxieties among Russian elites about political loyalty and social integration. Many conservatives identified a diverse population of some 20 million Muslim subjects—a total exceeding the number of Muslims under the rule of the Ottoman sultan—as a particular threat to the domestic order. Spread throughout the Volga River and Ural Mountains regions, the Crimea, Siberia, the Caucasus, the north Caspian steppe, and Transoxiana, Muslims appeared to present a danger to the stability and integrity of this vast empire.[1] Echoing earlier charges directed at Jews, critics such as E. N. Voronets claimed in 1891 that Muslims acted as a "state within a state."[2] Moreover, they maintained ties to millions of co-religionists in states adjoining Russia's southern borderlands. In an era when the Ottoman sultan Abdülhamid II asserted himself as the caliph of all Muslims, the Ministry of the Interior in St. Petersburg warned local Russian police to monitor Muslim subjects for signs of sympathy with the "idea of a world-wide Muslim kingdom with the sultan at the head" and for evidence that they "pray for the former, and not for the Sovereign Emperor."[3]

I am very grateful to Deborah Cohen, Laura Engelstein, Nancy Shields Kollmann, Stephen Kotkin, Olga Litvak, Margaret Sena, the editors of the *AHR*, and its anonymous reviewers, whose comments on earlier drafts of this essay improved the final version immeasurably. I would also like to thank the Fulbright-Hays Commission, the Working Group Modernity and Islam of the Wissenschaftskolleg zu Berlin, the Kennan Institute, and the Title VIII Funding Program for supporting the research for this article.

[1] In 1897, the first all-imperial census counted some 14 million Muslims (out of a total population of 150 million subjects), although officials conceded that they undercounted Muslims. While estimates ranged as high as 40 million, most Muslim commentators arrived at the figure of 20 million. See S. Rybakov, "Statistika musul'man v Rossii," *Mir Islama* 2, no. 11 (1913): 757–63. In the same year, the Ottoman census counted 14.1 million Muslims in the Ottoman Empire. Bilal Eryılmaz, *Osmanlı Devletinde Gayrimüslim Teb'anın Yönetimi* (Istanbul, 1990), 81.

[2] E. N. Voronets, *Nuzhnyi-li dlia Rossii mufti?* (Moscow, 1891), 4.

[3] See the warning of March 1893 to the governor of Kazan province in Natsional'nyi Arkhiv Respubliki Tatarstan (hereafter, NART), f. 1, op. 2, d. 9251, ll. 1–1 ob. On Abdülhamid, see Selim Deringil, *The Well-Protected Domains: Ideology and the Legitimation of Power in the Ottoman Empire, 1876–1909* (London, 1999).

Muslim intellectuals such as Ismail Bei Gasprinskii rejected charges of disloyalty but shared Russian conservatives' critique of an ostensibly isolated and inward-looking Muslim community, claiming that it "vegetates in the narrow, stifling realm of its old ideas and prejudices, as if isolated from the rest of humanity."[4] Appropriating the language of "reform" and "progress," Gasprinskii condemned his opponents as obscurantists and self-appointed guardians of Islam who rejected participation in the social and institutional life of the empire. The reformers set out to transform Islamic education and legal interpretation and looked to the state to advance science and the Russian language among Muslims. However, the regime remained suspicious of their overtures and continued to regard them as part of a broader scheme sponsored by foreign powers to weaken the Russian state in its Muslim regions.

The categories of these late nineteenth-century actors have largely determined how historians have approached the study of Islam in modern Russia. Reading these conflicts back into the distant past, scholars have tended to replicate the image of a conflict defined, on the one hand, by Muslim struggles against the regime and, on the other, by an internal tension between Muslim "reformers" and Muslim "traditionalists." Whereas internalist histories view the faith as an impregnable barrier against external threats to community and tradition, mainstream Russian historiography maintains that even Muslims who did not openly embrace jihad against the Russians nonetheless stood against, or apart from, the state. In most accounts, only the appearance of Muslim "modernist reformers" (Jadids) in the 1880s disrupts this story of cultural preservation and continuity.[5]

Such interpretations capture an important aspect of the controversies facing imperial and Muslim elites at the *fin de siècle* but obscure more complex patterns of interaction between Muslim communities and the tsarist regime in the long nineteenth century. From the reign of Catherine the Great, Muslims sometimes resisted or fled Russian military expansion under the banner of Islam. Many actors on both sides represented these clashes as essentially religious in nature. Yet resistance and flight to a neighboring Muslim land (the *hijra*) were not the only responses available to Muslims. Nor was the regime exclusively concerned with expelling or converting its Muslim subjects.[6] Even amid the brutal war waged for

---

[4] Ismail Bei Gasprinskii, *Russkoe musul'manstvo: Mysli, zametki i nabliudeniia musul'manina* (1881; rpt. edn., Oxford, 1985), 29.

[5] Accounts emphasizing unrelenting state hostility toward Muslims—and their resistance to the state—include J. G. Zäynullin, *XVIII yöz–XX yöz bashïnda tatar rukhani ädäbiyätï* (Kazan, 1998), 4–5; and Azade-Ayşe Rorlich, *The Volga Tatars: A Profile in National Resilience* (Stanford, Calif., 1986). For a valuable overview of Jadid ideology, see Edward J. Lazzerini, "Beyond Renewal: The Jadīd Response to Pressure for Change in the Modern Era," in *Muslims in Central Asia: Expressions of Identity and Change*, Jo-Ann Gross, ed. (Durham, N.C., 1992), 151–66. On the ideological concerns shared by reformers and their rivals, see the brilliant article by Stéphane A. Dudoignon, "Qu'est-ce que la 'qadīmiya'? Eléments pour une sociologie du traditionalisme musulman, en Islam de Russie et en Transoxiane (au tournant des XIXe et XIXe siècles)," *L'Islam de Russie: Conscience communautaire et autonomie politique chez les Tatars de la Volga et de l'Oural depuis le XVIIIe siècle*, Stéphane A. Dudoignon, Dämir Is'haqov, and Räfyq Möhämmätshin, eds. (Paris, 1997), 207–25.

[6] For a recent account of Russian military campaigns in the Caucasus that highlights the goal of mass expulsions, see Peter Holquist, "To Count, to Extract, and to Exterminate: Population Statistics and Population Politics in Late Imperial and Soviet Russia," in *A State of Nations: Empire and Nation-Making in the Age of Lenin and Stalin*, Ronald Grigor Suny and Terry Martin, eds. (Oxford, 2001), 111–44; on the Muslim resort to jihad, see Moshe Gammer, *Muslim Resistance to the Tsar:*

over a quarter century by tsarist forces against the mountain peoples of the north Caucasus, Russian administrators and Muslims frequently found themselves united against common foes.[7] Developed first, and most intensively, in the eastern provinces stretching from the Volga River and Ural Mountains into the steppe, these tactical alliances bound Muslims to tsarist institutions by offering protection to the defenders of "true religion" against "schismatics," "heretics," and others whose errors and innovations might corrupt the faithful. Over the course of the nineteenth century, the regime extended this patronage of Islamic orthodoxy to each newly conquered territory.

The tsarist regime achieved relative stability in managing these large Muslim populations on its southeastern frontiers not by repressing or ignoring Islam but by assuming responsibility for its policing. This article draws on court records, petitions, and denunciations from central and regional state archives as well as local Muslim accounts to show how the Russian state governed as patron and guardian of the faith of its Muslim subjects. Recent interpretations of the empire highlight the tensions between Russia's imperial and national identities, principally by exploring tsarist policy and educated Russians' images of non-Russians.[8] This article seeks to shift attention from questions of administration and representation to state-mediated conflicts among Muslims and other groups. The first part of this essay traces Russia's path to a confessional state committed to backing the construction and implementation of "orthodoxy" within each recognized religious community. Comparisons among Muslims, Protestants, Jews, Buddhists, and other groups suggest a broader pattern of interdependence between religious and state authorities. From the late eighteenth century, despite the close association between the Romanov dynasty and the Orthodox Church, these ties cut across confessional lines and endured into the early twentieth century, when they provided a crucial—but long overlooked—source of cohesion for a diverse polity confronted by divisive secular ideologies. The second part examines these developments more closely with respect to the Muslims of European and southeastern Russia, especially in the

---

Shamil and the Conquest of Chechnia and Daghestan (London, 1994); and Anna Zelkina, *In Quest for God and Freedom: The Sufi Response to the Russian Advance in the North Caucasus* (New York, 2000); and, more generally, the classic study by Rudolph Peters, *Islam and Colonialism: The Doctrine of Jihad in Modern History* (The Hague, 1979).

[7] In the Caucasus, Muslims also joined ranks with the Russians, sometimes directing tsarist formations against their enemies. See Firouzeh Mostashari, "Colonial Dilemmas: Russian Policies in the Muslim Caucasus," *Of Religion and Empire: Missions, Conversion, and Tolerance in Tsarist Russia*, Robert P. Geraci and Michael Khodarkovsky, eds. (Ithaca, N.Y., 2001), 229–49; V. O. Bobrovnikov, *Musul'mane Severnogo Kavkaza: Obychai, pravo, nasilie* (Moscow, 2002), esp. 46–51; and V. Lapin, "Natsional'nye formirovaniia v kavkazskoi voine," *Rossiia i Kavkaz skvoz' dva stoletiia*, G. G. Lisitsyna and Ia. A. Gordin, eds. (St. Petersburg, 2001), 108–25. On precedents for alliances between Muslims and Russian authorities aimed at other Muslims, see Michael Khodarkovsky, *Russia's Steppe Frontier: The Making of a Colonial Empire, 1500–1800* (Bloomington, Ind., 2002), esp. 37–39.

[8] See the innovative studies by Yuri Slezkine, *Arctic Mirrors: Russia and the Small Peoples of the North* (Ithaca, N.Y., 1994); Mark Bassin, *Imperial Visions: Nationalist Imagination and Geographical Expansion in the Russian Far East, 1840–1865* (Cambridge, 1999); Robert P. Geraci, *Window on the East: National and Imperial Identities in Late Tsarist Russia* (Ithaca, 2001); Theodore Weeks, *Nation and State in Late Imperial Russia: Nationalism and Russification on the Western Frontier, 1863–1914* (Dekalb, Ill., 1996); Austin Jersild, *Orientalism and Empire: North Caucasus Mountain Peoples and the Georgian Frontier, 1845–1917* (Montreal, 2002); and Andreas Kappeler, *Russland als Vielvölkerreich: Entstehung, Geschichte, Zerfall*, 2d edn. (Munich, 1993).

FIGURE 1: A mosque in the Bashkir village of Ekh'ia. Courtesy of the Prokudin-Gorskii Collection of the Library of Congress.

provinces straddling the Volga River and Ural Mountains.[9] It tells the story of how adherents of one religious tradition attempted to deploy the power of the state against their co-religionists to redefine the understanding of community and the content of religious orthodoxy. My aim is to illustrate how various actors understood—and competed to define—true religion and community in dynamic exchanges with the state, not prior to, or apart from, the imperial context but firmly within it.

Muslims seeking endorsement for their own views of religious orthodoxy found

[9] Valuable regional histories include Andreas Kappeler, *Russlands erste Nationalitäten: Das Zarenreich und die Völker der Mittleren Wolga vom 16. bis 19. Jahrhundert* (Cologne, 1982); Allen J. Frank, *Islamic Historiography and "Bulghar" Identity among the Tatars and Bashkirs of Russia* (Leiden, 1998); Paul W. Werth, *At the Margins of Orthodoxy: Mission, Governance, and Confessional Politics in Russia's Volga-Kama Region, 1827–1905* (Ithaca, N.Y., 2002); and Christian Noack, *Muslimischer Nationalismus im Russischen Reich: Nationsbildung und Nationalbewegung bei Tataren und Baschkiren, 1861–1917* (Stuttgart, 2000).

supporters in secular officials who valued Islam as a monotheistic source, albeit inferior to Orthodox Christianity, of stability, discipline, and order. Like the Muscovite litigation of honor disputes, the pursuit of religious struggles here forged a dynamic relationship between local communities and the judicial and policing institutions of the state.[10] But in the late eighteenth century, the state mediation of confessional differences formed a new instrumentality of imperial rule, not only over Muslims but over nearly all other non-Orthodox subjects.

While nationalist teleologies have tended to reduce imperial politics to a struggle between empire and the "nation," a closer examination of religious politics reveals a realm of imperial consciousness and state practice obscured by national frameworks and an anachronistic focus on "minorities." Diverse actors deployed police power to refashion non-Orthodox faiths as imperial traditions. Where non-Russians may have on occasion resisted tsarist taxation and conscription, the struggle for true religion established common interests between pious activists and the police. The faithful remade their communities by advancing new visions of religious orthodoxy and by deepening their integration in, and subordination to, the expanding institutions of the empire. Thus Muslims did not inhabit the static and isolated world depicted by Russian critics and reformers like Gasprinskii. Nor did they live within the confines of an unchanging Muslim tradition represented by clerics defending the faith against unlawful "innovation" (*bida*). The intense controversies that raged among Muslims over religious interpretation and identity extended beyond the elite circles that are so commonly the domain of Islamic history; indeed, as I will show, these conflicts not only engaged laypeople but also drew representatives of the tsarist regime into mediation of disputes over the meaning of Islamic tradition. The adjudication of intracommunal conflicts became a singularly important vehicle for the extension of state power into local life. Neither Islam nor any other religious tradition remained isolated or escaped entanglement with the regime, notwithstanding later nationalist claims that ethnicity served as a refuge against the incursions of the Russian government.

Tsarist religious politics took shape in the competitive international context of empire-building. Religious identities took on new meanings where states pursued imperial expansion as the extension of protection to co-religionists. Both the Orthodox tsar and Muslim sultan devised novel ways to accommodate subjects who shared the faith of their neighbors and European rivals. Ottoman attempts to counter European encroachment brought dramatic reforms in 1839 and 1856 designed to establish legal equality for Muslims and non-Muslims and to cultivate a supraconfessional loyalty to "Ottomanness" (*Osmanlılık*).[11] New European approaches to the utility of religion for state-building proved no less far-ranging in metropole and colony alike. Drawing on contemporary anthropology, many European elites shared the view that "religion" represented a universal determinant of human experience, which imposed certain moral constraints, to varying degrees, on its adherents everywhere. In the view of many late eighteenth and early nineteenth-

[10] Nancy Shields Kollmann, *By Honor Bound: State and Society in Early Modern Russia* (Ithaca, N.Y., 1999).
[11] See Bruce Masters, *Christians and Jews in the Ottoman Arab World: The Roots of Sectarianism* (Cambridge, 2001); and Gülnihâl Bozkurt, *Gayrimüslim Osmanlı Vatandaşlarının Hukuki Durumu (1839–1914)* (Ankara, 1989).

FIGURE 2: A scene depicting the environs of the town of Kazan on the Volga River, with a mosque and Orthodox Christian cathedrals in the background. Karl von Rechberg und Rothenlöwen, *Les peuples de la Russie*, vol. 1 (Paris, 1812). Courtesy of the Library of Congress.

century European officials, states could look to religious elites of diverse faiths as extensions of state authority, to instill moral behavior, social discipline, and submission to the general laws.[12]

Official backing for particular religious norms appeared to guarantee public order and personal morality, even while "superstitious" elements might simultaneously be selected for "reform." British Evangelicals sought out converts and the extirpation of "heathen" creeds in diverse imperial settings; however, many colonial administrators in India preferred to act as patrons of local shrines and mosques and undertook the scholarly study and codification of Hindu and Muslim legal traditions as the basis for personal status law.[13] Elsewhere, state recognition and incorporation of Jewish and Protestant consistories in France, the Jewish community in Habsburg Trieste, and the "four *millets*" in the Ottoman Empire provided these regimes with intermediary bodies that facilitated the expansion of centralizing regimes into local life and their colonization of the disciplinary functions of

[12] See Talal Asad, *Genealogies of Religion: Discipline and Reasons of Power in Christianity and Islam* (Baltimore, 1993), 27–54; and Lois C. Dubin, *The Port Jews of Habsburg Trieste: Absolutist Politics and Enlightenment Culture* (Stanford, Calif., 1999).

[13] The British remained implicated in the patronage of Muslim, Hindu, and other non-Christian religious institutions in India even *after* the colonial government responded to missionary pressure by affirming its policy of "non-interference" in law in 1863. See Peter van der Veer, *Imperial Encounters: Religion and Modernity in India and Britain* (Princeton, N.J., 2001), 21–23.

religious institutions.[14] Although the local configuration of these arrangements varied from state to state in the nineteenth century, the official institutionalization of religious difference frequently formed a useful modality of both imperial rule and nation-state formation. In turn, elites within these communities looked to the state to acquire new means to police communal boundaries and compel conformity. Where such overtures achieved official intervention, new conceptions of religious identity advanced with the expansion of the state.[15] In place of the romantic ideals of communal preservation and solidarity that historians tend to impose on their subjects, emerging notions of orthodoxy frequently forged ties between pious activists and the state and redrew the boundaries of community.

In Russia, these strategies inspired official sponsorship of an Islamic hierarchy. Drawing on the model of both the Orthodox Church and the Islamic establishment in the Ottoman Empire, Russian officials envisioned a domestic organizational structure for Islam that would lend religious authority to imperial policy and break Muslim ties to co-religionists abroad.[16] In 1788, Catherine founded the Orenburg Muhammadan Ecclesiastical Assembly, headed by a mufti (Islamic jurisconsult), in Ufa to assume responsibility for the administration of mosque communities throughout the Volga and Urals regions, Siberia, the capitals, and the steppe.[17] Muslim marriage, divorce, inheritance, clerical appointments, and other matters relating to Islamic law became objects of bureaucratic regulation. The regime looked to the Orenburg Assembly to bind Muslims through their faith to the Russian fatherland and Romanov dynasty but soon discovered that this hierarchy exercised authority over other Muslims *only* with the support of the state.

---

[14] Paula E. Hyman, *The Jews of Modern France* (Berkeley, Calif., 1998), 37–52; C. T. McIntire, "Changing Religious Establishments and Religious Liberty in France, Part I: 1787–1879," in *Freedom and Religion in the Nineteenth Century*, Richard Helmstadter, ed. (Stanford, Calif., 1997), 233–72; Dubin, *Port Jews*; Avigdor Levy, ed., *The Jews of the Ottoman Empire* (Princeton, N.J., 1994); and Kurt Nowak, *Geschichte des Christentums in Deutschland: Religion, Politik und Gesellschaft vom Ende der Aufklärung bis zur Mitte des 20. Jahrhunderts* (Munich, 1995), 64–93.

[15] See, for example, Bozkurt, *Gayrimüslim Osmanlı Vatandaşlarının Hukukî Durumu*, 24; David C. Itzkowitz, "The Jews of Europe and the Limits of Religious Freedom," in Helmstadter, *Freedom and Religion in the Nineteenth Century*, 150–71; and Lata Mani, "Contentious Traditions: The Debate on SATI in Colonial India," *Cultural Critique* 7 (Fall 1987): 119–56. Such contests for patronage and legitimacy for competing interpretations of "tradition" also resemble the elaboration of "customary law" analyzed in Martin Chanock, *Law, Custom and Social Order: The Colonial Experience in Malawi and Zambia* (Cambridge, 1985); and Ronald Robinson, "Non-European Foundations of European Imperialism: Sketch for a Theory of Collaboration," in *Studies in the Theory of Imperialism*, Roger Owen and Bob Sutcliffe, eds. (London, 1972), 117–42.

[16] Eighteenth-century Russian representations of Islam drew on Orthodox ecclesiology and, following European images, equated contemporary Ottoman institutions with Islamic norms. See F. A. Emin, *Kratkoe opisanie drevneishego i noveishogo sostoianiia Ottomanskoi Porty* (St. Petersburg, 1769); and an anonymous European work translated from Latin, *Sokrashchenie Magometanskoi very* (Moscow, 1784). Nineteenth-century Muslims also acknowledged the Ottoman model for the tsarist Islamic hierarchy. See Shihabetdin Märjani, *Möstäfadel-äkhbar fi äkhvali Kazan vä Bolgar (Kazan häm Bolgar khällere turinda faydalanılgan khäbärler)*, Ä. N. Khäyrullin, ed. (Kazan, 1989), 209.

[17] For a thorough study of this institution, see D. D. Azamatov, *Orenburgskoe Magometanskoe Dukhovnoe Sobranie v kontse XVIII–XIX vv.* (Ufa, 1999). Known in Russian as the *Orenburgskoe Magometanskoe Dukhovnoe Sobranie*, Tatar sources referred to it variously as the *Orenburg idare-i shariyya* (Orenburg Shari'a Administration), *Orenburg mahkemesi* (Orenburg Court), or *Orenburg sobraniesi* (Orenburg Assembly). It later served as a model for a regional hierarchy for the Crimea in 1794 and two separate administrations for Sunnis and Shi'ites in the Caucasus in the nineteenth century. On the latter institutions, see Mostashari, "Colonial Dilemmas." However, the regime retreated from this policy in the conquest and administration of the Muslims of Turkestan after 1865.

The formalization of these arrangements under Nicholas I yielded unintended consequences for Muslims and tsarist officials alike. Provisional alliances frequently rested on the imaginative translation of religious concepts from one tradition to another. Russians could see in Islam a familiar, if imperfect, faith that recognized "eight commandments" and the "Seven Deadly Sins," while Muslim petitioners could appeal to an image of a state that had offered them "protection" for 300 years and had always afforded them "freedom of religion, without the slightest constraint."[18] Muslim calls for state intervention in intracommunal disputes yielded a crucial mechanism for state expansion but also made Russian officials responsible for backing Islamic doctrine and propping up Muslim authorities whom they often mistrusted. Crossing confessional lines on behalf of true religion, Muslim activists drew the state deeper into local life. These exchanges among elites, laypeople, and state officials undermined and reconfigured the boundaries between state and society. Muslim subjects created novel forms of community not against but *with* the state. On occasion, Muslim villagers and townspeople warned that their Christian rulers threatened the survival of the faith by supporting Orthodox missions.[19] But more frequently, the threat to true religion came from within the camp of the believers themselves. Rather than disrupt imperial rule, the pursuit of Islamic orthodoxy formed an essential foundation of tsarist state-building on the southeastern frontiers of the empire.

FORMAL PROTECTIONS FOR ISLAM and other non-Orthodox faiths came only under Catherine II, who introduced a new paradigm of toleration designed to make religious discipline useful to the empire and to project imperial power on its frontiers. But this mode of toleration did not mean official indifference or neutrality toward non-Orthodox religious affairs. In the tradition of the "well-ordered police state" (*Polizeistaat*), the regime became directly involved in the regulation of central aspects of religious life in nearly every community.[20] For Catherine and her successors, the treatment of each faith depended on its utility to the state; its contribution to the maintenance of empire defined the scope of toleration. The tsars increasingly relied on Orthodoxy as a symbol of the national character of the monarchy, and some bureaucrats shared the church's view that conversion to the tsar's religion represented a testament of loyalty to the state.[21] But in the wake of

---

[18] *Sokrashchenie Magometanskoi very*; Rossiiskii Gosudarstvennyi Istoricheskii Arkhiv (hereafter, RGIA), f. 821, op. 8, d. 1078, ll. 445–445 ob. For similar language, see the petition reprinted in *Materialy po istorii Tatarii vtoroi poloviny XIX veka: Agrarnyi vopros i krest'ianskoe dvizhenie 50–70-kh godov XIX v.* (Moscow and Leningrad, 1936), 166.

[19] See Werth, *At the Margins of Orthodoxy*; and Geraci and Khodarkovsky, *Of Religion and Empire*.

[20] On this regulatory toleration, see Marc Raeff, *The Well-Ordered Police State: Social and Institutional Change through Law in the Germanies and Russia, 1600–1800* (New Haven, Conn., 1983), esp. 57; Karl Schwarz, "Vom Nutzen einer Christlichen Toleranz für den Staat: Bemerkungen zum Stellenwert der Religion bei den Spätkameralisten Justi und Sonnenfels," in *Im Zeichen der Toleranz: Aufsätze zur Toleranzgesetzgebung des 18. Jahrhunderts im Reiche Josephe II, ihren Voraussetzungen und ihren Folgen*, Peter F. Barton, ed. (Vienna, 1981), esp. 86–89; and Ole Peter Grell and Roy Porter, eds., *Toleration in Enlightenment Europe* (Cambridge, 2000).

[21] Tsarist law backed the monopoly of the Orthodox Church on proselytization and obliged its monarchs to profess Orthodoxy. It permitted only Protestants and Catholics to convert non-Christians under specific circumstances and with explicit state approval. See *Svod zakonov Rossiiskoi imperii,*

revolutionary events in Europe, the regime looked to compulsory submission to state-regulated religious institutions, even in non-Orthodox forms, as a safeguard against revolution in Russia, viewing religious conformity as the cornerstone of morality and public order and as a measure of its subjects' political attitudes.[22] Unlike elsewhere in Europe, tsarist law never permitted its subjects to renounce confessional allegiance and declare themselves "without a confession" (*konfessionslos*). Obligatory enrollment in a religious community brought nearly all subjects under the bureaucratic supervision of an official hierarchy.[23] The policing of morality thus remained the responsibility both of officially recognized ecclesiastical authorities and of the state. As Mikhail Speranskii, the influential adviser to Alexander I, noted in 1803, in ancient Rome, and "everywhere in well-ordered states," "preventive police" concerned themselves with censorship, public decorum, the suppression of "rumors and interpretations harmful to the government," and "the safeguarding of the rites of religion and the curbing of schisms."[24]

Under Nicholas I, new legal codes declared Orthodox Christianity the "preeminent and predominant" faith of the empire but also systematically backed other religions on the premise that "all peoples inhabiting Russia praise Almighty God in different languages according to the creed and confession of their forefathers, blessing the reign of the Russian Monarchs, and praying to the Creator of the universe for the increase of the prosperity and strengthening of the power of the Empire."[25] Court records, petitions, and denunciations reveal how, in largely secret proceedings, the state became deeply enmeshed in intraconfessional disputes as the guardian and patron of religious "orthodoxy" for the tolerated faiths of Islam, Catholicism, Protestantism, Judaism, Buddhism, and both branches of Armenian Christianity.[26] As Laura Engelstein has shown, Nicholas's government here acted as "the defender of absolute values in a world of revolutionary change." Like the regime's new efforts aimed at "disciplining the boundaries of true belief" among the

---

izdaniia 1857 goda, vol. 11, part 1 (St. Petersburg, 1857), 6. The state also backed Orthodox claims of church unity against the Uniate Church, which St. Petersburg absorbed into the state church in 1839; however, the Uniate Church in Poland was not affected until 1875. See Theodore R. Weeks, "Between Rome and Tsargrad: The Uniate Church in Imperial Russia," in Geraci and Khodarkovsky, *Of Religion and Empire*, 70–91.

[22] Paul I extended his patronage to the Jesuit order "to arrest the flood of impiety, illuminism, and ... Jacobinism." Without a Jesuit education for his subjects, the tsar warned, "everything will collapse, and there will not remain either religion or government." Quoted in William A. James, "The Jesuits' Role in Founding Schools in Late Tsarist Russia," in *Religious and Secular Forces in Late Tsarist Russia: Essays in Honor of Donald W. Treadgold*, Charles E. Timberlake, ed. (Seattle, 1992), 59.

[23] Tsarist law recognized "paganism" (*iazychestvo*) as a tolerated faith but declined to lend institutional support to these communities or protect them from Orthodox proselytism. Dissenters from the Orthodox Church also formed an exception to this pattern, although officials proposed various schemes to subject them to hierarchical organization. See also Laura Engelstein, "The Dream of Civil Society in Tsarist Russia: Law, State, and Religion," in *Civil Society before Democracy: Lessons from Nineteenth-Century Europe*, Nancy Bermeo and Philip Nord, eds. (Lanham, Md., 2000), 23–41.

[24] M. M. Speranskii, *Proekty i zapiski* (Moscow, 1961), 92–94.

[25] *Svod zakonov Rossiiskoi imperii*, vol. 1 (St. Petersburg, 1832), xvii–xviii.

[26] *Svod zakonov Rossiiskoi imperii*, xvi; and *Svod zakonov Rossiiskoi imperii*, 1857 edn., vol. 11, part 1 (St. Petersburg, 1857), 5. By 1858, Muslims (with a population well over 4.1 million) likely outnumbered Catholics as the largest non-Orthodox community in the empire. This conservative estimate includes partial figures on Kazakh nomads but largely excudes the Muslim population of the Caucasus, based on V. M. Kabuzan, *Narody Rossii v pervoi polovine XIX v.: Chislennost' i etnicheskii sostav* (Moscow, 1992).

Orthodox, its adoption of regulatory measures to ensure conformity in other communities made up another dimension of the tsarist "project of administrative modernization."[27]

Officials endorsed other faiths' capacity to order the family, instill morality, and guarantee the overlap of religious and worldly sanction for transgressions against temporal authority.[28] Confessional communities that subjected followers to divine as well as monarchical judgment provided useful forms of social discipline to complement the will of the sovereign. Despite rebellion in 1830–1831 in Poland, for example, F. F. Berg, the governor-general of the Kingdom of Poland and a Protestant, continued to regard Catholicism as "sometimes very useful for the government, because it helps it keep the people in check."[29] The *Digest of Laws* made this connection between religious orthodoxy and political loyalty clear in its instruction to rabbis "to explain to Jews their law . . . and make them understand . . . [its] true meaning" and to "direct Jews to observe moral obligations [and] to obey the general state laws and established authorities."[30] Moreover, the state appointed mullahs, priests, pastors, and rabbis to attend to the spiritual needs (and obligations) of non-Orthodox soldiers, sailors, and prisoners.

In extending toleration, Russian bureaucrats nonetheless retained the authority to intervene in areas that they claimed in the name of the state, including questions of dogma, ritual, and ecclesiastical organization. *Polizeistaat* toleration supported

---

[27] Laura Engelstein, *Castration and the Heavenly Kingdom: A Russian Folktale* (Ithaca, N.Y., 1999), 50–51. Even the architect of "Orthodoxy, Autocracy, and Nationality," Sergei Uvarov, viewed the major non-Orthodox traditions as essential supports of the political order. In a key proposal, Uvarov did not refer to "Orthodoxy" but to "religion" or *religion nationale*. Andrei Zorin, "Ideologiia 'Pravoslaviia—samoderzhaviia—narodnosti': Opyt rekonstruktsii," *Novoe literaturnoe obozrenie* 26 (1997): 71–104.

[28] The Orthodox leadership and some secular officials remained critical of state policy, but many Russians were inclined to stress the commonalities rather than the differences between Catholicism and Orthodoxy. The extent of rapprochement ranged from mixed marriages and the conversion of aristocratic men and women to Catholicism to proposals for union between the churches. A. I. Turgenev, the first director of the Department of Religious Affairs of Foreign Confessions and a graduate of the Protestant university at Göttingen, harbored aspirations to make Orthodox and Protestants feel themselves "citizens of one world, one church." Such sentiments found expression in Alexander I's decree directing all Protestants to commemorate the Reformation on the tercentenary of Martin Luther's Ninety-Five Theses in 1817; as in Prussia, the occasion marked the ascendancy of those in favor of unifying the Protestant churches. See L. E. Gorizontov, *Paradoksy imperskoi politiki: Poliaki v Rossii i russkie v Pol'she* (Moscow, 1999); Albert M. Ammann, *Abriss der ostslawischen Kirchengeschichte* (Vienna, 1950); Igor Smolitsch, *Geschichte der russischen Kirche*, vol. 2, Gregory L. Freeze, ed., *Forschungen zur Osteuropäischen Geschichte*, vol. 45 (1991); E. A. Vishlenkova, *Religioznaia politika: Ofitsial'nyi kurs i 'obshchee mnenie' Rossii aleksandrovskoi epokhi* (Kazan, 1997), 138; and Erik Amburger, *Geschichte des Protestantismus in Russland* (Stuttgart, 1961), 68.

[29] Blaming the "disturbances" of 1848 in Europe on "the lack of religion," Nicholas I encouraged Catholic bishops to "work to instill the faith" against the evils of civil unrest and divorce. "Ecclesiastical authority is separate from temporal [authority]," he added, "but I do not want to limit [the former], on the contrary I desire that it function in all of its power." Gorizontov, *Paradoksy*, 81–82, 238–39. After the government implicated Catholic clergy in the rebellion of 1863, repressions focused primarily on the "Polish element"; the Ministry of the Interior took care to restaff this clergy, though with German seminary students. *Izvlechenie iz otcheta Ministra vnutrennikh del za 1861, 1862 i 1863* (St. Petersburg, 1865), 187–88.

[30] *Svod zakonov*, vol. 11, part 1, 201. The 1836 statute for the Armenian Gregorian Church instructed its archbishops to "monitor the religious behavior of their subordinates and parishioners to assure that it corresponds to the teachings of the gospels" and to "encourage good acts among their subjects, filling them with the spirit of Christ." *Russia and the Armenians of Transcaucasia, 1797–1889: A Documentary Record*, trans. and commentary by George A. Bournoutian (Costa Mesa, Calif., 1998), 359.

religion only in its canonical and, where appropriate, "enlightened" forms. The law excluded sectarians, atheists, and "free-thinkers," as well as those who exceeded the boundaries of "moderation" in their piety.[31] The architects of the first Islamic hierarchy assigned it the task of monitoring the "Muhammadan law" so that "superstition and other abuses, which cannot be tolerated, do not creep into" its affairs.[32] The criminal code protected official non-Orthodox rites from interference, but religion that strayed beyond clerical direction and the approved canon of texts, prayers, and songs threatened the moral and social order.[33] Who determined the content of "orthodoxy" within each tradition and who figured as a "heretic" became a matter of critical importance for imperial officials, religious authorities, and laypeople.

Such policies of toleration figure prominently in analyses that attempt to account for the durability and relative strength of the empire. Andreas Kappeler argues that, from the Muscovite period well into the nineteenth century, the tsars maintained a pragmatic regard for the status quo by coopting indigenous elites into the ruling apparatus and accommodating local customs, beliefs, and laws.[34] Kappeler's influential view of the accommodationist imperial ethos reflects accurately the intentions of Russian authorities. But the perspective of the communities themselves suggests that the institutional and legal architecture for toleration did not simply confer and maintain the autonomy of established elites. Officials sought out for cooptation individuals whom they took to be the leaders of these communities; however, the search for cooperative elites embroiled them in questions of dogmatic, ritual, and legal interpretation. The prospect of support for particular positions initiated intense competition for patronage within these divided communities. Indigenous mediators between community and state who earned official backing often lacked legitimacy within their own communities. The state did not confirm religious notables in traditional roles as much as it created new elites. State backing confirmed some customary prerogatives, but many of the "traditional" rights for which clerics sought support were, in fact, novel. Patronage enabled Muhammadzhan Husainov, the first mufti, Stanislaus Siestrzeńcewicz, the Catholic metropolitan, and Iraklii Lisovskii and Joseph Semashko, metropolitans of the Uniate Church, as well as the Armenian primates Ep'rem and Hovhannēs to claim an unprecedented degree of power over their rivals and competing interpretations of their faiths. Confronted with the opposition of other clerics, laypeople, and

---

[31] In this vein, the state instructed official prelates to "avoid intolerance and undue strictness." See Bournoutian, *Russia and the Armenians*, 359. "Excessive" piety also met with police intervention elsewhere in Europe. See Ruth Harris, *Lourdes: Body and Spirit in the Secular Age* (New York, 1999); David Blackbourn, *Marpingen: Apparitions of the Virgin Mary in Bismarckian Germany* (Oxford, 1993); and, more generally, Werner Conze and Helga Reinhart, "Fanatismus," in *Geschichtliche Grundbegriffe: Historiches Lexicon zur politisch-sozialen Sprache in Deutschland*, Otto Brunner, Werner Conze, and Reinhart Kosseleck, eds., Band 2 (Stuttgart, 1975), 303–27.

[32] *Materialy po istorii Bashkirskoi ASSR*, vol. 5 (Moscow, 1960), 563–66.

[33] Thus Protestants could gather for "private prayer assemblies," but only with the permission of ecclesiastical and civil authorities. They had to forego preaching and sacraments and confine themselves to "the reading of Holy Scripture without any commentary . . . and the singing of religious songs, or the saying of prayers, . . . approved by the Consistories" to avoid giving cause to "reprehensible schisms in Christian society." *Svod zakonov*, vol. 11, part 1, 34.

[34] Kappeler maintains that the "closed social- and value-systems [of non-Russians] remained largely intact into the nineteenth century even after centuries of Russian rule and despite close interactions with Russians." *Russland als Vielvölkerreich*, 137.

superiors in Rome, Jerusalem, and elsewhere, the authority of these new elites rested less on clerical or lay consensus than on police power.[35]

The regime conferred new privileges on each confessional elite while subjecting it to more formal supervision. Following the consistorial model established in Napoleonic France, Russian officials sought to maximize the contribution of religion to morality and respect for authority by incorporating its leadership directly into the state. In 1810, Alexander I created the Main Administration of the Religious Affairs of Foreign Confessions. This office (later a department in the Ministry of the Interior) took on the arbitration of controversies within "foreign" faith communities and bolstered the authority of state-approved clerics as the guardians of morality, the presumed foundation of public order.[36] To this end, many members of these new "clergies" received exemption from corporal punishment. The state imposed financial obligations on them but also created new positions of power and cultural control, such as the censorship of religious literature.[37] It enlisted Jewish communal government, the *kahal*, in the enforcement of laws against the contraband, even permitting the imposition of the rabbinic ban (the *herem*, formally prohibited in 1804) against smugglers. In 1827, the government capitalized on religious and communal bonds by making the *kahal* responsible for the selection of recruits because, as Eli Lederhendler observes, the authorities assumed that Jews "could be expected to heed their own rabbis and leaders even when they disregarded the laws of the Christian state."[38] Like the Orthodox clergy, these clerics acted as adjuncts of state authority, discharging bureaucratic duties and performing the "useful" task of preaching submission to Russian law.

Under Nicholas I, the state consolidated a multiconfessional elite that shared significant resources and ambitious plans for amplifying the powers of central

[35] On the first mufti's efforts to overcome Muslim opposition to the authority of this new institution, see Gosudarstvennyi Arkhiv Orenburgskoi Oblasti (hereafter, GAOO), f. 6, op. 3, d. 4744, d. 2411, and d. 3277. See also Bournoutian, *Russia and the Armenians*, 74–77, 197–98, and 342–43; and N. Varadinov, *Istoriia Ministerstva vnutrennikh del*, part 2, book 1 (St. Petersburg, 1859), 411–14. Albert M. Ammann places Lisovskii alongside Siestrzeńcewicz as representatives of "Gallican-Josephinist" thought. *Abriss*, 467.

[36] In 1817, this body merged with the Ministry of Education to form the Ministry of Religious Affairs and Education; from 1832, it functioned as a department in the Ministry of the Interior. Erik Amburger, *Geschichte der Behördenorganisation Russlands von Peter dem Grossen bis 1917* (Leiden, 1966), 176–77; and Vishlenkova, *Religioznaia politika*. On challenges to established traditions, see Michael Kemper, *Sufis und Gelehrte in Tatarien und Baschkirien, 1789–1889: Der islamische Diskurs unter russischer Herrschaft* (Berlin, 1998); Werth, *At the Margins of Orthodoxy*; Eli Lederhendler, *The Road to Modern Jewish Politics: Political Tradition and Political Reconstruction in the Jewish Community of Tsarist Russia* (New York, 1989); and Amburger, *Geschichte des Protestantismus*.

[37] The privilege of exemption for Muslim clerics was limited to the mufti and highest officials of the Islamic hierarchies. In 1835, Jewish rabbis who had fulfilled their duties "without reproach" for a three-year period were freed from corporal punishment; however, in the Crimea, only the head of the Karaim (Turkic-speaking Jews) was exempt. From 1853, the Buddhist "clergy" was also freed from the knout. Even though few non-military clerics received a state salary, the regime made their communities responsible for paying taxes and other obligations for them. *Svod zakonov*, vol. 11, part 1, 203, 206. On censorship, see A. G. Karimullin, *U istokov tatarskoi knigi (ot nachala vozniknoveniia do 60-kh godov XIX veka)* (Kazan, 1971); NART, f. 1, op. 2, d. 483; Lederhendler, *Road to Modern Jewish Politics*, 49; and N. Barsov, "Katolicheskaia tserkov' v sovremennoi Rossii," *Entsiklopedicheskii slovar' Brokgauz-Efrona*, vol. 14 (1895), 740. Orthodox censors also monitored literature that polemicized with the Orthodox or supported proselytization. See A. Kotovich, *Dukhovnaia tsenzura v Rossii (1799–1855 gg.)* (St. Petersburg, 1909), 520–23.

[38] Lederhendler, *Road to Modern Jewish Politics*, 48–50; and Michael Stanislawski, *Tsar Nicholas I and the Jews: The Transformation of Jewish Society in Russia, 1825–1855* (Philadelphia, 1983).

authorities to discipline religious life through bureaucratic and police controls. The regime acquiesced to the mufti's claim that his judicial opinions (*fatwas*) bound all Muslims.[39] When the state empowered Jewish lay and rabbinic elites to implement the conscription of Jews, many used their new power to advance the cause of piety, targeting vagrants, poor families, as well as violators of Jewish law for the draft.[40] State-sponsored reorganization tended toward the centralization of ecclesiastical authority, religious opinion, and wealth, paralleling the institutional transformation under way in the Russian Orthodox establishment and in other churches throughout Europe.[41]

The state benefited from internal contests for religious authority and local initiatives for state patronage against rivals. The regime found Catholics willing to reorganize the church to resemble the French and Habsburg churches, which enjoyed significant independence from the Holy See.[42] Rivalries for supremacy within the Armenian Church involved clerics in Russia, the Ottoman Empire, India, and Iran. In supporting candidates to the office of the patriarchate at Etchmiadzin, tsarist diplomats saw an opportunity not only to cultivate notables with pro-Russian sympathies but also to create an institution with authority over Armenians in neighboring states. St. Petersburg backed local claims to represent "the entire Armenian nation" against skeptical subordinates in Russia and competitors in Jerusalem and Istanbul.[43]

Similarly, the regime assembled the varied Protestant churches in the empire under an "Evangelical Church," although it favored the Lutheranism of the Baltic German nobles. The statute of 1832 created a general consistorial regime but only intensified local doctrinal and social conflicts. Its endorsement of Lutheran dogma

---

[39] In 1815 and 1818, the first mufti, Muhammadzhan Husainov, asserted in reports to Russian authorities that "whoever scorns the decision and *fatwa* of a mufti should not be considered a Muslim." GAOO, f. 6, op. 4, d. 8085, ll. 49–49 ob. and 69 ob. See also the exhortations from Muslim authorities in *Sbornik tsirkuliariov i inykh rukovodiashchikh rasporiazhenii po okrugu Orenburgskogo Magometanskogo Dukhovnogo Sobraniia 1836–1903 g.* (Ufa, 1905).

[40] Stanislawski, *Tsar Nicholas I and the Jews*, 29.

[41] See David W. Edwards, "The System of Nicholas I in Church-State Relations," *Russian Orthodoxy under the Old Regime*, Robert L. Nichols and Theofanis George Stavrou, eds. (Minneapolis, 1978); and Paraskevas Konortas, "From Tâ'ife to Millet: Ottoman Terms for the Ottoman Greek Orthodox Community," in *Ottoman Greeks in the Age of Nationalism: Politics, Economy, and Society in the Nineteenth Century*, Dimitri Gondicas and Charles Issawi, eds. (Princeton, N.J., 1999), 169–79.

[42] Without consulting Rome, Catherine elevated Stanislaus Siestrzeńcewicz to the post of "bishop of all Catholics in Russia." She also ignored the papal decree of 1773 dissolving the Jesuit Order, making Russia a refuge for Jesuits fleeing other lands. In 1815, St. Petersburg expelled the order from the capitals and banned them from the empire in 1820 (with the exception of the Kingdom of Poland) after Orthodox nobles converted to Catholicism under their direction. Catholics also differed over the printing and distribution of vernacular editions of the Bible by the supra-confessional Russian Bible Society. Pius VII not only declined the tsar's invitation to join the Holy Alliance but also rebuked Siestrzeńcewicz for permitting Bibles in Polish without annotations prescribed by the Council of Trent. Dmitrii A. Tolstoi, *Rimskii Katolitsizm v Rossii: Istoricheskoe izsledovanie*, vol. 2 (St. Petersburg, 1876), 157–60; Vishlenkova, *Religioznaia politika*, 156–58; Ammann, *Abriss*, 440–41, 457–58, and 461–66; Smolitsch, *Geschichte der russischen Kirche*, 365; and Judith Cohen Zacek, "The Russian Bible Society and the Catholic Church," *Canadian Slavic Studies* 5, no. 1 (Spring 1971): 35–50.

[43] Bournoutian, *Russia and the Armenians*, 76–77, 456–61. In Georgia, by contrast, the Holy Synod claimed jurisdiction over the Orthodox, despite Georgian efforts to defend the church as a self-governing body. In 1811, the synod oversaw the absorption of the Georgian Church into the Russian Orthodox establishment. Nikolas K. Gvozdev, "The Russian Empire and the Georgian Orthodox Church in the First Decades of Imperial Rule, 1801–1830," *Central Asian Survey* 14, no. 3 (1995): 407–23.

sparked controversy in mixed Lutheran and Reformed communities on the Volga and in southern Russia, dividing congregations over the form of altars, crosses, and the singing of prayers.[44] Against this consistorial system and the standardizing texts and liturgy of the 1832 statute, charismatic preachers inspired movements that broke away in anticipation of Christ's imminent second coming and the end of the world. To counter these "separatists" and "superstitious sects," Nicholas backed the Protestant "orthodoxy" defined by the general consistory.[45]

And while the state supported Orthodox missions to dissenters, Muslims, and "pagans" from the late 1820s, conversionary efforts principally targeted apostates from Orthodoxy.[46] Buddhists, Muslims, and Jews who engaged in religious disputes with their co-religionists continued to seek—and receive—support for their views within the bureaucracy. In the case of Buddhism, alliances between officials searching for loyal authorities approximating a "church" and monastic elites seeking state backing transformed local hierarchies. In 1853, Nicholas I approved a centralized apparatus in Eastern Siberia to oversee these temples and their "clergy."[47]

The implications of such measures proved most dramatic for traditions that did not depend on an internally established hierarchical organization. For the Ministry of the Interior, determining what constituted "orthodox" opinion proved even more difficult when its officials could not look to an institution resembling a church structure. Judaism and Islam presented the state with very similar dilemmas. Officials scrutinized Jewish affairs with an eye to cultivating a form of Judaism that would be "useful" to both the Jews and the state. The Nicholaevan regime thus took steps to educate and institute an enlightened rabbinate. Reared in state institutions, "learned Jews" (*uchenye evrei*) and crown rabbis would supply officials with authoritative knowledge about Jewish law and perform some of the same disciplinary tasks as Muslim clerics. A Rabbinical Commission established in 1848 acted, like the Orenburg Assembly, as the highest authority on the religious law. In Muslim communities, legislation inspired by Orthodox ecclesiology set apart an ecclesiastical elite from lay society and extended the power of the former over the latter. In each "parish" (*prikhod*), the regime aimed at consolidating a formal "Muhammadan clergy" (*dukhovenstvo*) from among a group of men previously

---

[44] Amburger, *Geschichte des Protestantismus*, 88–89, 178–79.

[45] In the mid-1840s, the dependence of the Evangelical Church on the regime was demonstrated when the government broke from Lutheran opinion by accommodating separatists and by permitting the Orthodox archbishop of Riga to convert some 100,000 Latvian and Estonian peasants. Over the protests of the general consistory, the state recognized the Württembergers; it also confirmed toleration for Mennonites and extended it to the Baptists after 1879. Amburger, *Geschichte des Protestantismus*, 88–95; and *Izvlechenie iz otcheta Ministra vnutrennikh del za 1835 god* (St. Petersburg, 1836), 49–50.

[46] See the insightful Werth, *At the Margins of Orthodoxy*.

[47] In Transbaikal, the empress Anna had cultivated a church-like office, a "head" for Buriat lamas accountable to St. Petersburg rather than to Mongolia, Tibet, or China; the measure increased rivalries among local temples. See K. M. Gerasimova, *Lamaizm i natsional'no-kolonia'naia politika tsarizma v Zabaikal'e v XIX i nachale XX vekov* (Ulan-Ude, 1957), 44; E. S. Safronova, *Buddizm v Rossii* (Moscow, 1998), 44; Dittmar Schorkowitz, *Staat und Nationalitäten in Russland: Der Integrationsprozess der Burjaten und Kalmücken, 1822–1925* (Stuttgart, 2001); and Varadinov, *Istoriia Ministerstva vnutrennikh del*, part 3, book 2 (1862), 256–59. For criticism of state policy toward Buddhism, see Evstafii Voronets, *Russkim-li pravitel'stvom uzakoneno inozemnoe idolopoklonnicheskoe lamstvo v pravoslavnoi Rossii?* (Khar'kov, 1889).

distinguished only by their learning and their standing in the eyes of local communities.⁴⁸ The state assigned monopolies over the performance of marriage and divorce, the rites of burial, and the administration of oaths for state service, legal transactions, and witness testimony. Prohibitions against involvement in trade and other activities formalized and professionalized the clerical status of mullahs and rabbis. Some of these newly appointed clerics evaded attempts to limit their livelihoods, while others welcomed assistance against laypeople (and lower clerics) who performed marriages, burials, or other duties outside of their legal purview.⁴⁹

Non-Orthodox clerics likewise fulfilled a wide range of bureaucratic and social functions that complemented state undertakings in the realm of charity, welfare, and education, overseeing poorhouses, soup kitchens, orphanages, and hospitals.⁵⁰ Confessional schools and religious courts played a pivotal role in the imperial educational and judicial systems. Like Islamic courts, the Jewish *beth-din* dealt with marriage, divorce, inheritance, commerce, and contracts. Such institutions administered oaths to soldiers, witnesses, and litigants, demonstrating that the Orthodox creed was not the only pledge of political loyalty recognized by the state.⁵¹ For criminal offenses, subjects answered to both state and ecclesiastical officials; they were subject not only to secular punishment but to "penitence," "admonition," and other sanctions administered by religious personnel.⁵²

The non-Orthodox faiths played a critical role in disciplining the family. Just as the Orthodox Church regulated marriage to ensure domestic tranquility as a foundation of the political order, the Ministry of the Interior expected non-Orthodox leaders to exert similar controls.⁵³ Endowed with unprecedented police powers, the new clergies monitored compliance with statutes establishing minimum

---

⁴⁸ A system of licensing circumscribed membership in a male clerical estate. The hierarchy tested the qualifications of prayer-leaders, judges, teachers, and other mosque functionaries. Only clerics with a license (*ukaz*) from the assembly and the approval of Russian officials were permitted to perform these functions legally. Nonetheless, many itinerant prayer-leaders, preachers, and Sufi guides remained beyond the control of this system. In 1829, fewer than half of the imams in the 129 mosques of the district of Kazan had a license. Kemper, *Sufis und Gelehrte*, 43. Similar regulation came later to Jewish communities. From 1857, only graduates of government schools could be legally selected as rabbis, but unofficial rabbis continued to officiate.

⁴⁹ See Rizaeddin Fahreddinev, *Menasıb-ı diniye* (Orenburg, 1910), for an influential jurist's statement of the exclusive rights and duties of licensed Muslim clerics.

⁵⁰ Simon Dixon, "The Church's Social Role in St. Petersburg, 1880–1914," in *Church, Nation, and State in Russia and Ukraine*, Geoffrey A. Hosking, ed. (London, 1991), 167–92; Adele Lindenmeyr, *Poverty Is Not a Vice: Charity, Society, and the State in Imperial Russia* (Princeton, N.J., 1996); Amburger, *Geschichte des Protestantismus*, 166–70; and Heinz-Dietrich Löwe, "Von 'Mildtätigkeit' zu 'Sozialpolitik': Jüdische Selbsthilfe in Russland 1860–1917," in *Aufbruch der Gesellschaft im verordneten Staat: Russland in der Spätphase des Zarenreiches*, Heiko Haumann and Stefan Plaggenborg, eds. (Frankfurt am Main, 1994), 98–118.

⁵¹ Isaac Levitats, *The Jewish Community in Russia, 1772–1844* (New York, 1943), 200–04.

⁵² See, for example, the treatment of a Muslim woman found guilty of adultery in 1849 in Tsentral'nyi Gosudarstvennyi Istoricheskii Arkhiv Respubliki Bashkortostan (hereafter, TsGIARB), f. 1-295, op. 2, d. 43, ll. 755–56 ob. On the punishment of moral offenses in other communities, see Levitats, *Jewish Community in Russia*, 213–14; Gregory L. Freeze, "The Wages of Sin: The Decline of Public Penance in Imperial Russia," in Stephen K. Batalden, ed., *Seeking God: The Recovery of Religious Identity in Orthodox Russia, Ukraine, and Georgia* (Dekalb, Ill., 1993), 53–82; Laura Engelstein, *The Keys to Happiness: Sex and the Search for Modernity in Fin-de-Siècle Russia* (Ithaca, N.Y., 1992), 17–55; and for a contemporary critique of state involvement, M. A. Reisner, *Gosudarstvo i veruiushchaia lichnost': Sbornik statei* (St. Petersburg, 1905).

⁵³ Gregory Freeze, "Bringing Order to the Russian Family: Marriage and Divorce in Imperial Russia, 1760–1860," *Journal of Modern History* 62, no. 4 (December 1990): 709–46. The 1857 edition

ages for marriage, as well as questions of legitimacy, fidelity, incest, and the submission of children to parents. Far from autonomous actors, these authorities remained vulnerable to challenges from both the state and the laity. Officials intervened in marriage disputes at the request of dissatisfied litigants and overturned the rulings of these authorities.[54] Through these new instruments and the appellate mechanisms that linked them to central judicial organs, religious and secular authorities expanded their power to regulate family life. At the same time, this mediating role increased their knowledge about, and access to, local communities, enabling them to police many contacts between confessional groups and proscribe most kinds of intermarriage.[55]

While the administration provided new mechanisms of social control, the law reinforced clerical dependence on secular power by prohibiting existing mechanisms for compelling conformity, such as the rabbinic resort to punishment "by fines, curses, and expulsion from the community."[56] Similarly, the state denied Muslim clerics the use of corporal punishment, abrogating a range of Qur'anic punishments for theft, adultery, alcohol, and other offenses against religion.[57] Thus a basic tension marked sponsorship of non-Orthodox hierarchies and their disciplinary powers: the law forged interdependence between clerics and state officials by expanding clerical authority in some areas and limiting it in others.

While Russian officials thus sought to establish a clear chain of command running from St. Petersburg into the local parish, mosque, or synagogue community, they also remained responsive to challenges from below. Officials looked to lay initiative to keep clerical abuses in check. They proved sympathetic to lay reformers who admonished mullahs who drank wine or priests who seduced parishioners. Charges of "false teaching" and the exercise of miraculous powers suggested subversion and prompted police investigations.[58] Despite the many shortcomings of the tsarist legal system and threats from co-religionists ranging from social ostracism to murder, laypeople continued to look to the tsar's justice to overturn religious judgments. Clerical sanction alone remained insufficient to maintain the absolute power of informal religious courts, which relied on state authorities to implement controversial rulings.

Successful overtures to Russian officials depended on the litigants' ability to translate internal disputes into tsarist political categories. In constructing their

---

of the *Digest of Laws* compiled legislation on the organization of familial relations within each non-Orthodox confession.

[54] See, for example, RGIA, f. 821, op. 8, d. 951. ChaeRan Y. Freeze has richly documented this pattern of intervention in "The Litigious *Gerusha*: Jewish Women and Divorce in Imperial Russia," *Nationalities Papers* 25, no. 1 (1997): 89–101.

[55] See, for example, the intervention of the Ministry of the Interior in preventing marriages between Muslims and Christians in Orenburg province in 1821 in GAOO, f. 6, op. 4, d. 7601.

[56] *Svod zakonov*, vol. 11, part 1, 203.

[57] The practice continued in some communities in secret. See, for example, the accusations against a village imam in 1871 in TsGIARB, f. I-295, op. 2, d. 122, ll. 59 ob.–60.

[58] The first mufti solicited multiple police investigations of rival Sufis. See GAOO, f. 6, op. 2, d. 724 and d. 1026. For Jews, "complaints from the community" served as grounds for investigating rabbis charged with violating the prerogatives of their office. *Svod zakonov*, vol. 11, part 1, 203. Communal leaders in Minsk took on this challenge by discouraging appeals to outside powers: "No Jew is to testify in favor of a recalcitrant who brought his case to a non-Jewish court, but everyone is bound to testify all he knows in favor of his opponent." Levitats, *Jewish Community in Russia*, 202–03.

complaints and denunciations, contestants confronted the challenge of casting their opponents' views and actions as "heresy"—and thus beyond the scope of official toleration. Heresy in any community constituted a political issue in tsarist Russia: to the police, religious dissent and heterodoxy almost invariably involved a broader challenge to the existing order. When a new "rationalist" hymnal appeared among reformist Protestants in 1819, the tsar condemned the book, vowing to "protect" the Evangelical Church from "rules deviating from Christian morality."[59] In 1823, the Ministry of the Interior acquiesced to the Catholic hierarchy's request to suppress the champions of heterodox doctrine such as Ignace Lindl (who rejected the pope, the cult of the saints, and the Virgin Mary) by expelling the German mystic.[60] Jews, too, looked to tsarist police to aid them against opponents and often represented religious differences as political crimes. From the late eighteenth century, the Talmudic elite in Lithuania drew Russian police into conflicts between them and the *hasidim*, adherents of a new pietistic movement. Based on Jewish denunciations, police arrested some prominent Hasidic leaders and placed others under surveillance.[61] *Hasidim* such as the Jews of Rogachev of Mogilev province responded by warning the minister of the interior that their antagonists, such as the "learned Jew" Moisei Berlin, "not only did not come up to the goals and expectations of the government, but SERVED AS AN EXAMPLE OF DEPRAVITY and the slackening of the fulfillment of God's law and the dogma of our religion for youth."[62]

Concern for policing orthodoxy was not limited to the Ministry of the Interior or even to clerical elites. Laypeople also calculated that heresy left unchecked would undermine the community from within.[63] Spokesmen for the Jewish Enlightenment (Haskalah) turned to the regime, seeking patronage for their vision of a religion compatible with "civic responsibilities to the tsar and motherland" as well as "respectable and useful labor in all branches of the crafts, commerce, and

[59] When the tsar appointed Count Karl von Lieven to draw up plans for a Protestant consistory and bishopric, local constituencies petitioned to voice fears that the proposal would impose Orthodox and Catholic institutions and rites. However, the appearance of separatist movements, like the Württemberg Confession, persuaded Protestant elites in the 1820s to cooperate with plans for a hierarchy to combat such "sects." See Varadinov, *Istoriia Ministerstva vnutrennikh del*, part 2, book 1, 627–31, part 2, book 2, 149–50, and part 3, book 3, 110, 276.

[60] André Arvaldis Brumanis, *Aux origines de la hiérarchie latine en Russie: Mgr Stanislas Siestrzencewicz-Bohusz, Premier archevêque-metropolitain de Mohilev (1731–1826)* (Louvain, 1968), 333–36; and Vishlenkova, *Religioznaia politika*, 161–62.

[61] See Iulii Gessen, *Istoriia evreiskogo naroda v Rossii*, vol. 1, 2d rev. edn. (Leningrad, 1925), 103–13; and the denunciations and official correspondence on the "Hasidic sect" in G. Deich, *Tsarskoe pravitel'stvo i khasidskoe dvizhenie v Rossii: Arkhivnye dokumenty* (New York, 1994). The opponents of Hasidism invoked traditional Talmudic authority in calling on the tsar to intervene on their behalf, but officials eventually concluded that the *hasidim* formed a harmless "sect" that should be tolerated. See "Evreiskie religioznye sekty v Rossii," in *Zhurnal Ministerstva vnutrennikh del*, part 15 (1846): 3–49, 282–309, and part 16 (1846): 500–80. Nonetheless, official investigations continued into the late 1850s. On other overtures to the bureaucracy, see also Benjamin Nathans, "Conflict, Community, and the Jews of Late Nineteenth-Century St. Petersburg," *Jahrbücher für Geschichte Osteuropas* 44, no. 2 (1996): 178–215.

[62] Deich, *Tsarskoe pravitel'stvo*, 9.

[63] Some activists may have feared that such scandals would also endanger the reputation of the community and the privilege of toleration. On this fear in Europe, see Elisheva Carlebach, *The Pursuit of Heresy: Rabbi Moses Hagiz and the Sabbatian Controversies* (New York, 1990); and in Russia, Deich, *Tsarskoe pravitel'stvo*, esp. 20–21.

agriculture."⁶⁴ Like the *hasidim* and their foes, proponents and critics of the Haskalah did not shy away from denouncing their opponents.⁶⁵

For Jews and Muslims, toleration circumscribed religious autonomy while linking confessional disputes to state patronage and policing. Despite the conservative aims of officials, support for novel forms of bureaucratic organization and doctrinal emphasis brought change to every community. Ceremonies and liturgies integrated tsar and fatherland, while the rites of marriage, divorce, and death became the business of new hierarchies as well as of the Ministry of the Interior. Religious authorities adopted statistics, archives, examinations, and inspections as measures of internal social control. The recording of marriages, births, divorces, and deaths facilitated a more systematic and uniform application of canon law in Christian confessions, aided in establishing religious norms to govern the inner life of the family and community in others, and assisted the government in the levying of taxes and recruits. Police intervention became a dynamic agent of communal transformation, suppressing particular interpretations of the faith and advancing others. However, this kind of intervention did not emerge as a result of a concerted policy of "divide and rule" or a grand integrative strategy from above. Legislation and institutions governing the non-Orthodox often took shape as ad hoc responses to initiatives from members of these groups. Muslims, Jews, and others themselves shaped this process by initiating and placing limits on contacts with tsarist authorities.

A CLOSER EXAMINATION of the expansion of the state into the lives of Muslim men and women on the southeastern frontier reveals how the interdependence of Muslim communities and the regime grew out of the practice of *Polizeistaat* toleration and the collective pursuit of religious orthodoxy. From the fifteenth century, when Russia first acquired Muslim-populated lands, Muscovite rulers accommodated Muslims informally. In the next century, Russian expansion into the Volga and Urals regions put an end to local Muslim dynasties. Islamic institutions continued to exist beyond the purview of the state but remained subject to periodic assault at the hands of Orthodox militants, who leveled mosques and schools. As in other Muslim societies, learned men and women assumed positions of religious leadership outside the auspices of formal hierarchies. No single authority either defined or enforced a particular interpretation of Islamic orthodoxy, and Muslims

---

⁶⁴ Paul Mendes-Flohr and Jehuda Reinharz, eds., *The Jew in the Modern World*, 2d edn. (New York, 1995), 385. For Judah Leib Gordon, the Enlightenment educator and Hebrew poet, the government appeared as an ally of the Jews, who in turn had "the duty to obey in all sincerity . . . [the tsar's] orders and desire, and to be faithful and eager servants, so that the friends of the Jews will not be swayed from their course." Quoted in Michael Stanislawski, *For Whom Do I Toil? Judah Leib Gordon and the Crisis of Russian Jewry* (New York, 1988), 30. The pivotal role of the local administration in supporting the Haskalah is highlighted in Steven J. Zipperstein, *The Jews of Odessa: A Cultural History, 1794–1881* (Stanford, Calif., 1985), 41–69.

⁶⁵ In 1870, Moshe Rosensohn defended "upholders of the Torah of Moses" against reformist rivals who, he claimed, sinned "against justice, against God, against his king, against the Torah and his own faith." Lederhendler, *Road to Modern Jewish Politics*, 90–91, 95–100, 195.

engaged in debate largely without recourse to enforcement beyond the pressures of local, close-knit communal life.[66]

However, in the late eighteenth and early nineteenth centuries, the regime transformed the foundations of Islamic culture in the empire by extending its patronage to Islamic institutions, including generous state subsidies for mosques, the printing of the Qur'an and other religious texts, and, most important, the creation of a centralized hierarchy.[67] The Orenburg Assembly used its regulatory and investigative authority to oversee religious life in each mosque community by administering clerical examinations, licenses, visitations, and the archival recording of judicial decisions.[68] Through these new instruments, state-appointed Islamic authorities advanced novel understandings of the *shari'a*, which encompassed the norms, obligations, and rights enjoined by God's will for all the faithful. While following the directives of St. Petersburg, the mufti and judges (*kadis*) of the assembly capitalized on official support to pursue their own agenda. They relied on the police to secure the uniform application of a more narrow and, in their view, more "orthodox" range of opinions of the Hanafi school of law (one of the four established Sunni legal traditions) and Naqshbandi Sufi order.[69] Under Mufti Abdulvakhid Suleimanov, for example, the assembly utilized the Saratov provincial administration to pursue a disputed issue within Sufism about the legality of performing the rite of remembrance of the name of God (*zikr*) silently or vocally. In 1862, it ordered Muslims in the village of Tatarskie Kanadi to desist from "pronouncing prayers aloud," declaring that those who did not refrain from vocal *zikr* would be barred from the mosque as "apostates from the *shari'a*" (*otstupniki ot Sharigata*).[70] Armed with the tools of a modernizing regime, they combated similar departures from Naqshbandi positions and other regional variations in Islamic legal interpretation arising from the varied customs and social conditions of local

[66] On this pattern elsewhere, see Roy P. Mottahedeh, *Loyalty and Leadership in an Early Islamic Society* (Princeton, N.J., 1980); Ira M. Lapidus, *Muslim Cities in the Later Middle Ages* (Cambridge, Mass., 1967); and Richard W. Bulliet, *Islam: The View from the Edge* (New York, 1994). On Islam in eighteenth-century Russia, see Frank, *Islamic Historiography*, 21–46.

[67] Karimullin, *U istokov tatarskoi knigi*; İsmail Türkoğlu, *Rusya Türkleri Arasındaki Yenileşme Hareketinin Öncülerinden Rızaeddin Fahreddin (1858–1936)* (Istanbul, 2000), 83–84. Much of the relevant legislation appears in D. Iu. Arapov, ed., *Islam v Rossiiskoi imperii: Zakonodatel'nye akty, opisaniia, statistika* (Moscow, 2001).

[68] By 1835, the Orenburg Assembly administered 3,036 mosque communities and 4,781 licensed clerics serving a population of 1,034,976 Muslims in sixteen provinces. *Izvlechenie iz otcheta Ministra vnutrennikh del za 1835 god*, n.p. By 1849, these figures had increased to 3,233 mosques with 5,397 licensed clerics, and by 1858, 3,750 mosques, 1,569 schools, and more than 2 million Muslims. RGIA, f. 821, op. 8, d. 999, ll. 5 ob.–6; and Märjani, *Möstäfadel-äkhbar*, 210.

[69] Here, my interpretation differs from the excellent studies by Allen J. Frank, *Muslim Religious Institutions in Imperial Russia: The Islamic World of Novouzensk District and the Kazakh Inner Horde, 1780–1910* (Leiden, 2001); and Noack, *Muslimischer Nationalismus*, which tend to understand the Orenburg Assembly as a more autonomous institution and the expression of "toleration" in the modern liberal sense. One of its most controversial functions included the arbitration of conflicts about the timing of dawn, dusk, and nighttime prayers and holidays in the short winter days and white nights of the northern latitudes of Eurasia. In 1802, the assembly removed an imam for beginning holiday prayers before the time it had appointed. He nonetheless went on to become the second mufti. See Danil' Azamatov, "Gabdrakhimov, Gabdessaliam," in *Islam na territorii byvshei Rossiiskoi imperii: Entsiklopedicheskii slovar'*, vol. 1 (Moscow, 1998), 27. His name also appears in some sources as "Abdusalam Abdrakhimov," which I will use hereafter.

[70] TsGIARB, f. I-295, op. 3, d. 5048, ll. 9–9 ob.

communities, broad clerical discretion, and the circulation of diverse texts with a plurality of accepted opinions on particular issues.

In sponsoring the mufti, the state gained a voice who recognized the empire as the "House of Islam" (*dar al-Islam*), a territory where Muslims could fulfill their religious duties.[71] Muslim authorities represented such a potentially valuable resource for the government because they claimed guardianship of an array of legal matters that European jurisprudence would elsewhere break up into "civil," "criminal," "ecclesiastical," or "commercial" law. In determining the religious legality of personal behavior, the men of learning and piety (ulama) interpreted a vast body of sources, including the Qur'an, the sayings and acts of the Prophet, and various legal commentaries. The ulama claimed textual authority in the name of protecting the community against error and irreligion. Prayer-leaders exhorted villagers and townspeople who neglected communal prayer. They reconciled quarreling husbands and wives, educated the youth, and guided Muslims to live pious lives according to the *shari'a*. At the same time, the muftis cooperated with provincial officials who requested *fatwas* defining the instructions of secular officials as sacred obligations. *Fatwas* penned by the second mufti, Abdusalam Abdrakhimov, directed Muslims to send their children to Kazan University for medical training in 1831 and, wielding citations from the Qur'an and other sources, exhorted peasants in 1832 to labor diligently in the fields, sowing and harvesting at the appropriate times, as a defense against poverty and the pleasures of sin. Recognized by the tsar with the award of a gold medal, Abdrakhimov demonstrated his value again in 1836 when he reminded his charges that "each orthodox Muslim is obliged to obey the authorities and the laws" and to avoid sin, which invokes "God's anger and punishment."[72] In sermons, treatises, oaths, and prayers for the imperial family, official ulama enjoined obedience, loyalty, and patriotism. They aided the state in carrying out conscription and other administrative functions and preached the submission of children to their parents—and of Muslims to the regime.

Although officials expected the ulama to assist the insertion of the political order into each locale, these Muslim scholars did not necessarily enjoy unbounded authority in their own communities. Even after the introduction of the official hierarchy, their powers still depended on the opinion of the local lay community who elected them and could later petition the state for their removal. Contemporary biographical literature compiled by Muslim scholars celebrated the exemplary lives of those whose reputations for learning and piety empowered them to correct the religion of the people. Notable scholars gained renown for study in cosmopolitan centers of Islamic scholarship such as Bukhara, Kabul, Baghdad, Cairo, and Istanbul, or, closer to home, in the village of Tatarskaia Kargala on the steppe frontier of Orenburg province, and many imams earned (or inherited from their

---

[71] The first mufti actively campaigned in the borderlands to persuade his co-religionists to seek the protection of the empress. See his letters of 1801 to Kazakhs on the southeastern frontier in GAOO, f. 6, op. 2, d. 724; and on his activities on behalf of the empire in the north Caucasus, *V pamiat' stoletiia Orenburgskogo magometanskogo dukhovnogo sobraniia, uchrezhdennogo v gorode Ufe* (Ufa, 1891), 40–41.

[72] Kemper, *Sufis und Gelehrte*, 70–73; and *Sbornik tsirkuliariov*, 3–4.

fathers) a name for being "gentle and gracious" in their relations with members of the mosque community.[73] Still others were remembered for their acerbic wit. Gabbas b. Gabderräshid äl-Küshäri once confronted the prayer-leader of the village of Shashï, who had placed the niche marking the direction for prayer on the wrong side of the mosque. When the prayer-leader defended his mistake by citing a text of foreign origin (*A Collection of Signs*) pointing to Mecca in the West, Küshäri retorted, "Hey, stupid, was *A Collection of Signs* written in your Shashï?"[74] Clerics like the unfortunate imam of Shashï became increasingly exposed in the nineteenth century to ridicule and other challenges from scholars and laypeople who could now turn to state institutions to "correct" what they held to be unorthodox practices.

In turn, the fragile position of Muslim clerics forced them to seek out closer association with officials to back their authority. Village prayer-leaders combating debauchery, the refusal to attend prayers, the celebration of "un-Islamic" holidays, and competition from unlicensed rivals frequently had to resort to denouncing their parishioners not only to the Islamic hierarchy but to local police. As the imam Mukhamet'zhan Kuziakhmetov warned his flock in 1871, "for insubordination and non-fulfillment" of the *shari'a*, "[you] may be punished by God and the civil court."[75] The instruments of the modern state became essential to "orthodox" claims about the fulfillment of God's will.

Recent research has pointed to the intense debates among Muslim scholars in Russia about interpretation of the *shari'a*, or divine law. By tracing the contours of these conflicts among Muslim elites, these studies challenge the image of a monolithic and timeless Islam.[76] But the dynamism of these conflicts owed much to the fact that the contest for religious authority extended beyond the elites. Reformist Muslim scholars such as Rizaeddin Fahreddinev wrote numerous treatises defending clerical authority over lay Muslims and the power of men over women who stood to receive a "terrible punishment" in the afterlife for disobeying their husbands.[77] But the licensed keepers of Islamic knowledge were not the only ones committed to correcting those who had ostensibly strayed from the true path. Lay and clerical opponents of the interpretive monopoly of elites relied on a tradition in which interpretation of the *shari'a* potentially produced multiple solutions to a wide array of specific problems, ranging from divorce to commercial

---

[73] See the praise offered by one community for its imam in TsGIARB, f. I-295, op. 3, d. 5567, ll. 113 ob.-15 ob.; and on the biographies of regional scholars, Märjani, *Möstäfadel-äkhbar*.

[74] Märjani, *Möstäfadel-äkhbar*, 309-10.

[75] TsGIARB, f. I-295, op. 3, d. 122, l. 431 ob. See this file for further clerical denunciations of unruly parishes, including charges that parishioners regularly threatened the imam, became drunk, and refused to attend communal prayers. See also f. I-295, op. 3, d. 1830; and on a cleric's denunciation of an unlicensed preacher, f. I-295, op. 3, d. 5698.

[76] These conflicts pitted proponents of the exercise of independent reason (*ijtihad*) against defenders of the imitation (*taqlid*) of the sources of the law. See the learned studies by Stéphane A. Dudoignon, "Djadidisme, mirasisme, islamisme," *Cahiers du monde russe* 37, nos. 1-2 (1996): 13-40; and Kemper, *Sufis und Gelehrte*. Elsewhere, Wael B. Hallaq has questioned the tendency to treat *taqlid* and *ijtihad* as antithetical practices by identifying a wide range of interpretive activity in the exercise of *taqlid*, especially among Hanafis, the dominant legal school in the Russian Empire. Hallaq, *Authority, Continuity, and Change in Islamic Law* (Cambridge, 2001).

[77] Fahreddinev, *Menasıb-ı diniye*; and *Terbiyeli khatun* (Kazan, 1899), 6. See also the defense of clerics against the "slander" of laypeople in Märjani, *Möstäfadel-äkhbar*, 312-14.

FIGURE 3: The main mosque and the seat of the Orenburg mufti in the town of Ufa, constructed in 1830. Courtesy of the Prokudin-Gorskii Collection of the Library of Congress.

transactions.[78] Until the modern era of nation-states and legal codification, Islamic law did not reside in a single text or authority. Indeed, most Muslim scholars regarded *fatwas* as mere opinions—not binding rulings, except where temporal authorities backed their writ. In a legal tradition that relied on numerous authoritative sources and entertained the possibility of varied outcomes depending on the local social context, determining a *single*, uniform "orthodoxy" for police enforcement unleashed intense conflicts.

Official endorsement of orthodoxy meant that, in practice, the police became responsible for enforcing Islamic judicial decisions. In an influential study of Islamic law, Lawrence Rosen has highlighted the role of the Islamic judge as a mediator, a facilitator of "social bargaining," whose aim "is to put people back in the position of being able to negotiate their own permissible relationships without predetermining just what the outcome of those negotiations ought to be."[79] Under the Orenburg Assembly, prayer-leaders and judges assumed this role in formal legal proceedings and informally outside the mosque courtyard. Many of their decisions

[78] On criticism by regional ulama of the Orenburg Assembly and some of its muftis, see Kemper, *Sufis und Gelehrte*, 50–61, 66–70, 290–99; and TsGIARB, f. I-295, op. 2, d. 43.

[79] Lawrence Rosen, *The Anthropology of Justice: Law as Culture in Islamic Society* (Cambridge, 1989), 17.

FIGURE 4: A senior Tatar Muslim cleric (akhund). Karl von Rechberg und Rothenlöwen, *Les peuples de la Russie*, vol. 1 (Paris, 1812). Courtesy of the Library of Congress.

fitted with "the cultural concepts and social relations to which they were inextricably tied."[80] But, equally important, parties to disputes often eschewed mediation and opted for direct state intervention instead. When litigants turned to the police, debates over the *shari'a* shifted from the local social environment, where neighbors

[80] Rosen, *Anthropology of Justice*, 18.

and spouses might bargain and reconcile, toward coercive settlement of intractable differences under state control. Police involvement in returning wives who had fled their husbands, removing children from divorced spouses, or restraining controversial preachers did not facilitate negotiation but brought a bureaucratic finality to contested cases.

Lay Muslims thus looked to the institutions of the empire to insist on their own interpretations of God's law. Armed with knowledge acquired in a vast network of Qur'anic schools as well as through poetry, pilgrimage, sermons, and the circulation of printed and manuscript tracts, men and women pointed out the errors of clerics, relatives, and neighbors who avoided the mosque, drank wine, sang prayers, beat their wives, or committed adultery.[81] They even attacked prayer-leaders who failed to perform the rites, such as communal prayer, burial of the dead, and the celebration of holidays, that dramatized the bonds of community. Mediated by translators, scribes, and bilingual informants, calls for state involvement made explicit references to imperial statutes and decrees. Muslims developed novel rhetorical strategies to press their cases, integrating tsarist law codes, decrees, and procedure alongside appeals to the tsar and imperial family, the Qur'an, the sayings and acts of the Prophet, and other Islamic legal literature.[82] Denunciations that translated local conflicts over spiritual authority and theological interpretation into the vocabulary of tsarist law and the Orthodox Church proved most successful in launching police investigations. The criminal code became a valuable tool in the hands of Muslims who learned to cast their opponents as self-styled "saints," "pretenders," and "schismatics" (*raskol'niki*) or to connect them with inciting conversion to Islam.[83]

For the seekers of true religion, like the villagers of Bazitamak in Orenburg province who denounced their imam to Tsar Nicholas in 1849, intervention became a catalyst for strengthening the community and a guarantor of Islamic orthodoxy. They argued that the state, too, benefited from true religion and suffered from its neglect; in the absence of prayers led by the imam, "the Muhammadan people [had] almost begun to forget its faith," and youth strayed toward criminality "without reproach from the imam about fear of God."[84] In Kazan, Muslims tried to solicit police intervention "in accordance with both the *shari'a* and the civil law" against

---

[81] From the earliest period of Islamic history, Muslim scholars have identified the moral obligation to "command right and forbid wrong" as a duty incumbent on every Muslim. On the development of this doctrine, see Michael Cook, *Commanding Right and Forbidding Wrong in Islamic Thought* (Cambridge, 2000).

[82] See, for example, petitions that cited volume 11 of the *Digest of Laws* and other official texts in NART, f. 1, op. 3, d. 7615, ll. 12–12 ob.; RGIA, f. 821, op. 8, d. 775, ll. 1–8, d. 1078, ll. 445–47, and d. 614, ll. 15–82. On similar strategies among Russian peasants, see David Moon, *Russian Peasants and Tsarist Legislation on the Eve of Reform: Interaction between Peasants and Officialdom, 1825–1855* (Basingstoke, 1992).

[83] Mufti Husainov artfully employed this language in the early nineteenth century. GAOO, f. 6, op. 2, d. 724, ll. 135–135 ob. See also a representative case from the late 1850s; RGIA, f. 821, op. 8, d. 995. Articles 1159–64 of the criminal code defined such acts as offenses in *Polnoe sobranie zakonov Rossiiskoi imperii*, vol. 20, no. 19,283 (August 15, 1845) (St. Petersburg, 1846), 817–18. Tsarist officials also commented on Jewish knowledge of criminal law in making their accusations against co-religionists. See, for example, Deich, *Tsarskoe pravitel'stvo*, 46.

[84] TsGIARB, f. I-295, op. 2, d. 43, ll. 1215 ob.–1216.

Muslim women who appeared in public with "open faces" and engaged in prostitution.[85]

When Muslim peasants in Orenburg province addressed a petition to Nicholas I in 1833 to seek his help in ridding the village of their prayer-leader, they were motivated not by feelings of ethnic solidarity but by the conviction that the state would serve the cause of piety by punishing their imam, Sharafutdin Rakhimov. For these peasants, the conflict with Rakhimov represented a struggle to live according to God's law and to remove the polluting influence of an imam who refused to lead the community in worship, tormented the souls of the dead by neglecting their burial, and even beat one of his denouncers to a state of "great ill-health." Acting on their denunciation, the local police removed the imam from his position for "deeds carried out not only against the Muhammadan religion and its rules but also imperial statutes" and thereby affirmed these petitioners' vision of the regime as the disciplinary instrument of a community governed by the sacred law.[86]

Similarly, in February 1832, peasants in the district of Kazan gathered to condemn their mullah for provoking God's punishment, but they did not confine themselves to the rough justice of the village. The men of the community turned against Mullah Lupman Fatkullin to the township administration, seeking his removal and expulsion from the village. They informed local authorities that Fatkullin violated the *shari'a* by ignoring the five daily prayers, disregarding his obligation to instruct the children, and subjecting especially pious men—and even women—to "foul insults." The villagers echoed many Muslims who complained that the failings of their prayer-leaders had led to the decline of morals and the corruption of youth. Their denunciations drew on established anti-clerical tropes about greedy and self-interested mullahs. But pious concern for the collective obligations of the divine law may also have reflected local adaptation of new forms of Sufi thought transmitted orally by scholars and in manuscripts that circulated throughout the empire.[87] By appealing to authorities outside of their own village, and beyond the Muslim community, these locals effectively challenged the licensed ulama; they looked to the regime to restore "collective prayer" and spare the community from "the shudder of divine punishment," which the villagers saw in "the recent [outbreak of] the dangerous disease of cholera near our village."[88]

Notwithstanding the ambiguous status of appeal in the Islamic tradition, Muslims embraced the practice in Russia as a means to challenge the outcome of Islamic law court cases and safeguard the rights and obligations that they understood as essential components of the *shari'u*.[89] Laypeople challenged prayer-

---

[85] NART, f. 1, op. 3, d. 7615, l. 12 ob.

[86] TsGIARB, f. I-295, op. 3, d. 625, ll. 5 15. For further examples of tensions between prayer-leaders and parishioners, see RGIA, f. 821, op. 8, d. 615; TsGIARB, f. I-295, op. 3, d. 910, d. 5185, and d. 5698; and Frank, *Muslim Religious Institutions*, chap. 4.

[87] Dudoignon, "Djadidisme, mirasisme, islamisme"; and Kemper, *Sufis und Gelehrte*.

[88] TsGIARB, f. I-295, op. 3, d. 910, ll. 12 ob.–13.

[89] Evidence of appeal in other Muslim societies has emerged in a number of recent studies. See David S. Powers, "On Judicial Review in Islamic Law," *Law and Society Review* 26, no. 2 (1992): 315–41; and on women, Fariba Zarinebaf-Shahr, "Ottoman Women and the Tradition of Seeking Justice," in *Women in the Ottoman Empire: Middle Eastern Women in the Early Modern Era*, Madeline C. Zilfi, ed. (Leiden, 1997), 253–63. First introduced to Islamic law courts in the north Caucasus under Shamil's imamate, the principle of appeal became a central aspect of tsarist administration through "customary law" in the region as well as in Turkestan from the 1860s. Bobrovnikov, *Musul'mane*

leaders and judges by looking beyond the village or town mosque community to the police, the Orenburg Assembly, and the minister of the interior, whom a petition from mullahs in Orenburg province in 1863 styled the "Minister of Interior and Muslim Religious Affairs [sic]."[90] Similar appellate mechanisms appeared in other empires, but tsarist officials defended "orthodox" interpretation of the shari'a more consistently than their British or French counterparts. Where European judges incorporated considerations of "equity" and Roman legal principles, Russians looked almost exclusively to authoritative interpretation of the Islamic tradition.[91] In the tsarist setting, Muslims had access to two interrelated modes of appeal. In the first, aggrieved parties, as individuals or as kin groups, contested the resolution of divorce, inheritance, and other disputes by asking the Orenburg Assembly to review the case. In the second, litigants petitioned Russian officials ranging from the local bailiff to the emperor to overturn the rulings of local ulama, to compel husbands to refrain from beating their wives, or otherwise commit themselves to live "in accordance with the shari'a." In both types of appeal, the process began with the composition of a petition or complaint (usually on the basis of oral testimony) at the offices of the local police; the police investigated claims about the violation of the shari'a, gathered evidence, and then oversaw the execution of the final judgment. Litigants might simultaneously pursue both strategies or, after exhausting the first option, turn to the tsar with confidence that the laws of the empire supported God's law.

Both state archival records and Muslim historical sources show how contests over religious authority quietly transformed these small, face-to-face communities and their relationship to the state, as men and women adopted the practice of soliciting intervention to contest the outcomes of divorce, inheritance, and other cases involving the shari'a. In 1820, Bibi Kiz Bike petitioned the mufti to secure maintenance (nafaqa) from her husband.[92] In the same year, a villager named Sayyid from the Volga province of Simbirsk abrogated a marriage contract with his future son-in-law, Mecid, by refusing to permit his daughter Bibi Habibe to marry her fiancé. Mecid charged Sayyid with violating an agreement sanctioned by the shari'a and turned to the district police chief, who organized an investigation and gathered testimony from the villagers. After consulting the Orenburg Assembly, the police instructed local mullahs to assist in determining the legality of the contract on the basis of Islamic law. The mullahs apparently tried to reconcile the families of the betrothed, but, when mediation failed, the mufti Husainov put an end to the case by ruling that Sayyid was obliged to turn his daughter over to Mecid—a judgment to be delivered to the litigants and carried out jointly by the mullahs and the police. By the second quarter of the century, Muslims in over a dozen provinces had learned to act on the social and religious obligation to discipline co-religionists

---

Severnogo Kavkaza, 154–66; and Robert D. Crews, "Allies in God's Command: Muslim Communities and the State in Imperial Russia" (PhD dissertation, Princeton University, 1999), chap. 5.

[90] *Materialy po istorii Tatarii*, 166.

[91] See, for example, Michael R. Anderson, "Legal Scholarship and the Politics of Islam in British India," in R. S. Khare, ed., *Perspectives on Islamic Law, Justice, and Society* (Lanham, Md., 1999), 65–91.

[92] This paragraph is based on a reprint of the original correspondence of the mufti in Tatar and Persian in Rizaeddin Fahreddinev, *Asar*, vol. 4 (Orenburg, 1903), 190–91. The document refers to the official by his first name and patronymic, Nikolai Fedorovich.

by turning to the regime and its Islamic institutions to restore the communal religious standards and the purity of the faith commanded by God's law.

While recourse to tsarist law became an essential tool in the hands of Muslims whose competing visions of the *shari'a* animated clerical rivalries and village feuds, men and women also looked to the state to compel their spouses to live "according to the *shari'a*." As in other Muslim societies, women emerged as particularly active litigants. Often assisted by guardians and kin, they utilized courts and appeals to restrain abusive husbands, defend their honor, and even initiate divorce based on the claim that the *shari'a* accorded them these rights.[93] Women such as Khamida Salikhova, from the village of Novoe-Baltachevo in Orenburg province, turned to Nicholas I to protest the brutality of their husbands, asserting in petitions that physical abuse justified the awarding of a divorce "in accordance with the Muhammadan faith."[94] Invoking the protection of imperial law and officials, appeals from disgruntled wives, disappointed husbands, and frustrated prayer-leaders seeking justice and fulfillment of the divine will made the tsarist police arbiters of the most intimate of religious and familial disputes.

AT MID-CENTURY, the crisis of the Crimean War and fighting against the Ottomans provoked doubt in the minds of provincial officials and many Muslim peasants and townspeople about the continued convergence of interests between Muslims and their Christian rulers. Rumors of forced conversion on the Volga led some Muslim villagers to conclude, according to a local investigation of Muslim attitudes in Samara province, that the war with the Ottomans would endanger toleration, reckoning that, since "Christians suffer oppression in Turkey," then "our government, too, will do the same with the followers of Islam [*islamizm*]." Increasingly anxious about "fanaticism," provincial officials were also disconcerted by reports that Muslims collected money and offered prayers for the victory of the sultan, in addition to proselytizing among their non-Muslim neighbors and storing gunpowder for a rebellion.[95] But whereas the regime resorted to mass expulsions and encouraged flight from the militarily sensitive borderlands of the Caucasus and the Crimea in the wake of the war, it discouraged emigration from other regions and

---

[93] Allen Frank reconstructs the story of a communal defense of a woman's honor in *Muslim Religious Institutions*, 141–42. The criminal code also prohibited husbands' "cruel treatment" of their wives but left "injury," "blows," and "abuse" ill-defined. Mufti Suleimanov affirmed this representation of rights within the *shari'a* in his instructions to judges in 1840: "according to Islamic law, men are not permitted to subject their wives to beatings leading to the drawing of blood and the breaking of bones and pull their hair." TsGIARB, f. I-295, op. 3, d. 1096, ll. 29–29 ob. Women frequently initiated divorce by *khul'*, whereby they received the husband's permission to dissolve the marriage, often in exchange for the payment of a compensation. Of 3,836 recorded Muslim divorces in Ufa province between 1866 and 1868, 81 percent were by *khul'*. A. Z. Asfandiarov, *Bashkirskaia sem'ia v proshlom (XVIII–pervaia polovina XIX v.)* (Ufa, 1997), 72–73. On similar strategies in Ottoman courts, see Ronald C. Jennings, "Women in Early 17th Century Ottoman Judicial Records—The Sharia Court of Anatolian Kayseri," *Journal of the Economic and Social History of the Orient* 18 (1975): 53–114.

[94] TsGIARB, f. I-295, op. 3, d. 1749. Of the roughly 1,200 cases that the Orenburg Assembly handled annually in the 1880s, the largest number (200–250) involved inheritance disputes, followed by divorce cases (up to 150). *V pamiat'*, 36.

[95] *Materialy po istorii Tatarii*, 156–64.

attempted to dispel rumors that agitated mullahs and Orthodox priests alike.[96] Officials in St. Petersburg remained committed to the common moral language of sin and divine punishment that continued to make Islam useful in administering these provinces, despite warnings of "fanaticism" from local governors and bishops.

In the postwar reform era, the central government accommodated these protests by imposing more restrictions on the autonomy of Muslim authorities. The Ministry of the Interior increasingly subjected local appeals to the scrutiny of non-Muslim scholars trained in the newly established disciplines of Oriental studies. The regime took these figures to be not only more trustworthy in their devotion to the state but truer to the "correct" meaning of the Islamic tradition that they derived from their study of texts. Russian officials thus assumed greater responsibility for defining and enforcing Islamic "orthodoxy," even as they registered growing skepticism about the competence and reliability of its traditional spokesmen.[97] In reviewing appeals for the ministry, scholars such as the St. Petersburg University professor Alexander Kazem-Bek frequently called the decisions of the Orenburg Assembly into question. In 1865, the appointment of Selim-Girei Tevkelev to the post of Orenburg mufti bolstered the authority of Orientalist "experts." A retired staff cavalry captain, nobleman, and decorated veteran of campaigns against both the Ottomans and the rebellious Poles, Tevkelev lacked systematic training in the Islamic tradition. Through consultation on specific cases, Orientalists interpreted the *shariʿa* in new ways. Removing the process of disputation and discretionary interpretation from the social environment of the mosque community, they established binding precedents and limited the range and flexibility of Islamic interpretation by privileging a handful of legal texts that summarized major opinions of the Hanafi school of law. Scholars built on the "orthodox" agenda of the Orenburg Assembly by narrowing the latitude of Islamic jurisprudence but simultaneously undermined its authority by shifting final control over Islamic law judgments to the upper echelons of the appellate hierarchy in St. Petersburg. Kazem-Bek in particular contributed to the official redefinition of the *shariʿa* as a species of positive law, reducing the range of outcomes to a single judgment on a uniform basis.[98]

While Russian nationalists, Orthodox bishops, and Orientalists threatened the

[96] According to Bedri Habiçoğlu, between 1855 and 1907, some 600,000 emigrants from the Caucasus region reached Ottoman lands, and many hundreds of thousands more may have died on the way. Relocations and expulsions had been a strategy of Shamil's forces and, on a broader scale, those of the tsarist army in the northwest Caucasus. Like the Russian forces, Ottoman diplomats (including those whose families traced their origins to the region) encouraged the migrations, promising assistance in resettlement. The Ottoman press cast this development as the religious obligation of *hijra* to a Muslim land (*hicret etmiş*), a characterization that remains alive in popular memory. On the varied motivations of the migrants, or *muhacirs*, see Habiçoğlu, *Kafkasya'dan Anadolu'ya Göçler ve İskanlar* (Istanbul, 1993), esp. 67–73. On Muslim expulsions and transfers of other Muslims in the region, see Rukiya S. Šarafutdinova, "Zwei wiederentdeckte arabische Dokumente aus der Zeit des Kaukasuskrieges," in *Muslim Culture in Russia and Central Asia*, vol. 3, Anke von Kügelgen, Aširbek Muminov, and Michael Kemper, eds. (Berlin, 2000), 525–26; and Bobrovnikov, *Musul'mane Severnogo Kavkaza*, 17–19, 22–23.

[97] The position of Islamic clerics came to resemble that of Brahmin pundits in colonial India. Their authority, Lata Mani argues, "was problematic: the fact of being native simultaneously privileged and devalued them as reliable sources. The pundits were essential to 'unlocking' the scriptures for officials. But they were also believed by officials to be the 'devious minority' against which it was the mission of colonization to protect the 'simple majority.'" Mani, "Contentious Traditions," 135.

[98] *V pamiat'*, 43–45; and Danil' D. Azamatov, "The Muftis of the Orenburg Spiritual Assembly in the 18th and 19th Centuries: The Struggle for Power in Russia's Muslim Institution," in *Muslim Culture in Russia and Central Asia from the 18th to the Early 20th Centuries*, vol. 2, Anke von Kügelgen, Michael Kemper, and Allen J. Frank, eds. (Berlin, 1998), 355–84. See also M. Kazem-Bek, *Izbrannye*

power of the ulama, they did not displace Islamic law from its pivotal position at the nexus of state administration and the life of the local mosque community. Indeed, the rise of Orientalist scholarship gave laypeople new venues—and new languages—for advancing their understandings of the *shariʿa*. Despite the change in tone of many provincial officials, laypeople continued to look to the state as a force for salvation. In 1862, the peasant Khasan Ishmukhametev of Kazan province turned to the emperor "Alexander Nikolaevich" for justice. He sought his intervention in a bitter conflict with the local mullah, who refused to confer a name on his newly born son and pray for his sick daughter, who was also then absent at her burial, and, finally, who snubbed Ishmukhametev before the entire community at the celebration ending Ramadan.[99] Similarly, in 1865, the family of a Bashkir woman named Shagimardanova pursued a case against local ulama and the Orenburg Assembly all the way to the minister of the interior. In a petition to Peter Valuev, her father complained that her son-in-law had abused his daughter, accusing her of leading a "dissolute life" and cursing her mother with "impermissibly foul language." He argued that the "words of the Holy Law on the insulting [things said] in relation to my wife and daughter give me the boldness to ask Your Excellency to order the investigation of this case and to give my daughter a divorce according to our religion." Challenged by the scholar Kazem-Bek, who backed the ruling of the assembly, Shagimardanova and her father failed to win state backing for their views about the role of Islamic tradition in sanctifying the honor of their family.[100] Nonetheless, such appeals continued, guaranteeing the implication of the regime in the mediation of some of the most fundamental conflicts regarding religious authority and interpretation in Muslim communities.

The Muslim expectation that the tsarist police functioned as guardians of Islamic orthodoxy persisted despite challenges from provincial and church officials who sought to confine police support to the Orthodox faith alone as the pillar of the empire. In 1869, the governor-general of Orenburg province, N. A. Kryzhanovskii, protested a request to the police from the Orenburg mufti Tevkelev. The mufti had instructed the police in provinces inhabited by Muslims to distribute a circular requiring clerics to sign pledges that they would lead moral lives according to the *shariʿa*, root out sin, and "serve as an example [to parishioners] in their lives," inspiring them to fulfill "the obligations of a citizen, not only with respect to religion but in relation to obligations toward the authorities [*nachal'stvo*]."[101] Kryzhanovskii refused Tevkelev's request, claiming that none of the "foreign confessions" had this right, adding that "to compel the Russian police to affirm and spread the *shariʿa* in Russia, to drive the people into the mosques and invite parishioners to make monetary payments for the benefit of fanaticism [*izuverstvo*], in truth, may be taken for mockery of the Russian authorities." While Kryzhanovskii balked in the name of safeguarding the "state interest in relation to the Muhammadan religion," the governors of Astrakhan, Samara, Simbirsk, Viatka, Perm, Semipalatinsk, Nizhnyi Novgorod, and Tobol'sk provinces had already complied with Tevkelev's request, apparently in agreement with the mufti's representation of the mandate of his

---

proizvedeniia (Baku, 1985); and on his activities within the Ministry of the Interior, RGIA, f. 821, op. 8, d. 951, 964, 969.

[99] TsGIARB, f. I-295, op. 3, d. 5185.

[100] RGIA, f. 821, op. 8, d. 964, ll. 1 and 18–ob. 19.

[101] RGIA, f. 821, op. 8, d. 609, l. 7.

FIGURE 5: A lithograph representing the Tatars of Kazan. F. K. Pauli, *Description ethnographique des peuples de la Russe* (St. Petersburg, 1862). Courtesy of the Library of Congress.

FIGURES 6 and 7: A decree of 1844 established model mosque designs inspired by contemporary church architecture. However, this attempt to manage and contain the symbolic expression of Islam and impose a uniform imperial aesthetic on mosque construction proved impractical. In 1862, the government abandoned the obligatory model plans shown here but still required that drawings for mosque plans be approved in advance by Russian provincial officials. *Polnoe sobranie zakonov Rossiskoi imperii*, vol. 19 (St. Petersburg, 1845). Courtesy of the Library of Congress.

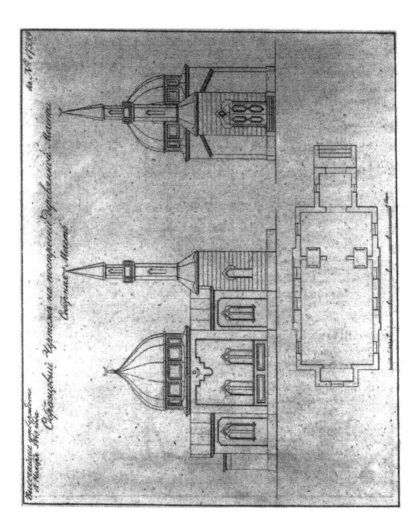

institution: "Strictly prosecuting the sins and constantly caring for the moral education of the people, it fufills its religious and civil duty, always with the view that good morality, following the path of the law, and irreproachable behavior serve as a pledge of the best civic virtues."[102]

The minister of the interior admonished Tevkelev to use "moral influence, and not police measures," but the assembly's own archival records show that resort to police intervention remained a basic component of its procedure.[103] Indeed, dependence on state institutions endured as a fundamental aspect of Islamic legal practice in the empire, even among Muslims who were divided on other questions of interpretation. In 1891, the same year that the critic of state policy E. N. Voronets charged Muslims with acting as a "state within a state," the reformer Gasprinskii published an editorial in his newspaper defending a recent decision by the Senate confirming Muslims' right to litigate inheritance disputes in state courts according to the *shari'a*. Responding to critics of the Senate's interpretation of the law, Gasprinskii argued against permitting Muslims to opt out of their religious law in state courts: "To grant Muslims the right to divide inheritance according to both civil and *shari'a* laws would mean purposefully to introduce discord into the Muslim family, and to make mandatory division only according to civil laws would be a restriction in the use and fulfillment of religion, and this is completely alien to the spirit and letter of Russian state laws."[104] Like their opponents, Gasprinskii and other reformers assimilated the legal language and bureaucratic practices of the state within their own competing interpretations of the faith, pressing the regime to stay true to its promise of toleration by safeguarding the divine law against its enemies both outside and within the Muslim community.

LIKE ALEXIS DE TOCQUEVILLE'S *ancien régime*, the tsarist state assumed an indispensable role in the minds of its Muslim subjects.[105] In turn, the adjudication of Islamic disputes shaped the basic legal and institutional structures of the state by linking the struggle for the *shari'a* to the expanding power of local policing and judicial institutions. The Islamic hierarchy experienced only relative success in mobilizing religious authority in support of empire. But a broader, and largely unintended, pattern of integration emerged from below: through the everyday mediation of Islamic legal disputes, Muslim litigants incorporated tsarist law and institutions into their pursuit of the obligation to "enjoin good and prohibit evil."

For Muslims and tsarist officials alike, imperial politics retained a critical confessional dimension into the early twentieth century. The "Muslim question" divided government ministers on the question of continued state patronage of Islam while supplying local Muslim factions with new labels such as "Pan-Islam" to castigate their foes before tsarist officials. But the state confronted in Islam neither a "minority" nor a "nationality" problem.[106] These concepts entered the vocabulary

---

[102] RGIA, f. 821, op. 8, d. 609, ll. 2 ob.–3, 6, and 13 ob.–15. See also ChaeRan Y. Freeze's discussion of like-minded Orthodox Jewish leaders, *Jewish Marriage and Divorce in Imperial Russia* (Hanover, N.H., 2002), esp. 247-55.

[103] RGIA, f. 821, op. 8, d. 609, l. 9 ob. But see also TsGIARB, f. I–295, op. 2, d. 122, l. 432 ob.

[104] *Tercüman/Perevodchik*, August 21, 1891. The Tatar version of this text is even more explicit, calling on Russian courts to guarantee "shares according to Islamic law" (*şer'î hisseleri*).

[105] Alexis de Tocqueville, *The Old Regime and the French Revolution*, Stuart Gilbert, trans. (New York, 1955).

[106] Concern with "minorities" and "minority rights" became a central constitutional issue in

of officialdom only in the last years of the regime and had a very limited impact on state policies and popular politics.[107] As in other communities, some educated Muslim elites imagined their co-religionists as a "nation" (*millet*). But relatively few Muslims adopted the language of nationality. From the perspective of the regime, too, religious affiliation endured, alongside "estate" (*soslovie*), as the most basic official social category.[108]

The story of Islam and other non-Orthodox faiths in nineteenth-century Russia suggests the extent to which the tsarist regime and empire rested on confessional foundations. Muslims and Jews shared more than legal disabilities such as restrictions on admission to the legal profession in the last decades of the old regime.[109] Religious institutions and personnel performed essential tasks on behalf of the local organs of government, administering justice, welfare, and education. In regulating the family and moral lives of the tsars' subjects and linking religious rituals to imperial themes, state-sponsored clerics constructed the moral order that underpinned the empire. A supraconfessional elite cultivated an imperial consciousness that cannot be reduced to "some other history," that of the "nation" or even of "ethnicity."[110] Imperial confessional identities were reshaped through the pursuit of religious goals within the framework of tsarist laws and institutions. By assuming the role of a confessional state and deploying police power on behalf of orthodoxy in each of the tolerated faiths, the regime deepened its regulatory and disciplinary reach into non-Orthodox communities. Religious controversies molded the local contours of the state, and pious activists succeeded in building the state from below. Police intervention on behalf of the state and true religion bound Muslims and other non-Orthodox to the tsarist political order, transforming both Islam and the empire.

European law only at the conclusion of World War I. On the incompatibility of "minorities" and imperial conceptual frameworks, see Aron Rodrigue, "Difference and Tolerance in the Ottoman Empire, Interview by Nancy Reynolds," *Stanford Humanities Review* 5, no. 1 (1995): 81–90. In Russia, Muslim elites first deployed the results of the census of 1897 in debates about representation in the Duma and the use of language in localities where Muslims formed the "predominant people" (*galip kavim*, also translated into Russian in a footnote as *preobladaiushchaia narodnost'*). See Musi Bigiief, *Rusya müslümanları ittifağının programı* (St. Petersburg, 1906), 18.

[107] On the persistent ambiguity of the categories of nationality and ethnicity in this context, see the excellent studies by Theodore R. Weeks, "Defending Our Own: Government and the Russian Minority in the Kingdom of Poland, 1905–1914," *Russian Review* 54, no. 4 (October 1995): 539–51; Charles Steinwedel, "To Make a Difference: The Category of Ethnicity in Late Imperial Russian Politics, 1861–1917," *Russian Modernity: Politics, Knowledge, Practices*, David L. Hoffmann and Yanni Kotsonis, eds. (New York, 2000), 67–86; and Noack, *Muslimischer Nationalismus*. For the broader intellectual context, see John W. Slocum, "Who, and When, Were the *Inorodtsy*? The Evolution of the Category of 'Aliens' in Imperial Russia," *Russian Review* 57 (April 1998): 173–90; and Nathaniel Knight, "Ethnicity, Nationality and the Masses: *Narodnost'* and Modernity in Imperial Russia," in Hoffmann and Kotsonis, *Russian Modernity*, 41–64.

[108] On "confession" as a primary category of nineteenth-century European censuses, see Brigitte Roth, "Religionen/Konfessionen," in *Die Nationalitäten des Russischen Reiches in der Volkszahlung von 1897*, Henning Bauer, Andreas Kappeler, and Brigitte Roth, eds., vol. A (Stuttgart, 1991), 285–323.

[109] S. M. Dubnow, *History of the Jews in Russia and Poland*, vol. 2 (Philadelphia, 1918), 352–53.

[110] Ranajit Guha, *Elementary Aspects of Peasant Insurgency in Colonial India* (Durham, N.C., 1999), 4.

Robert Crews is an assistant professor of history at Stanford University. He received his PhD in 1999 from Princeton University, where he studied with Laura Engelstein and Stephen Kotkin. Crews is completing a book on Islam and the politics of empire in Russia and Central Asia.

[20]
Kings of the Mountains
Mayréna, Missionaries, and French Colonial Divisions in 1880s Indochina[1]

JAMES P. DAUGHTON

In the late nineteenth century, the distance from Qui Nhon to Kontum – a trip of about two hundred kilometers – was nearly insurmountable. The route most travellers took led from the port town in southern Annam out across a narrow coastal plain of cultivated fields before crossing rivers and gorges, and ascending rocky mountains.[2] Then the path leveled out on a high plateau of extreme weather and dense forests where fever, tigers, and unwelcoming local communities intimidated even the hardiest of travellers. Though well within the borders of French-controlled Annam, there was little Vietnamese – and even less French – about these highlands. The region was inhabited almost exclusively by a variety of indigenous groups like the Sedang, the Bahnar, and the Jarai, who were both ethnically distinct from the majority Vietnamese population of Annam, and politically independent from the emperor in Hué as well as the French colonial administration. The region was so isolated from the rest of the colony that Frenchmen invoked the Vietnamese name for the area, calling it the *Pays Moï* – 'savages' country' – and even the missionaries, the only Europeans to live in the region until the early 1900s, referred to their headquarters in Kontum as the '*Mission des Sauvages*'.[3] It was an unlikely focal point for one of the most divisive controversies in the French empire.

In the late 1880s, few Frenchmen had heard of the *Pays Moï*, nor even knew of the Catholic mission at Kontum. But that changed in 1888, when Charles-David de Mayréna, a 'ne'er-do-well' adventurer and explorer, arrived in the central highlands claiming to be on an official mission for France.[4] Mayréna, with help from two local missionaries, Pères Guerlach and Irigoyen, spent over two months meeting with local chiefs, making agreements and signing constitutions which, among other things, submitted local populations to French authority, and regulated trade between the region and the rest of the colony.[5] But in June of 1888, Mayréna made a number of modifications to the agreements brokered up until that point.[6] In a constitution signed on 3 June at the Sedang village of Kon-Gung, Mayréna made one particularly significant amendment – a newly-crafted

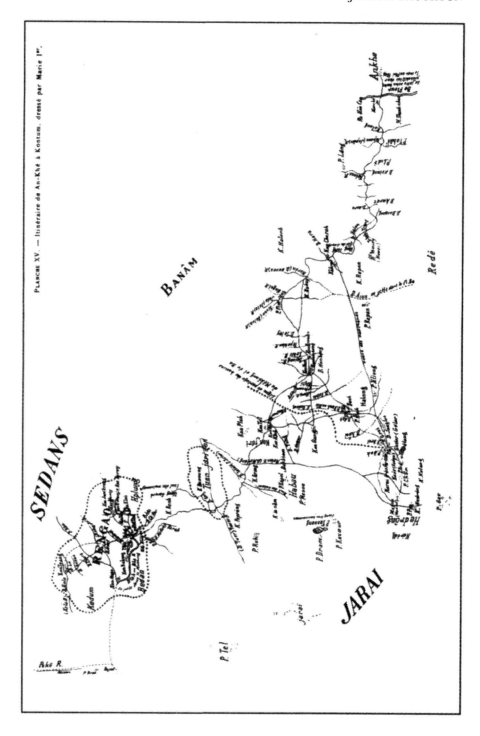

PLANCHE XV. — Itinéraire de An-Khé à Kontum, dressé par Marie 1er.

Article 3 that read: 'M. de Mayréna, already recognized chief, is elected King of the Sedangs.'[7]

Mayréna, who assumed the throne as Marie I, had a brief but notorious reign as King of the Sedangs. Though he had no aristocratic blood in his veins – 'de Mayréna' was an affectation – he was a master of royal pretensions and grandiose gestures. Shortly after naming himself king, Marie I had printed royal stationary, designed flags, medals of honour, and postage stamps, and even ordered military uniforms for his Sedang soldiers who traditionally did not wear European-style clothing.[8] To the embarrassment of some and the amusement of many, he gave interviews to French and British journalists, and wrote letters to the President of the French Republic in which he spoke about his commitment to defending his people – even though he could not communicate with his followers without an interpreter. Stories of his adventures were a hit in cafés from the Rue Catinat in Saigon to the boulevards of Paris, and filled columns in national and colonial papers.[9]

Not all, however, was harmless showmanship. Out of cash, Mayréna threatened to turn to Britain, Siam, or even Prussia (this, from a man awarded the Chevalier of the Legion of Honour for his part in the 1870 war) if the French failed to acknowledge and subsidise his Sedang kingdom. Concerned that the central highlands – a region outside of the administration's reach, part of which bordered lands controlled by Siam – could fall under the influence of France's adversaries, colonial officials monitored Mayréna's movements carefully, and treated him as a threat to colonial stability. The French government spurned his requests to meet with the Governor-General of Indochina and refused him an audience with the President of the Republic. Once he left Indochina – to go first to Hong Kong, then to Europe in search of investors in his new country – the French took steps to block Mayréna's return to his kingdom. In November of 1890, on the island of Tioman off the Malaysian peninsula, while plotting his reentry into the highlands, Mayréna died, reportedly from a snake bite.[10] 'I believe he was at the end of his resources', wrote the French consulate in Singapore. 'This adventure is therefore finally finished.'[11]

While the adventures of Mayréna represent a minor, if intriguing episode in the annals of French colonial history, the relative ease with which he founded his own kingdom within the borders of the French possession raised questions that took decades to answer. The central question in the affair that followed – how did this adventurer manage to name himself King of the Sedangs? – was answered with little effort by many in the French colonial community. Administrators and journalists alike fingered the French Catholic mission in Kontum, agreeing that Mayréna could not have accomplished what he did without the collaboration of missionary guides and translators. Less clear, however, was *why* the mission offered its services. The priests involved defended themselves by saying they were duped by a man who claimed to be working as an official envoy of France. Critics of the mission chose a different interpretation, asserting that the conniving Catholic mission had never supported the French colonial cause, and that Mayréna was an example of the lengths to which the mission would go to undermine French influence in the possession. The Catholic mission in Indochina, which realised the inevitability of French rule there, refused to accept such accusations, sparking debates both in official circles and the colonial press.

The Mayréna Affair offers a rare glimpse into the divided nature of French colonial society at an early stage of its development in Annam, Tonkin, and Cochinchina. Despite Jules Ferry's and other republicans' commitment to colonial expansion and fulfilling France's supposed '*mission civilisatrice*', the Mayréna Affair suggests that Frenchmen in the late 1880s in Indochina had little set programme or plan for bringing 'civilisation' to the '*sauvages*'.[12] Ironically, the job of civilising was left to the *least* republican members of the colonial society, Catholic missionaries. What held French colonial society together in the late 1880s was a vague concept of patriotism and a common desire to spread French 'influence'. But even definitions of these terms varied greatly according to Frenchmen's political and religious beliefs.

Mayréna's adventures and the 'affair' that followed have been the focus of a number of studies. Most of these have chronicled the events from Mayréna's assent to the mountains of the central highlands to his death as a fallen king, paying special attention to the question of why the administration approved the Mayréna expedition in the first place.[13] In his documentary survey of relations between French missionaries and the colonial administration, Patrick Tuck presents the Mayréna Affair as a key moment of division between the mission and the colonial community.[14] This article takes Tuck's work as a starting point, arguing not only that the Mayréna Affair exemplifies internal French colonial divisions, but that it reveals the extent to which many key colonial policies, such as how best to spread French 'influence' to regions outside the administration's reach, were still unformulated in the late 1880s. Rather than dictated from Paris or the Governor-General's office, these policies were shaped by conflict, debate, and collaboration of various sectors of the French colony – most notably the Catholic mission and its French critics in Indochina. The battle lines set in the conflict over Mayréna would shape other debates over proselytisation and 'civilisation' in Indochina for the following thirty years.

The Uncertain Borders of Indochina: Mayréna and the Politics of the Central Highlands

In 1888 when Mayréna announced his desire to lead an expedition to the interior of Annam, the colonial administration had recently taken interest in securing the central highlands. In the mid-1880s a number of events led to unease in Paris and Indochina about the security of Annam's western border in the central highlands. First, in 1884-1885 mandarins in Annam revolted, with widespread violence aimed at undermining French rule. In his history of Vietnamese anticolonialism, David Marr marks 5 July 1885 – the day Ham Nghi, the sitting emperor of Vietnam, fled his capital – as 'a turning point in the history of Vietnam's response to foreign intervention'.[15] The day signaled the intensification of the Can Vuong, or 'Loyalty to the King', movement of widespread, violent resistance by scholars and peasants. Can Vuong forces targeted Vietnamese Christians, killing between thirty and forty thousand; Christians retaliated, destroying pagodas and non-Christian villages, aiding the French cause. Northern Annam was particularly effected by the fighting, and General de Courcy, who led the French forces in Vietnam, realised he lacked the troops to deal effectively with the rebellion. Ham Nghi remained in hiding in the in-land mountains of northern Annam, seeking assistance from Muong minority villagers, until November 1888.[16]

The region directly surrounding the central highlands that Mayréna would eventually explore – south of Hué to Binh Dinh – witnessed episodic violence, though not on the scale of regions to the north. In central Annam, French administrators relied on collaborating mandarins to help put down local scholar-gentry rebellions. The relative security in this region, however, was undermined by international politics. While the French tried to bring the fighting under control, Siam increased its influence over territory east of the Mekong River – an encroachment that many Frenchmen thought was encouraged by the British. Suspicion grew even deeper in 1886 when the British moved into Upper Burma. Uncertain of their power over the colonial population, and worried by menacing neighbours, French colonialists saw their rule in Southeast Asia threatened from all sides.[17] By the mid-1880s, the '*Pays Moï*' ceased to be simply a *terra incognita*; now, many in the administration saw it as a vulnerable frontier where the Siamese, British, or even – as some rumors suggested – Prussians could stage an invasion of the French colony. The French were thoroughly unprepared to battle both foreign invaders and internal Can Vuong resistance fighters.

Though nominally a part of the French protectorate of Annam, the central highlands remained independent for all practical purposes. Local and regional mandarins – Vietnamese officials who administered much of the day-to-day functioning of the protectorate – were entirely absent from the region, with Vietnamese authority not stretching beyond An Khe, a town less than halfway to Kontum from Qui Nhon. Traditionally, highland minorities, especially the Sedang, Jarai, and Bahnar, fiercely defended their independence from the Vietnamese, occasionally fighting with and even enslaving Vietnamese who entered their territories. The French administration had little interest in challenging these groups' claims of independence; the mission was a powerful force in these communities, and until the 1880s, the administration accepted this as sufficient influence. But with the possibility of foreign powers entering the territory, France desired a more formal arrangement which would bring the highlands more directly under the protectorate, even if it meant by-passing Vietnamese authorities.

Mayréna may have been, in the words of a biographer, nothing more than a 'mediocre adventurer, a swindler, and worse still, nearly a traitor', but he was also an adept opportunist.[18] A suspected criminal with little money or connections, Mayréna ultimately succeeded in winning over the support of the colonial administration for his expedition to look for gold and silver in the central highlands.[19] Not all administrators were without reservation; the Director of the Interior in Cochinchina, for example, wrote, 'My confidence in the elder M. de Mayréna is [...] the most mediocre.' He suggested, nonetheless, that the government could help him organise an escort, but '*without arms*'.[20]

But the threat of Siamese and British activity near Annam's eastern edge clearly played a role in the government's decision to support Mayréna. Further complicating these international disputes were officials' fears that 'the rebel king [of Vietnam], his ministers, his partisans had taken refuge in the hinterland of Annam, and set out to raise the Moi [...] against us'.[21] Such preoccupations helped form the Lieutenant-Governor of Cochinchina's view that an expedition like Mayréna's could be beneficial under certain conditions. 'My opinion is that we have interest in developing French influence in this region. A mission of exploration, of reconnaissance, can only be advantageous, on the condition that it be entrusted to a man [...] of irreproachable morals and perfect honesty.' He added that he was unsure if Mayréna was such a man, but that another administrator – a M. Blanchy, President of the Conseil colonial – had recommended him for the mission.[22] In the early spring of 1888, the colonial government gave Mayréna permission to go, though without official recognition.

Mayréna boarded the *Haiphong*, a boat that took him from Saigon to Qui Nhon, capital of Binh Dinh province, from where he would start his travels to the interior. On board, he met both the Governor-General and the Secretary-General of the colony, the latter of whom wrote Mayréna a warm, if standard letter of introduction. The letter proved useful to Mayréna, as it helped him win the attention of the Resident-Superior in Qui Nhon, Charles Lemire. Lemire assisted in assembling the expedition, which at the time of its departure included Mayréna, his associate Alphonse Mercurol, their two Vietnamese concubines, a cook, four Chinese merchants to help locate gold deposits, an interpreter, eighteen *miliciens*, and eighty coolie porters.[23] In a letter written on the eve of Mayréna's departure, Lemire emphasised to the explorer that his trip was personal. But Lemire provided a number of goals for Mayréna to meet, such as opening a route from Annam into Laos. He also appealed to Mayréna's patriotism in asking him to collect flora, fauna, and minerals from the region for the Annam section of the Exposition de Paris. He also asked Mayréna and his Vietnamese interpreter to keep logs describing the expedition's activities, language usages of local inhabitants, the daily weather, and other information which might be presented to the Congrès géographique the following year. In closing, Lemire had only 'to say how much [Mayréna's] vast enterprise interests France and Annam'.[24]

While in Qui Nhon, Mayréna also impressed and apparently misled the bishop, Mgr Van Camelbeke. Believing Mayréna to be 'sent [...] by the French government', Van Camelbeke contacted the Kontum mission, and called on the missionaries' 'feeling of patriotism' to do whatever they could to facilitate the explorer's project.[25] Missionary assistance was crucial to Mayréna, for the priests were the only Europeans who had any prolonged experience in the highlands, having been permanently established there since 1852 after some ten years of trying.[26] Expeditions around Kontum had relied on missionary know-how before Mayréna. Père Guerlach, who would become embroiled in the Mayréna Affair, had personally assisted a number of important explorers, such as Administrator of Indigenous Affairs Navelle's in 1884, and Lieutenant Metz's three years later, as an interpreter and guide.[27] 'As Frenchmen, we were welcomed everywhere with open arms', Captain Cupet of the Pavie Mission wrote of his travels around Kontum with Guerlach in 1891. 'The savages recognized from afar our tri-colored flag which the Père had taught them to love.'[28]

Almost as soon as he arrived in the highlands, Mayréna needed missionary assistance. Most pressing was the fact that many of his porters abandoned him, claiming they had been brutalised and left unpaid.[29] He wrote to Guerlach asking the missionary to bring two elephants and some of his Christians to act as porters. Guerlach arrived at Mayréna's camp a few days later, elephants and porters in tow. In the meantime, Mayréna was already at work. He had signed two treaties of friendship with local chiefs, including a particularly influential one named Pim.[30] As Marquet pointed out in his study of Mayréna, if Guerlach ever doubted Mayréna's validity as an official representative of France, the adventurer had only to show the missionary his letters of introduction from the Secretary-General and the bishop, or to speak of the subvention he received from the government, or have him read the reports he regularly sent to the Ministry of the Interior and the Governor-General.[31] And in fact, Mayréna seemed to be carrying out work – that is, establishing 'amicable alliances between tribes' – that both missionaries and French administrators had championed for some time.[32] As he would later argue, Guerlach did what his bishop and his country asked him to: he helped a French explorer in need.

For much of the following three months, Mayréna travelled and lived 'side-by-side' with the missionaries of Kontum, particularly Père Guerlach, who, in addition to acting as interpreter, transcribed and translated the agreements Mayréna signed with local chiefs.[33] In his reports, Mayréna repeatedly spoke of the influence Guerlach and the missionaries held over the local population, stating that their involvement would be essential in any further negotiation.[34] Guerlach later reported that Mayréna increasingly spoke of founding a kingdom, asserting all along that the government had condoned the move. Guerlach claimed that he was placated by the adventurer's assurance that he did not plan 'to bury myself in these forests', but instead would turn over to French administrators the job of day-to-day control of the region.[35]

But what exactly happened during this time, especially what role the missionaries played in Mayréna's actions, remains, as *Le Temps* put it at the time, 'a little obscure'.[36] Later accounts by Guerlach, Mayréna, and others were starkly shaded by the accusations and defenses of the affair that followed. What is certain is that on 3 June 1888, in a Sedang village near the border with Laos, in a region of the French colony most vulnerable to foreign attack, an adventurer whose expedition had the consent, if not official sponsorship of the colonial regime named himself king.[37] Two facts would particularly call into question the missionaries' actions. On 1 July 1888, Mayréna reedited the constitution of the Sedang Kingdom, with an amended Article 12 stating that there would be freedom of religion, but that Catholicism would be 'the official religion' of the state.[38] Compounding the impression that the mission worked with Mayréna at every step was the fact that on nearly all the treaties Mayréna signed during his stay in the highlands were the signatures of missionaries – witnesses, if not collaborators of the King of the Sedangs.

Patriotism or Collaboration?
The Administration Investigates the Mission

If Mayréna himself did not appear particularly threatening to French colonists and administrators in Indochina – a number of works on him have argued that few took him seriously – his action did raise a number of important questions, primarily about the security of the French overseas possession. Mayréna's venture into a region beyond the reach of both Vietnamese and French authorities, yet within the borders of the protectorate revealed Annam's vulnerability to outside invasion as well as internal subversion. Still trying to win support from the French government, Mayréna himself wrote two letters published in the *Courrier d'Haiphong* in October and November of 1888 (the latter was addressed to the President of the Republic). In them, he addressed a number of controversial issues which would be anxiously debated by the administration as well as in the colonial and national press, such as the threat of foreign invasion, the fear of internal rebellion by the most 'savage' of the central highland groups, the mastery of the area by the mission, and the failure of the colony to meet its potential by neglecting the rich mining possibilities of the central highlands.

Mayréna started his article by claiming that his original expedition had been to undermine a Prussian mission looking to 'penetrate the land of the independent peoples of Indochina', and establish themselves there. In his first extensive statement to the French public after naming himself king of the Sedangs, Mayréna wrote that his expedition to stop Prussian invasion was without official government consent, though he strongly hinted that he secretly had France's blessing.[39] He went to the highlands, organised an army of Sedang warriors, and blocked the Prussians' route into Annam. 'The Prussians learned of the new state of things, and retreated to the right bank of the Mekong.' Upon reading his copy of the *Courrier d'Haiphong*, Père Guerlach scribbled one word in the margin of his newspaper next to this account of the run-in with the would-be invaders: 'False'.[40]

Once the Prussians were out of the way, Mayréna claimed to have gone after the Jarai, a highland group known for its fierceness on the battlefield. It was his successful campaign against the Jarai, he wrote, that won him the support of the Sedang, who as a result named him their king. (Again, Guerlach penned a 'False' in the margin.) His victories put at his disposal some twenty thousand men – both under his Sedang monarchy and as a result of an alliance with the Bahnar-Rungao confederation – which Mayréna could 'according to the needs of France, lead [*lancer*] into Annam or Cambodia in case of revolt'. Rather than a comment on France's relative strength and security, Mayréna's new-found army was a sign of the colonial administration's ineffectiveness in the more remote parts of Indochina.

Mayréna also detailed why this part of the French protectorate of Annam remained outside of the administration's reach:

> The independence of [the central highlands] is incontestable. It is affirmed by the missionaries, the people of the country who declare that they have never accepted foreign chiefs, it is incontestable due to the geographic configuration of the country, for three chains of high mountains, successive chains, protect it from Annam and Siam; these are natural and insurmountable walls, where, with one hundred men, an army would be stopped.[41]

The Vietnamese administration had achieved no more than France, not penetrating closer than a five days' walk from his kingdom. Mayréna stopped himself from saying that no Vietnamese had ever set foot in the region, claiming that those who did had been enslaved.[42] For any system of colonisation to arrive in the region, Mayréna declared, would take fifteen years of effort.[43]

In addition to the independence of the region, Mayréna raised a final point that was to concern many republican colonialists for nearly two decades to come. If Vietnamese and French authority were both powerless in the central highlands, who if anyone did have control? 'When you want to establish the limits between China and Annam', Mayréna asked, 'whom does one address? The Missions.' He continued: 'Who furnished the maps that the Ministry of Foreign Affairs has? The Missions. Who today can say where Annam ends? The Missions.'⁴⁴ A question that Mayréna needed not ask, but which was clearly in the minds of many French administrators was: Who helped Mayréna, a man now threatening to turn his allegiance to France's enemies, come to power as King of the Sedangs? The Missions.

The Resident of Qui Nhon, Charles Lemire, who initially showed great enthusiasm for Mayréna's project, and who was slow to condemn Mayréna after his unexpected ascendancy to the Sedang throne, was the first in the administration to point a finger at missionary wrong-doing. While Lemire's general attitude toward the mission is difficult to determine, in November of 1888 he claimed that the missionaries of the central highlands had not been duped, as they claimed, but rather had actively supported the work of Mayréna in the hope of establishing in the *Pays Moï* an independent kingdom like the Jesuits had in Paraguay.⁴⁵ As evidence of the mission's respect for the king, Lemire claimed that in the church in Qui Nhon they had given Mayréna a special *prie-Dieu* with red drapery and a cushion *after* he returned from the highlands as Marie I. And further Père Irigoyan – whose name appeared as translator of the famous Sedang constitution – allegedly gave a mass in honour of Mayréna.⁴⁶

Lemire was not the only member of the administration who questioned the mission's actions. Governor-General Richaud, in a report to Paris, wrote that the missionary's role in these events was 'very regrettable'. Emphasising the particular significance of these events which took place in a border region, the Governor-General added that it was 'gravely important [...] that the Mission should have chosen to side with a person who is claiming to detach from a country placed under our protectorate a region which is dependent on it'.⁴⁷ Paul Rheinart, Resident-Superior of Annam and Tonkin, also took Lemire's claims seriously, and oversaw the investigation of the mission's involvement in the affair. He demanded that Guerlach and Irigoyen be removed form their positions in the region – a request which drove Guerlach to travel to Hanoi to clear his name.⁴⁸ And he asked Mgr Van Camelbeke to explain the mission's position on French influence in the highlands. When Van Camelbeke expressed the belief that the region was largely independent of colonial administrative influence, Rheinart strongly rebuked him – 'the political map of Indochina contains no "blanks"' – and echoed the Governor-General's concern about why the mission 'took the side' of a man who planned to turn the region over to foreign domination.⁴⁹

Van Camelbeke responded quickly and repeatedly to the rumors and suggestions that the mission had knowingly collaborated with Mayréna. He dismissed as 'pure fable' Lemire's assertion that the Church had given a special mass in Mayréna's honour and outfitted a *prie-Dieu* for royal use. 'In the relations that I had to have with him, I let him know that neither my missionaries in Binh Dinh, nor I could take the least part in his projects and enterprises [...] We refused equally to give him the denominations of Sire, Majesty, King [...] etc.'⁵⁰ Lemire, in the bishop's view, believed too many of the extravagant things that came from Mayréna's mouth. Van Camelbeke also padded his denials with a healthy amount of patriotic fervor, reasserting what he called 'the correctness [*droiture*] of my sentiments' regarding the *patrie*.[51] 'France can, when it wants, recognize its protectorate over these savage tribes, since the missionaries displayed the French flag well before M. de Mayréna [...]'[52]

Guerlach's defense followed a similar tack. He pointed out that two important ethnic minorities, the Bahnar and Rungao, had formed a defensive confederation in 1885 under the direction of Père Vialleton, the superior of the Kontum mission. Though these chiefs were frightened by Mayréna's 'violent character', they signed a constitution with him in the hopes that it would lead to an agreement with France, under whose protectorate they wished to be. 'Wouldn't it be advantageous for our dear *Patrie* to assure itself the possession of all the country from the border of Annam to the Sedang territory?' Of course, he added, France had had representation in the form of the missionaries 'who planted the French flag' but who played no official political or diplomatic role. The Bahnar-Rungao confederation could now be dealt with directly, with the missionaries' help, and would form a buffer zone between Annam and Siam should Mayréna turn to Prussia or another adversary of France. 'Again, the missionaries are devoted to France', Guerlach concluded, but they could do little to help the nation as they had not been given an official political role. The missionary put himself at the Resident General's disposal should he decide to start talks with 'the savage chiefs' of the Bahnar-Rungao confederation.[53]

As far as Resident-General Rheinart was concerned, the declarations of patriotism made by Van Camelbeke and Guerlach cleared the mission from further suspicion. Writing to Van Camelbeke that he had 'always had much esteem and sympathy for our missions', Rheinart spoke of the 'sentiments of ardent patriotism' missionaries had shown 'many times in the face of danger'. Almost gushing, the Resident-General added, 'I am thus very happy, Monseigneur, to have to say that nowhere is more patriotism shown than in your beautiful mission'. Rather than simple reassurances, Van Camelbeke's 'so loyal declarations' had helped 'destroy and annul' all accusations made against Guerlach and Irigoyen.[54]

To Guerlach, Rheinart was no less laudatory. 'I thank you infinitely for this new sign of patriotism you have given us. Believe that I am very touched by it, and that I am very happy to have seen dissipate entirely the misunderstanding that had sprung up during the Mayréna Affair.' He also commended the missionary for his wise advice regarding the Bahnar-Rungao confederation, and for helping organise 'the defense of the country'.[55] Rheinart backed up his congratulations with administrative action. He instructed Lemire, whose behaviour he called 'tactless', to cease further investigation of missionary wrong-doing.[56] The following month, in January of 1889, Lemire was removed from his post, and reassigned to Vinh. Lemire left office still convinced the mission was guilty of duplicity, saying one missionary had supported Mayréna at Qui Nhon while another repudiated him at Hanoi.

Colonial Opinion and the Catholic Mission in the Wake of Mayréna

The mission had a considerably more difficult time clearing itself in the colonial press. In late June of 1888, Mayréna had a copy of the 3 June constitution of the Sedang kingdom turned over to the colonial newspaper *Courrier d'Haiphong*, thus beginning a rich exchange of articles reflecting an array of opinions about Mayréna, the French administration, the *Pays Moï*, and the mission. These articles also reflected the extent to which colonial public opinion in Indochina – particularly on issues concerning the mission – often diverged from, and even critiqued official administrative policy. Mayréna understood the potential of public opinion, and many of the subsequent articles he published on his kingdom were submitted in the hope that 'public opinion would provoke a solution'.[57]

In the colonial press, Guerlach was the most outspoken defender of the mission, a fitting role as his actions with Mayréna were perhaps the most suspicious. In December 1888, the same month that the missionary convinced Resident-General Rheinart of his limitless patriotism and absolute innocence, Guerlach published no fewer than three letters in the *Courrier d'Haiphong* explaining his role. On 20 December, the newspaper published Guerlach's first report on the events of the spring of 1888 in which the priest did little more than chronicle Mayréna's travel and work in the highlands. In this letter which tried to rewrite the inaccuracies of Mayréna's own account, the missionaries appear as relatively insignificant actors who simply offered their services – mainly as interpreters and translators – when the explorer needed them. Guerlach, lacking the combative ire that would later define his style, offered little explanation of why the missionaries continued to work with Mayréna after he named himself king.

Five days after the publication of his first letter, Guerlach wrote a second, this time responding to the many rumors he had heard since arriving in Hanoi where he had been summoned to explain his role to the Resident-General. Out of the seclusion of the highlands, Guerlach became aware of the suggestions of missionary collaboration that stretched from the possession to France. Even *Le Temps* was skeptical of missionary involvement, echoing Lemire's accusations that the Church had blessed the new-found kingdom. The newspaper, which took the entire affair light-heartedly, joked that, considering Mayréna's desire to find investors in Europe for his new enterprise, Guerlach might now bless dividends as well as the king's flags.[58] Guerlach flatly rejected any link to Mayréna: 'I assert that never did the missionaries give to M. de Mayréna any commercial or other mandate [...].' He also claimed that his and Père Irigoyen's signatures on Mayréna's agreements meant nothing: 'My signature, placed at the bottom of certain acts, does not imply at all any engagement nor cooperation whatsoever. I signed as an eye-witness, that's all.' Reminding his readers of the ways in which he had helped France in the past, Guerlach ended by defending the work of Navelle and Metz against the public criticisms of Mayréna; these official expeditions into the highlands both preceded Mayréna's and benefited from missionary assistance, and stood as evidence of Guerlach's goodwill to France.[59]

Three days after the *Courrier d'Haiphong* ran Guerlach's second letter, he penned yet another, much longer and more detailed, defense. He opened by wondering aloud if it would not have been better to let the rumors go unchecked until the affair had quieted down, but decided 'a longer delay would have given birth to a thousand suspicions some stranger than others [...]'. He said it was necessary to address 'the suspicions carried against the patriotism and honor of the missionaries' and the character of Mayréna as all these questions 'stir opinion and demand a prompt and decisive solution'. What emerged from Guerlach's long rebuttal was the template for how missionaries would define and defend their role in French Indochina for years to come.

Guerlach reiterated and in some cases expanded the same points of defense he made in previous letters to the editor. Again, he emphasised that from his position in the central highlands, Mayréna looked like a man on an official mission for the French Government, 'misleading [the missionaries] about the character of his mission'. There was no cause to suspect Mayréna had personal reasons to explore the area of the *Pays Moï*, as the missionary considered it under the protectorate of France. He did not deny the role he and Irigoyen played as translators and guides, but he strongly denied the suggestion – originating from Mayréna, and believed by Resident Lemire at Qui Nhon – that the mission was ready, at the explorer's signal, to turn on France. Lemire accused the mission 'of being hostile to our *patrie*', and yet, Guerlach wrote, the Resident received Mayréna at his table *after* the explorer threatened to turn his allegiances to England or Prussia. Guerlach thus turned on Lemire, the accuser of the Catholic mission, and suggested the Resident's own guilt by association. 'In this circumstance, as in many others, M. Lemire did not prove the qualities necessary of a Resident.'[60]

The missionary's argument went further, however, than denial and counter-accusation: his letter outlined a definition of commitment to France in moral terms. The bulk of his long letter touched on the many times Mayréna had lied, not simply in privately deceiving the mission or the Resident of Qui Nhon, but in his letters to the public, published in the colonial papers. Guerlach cast himself as the teller of truths, particularly in regards to Mayréna's own accounts of his travels in the highlands: 'Mayréna was able to invent everything at his ease, no one contradicted him.' The adventurer had lied about the presence of Prussians on the left bank of the Mekong river. He had told the *China Mail* in Hong Kong of meeting the Prussians in the highlands, and of threatening them into retreat; that too, Guerlach asserted, was false. Mayréna had claimed to lead an army of ten thousand soldiers, even though the total population of the villages that signed Mayréna's constitution was but twelve thousand. He had offered descriptions of the countryside, and of the inhabitants of the region, but all this information in reality had been supplied by the missionaries. He had spoken about rich mines of gold; of those, Guerlach 'knew absolutely nothing'. He had even gone so far as to invent an account of a trip to Hanoi, and to create 'an imaginary interview' with people he had never met.[61]

More than a condemnation of Mayréna, what is evident in Guerlach's letter is a recipe for French behaviour in the colonies. He alluded to the 'thousand' lies and exaggerations of Mayréna 'in order to edify the public about the morality of this character'. Against the deceptive ways of the notorious explorer, Guerlach contrasted the Resident-General 'whose rectitude, intention, and loyalty equals his intelligence and steadfastness'. The Resident-General's own upstanding character then shone benevolently on the mission: he knew 'that the missionaries established among the savages love France with all their heart and are disposed to serve it with all their power. May M. le Résident-Général receive here publicly evidence of my respectful devotion.'

Here, Guerlach's moral formula also had a distinctly racial element: repeatedly, he spoke of his work among 'the savages'. In so doing, he invoked an implicitly racial dimension to both morality and France's role in the colony, as well as a subtle critique of the less respectable elements of the colonial population. Though Guerlach was soon to be 'again on the route to the savages', he viewed his trip as a return 'to the calm of the apostolic life' in comparison to 'the agitations of these recent times'. As we will see in more detail later, Guerlach clearly found some 'savage' behaviour preferable to that of his compatriots. But morally questionable individuals to Guerlach were not simply undesirable neighbours in the colonies, they threatened to undermine the mission's and the nation's work among the savages:

> The missions in distant and unknown countries require serious people and not characters whom one wants to get rid of, who have much audacity but very little conscience and whose moral sense is obliterated. Such explorers harm the cause that they pretend to serve, and it would be desirable that serious missions be confined to serious and honorable men.[62]

What is perhaps most interesting about this passage is that Guerlach conflated Catholic missions with scientific and exploratory missions. He left 'the cause' which missions served as a vague concept – one that would become rhetorically the 'civilizing mission' in the 1890s. But clearly Guerlach was suggesting that French missions abroad, be they religious or laic, could only be conducted by the morally sound, and to be moral – a state Guerlach assumed inherent to all missionaries – was itself, in the colonies, commitment to France. Facing down this moral being was the savage, who could either benefit from the French presence or else threaten its very existence.

Guerlach ended his letter by saying that he considered the Mayréna Affair to be finished; and in fact debate in the colonial press did quiet down for a number of months. In the spring of 1889, Guerlach helped organise a number of meetings between local chiefs an official administrative representatives. In March, Resident-General Rheinart himself came to the highlands and met with a number of chiefs, such as a particularly influential chief named Krui who headed up the Bahnar-Rungao confederation. Rheinart assured the chiefs he met that Mayréna did not represent France, and that by entering the protectorate the individual minority groups would not be occupied by French forces.[63] In March and April, a further mission was undertaken by the new Vice-Resident of Qui Nhon, a M. Guiomar, met with the Hamong and Sedang chiefs who had signed the constitution with Mayréna.

In a letter in June 1889 to the *Courrier d'Haiphong* Guerlach updated the colony on the fate of the Mayréna Affair after Guiomar's trip. He was still combating what he called a number of 'very fantastical' stories published about him in the press. This, perhaps like all of his letters, was an attempt to put an end to the rumors. Guerlach's letter recounted how the Vice-Resident had explained to a number of local chiefs that Mayréna had duped both the mission and France. With the missionaries' assistance, Guiomar invited these groups to elect an indigenous chief and to join the Bahnar-Rungao confederation that had accepted France's protectorate.

Guiomar also tried to confiscate all reminders of the Sedang monarchy, such as the flags and banners that Mayréna had distributed. Guerlach made light of this project, recounting how one woman was hesitant to return a flag in her possession for she had made it into clothing. 'I must say that this national Sedang flag, transformed into a head-wrap, skirt, and wash rag, made me laugh hard.' He concluded by claiming that Mayréna's prestige in the highlands 'is reduced to zero'. The only thing left for the adventurer to do to improve his name in the colony was to repay some of the many debts he incurred. Guerlach signed off, 'That's my last word on this affair'.[64]

Criticism Renewed:
The Mission and Models of French Colonisation

But it was not. The following month, an anonymous article in the paper made passing reference to Guerlach's willingness, in helping Mayréna, to support a cause that was 'as royalist as [it was] ephemeral', provoking a fiery reply from Guerlach in October. But the anonymous article, entitled 'The New Confederation of the Bahnars-Rungaos-Sédangs', had far loftier goals than criticism of the mission. In fact, it proposed a programme for the future development of the highlands. Not particularly sympathetic to the mission, the author nonetheless saw its role as key in bringing about the Bahnar-Rungao confederation 'which can serve our cause and hasten the progress of French influence in the area'. Though the highlands were nominally part of Annam, the article argued that France must respect the autonomy of the region, with the protectorate remaining 'the political and commercial intermediary between the *Moi* and the Vietnamese'. Such a solution was 'acceptable for all and by all' – France, Annam, the *Moi*, and the Catholic mission.[65]

The plan set forth in 'The New Confederation' was both republican and tolerant of the role the mission could play to develop the protectorate in the highlands. The author of the article saw the confederation, and by extension the mission, as important to the political development of the highland minorities: 'Now the large tribes of the Sedangs and Hamongs join this confederation under the direction of the French *Pères*. The pseudo-kingdom of the Sedangs becomes a true Republic. That's not all: the President of this Moi republic is Krui, student of P. Vialleton, who has him by the hand, and who taught him to read and write in European characters.' This political progress, thus, would benefit the Moi as much as the French protectorate. But, the author warned, 'it's the tricolor flag that triumphs, but the work is still incomplete'. There remained for France the job of developing transportation throughout the highlands, from Qui Nhon to the Mekong, and south into Cochinchina. Such would protect the right bank of the Mekong, and would submit it to 'our influence' without question.[66] Such a dual plan – of political and commercial development – would become increasingly common in Indochina in the 1890s and 1900s.

Guerlach was misguided to unleash his anger on the anonymous author of 'The New Confederation'. The missionary's defense was growing stale more than a year after the affair began. Suggesting the author was not a 'man of honor' for remaining anonymous, Guerlach revisited old territory: he served his duty to France, etc. He again spoke of the work he had recently completed for Guiomar's visit, noting that the Vice-Resident 'had been able to see that the savages loved France'.[67] Ironically, in citing his work with Guiomar in order to defend himself against the anonymous author, Guerlach chose the wrong ally. For in May of 1889, apparently unbeknownst to Guerlach, Vice-Resident Guiomar filed a harsh report on the subject of his visit with the highland missionaries. Though he acknowledged being more or less at the mercy of the missionaries, as the highlands were nothing like the rest of Annam, Guiomar was skeptical throughout his visit of the mission's patriotism. For the Vice Resident's arrival in the village of Ro Hai, Guerlach's home, 'the priest had had flown in the middle of the village the French flag that I was going to see again in all the villages inhabited by the missionaries', but Guiomar was uncertain whether these were permanent displays, or simply put up for his benefit.[68]

Guiomar's inspection of the mission focused on the impact of its influence. In Kontum, he found that the mission had tremendous influence, over the pagan population as well as Christian. He did not say he thought that the influence was necessarily excessive, as he admitted the mission was useful in settling disputes between different parties. But one impression emerged: 'the missionaries consider the country they occupy as their property and they never voluntarily favor the settlement of any European whatsoever'. Their initial support of Mayréna helped convince Guiomar of this: in the Vice-Resident's opinion, the missionary found in Mayréna a man who would act at their discretion, 'a docile instrument' who would help them in 'the creation of a free state like that the Jesuits founded in Paraguay'. When it became apparent that Mayréna had ideas of his own, the mission turned on him because 'they preferred to abandon their projects before giving in to a master'.[69]

Patriotism, in Guiomar's estimation, had nothing to do with the missionaries' behaviour throughout the affair, and he even refused to believe that the mission ever thought Mayréna was a envoy of the French government. 'In the interest of their work and in order to justify their conduct that followed, they said and repeated that their patriotic sentiments had been abused.' The missionaries' show of concern over suggestions that they did not act in France's best interest worried them excessively. 'Why this fear if their conduct had not been dubious [*équivoque*]?' Finally, in a comment that rather ominously foreshadowed events in the highlands in the early 1900s, Guiomar questioned whether the mission would prove as helpful in the future, when the French administration slowly strengthened its presence in the highlands, and used its authority to regulate their own activities.[70]

Vice-Resident Guiomar's criticism struck at some basic truths about missionaries in Indochina. Guerlach's claims that he blindly followed Mayréna in the belief he was helping an official envoy of France simplified more complex motivations. From the outset, both Mgr Van Camelbeke and Père Guerlach saw potential benefits to Mayréna's expedition. Most appealing to the mission was that Mayréna offered a way in which the mission could, in the words of Van Camelbeke, 'try to find a solution to the famous Jarai affair'.[71] The Jarai were particularly aggressive neighbours of the Bahnar and had long menaced the proselytising efforts of the mission, attacking and pillaging villages and convoys. In a private letter, Guerlach candidly recounted how Mayréna's visit had a number of *positive* repercussions for the mission. Generally, by travelling with Mayréna across the region, Guerlach had 'an occasion to explore [some] foreign villages and to build with them relations of good friendship'.[72] As for the mission's enemies, Mayréna 'rendered us a great service by heading up an expedition against the *Jarai* of *Peleï Tring*', a group who had bothered the mission for over a year.

Mayréna led 1,400 Sedang-Bahnar-Rungao troops, with Guerlach going along 'as the chaplain', on a raid of the village. 'The Jarai received a severe lesson', wrote Guerlach; they were made to pay a ransom equivalent to the goods they had stolen, and they knew not to bother the mission again. The area secure, the mission could now 'more easily extend and develop our work'. In this instance, the missionary admitted, 'the *Mission des Sauvages* greatly prospered' from Mayréna's work.[73]

But the fact that Guerlach was willing, if not eager to use Mayréna's military power to benefit his mission does not suggest that the missionary supported the adventurer's monarchical aspirations. Guiomar's observation about the relative political and social power the mission enjoyed over the population greatly weakens his allegation that the mission hoped to use Mayréna to establish an independent Catholic state. European visitors were a rarity in the highlands, and the missionaries generally believed them to be an interference to their work. Also, missionaries throughout Indochina as a rule tried to remain as invisible to French administrators as possible; Guerlach was politically savvy enough to realise that claiming the central highlands an independent state would attract attention, especially at a time when the administration was intensely aware of security weaknesses. As the 'Pays Moï' were all but independent anyway, the mission had nothing to gain from taking drastic steps.

Though insightful and powerfully worded, Guiomar's report failed to change French policy toward the central highlands. The undertaking of developing an administrative presence in the region was too difficult and costly, and for many in the administration both in Indochina and in France, the missionaries were, at least for the time being, effective at spreading French influence. For much of the following decade, the mission continued its work, only interrupted by the occasional government mission or traveller. And in 1898, after years of informally relying on his help, the French government named Père Vialleton the official representative of the protectorate in the highlands.[74]

In naming Vialleton to the post, the Commandant-Superior of Lower Laos said that the priest, who was once implicated in the Mayréna Affair, had both civilised the savages of the region and used their influence to benefit the administration. The affair of 1888-1889 had died down. The protectorate had the representation they needed without building costly new posts; the mission was left to proselytise without outside interference; and the ethnic minorities held on to their relative autonomy from both French and Vietnamese administrators. It seemed that the anonymous author of 'The New Confederation' had been right to sum up his analysis with Shakespeare: 'all is well that ends well'.[75] But like a good Shakespearean drama, a ghost still wandered the hills and forests of the highlands, and that ghost was Mayréna.

Missionaries and the Colonial Regime: An Awkward Alliance

Regardless of the impact of his report, Guiomar raised an important question that Frenchmen across the empire were to debate throughout the 1890s and early 1900s: were French Catholic missionaries committed to France? Were they patriots fighting to extend the influence of the nation, or were they looking, as Guiomar and others suggested, to develop only their own power over local populations? To address such question requires an understanding of both long-term regional and colonial history, as well as the politics of patriotism, religion, and republicanism in late-nineteenth century France.

French Catholic missionaries in Indochina long predated French colonialism. In the mid-1800s when the French government started showing official interest in Southeast Asia, French missionaries – primarily either Jesuits or secular priests from the Société des Missions Etrangères de Paris – had been proselytising in the region for nearly two centuries. In fact, the French protectorate of the Catholic missions abroad – a commitment that dated from the Napoleonic era – justified French political and military involvement in Cochinchina, Annam, and Tonkin from the 1840s forward. Anti-Christian, anti-western movements, some of which led to the killing of thousands of Vietnamese converts, as well as the imprisonment, torture, and execution of many French missionaries, brought French ships into confrontation with Vietnamese forces throughout the 1840s and '50s. In the minds of both Vietnamese and French officials, the plight of indigenous Christians was closely associated with French colonial interests in the region, and in some cases, such as Francis Garnier's 1873-1874 invasion of Tonkin, Vietnamese Catholics played an important collaborative role.[76] As a prominent bishop in Hanoi put it in 1884 during one of the worst massacres of the century, Vietnamese mandarins killed Christians because they saw them as friends of France. 'Yes, I can say it, our neophytes have always loved and still love France', Mgr Puginier wrote.[77]

Throughout the 1890s, the assumption that French missionaries spread a love of both Christ *and* France remained the accepted wisdom of the foreign office in Paris and many colonial officials abroad. Missionaries usually taught some French – though not enough for some colonialists – and basic European social, economic and political skills. Until the 1890s, most colonialists considered missionary work a means of easing, if not paving the way for colonisation. For their troubles, the colonial governments regularly paid missionaries annual subventions to build and keep up schools, orphanages, hospitals, and other services.

Missionary *intentions*, however, did not always dovetail with appearances: many missionaries feared that the arrival of French administrators and colonists would be detrimental to their efforts of proselytisation. In 1890, for example, the bishop of West Cochinchina wondered in his *compte-rendu* why it seemed increasingly difficult to convert the local population. He attributed it in great part to the growing influence of Frenchmen in the colony, and 'the feeling of incredulity [*esprit d'incrédulité*] that penetrates the *indigènes* with knowledge of the French'; there existed among the local population 'everywhere, hate and contempt [...] for our compatriots'. He concluded his report, lamenting, '*Och!* If France had only sent honest and Christian men to Indochina!'[78]

Not all missionary criticism was of a moral kind; other reports argued that French policies in the possession led to hardship for the missionary and his followers. Taxes were especially contentious for they required an already poor Vietnamese to work harder, meaning 'he has neither the time, nor the leisure of studying prayers and Christian doctrine'.[79] Missionaries also worried about censuses, a necessary facet of effective colonial rule. A proposed 1905 census distinguished between Catholic and Buddhist Vietnamese populations, leading one bishop with memories of the 1884-85 massacre of Catholic converts to worry that the collected data could be used by mandarins to target Christian communities in future rebellions.[80] His concern was not without grounds: Vietnamese leaders throughout much of the second half of the nineteenth century used censuses to better locate and isolate Christians in times of unrest.

Missionaries in Indochina also regularly involved themselves in questions of justice when Christians were involved. In less divisive cases, the colonial government allowed missionaries to help settle local disputes. But often colonial officials found priests overstepping their bounds and threatening domestic order. For example, in 1891 a number of reports from Cambodia spoke of missionaries who overruled *balat* – local judicial officials – in order to impose punishments for crimes ranging from disputes over taxes to murder. 'The missionaries have in effect in Cambodia a very marked tendency to assume power that they do not have', wrote the Resident-Superior of Cambodia. Such interventions by missionaries there happened 'almost daily and always with impunity' in Christian villages which were like 'veritable independent states'.[81] Even in a case of murder, one local priest took it upon himself to pass sentence, excluding the local judge from the process, and failing to notify colonial officials but a few a miles away in Phnom Penh. According to one observer, the missionary's 'French nationality, his intelligence, and his instruction gives him a great prestige before the people and the mandarins, the latter of whom are not permitted to intervene in an affair in which the *Père* will be involved'.[82]

Missionaries' complaints about administration and the exercise of justice often stemmed from their troubled relations with Vietnamese mandarins. As Patrick Tuck has noted, the Treaty of 1874 – signed by the French and Vietnamese after France failed to establish a full-blown protectorate – guaranteed freedom of religion and proselytisation under Article 9. Under this article, written almost entirely by Mgr Colombert, Bishop of West Cochinchina, 'the mission received virtually unfettered sanction to purchase, inherit, and dispose of property', and Christians were to remain free of administrative harassment.[83] As the French administration saw Vietnamese Christians as allies to colonisation, it took an official stance of religious neutrality from the beginning of the protectorate. The administration refused to arm Christians, as many missionaries asked, but turned a blind eye on independent militias that some missionaries, including Guerlach, organised to defend their rights against mandarin threats.[84]

While the French administration tried to avoid involvement in religious conflict, it did play the part of mediator when conflicts became particularly heated. In 1889, the same year as the Mayréna affair, conflict between Christians and pagans in the troubled province of Nghê An threatened, as the Resident Superior of Annam put it, 'to lead to the return of the events of 1885'. Here, a number of priests attempted to oust mandarin leaders, and pursued charges against a Vietnamese army officer, despite calls from the French administration to back down. In a letter to the Governor-General, the Resident Superior argued that the Protectorate 'must without hesitation, remind the mission of the truth of their role to stop their encroachment in the domain of administrative authority'. In a proposed circular to Mgr Pinaud, the Resident Superior strongly advised the mission to respect the established chain of administration; the existing system, he said, was the best way to ensure the future safety of the mission, and tranquility of the region.[85]

Because of the seclusion of the central highlands in the 1880s and '90s, the missionaries in and around Kontum had little to worry about in the way of administrative interference or even criticism. Both before and after Mayréna, occasional travellers in the region required help and the mission usually offered its services as guides, interpreters, and cultural intermediaries. The highland missions did not, however, wish for more official French presence. In fact, in early 1893, Guerlach wrote a 204-page letter to a *curé* friend outside of Paris in which he showed himself at times strikingly antagonistic to the Governor-General, certain colonists, and his republican compatriots back in France.[86]

Equally interesting in this letter is how the priest used racial terminology to give weight and meaning to his claims about the weaknesses of *Frenchmen*; just as Guerlach invoked the image of the 'savage' during the Mayréna Affair to give import to the work he and the mission accomplished in the highlands, he now used the behaviour of his savages to show the relative decay of French society. Guerlach's letter is a fascinating document for a number of reasons. He offered extensive ethnographic information about a number of highland populations, as well as a picture of how lone missionaries functioned in societies geographically and culturally isolated from France. It also represented a stark critique of French republican society from a missionary who still felt scorned in the wake of both the triumph of republicanism in France, and a public debate over the mission's role in the Mayréna Affair in Indochina. And yet, in these pages, Guerlach also comes across as a zealous patriot, offering a glimpse of the complexity of allegiances held by missionaries in the 1880s and '90s at play, so to speak, in the fields of France.

In his long letter Guerlach tried to recapture his first impressions upon meeting the inhabitants of the central highlands, especially their behaviour, beliefs, and morals. Following a tradition of Catholic missionaries that stretched back to Alexandre de Rhodes, Guerlach arrived in the highlands convinced that 'the missionary must metamorphose himself and conform, *as much as possible,* to the mores and practices of the people he evangelizes'.[87] Though 'the human heart is [...] the same everywhere', he explained that the missionary must still, according to the local culture, 'use the most proper means to touch their hearts, to turn them towards God, and to ennoble them by rendering them truly Christian'.[88] This fundamental belief led Guerlach continually to compare the behaviour of the ethnic minorities with that of Frenchmen. For example, reminiscing about an episode shortly after his arrival in the early 1880s, the missionary noted that the drunken behaviour he encountered in his new home was not unlike that in France. When he criticised their love of fermented beverages, the 'savages' commonly told him, 'I am drunk, but I am not fighting with anyone, and I am not committing any immorality'. The missionary noted that he had heard the same words in France: 'the drunks of Blainville resemble those of Kon-Djeuri-Krong; depraved humanity is very much the same at all latitudes'.[89]

The temptation of drink and sex was also a subject that allowed Guerlach to make even stronger pronouncements about the morality of Frenchmen. At one point in his letter, the missionary told the story of Pierre, a young neophyte who fought the temptation of alcohol because the priest had taught him that a drunken man 'no longer has reason, and succumbs easily to temptations'.[90] But one day, while working in the hot sun, Pierre was offered some wine, sending him down a long and unfortunate path: 'it was then that a young pagan girl came to tempt him'. Pierre had been able to rebuke this woman's prior advances, Guerlach explained, but this time, having lost his head to drink, Pierre was doomed. 'My unfortunate young man', wrote Guerlach, ' "*let one thing lead to another*", as one vulgarly says, and he succumbed'.[91] When the wine vapors cleared, Pierre realised his mistake and wept; he swore never to drink again.

'How Europeans don't have this delicacy of conscience', bemoaned Guerlach. The French attitude veered sharply from Pierre's: '*One peccadillo more or less, what's that? Youth must have a good time!* Thus reasons the world; our Christians think differently.' The punishment for adultery in this highland society was harsh, and the guilty were made to pay a penalty of one buffalo to the village. Had the adultery resulted in 'complications', Guerlach added, the two would have been enslaved, or forced to pay five to nine buffalos. Rather than condemning this law outright, Guerlach took the opportunity it afforded to reflect on French 'civilization': 'Try then to pass this law in the Senate or in the chamber of deputies; our Honors would be wary of voting for it, and for good reason: Civilization is a beautiful thing; but how many of the civilized have a more obliterated moral sense than the Savages!'[92] Time and again, Guerlach detailed the ability of the 'savages' to understand and ameliorate their immoral behaviour, and compared it with Frenchmen's failure at this very task: 'Find me many drunks in France who correct themselves so rapidly and radically.' Guerlach was convinced 'that a good number of savages will have in heaven a higher place than many Frenchmen'.[93]

Such studies in comparative savagery – that is, observations that compared immoral behaviour among the populations of the highlands with similarly lamentable habits among Frenchmen – had political power, as well. For example, at one point the missionary turned a discussion of Sedang sorcerers into political commentary about Freemasonry. Guerlach explained how the devil intervened in sorcerers' work in order to keep the Sedang believing in witchcraft. Almost incongruously, Guerlach's description did not lead the missionary to condemn the Sedang, but rather led him to portray Freemasonry as demonic. He asked: 'don't our old cities of Europe and America offer worse scenes than those of the forests? [...] Our unfortunate savages are very much guilty of indulging in similar diabolical practices, but they are a thousand times less criminal than the Occultist Masons' who commit 'the most ignoble blasphemies and the most horrible profanations'.[94] Insinuations of savagery put a new colonial spin on a Catholic discourse of Freemasonry traditionally colored by anti-Semitism.

By condemning Masonic practices, Guerlach not only referenced a longstanding rivalry in French history between Freemasons and ardent Catholics, but also addressed a number of prevalent political issues in France and the colonies. Allusions to the impact Mason anticlericalism had not only on the mission, but on the well being of Vietnamese Christians appeared throughout Guerlach's letter. He showed particular scorn for Governor-General de Lanessen, a Mason and avid critic of Catholic proselytisation; and in so doing, Guerlach revealed the extent to which, even in his distant mission, he was still attuned to the political climate both in France and abroad. As Governor-General, Lanessan did not openly seek to limit the power of the mission, but nor did he help promote proselytisation. Rather, Lanessan represented a growing number of Radical masons in Indochina and other overseas possessions who were at odds with policies dictated from Paris which, because of both the *ralliement* and the power of moderate republicans, continued to support Catholic missionary work abroad.

Like much of his letter, Guerlach's critiques were incidental. On one occasion, Guerlach went to visit two Vietnamese 'princes' who had converted to Christianity and whom a regent had condemned to irons and exile because of his 'hatred of the Christian religion'. Guerlach charged Lanessan with complicity, as he had 'abandoned the Christian princes to the hatred of their persecutors in order to obtain concessions that were promised him and that he will never get'. Lanessan, a modern-day Pontius

Pilate, had veritably furnished the rod with which the mandarins beat the Vietnamese Christians.[95] With the deaths of Vietnamese Christians still fresh in the minds of many French Catholics, Lanessan's complicity was thus not only an egregious case of anticlericalism, but an indication of how Masonic hatred of religion could lead to truly savage behaviour.

But Guerlach did not liken all Frenchmen to savages, and in making a distinction he defined his own understanding of patriotism. He drew a sharp line between 'official' policies of Masonic administrators like Lanessan and the political and exploratory expeditions of French officers in the highlands such as the Navelle, Metz, and Pavie missions. Guerlach registered here strong similarities with his own work: 'missionary and soldier are brothers, especially when they meet so far from the *patrie*'.[96] Missionaries were the first 'to open the routes [in the region], and prepare the triumph of the French cause at the price of much fatigue and much suffering'; and these official missions took their work a step further. Guerlach took particular pleasure in helping the officers of the Pavie mission; in addition to 'serving the French cause' he helped 'men of heart whose energetic devotion I admired'. These officers committed great energy to fulfill their duty 'under the eye of God, in the service of the French Fatherland'. One of these men later died in the Sudan, and Guerlach mourned him as he would a missionary: 'I regret for France the loss of so good an officer, but I do not pity him, for he had the true death of a soldier, killed on the field of battle, facing the enemy. At the seminary on the rue de Bac, when we learned of the death of a missionary martyr, we did not cry, we sang the *Te Deum*'.[97]

French Influence and Patriotism, Missionary Style

The linking of missionary work with the conquest of soldiers had a tradition in France that stretched back long before Guerlach was born. But the missionary had personal reasons to see his own life in militaristic terms as well. His biography read as much like a Prime Minister's as a priest's: born on 14 *Juillet* 1858 in Metz, Lorraine, Guerlach took to the battlefield at age twelve to help defend his home against Prussian invasion in 1870.[98] He spent his youth in a '*patrie mutilée*', resentful of the Prussians, and praying to 'God the Protector' to 'save France in the name of the *Sacré Coeur*'.[99] Though he was keenly aware of the troubled plight of the Catholic Church in his republican home, Guerlach's decision to become a missionary was closely linked to his patriotism. By the very fact that he lived among the 'savages', learned their languages and customs, and made treaties with them, he believed he was fulfilling his duty to France.

Guerlach's work in the highlands often mirrored the efforts of French colonial officials to spread French influence. French official missions, like that of Navelle and Metz, were designed both to learn as much as possible about the geography and population of the region, as well as to negotiate agreements between the French protectorate and local chiefs. As we have seen, Guerlach and other missionaries proved helpful in these matters. But Guerlach acted on his own as well, securing treaties and agreements with local minorities, though he used methods of diplomacy all his own. The missionary wrought one such agreement in 1887 with the Sedang. In this era before Mayréna, Guerlach had worked primarily among the Bahnar, who had a history of conflict with the Sedang, since the early 1880s. In the spring of 1887, other conflicts made a Sedang attack on the Bahnar and their Catholic missionaries likely, so in an attempt to avoid violence Guerlach set out to broker an accord between the groups. In addition to minimising the chances of future bloodshed, Guerlach hoped that contact with the Sedang would bring them under the influence of the French mission.

Guerlach provided a remarkable description of how he – and many other Frenchmen in similar circumstances – interacted with local populations which on paper were 'colonized', but which in reality remained outside French administrative reach. First, he chose a man named Bat to help him make contact with the Sedang chiefs, and to organise a meeting. Once this was accomplished, Bat informed Guerlach that it would be necessary to make a blood pact to guarantee the union be indissoluble. 'That disgusted me a little', Guerlach admitted, 'but force made me submit to necessity. Thus after several discussions [...] my people went with Bat to find at Kon Run the two chiefs who would become my sons, and all the Sedangs who wanted to accompany them.' The Sedang arrived that night with Guerlach's village decked out '*à la mode* Bahnar' around a high bamboo pole decorated with colored paper and feathers.[100] Through the night the two groups drank 'wine of friendship' to the beat of drums; they slaughtered a buffalo 'with one blow' and feasted on it, reminding Guerlach of scenes from the *Iliad*. The missionary presented his new sons – 'one of whom could certainly have been my grandfather' – gifts of drums, bells, cotton, and pearls. Bat made a short speech saying that the two groups were now one village and one family, with one father – namely, Père Guerlach.[101]

The next morning, Guerlach set up an alter with a large crucifix surrounded by burning candles and a statuette of the Holy Virgin. Bahnars armed with lances and rifles formed an honour guard, and musicians played their gongs and drums. Guerlach stood between the two Sedang chiefs, and each of them placed a hand on the crucifix as the priest pronounced, 'Oh God [...] I make today an alliance of father and son with Peu and Léo of Kon Run'. The priest asked Jesus Christ to 'reward my sons if they are good and judge them according to your severe justice if they dare to break their promises'. The three men cut their thumbs and dripped blood into a cup of wine which Bat then stirred with a chicken bone. Closing his eyes, Guerlach took a sip of the blood and wine, and his two 'sons' finished it off. The cup was then refilled with wine so everyone present could drink from it. The drinking from the cup was a symbolic act of unity – one that drew on disparate traditions and histories: the cup from which the two groups sealed their blood union hung from a pole decorated with 'French flags, sabers, lances, arrows, a gun, and a *corne de guerre*' with the cross surmounting it.[102]

Guerlach's account of his securing an agreement with the Sedang was an example of how the missionary was required to accept – 'as much as possible' – the practices of the local culture. Guerlach's methods were not unorthodox for missionaries working in areas untouched by proselytisation. He mixed the pagan blood ritual with Christian prayer in order to establish relations which would lead the Sedang 'to quit the devil in order to give themselves over to the good God'. And just as the blood union was an odd concoction of animism and Christianity, so too was it a cocktail of local and colonial political symbolism. The fact that the cup from which Guerlach and the Sedang representatives drank dangled from a pole decorated with French flags reflected that the missionary believed his treaty had colonial significance.[103]

When critics of the mission's actions concerning Mayréna – from Lemire to Guiomar – asked whether Guerlach and the other highland missionaries were working to spread the influence of France, or simply the influence of God, they showed the extent to which republican officials' and missionaries' understanding of patriotism and duty to France differed in the late-1880s. For Guerlach, spreading Catholicism was in itself a patriotic act: the separation of French influence and the mission's influence was, in his mind, not possible.

This was most apparent in the concluding paragraphs of Guerlach's long letter to the *curé*. Though isolated in a group of small villages in one of the remotest parts of French Indochina, Guerlach wrote that he had read a number of commentaries and discussions which claimed that France 'is dead, that she is lost'. While he admitted that France seemed ill, he did not share the pessimism of these writers. Despite the rise to power of the republican left in French domestic politics, Guerlach remained convinced of France's overall moral impunity. Many terrible sins are committed in France, he wrote, but sins are committed in other European countries and elsewhere. 'If we scrutinized "*the conscience of nations*", what misery we would discover!'

> On the other hand, can other countries offer the same amount of goodness as France to counterbalance the evil done in their nations? God would have pardoned Sodom, if He had found only ten just men in that guilty town. How many tens of just men do you count in Paris and other large French towns? Moreover [...], France still remains the soldier of God and the kingdom of Mary. *Regnum Galliae, Regnum Mariae.* Count the missionaries evangelising Asia, Africa, and Oceania; the majority speak French.[104]

Guerlach's perspective on France's moral standing was both religious and international, a fact not surprising as he wrote his letter from a mission in a distant country under French rule. He did not doubt the seriousness of France's moral conflict at home, admitting that the lies and deception spread by republicans clearly brought great pain to Jesus' heart; but he underscored that 'this Heart [...] cannot be insensitive to the torture of thousands of little Angels and Saints who owe their salvation to the prayers, alms, and apostolic work of the sons of France'.[105]

In other words, France was in the throes of a moral crusade, though not one fought on French soil between politicians and writers. The battleground Guerlach had in mind encompassed the 'Kingdom of God' – that is, the entire world – and its primary soldiers were missionaries. Guerlach clearly saw himself as a warrior, fighting paganism and sin in his region. The struggle raged, not simply in the central highlands of Vietnam, but in every part of the world.[106] In this war, France, because of its missionaries, was the 'Soldier of God': 'No other nation can rob it of this title.'[107]

Conclusions

Guerlach's letter provided clear evidence that many missionaries did in fact define themselves as French patriots in the 1880s. Accusations from republican officials and colonists that questioned the mission's commitment to the nation were to some extent misguided when they accused missionaries of seeking the downfall of French colonialism in Indochina. But what is most evident in the debates spawned by the Mayréna Affair, and especially in the writing of Père Guerlach in the wake of the discord, is that missionaries' understanding of patriotism and commitment to the nation differed starkly from that of their republican compatriots. In fact, the two groups were guided by separate, even opposing historical traditions. As is apparent in Guerlach's long letter, missionaries grounded their love of *patrie* in the Crusades and the belief that France was 'the eldest daughter of the Church'.[108] Meanwhile, many republicans' located the origin of the nation in the Enlightenment and the French Revolution – two phenomena that sought to stamp out clericalism and 'superstition' in the name of reason.

When placed in the colonies, these differences posed a number of significant problems, especially for colonial officials. Most importantly, these views of patriotism shaped the goals and motivations of Frenchmen in Indochina. Republicans voiced their patriotism when they called for colonial programmes such as secular education, rational economic development, and the teaching of French to the indigenous populations. Missionaries on the other hand saw moral teaching and conversion to Christianity as the two most important steps to making the indigenous 'French'. As missionaries carried out the majority of the day-to-day civilising mission in the 1880s and '90s – the mission taught more students than secular schools, ran orphanages, leper facilities, and hospitals – the disparities of these two programmes increased the tension between the mission and its French critics. The colonial administration, at this time most concerned with minimising expenses, was happy to rely on the mission's work, but had to play an ever more active role in defusing potential controversies like those that made the colonial press in 1888 and 1889. But the Mayréna Affair was just a minor prelude to more serious conflicts to come.

Notes

1. I would like to thank Susanna Barrows, Hee Ko, Emanuel Rota, Greg Thomas, and Peter Zinoman for their helpful comments on earlier versions of this article. Research for this paper was made possible by financial support from the Fulbright Program and the Graduate Division of the University of California, Berkeley.
2. Annam was the central region of Vietnam that became a French protectorate in 1884, bordered by Tonkin to the north and Cochinchina to the south. 'Annam' was also often used by the French to refer to all of Vietnam, just as 'Annamites' signified ethnic Vietnamese people. In this article, I will use 'Annam' to refer to the French protectorate, and 'Vietnam' as a more general term, signifying the three regions together. Likewise, because of derogatory connotations of 'Annamite' in French, I will refer to the inhabitants of these areas as Vietnamese. Indochina – the union of which was created in 1887 – refers to the three Vietnamese regions, plus Cambodia and, in 1892, Laos. For a useful discussion of the colonial government structure of Indochina, see Truong Buu Lam, *Colonialism Experienced: Vietnamese Writings on Colonialism, 1900-1931* (Ann Arbor 2000) 'Chapter One: The Colonial Administrative Reality', 8-38.
3. A number of studies of the region reflect this usage. (M. l'Abbé) Pierre Dourisboure, *Les Sauvages Ba-Hnars, Souvenir d'un missionnaire* (Paris 1875); le Marquis Barthélémy, *Au Pays Moï* (Paris 1904); Henri Maître, *Les Jungles Moï* (Paris 1912); and for usage in French administrative documents and newspaper articles, see those collected in Jean Marquet, 'Un Aventurier du XIXe Siècle: Marie Ier, Roi des Sédangs (1888-1890)', *Bulletin des Amis du Vieux Hué* 14, 1 (January 1927) 107-128.
4. For the purposes of this article, the most useful of the works on Mayréna is Marquet's 'Marie Ier, Roi des Sédangs', as it reproduces a wide array of documents from government and missionary archives in Indochina and France that the author collected in the 1920s. Many of these archives have since been lost. A more romantic take on the Mayréna legend, published the same year as Marquet's, is Maurice Soulié, *Marie Ier, Roi des Sédangs, 1888-1890* (Paris 1927). Both of these texts were reviewed by Marcel Ner in *Bulletin de l'Ecole Française d'Extrême Orient* XXVII (1927) 308-350 in an article long and detailed enough to be considered a study in its own right. The only English-language source solely dedicated to Mayréna is Gerald Hickey, *Kingdom in the Morning Mist: Mayréna in the Highlands of Vietnam* (Philadelphia 1988). Hickey's clear account is based exclusively on these and other published French sources, and provides excellent detail of the events.
5. Centre d'Archives d'outre mer (Aix-en-Province) (CAOM): Indochina: Gouvernement Général de l'Indochine (GGI): 11890: Dossier Mayréna (8), 5 Janvier 1888 - 10 Août 1888: 'Traité avec Pim'.
6. Mayréna complained of severe fever at the time he became king, and his letters at times were nearly incomprehensible. See for example the rambling notes in CAOM: Indo: GGI: 11890: Letter from Mayréna à M. le Gouverneur-Général, Kon-Jeri-Krong, 25 July 1888.
7. Marquet, 'Un Aventurier du XIXe Siècle', 39.
8. Mayréna's army never received the uniforms because the king never paid for them. CAOM: Indo: GGI: 11894: Dossier Mayréna (12): Letter from M. Liébard à Père Guerlach. Haiphong, 23 January 1889.
9. Soulié claims that older Parisians in boulevard cafes still reminisced about Mayréna's exploits in the 1920s. *Marie Ier, Roi des Sédangs*, 5. And his legend lived on in Indochina for decades after his mysterious death in 1890: in the 1920s, the three studies appeared, and as late as 1967, Mayréna's antics even made their way into André Malraux's *Antimémoires*. Gerald Hickey provides a useful essay on printed sources dealing with the King of the Sedangs. *Kingdom in the Morning Mist*, xxi-xxix.
10. The bite of a poisonous snake was the official cause of death, though other possibilities abounded. Marquet suggested that rumors that Mayréna was killed in a duel seemed unfounded, but he did not rule out suicide by poisoning, as Mayréna's body had no sign of a bite. See 'Un Aventurier du XIXe Siècle', 101-105.

11 CAOM: Indo: GGI: 11897: Dossier Mayréna (15): Letter from the Consulat de France à Singapore to M. le Gouverneur-Général de l'Indochine, no. 145. Singapore, 24 November 1890.
12 On the role of republican ideology in French colonial expansion, see Raymond Betts, *Assimilation and Association in French Colonial Theory, 1890-1914* (New York 1961); and Alice Conklin, *A Mission to Civilize: The Republican Idea of Empire in France and West Africa, 1895-1930* (Stanford 1997) esp. 1-10.
13 This is especially true of the three main French sources on Mayréna, Marquet, 'Un Aventurier du XIXe Siècle'; Soulié, *Marie Ier: Roi des Sédangs*; and Ner's review. As Hickey's book relies heavily on these documents, he too examines in detail the relationship between Mayréna and the French colonial government. Hickey, however, also makes connections between Mayréna and the general position of the central highlands in Vietnamese history.
14 Patrick Tuck provides partial reproductions of a number of useful documents, as well as a handy historical overview: *French Catholic Missionaries and the Politics of Imperialism in Vietnam, 1857-1914: A Documentary Survey* (Liverpool 1987) 237-238; 241-247.
15 David Marr, *Vietnamese Anticolonialism, 1885-1925* (Berkeley 1971) 47.
16 Ibid., 54-55.
17 A useful discussion of the 'Siamese Question' and its relation to Mayréna is in Hickey, *Kingdom in the Morning Mist*, ch. 4.
18 Marquet, 'Un aventurier du XIXe Siècle', 9.
19 In 1887, a French administrator investigated Mayréna's home on suspicion of arms trafficking, found and impounded a number of weapons, but never – for reasons that remain unclear – brought charges against him. Marquet, 'Un Aventurier du XIXe Siècle', 18-19.
20 CAOM: Indo: GGI: 11883: Letter from le Directeur de l'Intérieur, Cochinchine Française, to M. le Gouverneur-Général, no. 19. Saigon (reçu), 15 June 1885. Emphasis in the original.
21 Ner, review, 326.
22 CAOM: Indo: GGI: 11890: Letter from the Cabinet Lieutenant-Gouverneur de Cochinchine Française to M. le Gouverneur-Général de l'Indochine, no. 9. Saigon, 7 January 1888.
23 For protection, Mayréna brought along 21 rifles, 4 revolvers, and 2,500 cartridges – an arsenal he thought rather too light for conquest. Marquet, 'Un Aventurier du XIXe Siècle', 25-26.
24 Letter from Lemire to Mayréna, no. 728. Qui Nhon, 15 April 1888, reproduced in Marquet, 'Un Aventurier du XIXe Siècle', 27-29.
25 The letter of 24 March 1888 is reproduced in Marquet, 'Un aventurier du XIXe Siècle', 25.
26 The first missionaries to try to proselytise in the highlands were captured in 1842 and sentenced to death by Vietnamese mandarins. Dourisboure, *Les Sauvages Ba-Hnars*, 3. In 1852 the Vicariate of East Cochinchina established a mission at Kon Trang. See Tuck, *French Catholic Missionaries*, 237-240.
27 Jean Marquet, 'Un aventurier du XIXe Siècle', 31; for a complete discussion of French expeditions in the highlands, see Gerald Hickey, *Sons of the Mountains: Ethnohistory of the Vietnamese Central Highlands to 1954* (New Haven 1982) 207-259.
28 The Pavie Mission was a sixteen-year expedition that explored the Mekong River and surrounding lands. Le Capitaine Cupet, *Mission Pavie, Indo-Chine 1879-1895. Géographie et voyages*, Vol. III: *Voyages au Laos et chez les sauvages du sud-est de l'Indo-Chine* (Paris 1900) 329.
29 Marquet, 'Un Aventurier du XIXe Siècle', 30.
30 The task of securing treaties had not been asked of Mayréna by the French government; he simply signed agreements which would later require official ratification by the French government. See the letter from Governor-General Richaud to Emile Jamais, Undersecretary for the Colonies (Hanoi, 14 December 1888) reproduced in Tuck, *French Catholic*

Missionaries, 241-242.
31 Marquet, 'Un Aventurier du XIXe Siècle', 34.
32 Lemire in 1888, in Marquet, 'Un Aventurier du XIXe Siècle', 111. Both Navelle, who travelled in the region in 1884, and Père Vialleton, the superior of the Mission at Kontum, discussed the benefits of such alliances.
33 Archives de la Société des Missions-Etrangères de Paris (ASME): 751 (Cochinchine Orientale), v. 2 (1887-1900); Folder 1889; Doc. 110: Letter from Marie I to Mgr Van Camelbeke, no. 939. Paris, 9 March 1889.
34 CAOM: Indo: GGI: 11890: Letter from Mayréna to M. le Gouverneur-Général, 15 May 1888; and Letter from Mayréna to M. le Gouverneur-Général. Kon-Jeri-Krong, 25 June 1888.
35 Hickey, *Kingdom in the Morning Mist*, 93.
36 'Lettres de l'Annam', *Le Temps*, 28 August 1888.
37 Mayréna was extremely busy during his first month in office, signing more treaties and decrees. For a full discussion, see Hickey, *Kingdom in the Morning Mist*, 99-104, and 106-107.
38 CAOM: Indo: GGI: 11892: Dossier Mayréna (10): Letter from the Résident de France à Qui Nhon to M. le Gouverneur de l'Indo-Chine, Saigon, no. 865. Qui Nhon, 20 Sept. 1888.
39 Marie I to Monsieur le Directeur du *Courrier d'Haiphong* (Qui Nhon, 8 October 1888) reproduced in Marquet, 'Un Aventurier du XIXe Siècle', 44-45.
40 Marquet, 'Un Aventurier du XIXe Siècle', 45; Marquet was able to see Guerlach's copy of the *Courrier d'Haiphong* at the archives of the Mission of Kontum.
41 Marquet, 'Un Aventurier du XIXe Siècle', 46.
42 Ibid., 46.
43 This prediction ended up being remarkably accurate. In Mayréna's letter to Monsieur le Président de la République Française (Haiphong, 4 November 1888) in Marquet, 'Un Aventurier du XIXe Siècle', 50.
44 Marquet, 'Un Aventurier du XIXe Siècle', 46.
45 For example, Ner rejects Marquet's assertion that Lemire was blinded by anti-clericalism; see Ner, review, 329-330.
46 Marquet, 'Un Aventurier du XIXe Siècle', 70-71.
47 Letter from Governor-General Richaud to Emile Jamais, Undersecretary for the colonies (Hanoi, 14 December 1888) reprinted in Tuck, *French Catholic Missionaries*, 241-242.
48 ASME: 751, v. 2; Folder 1889; Doc. 113: Letter from Guerlach to M. Pean. Kon-Jori-Krong, 9 April 1889.
49 Letter form Rheinart to Mgr Van Camelbeke (Hué, 27 November 1888) reprinted in Tuck, *French Catholic Missionaries*, 242.
50 CAOM: Indo: GGI: 11894: Extrait de la lettre de Mgr Van Camelbeke en date du 25 Décembre 1888 (à Qui Nhon).
51 CAOM. Indo: GGI: 11894: Extrait de la lettre de Mgr Van Camelbeke en date du 5 Décembre 1888 (à Qui Nhon).
52 Letter from Mgr Van Camelbeke to Resident General Rheinart (1 December 1888) reprinted in Marquet, 'Un Aventurier du XIXe Siècle', 72.
53 CAOM: Indo: GGI: 11894: Letter from Guerlach to the Résident-Général Rheinart. Hanoi, 28 December 1888.
54 ASME: 751, v. 2; Folder 1888; Doc. 109: Résident-Général en Annam et au Tonkin à Monseigneur Van Camelbeke à Qui Nhon, no. 86G. Hanoi, 27 December 1888.
55 Letter from Rheinart to Guerlach reprinted in J.-B. Guerlach, *'L'Oeuvre Néfaste': Les Missionnaires en Indo-Chine* (Saigon, Imprimerie Commerciale, 1906) 147-148.
56 ASME: 751, v. 2; Folder 1888; Doc. 109.
57 Mayréna in his letter to the editor, *Courrier d'Haiphong*, 8 October 1888, reproduced in Marquet, 'Un Aventurier du XIXe Siècle', 49.
58 'Lettres de l'Annam', *Le Temps*, 28 August 1888.
59 'Chez les Sédangs', *Courrier d'Haiphong* (27 December 1888) reprinted in Marquet, 'Un Aventurier du XIXe Siècle', 62-63.

60 'Chez les Sédangs', *Courrier d'Haiphong* (3 January 1889) reprinted in Marquet, 'Un Aventurier du XIXe Siècle', 66-67.
61 Marquet, 'Un Aventurier du XIXe Siècle', 68-69.
62 Ibid., 69.
63 Hickey, *Sons of the Mountains*, 236.
63 'Lettre d'Annam' (letter from Guerlach, 29 June 1889) in *Courrier d'Haiphong* (25 July 1889) reprinted in Marquet, 'Un Aventurier du XIXe Siècle', 117-120.
65 'La Nouvelle Confédération des Bahnars-Rongaos-Sédangs', by X.X.X. in *Courrier d'Haiphong* (8 Augustus 1889) reprinted in Marquet, 'Un Aventurier du XIXe Siècle', 110-111.
66 Marquet, 'Un Aventurier du XIXe Siècle', 112.
67 'Boite aux lettres', letter from Guerlach, 7 October 1889 in *Courrier d'Haiphong* (7 November 1889) reprinted in Marquet, 'Un Aventurier du XIXe Siècle', 121-122.
68 CAOM: Indo: GGI: 11894: Report from the Vice-Résident de France à Qui Nhon to M. le Résident-Général, Hué. Qui Nhon, 6 May 1889.
69 CAOM: Indo: GGI: 11894: Report from the Vice-Résident de France à Qui Nhon, 6 May 1889.
70 CAOM: Indo: GGI: 11894: Report from the Vice-Résident de France à Qui Nhon, 6 May 1889.
71 Van Camelbeke, quoted in Ner, review, 332.
72 ASME: 751: v. 2: Folder 1889: Doc. 115: Letter from Guerlach to 'Bien cher et Vénéré Père'. Mission des Sauvages, Kron-Jori-Krong, 21 June 1889.
73 ASME: 751: v. 2: Folder 1889: Doc. 115.
74 Tuck, *French Catholic Missionaries*, 245-46.
75 The original quote was in English. Marquet, 'Un Aventurier du XIXe Siècle', 112.
76 On this general subject, Tuck is indispensable: *French Catholic Missionaries*, 20-80; on Catholic collaboration in the 'Francis Garnier Affair' see Mark W. McLeod, *The Vietnamese Response to French Invasion, 1862-1874* (New York 1991) ch. 6.
77 CAOM: Indo: GGI: 11624: Rapport de Mgr Puginier sur les meurtres de missionnaires français et de chrétiens, et sur les pillages et incendies de chrétientés par des mandarins au Tonkin: Report from Puginier, Vic. Apostolique du Tonkin Occidental, to M. le Général de Division, Commandant en chef, le Corps expéditionnaire du Tonkin. Hanoi, 27 March 1884.
78 ASME: 759: Cochinchine Occidentale, 1888-1898; v. 2; Folder 1890: Doc. 367: Compte-Rendu, 1 September 1890.
79 ASME: 757: Folder 1901: Doc. 87: Compte-rendu, 1900-1901 from the Vicariat Apostolique de Cochinchine Occidentale. Saigon, 1 October 1901.
80 CAOM: Indo: GGI: 22548: A.S. d'une communication de Mgr Marcou relatif au recensement de la population de Ninh Binh, et des Chrétientés en particulier. 1904-05: Letter from Mgr Marcou, V.A. du Tonkin Maritime, to Résident-Supérieur. Phat Diem, 16 Décembre 1904.
81 CAOM: Indo: GGI: 22555: Enquête dur l'affaire de Banam (Cambodge): le père Pianet compromis dans une affaire d'assassinat, Avril-Mai 1891: Letter from the Résident-Supérieur au Cambodge à M. le Gouverneur-Général de l'Indochina, Hanoi, no. 25. Phnôm-Penh, 15 May 1891.
82 CAOM: Indo: GGI: 22555: Letter from Dr Hanh au Résident-Supérieur of Cambodia. Phnom Penh, 24 May 1891.
83 Tuck, *French Catholic Missionaries*, 166.
84 Ibid., 206-208.
85 CAOM: Indo: GGI: 9234: Affaire du Père Magat, 1889; Letter from M. Hector, Résident Supérieur en Annam à Monsieur le Gouverneur Général de l'Indo-Chine, Saigon, no. 614. Hué, 21 Août 1889; another case in 1896 resulted in a similar exchange of letters. See CAOM: Indo: GGI: 9800: Difficultés survenues entre MM Duranton et Guillet et la mission du Tonkin méridional.
86 ASME: 787: Lettres de M. Guerlach: Missions des Sauvages Bahnar - Sedang, District de Notre Dame de Lourdes, Pelei Maria, 29 Janvier 1893, à Mr l'Abbé Cauvigny, Curé,

Fontenay-le-Vicomte, par Mennacy (Seine-et-Oise).
87 For more on de Rhodes' work on missionary methods of 'inculturation', see Peter C. Phan, *Mission and Catechesis: Alexandre de Rhodes and Inculturation in Seventeenth-Century Vietnam* (Maryknoll, NY: Orbis Books, 1998): 75-81.
88 ASME: 787, 9; emphasis in original.
89 Ibid., 13.
90 Ibid., 35.
91 Ibid., 36; emphasis in the original.
92 Ibid., 38. In the manuscript, an editor as deleted these lines with a blue pen; as much of the letter was later published in *Missions Catholiques*, the editor was like a superior at the Missions Etrangères who wanted to clear out contentious material.
93 ASME: 787, 61, 64.
94 Ibid., 120; the anti-Masonic rant was marked for deletion.
95 Ibid., 157, 164.
96 Ibid., 199.
97 Ibid., 190, 191-193.
98 ASME: 785: Vie du Père Jean Baptiste Pierre Marie Guerlach des Missions-Etrangères de Paris, Provicaire de la Mission des Sauvages au Vicariat de la Cochinchine Orientale, 1858-1912. Par l'abbé Cauvigny, curé de campagne. Deux cahiers, 25 June 1913 to 12 September 1914. Notebook I: 6. According to another biography, Guerlach was an ambulance worker in 1870; see (no author), *Le Père Guerlach, Provicaire Apostolique, Supérieur de la Mission de Kontum (Sauvages Bahnars) (1858-1912)* (Quinhon 1912) 2.
99 ASME: 786: Lettres du Père Guerlach. Letter to his parents, 15 December 1874.
100 ASME: 787, 40.
101 Ibid., 41-43.
102 Ibid., 44-46.
103 His role of the common 'father' to a large family of Sedang 'sons' also mirrored French official attitudes vis-à-vis the Indochinese population. For example, French announcements to the Vietnamese population commonly referred to the local population in familial terms. At the declaration of the First World War, French officials described the Vietnamese as the 'preferred children' in the colonial family. See, for example, Trung Tam Luu Tru Quoc Gia 1 (National Archives of Vietnam, no. 1) (Hanoi): Résidence Supérieur du Tonkin (RST): 20,324: Proclamation au peuple annamite a.s. de la déclaration de la Grande Guerre. 1914.
104 ASME: 787, 200-201; emphasis is Guerlach's.
105 Ibid., 202.
106 For example, 'the battle that our soldiers fight in Africa is a holy war, as our compatriots destroy the empire of the devil, fetishism, and human sacrifices'. ASME: 787, 200.
107 ASME: 787, 200.
108 Réné Rémond, 'La Fille ainée de l'Eglise' in: Pierre Nora ed., *Les lieux de mémoire III: Les Frances, 3. De l'Archive à l'emblème* (Paris 1992) 540-581.

[21]

A Sentimental Journey: Mapping the Interior Frontier of Japanese Settlers in Colonial Korea

JUN UCHIDA

> *This article explores the role of affect and sentiment in shaping cross-cultural encounters in late colonial Korea, as seen and experienced through the eyes of Japanese men and women who grew up in Seoul. By interweaving the oral and written testimonies of former settlers who came of age on the peninsula between the late 1920s and the end of colonial rule in 1945, the paper attempts to reconstruct their emotional journey into adulthood as young offspring of empire: specifically, how they apprehended colonialism, what they felt when encountering different segments of the Korean population, and in what ways their understanding of the world and themselves changed as a result of these interactions. Focusing on the intimate and everyday zones of contact in family and school life, this study more broadly offers a way to understand colonialism without reducing complex local interactions to abstract mechanisms of capital and bureaucratic rule.*

IN WHAT WAYS CAN we talk about colonialism without reducing complex local human interactions to relations of power, dominance, and hegemony? In proposing emotion (see Reddy 2001; Haiyan Lee 2007) or "sensibility" (Wickberg 2007) as a lens through which to investigate the past, a number of studies have implicitly posed a new challenge for scholars of empire. Paying attention to sentiment and sensibility, they suggest, gets us beyond an analytical grid of race, gender, and class that has dominated cultural history—where colonial studies have reigned and thrived—and allows us to probe more subtle and sensory layers of experience (Wickberg 2007, 673–74). Heeding their insight, this article explores the role of affect and sentiment in shaping cross-cultural encounters in late colonial Korea, as seen and experienced through the eyes of young Japanese settlers who grew up in Seoul.

The centrality of affective matters to colonial governance is not new. Ann Stoler (2002), and a generation of scholars that followed her lead, have demonstrated how the state actively intervened in the private spheres of its subjects, in order to control what they felt and thought, and how they behaved—"matters of the intimate"—which were as important to the colonial order as macro processes of rule. While Stoler is chiefly concerned to show how the affective state of colonials, especially children, became subject to official surveillance, I am also interested in unpacking their emotional life itself: how they apprehended colonialism, what they felt when encountering different segments of the indigenous population, and in what ways their understanding of the world and themselves changed as a result of these interactions. For charting the world of settler youth, I will use sentiment and sensibility, inscribed in records of their sensory experience of Korea and its people, as an analytical prism through which to refract and reflect on the formation of selfhood, the process of socialization as "Japanese," and the dynamics of colonial encounter more broadly.[1]

In combing through a variety of literary sources for voices of the colonized, scholars of Korea have already shown how to anchor colonialism in the terrain of emotional life by attending to its broader registers, nuances, and resonances. But if the emotions of Koreans—as products of injustice, prejudice, and violence they suffered under Governor-General's rule—are deeply etched on the vernacular archive, it is somewhat difficult to identify and talk about emotions of Japanese colonists, who remain, for the most part, faceless.[2] Indeed, just as the colonizer seldom treated the colonized as thinking subjects, scholars have seldom treated the colonizer as an emotional being.

I propose to delve into the "murky worlds" of emotions, desires, beliefs, dispositions, and perceptions (Wickberg 2007, 670) that are largely absent from the existing accounts on colonizers by using what one might call sentimental texts: memoirs, letters, school alumni albums, and oral testimonies. My aim is to map the interior frontiers of settler youth—an affective geography of colonial encounter, as woven by the memories of those who came of age on the Korean peninsula, between the late 1920s and the end of colonial rule in 1945.[3] A focus on youth provides a particularly fruitful angle from which to explore the fluidity of colonial sensibilities in the embedded structures of power. It allows us to understand not only what it was like to grow up in the colony, but how young settlers felt about, perceived, and made sense of the

---

[1] For this approach, I have drawn much inspiration from Faier (2007).
[2] For a few pioneering works that have provided valuable profiles of settlers, see Kimura (1989), Duus (1995), and Takasaki (2002).
[3] The bulk of my data draws on oral and written testimonies of 87 former settlers (76 men, 13 women) collected from personal interviews, round-table discussions, school reunions, letters, and questionnaires distributed by myself to members of the Chūō Nikkan Kyōkai (Central Japan-Korea Association) and the following school alumni associations based in Tokyo: the Keijō Teikoku Daigaku Dōsōkai; the Rengyō no Kai; and the Higashi Nihon Dōsōkai. Personal interviews were conducted in the homes of my informants, and questionnaires were distributed at monthly meetings of school alumni associations or at annual school reunions, in the period from December 2001 to July 2003. The majority of my informants were born in Korea, raised in Seoul or other cities of major Japanese settlement, and were in their twenties when the war ended (most were students and some newly employed), and their families were engaged in commerce, business, and public service. Unless otherwise noted, the details of everyday life in this article draw on the information furnished by these informants.

larger colonial realities that constituted the context for their journeys into adulthood, indeed their process of becoming "Japanese."

For reconstructing settlers' life histories, memory offers but a mediated extension of the past—and it usually comes in fragments. A few oral and written accounts that document the lives of ordinary Japanese men and women who made Korea home provide only a string of impressions from their bygone youth. And though relics of the empire, they are hardly records of domination. Their narratives are replete with a sense of nostalgia which, as scholars have repeatedly noted, operates by a kind of self-censorship: an impulse to erase or mute aspects of experience that evoke "shame, guilt, or humiliation," leaving only those experiences one wants to remember (quoted in Tamanoi 2009, 6).

Nonetheless, these localized fragments of memory reveal a surprisingly diverse array of Japanese-Korean interactions that might have taken place in the skein of everyday life. Memoirs of former settlers teem with the colors, smells, tastes, and other sensory impressions of the local terrain they traversed and a multicultural milieu they inhabited as young offspring of empire. The minutiae of their day-to-day may not tell us how colonial rule was exercised through high politics, courts, and markets. But they show how ethnic boundaries and cultural identities were constituted, negotiated, policed, and transgressed through the quotidian rhythms and routines of daily life, where contact was absorbed into one's stream of consciousness. At times, fleeting impulses of emotion produced in these moments of encounter could capture the most enduring structures of colonial power, and the innermost contradictions of empire. Rather than residual and unreliable sources of history that are not worthy of study, oral and written testimonies of settlers are key repositories of knowledge about everyday life in colonial Korea. And insofar as each document embodies some elements of its author's sensibilities (Wickberg 2007, 676), they offer a rare window into the personal realms of feeling, perceiving, and experiencing the daily colonial realities that went unrecorded in official sources and wartime propaganda.

In taking the "emotional texts and utterances" (Reddy 2001) of settlers seriously, I employ the methodology of historical ethnography, as recently demonstrated by anthropologist Mariko Tamanoi (2009). In her seminal work on the Japanese agrarian settlers in Manchuria, Tamanoi has shown how to analyze and engage with memory, transmitted mostly in an oral form, while being mindful of its constructed, if not contorted, nature and a complex process of selection and narration—dictated by "who remembers and when, where, for whom, and how he or she remembers"—through which each memory is created. Following her approach I will interweave written and oral, published and unpublished, "past" and "present" accounts to reconstruct the everyday life of Japanese settlers in Korea, while also attending to moments when the informants interpolate their "intense subjectivity" in recounting their colonial experience (2009, 19–20).

In drawing "a memory map" of settler youth, I focus on two contact zones: family and school. These were formative sites where children developed a concrete sense of the self in relation to the other, learning of their "place and race" (Stoler 2002). Wherever the Japanese settled, family, and careful parenting, ensured that their children remained emotionally and culturally anchored in their Japanese identity. School was designed to cement this identity further by imbuing them with a sense of duty, superiority, and responsibility toward Korean charges as the future vanguard of empire. Through family life and proper education—central loci of official concern and social reform—settler youths were schooled to become and feel "truly Japanese."

But their cognitive development did not chart a neat trajectory envisioned by parents, policy makers, and pedagogical texts. As they moved up the educational ladder, their memories suggest, Japanese youth discovered Korea and Koreans they had previously not known in their familiar world, and developed more complex sensibilities that placed them neither fully in Japan nor in Korea but somewhere in-between.[4] Their rite of passage from childhood to adulthood was shaped and complicated at every stage by unexpected, and at times unsettling, encounters at home, in classrooms, and on most traveled streets and neighborhoods. It was in these intimate spaces where young settlers learned to communicate with Koreans through subtle cultural cues and gestures, including mere exchanges of glances, as well as to navigate the tension between the lofty colonial ideal of unity and the mundane reality of difference.

A topography of affect produced by these encounters, from fear and anxiety to empathy, affection, and kinship, was not a residual domain of colonial experience but rather central to the formation of settler sensibilities and selfhood. By teasing out such emotional and cognitive layers of experience that existed beneath the formalized structures of social control, I want to highlight the tacit and often unarticulated processes through which colonial relations were constituted. Paying attention to such relational dynamics allows us to see how colonialism was ultimately rooted in sensuous, visceral, and emotional human activity, which created a reservoir of potentialities for affective, if fragile, bonds to develop between the two worlds of settlers and Koreans.

GROWING UP IN KOREA

From the beginning of their migration in the closing decades of the nineteenth century, the Japanese in Korea constituted a socially diverse yet close-knit

---

[4]Outside my own work, the ambivalent identity and moral education of young settlers in this "in-between" space—a concept usually interrogated as a location for the formation of hybrid identities among the colonized (Bhabha 2004)—are richly explored by Cohen (2006) who focuses on the upbringing of children, Helen Lee (2008) who highlights the experience of women, and Inaba (2005) who provides a comprehensive overview of settler education. This article complements these studies by utilizing more oral testimonies and highlighting the dynamics of cross-cultural contact between Japanese and Korean students.

community. Dominated by natives from Kansai and Kyushu, early settlers managed their own daily affairs, from commerce to education and hygiene,[5] and invited carpenters from home to build shrines, temples, theaters and other community institutions to create a distinctly Japanese cultural milieu. By 1930, Japanese had become physically entrenched in cities and satellite towns, with a fully third of them born on the peninsula (Tange 1943, 2–3). Amid the heterogeneity, "a sense of equality" permeated the settler community, as one former resident of Seoul recounted, where government officials commingled with merchants and brothel owners, enjoying a bourgeois way of life inaccessible to most rural folks in the metropole (Keijō Nanzan 1996, 165–66).

The world of settlers did not remain completely sealed from the influence of Koreans who surrounded them, however. The process of acclimatization involved adopting certain aspects of the indigenous lifestyle, the extent of which varied widely among settlers depending on location, family occupation, social status, and length of stay.[6] While corporate and bureaucratic elites built Japanese- or Western-style homes, for instance, most settlers rented or remodeled existing Korean dwellings, typically keeping at least one room with *ondol* (Korean heated-floor), indispensable for what they described as the harsh "continental weather." Many former settlers had a tactile memory of living on *ondol*, where they "slept and studied in the winter," or "lay flat on its cold surface to cool down in the summer."[7] Settlers' diet mirrored the pattern of dwelling, to selectively incorporate local customs into an overall Japanese lifestyle. Except for those who lived in gated company housing communities and rarely ate Korean food, many of my informants grew up eating *kimch'i* on a daily basis. Some of their mothers learned from native housemaids or "omoni who lived nearby" how to make *kimch'i*, and customarily prepared it every autumn like local Korean families.

Nonetheless, settler children for the most part grew up in a protective cocoon of Japanese culture, where Korean was rarely spoken, and family and communal life evolved around the homeland throughout four seasons. Mothers played a central role in maintaining this culture as custodians of Japanese sensibilities in the colony. They kept themselves attuned to the latest trends and knowledge in home-making, family health, and child care as avid readers of women's magazines such as *Shufu no tomo* [Housewife's Companion] imported from the metropole. Full-time mothers rarely ventured beyond their neighborhood and a local Japanese commercial complex, where they shopped for groceries and sampled fabrics for kimono, which they often preferred to ready-made western dress.[8]

Mothers, too, were guardians of colonial hierarchy. Many Japanese women left their children in the care of Korean nursemaids—a luxury they could

---

[5]For the centrality of hygiene to the Japanese colonial project, see Henry 2005.
[6]For a detailed discussion of the internal diversity of settlers, see Cohen 2006, Chapter 2.
[7]Takeuchi Yoshirō, response to questionnaire, 12 August 2002; Osada 1982, 117.
[8]This information comes from my interviews and questionnaire surveys (see note 3).

afford due to wage differentials between Japanese and Koreans and overseas allowance (*zaikin kahō*) their husbands received in addition to regular salary. A Japanese family typically hired one young Korean girl as a babysitter (they called "kichibe" or "nēya") and one or two Korean women as housemaids (they called "omoni"), in addition to servant boys for miscellaneous chores such as laundry, heating a bath, and other forms of manual labor.[9] Although in-house Korean maids were often treated as family members, some were abused, for which upper-class Japanese women gained a notorious reputation.[10] In one incident recorded by the police in Seoul, a local Japanese housewife, upon seeing a teenage maid folding her husband's kimono left on the floor, scolded her for touching it "with such dirty hands" claiming that Koreans were "full of lice," an act of rewarding what was meant as a considerate gesture with racial insult (Chōsen Kenpeitai Shireibu 1933, 96–97).

Except for police officers and a few wealthy *yangban* families who lived on their streets, the categories of Koreans my informants grew up knowing largely belonged to "lower social orders": baby sitters, house servants, vegetable peddlers, fish mongers, store clerks, employees, and laborers. Japanese parents demonstrated to their children from very early on how to communicate with these Koreans as masters, not as social equals, including a habit of referring to them with a derogatory term, "*yobo*," passed onto children even as little as five years of age (Iwasaki 1966, 78). Indeed, it was in the comfort of home that Japanese children came to be embedded in asymmetrical relations of power: it was where they were schooled to acquire awareness as members of a ruling *minzoku* (ethnic group), and to form enduring images of Koreans as different, inferior, other.[11]

In the eyes of children, the outside world often appeared as segregated as inside their home. In the case of Seoul, many informants recalled, a rough division existed between the "Korean town" that sprawled around and north of the streets of Chongno and the "Japanese town" that grew around Honmachi in the southern part of the city. And yet, this fractured social geography did not always correspond with the lived experience of Japanese children. They frequently traversed the worlds of colonizer and colonized, taking detours en route to and from school and wandering into Korean neighborhoods, which were often declared off-limits by their parents. Even those who grew up in predominantly

---

[9]Interview with Aoki Etsuko, 21 December 2001. The wealthiest families employed as many as a dozen servants, including those they brought with them from Japan. According to one source, "kichibe" and "omoni" were given Japanese names, and paid a monthly wage of about 6 yen and 10 yen respectively, less than half the average salary Japanese maids received at the time (Kajiyama 1995, 167).

[10]*Chōsen oyobi Manshū*, February 1933: 119.

[11]A list of "Korean characteristics" enumerated by my informants indicate that since young age they had internalized many caricatures of Koreans, such as "propensity to lie," "toadyism," and "lack of hygiene."

Japanese neighborhoods recalled playing, and fighting, with Korean children, who taught them how to play a variety of traditional outdoor games such as Korean chess (*changgi*) and kite-flying.[12]

Although most of my informants grew up in an environment where Korean was not necessary for daily living, they also learned how to count and greet in the vernacular while being cradled by nursemaids, whose warmth they fondly remembered. Some picked up a few more phrases while shopping for fresh produce at local markets or helping their parents cater to Korean customers at the family storefront. In a few rare cases, where their families settled in Korean neighborhoods or in the countryside, Japanese children grew up speaking in Korean until they went onto primary school. One such former resident of the suburb of It'aewŏn, Sasaki Kuniyuki recounted how he used to masquerade as a Korean when gallivanting around Map'o with his childhood friend, Sin Wŏn-gyŏng, who would cautiously whisper in his ears, "Don't speak Japanese from this point on."[13] Childhood memories are full of such adventures of ethnic border crossing, through which snippets of Korean culture were seamlessly incorporated into the world of settler youth.

The mobility of their children made some Japanese parents very nervous. Privately they warned their kids against playing with Koreans, though their admonishments were often ignored.[14] Not unlike the Europeans who lived surrounded by natives in Africa and Asia, Japanese settlers feared the potentially harmful effects of ethnic proximity on their children's moral development. But, to borrow a keen observation made by Elizabeth Buettner on the British families in India, "parents often worried far more about children slipping into the realm *between* colonizer and colonized than they did about their possibly 'going native' through contact" (Buettner 2000, 292). Such fear, for instance, translated into widespread Japanese prejudice toward "mixed offspring (*konketsuji*)," though their number was too small to become a serious social threat. Of more immediate concern to Japanese parents was the perceived lack of cultural literacies among their offspring born and raised on Korean soil. This concern had already emerged around the time of annexation, when some predicted the birth of a new category of hybrids who were neither fully Japanese nor Korean (Aoyagi 1913, 146–47). Even as late as 1927, a veteran local Japanese teacher bemoaned that "some Japanese children in Korea, because they grew up in a land without a Shinto shrine or in a family that doesn't even have an amulet from Ise Shrine, have lesser comprehension of reverence for *kami* (gods) and ancestor worship than do children in *naichi* (mainland)" (Yasuda 1927,

---

[12]A round-table discussion with members of the Chūō Nikkan Kyōkai, Tokyo, 2 February and 23 February 2002; former student of Keijō Imperial University (Department of Law), letter to author, February 2002; Takenaka 2003, 116.

[13]Sasaki Kuniyuki, letter to author, 23 February 2002.

[14]Morita Kiyoshige, response to questionnaire, 12 May 2002.

224–25). Half-educated settlers were no less worrisome than educated native rebels against colonial rule.

Apart from family discipline, a sure defense against adverse effects of their children falling in this in-between space was school education. If hill stations in European colonies were "the nurseries of the ruling race" (Kennedy 1996, 130–146), Japanese primary schools in Korea were designed to serve precisely this role. Since annexation, the colonial government adopted a kind of "separate but equal" principle by creating "ordinary schools (*futsū gakkō*)" for Koreans and "primary schools (*shōgakkō*)" for Japanese, while absorbing or abolishing many native schools (*sŏdang*) in the process (Cohen 2006, 178; Tsurumi 1984, 296–301). Both ordinary and primary schools shared a pedagogical goal, first and foremost, to "nurture good and loyal *kokumin*"[15] by requiring their pupils, for instance, to daily recite the Imperial Rescript on Education—a pledge of allegiance to the emperor, which stressed loyalty, filial piety, and other "Confucian emotions" (Haiyan Lee 2008, 268) to foster affective ties to the patriarchal head of the Japanese family-state.

But their sentimental education was also differentiated along ethnic lines. The curriculum of Japanese primary schools closely conformed to the metropolitan system, placing particular emphasis on the students' future "responsibility to develop Korea and assimilate Koreans, and contribute to the fortune of the empire" (quoted in Kim 2005, 79). According to the guidelines for conducting an ethics class proposed by one school principal, local teachers were encouraged to pay utmost care in tutoring Japanese pupils "to show compassion toward living creatures, nurture a caring heart, and particularly be kind to Koreans and Chinese" (Morimoto 1917), sentiments deemed necessary for educating them in benevolent governance. Korean ordinary schools, by contrast, focused on the teaching of Japanese language and agricultural skills along with the values of industry, discipline, obedience, and love of labor, while "elevating the education of an [elite] minority."

For this latter purpose, in 1922 the colonial government replaced ethnicity with "regular use of Japanese" as a new criterion for sorting students' admission to colonial schools. Although this measure opened a way for a few Korean children with the necessary linguistic proficiency to enter Japanese primary schools, it did not fundamentally alter the ethnically separate patterns of enrollment (Caprio 2009, 130–32). Nor did it substantially raise the rate of Korean attendance; even in 1930, barely 20 percent of school-aged Korean children were in school, as opposed to almost all Japanese children by 1924 (Kim 2005, 70, 76). For most of the colonial period—at least until the second education rescript of 1938 moved toward unifying Japanese and Korean schools—primary schools remained all but a preserve of local settlers.

---

[15]"Kyōin kokoroe" (1916), repr., in Chōsen Kyōiku Kenkyūkai 1918, 74.

Schools and homes were expected to cooperate closely in monitoring the cognitive development of the child (Cohen 2006, 162–63). Local parents were encouraged to engage their children in activities that enhanced particularly "Japanese" aesthetic sensibilities at home. One 1941 article in a colonial educational journal proposed, for instance, utilizing Japan's traditional customs, such as *obon* for promoting ancestor worship, and the Boys' Festival (*tango no sekku*) and the Girls' Festival (*mono no sekku*) for fostering "valiance, military and warrior values, health, cheerfulness" as well as "gratitude to imperial Japan" (Takahashi Keiho 1941, 55–56). Like the case of "borderline Europeans" in the Indies whose citizenship was measured in terms of cultural competence (Stoler 2002, 118), Japanese identity was defined in terms of sentiments, values, and cognitive faculty, how one "felt" and "understood" what it meant to be "truly Japanese."

But the education of Japanese children presented a deep dilemma. While educators and policy makers expected them to stand at the frontline of contact with Korea, they also had to protect their fragile Japanese identity from the debilitating consequences of exposure.[16] This was further complicated by the tension between policy and parenting, which increased as the wartime regime after 1937 accelerated efforts to foster ethnic fusion in the name of *naisen ittai* (Japan and Korea as One). Nowhere did this contradiction become more manifest than in the issue of intermarriage. According to the recollection of Osada Kanako who lived in Korea until age twenty-one, "When I told my parents that it would be best to marry a Korean for the goal of '*naisen ittai*,' they reprimanded me severely, making me sulk" (Osada 1982, 117). Such an idea had not even crossed the minds of the former settlers I interviewed.[17] While the colonial state encouraged, and Japanese parents condemned, ethnic proximity, however, young settlers more often found themselves emotionally betwixt and between Japan and Korea. Such oscillation is vividly chronicled by their sentimental journey through school life in colonial Seoul, to which we now turn.

GOING TO SCHOOL

By the end of the colonial period, Seoul had seventeen Japanese primary schools, each of which admitted a handful of Korean children from well to do families every year. These students completely blended with Japanese pupils to be barely recognizable as "Korean," as one alumnus of Nanzan Primary School recounted: "our Korean classmates spoke perfect Japanese" and at the time "we assumed they were Japanese."[18] So assimilated they were, Fujimoto Hideo who graduated from Hinode Primary School confessed, that "it even

---

[16]Such ambivalence was reflected in one survey on the impact of cross-cultural contact on Japanese and Korean school pupils in North Hamgyŏng (see Chōsen Sōtokufu, *Chōsen*, August 1915: 140–45).
[17]Similar results were obtained by Kimura Kenji's survey on former settlers in Sinŭiju (2001).
[18]A round-table forum with graduates from Nanzan Primary School, 21 July 2003, Tokyo, Japan.

felt strange to a child's mind when visiting my friend's house to see him speak in Korean to his parents and brothers"[19]; only decades later did he realize how his innocent wonder underscored the brutal reality of a bilingual world in which Koreans were forced to live.[20] This demographic pattern carried over into Japanese middle schools (*chūgakkō*) or girls' schools (*jogakkō*),[21] where, as one Japanese alumnus of Ryūzan Middle School recalled, some of his Korean classmates were even "more Japanese than us."[22]

But the situation began to change dramatically as they moved onto higher learning. Instead of going back to Japan, as a few bright students of affluent families did, most former settlers I interviewed stayed in Korea for postsecondary education, an opportunity largely if not exclusively limited to male students. As part of the aforementioned educational revision in 1922, all vocational and post-secondary school facilities were made open to Korean and Japanese students alike (Chōsen Sōtokufu Gakumukyoku 1927). Among the dozen such schools included Keijō Higher Commercial School and Keijō Industrial School, elite-track colleges where local settler merchants would send their children with the hope that, instead of inheriting family business, they would land a white-collar job that promised them a higher social status. Two years later, moreover, Keijō Imperial University was created as a sixth imperial university in the Japanese empire, partly in response to nationalist pressure and partly as a means of preventing an exodus of colonial students to Japan. Although many of these schools ended up being dominated by Japanese, the ethnic ratio of students in public commercial schools in fifteen cities became more or less equal by 1937 (Chōsen Sōtokufu Gakumukyoku Gakumuka 1937, 33–34). Not an insignificant number of Koreans also entered Keijō Imperial University, especially in the department of law and letters (Tsūdō 2008, 221).[23]

For settler youth, going to higher school symbolized a rite of passage into adulthood. They were now allowed to drink and go to movies without school permission, and even smoke with the teachers' open knowledge. More important, it signaled the beginning of their journey of discovery, both of the self and the other. For most settlers who had known only babysitters and servants as the closest Koreans, it was in these institutions of higher learning where they for

---

[19]Fujimoto Hideo, response to questionnaire, n.d.
[20]According to two Korean graduates of Keijō Industrial School I interviewed (10 May 2002), they grew up speaking entirely in Japanese and could not read or write in Korean when the colonial rule ended in 1945.
[21]In the case of Keijō Middle School, between 1922 and 1943 the number of Korean pupils remained in the twenties and thirties, out of a student body of about 1,000 (Inaba 2005, 227–28).
[22]Takeuchi Yoshirō, response to questionnaire, 12 August 2002.
[23]Between 1929 and 1941, the department conferred a law degree on 196 Korean students, who represented forty-one percent of the total number of graduates. But the ethnic ratio in the department of medicine remained more unequal (Keijō Teikoku Daigaku 1927, 101; Chōsen Sōtokufu Gakumukyoku Gakumuka 1937, 67).

the first time began to interact with a large cohort of Koreans in their age range and treat them as social equals, at least on the level of formality.

One of the notable consequences of their daily interchange was to compel settler youths to revise, even overturn, the conventional images they had held about Koreans. Whatever sense of superiority they may have imbibed earlier was eclipsed by the brilliance of Korean classmates, who hailed from all provinces through a rigorous process of selection,[24] and invariably dominated the top rankings, while keeping their Japanese classmates in a permanent state of mediocrity. Senchimatsu Yatarō who attended Keijō Imperial University recalled how all ten Korean students in his class of forty studied extremely hard "as if competing" with Japanese students. To his amazement, they not only mastered Chinese texts such as *The Analects*, but interpreted literary allusions of such Japanese classics as *Tsurezure gusa* and *Genji monogatari* with effortless ease (Senchimatsu, 78–79). According to Takeshita Eigorō who attended Keijō Higher Commercial School, Korean students also excelled in foreign languages, whether English or German, while Japanese students struggled with simple Korean, a compulsory subject at vocational schools (Keijō Kōtō 1990, 375).

Multi-ethnic campus life also led to greater exposure to Korean culture. Since a tender age, most settler youths had gained only a glimpse of Korean ways of life—some from a distance (in the case of Takeda Tatsuya, over a fence that separated his house and a neighboring Korean village (Ryūzan 1988, 286)), some more closely, when visiting a friend's home (where they marveled at the "extreme hospitality" and "extravagant lifestyle" of their *yangban* host) or while attending a Korean neighbor's wedding where they watched with intense curiosity its solemn and intricate rituals.[25] Along with these moments of "culture shock," they occasionally stumbled onto the harsh rural realities of Korea, en route to a vacation spot or during a school excursion to the provinces where they witnessed in "amazement" the level of poverty among local farmers.[26] On the other hand, Satō Katsunori, while growing up in Taegu, became so accustomed to the stereotypical images of Koreans as "poor, dirty, vulgar," that he was "staggered" by the magnificence of the stone statue of Sŏkkulam he saw during a school trip to Kyŏngju.[27]

This frequently drawn contrast between "poor" living Koreans and "marvelous" Korean tradition, if a reminder of Japan's cultural debt to the peninsula, underscored a settler tendency to seldom treat Koreans as individuals. Instead they often dissolve into the nostalgic landscape as a mere collage of impressions, such as "*ajumoni* pounding their laundry at the well" and "the loud wailing of

---

[24]In the case of Zenrin Commercial School, only one out of 13.5 Korean applicants was offered admission in 1918 (Seiha 1992, 106–7).
[25]Takenaka Kiyoshi, response to questionnaire, 15 January 2002.
[26]Uehara Atsuo, response to questionnaire, n.d.
[27]Satō Katsunori, response to questionnaire, n.d.

'*aigō*' at a funeral" (Seiha 1992, 444–45). Still, accounts of campus life also illustrate how each interpersonal contact deepened young settlers' knowledge of Koreans and their culture. They discovered, for instance, that their Korean classmates were often several years older (and physically more well-built), and many already married due to the traditional custom of early marriages arranged by parents. For some settlers, their classroom turned into a space where they learned literally to "blend in the smell of Korea." Fujii Tsunao, who graduated from Zenrin Commercial School in 1939 as one of the only twelve Japanese out of fifty-two students in "B Class," recollected a typical scene of his classroom on a wintry day in Seoul:

> A *daruma* stove is burning. We place a shelf near the stove and line up our unwrapped lunch boxes to warm them up. As our lunch boxes warm up, the scent of *kimuchi* (K. *kimch'i*) begins to waft through the classroom. I felt it as the smell of B Class, not as a strange odor. Their lunch boxes are huge. They are packed with millet and red beans like pressed sushi. At the prime of my appetite I felt envious of their volume (Seiha 1992, 446).

For most Japanese pupils, their learning of Korean culture was less an intellectual appreciation of tradition than a visceral experience of its everyday forms, a string of small sensory discoveries buried in the routines of campus life.

On another level, however, settlers' encounter with Korean students could be unsettling. Unlike the few "docile" students whom they had known in primary and middle schools, their Korean classmates now were not only more visible but assertive. To hear Korean students speak in their native tongue during a break between classes was particularly "unpleasant," as many candidly recalled later. According to Fujii, "At times I felt irritated and somewhat looked down upon by the way they spoke in a language we did not understand while staring at us" (Seiha 1992, 446). Graduates of Keijō Imperial University similarly remembered feeling both "alienated" and "annoyed" by their Korean classmates who "would congregate among themselves and speak in Korean" especially when discussing what appeared to be "matters disadvantageous to them."[28]

For most Japanese students, their interactions with Korean students did not extend much beyond the classroom.[29] Their favorite activity after school was to amble up and down the streets of Honmachi, the hub of the "Japanese town." Students from Keijō Imperial University and Keijō Higher Commercial School especially relished the opportunity to take a *Honbura* (Honmachi-cruising) in their dashing "black school uniform and hat," some with a "gentleman's stick,"

---

[28] Yamaguchi Hisashi, response to questionnaire, 6 December 2001; Iijima Mitsutaka, letter to author, 2 August 2003.
[29] About a quarter of my sixty-four interviewees who attended post-secondary institutions said they had close Korean friends.

amid the admiring stares of girls' school students.[30] Winding past the crammed streets of Honmachi, some Japanese students ventured into Chongno to watch Hollywood movies or to eat and drink at local taverns (K. *sulchib*), food stalls, and restaurants where they even learned to play with *kisaeng* (Korean female entertainers).[31] But after-school clubs—what for most students constituted the most memorable part of campus life—tended to be ethnically separated. At Zenrin Commercial School, for instance, Japanese students dominated kendō, baseball, and archery clubs, while Korean students dominated table tennis and soccer (Seiha 1992, 229); as one Korean graduate of Keijō Higher Commercial School also evocatively reminisced, the soccer club "perhaps represented the only form of 'independence' Koreans could enjoy at the time" (Keijō Kōtō 1990, 170).

Such a division reflected ethnic politics growing out of cliquishness among Japanese and Korean students, who often kept each other at arms' length, and members of their own communities under mutual surveillance. Satō Katsunori, who attended Keijō Economic College, recollected how "Japanese friends would look at you from a biased viewpoint (*iromegane de miru*) if you became too close to Koreans."[32] Korean students appeared to be no less subject to peer pressure, as Yang Sŏng-dŏk recounted the atmosphere of his high school: "It was impossible to have friends among the Japanese students. If I did that, I would be branded pro-Japanese and persecuted by my classmates" (Kang 2001, 45). In the microcosm of campus life, outside the parents' purview indeed, Japanese and Korean students learned not only to gauge their distance from each other but also to police their identities among themselves. In so doing they effectively reproduced the boundaries of inclusion and exclusion that governed the larger colonial society, where one was not allowed to belong to both communities or remain amiably in-between.[33]

BETWIXT AND BETWEEN JAPAN AND KOREA

That campus life began to resemble the adult world may not be so surprising when considering the trajectory of co-education in colonial Korea. Far from laboratories of ethnic harmony as their architects had designed them, mixed vocational schools were continually beset with friction (Seiha 1992, 105, 152). Above all, students were key participants in Korean nationalist activities, including the most massive demonstrations for independence in March 1919, in the wake of which relations between Japanese and Korean students deteriorated to

---

[30]Keijō Kōtō 1990, 88; interview with 25 members of the Keijō Teikoku Daigaku/Yoka Dōsōkai, 5 December 2002, Tokyo.
[31]Responses to questionnaire; Sasamoto Hiroshi, Seiha 1992, 464–65.
[32]Satō Katsunori, response to questionnaire, n.d.
[33]See the example of one Japanese teacher in Morisaki 1984, 122.

a point where, as Yun Ch'i-ho reported on the Government Medical School, "they don't exchange even the simplest forms of common courtesies like 'Ohayo or Konichiwa'" (Kuksa P'yŏnch'an Wiwŏnhoe 1987, 141). Equally important to recognize is the fact that the March First movement, no less than the more numerous local incidents, stemmed from "trivial sentiments of animosity" that had accumulated in the minds of Koreans who daily endured settler abuse (Chōsen Sōtoku Kanbō 1925, 43–44). Such pent-up frustration galvanized some 54,000 Korean students into action a decade later, triggered by a "minor" incident in which Japanese middle-school students teased Korean female students on the train in Kwangju. From the nation-wide movements to local children's brawls, inter-ethnic conflicts, indeed, demonstrated how emotions became central loci for political contestation—and settlers of all ages were often primary targets of Korean ire.

Although the suppression of the Kwangju Student Demonstrations, and more decisively the outbreak of the war in 1937, spelled the end of organized resistance, nationalist sentiments by no means disappeared. Quite the contrary, former settlers' testimonies reveal how young Koreans, while studying side-by-side with Japanese, underwent their own rite of passage into selfhood and nationhood. Kaikyū Yoshihisa, who attended Keijō Imperial University during the last years of Japanese rule, observed first hand how Korean freshmen of various provincial origins became slowly "initiated into nationalism" by their *senpai* (senior students) and through a tight social network of Korean friends. "As months went by, a chasm [between Japanese and Korean freshmen] gradually developed," he recalled, "and after the first summer break it seemed to become permanent."[34]

It was also in the intimate spaces of classroom and tavern, where the most honest, if disturbing, confessions were uttered by Korean friends. "I heard for the first time Korean classmates rant about independence, but only when drinking," explained Kaikyū, admitting "I had to revise my understanding [about Koreans] significantly after that." Where such desires were not explicitly conveyed, Japanese students learned to interpret visual and linguistic cues of their Korean classmates as covert political gestures. Many of my informants stated how they simply "sensed" and "felt" Korean antipathy, for instance, every time their classmates said *"Ilbon saram* (Japanese person)" "while looking at us." Kitami Akira couldn't help but notice how one Korean classmate, who had graduated from the same Ryūzan Middle School, now made a point of slipping into Korean *hanbok* (traditional dress) everyday after school (Keijō Kōtō Shōgyō Gakkō 1990, 90)—what could be construed as a symbolic gesture of shedding his "Japanese" upbringing.

Even in the midst of war, several Korean students at Keijō Imperial University made a bolder gesture of defiance, recalled one Japanese alumnus, by failing

---

[34] Kaikyu Yoshihisa, response to questionnaire, n.d.

to turn in a class assignment to write out the Imperial Rescript on Education, an act that bordered on lèse-majesté.[35] Many also recounted how Korean students were not as enthusiastic as they were about participating in military drills and physical training. And during the infamous "name-changing campaign," Kiriyama Shin remembered feeling "odd" that his Korean classmates adopted such funny names as "Tokugawa" and "Toyotomi" (names of two "great unifiers" of Japan from the early modern era), only to realize that such a parody was "the sole form of resistance" they could present to the authorities (Keijō Kōtō Shōgyō Gakkō 1990, 85). When organized nationalist movement had all but disappeared in the peninsula, indeed, Japanese students became direct witnesses to how young Koreans continued to resist assimilation and subvert the hegemonic structures of rule in the indirect and non-confrontational ways available to them, that is, through language use, dress, and classroom conduct—the very cultural criteria by which their political attachments to the empire were measured.

Utterances as well as silences of Korean classmates continued to unsettle the interior world of settler youth in the course of war. As they began to learn of Korean desire for autonomy, outside the heavily censored textbooks, Japanese students developed a complex mixture of emotions, from "sympathy" and "understanding" to "fear," "danger," and "skepticism." Perhaps the most honest sentiment was conveyed by one graduate of Keijō Higher Commercial School who admitted, "even though I had understanding as a human being, as a Japanese I still did not want to see it,"[36] or in the words of a graduate of Keijō Imperial University, "I was equally sympathetic to the cause of Japanese colonization."[37] Uehara Atsuo who went to Keijō Commercial School "harbored a certain degree of fear about the Korean *han* (hatred) toward Japanese," while a fellow graduate, Satō Katsunori, recollected his internal conflict this way: "When Hitler came to power in Germany and the term 'national self-determination (*minzoku jiketsu*)' frequently appeared in newspaper headings, I constantly felt a sense of crisis by thinking how it must surely be swaying the mind of my Korean friend."[38]

Their fluid tangle of emotions illustrates how feeling and thought, far from discrete and isolated realms of human experience, remained inextricably entwined (Reddy 2001) in how settler youth experienced, comprehended, and grappled with distance from the world of Koreans. And as they encountered Korean national sentiments—their desires, frustrations, animosities—many Japanese students began to emotively straddle the colonizer-colonized divide, which

---

[35]Takenaka Kiyoshi, response to questionnaire, 15 January 2002.
[36]N. T., response to questionnaire, 5 February 2002.
[37]M. R., response to questionnaire, n.d.
[38]S. K., response to questionnaire, n.d. Although Hitler was calling for national self-determination of the Germans in their conquest of the Sudetenland, according to this informant, the idea of national self-determination itself had an immense appeal to the Korean intelligentsia.

compelled them to turn inward: to confront their own liminal status of being neither completely tied to Korea nor to the metropole.

The settlers' capacity to empathize, indeed, appears to have stemmed from their own ambivalent, interstitial being. In addition to displaying a remarkable lack of longing for their homeland, some of my interviewees claimed that they identified more closely with Koreans than with metropolitan Japanese,[39] as in the case of Aoki Etsuko, a graduate of Keijō Women Teachers' College who taught Korean children during the last years of war. While she could easily communicate with her Korean colleagues or parents of her pupils, Aoki told me, "I felt a cultural gap with Japanese who came from *naichi*. Because the Japanese at home had only seen Korean laborers, they also tended to disdain and belittle Koreans, which often enraged me as a resident of Korea."[40]

Many former settlers also confessed how they felt emotionally aloof from the emperor, a point corroborated by contemporary observers with much lament. To be sure, some of them avowedly became devoted "imperial youth (*kōkoku seinen*)," as they were mobilized for the public spectacle of lantern parades, military marches, and visits to Shinto shrines.[41] Mizuno Shin'ichi, a graduate of Ryūzan Middle School, proudly recounted the day in May 1939 when he joined the student representatives across the empire, from Karafuto to the South Seas, in marching from the Hibiya Park to the Imperial Palace where the august monarch "bestowed upon us a personal inspection" (Ryūzan 1988, 273–75).

Not all students appeared to be as moved by militarism as Mizuno, however. In the midst of war victory parades, as Ichikawa Hayao, a fellow Ryūzan alumnus, later recalled, "we felt neither the darkness of the wartime nor the opposite elevation of militarism," because "we were living as colonizers" and spared the hardship of metropolitan Japanese (Ryūzan 1988, 281–82). Morisaki Kazue, then a girls' school student in Taegu, similarly admitted that she had "less awareness as imperial subjects than the children in *naichi*," and the word "emperor did not evoke any special feelings" (Morisaki 1984, 42). To combat such apathy of Korea-born Japanese became the central vocation of a Keijō Imperial University Professor Tsuda Sakae and his followers, who founded the Ryokki Renmei in the early 1930s to propagate emperor-centered ideology (Takasaki 1982). They appear to have attracted only a small number of fellow settlers, however, and some of my interviewees who attended their meetings felt too "uncomfortable" to stay.[42]

---

[39] Also see Cohen 2006, Chapter 3.
[40] Interview with Aoki Etsuko, 21 December 2001, Tokyo, Japan.
[41] Interview with Hatae Kōsuke, 8 March 2002; also see his article in a school newspaper, *Suryō Gakuhō* (15 April 1944), reprinted in Keijō Kōtō 1990.
[42] Interviews and questionnaire survey with 25 members of the Keijō Teikoku Daigaku/Yoka Dōsōkai, distributed on 5 December 2002, Tokyo.

Settlers' emotional distance from home appears to have widened, as the thrust of militarism penetrated their campus life to transform classes into a daily regimen of military drills, physical training, and labor service. And as teachers who were labeled as "liberal" were gradually purged from faculty (Keijō Kōtō 1990, 80–81), some Japanese students developed a strong antipathy to the army. During his third year in Keijō Middle School, for instance, Takenaka Kiyoshi, with his best friend who was "antipathetic to Government-General's rule," played a prank on a signboard that read "*naisen ittai*" by adding a line to the character "*ichi* [one]" to make it read "*naisen nitai* [Japan and Korea as two]."[43] Anecdotes like this suggest a failure of affective education among some second-generation settlers, showing how Japanese children could subvert their learning.

Meanwhile, an atmosphere of anti-militarism forged empathetic, if fleeting, connections between some Japanese teachers and Korean pupils. According to one Japanese graduate of Keijō Commercial Higher School, during a students' debate one Korean classmate "boldly spoke about Toyotomi Hideyoshi and Yi Sun-sin," two rival military leaders during the ill-fated Japanese invasion of Korea in the late sixteenth century. Despite being a taboo subject, some Japanese professors apparently gave him an enthusiastic applause, which left a lasting impression on this observer as a sign of affirming their mutual resentment of the military (Keijō Kōtō Shōgyō Gakkō 1990, 86). Behind the closed doors of classrooms, a shared world of understanding also developed between an unlikely teacher and his Korean students, as one of them reminisced about Uesugi Jūjirō, a professor in charge of a "Japanese studies" seminar introduced in 1939. Though son of a right-leaning constitutional scholar who famously attacked Minobe Shunkichi's so-called "emperor-as-organ theory," Uesugi evidently "did not emphasize *kokutai* (national polity) very much" in his seminar. And when some Korean students complained that his phrase, "Koreans' plant-like existence," offended their sensibilities, Uesugi explained that he had meant to refer implicitly to their enduring condition of being colonized, to which the students responded with a satisfactory "smile" (Keijō Kōtō Shōgyō Gakkō 1990, 109, 168).

For most settlers, however, rarely did their animosity toward the army translate into criticism of their empire. According to Takenaka Kiyoshi, he consumed proletarian and socialist literature as voraciously as his Korean classmates did since middle school, but "strangely I never thought about Korea on the ground (*ashimoto*)." And while at Keijō Imperial University, he never obeyed the order to memorize the Imperial Rescript for Soldiers, "not because I thought about Korea, but because I had anti-army disposition" and most of all "wanted to avoid conscription."[44] A pioneering historian of Korea, Hatada Takashi who grew up in Masan similarly confessed that he had developed a precocious interest

---

[43] Takenaka Kiyoshi, letter to author, 7 January 2003.
[44] Takenaka Kiyoshi, letter to author, 7 January 2003.

in socialism and Marxism during high school and college in Japan, but that did not lead him to question Japanese colonial rule in Korea (Ko 2001, 72).

While conversant in the theoretical language of resistance, Japanese students remained surprisingly heedless of its local echoes. A sheer disconnect between what educated settlers embraced intellectually and what they could accept emotionally—a dissonance made plain precisely due to the interdependence of thought and feeling—poignantly reminds us that anti-militarism was ultimately not synonymous with anti-colonialism. Even as they resented army dominance, as Morisaki Kazue recounted later, settler youth like herself never doubted the legitimacy of their nation's empire, as convinced as their parents that the annexation of Korea "saved the country from its further internal conflict and decline" (Morisaki 1984, 138–39). Save for a few socialists who joined Korean workers and peasants in their anti-capitalist struggle (Sonobe 1989), settlers hardly, if ever, developed their empathy into self-criticism, far less into political action, ultimately confirming Albert Memmi's dictum that there can be no colonist revolutionary.

Limits of Japanese-Korean relations are rendered into psychological agony of young settler protagonists in autobiographical novels written by Kajiyama Toshiyuki, a second-generation *colon*.[45] Becoming an adult, as one character describes, meant not only to become aware of various "contradictions" and injustices of empire, occasioned by such moments as when feeling "cold glances as sharp as icicles pierced his body" on entering the Korean suburbs. It also meant to realize how enmeshed he himself had become in their daily operation, as another character explains: "I used to feel annoyed whenever our Korean maidservants spoke insolently to us after they'd become familiar with our household manners or when father's occasional Korean guests addressed him as if they were his equals. 'How dare you?' I wanted to ask them. In such instances, my antagonism was based only on the fact that they were Korean" (Kajiyama 1995, 116, 59).

More often, however, settler youths betrayed Koreans closest to them, while utterly unaware of their complicity with state violence. One former student of Keijō Middle School, who befriended a Korean student from Keijō Women Teachers' College, bitterly recalled an incident that would haunt him for decades. "One day she asked me for advice on how she ought to explain the meaning of '*hinomaru* (Japanese national flag)' to Korean primary school pupils. I casually brushed off the question by telling her something like, 'Why don't you just look at an encyclopedia.' I did not understand at the time her genuine worry and pain in dealing with what must have surely been an uncomfortable subject

---

[45] Along with Kajiyama, a number of writers—including Kobayashi Masaru, Muramatsu Takeshi, and Yuasa Katsuei (whose life and scholarship is deftly analyzed by Driscoll 2005)—self-consciously referred to themselves as second-generation colonists in Korea whose works constitute a distinct genre in the postwar Japanese literature.

to her."[46] Other memoirs also chronicle how a few true friendships that existed between Japanese and Korean students were severed rather than cemented by the wartime policy of *naisen ittai* (see Fujimoto 1994). All of these testimonies seem to converge on one message that consistently runs through Kajiyama's stories: insofar as the "Japanese" and "Koreans" could not exist outside of the colonial system, any relationship between the two was ultimately doomed.

IN THE EYES OF KOREAN STUDENTS

When looked from the perspective of Korean students, limits of inter-ethnic bonds seem to become even clearer. A few Korean voices featured in some school alumni albums allow us to access their experience studying alongside settlers. On the one hand, the Korean and Japanese memories of campus life are entangled with teachers they admired, shops they frequented, and notebooks they shared before school exams, and some of these experiences developed into life-long friendships they would cherish for decades after 1945. On the other hand, Korean reminiscences are littered with sentiments of loss, anger, frustration, resentment, alienation, and humiliation they felt, and held back, daily at school—memories that compete with the Japanese classmates' longing for their lost "home," claim to innocence, and remarkable silence on colonial violence.[47]

These emotions come alive in several essays that poignantly recapture the moments when Korean students confronted Japanese arrogance and prejudice, on and off campus. During a summer labor camp at an iron works in northern Korea, Kim Yŏng-ch'ŏl recalled for instance, he was "punched" by some Japanese classmates for speaking in Korean while playing *shōgi* with fellow Korean students (Kim Yŏng-ch'ŏl 2000, 28–29). A sense of outrage was palpable in another essay by Yi Wŏn-gap, a graduate of Keijo Higher Commercial School, who remembered how one Japanese professor of civil law abandoned any pretence of *naisen ittai* by habitually insulting Koreans during his lecture. His lack of sensitivity stirred Yi and other Korean students to lodge a protest, which evidently reached the ears of the education bureau chief (who most likely feared inflaming Korean hostility in the midst of war), and led to the teacher's dismissal from school (Keijō Kōtō 1990, 169–70).

Most Korean students found no redress, however. If they faced discrimination at school, more awaited them after graduation. Even those who finished at the top of class were not assured of a career, as local Japanese firms usually advertised jobs with a proviso that they were "for Japanese only" or hired few Koreans to fill their ethnic quotas "for formality's sake" (Keijō Kōtō 1990, 156). Kim Hyŏng-gŭn, an alumnus of Keijo Higher Commercial School, remembered

---

[46]Takenaka Kiyoshi, letter to author, 7 January 2003.
[47]Interview with three Korean alumni of Keijō Industrial School, 10 May 2002, Seoul.

when a few weeks before graduation the Japanese principal called only Korean students to his office and advised them to apply to Hwasin Department Store and other Korean-run firms, out of concern that Japanese companies would have few, if any, spots available to them. Upon hearing what was evidently meant as well-intentioned advice, Kim "felt to the bone the sorrow of a nation deprived of sovereignty" (Keijō Kōtō 1990, 209–11).

Their experiences were echoed by Korean graduates of Keijō Women Teachers' College, where they shared rooms, baths, and meals with Japanese students. According to a survey conducted by Sakimoto Kazuko, ethnic relations among the students were overall amicable, if only due to the nature of their training; as future educators they were "taught not to discriminate" in the spirit of *naisen ittai*, and to cultivate a different set of sensibilities such as grace, serenity, warmth, and strength (1999, 83–84). But Japanese students, while impressed by the "smart and well-mannered" Korean classmates, remained largely oblivious to their internal sufferings. As Ikeda Masae found out from her former classmates after war, Korean graduates not only incurred greater pressures to cooperate with the wartime policy—to cultivate affective ties with Korean pupils by serving as their "mothers," as an effective way to assimilate them as Japanese—but also faced discrimination at work place in terms of promotion and pay.[48] No wonder, Sakimoto points out, that Japanese students and teachers fell short of forming gender-based solidarity with Korean women to challenge the patriarchal structures of colonial society.

To be sure, many Korean graduates of elite-track vocational schools did land prestigious careers that prepared them as future business and political leaders in the post-liberation era (Song 2000; Cho 1999, 32–34). From the Korean testimonies, nevertheless, emerges a structure of discrimination so pervasive that it remained imperceptible to all but those who experienced it, that is, Koreans of all social classes. Colonialism was a tangible experience for Koreans who encountered its effects daily and "viscerally (*taikan teki*)," as journalist Sŏ Ch'un noted in 1939, such as at a local post office or a ticket gate in the train station, mundane spaces where no Korean would pass without at least once being insulted by a Japanese (quoted in Yi Sŭng-yŏp 2001, 39–40). That settler youth could be among the most unthinking offenders of Korean sensibilities makes it less difficult to fathom why they failed to emotionally connect with Korean classmates, even as they shared a common intellectual language, and in some cases a radical vision of social change.

CONCLUSION

"Our daily life (*seikatsu*) itself was an act of invasion (*shinryaku*)," wrote Morisaki Kazue in her memoir, years after she repatriated from Korea to the

---

[48]Ikeda Masae's testimony at the symposium on "Japanese settlers and Modernity" (14 June 2003, Hitotsubashi University, Tokyo); also Sakimoto 1999, 86.

home islands (1984). If Morisaki's confession disrupts the dominant settler narrative of nostalgia, it also powerfully resonates with the voices of a few like-minded offspring of empire, such as Takahashi Katsuo. A graduate of Nanzan Primary School, Takahashi injects his "intense subjectivity" in his school album to bridge the world of adults with the world of children. Children were no less culpable than adults in discriminating against Koreans, Takahashi writes, urging his fellow alumni "to speak and testify," instead of remaining silent and claiming that they were "too young to know." "Those of us who lived in Korea for thirteen years cannot even speak or write in Korean. This fact itself speaks to how, apart from violent persecution, fierce cultural discrimination was perpetrated. Discrimination performed by our everyday …. Unless we fully recognize this fact, our children will again become well-intentioned (*zen'i no*) perpetrators" (Keijō Nanzan 1996, 270, 272).

Takahashi's call, which also reverberates in novels authored by second- and third-generation *colons* like Kajiyama, raises a number of critical questions for scholars of empire. How is colonial power exercised and perpetuated through the rhythms and cycles of everyday life? How do "well-intentioned" teachers and "innocent" children become enmeshed in the structure of colonial violence? This article has made a preliminary step in answering these questions by tracing documentary trails of the emotional life of Japanese who grew up in colonial Korea. From their testimonies, we learn that colonialism operated not only through the state ruling apparatus but also in the realm of the unconscious—what Sakimoto Kazuko has called "*muishiki no sabetsu*"—where even children and naïve adolescents could participate in colonial domination through deeply ingrained habits of thought (caricatures about Koreans), language use ("*yobo*"), and sentiment (feeling of superiority). To anchor colonialism in emotional, mundane, and intimate spaces of encounter allows us to recognize, indeed, how the assumed boundaries separating the worlds of adults and children, the conscious and unconscious modalities of domination often blurred in the local operation of empire.

At the same time, settlers' journey into adulthood tells us not of a world so rigidly divided and fixed, but of a fluid and liminal space shaped by mundane and intimate encounters between Japanese and Koreans. Their emotional life vividly registers the effects of such encounter, showing how the everyday became the site for a dynamic cultural process where young settlers struggled to make sense of the new reality and tried to incorporate it into their worldview. Though most settlers lived in a monolingual environment and within the bounds of privilege, daily encounters forced them to relate to Koreans, and confront inner contradictions of empire as well as ambivalence about their own identity, intersubjectively. If settlers' tenuous, and often one-sided, moments of connection with Koreans reveal fundamental limits of their contact, they equally hint at the existence of the vast range of human and emotional experiences that can not be reduced to abstract mechanisms of capital and bureaucratic control.

Even as the state sought to control intimate matters and everyday practices, with a sense of urgency in the course of war, plural, marginal, and "differentiated" lived spaces (Certeau 1984, 188–89) emerged and existed between colonizer and colonized as they wittingly or unwittingly navigated across their divisions. Unearthing the horizon of sensibilities that emerged in this fluid zone of contact remains a challenge for scholars of empire.

Acknowledgement

I am grateful to Jordan Sand and Mariko Tamanoi for inviting me to explore rough ideas for this paper at the Symposium on "Imperial Japan and Colonial Sensibility: Affect, Object, Embodiment" (UCLA, December 2007) and to the participants for their comments and inspirations. I owe special thanks to Lieba Faeir and Mariko Tamanoi for pushing me to rethink some of the analytical categories used in the paper draft. For further comments and criticisms that helped give this paper its final form, I would like to thank J. P. Daughton, Julian Go, Sean Hanretta, Allyson Hobbs, Yumi Moon, Thomas Mullaney, Yukiko Shigeto, Laura Stokes, and three anonymous *JAS* reviewers. For invitations to present this paper at various stages of its evolution, I would also like to thank the Korea Institute and the Reischauer Institute of Harvard University, Henry Em at New York University, and Andre Schmid at Toronto University. Finally, I wish to thank all the former residents of colonial Korea who shared with me their personal experiences and memories, which form the basis for this paper.

List of References

AOYAGI NANMEI, ed. 1913. *Chōsen*, vol. 1. Keijō [Seoul]: Chōsen Kenkyūkai.

BHABHA, HOMI K. 2004. *The Location of Culture*. London; New York: Routledge.

BUETTNER, ELIZABETH. 2000. "Problematic Spaces, Problematic Races: Defining 'Europeans' in Late Colonial India." *Women's History Review* 9 (2): 277–97.

CAPRIO, MARK E. 2009. *Japanese Assimilation Policies in Colonial Korea, 1910–1945*. Seattle and London: University of Washington Press.

CERTEAU, MICHEL DE. 1984. *The Practice of Everyday Life*. trans. Steven Rendall. Berkeley and Los Angeles: University of California Press.

CHO IN-SŎK. 1999. "Keijō Kōtō Shōgyō Gakkō no ashiato." *Takushoku Daigaku hyakunenshi kenkyū* no. 3: 19–34.

CHŌSEN KENPEITAI SHIREIBU. 1933. *Chōsen dōhō ni taisuru naichijin hansei shiroku*. Keijō [Seoul].

CHŌSEN OYOBI MANSHŪ, 1933. Keijō [Seoul].

CHŌSEN SŌTOKUFU. *Chōsen*, 1915. Keijō [Seoul].

CHŌSEN SŌTOKUFU GAKUMUKYOKU. 1927. *Chōsen shogakkō ichiran*. Keijō [Seoul]: Chōsen Sōtokufu Gakumukyoku.

CHŌSEN SŌTOKUFU GAKUMUKYOKU GAKUMUKA. 1937. *Hi: Gakuji sankō shiryō*. Keijō [Seoul]: Chōsen Sōtokufu Gakumukyoku.

CHŌSEN SŌTOKU KANBŌ, SHOMUBU CHŌSAKA, ed. 1925. *Naisen mondai ni taisuru Chōsenjin no koe*. Keijō [Seoul]: Chōsen Sōtokufu.

728   Jun Uchida

COHEN, NICOLE. 2006. "Children of Empire: Growing up Japanese in Colonial Korea, 1876–1946." Ph.D. diss., Columbia University.
DRISCOLL, MARK. 2005. "Introduction" and "Conclusion." In *Kannai and Documents of Flames: Two Japanese Colonial Novels*. Durham and London: Duke University Press.
DUUS, PETER. 1995. *The Abacus and the Sword: The Japanese Penetration of Korea, 1895–1910*. Berkeley and Los Angles: University of California Press.
FAIER, LIEBA. 2007. "Filipina Migrants in Rural Japan and Their Professions of Love." *American Ethnologist* 34, no. 1 (February 2007): 148–62.
FUJIMOTO HIDEO. 1994. *Izumi Seiichi den: Andesu kara Saishūtō e*. Tokyo: Heibonsha.
HENRY, TODD A. 2005. "Sanitizing Empire: Japanese Articulations of Korean Otherness and the Construction of Early Colonial Seoul, 1905–19." *Journal of Asian Studies* 64, no. 3 (August 2005): 639–675.
INABA TSUGIO. 2005. *Kyū Kankoku, Chōsen no "Naichijin" kyōiku*. Fukuoka: Kyūshū Daigaku Shuppankai.
IWASAKI KIICHI. 1966. *Ondoru yawa*. Osaka: Kyōbunsha.
KAJIYAMA TOSHIYUKI. 1995. *The Clan Records: Five Stories of Korea*. trans. Yoshiko Dykstra. Honolulu: University of Hawai'i Press.
KANG, HILDI. 2001. *Under the Black Umbrella: Voices from Colonial Korea, 1910–1945*. Ithaca and London: Cornell University Press.
KEIJŌ NANZAN SHŌGAKKŌ DŌSŌKAI, ed. 1996. *Keijō Nanzan Shōgakkō 70 nen kinenshi: sakamichi to popura to aoisora to*. Tokyo: Keijō Nanzan Shōgakkō Dōsōkai.
KEIJŌ KŌTŌ SHŌGYŌ GAKKŌ (DŌ KEIZAI SENMON GAKKŌ) DŌSŌKAI SŪRYŌKAI, ed. 1990. *Hitotsubu no mugi: Keijō Kōtō Shōgyō Gakkō sōritsu 70 shūnen kinen bunshū*. Tokyo: Sūryōkai.
KEIJŌ TEIKOKU DAIGAKU. 1927. *Keijō Teikoku Daigaku ichiran*, 1926–1927. Keijō [Seoul]: Keijō Teikoku Daigaku.
KENNEDY, DANE. 1996. *The Magic Mountains: Hill Stations and the British Raj*. Berkeley and Los Angeles: University of California Press.
KIM PUJA. 2005. *Shokuminchiki Chōsen no kyōiku to gendā*. Yokohama: Seori Shobō.
KIM YŎNG-CH'ŎL. 2000. "Yūki aru kotoba." Sūryōkai, ed. *Sūryō*, vol. 44: 28–29.
KIMURA KENJI. 1989. *Zaichō Nihonjin no shakaishi*. Tokyo: Miraisha.
———. 2001. "Shokuminchika Shingishū zaijū Nihonjin no ibunka sesshoku." In *Kōsaku suru kokka, minzoku, shūkyō: imin no shakai tekiō*, ed. Togami Muneyoshi, 73–98. Tokyo: Fuji Shuppan.
KO KIL-HŬI. 2001. *'Zaichō Nihonjin nisei' no aidentitī keisei*. Tokyo: Kiri Shobō.
KUKSA P'YŎNCH'AN WIWŎNHOE, ed. 1987. *Yun Ch'iho ilgi*, vol. 8. Repr., Seoul: Kuksa P'yŏnch'an Wiwŏnhoe.
"KYOIN KOKOROE," Government-General kunrei no. 2 (January 1016). Reprinted in *Chōsen kyōikusha hikkei*, ed. Chōsen Kyōiku Kenkyūkai, 74. Keijō [Seoul]: Chōsen Kyōiku Kenkyūkai, 1918.
LEE, HAIYAN. 2007. *Revolution of the Heart: A Genealogy of Love in China, 1900–1950*. Stanford, Calif: Stanford University Press.
———. 2008. "Guest Editor's Introduction." *positions* 16:2: 263–78.
LEE, HELEN J.S. "Ch'eguk ŭi ttal rosŏ chungnŭndanŭn kŏt." *Asea yŏn'gu* 51:2 (2008): 80–105.
MORIMOTO TŌSUKE. 1917. "Chōsen kōritsu shōgakkō ni okeru shūshin kyōjujō tokuni chūi subeki yōkō narabini jikkōan." *Chōsen Kyōiku Kenkyūkai zasshi* vol. 18: 70–73.
MORISAKI KAZUE. 1984. *Keishū wa haha no yobigoe*. Tokyo: Shinchōsha.
OSADA KANAKO. 1982. "Yonjūgonen hachigatsu jūgonichi." *Kikan sanzenri* 31: 115–17.

REDDY, WILLIAM M. 2001. *The Navigation of Feeling: A Framework for the History of Emotions*. New York: Cambridge University Press.
RYŪZAN KŌRITSU CHŪGAKKŌ SŌRITSU 70 SHŪNEN KINENSHI HENSHŪ IINKAI, ed. 1988. *Ryūzan Kōritsu Chūgakkō sōritsu 70 shūnen kinenshi*. Tokyo: Ryūzan Kōritsu Chūgakkō Dōsōkai.
SAKIMOTO KAZUKO. 1999. "'Kōminka' seisakuki no zaichō Nihonjin: Keijō Joshi Shihan Gakkō o chūshin ni." *Kokusai kankeigaku kenkyū* (Tsudajuku Daigaku) 25: 79–94.
SEIHA KAIKO ZENRIN SHŌGYŌ HENSHŪ IINKAI, ed. 1992. *Seiha: kaiko, Zenrin Shōgyō*. Fukuoka: Zenrin Shōgyōgakkō Dōsōkai Seiha Kurabu.
SENCHIMATSU YATARŌ. n.d. "Manira no rakubi" (unpublished memoir).
SONG HŬNG-NYŎ. 2000. "Keijō Kōtō Shōgyō Gakkō ga Kankoku keizai kindaika ni hatashita yakuwari." *Takushoku Daigaku hyakunenshi kenkyū* no. 4: 74–97.
SONOBE HIROYUKI. 1989. "Zaichō Nihonjin no sanka shita kyōsanshugi undō." *Chōsenshi Kenkyūkai ronbunshū* 26: 213–39.
STOLER, ANN LAURA. 2002. *Carnal Knowledge and Imperial Power: Race and the Intimate in Colonial Rule*. Berkeley and Los Angeles: University of California Press.
TAKAHASHI KEIHO. 1941. "Tango no sekku shidō." *Chōsen no kyōiku kenkyū* 154: 55–56.
TAKASAKI SŌJI. 1982. "Ryokki Renmei to 'kōminka' undō." *Kikan sanzenri* 31: 64–72.
———. 2002. *Shokuminchiki Chōsen no Nihonjin*. Tokyo: Iwanami Shoten.
TAKENAKA KIYOSHI. 2003. "'Shokuminchi Chōsen no Nihonjin' to wakaki hi." *Bungei: umi* 67.
TAMANOI, MARIKO ASANO. 2009. *Memory Maps: The State and Manchuria in Postwar Japan*. Honolulu: University of Hawai'i Press.
TANGE IKUTARŌ, ed. 1943. *Chōsen ni okeru jinkō ni kansuru shotōkei*. Keijō [Seoul]: Chōsen Kōsei Kyōkai.
TSŪDŌ AYUMI. 2008. "Keijō Teikoku Daigaku hōbungakubu no saikentō." *Shigaku zasshi* 117(2): 58–84.
TSURUMI, PATRICIA. 1984. "Colonial Education in Korea and Taiwan." In *The Japanese Colonial Empire, 1895–1945*, ed. Ramon H. Myers and Mark R. Peattie, 275–311. Princeton N.J.: Princeton University Press.
WICKBERG, DANIEL. 2007. "What is the History of Sensibilities? On Cultural Histories, Old and New." *The American Historical Review* 112 (3): 661–84.
YASUDA YASUNORI. 1927. *Chōsen kyōiku ni anjū shite*. Keijō [Seoul]: Ōsakayagō Shoten.
YI SŬNG-YŎP. 2001. "Chōsenjin naisen ittai ronja no tenkō to dōka no ronri." *Nijusseiki kenkyū* 2: 25–46.

Name Index

Abbatucci, Serge 429
Abdülhamid II, Sultan 194, 203, 459
Abdülmecid, Sultan 196
Abraham, Collin E.R. 387
Abdrakhimov, Abdusalam 478
Abu-Lughod, Janet 140, 141
Adams, Kathleen 418, 424
Adamson, Walter 401
Aghā, Husayn 366
Aguinaldo, Emilio 329–30
Ahearne, Joseph 130–31
Akintoye, S.A. 8
Alatas, Hussein 400, 406
Alexander I, Tsar 467, 470
Alexander, C.W. 18
Alexandre, Pierre 277–8, 288
Al-Faruqi, Sami Pasha 215, 216
Al-Fayiz, Sattam 207–8
Al-Humud, Dhiyab 200–201
Ali, Hyder 254
Äl-Küshäri, Gabbas b. Gabderräshid 479
Allan, W.H. 7
Allen, J. de V. 399, 402
Al-Majali, Salih 203–4, 216
Al-Qadir, 'Abd 197
Al-Qasimi, Jamal al-Din 212, 213–14
Al-Sabah, Mubarak 194
Al-Tamimi, Muhammad Khalil 203
Ambler, Charles 8, 13
Amer, Sidi Ben 197
Andaya, Barbara 393, 394, 397
Andaya, Leonard Y. 392, 394
Anderson, David xiii, 4
Anderson, Warwick xiv, 125–38
Anthonisz, J.O. 176
Aoki, Etsuko 542
Aoyagi, Nanmei 533
Archinard, Louis 278
Ardener, Shirley 417
Arendt, Hannah 323
Aries, Philippe 162
Arnold, David 249, 428, 431

Asante, S.K.B. 17
Asiegbu, A.J. 5
Atanda, J.A. 8
Atmaprana, Pravrajika 449, 450, 454
Austin, Gareth xiv, 12, 19

Bailkin, Jordanna xvi
Ballhatchet, Kenneth 419
Bancroft, Joseph 135
Banks, Olive 446, 451
Banton, Michael 395
Baptista, Manuel 85
Baroli, Marc 425
Barr, Pat 445
Barrett, Sir James 125, 126, 134, 135–6, 138
Bashkow, Ira 142
Bates, Robert 3
Baud, J.C. 34
Bauduin, D.C.M. 433, 434
Bean, C.E.W. 138
Beardall, William 115
Begbie, P.J. 394, 397, 407
Behal, Rana xiii
Beidelman, Thomas 423
Beinart, William xiv, xvii, 4
Bell, J. Franklin 330
Bell, R.M. 112
Benn, W. Wedgwood 451
Bérenger-Féraud, L. 433
Berg, F.F. 468
Berlin, Moisei 475
Berman, Bruce 4, 7, 12, 20, 276
Berry, Richard 132
Berry, Sara xii, 3–31
Besant, Annie 450, 453
Betts, Raymond 140
Beveridge, Annette Akroyd 445, 448–9 passim, 453–4, 455
Beveridge, Henry 449
Beveridge, William H. 448
Bickers, Robert xviii
Bike, Bibi Kiz 484

Birch, J.W.W. 399
Bissell, William Cunningham xiv, 139–60
Blanchy, M. 498
Blanco, Ramón 329
Blumberger, J.Th. Petrus 431
Blussé, Leonard 420
Blyth, W.L. 404
Bock, Gisela 427, 432
Boeder, Gustav 113
Bolívar, Simón xx
Bonacich, Edna 386, 406
Bond, G.C. 22
Bonser, J.W. 180
Borthwick, Meredith 448, 449, 452, 454
Bose, J.C. 450, 453
Bosma, Ulbe xiii
Bourgeois, Léon 224
Boutilier, James 423, 424, 425
Boxer, C.R. 395
Braconier, A. de 420, 427, 430, 431
Breinl, Anton 135, 136–7, 138
Brink, K.B.M. 432
Brocheux, Pierre xiii
Brodrick, St. John 336
Brou, A.M.N. 430
Brown, Rebecca 141, 142–4
Brownfoot, Janice N. 422, 423
Buettner, Elizabeth 533
Bùi, Chiêu Quang 24–2
Bunge, Frederica M. 389
Burbank, Jane xvi
Burckhardt, John Lewis 212, 368
Burns, P.L. 399
Burroughs, Peter xii
Bush, Barbara xv
Butcher, John G. 391, 400, 409, 410, 420, 422
Butler, Nevile 452
Butler, R.A. 451

Caillié, Rene 278
Callan, Hilary 417
Callaway, Helen 417, 419, 420, 426, 434
Callwell, C.E. 338
Calmette, Albert 234
Cameron, John 399, 406
Campbell-Bannerman, Sir Henry 337
Campos, Arsenio Martínez 327
Cangi, Ellen Corwin xix
Cánovas del Castillo, Antonio 327

Canter, R.S. 22
Caprio, Mark E. xx, 534
Carney, Judith 4
Carpenter, J. Estlin 446, 452, 453
Carpenter, Mary 445–9 *passim*, 451, 453–4, 455
Carr, Henry 17
Catherine the Great 460, 465, 466
Çelik, Zeynep 142
Certeau, Michel de 548
Chadwick, Edwin 163
Chailley-Bert, M.J. 432
Cham, B.N. 387
Chandra, Siddharth 226–7
Chanock, Martin 4, 5, 8, 11, 16, 22, 299
Chatterjee, Partha 419
Chattopadhyay, Kamaladevi 450, 453, 455
Chattopadhyay, Swati 142–3
Chazan, Naomi 4
Cheah, Boon Kheng 407
Chenet, Ch. 431
Chilundo, Arlindo xiii, 69–101
Chivas-Baron, Clotide 420, 429
Cho, In-sŏk 546
Clammer, John R. 393
Clancy-Smith, Julia xviii
Clerkx, Lily 420, 422, 424
Clifford, Hugh 391, 402
Cohen, Nicole 534, 535
Cohen, William 420, 423
Coleman, James 8
Collier, Paul 23
Collyer, W.H. 161
Colombert, Isidore 512
Colson, Elizabeth 4
Comaroff, Jean 149
Comaroff, John 4, 13, 142, 149, 418
Comber, Leon 387
Confucius 174
Conklin, Alice L. xv
Connor, Walker 386
Conrad, Joseph 373
Cook, T.M. 374
Cooper, Frederick 418
Corneau, Grace 426
Cornwallis, Lord 247
Couillard, Marie-Andre 394
Cousins, James 450, 451, 452
Cousins, Margaret Gillespie 445, 450–51 *passim*, 452, 453–6

Cowan, C.D. 391, 399
Cowen, Michael 7
Cox, Jeffrey xix
Cox, Oliver C. 387
Cranworth, Bertram 433
Craven, Paul xiii
Crawfurd, John 37, 398
Crayssac, René 231
Crews, Robert D. xvi, xix, 459–92
Crofton, R.H. 155
Crook, Richard 11, 17, 18
Crosse-Upcott, A.R.W. 106–7
Cumpston, J.H.L. 137
Curtin, Philip D. 395, 396
Curwen, Henry 153–4
Curzon, Lord xiii

Dall, Charles 447
Darwin, Charles 395
Daughton, James P. xix, 493–525
Davin, Anna 427, 432
Davis, Diana K. xiv
De Bruyn, Feuilletau 433
De Courcy, Roussel 497
De Jesus, Edilberto C. 226
Dekker, Eduard Douwes 54
Delavignette, Robert 428, 432
De Lotbinière, G. 335
De Mayréna, Charles-David 493, 495–507 passim, 509–10, 518
De Montaigne, Michel 292
Denson, Alan 450
De Rhodes, Alexandre 514
Deringil, Selim xv
Descours-Gatin, Chantal 226
Dê Thám (Hoang Hoa Tham) 237
De Tocqueville, Alexis 491
Devi, Sarada 453
Devi, Sudhira 454
Diehl, F.W. 227
Dixon, C.J. 420
Dodge, N.H. 394
Dos Santos, João Ferreira 75
Dossal, Miriam 141
Douchet 430
Doumer, Paul 224–5, 231–2, 235, 237–8, 241
Dowd Hall, Jacquelyn 425
Drooglever, P. 418
D'Souza, Rohan xiv

Dufferin, Lord 370
Duignan, Peter 421, 423
Dunn, John 9, 11, 15, 19, 23
Du'o'ng Lâm, Tông đôc 239
Dupuy, Aimé 429, 430
Durand, H.M. 249

Echenberg, Myron xvi, xvii
Eliade, Mircea 161
Elkington, J.S.C. 135
Elphinstone, Lord 253
Elson, R.E. xiii, 33–68
Elton, Frederic 103, 106
Emerson, Rupert 400
Enes, António 94
Engels, Dagmar 453
Engelstein, Laura 467
Ernesto, Rosa 80, 81, 96
Etherington, Norman xix

Fahreddinev, Rizaeddin 479
Fall, Ousmane 281–2 passim, 293
Fanon, Frantz 145–6
Fatkullin, Mullah Lupman 483
Favre, J.L. 429, 432
Fawcett, Millicent Garrett 334
Feder, Gershon 23
Fernando, Merrenage Radin 55
Ferry, Jules xiv, 496
Fields, Karen 275–6
Fischbach, Michael R. 209
Fisher, Jeanne 13
Fodé 289–90, 291
Foner, P.S. 327
Fontaine, A.R. 221, 228, 233, 235, 236, 242
Foucault, Michel 138, 221, 222
Fourniau, Charles 226
Foxe, Barbara 449, 452
Frankel, S.H. 5
Fredrickson, George M. 387, 421
Freedman, Maurice 173, 188, 387
Fresnel, Fulgence 367
Frézouls, A. 235
Frobel, Friedrich 455
Fromm, Z.S. 115
Fujii, Tsunao 538
Fujimoto, Hideo 545

Gallieni, Joseph 281

Gandhi, M.K. xii
Gann, L.H. 16, 421, 423
Gantès, Gilles de 421, 426
García, Calixto 326
Garnier, Francis 511
Gartrell, Beverley 425
Gasprinskii, Ismail Bei 460, 463, 491
Gentle, Alex 176
Ghālib, Amīr 366
Ghose, Aurobindo 454
Ghose, Monomohan 446, 453
Gibbon, Edward xi, xx, 459
Gilman, Sander L. 418, 419, 429
Gilmartin, David xiv
Glazier, Jack 16
Gluckman, Max 10–11, 23
Go, Julian 330
Goering, Hermann 323
Gokhale, G.K. 259
Goldman, P.L.A. 332, 333
Goldsmith, Frederick 133, 135
Gómez, Máximo 326
Gordan, Linda 427
Gordon, R. 423
Gorgas, William C. 136
Gosling, L.A.P. 393
Gouda, Frances xviii
Gould, Stephen Jay 395
Goutalier, R. 417, 419, 424, 426, 431, 433
Grall, Ch. 423, 429, 432, 433
Greenstidel, Christine 453, 454
Gregory, J.W. 133
Grey, Earl 5
Grimshaw, Patricia 433, 434
Groff, David A. xiv
Grundlingh, A. 336
Guerlach, Père 493, 499–500, 501, 502–10
    passim, 513–19 passim
Guiomar, M. 507, 508–9, 510, 511
Gullick, J.M. 391, 406

Haeckel, Ernst 395
Hailey, Lord 5, 8, 10, 15
Haines, Sir Frederick 257
Hall, Catherine xix
Hall, D.G.E. 392
Ham, Nghi 497
Hammerton, James 427, 433
Hardy, George 432

Harland-Jacobs, Jessica xviii
Harris, Marvin 386, 395
Harrison, Brian 397
Hartenberg, Paul 429
Harwood, Dorothy 43
Hatada, Takashi 543
Hay, Douglas xiii
Hayford, J.C. 17
Hechter, Michael 386
Heiberg, Inge 350–51, 352
Heisler, Martin O. 385
Hellen, J.A. 16
Helmi, Hüseyin 204
Hémery, Daniel 222
Herbst, Jeffrey 276
Hermans, E.H. 432, 433
Hesselink, Liesbeth 420, 421, 422
Heyer, Judith 7
Hidalgo, Miguel xx
Hill, Leonard 131
Hill, Polly 12, 13, 19
Hirschman, Charles xvii, 385–416
Hitler, Adolf 541
Hoare, S. 452
Hobhouse, Emily 331, 334
Hobsbawm, Eric 427
Holland, Sir H.T. 171
Holleman, J.F. 298–9
Hopkins, A.G. 5, 7, 17
Horowitz, Donald 385
Hubback, A.B. xix
Hughes, Lotte xiv, xvii
Hunt, Nancy 432
Hunter, P.S. 183
Huntington, Ellsworth 132–3
Hurgronje, Christian Snouck 378
Husainov, Muhammadzhan 469
Husayn, Sharif 372
Huxley, Thomas 395
Hyam, Ronald 420, 434

Ibbetson, Denzil 262
Ibramji, Tayeb 366
Ichikawa, Hayao 542
Ikeda, Masae 546
Iliffe, John 112
Inglis, Amirah 424, 425
Irigoyen, Père 493, 502, 503, 504
Isaacman, Allen xiii, 69–101

Ishmukhametev, Khasan 487
Iskandar, Sultan 397
Isnard, H. xiv
Iwasaki, Kiichi 532

Jackson, James 391
Jackson, R.N. 404
Janmohamed, K.K. 21
Jasim, Shaykh 194
Jauréguiberry 429
Jeater, Diana xvi
Jenkins, G.D. 19
Jessop, Bob 3, 4
Jinarajadasa, Dorothy 450
Johnson, Samuel O. 8
Jones, Greta 395
Jordan, Winthrop 419, 422
Joseph, Richard 4
Joshi, Rama 453
Joyeux, Ch. 429

Kadru, Faris 201
Kaikyū, Yoshihisa 540
Kajiyama, Toshiyuki 544, 547
Kamissoko, 'Charles' 289–93 *passim*
Kang, Hildi 539
Kanogo, Tabitha 13, 20, 21
Kappeler, Andreas 469
Kaur, Rajkumari Amrit 450, 452, 453
Kavandame, Lázaro 91, 93
Kay, George 7, 16
Kazem-Bek, Alexander 486, 487
Keane, J.F. 378
Keating, J.H. 136
Kemasang, A.R.T. 393
Kendall, Henry 156
Kennedy, Dane xviii, 424, 425, 429, 433, 534
Kennedy, Raymond 409, 423
Kessler, S. 333
Kevles, Daniel 426
Khoo, Kay Kim 391, 394
Kibasira, Chief 113
Killingray, David xii
Kim, Hyŏng-gŭn 545–6
Kim, Puja 534
Kim, Yŏng-ch'ŏl 545
Kimble, David 11, 17
King, Anthony 139, 144, 429
King, Kenneth 20

Kiriyama, Shin 541
Kirkwood, Deborah 424
Kiswahili, Zanzibari 149
Kitami, Akira 540
Kitchener, Lord 325, 332
Kitching, Gavin 3, 16
Klamroth, Martin 106
Klein, Martin A. xiii
Klobukowski, Antony 232
Knibiehler, Y. 417, 419, 424, 426, 431, 433
Ko, Kil-Hŭi 544
Koch, Robert 375
Koks, J.Th. 427
Konkonko, Fátima 98
Kratoska, Paul H. 399, 402, 408
Krui, Chief 507
Kryzhanovskii, N.A. 487
Kuklick, Henrika 11, 434
Kuziakhmetov, Mukhamet'zhan 479
Kyaa, Yaa 9

Labouret, H. 293
La Fontaine, Jean 141
Lahiri, Krishna 446, 447
Lamb, Alastair 388
Lanchester, H.V. 154–6 *passim*
Lanessan, Jean Marie Antoine 515–16
Lavan, Spencer 447
Law, Robin xiii
Lawrence, Sir John 250
Lawrance, Benjamin N. xvi
Lawrence, Sir Henry 245, 248
Le Bras, Hervé 426
Le Conte, A. 228–9
Lederhendler, Eli 470
Lee, Haiyan 527, 534
Lemire, Charles 498–9, 502, 503, 504, 505, 518
Leopold II 345, 346, 354
Levine, Philippa xviii
Lewis, Dianne 392
Liddle, Joanne 453
Lieberson, Stanley 386
Lim, Boon Keng 185
Lim, C.Y. 405
Lim, T.G. 405, 408
Lind, Mary Ann 445
Lindl, Ignace 475
Lisovskii, Iraklii 469

Lloyd, Peter C. 19
Lofchie, Michael 148
Loh, Philip Fook Sen 387, 399, 405
Lonsdale, John 3, 4, 7, 12, 20, 276
Loutfi, Martine Astier 418, 428, 432
Low, Hugh 399
Low, Michael Christopher xvii
Low, Ngiong Ing 177
Lucas, Nicole 420, 421, 424
Lugard, Frederick D. xii, 8
Lunn, Joe xvi
Lyautey, Hubert 140
Lyons, Maryinez xvii, 345–64
Lytton, Lord 451

McCallum, H.E. 182
McCaskie, Thomas 9, 11
Maceo, Antonio 326
MacGaffey, Wyatt 5, 22
McGregor, Sir William 136
McKinley, William 325
Mackinnon, Murdoch 433
MacMunn, George 251, 261–2, 264
McNair, J.F. 400
Madamombe, Emelda 315
Makalawila, Licúrio 98
Makassouba, Chief 281, 283, 284–6 *passim*
Malleret, Louis 418, 420, 423, 431, 434
Maltby, Josephine xv
Malvar, Miguel 329
Mamdani, Mahmood 276
Mann, Gregory xvi
Mannoni, Octavio 423
Mansfield, W. 253
Mansvelt, W. 430, 431
Manton, Jo 446, 447
Mapanda, Abdullah 112, 113
Marr, David 497
Marti, José 326
Martin, Phyllis 141
Martinez-Alier, Verena 418
Marwodzi, Elijah 304, 314–15
Mason, Philip 248, 424, 425
Master, Robert 250
Mataquenha, Romeu 86
Maugham, Somerset 161
Maunier, M. René 429, 430
Maxwell, CJ 18
Maxwell, George 408

Maxwell, Walter 130
May, G.A. 330
Mayo, Katherine 451, 453
Mazet, Jacques 430
Medhurst, Walter H. 402
Meebelo, H.S. 16
Meek, C.K. 10
Megama, Chief 93
Meggitt, M. 423
Mehta, Hansa 450
Meilink-Roelofsz, M.A.P. 392
Memmi, Albert 544
Mencius 174
Menon, Lakshmi 453
Menon, Ramachandran 148
Mercier, Paul 425
Mercurol, Alphonse 498
Merrillees, James 131
Metcalf, Thomas R. xvi, xix
Midhat, Pasha 202, 206, 207, 208
Mikhail, Alan xv
Mille, Pierre 432
Miller, Michael B. xvii
Millis, W. 327
Milner, Sir Alfred 332, 333, 406
Ming, Hanneke 418, 420, 430
Minobe, Shunkichi 543
Mizuno, Shin'ichi 542
Model, John 386
Moore, Sally Falk 4
Moore-Gilbert, B.J. 421
Morimoto, Tōsuke 534
Morisaki, Kazue 542, 544, 546–7
Mosse, George 426, 427, 432
Mpemo, Murinvona 87, 96
Mukherjee, S.N. 453
Mundy, Martha 208
Munro, J. Forbes 5
Muzonde 310–11
Myers, Garth 146, 148, 154

Nagata, Judith 393
Nandy, Ashis 423
Nankoe, Hakiem 227, 234
Napier, Lord 447
Navelle, F.-A. 505
Nehru, Rameshwari 451
Newbold, T.J. 401, 407
Ngô, Long Vinh 220

Nguyên, Ái Quôc (Hô Chi Minh) 242
Nicholas I, Tsar 466, 467, 470, 472, 482–3, 485
Nieuwenhuys, Roger 422
Nightingale, Florence 448
Nikolaevich, Alexander 487
Niquaria, Chief 93
Nivedita, Sister see Margaret Noble
Noble, Margaret (Sister Nivedita) 445, 449–50, 452, 453–4, 455–6
Nora, Pierre 423
Noronha, R. 23
Northrup, David xiii

O'Brien, Rita Cruise 425
Ochieng, W.R. 21
Ogilvie, Alexander 367
Omissi, David xv, 245–71
Osada, Kanako 535
Osborn, Emily Lynn xvi, 273–94
Osborne, W.A. 137
Osman, Nuri 203
Oularé, Lassana 273, 281, 283–6 passim, 293
Oyediran, O.O. 19

Paasche, Hans 108, 112, 114, 115
Pakenham, T. 335
Parkinson, C. Northcote 391
Parsons, J. Langdon 125
Pasha, Muhammad 'Alī 366, 367
Pearce, F.B. 153, 154
Peel, Sir Robert 249
Perak 397
Perham, Margery 8
Péroz, Étienne 278
Pestalozzi, Johann 455
Peters, Pauline 4, 12
Phạm, Quỳnh 242
Phérivong, Charles 228
Philliou, Christine M. xv
Pickering, W.A. 175
Pim, Alan 5
Pim, Chief 499
Pinaud, Pierre François 513
Polavieja, Camilo Garcia 329
Pollman, Tessel 420
Popham, Sir Home 366
Pottier, Johan 13
Pouvourville, Albert de 431
Prempe, Agyeman I. 9

Price, Grenfell A. 429, 433
Prochaska, David 418
Prochaska, Frank K. 446
Proust, Achille 368, 374
Puginier, Paul-François 511
Pujarniscle, E. 418, 428, 429, 430
Purcell, Victor 393, 409

Rabinow, Paul 222
Raffles, Sir Thomas Stamford 398
Rakhimov, Sharafutdin 483
Ramakrishna 449
Ramusack, Barbara N. xix, 445–57
Ranger, Terence 4, 5, 7, 16
Raptchinsky, B. 429
Rashid, Mehmet 199–201 passim, 202
Rasoul, Abd-er- 366
Rathbone, Eleanor xix, 445, 451–2, 453–4, 455
Rattray, R.S. 10–11
Rau, Dhanvanthi Rama 451
Ray, Sarala 451
Razzack, Abdur 369–70, 374, 375, 377, 378
Reddy, Muthulakshmi 453
Reddy, William M. 527, 529, 541
Reid, Anthony 388
Reid, Thomas H. 401
Reijs, J. 417
Reymond, Lizelle 449
Rheinart, Paul 502, 503, 504, 507
Richards, A.I. 13, 22
Richards, S.J. 131
Richaud, Étienne 502
Ridley, Hugh 418, 427, 428, 432
Rihambe, Jumbe 112
Riley, James 162
Ritter, W.L. 420
Roberts, Andrew 9
Roberts, Lord 257–8, 332
Roberts, Richard xiii, xiv, 276
Robertson, A.F. 9, 11, 15, 19, 23
Robinson, Ronald 275
Rodenwaldt, Ernest 427, 433
Roff, William R. xvii, 365–82, 393, 405, 410
Rogan, Eugene L. xv, 193–218
Roosevelt, Theodore 331
Rosen, Lawrence 480
Rousseau, Armand 235
Roy, Rammuhan 446, 451, 453
Rudner, Martin 405

Rush, James 44

Sack, Robert David 180
Sadka, Emily 393, 399
Said, Edward 418, 428
Sa'id, Muhammad 195–6, 197
Sakimoto, Kazuko 546, 547
Salazar, António 74
Salem, Ben (Ahmet Salim) 196–7
Salikhova, Khamida 485
Sambuc, Henri 431
Sandhu, Kernial Singh 393, 404
Sarbah, J. Mensah 17
Sasaki, Kuniyuki 533
Sasges, Gerard xv, 219–43
Satō, Katsunori 537, 539, 541
Saw, Swee Hock 391
Schmidt, Elizabeth xvi, 295–321, 424, 425
Schoevers, T. 421
Schupf, Harriet Warm 446, 452
Seah, Seah Liang 170
See, Tiong Wah 186
Seki, Chief 314–15
Semashko, Joseph 469
Sen, Keshub Chandra 448–9, 453
Sen, Sushama 450
Senchimatsu, Yatarō 537
Shakespeare, William 510
Sheriff, Abdul 150, 154–5
Siestrzeńcewicz, Stanislaus 469
Sillitoe, K.K. 16
Simon, David 141
Simpson, W.J.R. 150, 152–3, 154
Sin, Wŏngyŏng 533
Singh, Ajit 252
Singh, Gobind 251
Singh, Raja Rampal 259
Singh, Ranjit 251
Sinha, Mrinalini xviii, 453
Sivan, Emmanuel 424
Skelton, Dudley 150–52
Skinner, G. William 386
Slimming, John 401
Smith, Andrea L. xv
Smith, Iain R. xvii, 323–43
Smith-Rosenberg, Carroll 432
Snyder, Francis G. 4, 5, 22
Sŏ, Ch'un 546
Somers-Heidhues, Mary F. 386

Song, Hŭng-nyŏ 546
Sonobe, Hiroyuke 544
Sorrenson, M.P.K. 12, 13, 16, 20, 21
Spaneke, Fátima 98
Spear, Percival 423
Spear, Thomas xii
Spencer, Herbert 395
Spengler, Oswald 172
Speranskii, Mikhail 467
Spies, S.B. 333
Stenson, Michael 387
Stephens, A.G. 131
Stevenson, Rex 405
Stocks, Mary D. 451
Stockwell, A.J. 400
Stoler, Ann L. xviii, 417–43, 527, 530, 535
Stollowsky, Otto 107
Streets, Heather xvi
Strobel, Margaret 417, 424, 425
Stucki, Andreas xvii, 323–43
Stuurman, Siep 432
Subhi, Abdülletif 202
Suleimanov, Abdulvakhid 477
Sunseri, Thaddeus xiv, 103–24
Sutherland, Heather 428
Sutton, Inez 11, 19, 22
Swanson, Maynard 141
Swettenham, Frank 399, 400, 401, 402

Tahir, Mehmet 216
Takahashi, Katsuo 547
Takahashi, Keiho 535
Takaki, Ronald 419
Takasaki, Sōji 542
Takenaka, Kiyoshi 543
Takeda, Tatsuya 537
Takeshita, Eigorō 537
Tamanoi, Mariko 529
Tan, Chee Beng 393
Tan, Jiak Kim 184
Tan, Kheam Hock 186
Tange, Ikutarō 531
Taylor, Griffith 133, 135
Taylor, Jean 418, 420, 421, 422, 424, 427, 428, 431
Tevkelev, Selim-Girei 486
Thompson, Edgar T. 385, 387, 392
Thomson, J.T. 163
Thoreau-Levaré, Abdel 290–91
Throup, David 21

Tiffany, Sharon 418, 424
Tirefort, A. 421, 425
Tocola, Muariri 98
Tordoff, William 9
Toyotomi, Hideyoshi 543
Tredgold, C.H. 305
Trocki, Carl A. 394
Tru'o'ng, Lâm Bu'u 220
Tsuda, Sakae 542
Tsūdō, Ayumi 536
Tsurumi, Patricia 534
Tuck, Patrick 496, 512
Tự Đú'c, Emperor 223
Turé, Samori 283–4

Uchida, Jun xix, 527–50
Uesugi, Jūjirō 543

Valuev, Peter 487
Vambe, Lawrence 314
Van Arbeid, Kantoor 428
Van Camelbeke, François Xavier 499, 502–3, 509
Van Campenhout, Emile 361
Van den Berghe, Pierre L. 385, 386
Van den Bosch, Johannes 33–4, 36–8 passim
Van Donge, J.Kees 22
Van Doorn, Jacques 427
Van Helten, J. 419
Van Marle, A. 420
Van Onselen, Charles 425
Vaughan, Megan 4
Veerde, A.G. 428
Vellut, Jean-Luc 425, 428, 431, 433
Vere Allen, J. de 423
Vialleton, Père 503, 508, 510
Victoria, Queen 448
Vivekananda, Swami 449, 450, 453, 454
Von Götzen, Adolf 110, 111, 112, 114
Von Liebert, Eduard 112
Von Rechenberg, Albrecht 114
Voronets, E.N. 459, 491

Wallace, Alfred Russel 395, 398–9
Wambaa, Rebman 20
Wanderken, P. 433
Wang, Gungwu 393
Warnford-Lock, C.G. 412
Warwick, P. 333
Washington, George xx
Watson, William 13
Watts, Michael 4
Weiskel, Timothy 5
Weld, Frederick 402
Weyler, Valeriano 327–9, 331
Whaley, Gray xviii
Wheatley, Paul 161, 388
White, Owen xv, xviii, xix
Wickberg, Daniel 527, 528, 529
Wilks, Ivor 9
Williams, K. 419
Willingdon, Lord 452
Winckel, Ch.W.F. 429, 433
Wolters, O.W. 392
Wong, Lin Ken 391
Wong, Toh 181
Woodcock, George 421, 423
Woodside, Alexander 222
Wright, Arnold 401

Yang, Sŏng-dŏk 539
Yasuda, Yasunori 533
Yeats, W.B. 450
Yeoh, Brenda S.A. xiv, 142, 161–91
Y Guinart, Echauz 326
Yi, Sun-sin 543
Yi, Sŭng-yŏp 546
Yi, Wŏn-gap 545
Young, Crawford 14, 276
Yun, Ch'i-ho 540
Yūsuf, Abim 366

Zinoman, Peter xvii, 222
Zohrab, J.N.E. 369, 370